To Vicki
Merry Christmas

Love
Mona

MILLER'S

COLLECTIBLES PRICE GUIDE 2007

To Cicely

MILLER'S COLLECTIBLES PRICE GUIDE 2007

Created and designed by
Miller's
The Cellars, High Street
Tenterden, Kent, TN30 6BN
Tel: +44 (0)1580 766411
Fax: +44 (0)1580 766100

First published in Great Britain in 2006
by Miller's, a division of Mitchell Beazley,
imprints of Octopus Publishing Group Ltd,
2–4 Heron Quays, London E14 4JP
Miller's is a registered trademark of
Octopus Publishing Group Ltd

ISBN-13: 978-1-84533-135-1

ISBN-10: 1-84533-135-4

A CIP record for this book is
available from the British Library

Set in Frutiger

Colour origination by Apex Press Ltd, Whitstable, Kent, England
Advert reproduction: Ian Williamson, Pevensey Scanning
Printed and bound by LEGO, Italy

Consultant Editor: Jonty Hearnden

General Editor: Katherine Higgins
Managing Editor: Valerie Lewis
Production Co-ordinator: Philip Hannath
Editorial Co-ordinator: Deborah Wanstall
Editorial Assistants: Melissa Hall, Joanna Hill
Production Assistants: Charlotte Smith, Ethne Tragett
Advertising Co-ordinator & Administrator: Melinda Williams
Advertising Executives: Michael Webb, Carol Woodcock
Designer: Kari Moody
Indexer: Hilary Bird
Production: Jane Rogers
Jacket Design: Rhonda Summerbell
Additional Photography: Paul Harding, Jeremy Martin, Dennis O'Reilly, Robin Saker
North American Consultants: Marilynn and Sheila Brass

Front Cover Illustrations:
A pair of Whitefrairs glass Drunken Bricklayer vases, by Geoffrey Baxter, 1967, 8in (20.5cm) high. **$320–380** G(L)
A GEAG robot, Japan, 1979, 9½in (24cm) high. **$470–520** **HUX**
The Beatles Scrapbook, published by Whitman, America, 1960s, 13½in (34.5cm) high. **$100–120** **KA**
A Royal Doulton Baseball Player prototype character jug, by David Briggs, 1970, 8½in (21.5cm) high. **$11,200–13,500** P

Photographs of Jonty Hearnden and Katherine Higgins by Adrian Pope
Introduction photograph of Katherine Higgins courtesy of the *BBC Homes & Antiques* magazine

MILLER'S

COLLECTIBLES PRICE GUIDE 2007

KATHERINE HIGGINS *General Editor*

JONTY HEARNDEN
Consultant Editor

HOW TO USE

To find a particular item, consult the contents list on page 5 to determine the main heading – for example, Advertising & Packaging. You will find that larger sections have been sub-divided into more focused collecting areas. If you are looking for a particular factory, designer or craftsman, consult the index which starts on page 454.

16 **ADVERTISING & PACKAGING**

TINS

TINS

A Hudson's Soap tin string dispenser, c1850, 8in (20.5cm) high.

£220–250 SMI

Robert Spear Hudson invented the first dry soap powder in his small pharmacy in West Bromwich, England in 1837. It was largely thanks to Hudson's flair for advertising that his soap became a household name. One of the brand's earliest slogans, 'A little of Hudson's goes a long way', was emblazoned on the coach that made the twice-weekly journey from Liverpool to York. In the early 20th century the enterprising firm used giant balloons painted with the words 'Hudson's Soap' that could be seen from the ground.

MILLER'S COMPARES

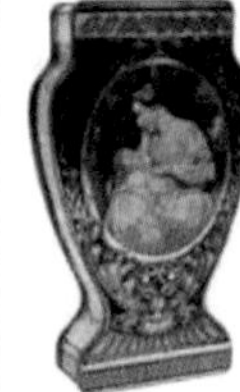

(L) A Rowntree's Chocolate tin, c1920, 8in (20.5cm) high.

£15–20 SAFF

(R) A Huntley & Palmers Pompeii biscuit tin, c1893, 6½in (16.5cm) high.

£180–200 SAFF

Both these tins are unusual in terms of their shape, but the Huntley & Palmer's tin on the right is far more decorative. It is printed with four detailed scenes – a level of workmanship typical of the so-called 'Golden Era', roughly 1880 to 1930, and relatively few early Huntley & Palmer's tins of this type exist today. The Rowntrees tin on the left, made some 30 years on, is plainer and as a product of a fully mechanized age, it was far easier and therefore cheaper to make and sell. Big sales mean more survivors today and a lower overall value.

Miller's Compares
an expert looks at why two items which appear similar have realized very different prices.

Caption
provides a brief description of the item including the maker's name, medium, size, year it was made and in some cases condition.

SAMPLE/VESTA TINS

Three Cadbury's Cocoa sample tins, re-used as vestas, 1905, 2in (5cm) wide.

£40–45 HUX

- Sample tins let customers have a mouthwatering taste of chocolate or biscuits but no more. They were some of the earliest premiums – namely items given away free to promote a new line.
- Often these doubled as vesta cases with a striking surface beneath, making them too useful to throw away.
- When the customer returned to buy the product, there in their pocket was a neatly branded tin that acted as an *aide-mémoire*. You couldn't fail to get it wrong!

A Victory V sweets tin, c1910, 11in (28cm) high.

£55–65 WAC

Information Box
is a quick reference guide to the collecting area packed with information about makers, products, history and designers.

Source code
refers to the Key to Illustrations on page 443 that lists the details of where the item was photographed. The icon indicates the item was sold at auction. The icon indicates the item originated from a dealer.

Price guide
this is based on actual prices realized. Remember that Miller's is a price guide not a price list and prices are affected by many variables such as location, condition, desirability and so on. Don't forget that if you are selling it is quite likely you will be offered less than the price range. Price ranges for items sold at auction tend to include the buyer's premium and VAT if applicable.

contents

MEET THE EXPERTS

The publishers would like to acknowledge the great assistance given by our consultants. We would also like to extend our thanks to all auction houses and their press offices, as well as dealers and collectors, who have assisted us in the production of this book.

GENERAL EDITOR: **Katherine Higgins** is an author, writer and broadcaster specializing in collectables. Current TV and radio credits include BBC TV's *Antiques Roadshow* (currently filming the 29th series) and ITV's *Christmas Show*. Katherine writes for *Woman & Home* magazine, *BBC Homes & Antiques* as well as the *Sunday Times*, *Daily Mail*, the *Express*, *The Times* and the *Daily Telegraph*. She has also worked extensively for Sky News. Katherine started her career in antiques as a Press Officer for Christie's and was antiques correspondent at the *Express*. She is passionate about modern collectables, especially Whitefriars glass, vintage fashion and all things plastic. Her first book, *Are You Rich?* was published by Andre Deutsch/Carlton Books in 1999.
www.higginsworld.co.uk
katherine@higgins-world.co.uk

CHILDREN'S BOOKS: **Anne Excell** founded Bookmark in 1973, and ten years later her daughter Leonora joined in partnership. They specialise in antiquarian and modern children's books, associated juvenilia and nursery china; it is a mail order business but they also exhibit at book fairs in London and Bath, Harrogate and Oxford. Anne writes the catalogues, but if you email or telephone you are most likely to be answered by Leonora, and at book fairs you will see them both together.
Bookmark Children's Books, Fortnight, Wick Down, Broadhinton, Nr Swindon, Wilts SN4 9NR

COOKERY BOOKS: **Marilynn & Sheila Brass** are North American Consultants for *Miller's Antiques Price Guides* and *Miller's Collectables Price Guide*. They also consult to universities, publications, television stations and dealers. Antique dealers for 30 years, they are also design consultants. Their collection of antique kitchenware, food moulds and cookbooks is considered one of the best in the US. They are the authors of *Heirloom Baking with the Brass Sisters*, published in 2006 by Black Dog & Leventhal Publishers.
Mpbkitty@aol.com

MILK BOTTLES: **Jim Call** began collecting milk bottles and African art about 35 years ago and sells at collectors' shows, flea markets and on the internet. Since retiring he has become the webmaster for all three of his websites. He lives in Colorado, USA.
tribalam@3Gsmilkbottles.com

CERAMICS: **Steven Moore's** passion for collecting started as a child, beginning with curios begged or borrowed from his grandmother's attic. By the age of 16, he had curated his first exhibition at Newcastle's Laing Art Gallery and he had written his first book by 21. After studying to be an archaeologist he moved into antique dealing and writing. He is curator for CT Maling & Sons and Chairman of the Maling Collectors Society. He currently works as a freelance arts and antiques consultant, writer and broadcaster. Steven is a member of the *Antiques Roadshow* experts team and is currently filming the 29th season of the programme.

FILM & ENTERTAINMENT: **Stephen Lane** has been an avid collector of movie props and costumes for over 15 years and in 1999 set up the The Prop Store of London. Operating predominantly through a web site, The Prop Store is recognized as one of the world's leading vendors of film memorabilia. Stephen's opinion is often sought for TV shows, books, magazines, newspapers and web articles. He has also acted as an adviser to some of the world's leading auction houses.
www.propstore.com

GLASS: **Jeanette Hayhurst** was European fine art photographer for Sotheby's and a collector of 18th-century drinking glasses. Together with her husband Malcolm they established their business in 1980 when their collecting habit got out of control and opened their present shop in 1986, specializing in most aspects and periods of British and European antique glass together with post-war design. Jeanette has lectured extensively on the identification of glass, appeared on television and radio, written and edited articles and books and was Special Consultant for *Miller's Glass of the '20s and '30s*. She has also curated several innovative exhibitions.
Jeanette Hayhurst, 32a Kensington Church Street, London W8 4HA

BLENKO GLASS: **Damon Crain** is a decorative arts consultant, Director of the Blenko Museum and Vice-President of the New York Metropolitan Glass Club. He has contributed to numerous publications including *Glass Quarterly*, *The Journal of Antiques*, and *ID Magazine* and has worked with such museums as the Corning Museum of Glass and the Chrysler Museum. Damon holds a degree in Fine Arts from the Emily Carr Institute of Art, Vancouver, Canada, and studied at the Pratt Institute in New York.
www.VMglasshouse.com
info@VMglasshouse.com

MILITARY & NAVAL: **Graham Lay** worked for auctioneers King & Chasemore from 1975 until they were taken over by Sotheby's in 1980. He then worked for Sotheby's both in London and Billingshurst, Sussex, until 1988 when he joined Bonham's. He was appointed to the main Board in 1992 and in 2002 became a Senior Director responsible for the Regional Operations of the Company. In 2004 he resigned from Bonham's to write and finally enjoy life and has been an Expert on the *Antiques Roadshow* since 1989.
g.l@virgin.net

MODERN TECHNOLOGY: **Pepe Tozzo** has a background in healthcare and financial IT systems. His career started with the National Blood Transfusion Service as a medical scientist, after which he moved into IT in healthcare and financial markets. His interest in technology dates back to the early 1970s when the brilliance of Clive Sinclair's early jewel-like calculators fired his imagination. The technology explosion that followed heightened this interest. Pepe is the author of *Collectable Technology*, published by Carlton Books in 2005, and appears on both television and radio.
www.tozzo.co.uk

ROCK & POP: **Garry Shrum's** education in recorded music started early – when just five years old he was listening to his brother's records and in 1964 he was playing in his first band and attending his first rock concert (The Rolling Stones). After a stint in the corporate world, Garry started his own successful record store, Blue Meanie Records, in 1976. Attending many record shows in the United States and Europe over the years, Garry has become an expert on imports, especially those of the 1960s. He has been providing expertise for Heritage's Music and Entertainment Auctions since 2004.
Heritage Auction Galleries,
3500 Maple Ave, 17th Floor, Dallas, Texas 75219-3941, USA
www.heritageauctions.com

SPORT: **Graham Budd** worked for Sotheby's for 25 years where he was a Deputy Director and Head of Sporting Memorabilia. High profile auctions he curated include the Lester Piggott Collection and the auction for the late Sir Stanley Matthews. In 2004 he founded his own company, Graham Budd Auctions, a specialist firm of auctioneers in the sporting memorabilia market. Graham Budd Auctions and Sotheby's still maintain a close association and the auctions are held at Sotheby's Olympia in London. Graham Budd is the author of two books, *Racing Art and Memorabilia, A Celebration of the Turf* (Philip Wilson, 1997) and *Soccer Memorabilia, A Collectors' Guide* (Philip Wilson, 1999). He is also a regular contributor to television and radio, including BBC TV's *20th Century Roadshow*.
gb@grahambuddauctions.co.uk
Tel: 020 8366 2525

Special thanks go to the following people for their help in the production of this book: Graham Budd, Peter Golding, Colin Lewis at The Magic Toy Box, Steven Moore, Colin Narbeth at Colin Narbeth & Son Ltd, Clive Parks & Philip Parfitt at Wardrobe/First Call, Mark Ray at Collectors World, Mike Richardson at Retroselect, Alexander von Tutschek and Pepe Tozzo.

Katherine Higgins
General Editor

AT SOME POINT in our lives we all seem to be struck by the collecting bug. Take my early years: at the age of five I was passionate about badges. Saturday morning jumble and garage sales, way before car boots and eBay existed, were the place to find such collectables.

In my twenties, with a bit more than pocket money behind me, I got into glass, the ribbon-trailed inter-war pieces that hailed from Britain's Whitefriars factory. In those days I went shopping at auctions and haggled hard with the dealers. More recently it's been vintage fashion, costume jewellery and period 1950s kitchenware, which I wear and use whenever the mood takes me.

Collecting these days is a surprisingly broad affair; like me you can start with one thing and it leads to another, rather like surfing the internet. And faced with an open-ended pursuit like spotting collectables it's vital to have an all-round sourcebook to turn to. Way before I took on the role of General Editor of this title, *Miller's Collectables Price Guide* was my backstop to buying. As a one stop shop that takes you from Advertising to Watches with the turn of a page it's always been the ultimate collector's tool.

A Scheurich vase, with lava glaze and handle, West Germany, 1970s, 10in (25.5cm) high.

£20–25 ⊞ RETC

See page 82 for more Scheurich ceramics.

For our new and updated 2007 edition we've made it even better. Reflecting current worldwide trends is something I'm passionate about so this year we've gone 'big' on Modern Technology, Fashion and Ceramics. It hardly seems like 30 years have passed since the world's first pocket calculator appeared but vintage examples from the Disco decade are busy changing hands for serious sums. Perhaps even more astonishing is the level of interest that surrounds mobile telephones. Sets that were in our jacket pockets just last year are classed now as desirable rather than disposable.

The key to getting into a new area like this is to bring yourself up to speed with the market. For the first time we lend you an expert hand in the shape of our team of Miller's authenticators – well-known collectables specialists and faces you'll recognize from TV and broadcasting who give you their tips on what to look for. The Miller's experts lead you into emerging areas like post-war West German ceramics, which litter thrift shops in the UK but are climbing in price in the US.

I think one of the most popular queries I have when assessing collectables is 'What should I be looking for?' Tackling this head on we've introduced a new feature for 2007 – Miller's Compares. Taking two seemingly identical objects, our expert authenticators show you exactly how to look at a collectable and spot the best example.

In some cases they separate real from reproduction to help train your eye even further.

Every collector is reliant on knowing up-to-date prices and *Miller's Collectables Price Guide* gives you over 4,000 to choose from, gathered over the course of a year. The unrivalled range of sources (auction houses, dealers and the internet) means you're party to the bigger picture – the collecting market worldwide.

And this is a real bonus in a world where we spend more time surfing for collectables than anything else online. So there's only one message that remains – enjoy the hunt and keep ahead with your Miller's!

ADVERTISING & PACKAGING

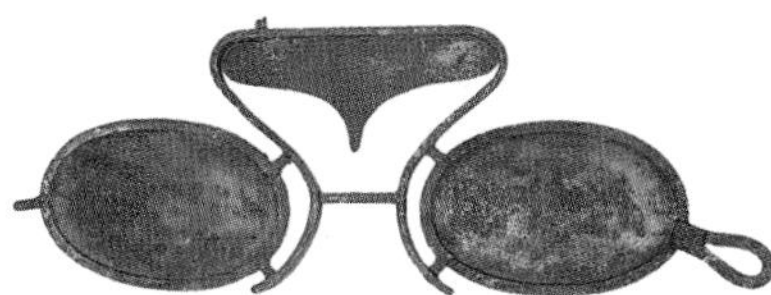

An optician's sign, cast-iron, in the form of a pair of spectacles, France, c1880, 29in (73.5cm) wide.

$740–840 PICA

This sign would originally have had painted eyes within the frames.

► **A Lance advertising figure,** papier-mâché and felt, c1910, 31in (78.5cm) high.

$1,200–1,350 PICA

A blacksmith's sign, metal, Germany, c1920, 51in (129.5cm) wide.

$530–600 PICA

In Germany, blacksmith's forges were often situated on highways and signs like this were helpful in identifying them.

A Reid, Murdoch & Co candied peel box, wood, America, early 20thC, 14in (35.5cm) wide.

$40–50 JAA

Reid, Murdoch & Co was an American wholesale grocery company. Their waterside warehouse was built in 1914 and is one of the best known buildings along the Chicago river. Reid, Murdoch & Co items are popular collectables today.

A Walter Barnard & Son hat box, cardboard, 1920s, 13in (33cm) wide.

$25–30 OH

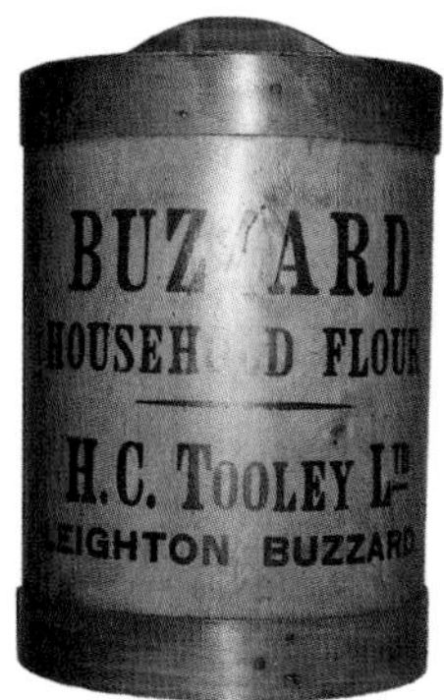

An H. C. Tooley Buzzard Household Flour barrel, wood, c1920, 15in (38cm) high.

$230–260 B&R

◄ **A W. T. Wright cream container,** printed paper, America, 1920s, 3¾in (9.5cm) high.

$25–30 MSB

American dairies adopted paper cartons for milk and cream long before their European counterparts. Although the first waxed paper milk cartons were patented in the early 1900s it was not until c1938 that they were put into general use in the US and the 1960s in the UK. Cartons had distinct advantages over bottles; they weighed less, were space-saving and didn't need to be returned so the dairies could service a wider audience. The slow take-up of paper cartons in Britain links with the pace of change in domestic refrigeration.

COCA-COLA

A Coca-Cola tip tray, painted with a beauty girl, slight damage, 1907, 16½in (42cm) high.

$950–1,100 JDJ

A Coca-Cola sign, tin, 1934, 36in (91.5cm) wide.

$200–230 JDJ

A Coca-Cola sign, cardboard, 1950, 34in (86.5cm) wide.

$390–440 Do

A Coca-Cola Vendorlator 3D-33 machine, holds 33 bottles, slight damage, c1955, 52in (132cm) high.

$910–1,050 JDJ

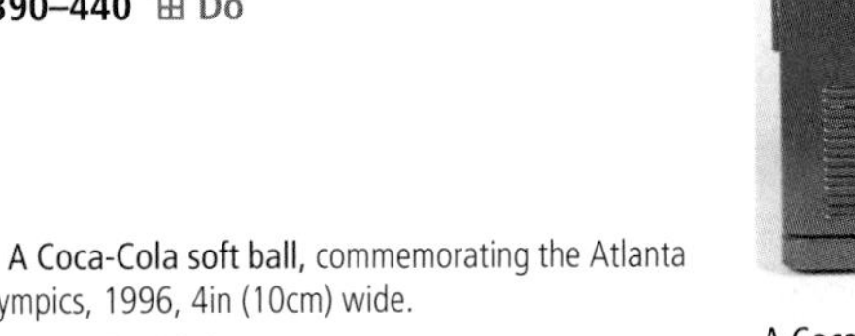

◄ A Coca-Cola soft ball, commemorating the Atlanta Olympics, 1996, 4in (10cm) wide.

$5–10 M&C

- Coca-Cola was the brainchild of American pharmacist Dr John Stith Pemberton. It was first served as a 'delicious and refreshing' syrup for mixing with soda in 1886. It cost five cents a glass and in its first year around nine glasses a day were consumed.
- Advertisements in the unique Coca-Cola script were quick to appear and in 1893 the Coca-Cola trademark was registered.
- In 1894 the first bottled Coca-Cola appeared. The straight-sided 'Hutchinson' bottles with script lettering and metal stoppers are real rarities today. With only 12 or so varieties to collect they can be worth as much as £2,300 a piece.
- The hallmark embossed contour or 'hobble skirt' bottle was trademarked in 1915 to combat copycat beverages. Because they were mass-produced, made to last and available for over 40 years, these Coke bottles are low-value collectables today.
- All manner of items from clocks and tip trays to games feature the Coca-Cola logo making this a fantastically broad area for collecting.
- Paper items are among the most desirable Coca-Cola treasures. A 1912 calendar illustrated with Coca-Cola beauties could be worth £4,600.
- Look out for cross-over collectables – like a Coca-Cola bottle with the Olympic logo – which are sought after by two collecting groups.

A Coca-Cola glass bottle and case, commemorating 100 years of Magic at Disney, Florida, 2001, 8in (15cm) high.

$5–10 HeA

A Parker & Sons Invalid Jelly jar, ceramic, transfer-printed, 1920s, 3¼in (8.5cm) high.

$65–75 ⊞ **BS**

◀ A shoe shine box, painted wood, with a brass footrest, America, 1920s, 9in (23cm) wide.

$135–155
⊞ **OCA**

▶ A Uneeda Biscuits letter opener, lithographed metal, America, c1920, 8½in (21.5cm) long.

$25–20 ⊞ **SAFF**

A Rothwell's Milk Chocolate Wafers dummy chocolate bar, c1930, 5in (12.5cm) long.

$15–25 ⊞ **HUX**

◀ A Koray pill box, Bakelite, inscribed 'For All Pain', 1930s, 1½in (4cm) diam.

$5–10 ⊞ **RTT**

◀ A Planters Salted Peanuts shelf display, in the form of a woman, lithographed die-cut cardboard, America, New York, c1938, 25in (63.5cm) high.

$790–950 **JDJ**

The Planters Peanut Company was founded in America in 1906. Their icon is still Mr Peanut, seen here on the tray with his hallmark top hat, monocle and cane. He was created in 1916 after a national drawing contest was won by a schoolboy.
This store display is remarkably well preserved and the printed colour shows little fading, which is key to its value.

A Virol spoon, metal, 1940s, 8in (20.5cm) long.

$10–15 ⊞ **WeA**

Virol was a thick brown liquid health supplement made from malt extract and cod liver oil. During WWII, British children were given a weekly dose to make sure they got their vitamins.

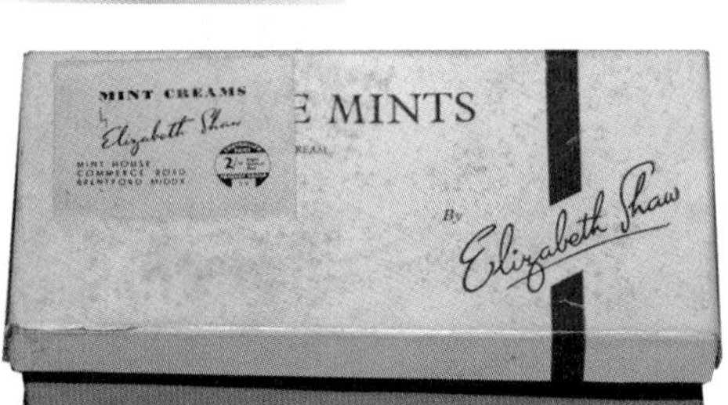

A box of Elizabeth Shaw mint creams, 1939–45, 6¾in (17cm) wide.

$5–10 ⊞ **HUX**

A Silverthorn Surekill DDT hanging fly paper, in the form of a rabbit, 1940s, 9in (23cm) high.

$5–10 ⊞ **POS**

An OXO promotional barometer, mahogany with inlaid decoration, 1950s, 12in (30.5cm) high.

$260–290 ⊞ **RTW**

A US Quarry Tile Co advertising tile, inscribed 'Romany Spartan', c1950, 4in (10cm) square.

$40–50 ⊞ KMG

A Bulmer's Cider weather house, cardboard, c1950, 9in (23cm) wide.

$75–85 ⊞ IQ

A Wall's Double Delight advertising sign, cardboard, 1957, 7in (18cm) wide.

$25–30 ⊞ RUSS

A Lifebuoy Health Soap box, 1950s, 3in (7.5cm) wide.

$5–10 ⊞ Do

A box of Bird's Blancmange Powder, c1960, 4in (10cm) high.

$5–10 ⊞ M&C

A box of Bronco Toilet Tissue, c1960, 5in (12.5cm) wide.

$5–10 ⊞ M&C

PAPER BAGS – THE THROW-AWAY COLLECTABLES

- Commercial paper bags were first manufactured in the 1840s. They were largely hand-made with either one centre or two side seams, and a bottom seam.
- Industrialization brought the first paper bag-making machine in the 1850s, which simply folded, pasted then cut a continuous flat tube. One end was then stuck by hand.
- Firms were quick to realize the advantages of branding bags and improved printing techniques in the 20th century saw fancy designs and overlay colour.
- Bags printed with well-known brands such as American Moxie soda or the UK's Biba store will always be sought after.
- Even today's paper bags are worth keeping. With four out of five grocery bags being plastic and our rates of recycling increasing it means the humble paper bag will be a rarity in years to come.

An ANCO paper bag, Belgium, 1950s, 10 x 7in (25.5 x 18cm).

$5–10 ⊞ TWI

A Robertson's Mincemeat paper bag, 1960s, 7in (18cm) high.

$10–15 ⊞ UD

◄ **An Express Dairy paper bag,** 1970s, 12¾ x 8½in (32.5 x 21.5cm).

$5–10 ⊞ TWI

ADVERTISEMENTS & SHOWCARDS

An Argosy Cigarettes showcard, c1900,19 x 14in (48.5 x 35.5cm), framed.

$930–1,100 CAG

A Henderson's Biscuits showcard, c1900, 19 x 14in (48.5 x 35.5cm), framed.

$720–860 CAG

▶ A Greensmith's Derby Dog Biscuits sign, cardboard, 1920, 24in (61cm) wide.

$260–300 Do

A Camp Coffee advertising postcard, c1907, 5in (12.5cm) wide.

$25–30 M&C

A Fry's Cocoa advertising postcard, c1910, 5in (12.5cm) wide.

$30–40 M&C

IMAGES OF EMPIRE

- The British Empire was the largest formal empire the world had ever known. In 1921 about a quarter of the earth's total land area was under British control.
- Manufacturers and advertisers realized that any association with this powerful Empire would boost sales and they incorporated familiar imagery into their packaging designs.
- Horniman's used an image of King Edward VII to promote their tea. By inference, if it was good enough for the Monarch to drink it was good enough for his subjects.
- Refined drinkers would have been drawn to the image of the genteel lady on the Mazawattee Tea showcard. Her obvious authority over her servant boy perpetuates the Victorian notion of colonial superiority.

A Mazawattee Tea hanging showcard, printed tin, c1900, 19 x 12in (48.5 x 30.5cm), framed.

$380–430 AAA

For more Empire related items, please see the Tins section on pages 16–18.

A Horniman's Tea advertising postcard, 1905, 5in (12.5cm) high.

$15–25 M&C

A Brook's Sewing Machine Cotton showcard, c1920, 24 x 18in (61 x 45.5cm).

$75–85 RTT

Thanks to Isaac Singer, the sewing machine was an essential household item in Victorian homes. Jonas Brook & Bros (based at Meltham Mills, Yorkshire) was one of Britain's leading cotton thread manufacturers. The firm won countless international awards for their high quality threads, which they claimed were 'the best for hand and machine use'. The Brook's goat's head trademark, also used on their reels, appears at the top of this tradecard.

A Richmond Gem Cigarettes showcard, by Allen & Ginter, depicting a Native American woman, c1920, 19 x 13in (48.5 x 33cm), in a later frame.

$380–440 CAG

A Wright's Shampoo Powder advertising postcard, c1920, 5in (12.5cm) high.

$40–50 M&C

A Bobby Lou Lithiated-Lemon advertising poster, 1920, 18 x 15in (45.5 x 38cm).

$250–290 Do

A Lyon's Custard Powder showcard, 1930, 18in (45.5cm) high.

$170–195 Do

A Mackintosh's magazine advertisement, 1930s, 7 x 5in (18 x 12.5cm).

$2–10 POS

► An Ovaltine showcard, 1950, 14in (35.5cm) high.

$95–110 Do

A Nelson Tipped Cigarettes showcard, 1950s, 10 x 8¾in (25.5 x 22cm).

$30–40 RTT

SIGNS

An R. W. Forsyth sign, enamel, depicting the Glasgow department store, Scotland, 1890s, 48 x 36in (122 x 91.5cm).

$340–410 DW

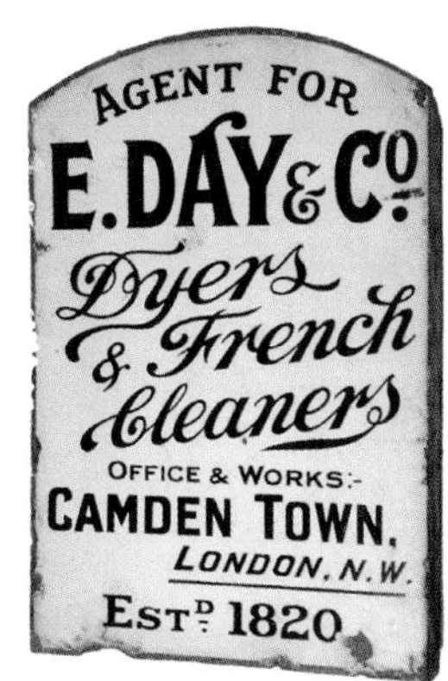

An E. Day & Co Dyers and French Cleaners sign, enamel, c1900, 18in (45.5cm) high.

$120–135 COB

A Bell Telephone Co hanging sign, painted porcelain, 1895–1908, 23 x 22½in (58.5 x 57cm), in a wrought-iron frame.

$650–770 JDJ

The Bell Telephone Company was formed in America in 1877 to exploit Alexander Graham Bell's new invention – the telephone. The first Bell logo appeared in 1889 and simply promoted their long distance telephone services. A few years later the words 'local' (shown here) were added. Bell initially imported their signs from England but by 1895 most of the porcelain signs were made in the United States by Ingraham-Richardson and The Burdick Sign Company. This is one of the early British rarities made even more exciting by the seldom seen wrought-iron frame that surrounds it.

PRICE SIGNS

- A century ago, way before refrigerators were commonplace, homes had limited food storage. Grocery shopping was a daily rather than weekly affair.
- Toleware (painted tinplate) signs like these remind us how everything was individually weighed.
- Today, the most sought after are those with unusual outlines and lavish colourful script.

Four grocery shop price signs, c1910, largest 8in (20.5cm) wide.

$60–70 each SMI

◄ **Two fish shop display signs,** tin, c1910, 8in (20.5cm) wide.

$85–100 each SMI

A Fry's Chocolate sign, enamel, c1915, 22 x 30in (56 x 76cm).

$1,200–1,350 AAA

The Fry's Five Boys advertisement was first used in 1885. In keeping with the Victorian vogue for photographic portraits, the British confectionery firm, J. S. Fry & Sons asked Poulton & Son, well known photographers in their day, to take the pictures. The young boy was the photographer's son, Lindsay, who had to endure a rag soaked in ammonia to ensure he made the 'desperation face'. When Fry's milk chocolate was launched in 1902 this picture was printed on the label and it became known as 'Five Boys Chocolate'.

◄ **A Huntley & Palmers Biscuits sign,** enamel, 1960s, 36in (91.5cm) wide.

$95–110 TRA

TINS

A Hudson's Soap tin string dispenser, c1850, 8in (20.5cm) high.

$380–440 SMI

Robert Spear Hudson invented the first dry soap powder in his small pharmacy in West Bromwich, England in 1837. It was largely thanks to Hudson's flair for advertising that his soap became a household name. One of the brand's earliest slogans, 'A little of Hudson's goes a long way', was emblazoned on the coach that made the twice-weekly journey from Liverpool to York. In the early 20th century the enterprising firm used giant balloons painted with the words 'Hudson's Soap' that could be seen from the ground.

A Colman's Mustard tin, c1895, 8in (20.5cm) wide.

$85–100 SAFF

A Huntley & Palmer's Ivory biscuit tin, 1899–1901, 8¼in (21cm) wide.

$135–150 HUX

MILLER'S COMPARES

(L) A Rowntree's Chocolate tin, c1920, 8in (20.5cm) high.

$25–30 SAFF

(R) A Huntley & Palmers Pompeii biscuit tin, c1893, 6½in (16.5cm) high.

$310–340 SAFF

Both these tins are unusual in terms of their shape, but the Huntley & Palmer's tin on the right is far more decorative. It is printed with four detailed scenes – a level of workmanship typical of the so-called 'Golden Era', roughly 1880 to 1930, and relatively few early Huntley & Palmer's tins of this type exist today. The Rowntrees tin on the left, made some 30 years on, is plainer and as a product of a fully mechanized age, it was far easier and therefore cheaper to make and sell. Big sales mean more survivors today and a lower overall value.

A Huntley & Palmer's biscuit tin, in the form of a post box, c1910, 7in (18cm) high.

$110–125 M&C

► A Perry & Co Naval Series Pens samples tin, c1910, 1¾in (4.5cm) wide.

$15–25 SAFF

A Mazawattee Tea tin glove box, c1910, 10in (25.5cm) wide.

$25–30 SAFF

A Victory V sweets tin, c1910, 11in (28cm) high.

$95–110 ⊞ WAC

A Princess Mary embossed brass chocolate/tobacco tin, 1914, 5in (12.5cm) wide.

$30–40 ⊞ SAFF

The idea behind this box came from Princess Mary, the 17-year- old daughter of Britain's King George V and Queen Mary. As the first Christmas of WWI approached, she thought of giving a 'present from the nation to every sailor afloat and every soldier at the front'. A public fund was set up and more than £162,500 was raised. This embossed brass box was central to the gift. Smokers also received one ounce of tobacco, 20 cigarettes, a pipe, a tinder lighter, a Christmas card and a photograph of the Princess. For non-smokers the contents was adjusted to include acid tablets and a writing case. Indian Sikh troops had their box filled with sugar candy while nurses at the front were given a packet of chocolate. Close to 500,000 of these boxes were made and many were re-used by the soldiers to send their own families Christmas presents. Check the quality of the brass carefully. Boxes distributed before Christmas 1914 are made from better quality brass strip. You can see that late New Year arrivals use an inferior plated alloy.

A Turnwright's De-Light Toffee tin, in the form of a bucket, 1920s, 9in (23cm) high.

$85–100 ⊞ HUX

To make sure memories of their toffee lasted beyond the last sweet, British-based confectioners Turnwright's made this clever tin. It doubled as a children's sand or water bucket. Watch out for chips and scratches as most were used as playthings.

◀ **A Jacob's biscuit tin,** in the form of a humming top, c1928, 9in (23cm) high.

$240–280 ⊞ SAFF

SAMPLE/VESTA TINS

Three Cadbury's Cocoa sample tins, re-used as vestas, 1905, 2in (5cm) wide.

$65–75 ⊞ HUX

- Sample tins let customers have a mouthwatering taste of chocolate or biscuits but no more. They were some of the earliest premiums – namely items given away free to promote a new line.
- Often these doubled as vesta cases with a striking surface beneath, making them too useful to throw away.
- When the customer returned to buy the product, there in their pocket was a neatly branded tin that acted as an *aide-mémoire*. You couldn't fail to get it wrong!

An Embassy gramophone needles tin, c1925, 1½in (4cm) wide.

$15–25 ⊞ SAFF

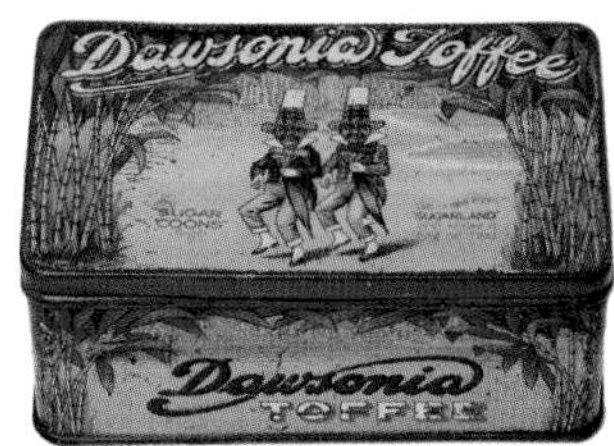

A Dawsonia Toffee tin, c1930, 5½in (14cm) wide.

$155–170 ⊞ HUX

A Peacock gramophone needles tin, 1950s, 2½in (6.5cm) wide.

$75–85 ⊞ HUX

A Peek Frean & Co biscuit tin, inscribed 'A Stitch in Time Saves Nine', c1936, 7in (18cm) wide.

$65–75 ⊞ TMa

► **A Tate & Lyle Golden Syrup tin,** 1939–45, 4in (10cm) high.

$10–15 ⊞ HUX

During WWII Britain's food manufacturers scaled down the decoration on their packaging in a bid to conserve materials and labour. Before the war, Tate & Lyle's tins of syrup would have been lavishly printed with the firm's lion and bee trademark but this wartime version is far plainer. Golden syrup was rationed along with jam and marmalade in 1941.

An Ostermilk powdered milk tin, c1950, 6in (15cm) high.

$30–40 ⊞ DaM

A Sharp's Super-Kreem Toffee tin, c1930, 8in (20.5cm) wide.

$30–40 ⊞ M&C

Sir Kreemy Knut, the distinctive monocled character, became a brand icon for British confectionery firm Edward Sharp & Sons Ltd who began making toffee in the 1880s. From the 1920s he appeared on the firm's toffee tins either with or without his partner, a macaw, to link with the firm's slogan 'Speaks for itself.' He became so well known that even a car mascot was modelled after him.

A Bisto Gravy tin, c1960, 8in (20.5cm) high.

$15–25 ⊞ M&C

A Dissmal sweet tin, 1930s, 5in (12.5cm) wide.

$75–85 ⊞ Do

A Lane's Superfine Wax Boot Polish tin, 1939–45, 2½in (6.5cm) wide.

$4–8 ⊞ HUX

A Thorn's Toffee tin, c1950, 6in (15cm) wide.

$15–25 ⊞ TMa

A Jacob's biscuit tin, in the form of a drum, c1980, 10in (20.5cm) wide.

$25–30 ⊞ TMa

AERONAUTICA

Flying, The Why & Wherefore, published by The Aero, London, c1910, 7½ x 4¾in (19 x 12cm).

$80–90 ⊞ BB

A Royal Flying Corps silk postcard, with the motto 'Per Ardua ad Astra', 1914, 3½ x 5½in (9 x 14cm).

$45–50 ⊞ J&S

Embroidered by Belgian and French women during WWI, these were sold through military canteens and sent home to mothers, sweethearts and wives. Try to find cards with original colours and avoid ones that are faded.

A brass lighter, decorated with Louis Blériot's monoplane, France, c1914, 2in (5cm) diam.

$85–95 ⊞ RUSS

AIRSHIPS

- Development of airships followed the invention of hot air balloons in the 1780s by Frenchmen Joseph and Jacques Montgolfier.
- Commercial travel by airship was luxurious but expensive; it was not viable and was unsafe if hydrogen was used instead of nitrogen.
- 1852: Henri Giffard steered the first manned steam-powered dirigible.
- 1883: The first electric-powered airship flight was made by Gaston Tissandier.
- 1900: Ferdinand Graf von Zeppelin built his first airship, the LZ-1.
- 1911: The Mayfly was the first British airship to be built but it was irreparably damaged while being taken out of its shed.
- WWI: Zeppelins were used to bomb England, but many were shot down.
- 1919: The British R-series of airships first built in Cardington, Bedfordshire, with the R34 the first aircraft to complete a double crossing of the Atlantic.
- 1937: The Luxury airship Hindenburg crashed in New York, killing 36 people and brings to an end commercial airship travel.

Harry Delacombe, *The Boy's Book of Airships and other Aerial Craft*, published by Grant Richards, 1910, 8in (20.5cm) high.

$70–80 ⊞ COB

A ceramic table lamp, in the form of an airship surmounted by cherubs, Germany, c1930, 9½in (24cm) wide.

$700–780 ⊞ AU

A Graf Zeppelin postal cover, commemorating a flight over England, 1931, 4 x 6in (10 x 15cm).

$85–95 ⊞ J&S

A Graf Zeppelin calendar, with 54 photographs, 1933, 6½ x 8¾in (16.5 x 22cm).

$950–1,050 ⊞ ET

A gold presentation clock, inscribed 'Congratulations to the Schneider Cup Winner from a few of his Comrades at Butts School', 1927, 2in (5cm) high.

$1,100–1,250 ⊞ COB

Frenchman Jacques Schneider initiated the idea of a race for seaplanes in 1912. During the 1920s and '30s the quest for ever higher speeds flamed public imagination. Flying a combination of Rolls-Royce engines and streamlined airframes by Supermarine's Chief Designer R. J. Mitchell, heroic RAF officers such as Flt Lt Sidney Webster outshone pilots from most competing countries. Italy nearly won the trophy outright by winning three times in a row but Britain finally achieved that feat in 1931, effectively ending the competition. The winning aircraft included the Supermarine S5 and S6, forerunners of the Spitfire.

A Schneider Trophy print block, depicting a Supermarine S5 or S6, 1929, 4 x 7in (10 x 18cm).

$230–260 ⊞ COB

A set of four watercolour paintings, depicting pre-WWII aircraft, c1930, 7 x 12in (18 x 30.5cm).

$240–270 ⊞ COB

A print of a de Havilland Dragon Rapide DH89 passenger plane, 1930s, 8 x 10in (20.5 x 25.5cm).

$20–25 ⊞ RTT

The de Havilland Dragon Rapide (DH89) was a well-made British short distance passenger aircraft that used modern materials in its construction, including aluminium propellers. It featured tapered wings and streamlined undercarriage fairings. In 1936, General Franco was carried in a DH89 on his escape from Africa to Spain at the start of the Spanish Civil War. At the outbreak of WWII the RAF commandeered many Dragon Rapides which were used for passenger duties and navigation training. A total of 731 were built, many of which are still in use, and two currently fly from the Imperial War Museum at Duxford.

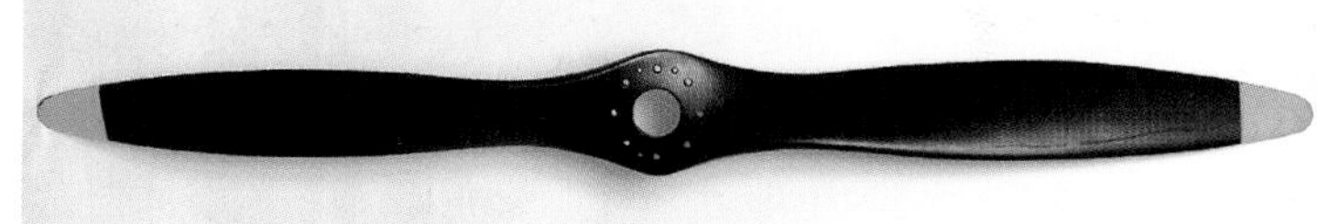

A de Havilland Dragon Rapide aluminium propeller, c1939, 71in (180.5cm) long.

$700–800 ⊞ OLD

An RAF Air Ministry gun metal scramble bell, 1937, 10in (25.5cm) high.

$1,250–1,500 ⊞ OLD

A Luftwaffe aluminium and wood lamp base, converted from a pilot's oxygen bottle, c1938.

$80–90 ⊞ OLD

A model of a Spitfire, made from aircraft alloy, c1943, 6in (15cm) wide.

$70–80 ⊞ COB

◄ **A photograph of a Luftwaffe pilot,** Major Hermann Graf, stamped, 1943, 6 x 4in (15 x 10cm).

$45–50 ⊞ **S&D**

► **An RAF officer's aluminium cigarette case,** decorated with a seaplane, Egypt, 1943, 6in (15cm) wide.

$70–80 ⊞ **COB**

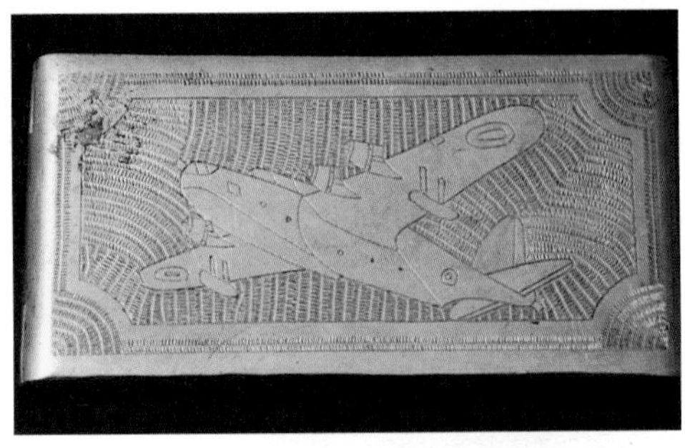

◄ **An RAAF squadron leader's flying log book,** with wings and related ephemera, 1944–45, book 10in (25.5cm) high.

$800–900 ⊞ **OLD**

► **A Luftwaffe bubble sextant,** in an aluminium case, 1944, 13in (33cm) wide.

$540–600 ⊞ **OLD**

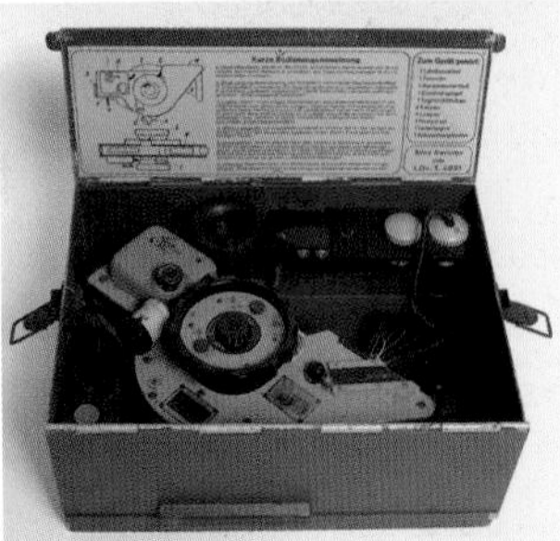

An Air Ministry issue pilot's first aid bag, with contents, 1940s, 8in (20.5cm) wide.

$180–200 ⊞ **OLD**

Guide to Madeira, published by Aquila Airways, 1958, 9in (23cm) high.

$20–25 ⊞ **COB**

A BEA Benson & Hedges cigarette tin, c1960, 3in (7.5cm) wide.

$5–10 ⊞ **M&C**

A chrome cruet set, in the form of an aeroplane, c1960, 6in (15cm) high.

$80–90 ⊞ **TOP**

A BOAC VC10 in-flight menu, 1962, 11in (28cm) high.

$10–15 ⊞ **COB**

A BOAC aluminium ashtray, 1960s, 5in (12.5cm) diam.

$10–15 ⊞ **UD**

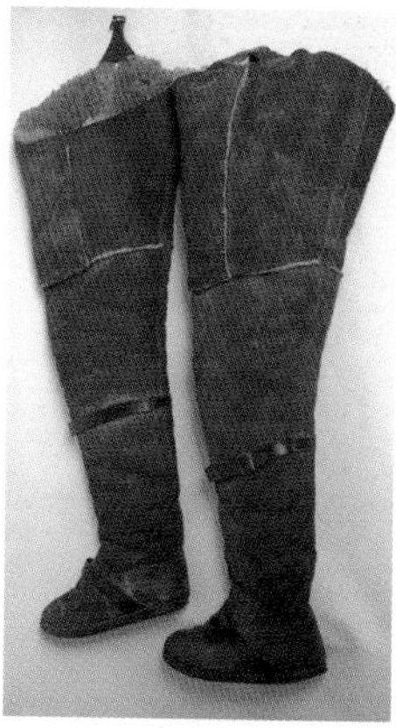

A pair of Royal Flying Corps **suede Fug boots,** with fur lining and rubber soles, c1915, 35in (89cm) high.

$1,800–2,000 ⊞ OLD

These thigh-length flying boots were standard issue to aircrew of the RNAS, RFC and the newly formed RAF (1 April 1918). Early boots had leather soles; the pair shown has V-shaped leather straps and buckles to the top and both foot and leg straps. Boots were often cut down for greater comfort but this pair is original. WWI flying clothing is scarce and if in good condition will fetch high prices.

A flying suit, with fur lining and collar, Japan, 1942.

$750–830 ⊞ OLD

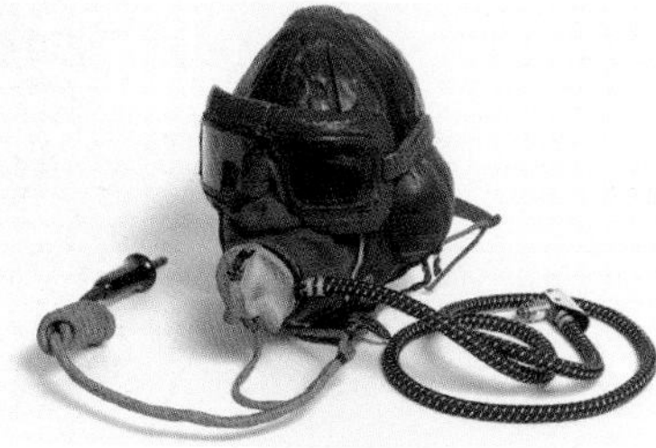

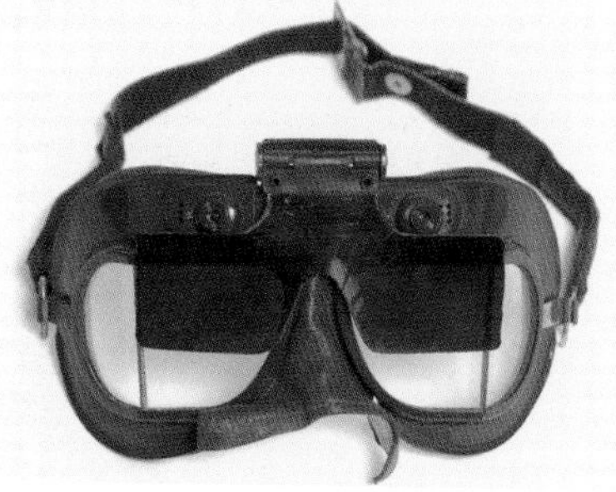

A pair of RAF Mk VII glass and leather flying goggles, with polarizing filter, c1942, 8in (20.5cm) wide.

$410–460 ⊞ OLD

WWII RAF goggles are sought after, especially if they were worn by a well-known fighter pilot.

An RAF Irvin flying jacket, decorated with a De Havilland Mosquito aeroplane, 1942.

$640–710 ⊞ OLD

A USN G-1 leather flying jacket, with rayon lining, America, c1950.

$540–600 ⊞ OLD

◀ **An RAF B-type flying helmet,** with D-type oxygen mask and Mark VIII goggles, c1940.

$3,400–3,800 ⊞ OLD

An RAF officer's leather and cloth cap, by Bates Service Caps, c1940.

$300–330 ⊞ OLD

An MA-1 flying jacket, by Skyline Clothing Corporation, with wool collar, cuffs and waistband, with Crown zips, 1961.

$210–240 ⊞ DeJ

The development of the the jet engine in the late 1940s meant higher and therefore colder flying conditions, resulting in a need for better comfort and safety. The new cockpits were too confined for the old leather jackets which were bulky and heavy. The first nylon jacket was called B-15 and had a fur collar, and the first MA-1s were issued in 1949 to the USAF and USNAS. In the early 1960s Alpha Industries were the largest supplier of flight jackets and exported to Europe. Early models had a front tab where the pilot could clip his oxygen mask when not in use and had sewn loops to hold the wires running from the radio to the pilot's helmet. They were worn by the Air Force and had the United States Air Force decal on each sleeve. They were originally coloured either green or dark blue but the the latter was phased out in the 1950s. The designs were often copied so look out for reinforced stitching and the Alpha logo and specification label sewn inside the left pocket. The jacket above is a late model which is reversible, with an orange lining for high visibility during rescue.

AMUSEMENT & SLOT MACHINES

A slot machine, 'The Clown', France, 1900s, 28in (71cm) high.

$1,250–1,400 ⊞ **PMa**

An Original-Musikwerke game-shooting slot machine, 'Winter Sports – The Running Hare', Germany, 1910, 21in (53.5cm) high.

$3,100–3,450 ⊞ **PMa**

A Mills Novelty Co oak and enamel baseball one-armed bandit, with lithographed front panel and cast-metal players, slight damage, America, 1920s, 26in (66cm) high.

$8,000–9,600 ⚒ **JDJ**

An Essex Auto Manufacturing Co slot machine, 'Electric Exchange', 1929, 30in (76cm) high.

$800–900 ⊞ **PMa**

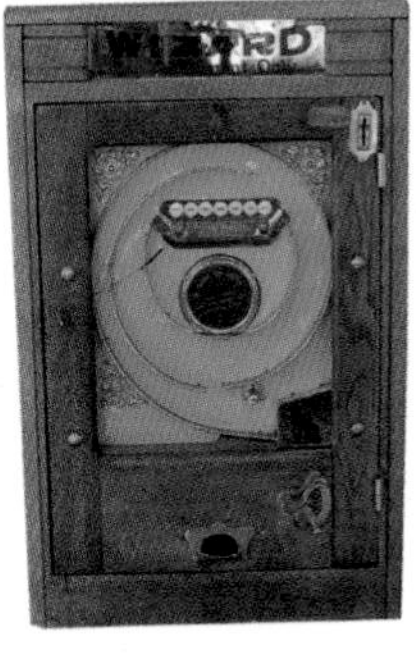

A British Manufacturing Co Wizard slot machine, 1933, 29in (73.5cm) high.

$1,100–1,250 ⊞ **PMa**

A Brenner slot machine, 'Get the Ball Past the Arrow', 1937, 29in (73.5cm) high.

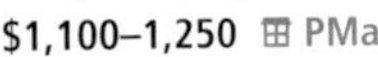

$1,100–1,250 ⊞ **PMa**

◄ A Stephenson & Lovett slot machine, 'Conveyor', 1948, 35in (89cm) high.

$1,550–1,750 ⊞ **PMa**

A Manhattan one-armed bandit, c1950, 29½in (75cm) high.

$350–420 ⚒ **ROS**

◄ A peep-show slot machine stereo viewer, '3-D Show-Show', showing 40 glamour model slides, West Germany, late 1950s, 27in (68.5cm) high.

$950–1,050 ⊞ **PMa**

◄ A Bally Super Blue one-armed bandit, 1960s, 44in (112cm) high.

$950–1,050 ⊞ **Pin**

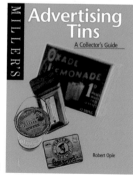

AUTOGRAPHS

LETTERS

Signed letters are popular with collectors as they often provide more background and details relating to the autograph.

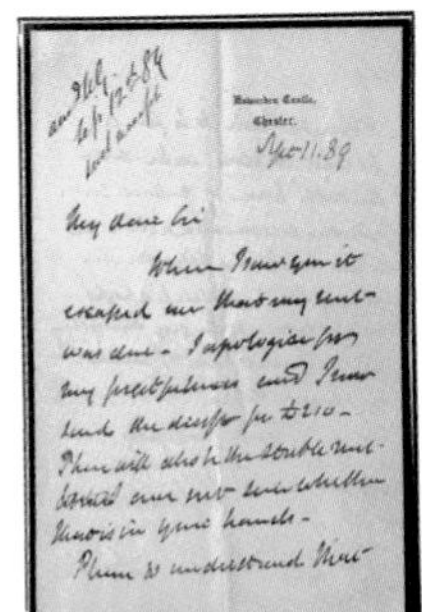

► **William Ewart Gladstone,** a signed letter, 1889, 8 x 5in (20.5 x 12.5cm).

$95–105 ⊞ **AEL**

Dwight D. Eisenhower, a signed photograph, in a silver frame engraved with the seal of the President of the United States, 1953–61, framed, 15 x 10in (38 x 25.5cm).

$450–540 ⚒ **MCA**

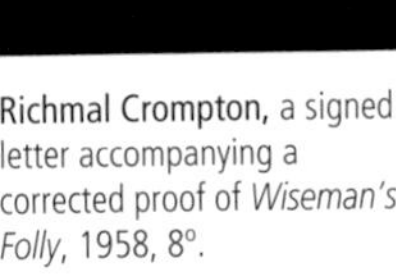

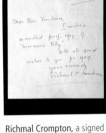

Richmal Crompton, a signed letter accompanying a corrected proof of *Wiseman's Folly*, 1958, 8°.

$95–105 ⊞ **CFSD**

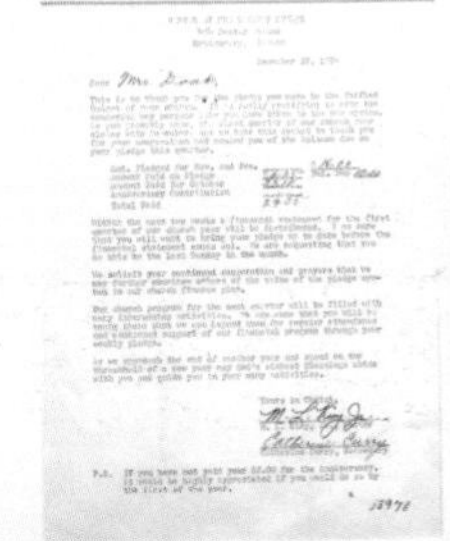

◄ **Martin Luther King,** a signed letter mounted with a photograph, 1954, 10 x 8in (25.5 x 20.5cm).

$4,700–5,200 ⊞ **IQ**

For children's books written by Richmal Crompton, please see the Books section on pages 34–43.

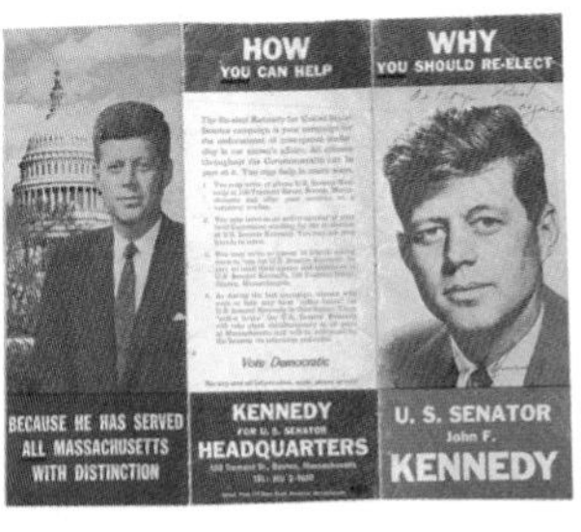

◄ **John F. Kennedy,** a signed campaign leaflet, inscribed in blue ink 'To Roy Best regards', 1958, 3¾ x 9in (9.5 x 23cm) high.

$4,600–5,100 ⊞ **FRa**

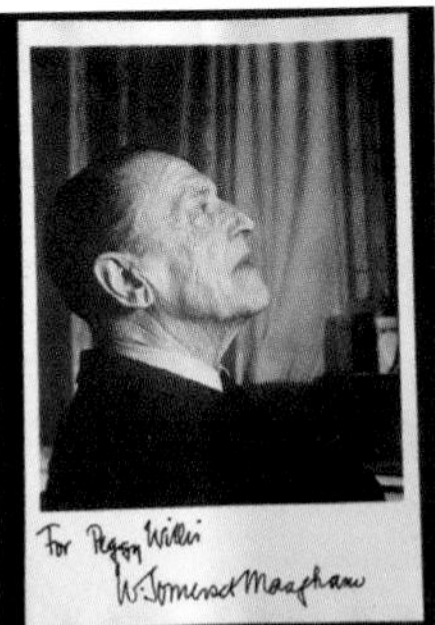

William Somerset Maugham, a signed photograph, inscribed 'For Peggy Willis', 1950s–60s, 6 x 4in (15 x 10cm).

$430–480 ⊞ **CFSD**

Marlene Dietrich, a signed photograph, 1950–60, 9 x 7in (23 x 18cm).

$250–280 ⊞ **HOM**

◄ **The Beatles, a set of four autographs,** signed in ball point pen, in album, with informal photograph of Paul McCartney, 1960s, 4½ x 5½in (11.5 x 14cm).

$3,400–3,800 ⊞ **ROS**

James Bond 007, a collection of five signed photographs of the actors Sean Connery, George Lazenby, Roger Moore, Timothy Dalton and Pierce Brosnan, 1962–99, each 10 x 8in (25.5 x 20.5cm), mounted, framed and glazed.

$1,500–1,650 ⊞ FRa

Russ Abbot, a signed photograph, late 1970s, 6 x 3in (15 x 7.5cm).

$5–10 ⊞ S&D

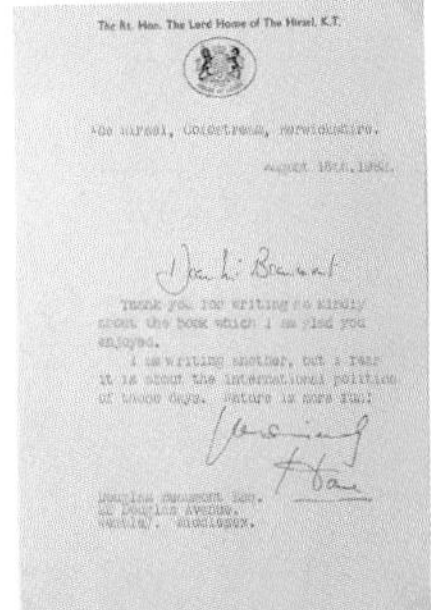
The Rt. Hon. The Lord Home of The Hirsel, K.T.

Sir Alec Douglas-Home, a signed letter to Douglas Beaumont, 1982, 10 x 8in (25.5 x 20.5cm).

$80–90 ⊞ AEL

Pete Best, a signed photograph, signed 1995, 8 x 10in (20.5 x 25.5cm).

$60–70 ⊞ ACOG

▶ **Brigitte Bardot,** a signed photograph, signed 2001, 10 x 8in (25.5 x 8in).

$80–90 ⊞ ACOG

MILLER'S COMPARES

(L) Paddy Ashdown, a signed photograph, 1990s, framed, 7 x 5in (18 x 12.5cm).

$130–145 ⊞ POL

(R) Margaret Thatcher, a signed photograph, 1990s, framed, 30 x 23in (76 x 58.5cm).

$310–350 ⊞ POL

Both these items are collectable autographs. However, the Margaret Thatcher signed photograph on the right is of a very well-known political figure whose position as Britain's first woman Prime Minister from 1979 to 1999 has resulted in items relating to her being very sought after, especially with collectors in the US and Japan.

The Paddy Ashdown signed photograph on the left is also of a British politician and although he was leader of the Liberal Democrats from 1988 to 1999 he was never elected Prime Minister. Items relating to him are therefore not as collectable and do not command such a high price.

Fakes

Buyers should be aware that there are many fake political autographs on the market and, as a rule, items signed in blue felt tip are less likely to be forged.

Tony Curtis, a photograph, signed 2002, 10 x 8in (25.5 x 20.5cm).

$80–90 ⊞ ACOG

AUTOMOBILIA

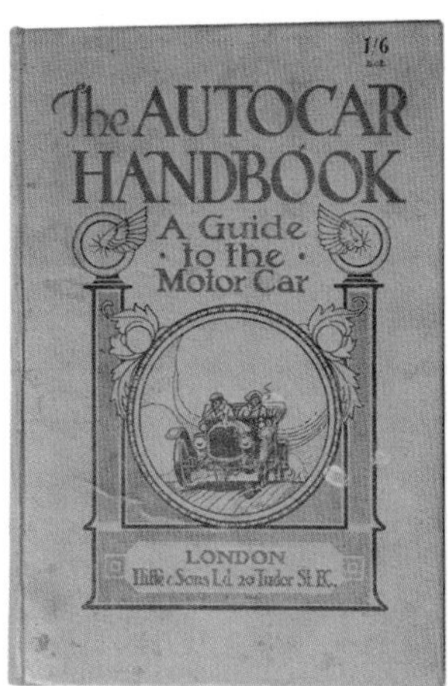

Douglas Leechman, *The Autocar Handbook*, third edition, published by Iliffe & Sons, London, c1911, 21 x 14in (53.5 x 35.5cm).

$105–120 BB

AUTOMOBILE ASSOCIATION KEYS

A steel AA key, c1920, 2in (5cm) long.

$50–55 BS

A nickel-plated AA key, 1920, 3in (7.5cm) long.

$95–105 BS

A nickel-plated AA key, 1950s, 3in (7.5cm) long.

$35–40 BS

- AA roadside boxes with a 24-hour telephone service were introduced in 1920. Manufactured by H&T Vaughan of Willenhall the keys issued enabled members to access any box at any time.
- Each was embossed 'AA The Key to the Open Road', 'H&TV 1921' and the member's registration number was impressed.
- By 1935 Yale & Towne had taken over H&T Vaughan and the head changed to a hexagon, a shape which was in use until 1967, when the latest design was introduced.
- The keys are now collected by enthusiasts of both the AA and keys.

◄ **A bronze car mascot,** in the form of Bonzo the dog, 1920s, 2¾in (7cm) high.

$260–290 MCA

A Shell Oil and Petrol poster, by Jean d'Ylen, published by Shell-Mex, slight damage, 1926, 26¾ x 42¼in (68 x 107.5cm).

$750–900 ONS

Jean d'Ylen was a renowned international poster artist during the 1920s and 1930s. He created designs for Esso, BP, Waterman, Ripolin, Bally, Daily Herald *and* Power Ethyl *as well as many others.*

A Dunlop enamel advertising sign, 1927, 48 x 72in (122 x 183cm).

$350–390 JUN

A Frames Tours cardboard ticket folder, 1927, 5 x 4½in (12.5 x 11.5cm).

$10–15 RTT

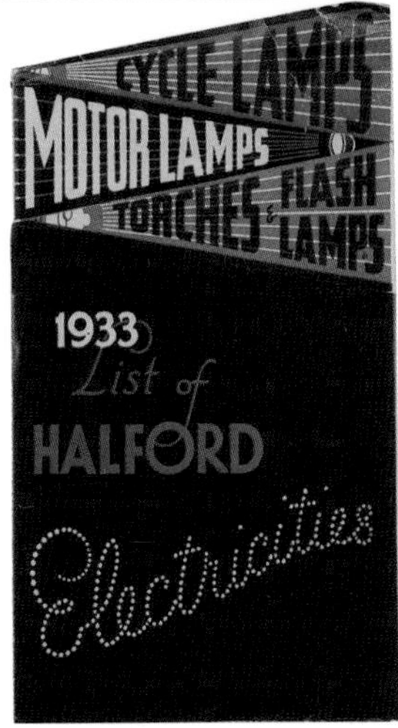

A Halford list of electrical products, 1933, 8in (20.5cm) high.

$10–15 ⊞ COB

Founded in Birmingham in 1892 by F. W. Rushbrooke, it was not until the 1960s that the business became known as Halfords. It is now the leading UK retailer of car parts, bicycles and travel items.

A map of the Grossglockner Alpine Road, Austria, 1938, 9½ x 5½in (24 x 14cm).

$5–10 ⊞ RTT

A silver Viscount Wakefield trophy, 1938, 8in (20.5cm) high.

$1,300–1,450 ⊞ AU

An enamel bus stop sign, 1950s, 12in (30.5cm) wide.

$60–70 ⊞ COB

A Route 66 plastic sign, fitted for electricity, c1950, 15½in (39.5cm) wide.

$120–135 ⊞ DuM

***The Autocar* magazine,** 1950, 11 x 9in (28 x 23cm).

$5–10 ⊞ HOM

A Sprinkleen car cleaner, 1950–60, with box, 8in (20.5cm) wide.

$10–15 ⊞ RTT

▶ **A James Cycle Co instruction manual,** for Captain, Cotswold and Commando motorcycle models, 1954, 8in (20.5cm) high.

$25–30 ⊞ COB

The James Cycle Co was formed in 1897 in Birmingham. It began by specializing in bicycles, tricycles and tandems and encouraged the development of carrier bicycles for tradesmen. From 1900 the company began manufacturing motorcycles.

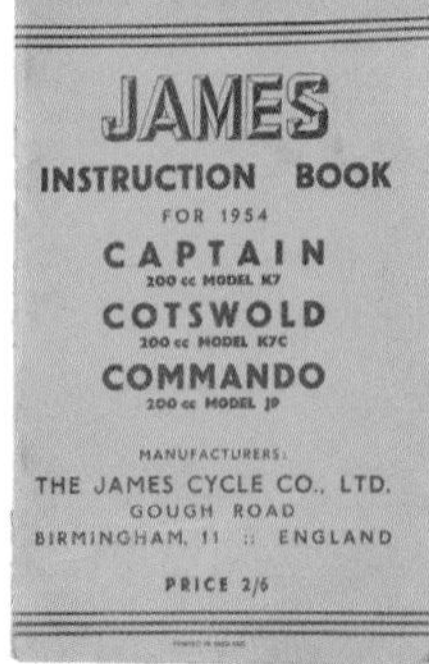

An oil painting, depicting Juan Manuel Fangio leading Stirling Moss at the Zandvoort Grand Prix, signed and dated, 1955, 23¾ x 36in (60.5 x 91.5cm).

$1,350–1,550 WW

► **An Aintree Grand Prix d'Europe programme,** signed by Jack Brabham, 1957, 9 x 6in (23 x 15cm).

$50–60 WAC

A John Bartholomew & Son revised map of Ñorth Somerset, 1957, 7½ x 4in (19 x 10cm).

$5–10 HOM

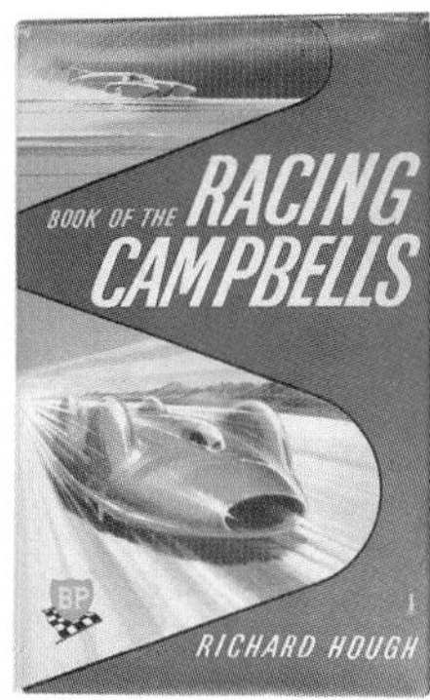

◄ **An RAC British Grand Prix Silverstone pass,** 1963, 3in (7.5cm) high.

$5–10 WAC

► **A wood and metal Ferrari 250 GTO steering wheel,** c1963, 16in (40.5cm) diam.

$3,100–3,450 RS

Richard Hough, *A Book of the Racing Campbells*, **first edition, published by Stanley Paul, London,** 1960, 9 x 6in (23 x 15cm).

$20–25 WAC

Malcolm Campbell and his son, Donald, pushed the boundaries of speed on land and water. Between them they achieved many world speed records from the 1920s to the 1960s.

► **A 35th Monaco Grand Prix programme,** signed, 1977, 9 x 6in (23 x 15cm).

$45–50 WAC

A Jordan 199 Formula 1 steering wheel, 1999, 11in (28cm) wide.

$7,800–8,600 RS

◄ **A Minardi Formula 1 Cosworth V10 titanium piston and connecting rod,** c2000, 6in (15cm) high.

$115–130 RS

A Jordan Formula 1 EJ10 car wing, 2000, 50in (127cm) wide.

$380–420 RS

BADGES/PINS

OWING TO THE HUGE QUANTITY of badges (knowns as pins in the US) produced in most countries from the 19th century to the present day, it is impossible for the collector to generalize. The novice collector would do best to choose a favourite subject and concentrate on that area – this will provide ample scope for the thrill of the hunt and the buzz to be had from finding a variation of a badge that your fellow collectors are desperately seeking.

Although limited edition badges are now being produced with the intention of attracting collectors, it is the earlier examples, mainly pre-1960s, that are more sought after and therefore of greater value. Many collectors are so proud of their collection that they set up websites illustrating their badges and these can be a great source of information for the new collector.

In the UK there is a tradition of manufacturing vitreous enamel badges, mainly by makers in Birmingham and London. In the US, however, celluloid-covered badges are more traditional and feature subjects such as politics, advertising and patriotism.

With the rising value of badges fakes or reproductions of early or scarce badges from countries in the Far East is inevitable. These will have a cheaper look and feel and copies of gilt badges will be bright and gaudy. It is a good idea to buy a common or damaged version of an early badge and carry it with you to compare with rare versions of a similar age.

Graham Lay

A celluloid Pepsin Gum Co badge, America, dated 1894, 1in (2.5cm) diam.

$10–15 ⊞ Mel

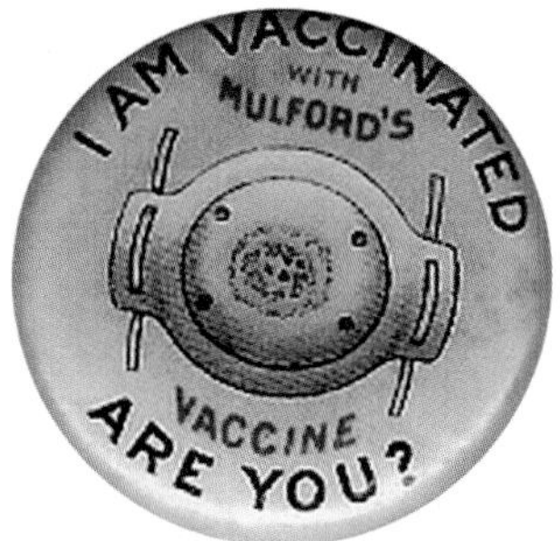

A celluloid Mulfords Vaccine badge, America, c1896.

$50–55 ⊞ KBE

A celluloid Dr L. D. Le Gear Medicine Co badge, America, c1910, 1¼in (3cm) diam.

$50–55 ⊞ KBE

This badge is advertising animal feed and shows Dr Le Gear, the 'largest horse in the world' owned by the Dr L. D. Le Gear Medicine Co, who made stock and poultry related products.

◀ **Two enamel Olympic Games key fob badges,** commemorating the Mexico City Games, 1968, 1½in (4cm) wide.

$25–30 each ⊞ MRW

Each Olympic Games generated huge quanitities of merchandise, particularly enamel badges, to sell to the spectators and athletes who wanted a souvenir to take home. Earlier badges are more desirable and usually more valuable. Although the Olympic Games began in 776 BC in Greece, the first modern games were organized by Baron Pierre de Coubertin in 1896. In honour of the ancient games the first of these modern Olympics was held in Athens.

▶ **A Beatles badge,** 1982, 1in (2.5cm) diam.

$10–15 ⊞ KA

BUTLIN'S

An enamel Butlin's Albert Hall Reunion badge, 1946, 1in (2.5cm) diam.

$35–40 WAC

An enamel Butlin's Clacton badge, 1950, 1in (2.5cm) high.

$25–30 WAC

An enamel Butlin's Skegness badge, 1957, 1in (2.5cm) high.

$25–30 WAC

An enamel Butlin's Filey key badge, 1959, 1in (2.5cm) wide.

$5–10 TAC

ROBERTSON'S

A brass and enamel Robertson's Raspberry badge, 1950, 1in (2.5cm) wide.

$45–50 TAC

There are two variations of this badge. One reads 'Robertson' and was made by Fattorini, the other reads 'Robertson's', and was made by Miller.

A brass and enamel Robertson's golly badge, Cricketer, 1970s, 1½in (4cm) high.

$45–50 TASV

A brass and enamel Robertson's golly badge, Bank It, 1988, 1½in (4cm) high.

$250–280 WAC

A brass and enamel Robertson's golly badge, Clown, limited edition, c1990, 1in (2.5cm) high.

$60–70 MRW

- Robertson's started making marmalade in Britain in about 1864.
- By 1914 the factories were producing vast quantities of jam and marmalade for sale around the world.
- In 1910 James Robertson's son brought a golly back from the US.
- The golly figure was used on the advertising price lists from 1910.
- The golly was was only used in certain parts of the world, not the USA or Canada, for example.
- Used as loyalty scheme with badges since 1928.
- Special promotional badges, such as Bank It badge, are worth more.
- Buy rare badges first as they will go up in value faster than common ones.
- The golly badge scheme is the longest running in the UK.
- More than 20 million golly badges have been issued.
- Robertson's stopped issuing golly badges in 2001.

A brass and enamel Robertson's golly badge, Surfer, 1993–4, 1½in (4cm) high.

$20–25 KA

BICYCLES

A Doulton Lambeth jug, decorated with cyclists, c1900, 9in (23cm) high.

$950–1,050 ⊞ MSh

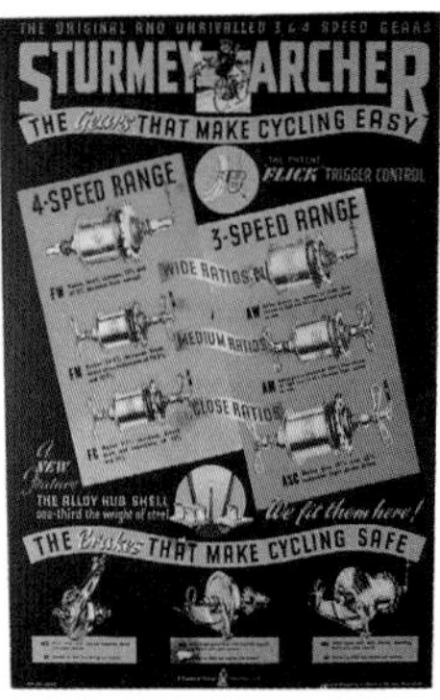

A Sturmey Archer card sign, advertising hub gears, 1951, 28 x 19in (71 x 48.5cm).

$60–70 ⊞ AVT

Sturmey Archer and the Raleigh Cycle Co in Nottingham were effectively one and the same company. Famous for making three- and four-speed cycle hub gears, most of which have little value. The desirable gears are the sporting versions, the two- and three-speed fixed-wheel TF and ASC, and the close ratio versions AC, FC, FM, sometimes with an alloy barrel. These hub gears were made in the period between 1933 and 1956.

A Chater-Lea chrome chain set, with a 44-tooth chainwheel and cranks, 1930–60, 6¾in (17cm) diam.

$115–130 ⊞ AVT

Chater-Lea began in the late 19th century as a London maker of top-quality English cycle components such as cycle bearings, hubs, chainsets, pedals and lamp brackets and were a dominant force from the 1930s to 1950s. They moved over to general engineering as the cycle market faded with growing car ownership in the mid-1950s. Chater-Lea components are very collectable if in good condition.

A photograph of Marguerite Wilson, 1940s, 16 x 15in (40.5 x 38cm), framed.

$45–50 ⊞ AVT

Marguerite Wilson, also known as the 'blonde bombshell' was a successful racing cyclist. She started with the Bournemouth Arrow Cycling Club and was at her peak from the 1920s to the 1940s when she broke most English road records. Marguerite later became quite a successful golfer.

MILLER'S COMPARES

(L) A Viking Severn Valley bicycle, with original paintwork and components, 1963.

$340–380 ⊞ AVT

(R) A Hetchins Magnum Opus bicycle, with curly stays and period components, repainted, 1954.

$1,150–1,300 ⊞ AVT

The Viking Severn Valley, on the left, has its very attractive original paint finish which has survived in remarkably good condition. It has had one owner from new and is probably the finest surviving example of this bicycle. However, Viking made lightweight cycles in large quantities in a factory setting and this bicycle is not as rare as the bicycle on the right. Hymie Hetchins opened his shop in Severn Sisters Road, London in the early 1930s and it became synonomous with top-quality hand-made cycle frames, elaborate hand-cut fancy lugwork and their 'curly' stays. The Magnum Opus bicycle was introduced in 1950 and became their top-of-the-range model. It is now quite rare and a very desirable bicycle that is collected worldwide.

BOOKS

MODERN FIRST EDITIONS

John Steinbeck, *The Long Valley*, published by Viking, New York, first edition, 1938, 8°, cloth, dust jacket.

$830–990 FFAP

William Faulkner, *The Wild Palms*, published by Random House, New York, first edition, 1939, 8°, cloth, dust jacket, slight damage.

$900–1,050 FFAP

P. G. Wodehouse, *Full Moon*, published by Herbert Jenkins, London, first edition, 1947, 7½ x 5in (19 x 12.5cm), dust jacket.

$100–110 BAY

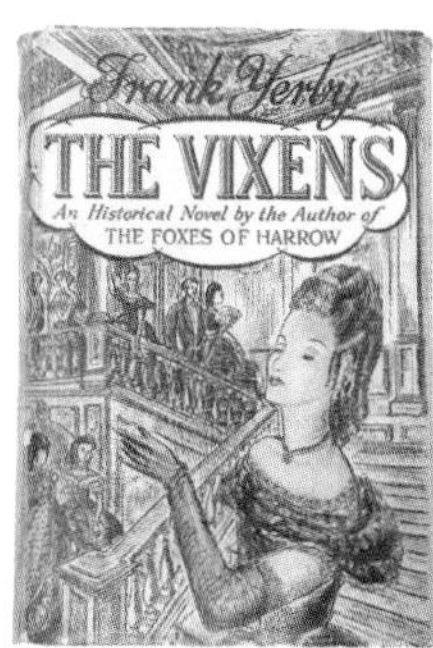

Frank Yerby, *The Vixens*, published by William Heinemann, London, first edition, 1948, 8 x 5½in (20.5 x 14cm), dust jacket.

$45–50 BB

Frank Yerby (1916–91) was born in Georgia, USA. The son of a racially mixed couple, he identified himself as black. His early life was marked by racial conflict, a theme which would dominate his fiction although his early works were often criticized by blacks for either the lack of focus on, or stereotypical treatment of his African American characters. Thus Yerby held the distinction of being the first best-selling black novelist while also being one of the most disparaged for his lack of racial consciousness. He redressed this in his later works, however.

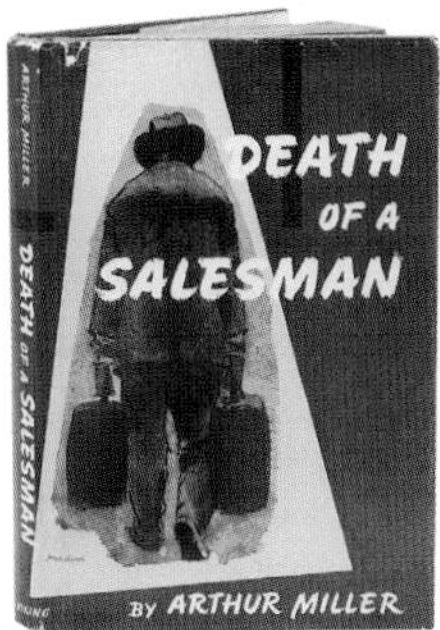

Arthur Miller, *Death of a Salesman*, published by Viking, New York, first edition, signed, 1949, 8°, cloth, dust jacket, slight damage.

$1,800–2,150 FFAP

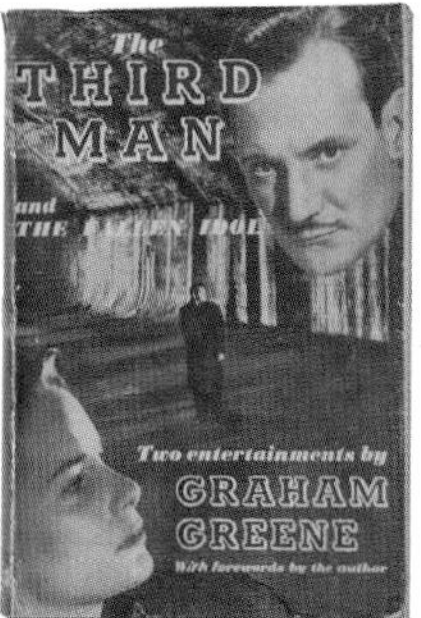

Graham Greene, *The Third Man* and *The Fallen Idol*, published by William Heinemann, first edition, 1950, 7 x 5in (18 x 12.5cm), dust jacket.

$270–300 BAY

Agatha Christie, *A Pocket Full of Rye*, published by The Crime Club, Collins, London, first edition, 1953, 7 x 5in (18 x 12.5cm), dust jacket.

$190–210 BAY

► Fredric Wertham, *Seduction of the Innocent*, published by Rinehart, first edition, 1954, 8½ x 5¾in (21.5 x 14.5cm), dust jacket.

$430–510 VAU

Frederic Wertham (1895–1981) specialized in psychiatry. He moved from Germany to the US in 1922, where he had an impressive career in mental hygiene. In his work with juvenile offenders Wertham observed that many of them avidly read comic books and concluded that they were a major influence that led the youngsters to crime and violence. Wertham found that the comic books of the day were crude, violent and tasteless, depicting graphic crime and horror. Seduction of the Innocent *is the culmination of years of lectures, articles and his experience as an expert witness before legislative committees investigating the comic book menace. As a result of Wertham's crusade the Comics Code appeared c1955 and gradually, under the code's restrictive rules, violent and gory comics disappeared from the newsstands.*

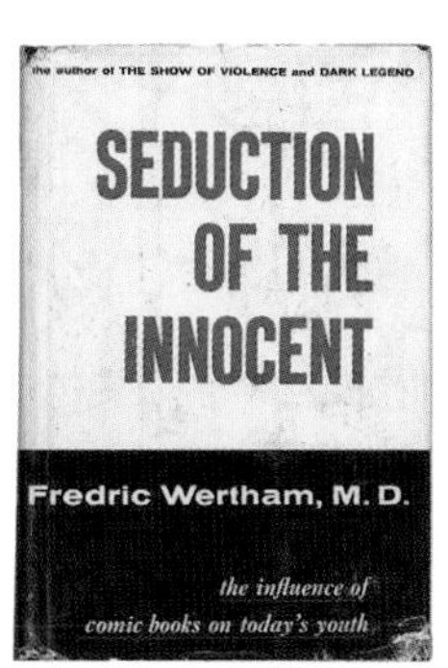

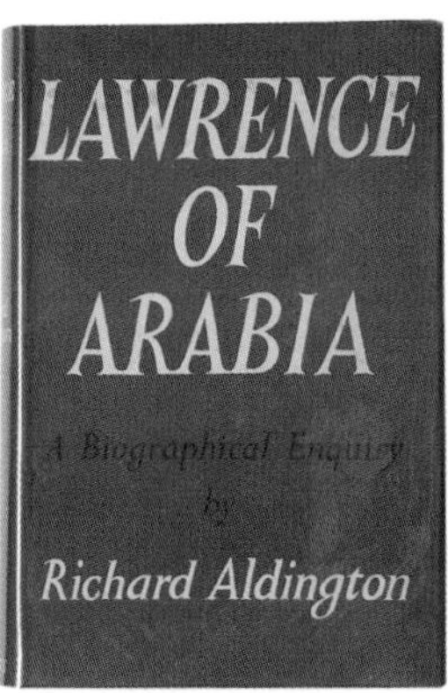

Richard Aldington, *Lawrence of Arabia*, published by Collins, London, first edition, 1955, 9 x 6in (23 x 15cm), dust jacket.

$75–85 BAY

Truman Capote, *Breakfast at Tiffany's*, published by Hamish Hamilton, first edition, 1958, 8°, original cloth, dust jacket.

$570–630 PHa

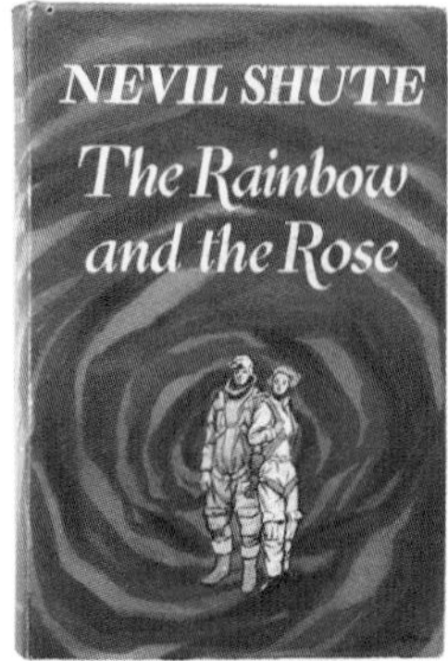

Nevil Shute, *The Rainbow and the Rose*, published by William Heinemann, London, first edition, 1958, 8 x 4¼in (20.5 x 11cm), dust jacket.

$60–70 BB

Henry Miller, *Reunion in Barcelona*, published by Scorpion Press, London, limited edition, 1959, 8¾ x 5¾in (22 x 14.5cm).

$150–170 BB

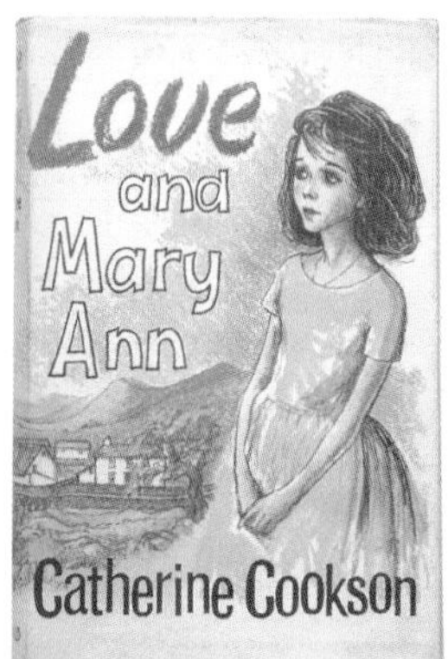

Catherine Cookson, *Love and Mary Ann*, published by Macdonald, London, first edition, 1961, 8 x 5½in (20.5 x 14cm), dust jacket.

$80–90 BB

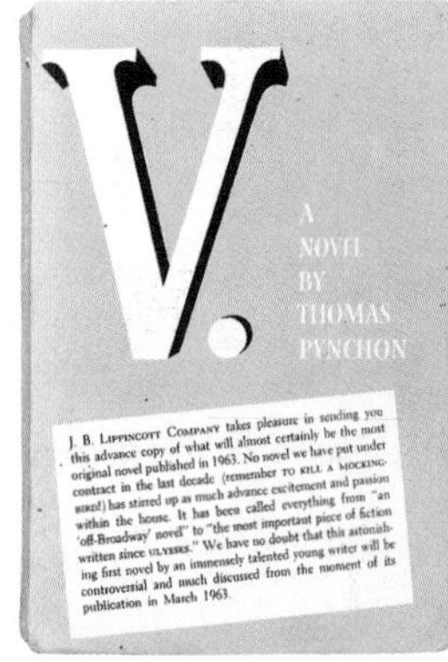

Thomas Pynchon, *V.*, published by J. B. Lippincott, Philadelphia, advance proof copy, 1963, 8°, original wrappers.

$700–840 FFAP

Nigel Tranter, *Past Master*, published by Hodder & Stoughton, London, first edition, 1965, 8 x 5¼in (20.5 x 13.5cm), dust jacket.

$100–110 BB

Arthur C. Clarke, *Rendezvous with Rama*, published by Victor Gollancz, London, first edition, 1973, 8 x 5¼in (20.5 x 13.5cm), dust jacket.

$120–135 BB

Craig Thomas, *Rat Trap*, published by Michael Joseph, London, first edition, 1976, 8 x 5¼in (20.5 x 13.5cm), dust jacket.

$120–135 BB

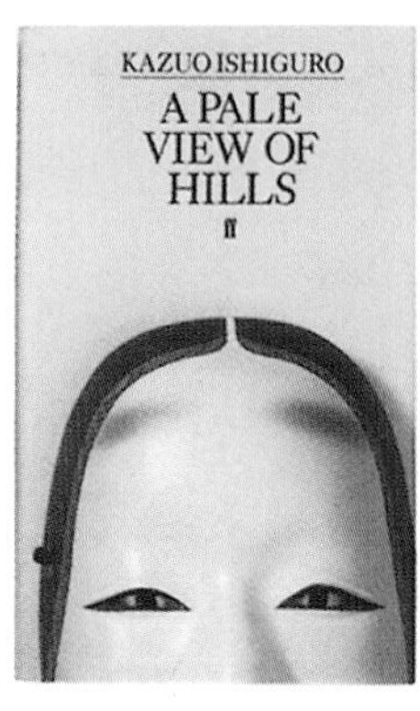

◀ Kazuo Ishiguro, *A Pale View of Hills*, first edition, 1982, 8°, dust jacket.

$1,000–1,200 BBA

This is Ishiguro's first novel, which was awarded the Winifred Holtby Memorial Prize. His third novel, Remains of the Day, *was made into an award-winning film starring Anthony Hopkins and Emma Thompson.*

Thomas Keneally, *Schindler's Ark*, published by Hodder & Stoughton, London, first edition, 1982, 9 x 6in (23 x 15cm), dust jacket.

$70–80 BAY

Anthony Powell, *The Fisher King*, published by William Heinemann, London, first edition, 1986, 8½ x 5¼in (21.5 x 13.5cm), dust jacket.

$25–30 BAY

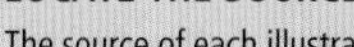

LOCATE THE SOURCE

The source of each illustration in Miller's can be found by checking the code letters below each caption with the Key to Illustrations, pages 444–452.

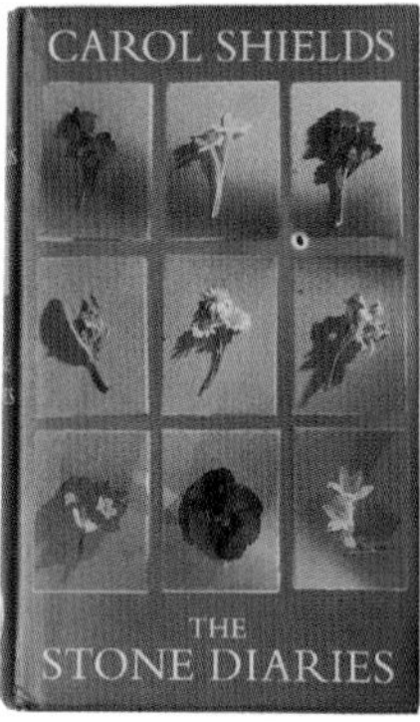

Carol Shields, *The Stone Diaries*, published by Random House, first edition, 1993, 7 x 5in (18 x 12.5cm).

$150–165 BA

Philip Pullman, *Northern Lights*, published by Scholastic, first edition, 1995, 8°, original boards, dust jacket.

$2,400–2,900 BBA

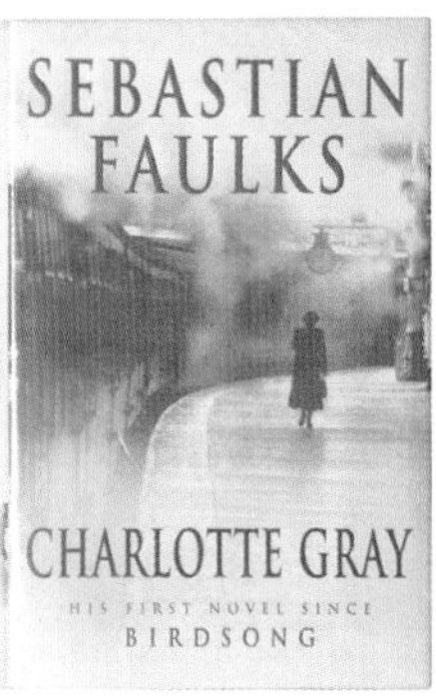

Sebastian Faulks, *Charlotte Gray*, published by Hutchinson, London, first edition, 1998, 9 x 6in (23 x 15cm), dust jacket.

$40–45 BAY

Patrick O'Brian, *The Hundred Days*, published by Harper Collins, first edition, 1998, 9 x 6in (23 x 15cm), dust jacket.

$60–70 BAY

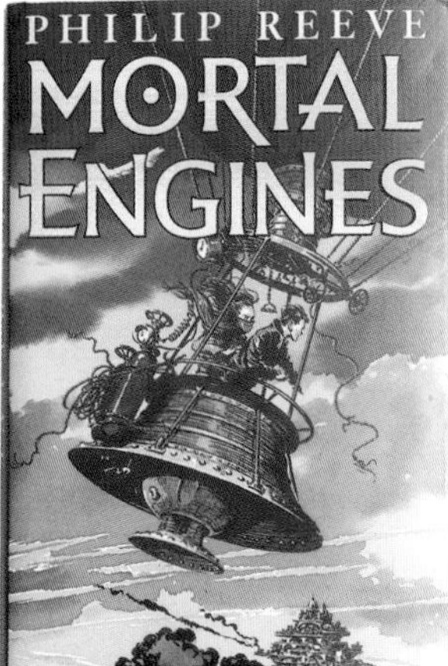

◀ Philip Reeve, *Mortal Engines*, published by Scholastic Press, first edition, 2001, 8¾ x 5¾in (22 x 14.5cm), dust jacket.

$70–80 BIB

▶ Karen Joy Fowler, *The Jane Austin Book Club*, published by Viking, first edition, 2004, 8 x 5½in (20.5 x 14cm).

$25–30 BIB

This is a novel about a book club, of which each member identifies with an Austen character. It was written for book clubs and treats modern western preoccupations in similar ways to which Austen portrayed 19th-century English manners.

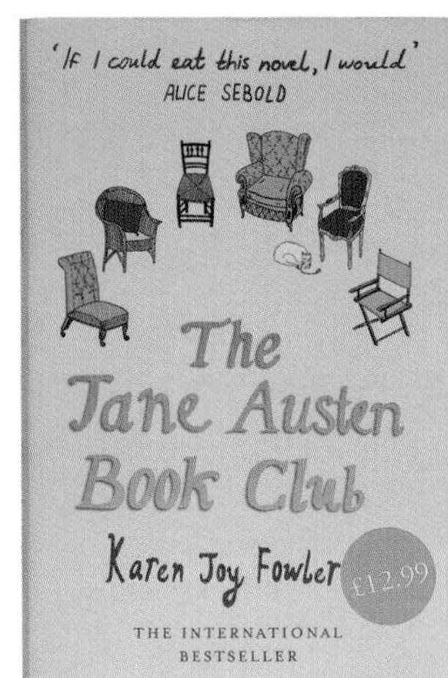

CHILDREN'S BOOKS

SEASONED COLLECTORS know that children's books are both great fun and very interesting. Beginners often wonder where to start and one way would be to rediscover some half-forgotten favourites from childhood. Ask older relatives about the books they read, look at reference books, send for specialist booksellers' catalogues, visit shops and book fairs and see some of the books yourself – you'll soon find where your interests lie.

One category is Victorian books with pictorial cloth bindings. Some were written by famous authors including Hans Christian Andersen, R. M. Ballantyne and Frances Hodgson Burnett; many are by lesser-known authors, so there is a wide range of values for the collector. Annuals are always popular, such as *Boy's Own*, *The Children's Friend*, *Rupert*, and *Little Folks*, through to *Dr Who* and other modern annuals. Books illustrated by Edmund Dulac, Arthur Rackham, Walter Crane, Kate Greenaway, Louis Wain, Beatrix Potter and other top artists are sought after. Moveable and pop-up books are entertaining and span a fairly wide date range – early books are rare and valuable but the more modern ones can be found at moderate prices. There is a huge assortment of wonderful picture books, some of which are extremely well printed by notable firms such as Marcus Ward, Ernest Nister and Raphael Tuck. Many are highly decorative and look beautiful on the shelf. If you enjoy reading, a collection of books by highly regarded authors from different eras would be worthwhile, as would books by modern authors and illustrators such as Quentin Blake, Roald Dahl, Charles Keeping and Raymond Briggs.

Market trends indicate that some of the books from the 1940s and '50s are currently rising in value and so are books that have been made into films, such as *The Secret Garden* and *The Lion, the Witch and the Wardrobe*. Also worth noting is that *Charlie and the Chocolate Factory* has recently been filmed, and rights to *Rupert Bear* and Enid Blyton's *Noddy* have been bought for future TV cartoons in the US and Britain.

The value of any book depends greatly on rarity, edition and condition. You may need a specialist dealer to lead you through the intricacies of dating editions. Values can be daunting – and this is where we hope *Miller's Collectables Price Guide* will help.

Anne Excell

Toyland Treasures ABC, Father Tuck's Nursery Series, 1890–1900, 11 x 8½in (28 x 21.5cm).

$10–15 GAZE

◄ Robert Louis Stevenson, *A Child's Garden of Verses*, illustrated by Millicent Sowerby, published by Longmans, Green & Co, London, 1910, 9in (23cm) high.

$85–95 VAN

► *Our Little People's Book*, published by Ernest Nister, c1915, 11x 12in (28 x 30.5cm).

$200–220 BIB

Laurence Housman, *Princess Badoura*, illustrated by Edmund Dulac, published by Hodder & Stoughton, first edition, 1913, 10¼ x 8in (26 x 20.5cm).

$950–1,050 BI

Verses for Children, 48 coloured plates by Margaret W. Tarrant, published by Ward, Lock & Co, 1920–30, 8½in (21.5cm) high.

$130–145 VAN

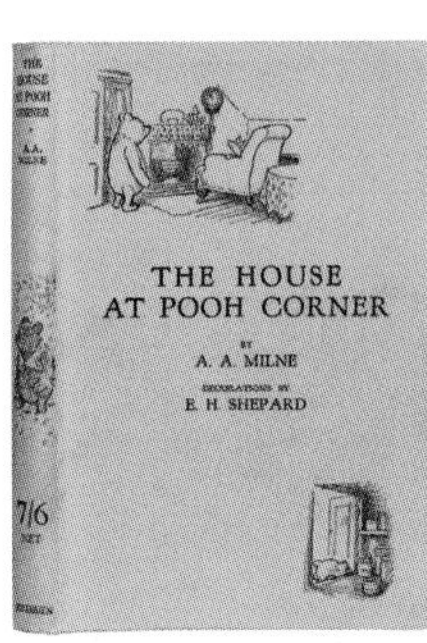

A. A. Milne, *The House at Pooh Corner*, published by Methuen & Co, illustrated by E. H. Shepard, first edition, 1928, 8°, dust jacket.

$2,350–2,550 ⊞ PHa

Hans Christian Andersen, *Andersen's Fairy Tales*, illustrated by Mabel Lucie Attwell, published by Raphael Tuck & Sons, London, 1930, 7½in (19cm) high.

$90–100 ⊞ VAN

Jessie Pope, *The Cat Scouts*, illustrated by Louis Wain, published by Blackie & Son, London, c1930, 10 x 7in (25.5 x 18cm).

$850–940 ⊞ BIB

Monster Book for Tinies, published by Dean, c1930, 10 x 8in (25.5 x 20.5cm).

$10–15 ⊞ TOP

▶ Beatrix Potter, *The Tale of Little Pig Robinson*, published by Frederick Warne & Co, London, first edition, 1930, 8 x 7in (20.5 x 18cm).

$300–330 ⊞ BIB

The Tale of Little Pig Robinson *was one of the first stories Beatrix Potter ever wrote – and almost the last to be published. In 1902 the story was set aside, only half finished, after three attempts at writing it. After the success of* The Tale of Peter Rabbit *Beatrix was too busy writing her other books to think of Pig Robinson. Just as she thought she would be able to retire, her publishers begged her to write one more book and so, in 1930,* The Tale of Little Pig Robinson *was finally completed. It was published simultaneously in London by Frederick Warne and the US by McKay (this edition had 13 more black and white illustrations than its English counterpart). The UK edition is a much larger format than Potter's previous books, is bound in blue coth and has a blue dust jacket on which is mounted a coloured pictorial onlay. The presence of the dust jacket significantly increases the value of this title – expect to pay up to $560 if the jacket is in very good condition.*

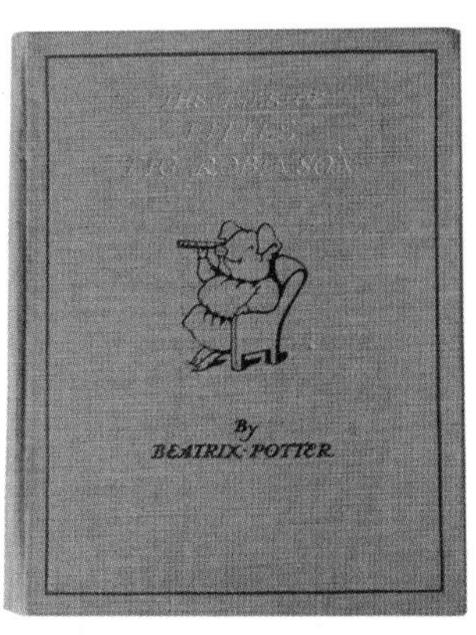

Hugh Lofting, *The Twilight of Magic*, illustrated by Ois Lenski, published by Jonathan Cape, London, first edition, 1931, 8 x 6in (20.5 x 15cm).

$470–520 ⊞ NW

The New Adventures of Rupert, first edition, published by the Daily Express, 1936, 4°, dust jacket.

$3,000–3,600 ⚒ BBA

◀ Kathleen Hale, *Orlando, The Marmalade Cat, A Trip Abroad*, published by Country Life, London, 1943, 14 x 10in (35.5 x 25.5cm).

$80–90 ⊞ J&J

▶ C. S. Lewis, *The Lion, The Witch and The Wardrobe*, published by Geoffrey Bles, London, first edition, 1950, 8°.

$9,000–10,000 ⊞ PHa

There is currently renewed interest in this title due to the recent film. As a result values have risen markedly and you could pay over $10,400 for a copy with a dust jacket in perfect condition.

Enid Blyton, *Teddy Bear's Party*, 'Little' Book No. 5, published by Brockhampton Press, Leicester, c1950, 6 x 5in (15 x 12.5cm).

$25–30 ⊞ J&J

Susan Coolidge, *What Katy Did* and *What Katy Did Next*, published by Blackie & Son, c1950, 8 x 5in (20.5 x 12.5cm), dust jackets.

$5–10 each ⊞ ADD

Dan Dare, Pilot of the Future, pop-up book, published by Juvenile Productions, London, 1950s, 8 x 10in (20.5 x 25.5cm).

$70–80 ⊞ J&J

C. S. Lewis, *The Magician's Nephew*, illustrated by Pauline Baynes, first edition, 1955, 8°, dust jacket.

$980–1,150 BBA

The Rover Book for Boys, published by D. C. Thomson, London, 1957, 11 x 7½in (28 x 19cm), dust jacket.

$25–30 ⊞ BB

Dr Seuss, *The Cat in the Hat*, published by Random House, New York, first edition, 1957, 4°, dust jacket.

$3,900–4,300 ⊞ PHa

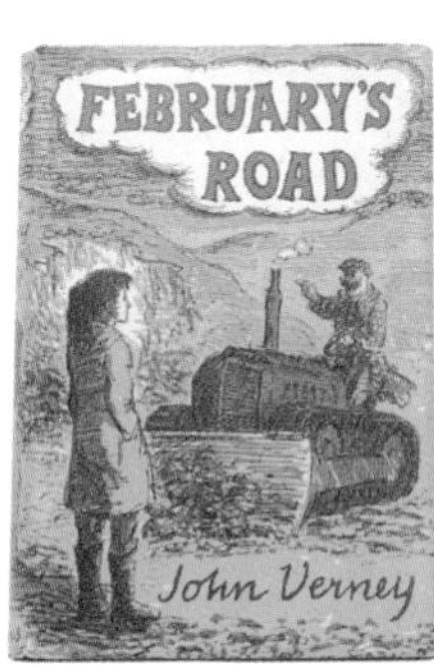

John Verney, *February's Road*, published by Collins, London, first edition, 1961, 8¼ x 6in (21 x 15cm), dust jacket.

$70–80 ⊞ BB

Nicholas Stewart Gray, *Down in the Cellar*, illustrated by Edward Ardizzone, published by Dennis Dobson, London, first edition, 1961, 8 x 5¼in (20.5 x 13.5cm), dust jacket.

$60–70 ⊞ BB

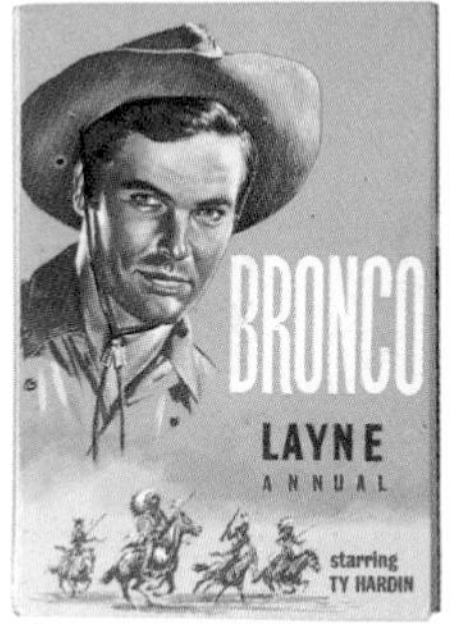

Bronco Layne Annual, published by Warner Bros, 1963, 11 x 8in (28 x 20.5cm).

$10–15 ⊞ J&J

Enid Blyton, *Five Go to Mystery Moor*, illustrated by Eileen Sper, published by Hodder & Stoughton, 1964, 7½ x 5in (19 x 12.5cm), dust jacket.

$30–35 ⊞ NW

David Whitaker, *Dr Who*, published by Armada, 1965, 7 x 5in (18 x 12.5cm).

$5–10 ⊞ HeA

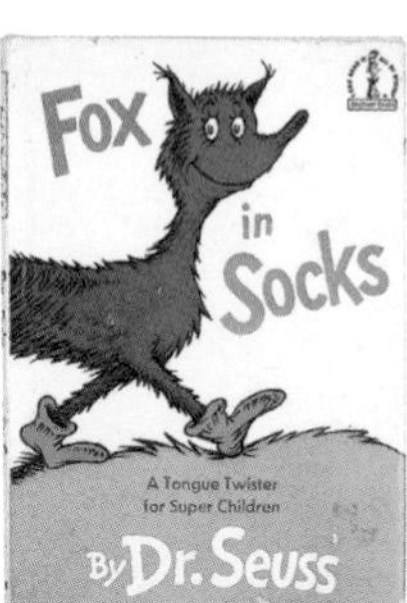

Dr Seuss, *Fox in Socks*, published by Random House, New York, first edition, 1965, 8°, matt boards.

$2,350–2,600 ⊞ PHa

Philip Pullman, *Count Karlstein*, published by Oxford University Press, signed, 1986, 8¾ x 6in (22 x 15cm).

$80–90 ⊞ BB

Roald Dahl, *Esio Trot*, illustrated by Quentin Blake, published by Jonathan Cape, first edition, 1990, 9½ x 6in (24 x 15cm).

$45–50 ⊞ BAY

Roald Dahl has been voted a favourite author by a great many children who love his intriguing stories and wicked sense of humour. Quentin Blake's lively illustrations are exactly right for this book.

► Richmal Crompton, *William The Detective*, illustrated by Thomas Henry, published by George Newnes, London, 1967, 7 x 6in (18 x 15cm).

$25–30 ⊞ NW

Charles M. Schulz, *Peanuts Jubilee, My Life and Art with Charlie Brown and Others*, 1976, 8 x 11in (20.5 x 28cm).

$5–10 ⊞ SPRI

The Peanuts comic strip by the gifted American artist and writer Charles Monroe Schulz first appeared in 1950. The chief characters are Charlie Brown, a kind-hearted boy; Snoopy, a dog who daydreams of becoming a great writer; Woodstock, a tiny bird who tries to be helpful and Lucy, a rather short tempered girl. They all appear in a great many books by Schulz, published in America, where there is huge demand with prices ranging from $130 to $260. English editions were published later, and these can now be found from $25 to $80, according to title, date and condition.

David Pelham, *Say Cheese*, 1996, 6in (15cm) high.

$25–30 ⊞ LAS

► J. K. Rowling, *Harry Potter*, boxed set of the first four paperbacks, published by Bloomsbury, 2001, 8in (20.5cm) high, in original packaging.

$20–25 ⊞ KA

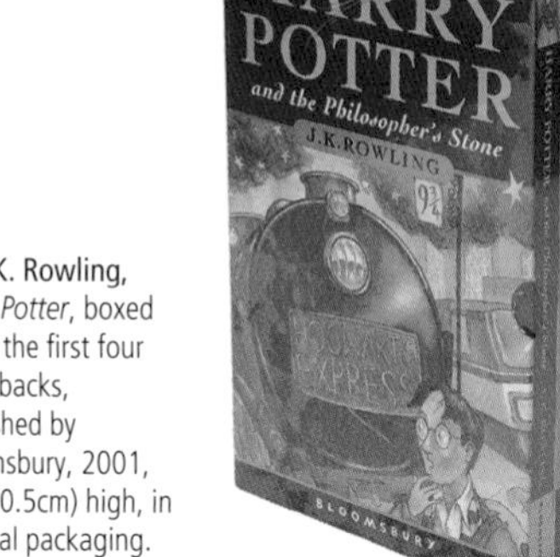

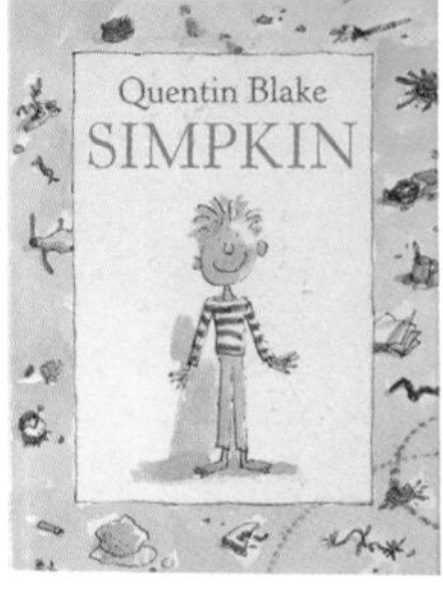

Quentin Blake, *Simpkin*, published by Viking, America, first edition, 1994, 11 x 8in (28 x 20.5cm), printed paper boards.

$45–50 ⊞ BIB

Quentin Blake's illustrations are always tremendously appealing, exuberant and extraordinarily lively. His first published illustrations were cartoons for Punch *and other magazines, as well as some drawings for Penguin book covers. He then began to provide illustrations for Patrick Campbell's* Come here Till I Tell You *(1960) and J. P. Martin's* Uncle *(1964) as well as books by many other authors. The first book that he wrote and illustrated himself was* Patrick *(1968). In 1980 he was awarded the Kate Greenaway medal for* Mr Magnolia *and has subsequently won other awards for* All Join In *and* Clown. *He was awarded the OBE in 1988 and appointed the very first Children's Laureate in 1999. Quentin Blake's work is not only great fun to collect but also highly desirable. Prices depend on many factors, but expect to pay up to about $130.*

Bunnikin's Picnic Party, illustrated by A. J. McGregor, published by Wills & Hepworth, first edition, 7 x 4¾in (18 x 12cm), 1940, dust jacket.

$400–440 ⊞ WWB

Muriel Levy, *The Snowman, The Adventures of Wonk*, illustrated by Kiddell Monroe, published by Ladybird, 1949, 7 x 4¾in (18 x 12cm).

$130–145 ⊞ J&J

Uncle Mac's ABC Book, published by Ladybird, first edition, 1950, 7 x 4¾in (18 x 12cm), dust jacket.

$180–200 ⊞ WWB

Uncle Mac, alias Derek McCulloch was a children's entertainer, author and radio broadcaster for the BBC.

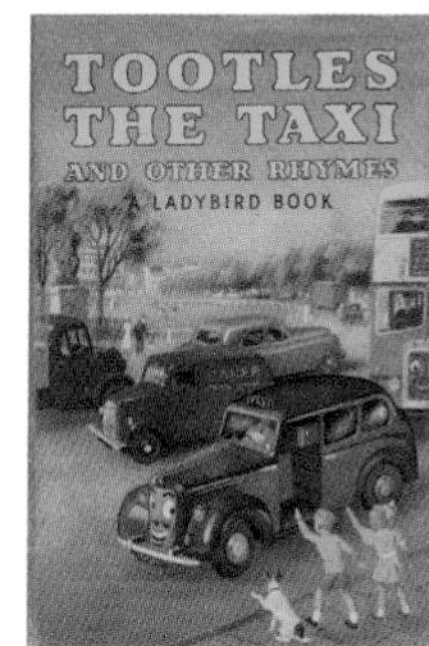

Tootles The Taxi and Other Rhymes, by Joyce. B. Clegg, illustrated by John Kenney, published by Ladybird, first edition, 1956, dust jacket.

$350–390 ⊞ WWB

The front boards of Series 413 – 'Fairy Tales and Rhymes', were printed with the same illustration as that on the dust jackets. The exceptions were Tootles the Taxi, The Circus came to Town, Red Riding Hood *and* Goldilocks and the Three Bears *which had line drawings instead.*

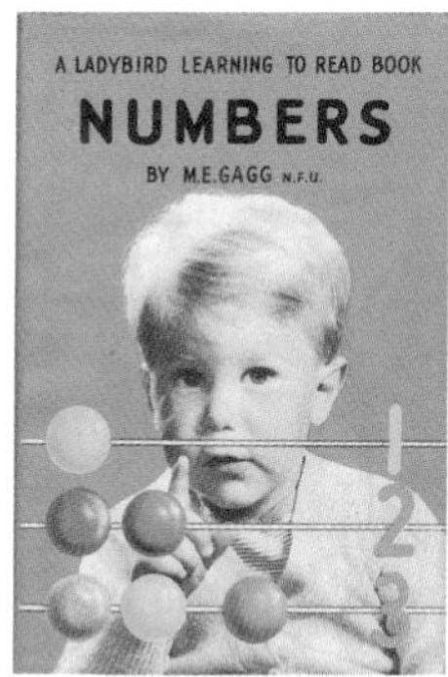

Numbers, Learning to Read, published by Ladybird, first edition, 1959, 7 x 4¾in (18 x 12cm), dust jacket.

$200–220 ⊞ WWB

Two books in the Learning to Read Series are particularly rare and sought after. These are Numbers *and* Telling the Time.

Play With Us, Keywords Reading Scheme, 1a, published by Ladybird, first edition, 1964, 7 x 4¾in (18 x 12cm), matt boards.

$45–50 ⊞ WWB

The Keywords Reading Scheme series was divided into three grades: grade a, grade b and grade c with each having 12 books.

Well-Loved Tales, Cinderella, retold by Vera Southgate, illustrated by Eric Winter, published by Ladybird, first edition, 1964, 7 x 4¾in (18 x 12cm), dust jacket.

$310–350 ⊞ WWB

Cinderella, *the first and most popular book of series 606d was the only title from this series to be issued with a dust jacket. In 1965 Ladybird began producing matt boards instead. This was to save on cost at a time when production was being increased.*

Well-Loved Tales, The Three Little Pigs, published by Ladybird, first edition, 1965, 7 x 4¾in (18 x 12cm), matt boards.

$45–50 ⊞ WWB

◀ ***Well-Loved Tales, The Magic Porridge Pot,*** retold by Vera Southgate, illustrated by Robert Lumley, published by Ladybird, first edition 1971, 7 x 4¾in (18 x 12cm), matt boards.

$80–90 ⊞ WWB

▶ ***People at work, The Customs Officer,*** by Max Dunstone, illustrated by John Berry, published by Ladybird, first edition, 1972, 7 x 4¾in (18 x 12cm), matt boards.

$70–80 ⊞ WWB

Series 606b – 'People At Work', consisted of 30 titles with The Customs Officer, In a Hotel *and* In a big Store *being the hardest to find.*

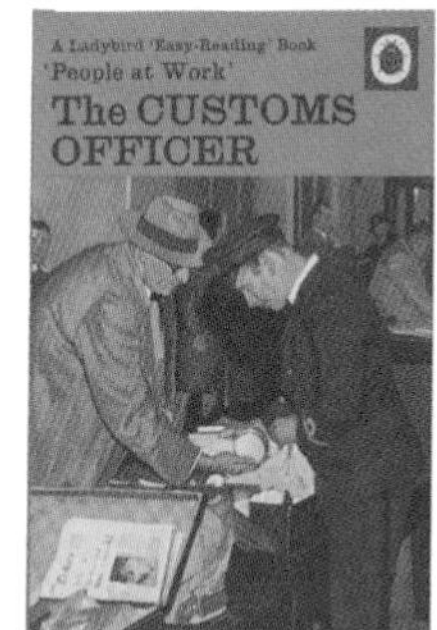

COOKERY BOOKS

Mrs Isabella Beeton, *Mrs Beeton's Cookery Book*, published by Ward, Lock & Co, London, 1902, 7½ x 5½in (19 x 14cm).

$80–90 ⊞ BIB

Mrs Isabella Beeton, *Mrs Beeton's Hints to Housewives, Home-Running on Labour-Saving Lines*, published by Ward, Lock & Co, London, first edition, 1928, 7½ x 5in (19.5 x 12.5cm), dust jacket.

$180–200 ⊞ BIB

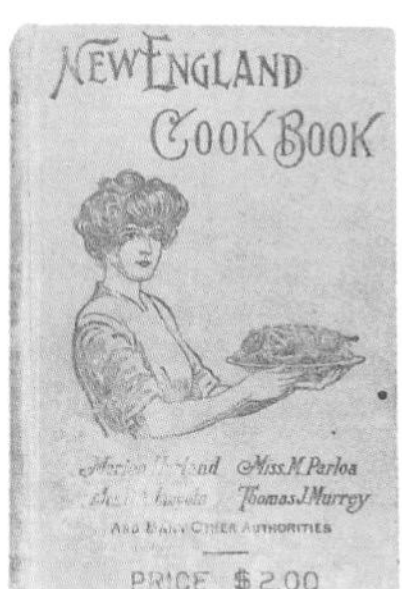

Marion Harland, Miss M. Parloa, Mrs D. A. Lincoln, Thomas J. Murrey, *New England Cookbook*, published by Charles E. Brown Publishing Co, Boston, 1906, 7¾ x 5¼in (19.5 x 13.5cm).

$70–80 ⊞ MSB

Miss Parloa and Mrs Hill, *Choice Recipes*, published by Walter Baker & Co, Massachusetts, 1916, 6½ x 3¾in (16.5 x 9.5cm).

$60–70 ⊞ MSB

THE BOOK OF HOUSEHOLD MANAGEMENT

- Written by Isabella Beeton (1836–65) and published in 1861 by her husband, Samuel O. Beeton.
- Sold 60,000 copies in its first year.
- First editions are rare and sought after as they are often handed down in families.
- The book was derived from articles Isabella wrote for *The English Woman's Domestic Magazine*, also published by Samuel Beeton.
- Its aim was to assist the new middle classes in adjusting to the challenges of society and managing a home; it provided information for mistress, housekeeper, cook and household staff and gave sanitary, medical and legal advice.
- The publishing rights were sold to Ward, Lock & Co after Isabella's death.
- *Mrs Beeton's Cookery Book* and *Hints to Housewives* were aimed at running smaller homes with reduced staff.

Mrs Isabella Beeton, *Mrs Beeton's Household Management*, published by Ward, Lock & Co, London, c1930, 8½ x 6in (21.5 x 15cm).

$250–280 ⊞ BAY

Walter Baker & Co was a chocolate manufacturer founded in Dorchester, Massachusetts by Dr James Baker and John Hannon in the mid-1760s. Among the many products produced was German's Sweet Chocolate, named after Samuel German who created it in 1852. In 1883, the company adopted the image of La Belle Chocolatière *as their trademark and the lady serving chocolate appears on all Baker's packaging and publications. The company found that pamphlets such as* Chocolate and Cocoa Recipes, *written by local cooking authority Maria Parloa in 1909, were helpful in promoting their products. Baker's Chocolate was purchased in 1927 by General Foods and subsequently Kraft Foods. Any pamphlets or premiums distributed by Walter Baker & Co are highly desirable.*

Further reading

Miller's Collecting Modern Books, Mitchell Beazley, 2003

▶ Captain L. L. Deitrick, *Manual for Army Bakers*, published by Military Publishing Co, America, 1916, 5¾ x 4¼in (14.5 x 11cm).

$50–60 ⊞ MSB

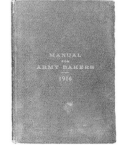

Hecker Products Corporation (publisher), *The Presto Recipe Book*, 1937, 7½ x 5½in (19 x 14cm).

$10–15 MSB

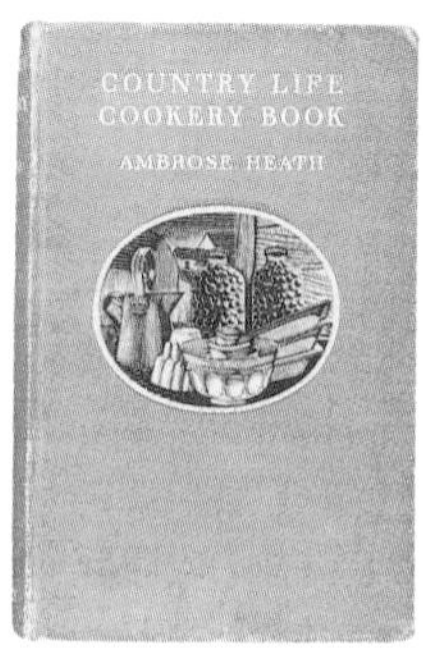

Ambrose Heath, *Country Life Cookery Book*, 8½ x 5½in (21.5 x 14cm).

$35–40 MSB

Aunt Jenny, *Good Cooking Made Easy*, published by Lever Brothers Co, Massachusetts, 1942, 7¼ x 5¾in (18.5 x 14.5 cm).

$20–25 MSB

Baker's Favorite Chocolate Recipes, published by General Food's Corporation, 1950, 6¾ x 4¼in (17 x 11cm).

$20–25 MSB

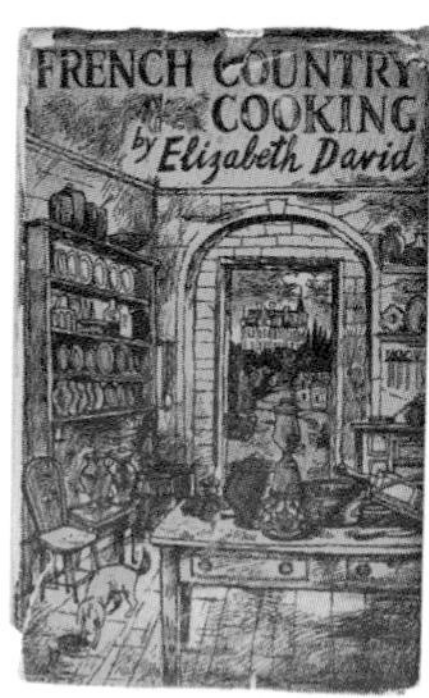

Elizabeth David, *French Country Cooking*, published by John Lehmann, London, first edition, 1951, 8 x 5½in (20.5 x 14cm).

$115–130 BIB

Elizabeth David (1913–92) was one of the first modern food writers to view food as both nourishing and enjoyable to eat. Her recipes reflect the use of good simple fresh foods, properly seasoned and beautifully presented. She started writing in 1946, focusing on the food she had cooked and eaten using local ingredients while living and travelling in Europe and the Mediterranean. Her titles reflect this interest: French Country Cooking, French Provincial Cooking, Italian Cooking, Spices, Salt and Aromatics in the English Kitchen *and* Bread and Yeast Cookery. Harvest of the Cold Months *was published posthumously. David was a Fellow of the Royal Society of Literature and among her many honours are the OBE, presented in 1976.*

McDougall's Cookery Book, 1950s, 7in (18cm) high.

$5–10 DaM

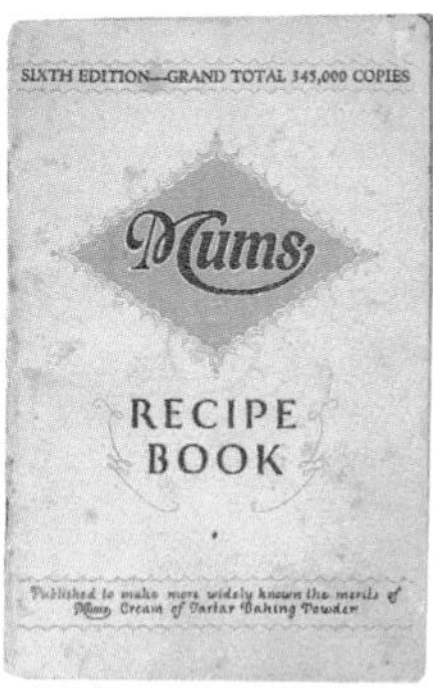

Mums Recipe Book, sixth edition, Australia, 1950s, 7in (18cm) high.

$5–10 DaM

A set of Cadbury's Bournville Chocolate recipe cards, c1970, 6in (15cm) wide.

$10–15 M&C

Sharon Cadwallader and Judi Ohr, *Whole Earth Cookbook*, published by Penguin Books and André Deutsch, 1973, 7in (18cm) high.

$10–15 LBM

In the 1970s there was a drive to educate consumers about the importance of responsible farming and healthy eating. The natural food movement is a term for a style of eating that became popular in America and western Europe that included avoiding artificial ingredients and processed foods. Whole Earth Cookery emphasizes the consumption of fresh fruits and vegetables and the use of whole grains. Continued interest in nutrition, coupled with a respect for maintaining the resources of the planet, have resulted in the collecting and re-issuing of cookbooks with a healthy theme.

► Anna Paziena, *Cooking Broccoli and Cauliflower*, c1970, 4½in (11.5cm) high.

$5–10 LBM

BOTTLES

A glass Stafford's Ink bottle, America, c1870, 7in (18cm) high.

$5–10 OIA

▶ **A glass Codd bottle,** embossed 'A. Poore & Son, Andover', c1880, 9in (23cm) high.

$35–40 OIA

Codd bottles take their name from Suffolk-born Hiram Codd (1830–87) who, c1870, designed and patented a system for keeping fizzy drinks in bottles with a glass marble stopper. When the bottle is filled, pressure in the bottle keeps the marble against a rubber washer at the top making a seal. To open the bottle, the marble had to be pressed down into the neck chamber. The Codd bottle was very successful across Europe and throughout the British Empire and was used until about 1930.

A London glass beer bottle, 19thC, 7in (18cm) high.

$20–25 BoC

A glass grape storage bottle, embossed 'Copped Hall', c1910, 12in (30.5cm) long.

$90–100 HOP

▶ **A glass bottle,** embossed 'Cheltenham Natural Aperient Water', c1910, 11in (28cm) high.

$10–15 OIA

GINGER BEER BOTTLES

A stoneware ginger beer bottle, with a transfer-printed label, c1920, 7in (18cm) high.

$35–40 OIA

A stoneware ginger beer bottle, with a transfer-printed label, c1920, 7½in (19cm) high.

$35–40 JAM

A stoneware ginger beer bottle, impressed 'Schweppes to H. M. King', 1920–30, 6¾in (17cm) high.

$20–25 JAM

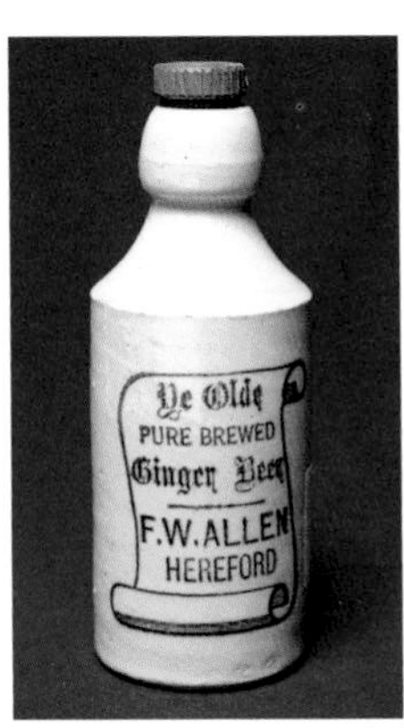

A stoneware ginger beer bottle, with a transfer-printed label, c1920, 7in (18cm) high.

$20–25 JAM

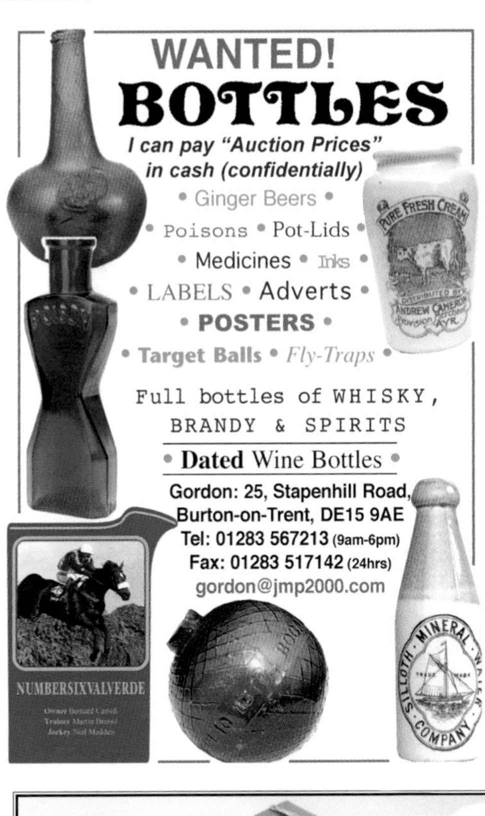
WANTED!
BOTTLES
I can pay "Auction Prices" in cash (confidentially)
• Ginger Beers •
• Poisons • Pot-Lids •
• Medicines • Inks •
• LABELS • Adverts •
• POSTERS •
• Target Balls • Fly-Traps •
Full bottles of WHISKY, BRANDY & SPIRITS
• Dated Wine Bottles •
Gordon: 25, Stapenhill Road, Burton-on-Trent, DE15 9AE
Tel: 01283 567213 (9am-6pm)
Fax: 01283 517142 (24hrs)
gordon@jmp2000.com
NUMBERSIXVALVERDE
PURE FRESH CREAM
ANDREW CAMERON
AYR
SILLOTH MINERAL WATER COMPANY

PUB-JUGS
BREWERIANA & WHISKY
FOR SALE / WANTED !!!
Send for FREE Pub Jug List!
PRICE GUIDE BOOK for sale
Grand National
Jug Book For Sale
• ADVERTS • Mirrors •
• Labels • GUINNESS •
POSTERS all subjects
Travel, sport, entertainment etc.
• FIGURES etc. •
• Playing Cards •
Full bottles of Whisky, Brandy, Spirits etc
Gordon: 25, Stapenhill Road, Burton-on-Trent, Staffs DE15 9AE
Tel: 01283 567 213 (9am-7pm)
Fax: 01283 517 142 (24hrs)
Email: gordon@jmp2000.com
NUMBERSIXVALVERDE
'BLACK & WHITE'

MILK BOTTLES

A Meredith Dairies glass milk bottle, 1920–50, 8½in (21.5cm) high.

$20–25 ⊞ BS

A Szep's Dairy glass milk bottle, America, Pennsylvania, c1949, 7¼in (18.5cm) high.

$20–25 ⊞ JTB

An Owensboro Dairy Products glass milk bottle, America, Kentucky, 1950s, 9¼in (23.5cm) high.

$25–30 ⊞ JTB

A Daisy Dairy glass milk bottle, 1970s, 8½in (21.5cm) high.

$20–25 ⊞ JTB

• Milk bottles were produced in clear glass. Early manufacturers embossed their bottles using slug plates, which produced a raised lettering 'label'. Next came pyro glazing (paint with fibreglass), popular from the 1940s to the 1960s.

• The early embossed milk bottles in the UK were mostly replaced by those with ACL (applied colour labelling) and one pint advertising bottles (568 ml) of the 1970s and 1980s are now highly collectable and very much in demand.

• Many enthusiasts collect by region, such as bottles from specific UK villages or parishes or US states.

• A bottle that has good graphics as well as the name of the county (or city and state if it is American), has multiple colours and is a specific shape – for example a tall round quart – will fetch a high price.

• A good milk bottle will be clear, have no chips or cracks, be stamped with a date and the pyro will not be scratched; prices range from $1 to $3,000. Please note that care should be taken when trying to clean milk bottles as the glass can be scratched by abrasives.

Jim Call

SODA SYPHONS

◄ **A glass soda syphon,** with a wicker cover, c1900, 13in (33cm) high.

$85–95 ⊞ HO

► **A glass soda syphon,** 1920–30, 13in (33cm) high.

$35–40 ⊞ HO

A glass soda syphon, with a metal syphon holder, 1930s, 6½in (16.5cm) high.

$85–95 ⊞ JAM

BREWERIANA

A brass-bound oak scrumpy jug, 1855, 7½in (19cm) high.

$140–155 ⊞ F&F

Four mahogany and brass spirit seals, c1880, 4in (10cm) high.

$150–170 each ⊞ GAU

A Salamander Brandy advertising card, 1920, 16in (40.5cm) high.

$220–250 ⊞ Do

◄ A Royal Doulton Sandeman ashtray, 1930s, 3in (7.5cm) high.

$85–95 ⊞ BS

► A glass Suze carafe, 1930, 8in (20.5cm) high.

$20–25 ⊞ HUX

◄ A celluloid Sportsman Gin sign, 1930s, 12 x 9in (30.5 x 23cm).

$310–350 ⊞ MURR

► A ceramic Casanis water jug, 1950s, 7in (18cm) high.

$50–55 ⊞ HUX

A Recipe glass cocktail shaker, 1950s, 8in (20.5cm) high.

$20–25 ⊞ UD

A Babycham clock, 1970s, 12 x 10in (30.5 x 25.5cm).

$200–220 ⊞ MURR

Babycham, the sparkling alcoholic drink made from pears, was first developed in the 1940s by Francis Showering in Shepton Mallet, Somerset, where it is still in production today.

An Embassy glass Cocktail Bar set, 1950s, in original box, 16in (40.5cm) wide.

$25–30 ⊞ UD

BEER

A copper public house sign, inscribed 'Farmer's Arms', in a brass frame, c1890, 44 x 30in (112 x 76cm).

$1,450–1,600 PICA

◄ **A wooden public house sign,** inscribed 'The George', c1900, in a wooden frame, 42 x 36in (106.5 x 91.5cm).

$430–480 PICA

A Geo. Younger & Sons Pale & Mild Ales advertising mirror, by Forrest & Sons, Scotland, c1900, in an oak frame, 36in (91.5cm) wide.

$950–1,050 GEO

◄ **An Usher's Pale Ale advertising mirror,** Scotland, 1900s, in a mahogany frame, 36in (91.5cm) wide.

$1,900–2,100 GEO

◄ **An Anheuser-Busch Brewing Association Budweiser Girl printed cardboard sign,** by Kaufmann & Strauss Co, America, c1907, in an oak frame, 38½ x 23in (98 x 58.5cm).

$2,300–2,600 JDJ

The Anheuser-Busch advertising campaign in the late 1800s featured a series of girls holding a bottle of Budweiser beer. The campaign began with a girl in pink but her appearance changed in 1907 when Budweiser introduced a girl with a red dress and a different hairstyle.

A wooden public house sign, inscribed 'The Green Man' and 'Old Green Man', c1920, in a wooden frame, 40 x 42in (101.5 x 106.5cm).

$410–460 PICA

A Rhymney Brewery wooden figure, in the form of a huntsman on a hobby horse, 1920–30, 14½in (37cm) wide.

$160–190 BWL

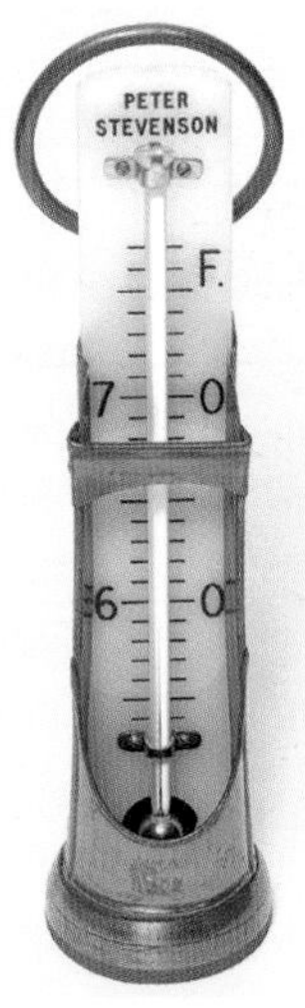

► **A Peter Stevenson brass and copper mercury brewery thermometer,** 1950, 11in (28cm) high.

$25–30 ET

A Beck's Beer ceramic ashtray, Germany, 1950s, 4in (10cm) diam.

$10–15 HUX

GUINNESS

A Guinness advertising plaque, inscribed 'Guinness is good for you', 1930s, framed and glazed, 20 x 11in (51 x 28cm).

$350–420 BWL

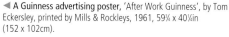

A Guinness printed advertising sign, 'Opening Time is Guinness Time', by John Gilroy, printed by Sanders Phillips, 1952, 30 x 40¼in (76 x 102cm).

$660–780 ONS

Two packs of Guinness playing cards, c1960, 3½in (9cm) high.

$20–25 M&C

◄ **A Guinness advertising poster,** 'After Work Guinness', by Tom Eckersley, printed by Mills & Rockleys, 1961, 59¾ x 40¼in (152 x 102cm).

$520–620 ONS

A set of four Wade Guinness peanut dishes, in a Christmas presentation box, c1962, 12in (24cm) square.

$540–600 MURR

A Carlton Ware Guinness model of a penguin, 'Draught Guinness', c1964, 3¾in (9.5cm) high.

$175–210 BBR

Carlton produced a range of Guinness-related items in the 1960s including toucans and small animal figures.

A Wade Guinness plate, inscribed 'Sam Weller Composing his Valentine. From an illustration by Phiz which includes a contemporary Guinness advertisement', 1960s, 10in (25.5cm) diam.

$110–125 MURR

Hablot Knight Browne, also known as Phiz, was a famous English artist during the 19th century. He illustrated some of the best-known books by Charles Dickens, Charles Lever and Harrison Ainsworth.

A Guinness three-handled commemorative mug, with Licensed Victualler's School shield, c1983, 5½in (14cm) diam.

$120–135 M&C

The Society of Licensed Victuallers was a charity whose remit was the charitable support of the young, elderly and sick within the licensed drinks industry. To support the children of those working in the trade, the Licensed Victualler's School was founded in Kennington in Lambeth in 1803 and subsequently moved to Ascot where it is still active today.

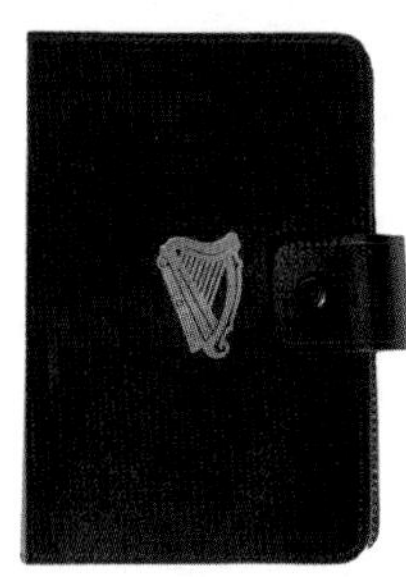

A Guinness leather Filofax, 1988, 6in (15cm) high.

$20–25 M&C

WHISKY

A Case's B Blend Special Scotch Whisky advertising mirror, 1900–10, 2½ x 1¼in (6.5 x 3cm), framed.

$430–480 MURR

A Glenfiddich Whisky ceramic jug, 1960s, 5½in (14cm) high.

$25–30 HUX

A Royal Doulton John Dewar & Sons whisky jug, decorated with hunting motifs, 7in (18cm) high.

$280–310 OD

◄ A Dandie Dinmont Special Blended Scotch Whisky ceramic jug, transfer-printed, Scotland, 1920s, 8in (20.5cm) high.

$280–330 BBR

A Johnnie Walker Scotch Whisky glass ashtray, 1950s, 4in (10cm) square.

$10–15 HUX

A King George IV Old Scotch Whisky ceramic water jug, 1920s, 6½in (16.5cm) high.

$150–165 MURR

A Johnnie Walker Scotch Whisky ceramic water jug, 1930, 7in (18cm) high.

$310–350 HUX

John Walker developed his famous brand of blended Scotch Whisky in 1820 in the west of Scotland. The famous Johnnie Walker striding man was first drawn by popular cartoonist Tom Browne, and has been redrawn over the years by a succession of leading artists such as Basil Partridge, Leo Cheney, Clive Upton and Michael Peters.

◄ A Royal Doulton Jim Beam Whiskey character jug, by Harry Sales, in the form of Mr Pickwick, 1984, 4in (10cm) high.

$35–45 BBR

Jacob Beam sold his first barrel of 'Old Jake Beam Sour Mash' in 1795 in Kentucky, US. The recipe has been handed down through the Beam family generations and the company filled its nine-millionth barrel of Jim Beam Whiskey in 2002. Production continues today.

CAMERAS

FOLDING CAMERAS

A Kodak No. 3 Kodet folding teak and brass camera, 1896, 10¼in (26cm) wide.

$630–700 ⊞ **OACC**

A Kodak 1A metal and leather camera, with autographic feature, 1914, 8in (20.5cm) high.

$10–15 ⊞ **OACC**

A Certo Dollina II enamel and chrome camera, with rangefinder and focus knob, 1936, 4¾in (12cm) wide.

$140–155 ⊞ **OACC**

35MM CAMERAS

A FED 1 camera, Russia, 1936, 5¼in (13.5cm) wide.

$240–270 ⊞ **APC**

After the Russian Revolution, the Soviet Union focused on becoming self-sufficient at every turn. Imports of Leica cameras ceased in the early 1930s and instead Russian camera firms like FED (derived from the F. E. Dzerzhinsky Labour Commune who made the cameras), based in the Ukraine, concentrated on making high quality copies. Their FED 1 is a direct clone of the Leica II and production ran from 1934 up to about 1955. Around 150,000 pre-war examples like this were made and over 470,000 were made post-war. Fakes of the early cameras do exist so avoid anything that claims to be a special 'Red Army Issue'.

A Zeiss Ikon Contaflex Super Synchro Compur metal and leather camera, with Tessar lens, c1960, 5¼in (13.5cm) wide.

$105–120 ⊞ **OACC**

An Alpha Reflex 9d camera, with fitted Kern-Macro-Switar 50mm f1.8 lens, with E.R. case, c1964.

$760–910 **AG**

At its launch in 1964, this camera's Swiss makers described it as being 'in a class of its own'. On the outside the smooth lines and attractive well-balanced body made it cutting edge at the time. But the key to its innovation was inside. This was one of the first cameras to incorporate a TTL (through the lens) exposure meter.

◀ **A Voigtlander Bessa-T camera,** with rangefinder and Heliar lens, 2001, 5½in (14cm) wide.

$930–1,050 ⊞ **OACC**

ROLL FILM CAMERAS

A Bencini Comet III metal and plastic camera, fixed focus, 3 x 4cm roll film, 1953, 4¼in (11cm) high.

$45–50 ⊞ OACC

A Mamiyaflex C2 metal and leather camera, twin lens reflex, 6 x 6cm film, removable viewing hood, c1958, 6¾in (17cm) high.

$175–195 ⊞ OACC

A Kowa Six camera, single lens reflex, interchangeable lens, viewing hood, c1968, 5in (12cm) high.

$430–480 ⊞ OACC

SUB-MINIATURE CAMERAS

An Ensign Midget model 22 camera, with case, c1935, 2in (5cm) wide.

$95–105 ⊞ APC

A Narciss 16mm metal and plastic camera, single lens reflex, Vega-M-1 lens, 35mm thread, Russia, c1960, 4in (10cm) wide.

$175–195 ⊞ OACC

A Yashica Atoron camera, c1965, 4¼in (11cm) wide.

$50–55 ⊞ APC

- Sub-miniature generally refers to cameras with a film size of less than 35mm.
- Victorian camera enthusiasts were the first to explore the merits of small, unobtrusive 'spy' cameras, made initially for plates and then roll film.
- Around 1905 a pocket watch camera appeared in both the UK (the Ticka), and in the US (the Watch Camera). It was capable of taking 25 pictures measuring just 6¼ x 8¾in (16 x 22mm).
- One sought-after UK sub-miniature is the tiny Bakelite-cased Coronet 'Midget'. Collectors like to have an example of all five colours, with blue being the most desirable.
- The 1930s was a period of ingenuity when one of the most famous names in sub-miniature cameras was born – the Minox. Made in Latvia, it took pictures of 3 x 4¼in (8 x 11mm) on special film cassettes. It was widely used on both sides of the Iron Curtain as a real 'spy' camera and popularized in the 1960s by fictional British agent, James Bond. This is a good camera to collect as the film is still available.
- The small sizes, intriguing shapes and diverse array of accessories make them ideal collectables, which are easy to display.

CERAMICS

CERAMICS ARE THE CORNERSTONE of the collecting world and today's collectors really are spoilt for choice. The range of items is so vast that clever collectors can still seek out a bargain if they are well informed and know where to look. Fads and fashions seem to come and go with their associated increases in price but quality always finds a way of being sought out. The market seems to be controlled by collectors seeking new trends, rather than by dealers or the salerooms.

Online auction sites like eBay are now one of the main sources to find modern collectables. Serious money can be paid for some items, as was proved recently by the sale of a Susie Cooper vase that reached $6,650. In the pre-internet age this would have been the highlight of a London sale but in today's diverse collecting world buyer and seller made direct contact and the vase changed hands. A further consequence of internet sales is that the globe is shrinking and pieces originally intended for home markets are now available to collectors worldwide. Ten years ago, a UK-based collector looking for American ceramics by Raymond Lowey or Eva Zeisel would be required to make annual trips to the USA. Today these are just a click away. I know of at least one collector of Clarice Cliff on the Falkland Islands – an impossibility without the internet.

Auction houses are not losing out by the new technology. The clever ones have a large online presence and see the increased business potential in collectors using their site. Once the smaller relation to the traditional ceramics department, modern-day ceramic collectables are now bringing in rewards for auctioneers who target collectors and take the time to research and market properly. A stunning example of this is the record-breaking hammer price of $22,500 at Bonham's London Sally Tuffin's March of the Penguins vase.

The internet can also flush ceramics out and saturate the market. For instance, prices of the more common pieces of Troika have settled down as a consequence of items that would once have gathered dust at home coming to the market via the home computer. Good Troika still sells well, such as large wheel vases, face masks and plaques, which are still making high prices, but smaller pieces are falling back in value.

For me quality is always paramount, be it of design (essential) or condition (flexible). Yet the market seems to love certain things. Clarice Cliff's ever-popular designs seem to be unstoppable. However, as collectors become more sophisticated they also become more choosy. Condition plays an important part, but so does shape and pattern – get all three right and the big bucks roll in. Clarice Cliff's May Avenue pattern still seems to be a winner with collectors – a recent private sale of a Stamford shape morning set achieved $34,500.

So what will my tips be for the coming year? I think there are still plenty of bargains out there. Colin Melbourne's fantastic designs for Crown Devon and Beswick are massively undervalued, in my opinion. Great examples can be found for under $175 – but for how much longer? John Clappison's Hornsea designs deserve to be more widely appreciated as do Myott's funky hand-painted Art Deco pieces that are gaining popularity (especially as Clarice Cliff gets more expensive). In America, post-war West German ceramics are greatly appreciated. Good examples by Ruscha, Bay Keramik and Scheurich bring decent prices; in the UK they can still be found in charity shops.

Remember that the 1950s are over half a century ago now, a fact that makes later pieces from the '70s, '80s and '90s even more collectable, although still fairly easy to find. Think of when you last saw a wonderful Midwinter studio vase for under $10; well designed and speaking strongly of its period, it is still undervalued.

Steven Moore

ART POTTERY

A C. H. Brannam planter, slight damage, signed, dated 1901, 12½in (32cm) wide.

$140–165 SWO

▶ A C. H. Brannam Bittern jug, c1910, 11in (28cm) high.

$540–600 BKJL

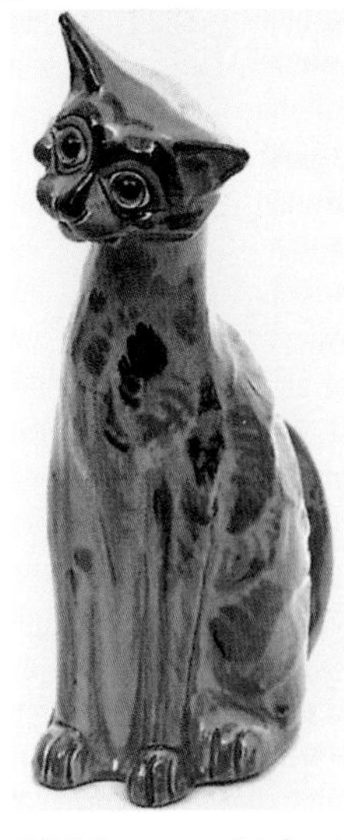

A C. H. Brannam model of a cat, with glass eyes, incised marks, 1911, 13½in (34.5cm) high.

$1,100–1,300 Bea

A C. H. Brannam jug, with cold-painted decoration, 1920–30, 7in (18cm) high.

$45–50 IW

A C. H. Brannam jug, c1928, 10in (25.5cm) high.

$70–80 WAC

A Bretby model of an eagle, c1900, 11in (28cm) high.

$1,100–1,250 HUN

◀ A pair of Bretby jugs, c1885, 9in (23cm) high.

$600–660 HUN

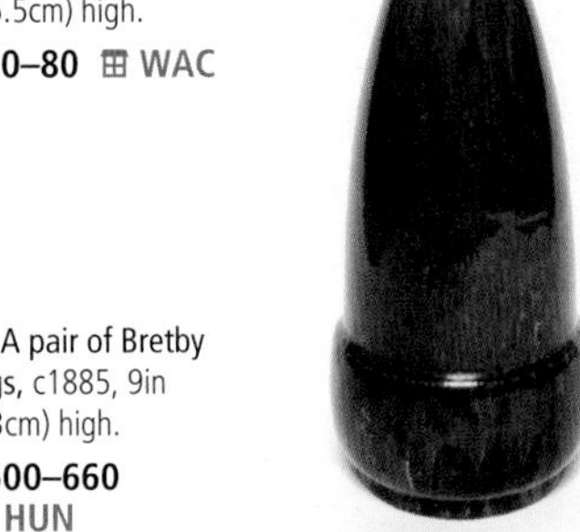

◀ A Bretby vase, c1910, 9½in (24cm) high.

$780–860 HUN

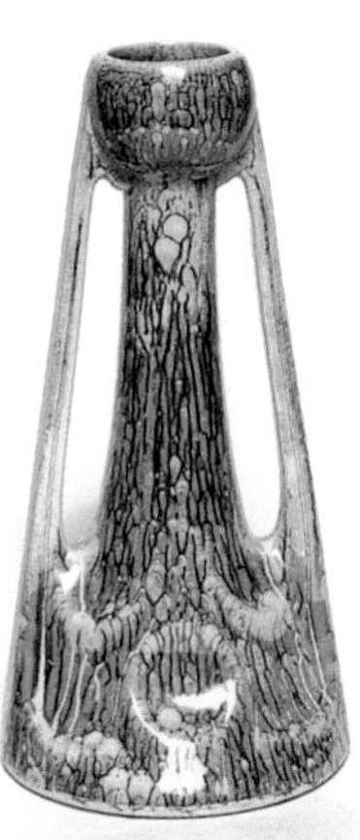

◀ **A pair of Bretby vases,** c1910, 9in (23cm) high.

$600–660 HUN

A Bretby earthenware model of a cat, with cold-painted glaze, 1920s, 9½in (24cm) wide.

$70–80 SAA

▶ **A Bretby figure of Ragged Dick,** 1930s, 9in (23cm) high.

$85–95 HeA

Ragged Dick is the central character in Horatio Alger's book Ragged Dick, *an account of the neglected and abandoned children in mid-19th-century New York, first published in 1866.*

◀ **A Minton Secessionist vase,** designed by Léon Solon, shape No. 42, pattern No. 3547, 1902–14, 5in (12.5cm) high.

$220–250 WAC

▶ **A Newcomb College vase,** by Joseph Fortune Meyer, decorated by Sarah Agnes Estelle Irvine with Flowering Quince pattern, America, signed, 1927, 6in (15cm) high.

$1,300–1,550 NOA

A Newcomb College vase, by Jonathan Browne Hunt, decorated by Sarah Agnes Estelle Irving with Moon and Moss pattern, signed, America, 1932, 5¼in (13.5cm) high.

$1,700–2,000 NOA

A Roseville vase, decorated with Bleeding Heart pattern, shape No. 973, marked, America, early–mid 20thC, 10½in (26.5cm) high.

$220–260 JAA

A Ruskin footed bowl, with soufflé glaze, 1928–29, 3½in (9cm).

$330–370 SAT

BELLEEK

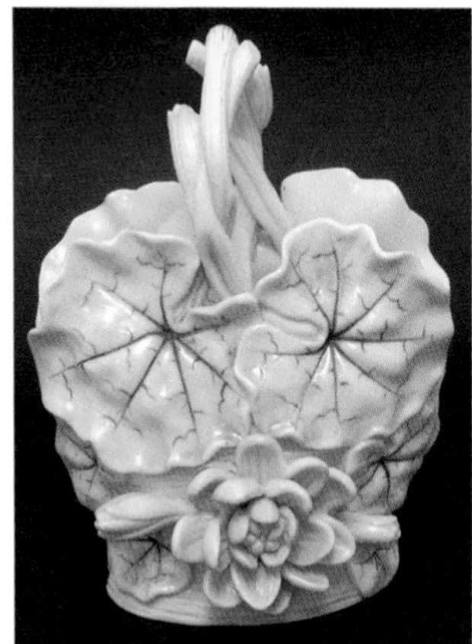

A Belleek **Water Lily basket,** Irish, First Period, 1863–90, 8¼in (21cm) high.

$1,100–1,300 G(L)

A Belleek **Rathmore jardinière,** decorated with flowers and finches, Irish, Second Period, 1891–1926, 10¼in (26cm) diam.

$1,050–1,250 JAd

A Belleek **salt,** in the shape of a shamrock, Second Period, 1891–1926, 3in (7.5cm) wide.

$85–95 SAAC

A Belleek **Aberdeen left-handed jug,** Irish, Third Period, 1926–46, 7½in (19cm) high.

$600–660 DeA

Named after Sir James Campbell Hamilton Gordon, the 7th Earl and 1st Marquis of Aberdeen, these jugs were made both with and without flowers and came in three sizes. Right- and left-handed versions are available and a pair of right- and left-handed jugs is more desirable than a single jug.

A Belleek **Limpet cup, saucer and plate,** Irish, Third Period, 1926–46, plate 7in (18cm) diam.

$200–220 BtoB

A Belleek **Limpet sugar bowl and cream jug,** Irish, Third Period, 1926–46, bowl 5in (12.5cm) diam.

$210–240 BtoB

► A Belleek **Shamrock cream jug,** Irish, Third Period, 1926–46, 10in (25.5cm) diam.

$85–95 BtoB

DATING BELLEEK

The Belleek mark has always contained the same main elements: an Irish harp, a wolfhound and a tower, seated on a scroll with the word Belleek.

First Period: black mark	1863–90
Second Period: black mark	1891–1926
Third Period: black mark	1926–46
Fourth Period: green mark	1946–55
Fifth Period: green mark	1955–65
Sixth Period: green mark	1965–80
Seventh Period: gold mark	1980–92
Eighth Period: blue mark	1993–97
Ninth Period from: blue mark	1997–99

A Belleek Tridacna cream jug, with gilt rim, Irish, Second Period, 1891–1926, 4½in (11.5cm) wide.

$130–145 ⊞ BtoB

A Belleek Limpet bread plate, Irish, Third Period, 1926–46, 10in (25.5cm) diam.

$220–250 ⊞ BtoB

A Belleek cream jug and sugar bowl, c1940, 4in (10cm) high.

$190–210 ⊞ DeA

- Belleek was established in 1857 to produce fine porcelain using local clay.
- Initially pottery was produced, followed by Parian wares from 1863.
- Well modelled Parian busts were produced similar to those made by Goss (where some of the skilled Belleek workers were recruited) and finely modelled glazed Parian wares with intricate flowers and basketwork.
- The finest pieces were produced during the First Period, 1863–90.
- The factory is still in production today.
- Later pieces lack the quality of earlier examples.

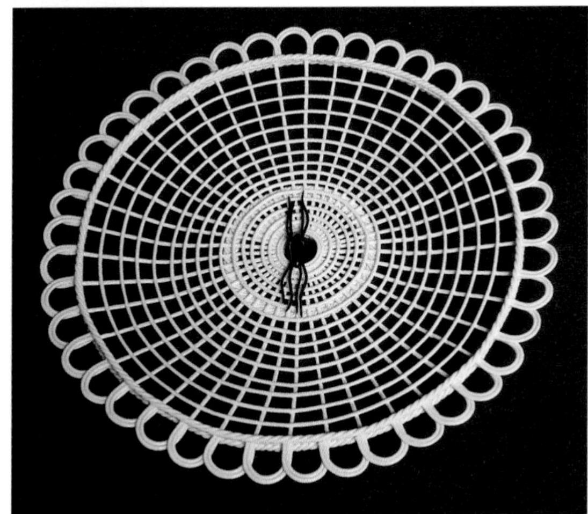

A Belleek wall plaque, in the form of a spider on a web, Irish, 10in (25.5cm) diam.

$3,800–4,200 ⊞ DeA

BESWICK

A Beswick vase, by Mr Symcox, shape No. 30, with satin matt glaze, c1934, 7in (18cm) high.

$45–50 ⊞ WAC

A Beswick wall vase, by James Hayward, shape No. 1063, 1946, 9in (23cm) high.

$90–100 ⊞ HEW

A Beswick jug, by Albert Hallam, shape No. 1367, 1955, 10½in (26.5cm) high.

$35–40 ⊞ RETO

◀ **A Beswick tripod bowl,** designed by Albert Hallam, No. 1387, two legs restored, 1955–62, 4½in (11.5cm) high.

$35–40 ⊞ RETO

Examples of tripod wares are rare, mainly due to the fact that the three legs are easily broken and many damaged items have been thrown away.

A Beswick vase, shape No. 1371, 1955, 6in (15cm) high.

$110–130 ⊞ RETO

A Beswick jug, designed by Albert Hallam, shape No. 1367, 1955–69, 10½in (26.5cm) high.

$175–195 ⊞ RETO

A Beswick vase, designed by Albert Hallam, 1954–62, 6in (15cm) high.

$35–40 ⊞ RETO

A Beswick vase, shape No. 1888, impressed mark, 1963–65, 6in (15cm) high.

$25–30 BBR

◀ **A Beswick vase,** designed by Colin Melbourne, shape No. 1392, 1956–63, 9½in (24cm) high.

$540–600 RETO

A Beswick Ballet preserve pot, designed by Albert Hallam, shape No. 1422, 1965–61, 4in (10cm) high.

$10–15 RETO

COLIN MELBOURNE

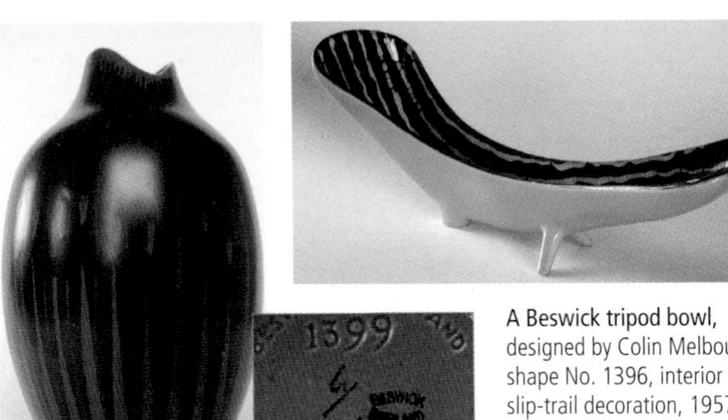

A Beswick vase, designed by Colin Melbourne, shape No. 1399, 1956, 6in (15cm) high.

$85–95 RETO

Colin Melbourne produced some of the most innovative designs of the 1950s and '60s. His work for Beswick is usually marked with a facsimile signature.

A Beswick tripod bowl, designed by Colin Melbourne, shape No. 1396, interior with slip-trail decoration, 1957–63, 10½in (26.5cm) wide.

$60–70 RETO

A W. H. Bossons Bullfight plaque, designed by Colin Melbourne, with hand-painted detail, marked 'Bossons, Bullfight 6', 1959, 9in (23cm) wide.

$115–130 RETO

Bossons, established in Congleton, Cheshire in 1946, are well known for their 'vitreplas' chalk ware face masks, as well as a number of well-designed earthenware items, including this great piece designed by Colin Melbourne.

- Colin Melbourne is one of the most gifted ceramics designers working in post-war Britain.
- His CM series is now highly regarded, but in its time was considered too modern and was not a commercial success.
- Not all the pieces he designed for Beswick have the Colin Melbourne facsimile signature or CM monogram, although they do carry the Beswick mark.
- He also designed for other companies including Bossons, Midwinter, Royal Norfolk and Crown Devon.
- In 1954 he formed a design consultancy with David Queensberry called Drumlanrig Melbourne, and some pieces from this era can still be found.

ARTHUR GREDINGTON

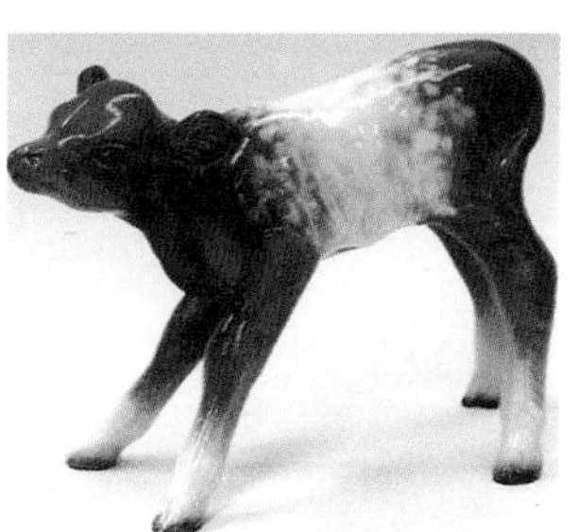

A Beswick model of a Hereford calf, designed by Arthur Gredington, shape No. 854, restored, 1940–57, 4½in (11.5cm) high.

$700–840 BBR

A Beswick model of a blue tit, designed by Arthur Gredington, shape No. 922A, 1943–73, 2¾in (7cm) high.

$35–40 BBR

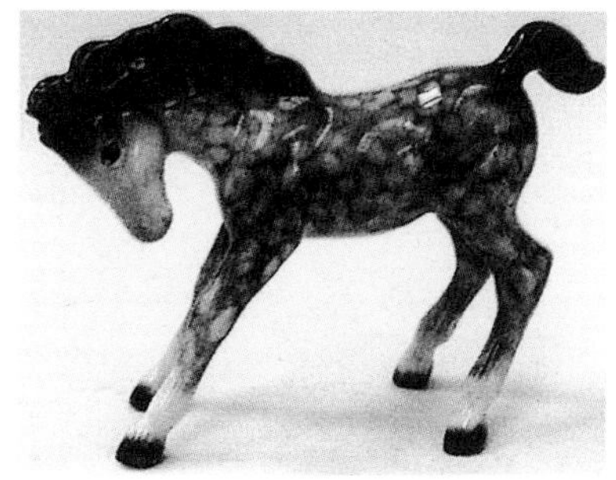

A Beswick model of a foal, by Arthur Gredington, shape No. 1085, 1961–71, 3½in (9cm) high.

$550–650 BBR

- Beswick introduced animal models in 1934, many of the best being modelled by Arthur Gredington.
- Gredington pioneered the use of real champion horses and the best of breeds on which to base designs – these have captured collectors' hearts since the 1930s.
- Many of Gredington's models remain in production – a testament to his skill and popularity.

◄ **A Beswick model of pig,** by Colin Melbourne, shape No. 1473, stamped mark, 1957–66, 5½in (14cm) wide.

$780–860 RETO

A Beswick model of a poodle, 1953, 4½in (11.5cm) high.

$100–110 TASV

► **A Beswick model of a Persian cat,** designed by Albert Hallam, shape No. 1867, 1963–70, 8½in (21.5cm) high.

$70–80 BBR

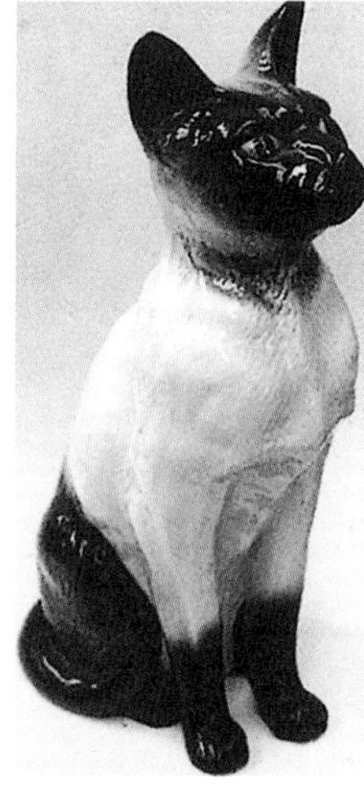

A Beswick model of a Siamese cat, designed by Mr Garbet, shape No. 2139, 1967–1989, 13½in (34.5cm) high.

$85–95 BBR

◀ **A Beswick model of a fox,** designed by Graham Tongue, shape No. 2348, 1970–84, 12¼in (31cm) high.

$470–560 BBR

A Beswick Thelwell group, designed by Harry Sales, entitled 'Kick Start', 1982–89, 3¼in (8.5cm) high.

$175–210 BBR

Although relatively recent, these Thelwell figures are highly collectable.

A Beswick model of Christopher the Guitar Player, designed by Warren Platt, 1996, 5in (12.5cm) high.

$50–55 KA

Originally one of 12 in the Pig Promenade series, Christopher the Guitar Player is relatively common. However, rarer models such as George, Thomas and Benjamin, the last three in the series and issued as limited editions, can be expected to command twice as much the model shown above.

◀ **A Beswick model of Richard the French Horn Player,** designed by Shane Ridge, 1996, 6in (15cm) high.

$50–55 KA

BEATRIX POTTER FIGURES

- Introduced in 1947, many models are still in production.
- Over 130 different models have been produced, early examples being the most collectable.
- Recently retired pieces can still command high prices, especially in the US.
- The rarest model is Duchess With Flowers, a standing dog holding a bouquet of flowers, produced from 1954 to 1967. Unpopular at the time, it now sells for $2,100–2,750.
- Beswick was taken over by Royal Doulton in 1969 and later pieces either mention the Doulton brand or are issued under Royal Albert.
- New figures are marked 'Beswick Ware'.

◀ **A Beswick model of Beatrix Potter's Mr Alderman Ptolmey,** modelled by Graham Tongue, 1973–97, 3½in (9cm) high.

$60–70 BBR

▶ **A Beswick model of Beatrix Potter's Mrs Rabbit,** modelled by Arthur Gredington, 1975–2002, 4in (10cm) high.

$45–50 BBR

◀ **A Royal Albert model of Beatrix Potter's Mrs Tiggywinkle Takes Tea,** c1989, 3in (7.5cm) high, with box.

$45–50 TAC

The Beswick factory was purchased by Royal Doulton in 1989, and from then onwards Beatrix Potter figures were produced with a Royal Albert stamp.

BURLEIGH WARE

A Burleigh Ware vase, by Harold Bennett, with tube-lined decoration, c1935, 5in (12.5cm) high.

$130–145 ⊞ MARK

A Burleigh Ware Pied Piper jug, 1930–35, 8in (20.5cm) high.

$240–270 ⊞ OD

A Burleigh Ware vase, by Harold Bennett, pattern No. 5199, tube-lined with leaves, printed mark, 1926–39, 8in (20.5cm) high.

$25–30 WW

Tube lining is a decorative process where liquid clay is squeezed out of a rubber bag, rather like icing a cake. It leaves raised lines which are often filled in by decoration. It was much used by many factories including Charlotte Rhead and Moorcroft.

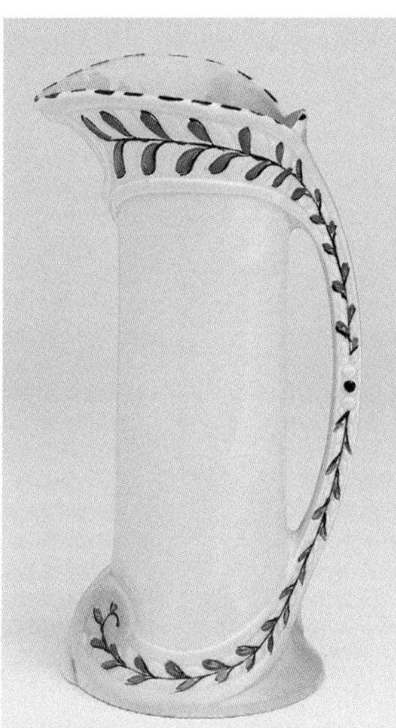

A Burleigh Ware jug, 1930s, 8in (20.5cm) high.

$200–220 ⊞ BEV

◄ **A Burleigh Ware Parrot jug,** 1930s, 9in (23cm) high.

$175–195 ⊞ BEV

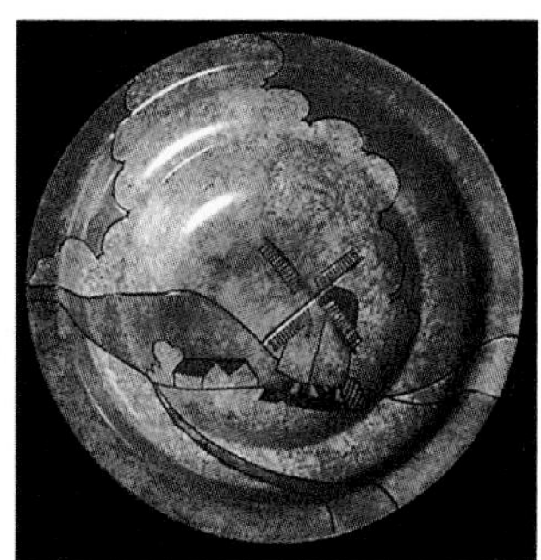

A Burleigh Ware pedestal bowl, by Harold Bennett, tube-lined with a windmill, printed mark, 1926–39, 10¾in (27.5cm) diam.

$155–180 WW

A Burleigh Ware Dragon jug, 1930s, 10in (25.5cm) high.

$130–145 ⊞ OD

A Burleigh Ware Sloth jug, 1930s, 3in (7.5cm) high.

$175–195 ⊞ BEV

A Burleigh Ware Golf jug, 1930s, 9in (23cm) high.

$1,750–1,950 ⊞ **BEV**

◀ A Burleigh Ware Butterflies jug, 1930s, 8in (20.5cm) high.

$600–660 ⊞ **HOM**

A Burleigh Ware Harvest jug, 1930s, 9in (23cm) high.

$150–165 ⊞ **BEV**

A Burleigh Ware vase, designed by Harold Bennett, 1950s, 14in (35.5cm) high.

$35–40 ⊞ **RETO**

A Burleigh Ware vase, designed by Harold Bennett, 1950s, 10½in (26.5cm) high.

$35–40 ⊞ **RETO**

A Burleigh Ware dish, designed by Harold Bennett, 1950s, 10in (25.5cm) wide.

$20–25 ⊞ **RETO**

A set of four Burleigh Ware coffee cups and saucers, c1960, 2½in (6.5cm) diam.

$85–95 ⊞ **KA**

CARLTON WARE

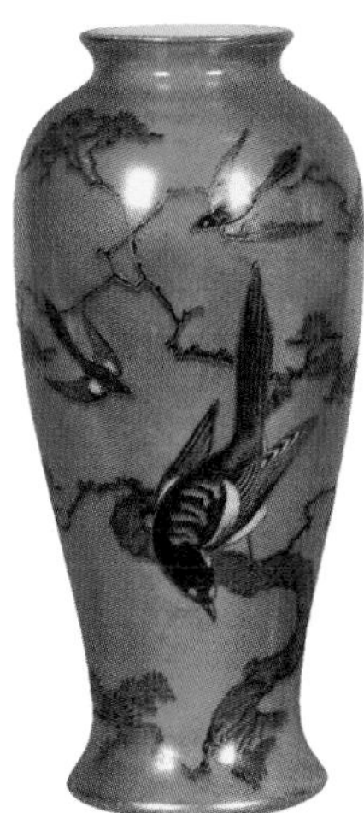

A pair of Carlton Ware vases, decorated with Magpie pattern, No. 2911, stamped mark, 1920–26, 10½in (26.5cm) high.

$300–360 Mit

A pair of Carlton Ware Vert Royale candlesticks, 4in (10cm) high.

$380–420 BEV

A Carlton Ware jam pot, in the form of a pineapple, mid-1920s, 3in (7.5cm) high.

$190–210 BEV

A Carlton Ware bowl, gilded and decorated with Chinese Figures pattern, No. 3199, printed mark, c1930.

$110–130 Mit

A Carlton Ware Velox bowl, decorated with Hollyhocks pattern, No. 3820, on three bun feet, stamped mark, 1935–40, 9¼in (23.5cm) diam.

$280–330 Mit

CARLTON WARE

- The company was founded as Wiltshaw & Robinson in 1890 at the Carlton Works, Stoke-on-Trent.
- Wiltshaw & Robinson became Carlton Ware Ltd in 1958 and the firm continued production until 1992.
- Carlton lustre is highly collectable. Pre-war pieces bring high prices but the post-ware Vert, Rouge and Bleu Royale wares are also making good ground.

A Carlton Ware coffee service, comprising 15 pieces, printed and painted with Nightingale pattern, No. 3562, c1930, coffee pot 8in (20.5cm) high.

$4,500–5,400 BAM(M)

The value of this set lies in its good condition and the fact that it is complete.

A Carlton Ware dish, decorated with Apple Blossom pattern, 1935–61, 9½in (24cm) wide.

$50–55 KA

A Carlton Ware bonbon dish, decorated with Foxglove pattern, 1935–61, 6in (15cm) wide.

$60–70 KA

A Carlton Ware basket, decorated with Waterlily pattern , 1937–38, 11in (28cm) wide.

$330–370 BEV

A Carlton Ware Poppy wall vase, impressed No. 1746, 1939, 10¼in (26cm) high.

$85–100 DA

A Carlton Ware lustre cruet set, 5in (12.5cm) wide.

$140–155 BEV

A Carlton Ware vase, decorated with Sketching Bird pattern, printed and painted marks, 1930s, 5¾in (14.5cm) high.

$220–260 WAD

A Carlton Ware Bleu Royale dish, 9in (23cm) diam.

$95–115 WAD

A Carlton Ware Vert Royale bowl, 9½in (24cm) diam.

$155–185 WAD

A Carlton Ware jug, in the form of a pig, c1950, 10in (25.5cm) high.

$95–105 ⊞ WAC

A Carlton Ware coffee pot, designed by Peter Foster, decorated with Orbit pattern, 1950s, 11in (28cm) high.

$85–95 ⊞ RETO

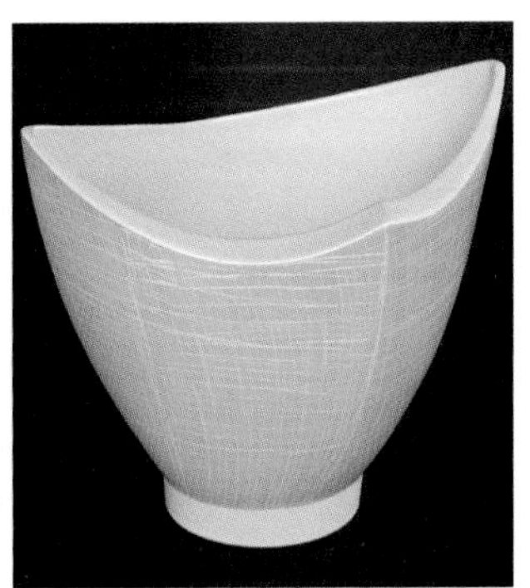

A Carlton Ware vase, sgraffito-decorated with Linen pattern, 1958–59.

$35–40 ⊞ RETO

A Carlton Ware jam pot, in the form of an apple, 1960s, 3in (7.5cm) high.

$90–100 ⊞ BEV

A Carlton Ware money box, in the form of a bird, 1960s, 5½in (14cm) high.

$80–90 ⊞ RETO

► **A Carlton Ware Wellington coffee pot,** early 1970s, 13in (33cm) high.

$45–50 ⊞ UD

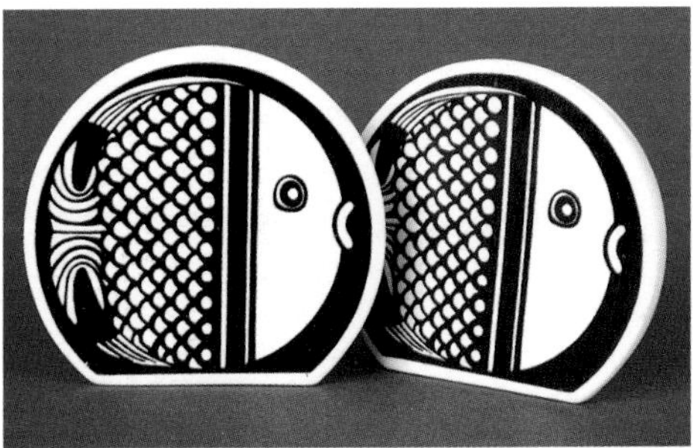

A Carlton Ware cruet set, decorated with fish, c1970, 3in (7.5cm) high.

$30–35 ⊞ RETO

A Carlton Ware cruet set, decorated with cats, c1970, 3in (7.5cm) high.

$30–35 ⊞ RETO

A Carlton Ware jam pot, in the form of a raspberry, 1971–72, 4¾in (12cm) high.

$25–30 ⊞ RETO

A Carlton Ware jam pot, in the form of a blackberry, 1971–72, 4¾in (12cm) high.

$25–30 ⊞ RETO

A Carlton Ware jam pot, in the form of a pineapple, 1971–72, 4¾in (12cm) high.

$25–30 ⊞ RETO

WELLINGTON RANGE

A Carlton Ware Wellington cruet set, 1971, 5in (12.5cm) high.

$10–15 ⊞ RETO

- The Wellington range was introduced in 1971.
- The ribbed and flanged design resembles the electrical insulators on power lines.
- Colours included bright yellow, lime green, orange, brown and white or dark blue with floral patterns.
- Coffee sets, vases and candlesticks are commonly found, but butter dishes are very rare.
- This range was not very popular when first produced.

A pair of Carlton Ware Wellington candlesticks, 1971, 4½in (11.5cm) high.

$20–25 ⊞ RETO

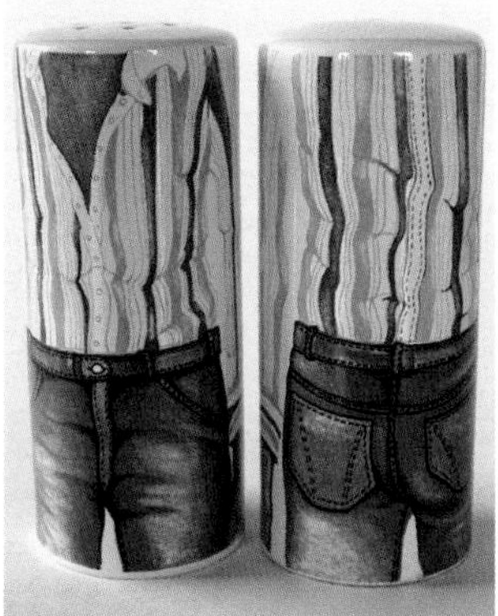

◄ **A Carlton Ware Denim ware cruet set,** c1978, 4in (10cm) high.

$25–30 ⊞ RETO

This range, introduced in 1978, was not a big seller in its day. Its appeal with collectors seems to stem from its ambiguity – whose hand is in whose pocket?

A Carlton Ware cruet set, Bean Bag range, in the form of beans on toast, 1980, 5in (12.5cm) wide.

$60–70 ⊞ RETO

CHINTZ WARE

INSPIRED BY CHINTZ FABRIC DESIGNS, chintz ware incorporates an all-over pattern using a sheet lithographic printing technique. The first modern chintz design, 'Marguerite' was introduced by Royal Winton in 1928 and was quickly followed by many others. Manufacturers to look out for include Royal Winton, Crown Ducal and James Kent. Collectors of chintz pieces are looking for how well the pattern fits the shape and that the print is clean and well defined.

A Crown Ducal Ivory Chintz centrepiece, decorated with Ivory Chintz pattern, 1920s, 10in (25.5cm) diam.

$350–390 BEV

A Crown Ducal sweet dish, decorated with Peony pattern, late 1920s, 7in (18cm) diam.

$200–220 BEV

An Elijah Cotton Lord Nelson Ware butter dish, decorated with Marina pattern, c1930, 6in (15cm) wide.

$210–250 DHA

Lord Nelson Ware was produced by Elijah Cotton. Their wares tend to be chunkier and have less well applied transfers. The undecorated handle seen on this item is a typical feature. Rare patterns such as Black Beauty and Green Tulip are highly sought after, particularly in the USA as they were mainly made for Australia and New Zealand.

A Royal Winton breakfast set, comprising teapot, creamer, sugar bowl, tea cup and tray, decorated with Marguerite pattern, early 20thC, tray 8¾in (22cm) wide.

$190–220 ROS

Introduced in 1928, the Marguerite pattern proved very popular and was in production well into the 1980s.

► **A Royal Winton breakfast set,** comprising teapot, creamer, sugar bowl, tea cup and tray, decorated with Somerset pattern, jug damaged, c1930, tray 10in (25.5cm) wide.

$1,000–1,200 DHA

A Royal Winton bonbon dish, decorated with Marguerite pattern, c1930, 6in (15cm) wide.

$110–130 DHA

A Royal Winton tennis set, decorated with Summertime pattern, 1930s, cup 3in (7.5cm) high.

$105–120 SAT

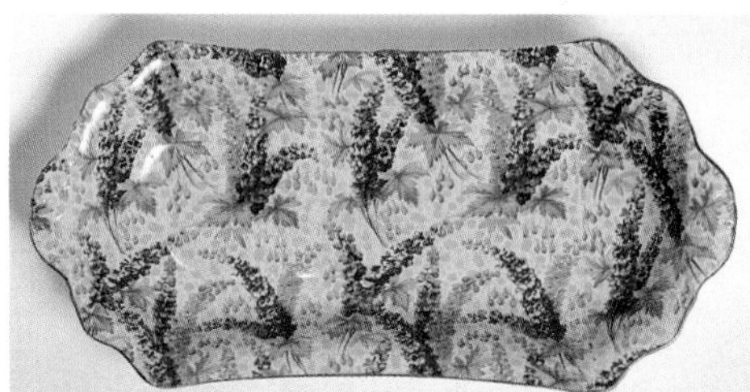

A Royal Winton sweet dish, decorated with Somerset pattern, 1932, 3in (7.5cm) high.

$470–520 BEV

A Royal Winton tennis set, decorated with Kew pattern, c1930, 8in (20.5cm) wide.

$150–180 DHA

A Crown Ducal jam pot, decorated with Du Barry pattern, 1930s, 3¾in (9.5cm) high.

$280–310 BEV

◄ **A Royal Winton sandwich plate,** decorated with Delphinium pattern, 1930s, 11in (28cm) wide.

$155–185 DHA

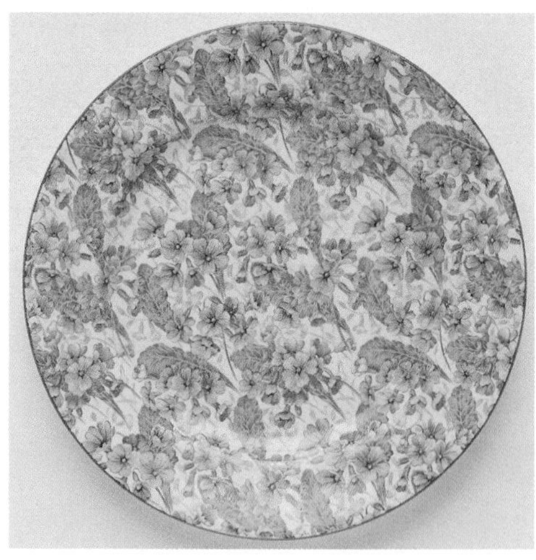

A Crown Ducal plate, decorated with Primrose pattern, 1930s, 3¾in (9.5cm) high.

$150–165 BEV

A Royal Winton teapot, decorated with Hazel pattern, 1934, 5in (12.5cm) high.

$780–860 ⊞ BEV

A Royal Winton nut dish, decorated with Sweet Pea pattern, 1936, 10in (25.5cm) wide.

$310–350 ⊞ BEV

A Royal Winton toast rack, decorated with Richmond pattern, 1938, 7in (18cm) wide.

$260–290 ⊞ BEV

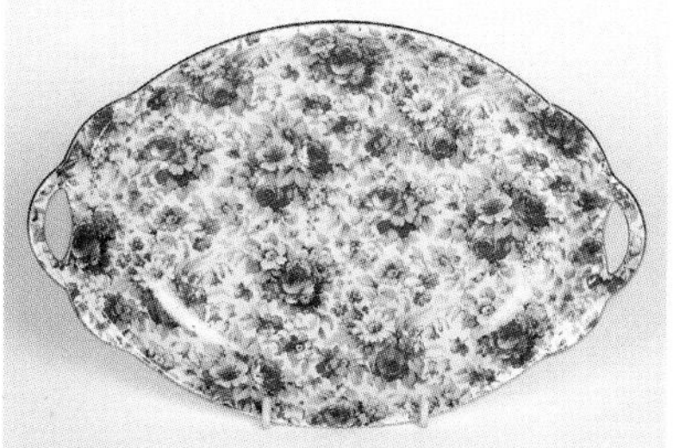

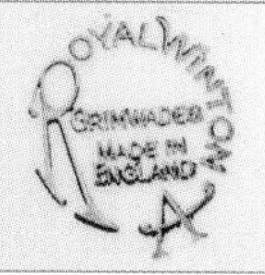

A Royal Winton dish, decorated with Summertime pattern, 1930–40, 10¾in (27.5cm) wide.

$45–50 ⊞ OACC

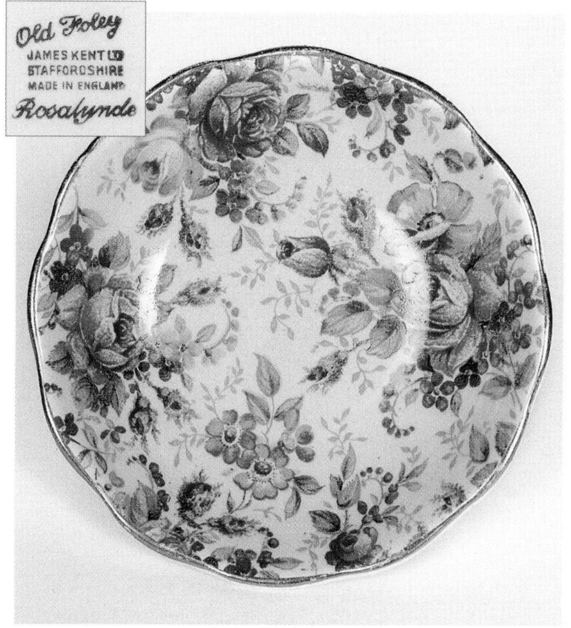

An Old Foley dish, 1950s, 3¼in (8.5cm) diam.

$10–15 ⊞ OACC

► **A Wade vase,** 1970s, 8in (20.5cm) high.

$45–50 ⊞ OACC

CLARICE CLIFF

A Clarice Cliff Fantasque plate, decorated with Trees and House pattern, 1929–30, 8¾in (22cm) diam.

$280–330 HAD

A Clarice Cliff Fantasque tea cup and saucer, decorated with Fruit pattern, c1930, saucer 5½in (12.5cm) diam.

$140–165 WAD

A Clarice Cliff Original Bizarre fern pot, c1930, 4in (10cm) diam.

$260–310 G(L)

A Clarice Cliff Bizarre plate, decorated with Oranges and Lemons pattern, painted marks, 1931, 10in (5.5cm) diam.

$870–1,000 G(L)

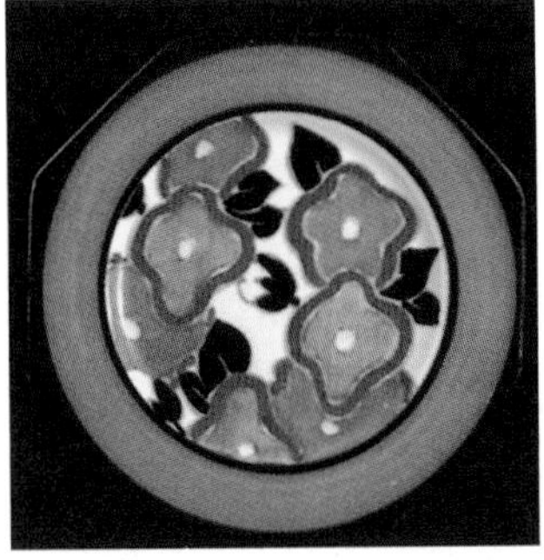

A Clarice Cliff Fantasque Bizarre plate, decorated with Orange Chintz pattern, printed mark, 1932, 7½in (19cm) diam.

$220–260 WW

A Clarice Cliff plate, decorated with Taormina pattern, 1936–37, 9¾in (25cm) diam.

$480–570 HAD

A Clarice Cliff wall medallion, 1932, 13in (33cm) diam.

$250–300 LAY

A Clarice Cliff Athens jug, decorated with Oranges pattern, 1931–32, 8in (20.5cm) high.

$700–840 DA

A Clarice Cliff Athens jug, decorated with Capri pattern, printed mark, 1935–36, 7in (18cm) high.

$400–480 BAM

A Clarice Cliff Fantastique Bizarre vase, decorated with Orange Gardenia pattern, shape No. 341, printed mark, 1931–32, 5¼in (13.5cm) high.

$520–620 N

◀ **A Clarice Cliff vase,** decorated with Rhodanthe pattern, shape No. 452, 1934–41, 8¼in (21cm) high.

$350–420 G(L)

A Clarice Cliff vase, decorated with Umbrellas and Rain pattern, shape No. 362, 1929–30, 8in (20.5cm) high.

$640–760 SPF

◀ **A Clarice Cliff Fantasque bowl,** decorated with Windbells pattern, printed marks, c1930, 8¼in (21cm) diam.

$480–570 CHTR

A Clarice Cliff Fantasque Bizarre cachepot, decorated with Alton pattern, 1934, 4in (10cm) diam.

$165–200 Holl

This pattern was named after the Alton Towers Mansion and Gardens in Staffordshire, which opened in 1880.

A Clarice Cliff Bizarre bowl, decorated with Summerhouse pattern on a Café-au-Lait ground, 1931–33, 8¾in (22cm) diam.

$165–200 HAD

◀ **A Clarice Cliff vase,** decorated with Gardenia pattern, shape No. 279, 1931–32, 8in (20.5cm) high.

$950–1,100 BWL

▶ **A Clarice Cliff Bizarre Stamford jardinière,** decorated with Nasturtium pattern, on a Café-au-Lait ground, printed marks, 1932–40, 6¼in (16cm) high.

$400–480 Bea

A Clarice Cliff Bizarre honey pot, decorated with Crocus pattern, 1928–63, 3in (7.5cm) high.

$230–260 HUM

A Clarice Cliff honey pot, decorated with Gayday pattern, 1930–34, 9in (23cm) diam.

$350–420 G(B)

A Clarice Cliff Lynton honey pot, decorated with Honeydew pattern, 1935–36, 4½in (11.5cm) high.

$380–420 HUM

MILLER'S COMPARES

(L) A Clarice Cliff Conical sugar sifter, decorated with Capri pattern, marked, 1933–34, 5¾in (14.5cm) high.

$550–650 G(B)

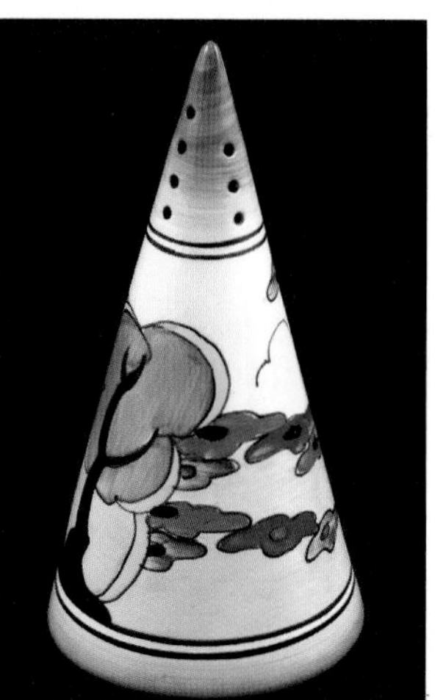

(R) A Clarice Cliff Bizarre Conical sugar sifter, decorated with Erin pattern, printed marks, 1933–34, 5½in (14cm) high.

$1,400–1,650 G(L)

Clarice Cliff Conical sugar sifters are archetypal of the Art Deco period and highly prized by collectors. However, the more desirable the painted pattern, the higher the price. The sugar sifter on the left is decorated with Capri pattern in the green colourway, which is a rather fussy design with muted colours, which are less popular. The item on the right, however, is decorated with Erin pattern in the green colourway which is far more typical of the Art Deco period. With its clear design and bright colours it achieved a substantially higher price than the item on the left.

A Clarice Cliff Bizarre coffee pot, decorated with Secrets pattern, damaged, 1933–37, 7¾in (19.5cm) high.

$410–490 HAD

Had this coffee pot been in good condition it could have made $350–500 more. However, a rarer pattern in this shape could achieve over $1,700 in perfect condition.

A Clarice Cliff teapot, in the form of a rooster, late 1930s, 7in (18cm) high.

$380–420 BEV

A Clarice Cliff teapot, decorated with Harvest pattern, printed marks, 1937–41, 6½in (16.5cm) high.

$175–200 PF

This design was introduced in 1937 and seen with a black printed mark up until 1941 after which the green mark was used.

A Clarice Cliff jug, c1932, 6in (15cm) high.

$1,000–1,100 HEW

A Clarice Cliff Bon Jour tea service, comprising four pieces, decorated with Rhodanthe pattern, 1934–41, teapot 5¼in (13.5cm) high.

$830–990 MA&I

Introduced in 1933, this shape was based on the work of French designer Jean Tetard, who also provided the inspiration for Stamford and Biarritz.

► **A Clarice Cliff cake stand,** decorated with Celtic Harvest pattern, post-WWII, 8¾in (22cm) diam.

$140–165 G(B)

With rising prices for Clarice Cliff painted wares, the once neglected moulded designs are increasing in value.

A Clarice Cliff model of a sabot, decorated with Crocus pattern, c1930, 5¼in (13.5cm) wide.

$280–330 G(L)

A Clarice Cliff Stamford early morning set, decorated with Sunshine pattern, c1930, teapot 5in (12.5cm) high.

$870–1,000 AH

A Clarice Cliff Bizarre Lynton coffee service, comprising 15 pieces, decorated with Tulip pattern, damaged, c1930.

$780–930 DA

◀ **A Clarice Cliff bowl,** decorated with Opalesque Bruna pattern, shape No. 450, 1934, 4¾in (12cm) high.

$140–155 ⊞ ROS

A **Clarice Cliff cake stand,** decorated with Applique Idyll pattern, 1931–36, 10¼in (26cm) high.

$250–280 ⊞ ROS

▶ **A matched Clarice Cliff coffee service,** decorated with Autumn Crocus pattern, with two Windsor coffee pots and cream jug, slight damage, 1930s.

$830–990 Bea

A Clarice Cliff Original Bizarre ginger jar, cover missing, c1930, 7¼in (18.5cm) high.

$45–50 ⊞ ROS

COLLECTING CROCUS

A Clarice Cliff honey pot, decorated with Crocus pattern, 1930s, 4½in (11.5cm) high.

$240–270 ⊞ TASV

A Clarice Cliff water jug, decorated with Crocus pattern, Royal Staffordshire mark, post-WWII, 3½in (9cm) high.

$300–330 ⊞ TASV

A Clarice Cliff water jug, decorated with Crocus pattern, 1930s, 4in (10cm) high.

$380–420 ⊞ TAC

- In 1928 Clarice Cliff wanted to introduce a floral design into her Bizarre range. Her first choice, a painted lupin design, proved too complex to reproduce and was abandoned.
- The Autumn Crocus pattern began when John Butler, Cliff's mentor at Wilkinson's Pottery, taught her the simple strokes needed to produce an orange, blue or purple crocus-like flower with thin green 'flicks' to represent leaves. A brown band was added symbolizing the earth, with a yellow one above representing the sun.
- Autumn Crocus pattern was easy to mass-produce and remained popular until 1963.
- Other versions exist including Blue and Purple Crocus, produced from 1935.
- Spring Crocus incorporated pink, yellow and blue flowers and was in production from 1933 to 1963.
- Sungleam Crocus incorporated orange and yellow flowers and was in production from 1931 to 1934.
- Awakening is a rare design which incorporates a silhouette of a tree and rabbits against a miniature version of Autumn Crocus. Introduced in 1930, it was soon discontinued due to poor sales.

CONTINENTAL

BOCH FRÈRES

◄ **A Boch Frères vase,** Belgium, c1910, 7in (18cm) high.

$95–115 WAD

► **A Boch Frères vase,** Belgium, c1910, 7in (18cm) high.

$270–300 MARK

This vase illustrates the cloisonné technique much used at the Boch Frères pottery. The pattern is cut through the glaze to form cells which are filled with enamel colour and then fired. The best examples have many colours, all fired at different temperatures.

- Originally founded in Luxemburg in 1841, Boch Frères was re-established in Belgium at La Louvière in 1844.
- They produced stunning Art Deco ceramics, many designed by Charles Catteau (active 1922–45) whose facsimile signature can be found on his designs.
- Items are highly collectable with good examples achieving four-figure sums, especially in the USA.
- Boch Frères pieces are collected by the Belgian Royal Family.
- The 'Keramis' mark introduced in 1927 is often associated with the best Art Deco period pieces.

► **A pottery bust of a woman,** slight damage, impressed marks, Czechoslovakia, c1920, 10½in (26.5cm) high.

$140–165 WAD

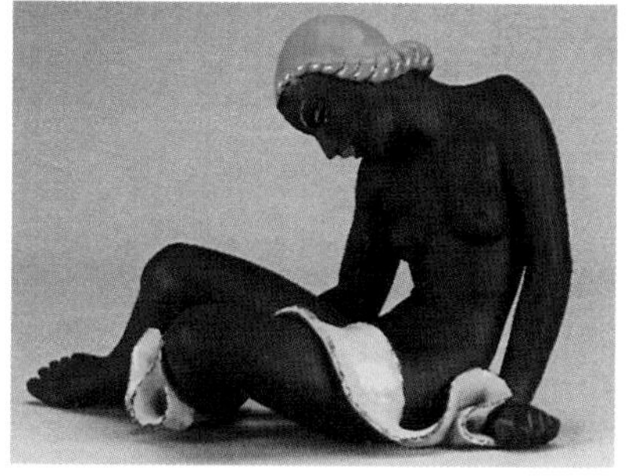

A terracotta figure of a woman, slight damage, impressed marks, Czechoslovakia, 1950s, 10½in (26.5cm) high.

$280–330 WAD

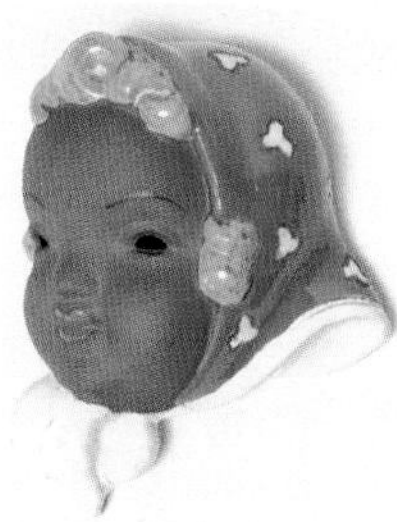

A pottery terracotta wall mask, Czechoslovakia, 1930s, 8in (20.5cm) high.

$95–105 WAC

► **A Ditmar Urbach jug,** in the form of a cockerel, Czechoslovakia, c1925, 10in (25.5cm) high.

$130–145 LLD

► **A Ditmar Urbach jug,** Czechoslovakia, c1925, 6in (15cm) high.

$60–70 LLD

A Dresden figure of a young woman with a basket of flowers, Germany, c1930, 7in (18cm) high.

$130–145 MRA

A pair of Dresden figures, Germany, c1940, 9in (23cm) high.

$300–330 MRA

A Goldscheider group of two foals, factory marks, impressed 'Melsner', Austrian, 1930s, 9in (23cm) high.

$180–200 ROS

A pair of Gouda vases and covers, Holland, 1910, 12in (30.5cm) high.

$3,300–3,600 CARA

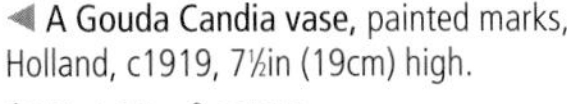

◀ **A Gouda Candia vase,** painted marks, Holland, c1919, 7½in (19cm) high.

$95–115 WAD

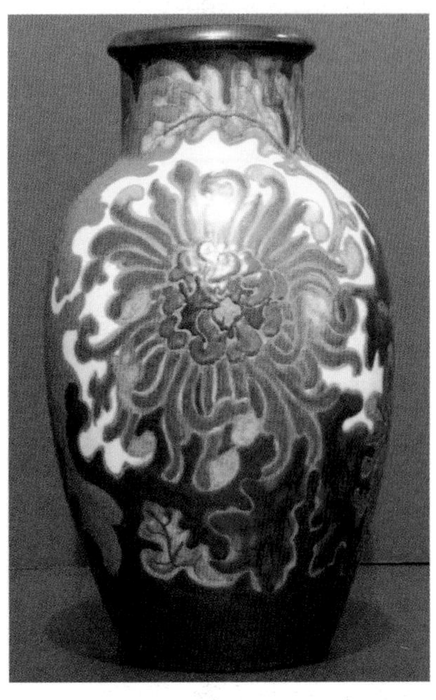

A Gouda Amphora vase, Holland, c1920, 10in (25.5cm) high.

$1,100–1,250 CARA

A Gouda Lody vase, painted marks, Holland, c1928, 12½in (32cm) high.

$230–270 WAD

A Gouda Auwet jug, painted marks, Holland, c1928, 8in (20.5cm) high.

$95–115 WAD

A pair of Gouda Imans chambersticks, painted marks, Holland, c1928, 7in (18cm) high.

$220–260 WAD

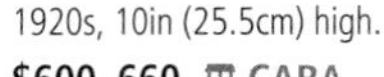

A Gouda vase, Holland, Schoonhoven, 1920s, 10in (25.5cm) high.

$600–660 ⊞ CARA

A Gouda Anjer pot, Holland, 1920s, 4in (10cm) high.

$220–250 ⊞ CARA

A Lladro figure of a girl, from the Inspiration Millennium range, Spain, 1998, 15¾in (40cm) high.

$240–280 G(B)

A Lladro figure of a ballerina, by Vicente Martínez, entitled 'Death of a Swan', Spain, 1973–91, 9¾in (25cm) long.

$210–240 ⊞ OACC

A Lladro figure of a ballerina, Spain, 1987, 5¼in (13.5cm) high.

$180–200 ⊞ OACC

A Lladro figure of a ballerina, Spain, 1987, 5¼in (13.5cm) high.

$180–200 ⊞ OACC

A Rosenthal model, by T. Karner, entitled 'Squirrel', Germany, c1920, 4in (10cm) high.

$180–200 ⊞ CHO

A Rosenthal figure, by Richard Aigner, entitled 'Spring of Love', Germany, dated 1923, 10in (25.5cm) high.

$620–700 ⊞ CHO

► A Rosenthal group of a woman and a duck, by Ferdinand Liebermann, entitled 'The Two Princesses', Germany, c1940, 5in (12.5cm) high.

$780–860 ⊞ CHO

◄ A Rosenthal model of a fox, Germany, c1940, 16in (40.5cm) high.

$880–970 ⊞ Scot

A Rosenthal group, impressed, printed and painted marks, Germany, mid-20thC, 8¼in (21cm) high.

$140–165 WAD

A Rosenthal 25 Jahre Suomi vase, by Timo Sarpaneva, printed marks, Germany, late 20thC, 10½in (26.5cm) high, with a fitted wooden presentation case.

$480–570 WAD

A Royal Dux figural group, impressed and painted marks, Czechoslovakia, c1930, 18¾in (47.5cm) high.

$280–330 WAD

SCHEURICH

- Scheurich Keramik was founded in 1927 by Alois Scheurich as a wholesale firm.
- The business began manufacturing its own products in the late 1950s and became the largest producer of commercial art pottery in Germany.
- Scheurich excelled at producing the type of later wares shown here – some of the most fantastic glazes are associated with them.
- No colour combination seemed off-limits, making these shockingly bright wares totally at home in modern minimalist interiors.
- Where the colours work well and the glazes have reacted in an interesting way the pieces can be stunning; at worst they can look like rejects from the set of *Star Trek*!

A Scheurich vase, with lava glaze, West Germany, 1960s, 12in (30.5cm) high.

$60–70 RETC

A Scheurich handled vase, with lava gaze, West Germany, 1960–70, 8in (20.5cm) high.

$35–40 RETC

A Scheurich floor vase, No. 286–52, West Germany, 1970s, 10in (25.5cm) high.

$155–175 RETC

◄ **A Scheurich vase,** with lava glaze, West Germany, c1970, 13in (33cm) high.

$50–55 RETC

► **A Scheurich vase,** with lava glaze and handle, West Germany, 1970s, 10in (25.5cm) high.

$35–40 RETC

A Volkstedt figure of a cherub, Germany, c1920, 5in (12.5cm) high.

$270–300 ⊞ OAK

A Karl Ens, Volkstedt model of a dog, Germany, c1930, 6in (15cm) high.

$140–155 ⊞ EAn

◄ A Karl Ens, Volkstedt figure of a child, Germany 1930s, 6in (15cm) high.

$700–770 ⊞ EAn

A Karl Ens, Volkstedt figure of a child, Germany, 1930s, 6in (15cm) high.

$850–940 ⊞ EAn

The Karl Ens factory in Volkstedt was founded in 1890 in what was later to become East Germany. The Government became a shareholder in 1959 and it managed to continue until 1972 when it was fully nationalized. It was known for producing charming figures and bird models.

A figure of a girl, signed 'Volkhov & Morjantseva', Russia, dated 1924, 8in (20.5cm) high.

$4,150–4,950 G(L)

ZSOLNAY PECS

A Zsolnay Pecs model of a dachschund, Hungary, c1950, 5in (12.5cm) long.

$165–185 ⊞ DSG

► A Zsolnay Pecs model of an owl, Hungary, c1950, 3in (7.5cm) high.

$110–120 ⊞ DSG

- The firm was founded in 1851 and is still in production.
- It became famous for its gold-based eosin lustre glazes introduced from 1891, giving the effect of metal.
- Initially Zoslnay Pecs struggled under communism but flourished again in the 1950s.

SUSIE COOPER

SUSIE COOPER (1902–95) was unique; a determined and highly skilled designer, she was so frustrated with the restrictions of designing for someone else that she set up her own factory. After being granted a scholarship in 1919 she studied for three years at Burslem School of Art. In 1922 she joined Gray's pottery, where she began as a paintress, rising quickly to designer; she summed up her style as 'elegance with utility'. Some of the items produced at Gray's bear the mark 'designed by Susie Cooper'.

In 1929 she left secure employment to establish her own factory called The Susie Cooper Pottery. As with Gray's, she began by buying in blank wares to be decorated, but from 1931 she designed her own shapes, which were made at Woods pottery, next door. Her first mark is the rarely seen 'triangle' mark used from 1929–31 with the simple words 'A Susie Cooper production'. This was followed in 1932 by a lithographed mark of a leaping stag, used until just after WWII. Many items bear her signature, which denotes that she designed, but did not necessarily decorate, the pieces. From 1950 she designed new shapes for production in bone china and in 1966 her firm was taken over by Wedgwood.

Susie Cooper's work has never achieved the large sums attracted by Clarice Cliff pieces, but recently a large vase dating to c1932 and hand-painted with a hunter stalking an ibex, sold for $6,650 on a well-known internet auction site.

A Susie Cooper chamberstick, decorated with Cubist pattern, 1929–30, 5in (12.5cm) diam.

$380–420 ⊞ BEV

A Susie Cooper sandwich tray, decorated with Homestead pattern, 1931–32, 5in (12.5cm) diam.

$310–350 ⊞ BEV

A Susie Cooper vase, carved with tulips, signed and dated 1932, 5¼in (13.5cm) high.

$175–210 PFK

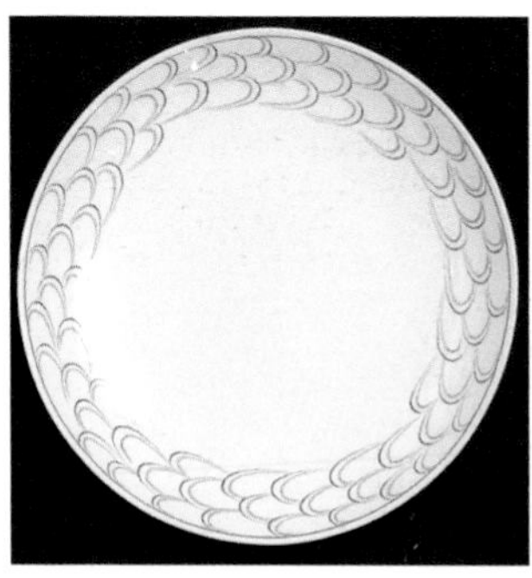

A Susie Cooper plate, decorated with Crayon Loop pattern, c1936, 9in (23cm) diam.

$70–80 ⊞ BEV

Susie Cooper was always looking for new techniques. When she saw her kiln workers using a solid lump of colour to mark trials, she tested it herself and found that by making the solid colour into more manageable 'crayons' many softer looking designs could be produced.

◄ **A Susie Cooper teapot,** triangle mark, c1930, 7in (18cm) wide.

$1,000–1,100 ⊞ BEV

A Susie Cooper plate, decorated with Patricia Rose pattern, c1930, 8in (20.5cm) diam.

$50–55 ⊞ BEV

A Susie Cooper cheese dish, decorated with Gentian pattern, 1930s, 8in (20.5cm) wide.

$50–55 ⊞ HO

PEGGY DAVIES CERAMICS

INCORPORATING

Francis

Tea with Clarice Cliff
Released February
1997. **SOLD OUT**

Young Clarice
SOLD OUT
Issue Price £130.00

Lo La Palooza
Released June '97
SOLD OUT
Issue Price £149.00

Persian Dancer
Issue Price £115.00
SOLD OUT

Susie Cooper
Issue Price £145.00
SOLD OUT

Pyjama Girl
Released November 1998
Issue Price £175.00

D-Day Landings
Limited Edition 750
£147.00

Charlotte Rhead figurine
Limited Edition of 950 worldwide
SOLD OUT
Issue Price £195.00

Approximate average height is 9 inches.

PEGGY DAVIES CERAMICS

Peggy Davies Ceramics, the sole producers of Kevin Francis ware, established by the world renowned ceramic artist Peggy Davies, is at the forefront when it comes to design and quality in the world of Limited Edition, hand crafted, hand painted ceramic art.

Celebrating ten years of producing the world's most intricate pieces in 1997, the Kevin Francis range has become much sought after, so much so that there is now an investment label on these quality items. Our range is being added to approximately four times a year. To join our free register of Collectors for regular brochures, or to find out more about the thriving Kevin Francis Collectors Guild, write, phone or fax Rod Davies or Rhys Davies

Peggy Davies Ceramics
Formerly St Luke's School Lower, Wellington Road, Hanley ST1 3QH
Tel: +44(0)1782 262002 Fax: +44 (0)1782 284681
Email: rhys@peggydavies.com Website: www.peggydavies.com

www.bulldogs.co.uk

A Susie Cooper cup and saucer, decorated with bands and polka dots, c1934, cup 3in (7.5cm) diam.

$110–125 ⊞ BEV

A Susie Cooper cup and saucer, decorated with sgraffito Crescents pattern, 1938, cup 2in (5cm) diam.

$80–90 ⊞ BEV

The sgraffito technique was widely used by Susie Cooper. The design is scratched through a painted layer, revealing the white body underneath.

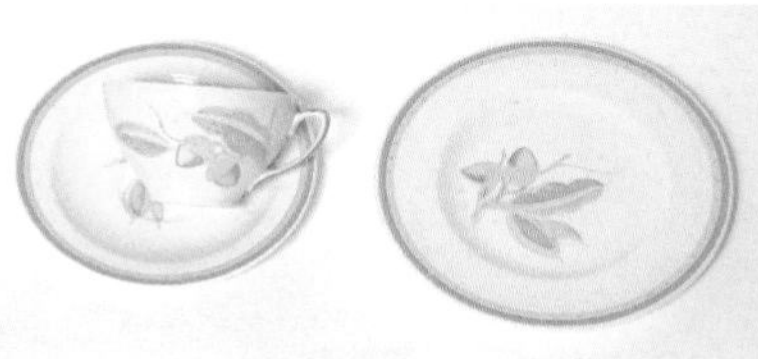

A Susie Cooper cup, saucer and plate, decorated with Acorn pattern, 1930s, plate 7in (18cm) diam.

$45–50 ⊞ UD

A Susie Cooper Kestrel cup, saucer and plate, decorated with Dresden Spray pattern, 1935, saucer 6in (15cm) diam.

$95–105 ⊞ BEV

◄ A Susie Cooper Kestrel tea-for-one set, decorated with Circle and Dash pattern, c1935, teapot 5in (12.5cm) high.

$660–740 ⊞ BEV

A Susie Cooper Kestrel coffee service, comprising 13 pieces, decorated with Nosegay pattern, c1940.

$220–260 G(B)

A Susie Cooper vase, carved with tulips, c1933, 7in (18cm) high.

$50–55 ⊞ OACC

A Susie Cooper vase, 1930s, 8¾in (22cm) high.

$95–105 ⊞ OACC

A Susie Cooper Quail sugar bowl and milk jug, decorated with Carnation pattern, 1960s, jug 4in (10cm) high.

$90–100 ⊞ CHI

► A Wedgwood coffee cup, saucer and side plate, by Susie Cooper, decorated with Applegay pattern, 1964, cup 3in (7.5cm) high.

$80–90 ⊞ CHI

A Wedgwood cup and saucer, designed by Susie Cooper, decorated with Camellia pattern, late 1960s, cup 2in (5cm) diam.

$45–50 ⊞ BEV

The Susie Cooper Pottery was taken over by Wedgwood in 1966 and Camellia is typical of the patterns produced at that time.

COTTAGE WARES

A W. H. Goss model of Ellen Terry's house, c1920, 3in (17.5cm) wide.

$380–420 SAAC

Ellen Alice Terry was a Victorian actress who resided at Smallhythe Place, Tenterden, Kent between 1899 and 1928.

A W. H. Goss model of William Wordsworth's birthplace, c1920, 3in (7.5cm) wide.

$220–250 SAAC

HAZLE CERAMICS

◄ A Hazle Ceramics model of a dress shop, 2001, 3¾in (9.5cm) wide.

$350–390 JEG

This model of a dress shop was issued by Pink Ribbon Crusade, a US breast cancer charity formed to continue the work of Diana, Princess of Wales. It was issued in a limited edition of 500 and was produced by Hazle Ceramics in England. Each house is numbered and signed by the artist.

A Hazle Ceramics model of Painswick Post Office, 1999–2001, 5½in (14cm) wide.

$220–250 JEG

This building in Gloucestershire is thought to be the oldest working Post Office in England.

A Hazle Ceramics model of Bear Necessities, Windsor, artist's sample, 1999–2004, 3¾in (9.5cm) wide.

$230–270 HCE

- Hazle Ceramics produce a popular range of collectable wall plaques called 'A Nation of Shopkeepers'.
- These capture the nostalgia of the British high street with its mixture of architectural styles and bustling activity.
- The plaques can be hung together to create a unique high street.

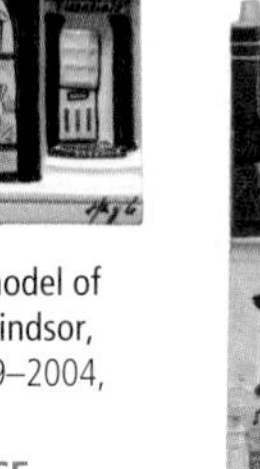

A Hazle Ceramics model of Greensleeves Music shop, original Seaford Edwardian Building mould 1999–2005, limited painting 2004, 3¾in (9.5cm) wide.

$300–360 ROA

A Hazle Ceramics model of an Organic Farmshop, limited edition, 2003, 6½in (16.5cm) wide.

$430–500 ROA

This Organic Farmshop is a limited edition painting on a blank model of Master Saddler, which was in production from 1997 to 2001.

A Lilliput Lane model of Spring Bank Cottage, 1986, 2½in (6.5cm) high, with box.

$25–30 ⊞ KA

Spring Bank Cottage was inspired by the cottages in the hills surrounding Lyme Regis in Dorset. Lilliput Lane models have remained popular but prices have fallen in the last five years.

A Willow Art model of the Old Mint House, c1907, 5in (12.5cm) wide.

$270–300 ⊞ SAAC

The Old Mint House is situated in Pevensey, E Sussex.

◀ **A Willow Art model of Robert Burn's cottage,** 1925–30, 4in (10cm) wide.

$70–80 ⊞ SAAC

A Willow Art model of Shakespeare's house, c1920, 7in (18cm) wide.

$90–100 ⊞ SAAC

DAVID WINTER

- David Winter was born in Yorkshire in 1958.
- In partnership with John Hine, David Winter made his first cottage, The Mill House, in 1979. In the early days production took place in the coal shed at David's parents' house.
- Inspiration came from real buildings and he studied a variety of houses to ensure accuracy on a miniature scale.
- Cottages are particularly sought after in the US and there is an active collector's guild.

A David Winter model of the Architect's House, by Enesco, 1999, 6in (15cm) high.

$80–90 ⊞ BCC

A David Winter model of Pickwick's Parlour, Christmas Cottage Collection, 2004, 7¾in (19.5cm) wide.

$155–175 ⊞ BCC

GOSS & CRESTED CHINA

MILLER'S COMPARES

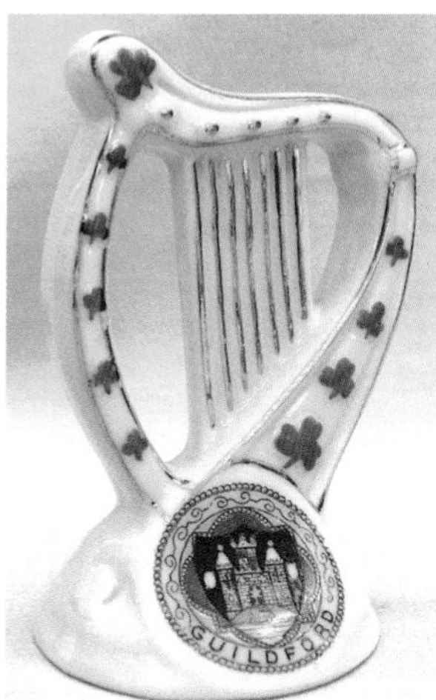

(L) **A Carlton model of an Irish harp,** with Guildford crest, 1902–30, 3¾in (9.5cm) high.

$20–25 G&CC

(R) **A Goss model of a Letchworth cinerary urn,** with Maidenhead crest, 1881–1929, 3¾in (9.5cm) high.

$120–135 G&CC

The ornate Carlton harp on the left might be expected to achieve more than the plainer Goss vase on the right. However, Goss is generally more collectable as it was the first factory to produce crested wares. Carlton was a latecomer to the industry and is less collectable. It is worth looking out for rarer WWI models of tanks, battleships and soldiers by minor factories such as Arcadian and Willow Art which are also very collectable.

An Arcadian model of Beachy Head lighthouse, with Eastbourne crest, c1920, 4in (10cm) high.

$20–25 SAAC

An Arcadian model of a hen, with Ramsgate crest, 1920, 3in (7.5cm) high.

$35–40 SAAC

An Arcadian model of a Sussex pig, with City of London crest, 1920s–30s, 2in (5cm) high.

$10–15 JMC

◄ **An Arcadian model of a guitar,** with Maidstone crest, 1903–33, 6¼in (16cm) high.

$25–30 G&CC

A Carlton model of a basket of fruit, one side decorated with lucky white heather, c1925, 3½in (9cm) high.

$50–55 ⊞ G&CC

A Carlton Pears advertising boy, inscribed 'I'm Forever Blowing Bubbles', with Bournemouth crest, 1902–30, 4¼in (11cm) high.

$50–55 ⊞ G&CC

A Carlton jug, decorated and inscribed 'Lucky White Heather from Worthing', 1920s–30s, 2¼in (5.5cm) high.

$20–25 ⊞ JMC

A Goss model of a melon jug, with Blankenberghe, Belgium, crest, 1900–14, 3¼in (8.5cm) high.

$35–40 ⊞ G&CC

A Goss model of a Welsh leek, with Chichester crest, 1881–1939, 3½in (9cm) high.

$25–30 ⊞ G&CC

A Goss model of an Oxford Ashmolean ewer, with Devon crests, 1880–1920, 5in (12.5cm) high.

$50–55 ⊞ G&CC

◀ **A Goss model of whiskey and soda on a thistle tray,** with Land's End crest, 1920s–30s, 2in (5cm) high.

$70–80 ⊞ G&CC

▶ **A Goss model of a Swiss cow bell with a clapper,** with Paisley crest, 1900–28, 2¾in (7cm) high.

$35–40 ⊞ G&CC

CROWN DEVON

THE STAFFORDSHIRE FIRM S(imon) Fielding & Co began as an investor in pottery rather than a manufacturer. The company ran into difficulties, however, and Abraham Fielding, Simon Fielding's son, paid off the debt and took over the firm in 1879. Originally called the Railway Pottery, it was renamed the Devon Pottery in 1911 and then Crown Devon after a Royal visit in 1913.

Trading until 1986, they produced many quality mid-range goods. Their wares reflected current taste and were similar to designs by other market leaders of the time. Thus when Royal Worcester Blush porcelain was all the rage Fielding's produced similar wares in pottery.

The firm produced majolica wares, most of which were made for export to the US and, as it is seldom seen in the UK, prices are correspondingly high. Good Art Deco lustre pieces were also made. The 'mattajade' ground, launched at the 1932 British Industries Fair was a great success and the Fairy Castle pattern on this ground is highly collectable. Well-made figures were produced too, often modelled by Kathleen Parsons as well as a popular series of musical jugs.

A Crown Devon Sylvan Lustrine Butterflies vase, gold-printed mark, pattern No. 2296, impressed marks, 1925–30, 11½in (29cm) high.

$175–210 PFK

A Crown Devon Mattia cruet set, modelled as a pixie and mushrooms, c1930, 5in (12.5cm) diam.

$210–240 BEV

Further reading

Miller's Ceramics Buyer's Guide, Miller's Publications, 2006

A Fielding Crown Devon Sarie Marais tankard, 1930s, 7in (18cm) high.

$930–1,050 EAn

The Sarie Marais tankard was introduced in 1935 to coincide with Reginald Fielding's trip to South Africa; it was made exclusively for the South African market. Saire Marais is a popular South African campfire song, written at the time of the Boer War.

A Crown Devon Sarie Marais musical jug, 1930s, 8in (20.5cm) high.

$1,400–1,550 EAn

A Crown Devon triple tray, 1930s, 11in (28cm) wide.

$105–120 SAT

A Crown Devon plate, decorated with Riviera pattern, 1950s, 8in (20.5cm) diam.

$10–15 RETO

DENBY

FOUNDED IN 1809 by the Bourne family in Denby, Derbyshire, the firm began by making stoneware bottles. In the 20th century that tradition continued but new art wares were added to the existing range. Home-grown talents like Albert and Glyn Colledge were supplemented by designers such as Alice Teichtner and Tibor Reich. Reich's post-war designs are now highly collectable and good pieces are becoming hard to find as they were made in smaller quantities.

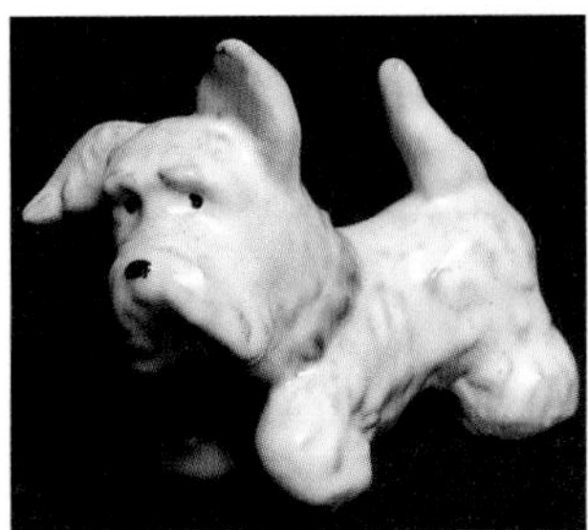

A Denby model of a Scottie dog, designed by Alice Teichtner, 1930s, 5in (12.5cm) wide.

$180–200 ⊞ StB

Fleeing Nazi Oppression in her home country of Austria , Alice Teichtner, from the Weiner Werkstatte, brought a new direction to Denby from 1936 to 1939. As an Austrian she was forced to register as an Alien in 1939 and therefore could not work. She left for a new life in Canada in 1943.

A Denby figure of a caddy with golf clubs, c1935, 5in (12.5cm) high.

$280–310 ⊞ JSG

A Bourne Denby Orient ware vase, 1930s, 4in (10cm) high.

$130–145 ⊞ MARK

Introduced by Albert Colledge in 1926, this distinctive range used matt crystalline glazes to great effect.

A pair of Denby Burlington vases, 1956, 11in (28cm) high.

$90–100 ⊞ RETO

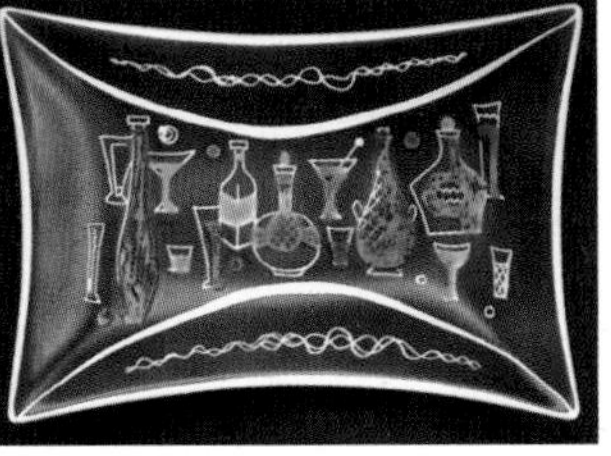

A Denby Cloisonné dish, designed by Glyn and Albert Colledge, 1956, 9½in (24cm) wide.

$60–70 ⊞ RETO

A Denby Shamrock lidded casserole, by Albert Colledge, early 1960s, 7in (18cm) diam.

$70–80 ⊞ CHI

► A Denby Falstaff plate, 1971, 8in (20.5cm) diam.

$35–40 ⊞ CHI

Designed by Glynn Colledge and marketed in 1971–72, this freely painted pattern typifies Glynn's later designs, showing as much freshness as his earlier work.

A Denby Sonnet milk jug, c1977, 2½in (6.5cm) high.

$25–30 ⊞ CHI

GOEBEL

A Goebel owl napkin ring, Germany, c1930, 3in (7.5cm) diam.

$80–90 BEV

A Goebel table brush, the handle modelled as a cat, Germany, c1930, 6in (15cm) long.

$130–145 BEV

► A Goebel umbrella wall vase, Germany, 1930s, 6in (15cm) high.

$110–125 BEV

A Goebel Hummel figure, 'Little Goat Herder', Germany, c1970, 4¾in (12cm) high.

$220–250 OACC

A Goebel Hummel figure, 'Little Shopper', Germany, c1970, 4¾in (12cm) high.

$150–165 OACC

A Goebel Hummel figure, 'Little Gardener', Germany, c1970, 4½in (11cm) high.

$105–120 OACC

A Goebel Hummel figure, 'Merry Wanderer', Germany, c1970, 4in (10cm) high.

$105–120 OACC

A Goebel Hummel figure, 'Baker', Germany, c1980, 4¾in (12cm) high.

$190–210 OACC

A Goebel Hummel figure, 'Wayside Harmony', Germany, c1980, 4in (10cm) high.

$130–145 OACC

A Goebel Hummel figure, 'Goose Girl', Germany, c1980, 4½in (11cm) high.

$150–165 OACC

T. G. GREEN

◀ A T. G. Green Mocha ware mug, c1870, 6in (15cm) high.

$230–260 ⊞ OD

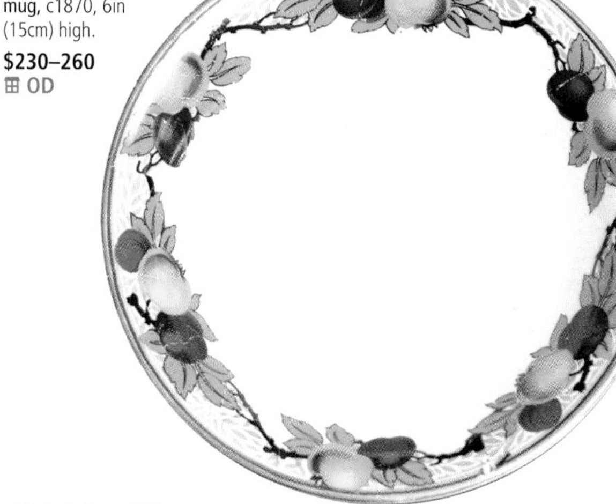

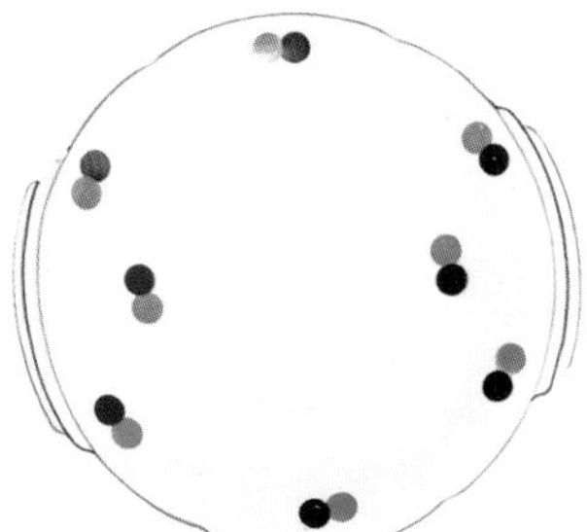

◀ A T. G. Green Eclipse tea plate, c1930, 9in (23cm) diam.

$25–30 ⊞ CAL

A T. G. Green dish, decorated with Peach and Plum pattern border, c1925, 5½in (14cm) diam.

$5–10 ⊞ CAL

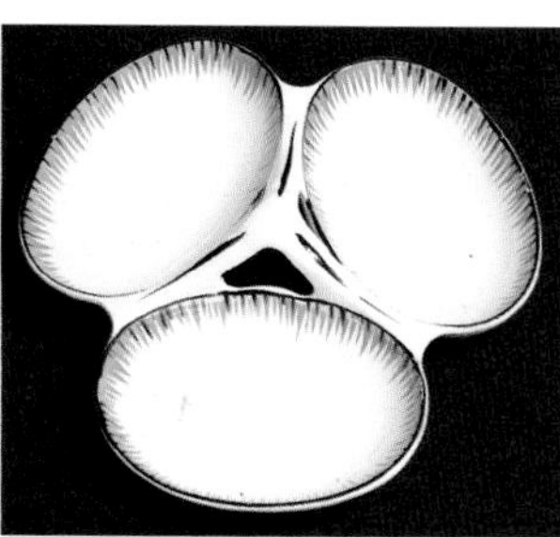

A T. G. Green Grassmere triple tray, 1930, 8in (20.5cm) wide.

$85–95 ⊞ CAL

A T. G. Green Streamline storage jar, inscribed 'Custard Powder', c1935, 5in (12.5cm) high.

$240–270 ⊞ SCH

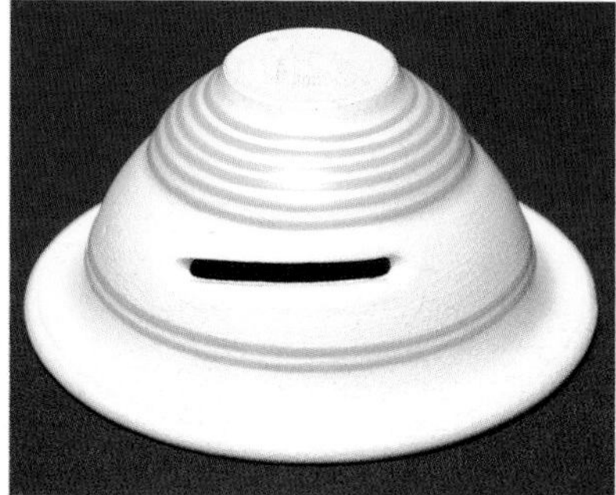

A T. G. Green Streamline egg separator, c1935, 4in (10cm) diam.

$180–200 ⊞ SCH

A T. G. Green Streamline jug, c1935, 5½in (14cm) high.

$120–135 ⊞ SCH

A T. G. Green banded jug, 1930s–50s, 5in (12.5cm) high.

$45–50 ⊞ CAL

A T. G. Green Green Polka Dot milk jug, 1930s, 4in (10cm) high.

$25–30 ⊞ CAL

CORNISH WARE

A T. G. Green Cornish Ware suet dish, 1930s, 5in (12.5cm) diam.

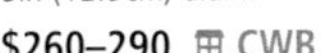

$260–290 ⊞ CWB

A T. G. Green Cornish Ware flour shaker, 1930s, 5in (12.5cm) high.

$70–80 ⊞ CWB

A T. G. Green Cornish Ware storage jar, inscribed 'Nutmegs', 1930s, 3½in (9cm) high.

$155–175 ⊞ CWB

- Established in 1862 T. G. Green is famous for its Cornish Ware that has been in production since the 1920s.
- Genuine Cornish Ware is turned on a lathe, cutting sharp edged bands though blue slip revealing the white underneath – the blue and white design is said to represent the blue sky and white clouds of Cornwall.
- Other T. G. Green designs include Gingham, Domino and Streamline.
- Storage jars inscribed with rare names such as 'Borax', 'Curry' and 'Apricots' command huge prices.
- Beware of genuine items with fake names added under cold glaze. Unlike genuine examples, these rogue names can be scraped off.

A T. G. Green Cornish Ware storage jar, inscribed 'Custard Powder', 1930s, 5in (12.5cm) high.

$240–270 ⊞ CWB

A T. G. Green Green Polka Dot teapot, early 1930s, 5in (12.5cm) high.

$70–80 ⊞ CAL

This pattern also appeared in red and white. It predates T. G. Green's well-known Blue Domino Ware.

A T. G. Green Cornish Ware double eggcup, 1940s, 4in (10cm) high.

$80–90 ⊞ CWB

◀ A T. G. Green Cornish Ware tea pot, 1950s, 4½in (11.5cm) high.

$230–260 ⊞ CWB

▶ A T. G. Green sauce boat, 1950s, 7½in (19cm) wide.

$20–25 ⊞ CAL

A T. G. Green Yellow Cornish Ware tea cup and saucer, c1960, 8in (20.5cm) high.

$25–30 ⊞ CWB

A T. G. Green Yellow Cornish Ware coffee pot, 1960s, 8in (20.5cm) high.

$190–210 ⊞ CAL

Promoted as 'A new sunlit yellow for Spring', yellow Cornish Ware first appeared in April 1960.

A T. G. Green Gold Cornish Ware sugar shaker, Judith Onions backstamp, c1970, 5¼in (13.5cm) high.

$50–55 ⊞ CWB

A T. G. Green Yellow Cornish Ware jug, 1960s, 4¼in (11cm) high.

$45–50 ⊞ CWB

► A T. G. Green Cornish Ware bowl, with pouring spout, Judith Onions backstamp, c1970, 5½in (14cm) high.

$80–90 ⊞ CWB

A T. G. Green Cornish Ware milk jug, Judith Onions backstamp, c1970, 4¾in (12cm) high.

$70–80 ⊞ CWB

A T. G. Green jug, 1970, 6in (15cm) high.

$80–90 ⊞ CAL

A T. G. Green Cornish Ware measure, limited edition for Collectors' Club, c1998, 3¼in (8.5cm) high.

$120–135 ⊞ CWB

HORNSEA

SET UP IN A TERRACED HOUSE on the sea front at Hornsea, Humberside, by brothers Colin and Desmond Rawson in 1949 Hornsea Pottery was initially a cottage industry. Gradually they expanded and in 1954 they moved to a nearby former brick works in the town.

At first, small 'fancies' such as toby jugs, boots and animal figures were made. Things began to change in 1955 when John Clappison became involved with the firm, moving the wares in a more 'artistic' direction.

Clappison's moulded Studio Craft range from 1960 to 1962 includes designs such as White Thorn, White Frost and Bud, which were revolutionary at the time and are now highly sought after. A move into tableware and kitchen storage jars in the late 1960s kept the pottery's furnaces going until 1989.

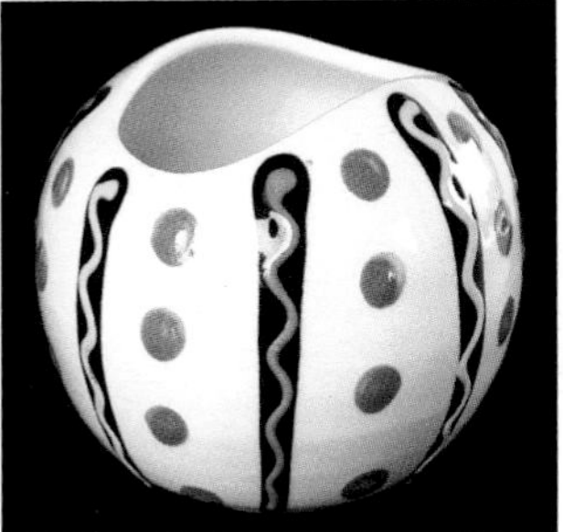

A Hornsea Studio Slipware sugar bowl, 1954–56, 3in (7.5cm) high.

$45–50 ⊞ RETO

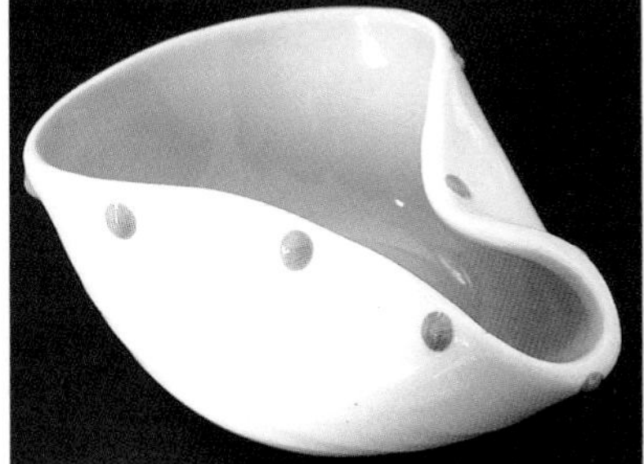

A Hornsea Studio Slipware dish, 1955–56, 4in (10cm) wide.

$10–15 ⊞ RETO

A Hornsea Elegance cruet, 1955, 4¾in (12cm) high.

$25–30 ⊞ RETO

Elegance was John Clappison's first design for Hornsea. Employed by the firm until 1972 he continued to work freelance after he began to design for Ravenshead glass.

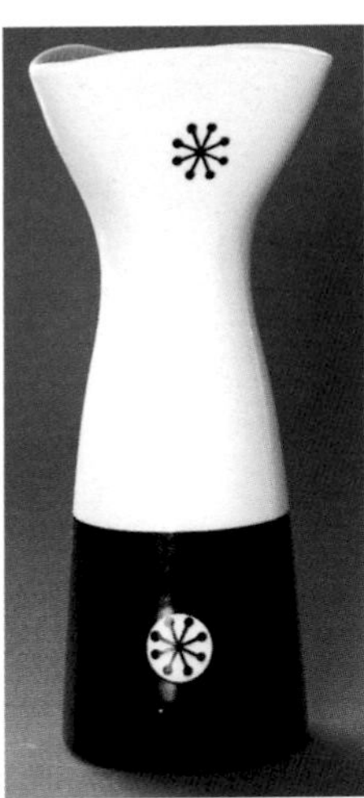

A Hornsea Tricorn vase, 1958, 7½in (19cm) high.

$105–120 ⊞ RETO

Tricorn was designed by John Clappison while he was still at college. It is rarely seen on the market and is very popular with collectors.

A Hornsea Tricorn sugar bowl, 1958, 3in (7.5cm) high.

$85–95 ⊞ RETO

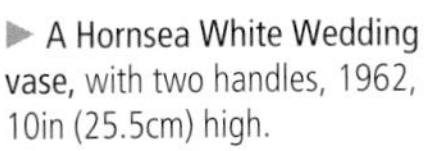

► **A Hornsea White Wedding vase,** with two handles, 1962, 10in (25.5cm) high.

$50–55 ⊞ MARK

◄ **A Hornsea White Wedding planter,** 1962, 10in (25.5cm) high.

$25–30 ⊞ MARK

A Hornsea Slipware vase, 1963, 6in (15cm) high.

$60–70 ⊞ RETO

A Hornsea Gaiety anvil vase, 1964–65, 6½in (16.5cm) high.

$85–95 ⊞ RETO

A Hornsea Sunflower plant pot, 1965, 5in (16cm) high.

$70–80 ⊞ RETO

A Hornsea Springtime canister and cover, 1964–65, 5½in (14cm) high.

$25–30 ⊞ RETO

◀ A Hornsea Muramic wall decoration, 1960s, 17in (43cm) wide.

$280–330 DA

Produced by hand in small quantities between 1971 and 1972, Hornsea's Muramic Art was, in their opinion, the best work of the pottery. Designed by John Clappison, small red clay slabs are individuallly decorated to form a picture that is mounted on a linen backgrond, framed and mounted on an afformosia wood panel. John Clappison produced a number of earlier 'Muramics' as one-offs in the late 1960s; these are made from white clay and tied together. Decorated in oxides they are now very rare.

A Hornsea jam pot, screen-printed with a geometric pattern, early 1970s, 4in (10cm) high.

$25–30 ⊞ RETO

▶ A pair of Hornsea salt and pepper pots, screen-printed with apples, 1971, 2½in (6.5cm) high.

$5–10 ⊞ RETO

A pair of Hornsea salt and pepper pots, decorated with Rondel pattern, 1971, 2½in (6.5cm) high.

$10–15 ⊞ RETO

A Hornsea preserve pot, screen-printed with owls, 1972, 4in (10cm) high.

$20–25 ⊞ RETO

A special technique much used by Hornsea was mechanical screen-printing. In the unglazed 'biscuit' state the piece was mounted onto a machine that screen-printed a coloured design that resisted the glaze. This was a technique developed and patented by Hornsea. When the glaze was applied (usually in a contrasting colour) the screen-printed area resisted the glaze and gave it an 'embossed' effect.

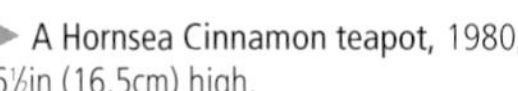

▶ A Hornsea Cinnamon teapot, 1980, 6½in (16.5cm) high.

$10–15 ⊞ RETO

MIDWINTER

ESTABLISHED IN 1910 Midwinter came to the fore in the 1950s. Heavily influenced by American design, Roy Midwinter introduced the ground-breaking Stylecraft range in 1953. A combination of hand-painted and printed designs by in-house designer Jessie Tait kept the firm well ahead of the competition throughout the 1950s and '60s.

In the 1970s Eve Midwinter's Creation glaze, along with her Earth, Day and Sun designs broke new ground on the Stonehenge shape, introduced in 1971 by Roy Midwinter. Designs from the 1950s such as Plant life, Nature study and Salad Ware by Terence Conran, and Cannes by Hugh Casson are highly collectable.

A Midwinter model of Larry the Lamb, 1930s, 6in (15cm) high.

$80–90 ⊞ WAC

A Midwinter Homespun canister and cover, designed by Jessie Tait, c1960, 7in (18cm) high.

$70–80 ⊞ CHI

A Midwinter Cannes coffee pot, decorated by Hugh Casson, 1955, 7½in (19cm) high.

$155–175 ⊞ RETO

A Midwinter dish, c1960, 7in (18cm) wide.

$10–15 ⊞ RETO

A Midwinter Fine dish, by David Queensbury, decorated with Sienna pattern by Jessie Tait, 1960s, 7in (18cm) wide.

$10–15 ⊞ KA

A Midwinter Cheese Plant plate, 1960, 8in (20.5cm) square.

$25–30 ⊞ RETO

A Midwinter Creation tea cup and saucer, by Eve Midwinter, c1972, cup 3in (7.5cm) high.

$20–25 CHI

A Midwinter Stonehenge plate, decorated with Seascape pattern designed by Eve Midwinter, 1980s, 10½in (26.5cm) diam.

$20–25 CHI

A Midwinter Stonehenge plate, decorated with Wild Oats pattern designed by Eve Midwinter, 1974, 7in (18cm) diam.

$20–25 CHI

◀ **A Midwinter Stonehenge coffee pot,** decorated with Green Leaves pattern designed by Eve Midwinter, 1974–83, 8in (20.5cm) high.

$10–15 CCO

A Midwinter Day teapot, designed by Eve Midwinter, 1977–79, 7in (18cm) high.

$50–55 CHI

Earth, Sun and Day are Eve Midwinter's most collected designs.

A Midwinter Stonehenge tureen, decorated with Rangoon pattern designed by Eve Midwinter, 1970s, 9½in (24cm) diam.

$70–80 CHI

The Stonehenge shape, designed by Roy Midwinter, was introduced in 1971. The design broke new ground when coupled with Eve Midwinter's Creation glaze and her Earth, Day and Sun patterns.

A Midwinter coffee pot and milk jug, designed by Jessie Tait, decorated with Hazelwood pattern, 1973–76, 8in (20.5cm) high.

$60–70 CHI

MOORCROFT

A Moorcroft Macintyre Florian Ware vase, with tube-lined decoration, painted marks, c1900, 8¾in (22cm) high.

$3,000–3,600 Bea

So-called Moorcroft Macintyre was designed by William Moorcroft but manufactured from 1897 by James Macintyre & Co of Burslem. After a fall-out in 1913 Moorcroft left with his staff and set up his own pottery just across the park in Sandbach Road, with support from Liberty.

A Moorcroft Macintyre Florian Ware vase, 1900–13, 4¾in (12cm) high.

$2,100–2,500 G(L)

Florian was William Moorcroft's first range and was launched at Liberty's in 1898. Stylized organic and floral forms anticipate Art Nouveau and have been collected from the start.

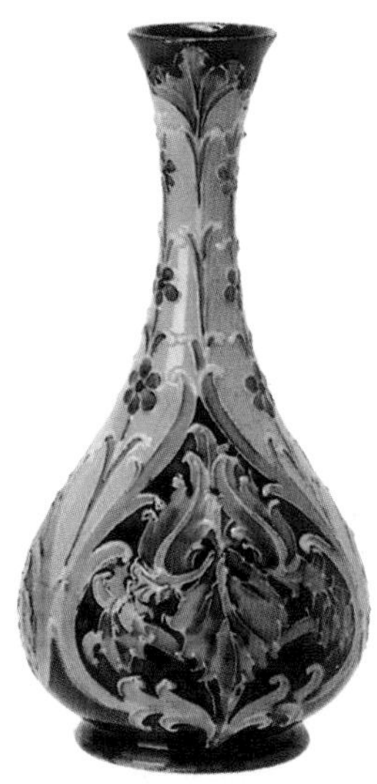

A Moorcroft Macintyre Florian Ware vase, made for Liberty & Co, slight damage, printed mark and impressed signature, 1898–1906, 8in (20.5cm) high.

$620–740 AG

A Moorcroft Flamminian ware bowl, made for Liberty & Co, early 20thC, 8in (20.5cm) diam.

$330–390 L&E

A Moorcroft vase, decorated with bands of peacock feathers, impressed marks, signed, c1915, 9in (23cm) high.

$1,550–1,850 SWO

◄ **A Moorcroft two-handled Flamminian ware vase,** incised signature, early 20thC, 7in (18cm) high.

$200–240 BWL

A Moorcroft vase, made for Liberty & Co, with a Tudric pewter base, c1915, 9in (18cm) high.

$155–185 BWL

Liberty of London and Moorcroft are so strongly associated that collectors pay a premium for pieces produced especially for this famous London store. Many were designed to be mounted in Liberty's Tudric pewter range and are highly desirable.

MOOCROFT: SIXTY YEARS WITH JUST TWO DESIGNERS

A Moorcroft pot pourri vase, made for Liberty & Co, decorated with Claremont pattern, 1915, 5in (12.5cm) high.

$2,400–2,800 AG

A Moorcroft salt-glazed jug, decorated with fish, early 1920s, 8in (20.5cm) high.

$2,750–3,050 BWDA

A Moorcroft plate, decorated with Leaves and Fruit pattern, signed, impressed mark, c1930, 9¼in (23.5cm) diam.

$410–490 TMA

A Moorcroft vase, decorated with Leaves and Fruit pattern, impressed mark, c1930, 9in (23cm) high.

$470–560 Hal

A Moorcroft vase, decorated with Frilled and Slipper Orchid pattern, impressed factory mark, mid-20thC, 5¼in (13.5cm) high.

$250–280 ROS

A Moorcroft vase, decorated by Rachael Bishop, printed marks, signed, c1996, 11½in (29cm) high.

$250–280 ROS

- Between 1897 and 1987 Moorcroft was designed by just two people: father and son team William and Walter Moorcroft. The controlling share was owned by Liberty of London from 1913 until 1962, when the Moorcroft family acquired the major shareholding.
- New owners, the Roper brothers, came in 1984 and soon afterwards the firm looked set to close until Richard Dennis and Hugh Edwards stepped in in 1986.
- Sally Tuffin, a ceramics and fashion designer famed for bring half of the 1960s clothes partnership Foale and Tuffin (see p180), became the third designer in 1987, followed by Rachel Bishop in 1993, after Hugh Edwards became majority shareholder.
- These new owners and designers brought about a massive revival, putting Moorcroft back in the position it has held with collectors for over a century. Today Moorcroft holds regular new design launches at Liberty, bringing its history full circle.

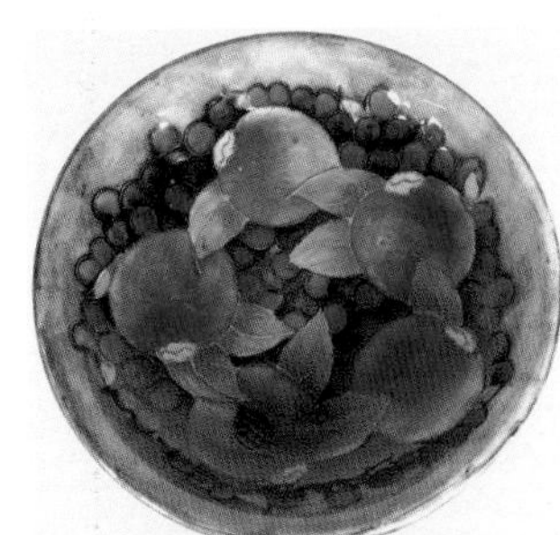

A Moorcroft plate, decorated with Pomegranate pattern, impressed mark, signed, c1920, 8½in (21.5cm) diam.

$430–510 Hal

A Moorcroft vase, with tube-lined decoration, decorated with Honesty pattern, slight damage, painted and impressed marks, c1935, 8¼in (21cm) high.

$700–840 DN(HAM)

► A Moorcroft dish, decorated with Leaves and Fruit pattern, painted and impressed marks, 1930s, 7¼in (18.5cm) diam.

$105–120 CGC

A Walter Moorcroft flambé bowl, decorated with African Lily pattern, c1947, 10½in (26.5cm) diam.

$2,350–2,600 GOv

A Moorcroft dish, decorated with Hibiscus pattern, impressed mark, signed, c1960, 7¼in (18.5cm) diam.

$190–220 GTH

◄ A Moorcroft vase, decorated with Anemone pattern, signed, 1970s, 4in (10cm) high.

$120–135 ROS

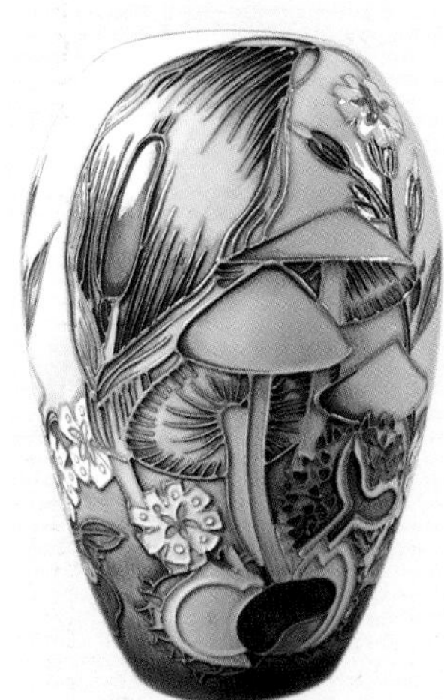

A Moorcroft vase, decorated in Underwood pattern by Debbie Hancock, No. 240 of edition of 350, marked, artist's monogram, signed, c1998, (18.5cm) high.

$175–195 ROS

► A Moorcroft vase, decorated with the 'Andalucia' design by Beverley Wilkes, printed marks, artist's initials, dated 1998, 8½in (21.5cm) high.

$190–210 ROS

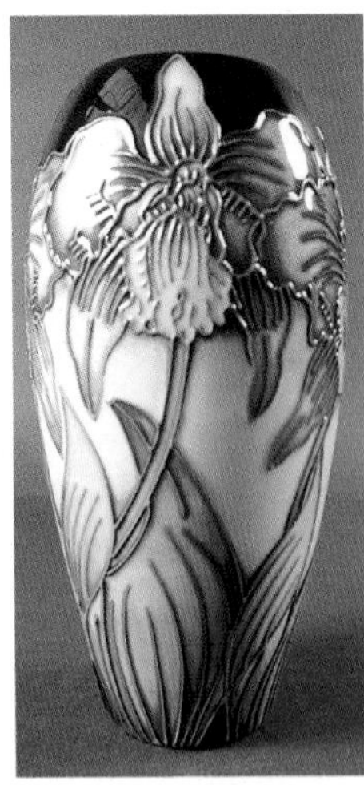

A Moorcroft vase, decorated in Pink Orchid pattern by Nicola Slaney, No. 18 of edition of 100, marked, artist's monogram, signed, 1998, 7½in (19cm) high.

$175–195 ROS

KEITH MURRAY

A Wedgwood vase, by Keith Murray, printed marks and signature, 1932, 10¾in (27.5cm) high.

$430–510 WAD

A Wedgwood vase, by Keith Murray, shape No. 3801, with incised decoration, printed mark, c1933, 6¼in (16cm) high.

$280–330 WW

A Wedgwood vase, by Keith Murray, shape No. 3765, printed mark, c1933, 6¼in (16cm) high.

$350–420 WW

A Wedgwood coffee can and saucer, by Keith Murray, with a silver handle, 1933, coffee can, 2in (5cm) high.

$105–120 BEV

A Wedgwood bowl, by Keith Murray, shape No. 3813, with incised decoration, printed mark, c1935, 6½in (16.5cm) diam.

$310–370 WW

◄ **A Wedgwood top hat bowl,** by Keith Murray, impressed and printed mark, c1935, 9½in (24cm) high.

$280–330 WW

A Wedgwood bowl, by Keith Murray, with a celadon glaze, printed mark, c1935, 9½in (24cm) high.

$380–450 WW

A Wedgwood vase, by Keith Murray, with engine-turned decoration, 1935, 10¾in (27.5cm) high.

$800–880 BEV

A Wedgwood vase, by Keith Murray, with incised decoration and a celadon glaze, printed mark, c1936, 7¼in (18.5cm) high.

$380–450 WW

A Wedgwood dish and cover, by Keith Murray, printed mark, signed, c1936, 4½in (11.5cm) diam.

$105–120 WW

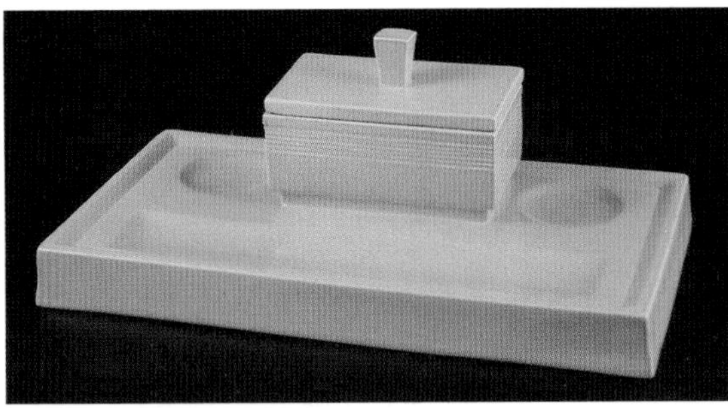

A Wedgwood ink stand, by Keith Murray, No. 3873, slight damage, impressed and painted marks, c1936, signed, 9¾in (25cm) wide.

$650–780 WW

A Wedgwood coffee service, by Keith Murray, comprising 15 pieces, c1937, shape No. 3901, coffee pot 8¼in (21cm) high.

$1,050–1,250 WW

◄ **A Wedgwood bowl,** by Keith Murray, 1937, 4in (10cm) diam.

$340–380 BEV

A Wedgwood vase, by Keith Murray, printed mark, 1930s, 7in (18cm) high.

$300–360 HYD

◄ **A Wedgwood vase,** by Keith Murray, printed marks and signature, 1930s, 6¼in (16cm) high.

$280–330 G(B)

A Wedgwood vase, by Keith Murray, with a celadon glaze and incised decoration, 1938, 7in (12cm) high.

$340–380 BEV

MYOTT

A Myott jug, with hand-painted decoration, 1930, 6in (15cm) high.

$175–195 BEV

A Myott dish, with hand-painted decoration, c1936, 5in (12.5cm) diam.

$10–15 OIA

A Myott jug, with hand-painted decoration, 1930s, 6in (15cm) high.

$120–135 BEV

A Myott Bowtie vase, with hand-painted decoration, 1930s, 8in (20.5cm) high.

$260–290 BEV

◄ A Myott jug, with hand-painted decoration, 1930s, 6¾in (17cm) high.

$175–195 BEV

A Myott jug, with hand-painted decoration, 1930s, 8in (20.5cm) high.

$175–195 BEV

◄ A Myott vase, with hand-painted decoration, ceramic flower holder missing, 1930s, 6in (15cm) high.

$120–135 OIA

NURSERY WARE

MABEL LUCIE ATTWELL

A Shelley figure, designed by Mabel Lucie Attwell, entitled 'The Bride', 1926–40, 6¼in (16cm) high.

$1,100–1,300 LT

A Shelley cup and saucer, designed by Mabel Lucie Attwell, 1926–40, plate 5½in (14cm) diam.

$310–350 GaL

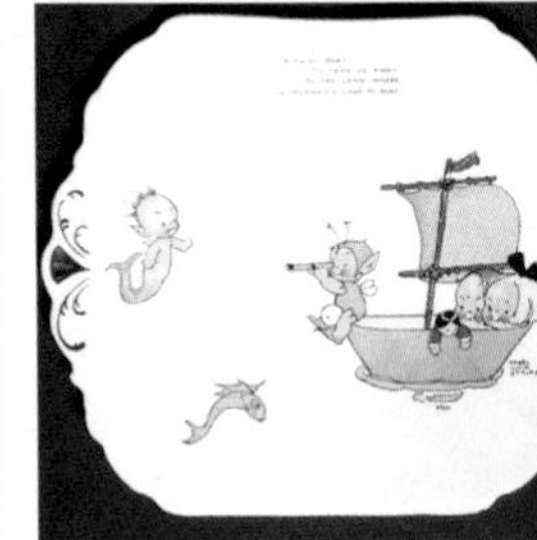

A Shelley serving plate, designed by Mabel Lucie Attwell, 1926–40, 9½in (24cm) wide.

$470–520 GaL

- Mabel Lucie Attwell (1879–1964) was born in London, the ninth child of ten. She studied at art school but did not complete her course because she grew bored of copying, preferring instead to illustrate her own fantasies.
- A popular illustrator, her work was applied to a variety of media, including pottery and postcards. Shelley introduced patterns based on her designs from 1926.
- Her illustrations of chubby-faced children were based on her daughter Peggy; the small pixies seen in her work are called Boo Boos.
- In 1937 Princess Margaret commissioned her to do a personal Christmas card and sets of her china (for Shelley) were used in the Royal nursery.

► **A Staffordshire porridge bowl,** c1910, 9in (23cm) diam.

$155–175 SMI

A Staffordshire cup, saucer and plate, decorated with Pinky and Perky, c1960, plate 7in (18cm) diam.

$50–55 CTO

Pinky and Perky were a pair of British singing puppets in the form of piglets. Created by in 1956 by Czechoslovakian-born Jan and Vlasta Dalibor, they had their own extremely popular TV show from 1957 until the early 1970s and released many popular records, mostly covers of pop tunes.

A Carlton Ware child's tea service, comprising 15 pieces, decorated with ducks, c1930, teapot 4in (10cm) high.

$600–660 EAn

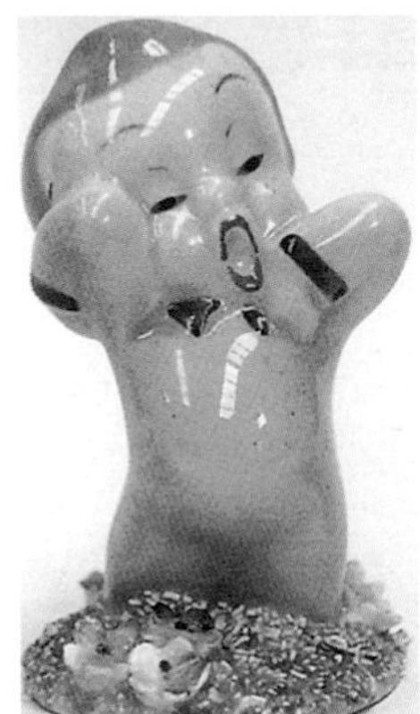

◄ **A Wade figure,** entitled 'Nod', 1948–58, 2¾in (7cm) high.

$90–105 BBR

Wynken, Blynken and Nod were based on characters from a poem written in 1889 by an American, Eugene Field. Walt Disney made a cartoon of the characters in 1938 and the pyjama-clad figure seen here is inspired by that interpretation.

PEN DELFIN

A Pen Delfin Little Bo Peep wall plaque, 1956–59, 5in (12.5cm) high.

$350–420 ASHB

A Pen Delfin Mother rabbit model, with thin neck, 1956, 8in (20.5cm) high.

$175–210 ASHB

A Pen Delfin Margot Rabbit model, with pleated skirt, 1956–57, 4in (10.5cm) high.

$330–390 ASHB

A Pen Delfin Pieface model, No. 924984, 1966–87, 4½in (11.5cm) high.

$120–135 TA

A Pen Delfin Dandy model, designed by Noel Roberts, No. 1002814, 1981, 4in (10cm) high.

$35–40 TA

A Pen Delfin Clanger model, designed by Jean Walmsley Heap, No. 1012146, 1983–98, 8½in (21.5cm) high.

$80–90 TA

A Pen Delfin Tidy Patch model, Collectors' Club piece, 1998, 3¾in (9.5cm) high.

$25–30 TA

A Pen Delfin Barrow Boy model, withdrawn 2001, 4in (10cm) high.

$35–40 TA

A Pen Delfin Nightingale Red Cross model, 2003, 4in (10cm) high.

$200–240 ASHB

PLICHTA / WEMYSS

MILLER'S COMPARES

(L) A **Plichta pig**, decorated with shamrocks, c1935, 6in (15cm) long.

$670–740 ⊞ **Fai**

(R) A **Wemyss pig**, impressed mark, c1900, 6½in (16.5cm) long.

$1,400–1,550 ⊞ **Fai**

The dowdy looking black-sponged pig on the right is by Scotland's Wemyss pottery and dates to c1900. When the pottery closed in 1930 the name and moulds were acquired and made at the Bovey Tracey pottery in Devon and retailed by Jan Plichta in London. The more decorative pig on the left is a later Plichta example, hence the lower price. An original Wemyss pig decorated in shamrocks would be worth between $2,600 and $3,500.

A **Plichta model of a cockerel**, 1930–50, 5in (12.5cm) high.

$380–420 ⊞ **BKJL**

A **Plichta model of a cat**, decorated with roses, 1930s, 11in (28cm) high.

$2,400–2,650 ⊞ **SDD**

This is a rare Plichta shape and with well-painted decoration.

A **Plichta pot and cover**, decorated with plums, 1930–50, 4½in (11.5cm) diam.

$85–95 ⊞ **OD**

A **Wemyss Stuart pot**, painted by Sharp, decorated with daffodils, c1900, 7in (18cm) high.

$2,000–2,200 ⊞ **Fai**

◀ A **Wemyss bowl**, painted with cherries, impressed mark, slight damage, early 20thC, 6¾in (17cm) high.

$150–180 **BWL**

A **Wemyss basket**, painted with roses, early 20thC, 8in (20.5cm) wide.

$550–610 ⊞ **OD**

POOLE

A Carter, Stabler & Adams vase, 1920s, 2¾in (7cm) high.

$20–25 OACC

A Carter, Stabler & Adams vase, by Truda Carter, decorated with stylized flowers, impressed mark, c1930, 10in (25.5cm) high.

$380–450 PFK

A Carter, Stabler & Adams vase, by Eileen Prangnell, decorated with YO pattern, painted with stylized flowers, impressed and painted marks, c1930, 7in (18cm) high.

$175–210 WW

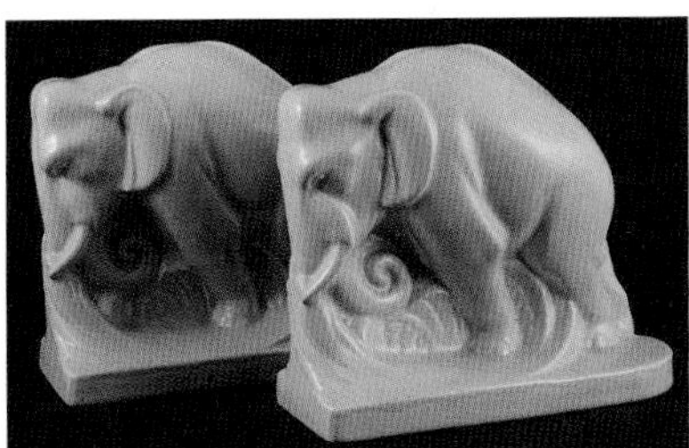

A pair of Carter, Stabler & Adams bookends, by Harold Brownsword, model No. 813, in the form of elephants, impressed and painted marks, c1930, 6in (15cm) high.

$350–420 WW

A Carter, Stabler & Adams vase, painted with sprays of flowers, c1930, 12in (30.5cm) high.

$280–330 Holl

A Carter, Stabler & Adams plate, designed by Arthur Bradbury, painted by Gwen Haskins, inscribed 'Brig General Wolfe Newfoundland Trader Poole 1797', c1939, 9¾in (25cm) diam.

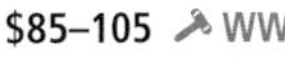

$85–105 WW

A Carter, Stabler & Adams vase, by Truda Rivers, decorated with CI pattern, impressed mark, painted monogram, 1930s, 9in (23cm) high.

$780–930 WW

A Carter, Stabler & Adams vase, decorated with TV pattern, printed and painted marks, slight damage, 1930s, 9¾in (25cm) high.

$350–420 WW

A Carter, Stabler & Adams vase, by Ann Hatchard, decorated with CE pattern, impressed and painted marks, 1930s, 9½in (24cm) high.

$520–620 WW

POOLE POTTERY

A Carter, Stabler & Adams Plane Ware vase, by John Adams, model No. 164P, printed, impressed and incised marks, c1930, 8¼in (21cm) high.

$520–620 WW

A Carter, Stabler & Adams miniature vase, painted with sprays of flowers, printed and painted marks, c1935, 4¼in (11cm) high.

$105–120 WW

A Poole Studio ware Atlantis vase, by Guy Sydenham, decorated with Atlantis pattern, impressed mark and artist's monogram, 1970s, 6¾in (17cm) high.

$360–400 ROS

- In 1873 a builder's merchant and ironmonger, Jesse Carter, bought a near derelict pottery in Poole, Dorset, calling it Carter & Co. It primarily made tiling and architectural products.
- By 1921 a subsidiary of Carter & Co, Carter, Stabler & Adams, was set up to produce ornamental pottery.
- In 1963 the name was changed to Poole Pottery Ltd when it came under the control of the Pilkington group.

A Carter, Stabler & Adams vase, decorated with EP pattern, slight damage, impressed and painted marks, 1930s, 9¾in (25cm) high.

$350–420 WW

◄ **A Carter, Stabler & Adams jug,** shape No. 303, decorated with DR pattern, painted with flowers and foliage, impressed and painted marks, handle restored, 1930s, 7¾in (19.5cm) high.

$260–310 WW

► **A Carter, Stabler & Adams vase,** by Doris Marshall, decorated with TJ pattern, impressed and painted marks, 1930s, 8in (20.5cm) high.

$260–310 WW

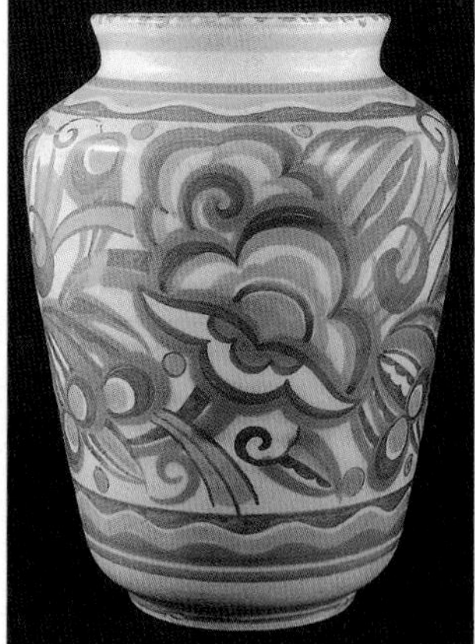

A Carter, Stabler & Adams vase, by Ann Hatchard, decorated with TV pattern, impressed and painted marks, 1930s, 10¼in (26cm) high.

$1,100–1,300 WW

A Carter, Stabler & Adams vase, by Iris Skinner, decorated with KK pattern, impressed and painted marks, 1930s, 7¼in (18.5cm) high.

$260–310 WW

A Carter, Stabler & Adams vase, decorated with KW pattern, 1950s, 4in (10cm) high.

$10–20 KA

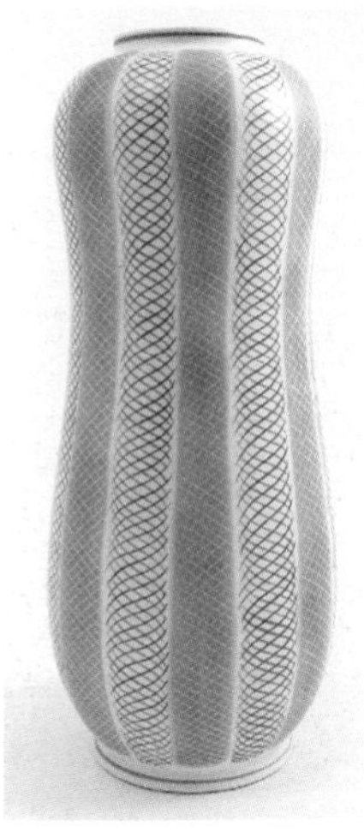

A Carter, Stabler & Adams vase, by Alfred Read, decorated with PKT pattern, 1955–59, 17in (43cm) high.

$650–780 G(L)

A Carter, Stabler & Adams vase, designed by Alfred Read and Guy Sydenham, painted by Dianne Holloway, shape No. 697, decorated with PRP pattern, marked, c1954, 10¾in (27.5cm) high.

$105–120 ROS

A Poole Studio ware pedestal vase, impressed mark, 1962–64, 4in (10cm) high.

$380–410 POI

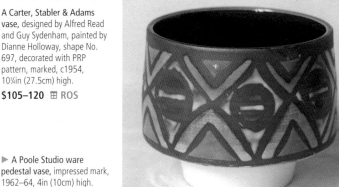

A Poole Pottery vase, by Guy Sydenham, 1960s, 11in (28cm) high.

$310–350 OD

► **A Poole Studio ware pedestal vase,** impressed mark, 1962–64, 4in (10cm) high.

$410–460 POI

A Poole Studio ware vase, 1962–64, 5in (12.5cm) high.

$700–770 POI

A Poole Studio ware vase, 1964–66, 4in (10cm) high.
$280–310 POI

◄ A Poole Studio ware vase, shape No. 27, incised and printed mark, 1962–64, 12in (30.5cm) high.
$1,900–2,100 POI

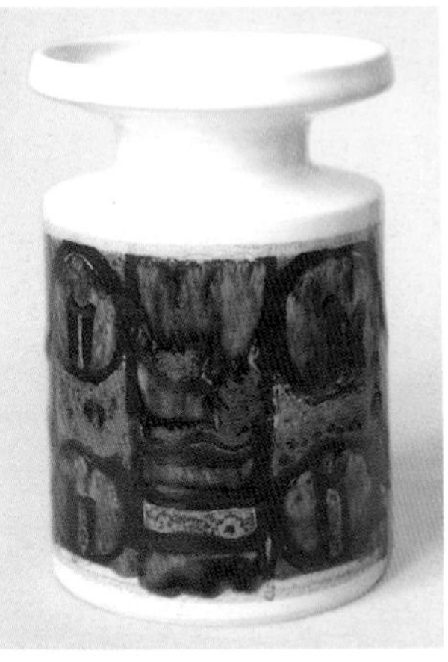

A Poole Studio ware vase, shape No. 67, 1964–66, 5in (12.5cm) high.
$240–270 POI

A Poole Studio ware vase, No. 60, 1964–66, 8in (20.5cm) high.
$470–520 POI

A Poole Pottery bowl, by Mary Stainer, 1975, 7in (18cm) wide.
$55–60 OACC

A Poole Pottery vase, by Mary Stainer, 1975, 6in (15cm) high.
$45–50 OACC

◄ A Poole Studio ware Atlantis vase, by Jenny Haigh, impressed mark and artist's monogram, 1970s, 13in (33cm) high.
$540–600 ROS

► A Poole Studio ware vase, by Alan White, printed mark, c2000, 15½in (39.5cm) high.
$190–210 ROS

PORTMEIRION

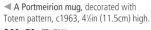

◀ **A Portmeirion mug,** decorated with Totem pattern, c1963, 4½in (11.5cm) high.

$60–70 ⊞ CHI

Launched in 1963 the Totem design put the firm on the map. Susan Williams-Ellis took inspiration from primitive art to create her design.

A Portmeirion goblet, decorated with Totem pattern, c1963, 5in (12.5cm) high.

$60–70 ⊞ CHI

A Portmeirion storage jar, decorated with Totem pattern, c1963, 8in (20.5cm) high.

$165–185 ⊞ CHI

▶ **A Portmeirion teapot,** decorated with Totem pattern, c1970, 6in (15cm) high.

$50–55 ⊞ LUNA

◀ **A Portmeirion coffee set,** decorated with Totem pattern, 1960s, coffee pot 13in (33cm) high.

$110–125 ⊞ MARK

A Portmeirion storage jar, decorated with Talisman pattern, c1962, 6in (15cm) high.

$220–250 ⊞ CHI

A Portmeirion storage jar, decorated with Variations pattern, c1964, 6in (15cm) high.

$130–145 ⊞ CHI

A Portmeirion storage jar, decorated with Variations pattern, c1964, 7½in (20.5cm) high.

$25–30 ⊞ CHI

A Portmeirion storage jar, decorated with Monte Sol pattern, c1965, 6in (15cm) high.

$130–145 ⊞ CHI

This pattern was designed by Susan Williams-Ellis while breakfasting in the Monte Sol Hotel in Ibiza, Spain.

A Portmeirion storage jar, decorated with vegetables, c1963, 5in (12.5cm) high.

$25–30 TAC

A Portmeirion coffee pot, decorated with Phoenix pattern, 1960s, 13in (33cm) high.

$50–55 CHI

A set of six Portmeirion spice jars, decorated with Dolphin pattern, c1965, 4in (10cm) high.

$80–90 CHI

Dolphin pattern, designed by Susan Williams-Ellis, was originally introduced in 1959 to be an exclusive design sold in the gift shop within Portmerion, the village designed by her father, Clough Williams-Ellis. Later it was adapted and added to the widely sold Portmerion range.

A Portmeirion teacup and saucer, decorated with Sailing Ships pattern, 1960s, saucer 5in (12.5cm) diam.

$70–80 CHI

A Portmeirion mug, decorated with *The Mayflower*, Collectors Series of 10,000, 1960s, 4in (10cm) high.

$70–80 CHI

A Portmeirion mug, decorated with Sailing Ships pattern, 1960s, 5in (12.5cm) high.

$45–50 CHI

◄ A Portmeirion coffee pot, decorated with Magic Garden pattern, c1966, 13in (33cm) diam.

$155–175 CHI

The Magic Garden pattern was introduced in 1970 and was based on how a garden might look on another planet.

A Portmeirion mug, decorated with Magic City pattern, c1966, 4½in (11.5cm) diam.

$60–70 CHI

The Magic City pattern, launched at Christmas in 1966, was inspired by a firework display. Tall, slender coffee pots show off the design well and are highly sought after, especially as they are prone to damage and rarely appear on the market in good condition.

A Portmeirion Meridian sugar bowl, c1971, 2in (5cm) high.

$10–15 ⊞ CHI

► A Portmeirion **Meridian jug,** c1971, 3in (10cm) high.

$25–30 ⊞ CHI

► **A Portmeirion trio,** decorated with Blue Garland pattern, c1974, 2½in (6.5cm) high.

$35–40 ⊞ CHI

BOTANIC GARDEN

A Portmeirion Botanic Garden plate, decorated with Venus Fly Trap pattern, 1972, 10in (25.5cm) diam.

$50–55 ⊞ CHI

A Portmeirion Botanic Garden plate, decorated with Christmas Rose pattern, 1972, 10in (25.5cm) diam.

$15–20 ⊞ CHI

A Portmeirion Botanic Garden plate, decorated with Convolvulus pattern, 1972, 10in (25.5cm) diam.

$25–30 ⊞ CHI

- Susan Williams-Ellis's Botanic Garden design was introduced in 1972 and used botanical illustrations from a book as the basis of her new multi-motif floral design.
- The original launch included 28 different plant motifs.
- Botanic Garden is one of Susan Williams-Ellis's most popular designs forming up to 60 per cent of current production.
- From 1982 the mark includes 'dishwasher and microwave oven safe'.

► **A Portmeirion Botanic Garden Parmesan pot,** 1975–82, 5½in (14cm) diam.

$10–15 ⊞ TAC

CHARLOTTE RHEAD

CHARLOTTE RHEAD (1885–1947)

A Charlotte Rhead Bursley ware vase, 1922–26, 6in (15cm) high.

$620–690 HEW

A Charlotte Rhead vase, signed, c1930, 7in (18cm) high.

$120–140 GTH

A Charlotte Rhead Crown Ducal vase, 1932–42, 10¼in (26cm) high.

$170–200 DA

- Charlotte was the talented daughter of pottery designer Frederick Rhead.
- She designed for a number of firms including Bursley (H. J. Wood), Crown Ducal and Burgess & Leigh.
- Tube lining became her signature method of decoration. It is the ceramic equivalent to icing a cake. Liquid clay is piped onto the pottery piece with a rubber bag and fine glass nozzle, using an outline as a guide. Moorcroft used the same techniques extensively.
- In 1922 Charlotte joined her father at the Bursley works.
- In 1926 she joined Burgess & Leigh.
- Between 1932 and 1942 she designed for Crown Ducal (A. G. Richardson).
- In 1942 she again designed for H. J. Wood; Bursley trademark reintroduced.
- Many patterns designed for Woods between 1942 and 1947 (the year she died) were not produced until 1952 due to wartime restrictions. Her late Bursley patterns all have the prefix TL for tube lined. Numbers after TL 105 are not by Charlotte Rhead.

◄ A Charlotte Rhead Crown Ducal vase, 1932–42, 7in (18cm) high.

$170–190 HEW

► A Charlotte Rhead Crown Ducal vase, 1932–42, 7in (18cm) high.

$470–520 HEW

A Charlotte Rhead Crown Ducal vase, pattern No. 6189, signed, 1932–42, 7½in (19cm) high.

$240–280 G(B)

◄ **A Charlotte Rhead Crown Ducal vase,** decorated with Persian Rose pattern, c1935, 5¾in (14.5cm) high.

$380–420 BEV

A Charlotte Rhead Crown Ducal coffee pot, decorated with Padua patttern, c1930, 8in (20.5cm) diam.

$1,000–1,100 BEV

◄ **A Charlotte Rhead Crown Ducal jug,** decorated with Persian Rose pattern, 1932–42, 9in (23cm) high.

$540–600 HEW

A Charlotte Rhead Bursley vase and cover, pattern No. TL76, printed and painted marks, 1954, 5½in (14cm) high.

$175–210 WAD

A Charlotte Rhead Bursley jug, 1954, 5in (12.5cm) high.

$150–170 HEW

A pair of Charlotte Rhead chargers, tube-lined with leaves and flowerheads, pattern No. 4921, 1932–42, 12¼in (31cm) diam.

$260–310 DA

A Charlotte Rhead Crown Ducal charger, printed and painted marks, 1933–38, 17½in (44.5cm) diam.

$105–120 WAD

ROYAL DOULTON

A Royal Doulton model of an elephant, 1926–62, 7½in (19cm) wide.
$95–115 G(L)

A Royal Doulton model of a terrier, No. HN997, restored, 1930–46, 5in (12.5cm) high.
$1,300–1,450 PASC

A Royal Doulton model of a Sealyham terrier, No. HN1030, slight damage, 1931–55, 5in (12.5cm) high.
$175–210 POTT

A Royal Doulton model of a seagull, No. HN1196, 1937–46, 9in (23cm) long.
$330–390 POTT

A Royal Doulton model of a greyhound, No. HN1075, 1932–55, 8½in (21.5cm) high.
$1,600–1,750 PASC

A Royal Doulton model of an Alsation, Champion Benign of Picardy, No. HN1115, 1937–60, 9in (23cm) high.
$1,100–1,250 PASC

A Royal Doulton model of a cocker spaniel with a pheasant, designed by Frederick Daws, No. HN1138, marked, 1937–85, 5¼in (13.5cm) high.
$260–310 BBR

BUNNYKINS

A Royal Doulton Reggie **Bunnykins,** by Charles Noke, No. D6025, printed mark, 1939–40, 3¾in (9.5cm) high.

$2,100–2,500 BBR

A Royal Doulton Carol Singer **Bunnykins,** by David Lyttleton, No. DB104, marked, 1991, 4in (10cm) high, with box.

$150–180 BBR

A Royal Doulton Mystic **Bunnykins,** No. DB197, 1999, 4½in (11.5cm) high.

$35–40 KA

A Royal Doulton Sundial **Bunnykins,** No. DB213, Time Series, Bunnykins of the Year, 2000, 5in (12.5cm) high.

$35–40 KA

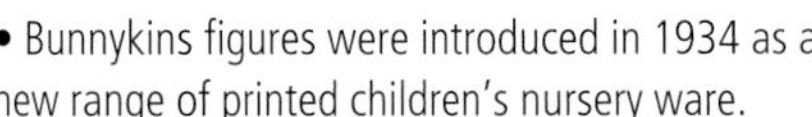

- Bunnykins figures were introduced in 1934 as a new range of printed children's nursery ware.

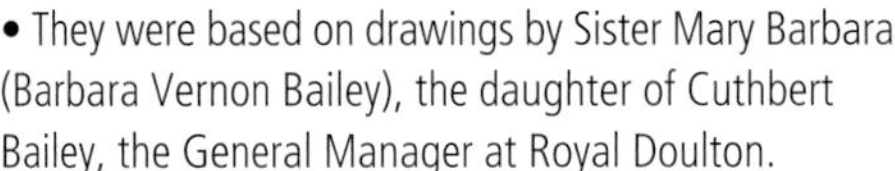

- They were based on drawings by Sister Mary Barbara (Barbara Vernon Bailey), the daughter of Cuthbert Bailey, the General Manager at Royal Doulton.

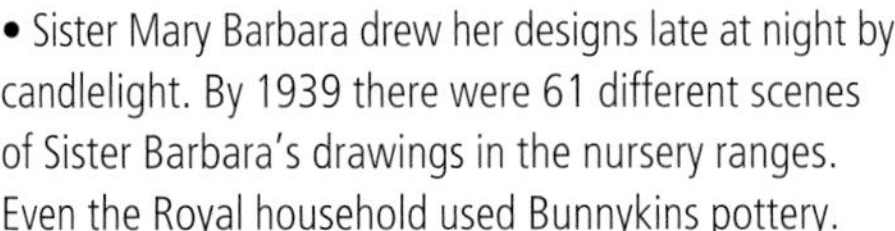

- Sister Mary Barbara drew her designs late at night by candlelight. By 1939 there were 61 different scenes of Sister Barbara's drawings in the nursery ranges. Even the Royal household used Bunnykins pottery.

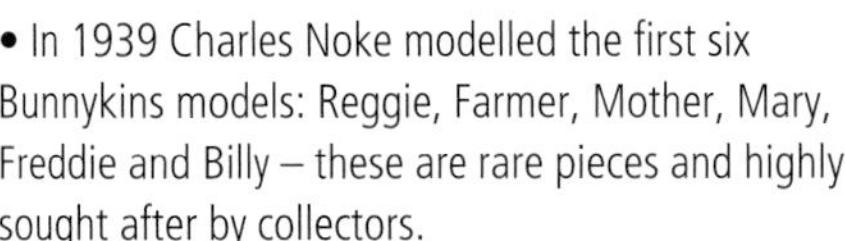

- In 1939 Charles Noke modelled the first six Bunnykins models: Reggie, Farmer, Mother, Mary, Freddie and Billy – these are rare pieces and highly sought after by collectors.

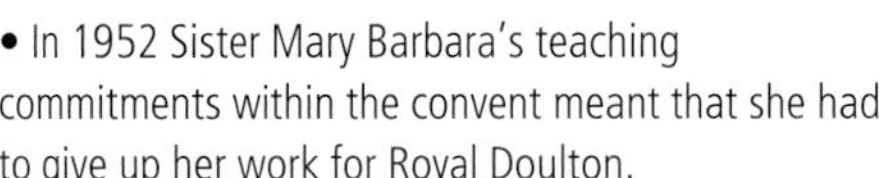

- In 1952 Sister Mary Barbara's teaching commitments within the convent meant that she had to give up her work for Royal Doulton.
- In 1972 the DB Bunnykins range was launched, shortly after Royal Doulton took over the Beswick factory.
- DB Bunnykins are smaller, busier figures. Originally just nine, there are now hundreds to collect.
- The rarest Bunnykins are the six original Charles Noke models from 1939. Examples from the early '70s to the '90s can command high prices, such as 'Trick or Treat' and the two variations of 'Clown'.
- 2003 Barbara Vernon died, aged 92.

A Royal Doulton Betsy Ross **Bunnykins,** No. DB313, American Heritage Collection, 2003, 4¼in (11cm) high.

$70–80 PASC

A Royal Doulton George **Washington Bunnykins,** by Caroline Dadd, No. DB367, American Heritage Collection, 2005, 5in (12.5cm) high.

$80–90 PASC

A Royal Doulton Sister Mary **Barbara Bunnykins,** No. DB334, 2005.

$35–40 PASC

A Royal Doulton Balloon **Man Bunnykins,** No. DB366, limited edition of 2000, 2005.

$80–90 PASC

A Royal Doulton figure, entitled 'One of the Forty', 1924–38, 7¾in (19.5cm) high.

$730–870 HAD

This is the tenth version of this popular figure originally produced in 1920 and designed by Harry Tittensor. It was inspired by the operetta Chu Chin Chow, *later to become* Ali Baba and the Forty Thieves. *Never to be outdone, Doulton produced well over forty thieves!*

A Royal Doulton figure, by Leslie Harradine, entitled 'Lady Fayre', No. HN1265, 1928–38, 5¼in (13.5cm) high.

$2,250–2,500 PASC

A Royal Doulton figure, entitled 'Priscilla', No. HN1340, printed mark, 1933, 8in (20.5cm) high.

$240–280 CAG

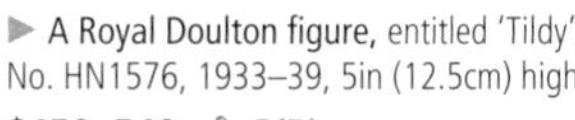

► **A Royal Doulton figure,** entitled 'Tildy', No. HN1576, 1933–39, 5in (12.5cm) high.

$450–540 G(B)

A Royal Doulton figure, by Leslie Harradine, entitled 'Marion', No. HN1582, 1933–40, 6½in (16.5cm) high.

$3,200–3,550 PASC

Although many copies of 'Marion' were produced, this particular model is a rare colourway, which explains the high price.

A Royal Doulton figure, entitled 'Called Love, A Little Boy', restored, 1933–49, 3½in (9cm) high.

$175–210 G(B)

◄ **A Royal Doulton figure,** entitled 'Modena', No. HN1846, printed mark, c1938, 7in (18cm) high.

$1,550–1,850 CAG

ROYAL DOULTON FIGURES

A Royal Doulton figure, by Leslie Harradine, entitled 'Toinette', No. HN1940, 1940–49, 6¾in (17cm) high.

$2,200–2,450 PASC

A Royal Doulton figure, entitled 'Columbine', 1982, 12¼in (31cm) high.

$520–620 HAD

A Royal Doulton figure, entitled 'Harlequin', 1982, 12¼in (31cm) high.

$480–570 HAD

- Royal Doulton figures are highly collectable. The modern range dates back to 1913.
- Most have an HN prefix – the initials of Harry Nixon, the first manager of the figure making shop.
- HN1 was the first figure. Originally named 'Bedtime' this small figure of a tired child was renamed 'Darling' after Queen Mary declared the figure to be 'a darling'.
- Current HN numbers are in the 4000s. Looking up the HN number will date the figure to the period when it was produced.
- Early figures and those produced for short periods are more collectable.
- Rare colourways and anomalies add value.

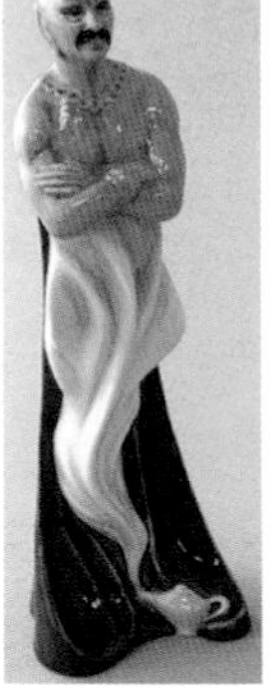

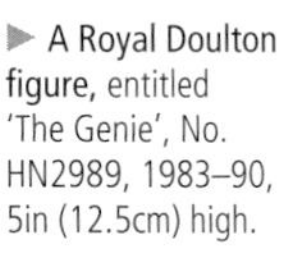

► **A Royal Doulton figure,** entitled 'The Genie', No. HN2989, 1983–90, 5in (12.5cm) high.

$140–165 G(B)

A Royal Doulton jug, by Fenton and Noke, limited edition of 600, 1932, 7in (18cm) high.

$1,100–1,250 BWDA

► **A Royal Doulton character jug,** by Gary Sharpe, entitled 'Captain Ahab', 1959–84, 8in (20.5cm) high.

$95–105 KA

A Royal Doulton character jug, by David B. Biggs, entitled 'Bootmaker', Williamsburg Series, 1963–83, 8in (20.5cm) high.

$105–120 ⊞ KA

A Royal Doulton character jug, by Max Henk and David B. Biggs, entitled 'Captain Hook', No. D6597, marked, 1965–71, 7¼in (18.5cm) high.

$330–390 BBR

A Royal Doulton character jug, by Colin M. Davidson, entitled 'Mae West', No. D6688, marked, 1983–86, 7½in (19cm) high, with box.

$105–120 BBR

◀ **A Royal Doulton character jug,** by Harry Sales, entitled 'Uncle Sam', limited edition of 500, marked, 1986, 5½in (14cm) high.

$60–70 BBR

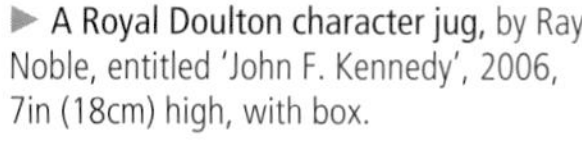

▶ **A Royal Doulton character jug,** by Ray Noble, entitled 'John F. Kennedy', 2006, 7in (18cm) high, with box.

$200–220 ⊞ PASC

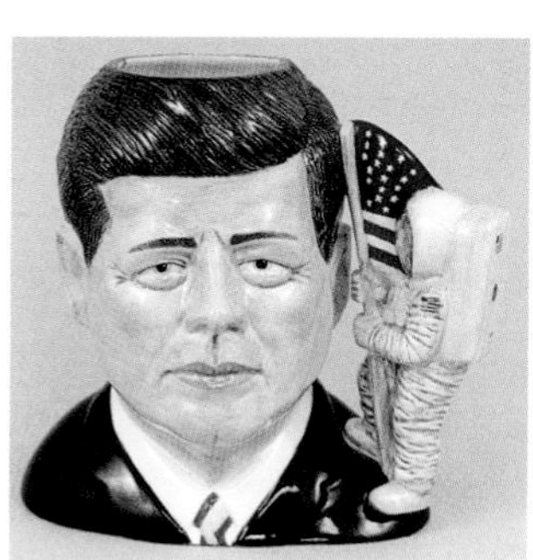

SERIES WARE

A Royal Doulton Series Ware Gaffers sandwich tray, inscribed 'I be all the way from Zummerset', 1972, 14in (35.5cm) wide.

$165–185 ⊞ PASC

- Series Ware was a popular line introduced by Doulton's senior designer, Charles Noke.
- It ran from 1899 to the 1950s.
- Each group or series of designs are linked by style and theme so they were ideal to give as gifts or display as well as to use.
- The themes cover many different subjects, from sports and hobbies to folklore and literature – including every popular Dickens series.
- According to Noke, these wares were 'Made to adorn yet serve some useful purpose'.

A Royal Doulton Series Ware jug, entitled 'Oliver Twist', 1925–50, 5¾in (14.5cm) high.

$175–195 ⊞ PASC

RYE POTTERIES

A Rye Pottery dish, impressed 'Rye' 1949–52, 5¾in (14.5cm) wide.

$50–55 MARK

A Cinque Ports Pottery jug, 1956–60, 6in (15cm) high.

$70–80 TAC

A Rye Pottery Tulip vase, printed mark, 1957–71, 6¼in (16cm) high.

$35–40 MARK

An Iden Pottery candlestick, by Dennis Townsend, entitled 'Candle Woman', printed mark 1959–70, (24cm) high.

$110–125 MARK

An Iden Pottery vase, by Dennis Townsend, marked, 1959–70, 11in (28cm) high.

$80–90 MARK

A Rye Pottery vase, printed mark, 1957–71, 5¼in (13.5cm) high.

$60–70 MARK

◄ A Rye Pottery vase, by Dennis Townsend, 1957–59, 5in (12.5cm) high.

$70–80 MARK

Dennis Townsend's hands are famous. During the late 1950s BBC TV used short films to fill in the spaces between programmes or plays. These consisted of tranquil films accompanied by music and subjects included a spinning wheel, a kitten, a windmill and a potter using a wheel. Dennis Townsend was the potter but he was never identified as you could only see his hands.

A Rye Art Pottery footed bowl, by David Sharp, 1960s, 3in (7.5cm) high.

$80–90 MARK

A Cinque Ports Pottery mug, 1964–88, 8¾in (22cm) high.

$50–55 MARK

A Rye Art Pottery jug, by David Sharp, c1964, 3¼in (8.5cm) high.

$350–40 MARK

A Cinque Ports Pottery cruet set, in the form of a pair of monks, 1965–75, 8in (20.5cm) high.

$70–80 MARK

A David Sharp money box, in the form of a rabbit, c1970, 6in (15cm) high.

$95–105 MARK

A Cinque Ports Pottery vase, 1970s, 6in (15cm) high.

$25–30 MARK

A David Sharp model of a lion cub, 1970s, 8in (20.5cm) high.

$80–90 MARK

A David Sharp model of a dog, 1974–80, 7in (18cm) high.

$70–80 MARK

A Cinque Ports Pottery coffee pot, printed mark, c1988, 10½in (26.5cm) high.

$50–55 MARK

SCANDINAVIAN POTTERY

A **Björn Wiinblad bowl,** painted signature, Denmark, dated 1961, 20½in (52cm) diam.

$710–850 WAD

A **pair of Björn Wiinblad candelabra,** repaired, painted marks, Denmark, dated 1963, 14½in (37cm) high.

$140–165 WAD

A **Björn Wiinblad face vase,** painted marks, Denmark, dated 1979, 6½in (16.5cm) high.

$190–220 WAD

Further reading

Miller's Ceramics Buyers Guide, Miller's Publications, 2006

An **Egersund Fayancefabrik dish and cover,** Norway, 1950s, 9in (23cm) diam.

$20–25 UD

A **Gustavsberg Argenta dish,** painted marks, Sweden, 1930s, 14in (35.5cm) square.

$360–430 WAD

Introduced in 1930, the Argenta range was designed by Wilhelm Kåge (1889–1960).

An **Egersund Fayancefabrik dish,** Norway, 1950s, 8in (20.5cm) diam.

$20–25 UD

STIG LINDBERG

A Gustavsberg cup and saucer, by Stig Lindberg, Sweden, c1955, 2in (5cm) high.

$20–25 MARK

A Gustavsberg stoneware model of a horse, by Stig Lindberg, entitled 'Springare', signed, Sweden, 1952–72, 4¼in (11cm) high.

$1,900–2,250 SEK

A Gustavsberg Domino ashtray, by Stig Lindberg, Sweden, 1955, 8in (20.5cm) square.

$85–95 RETO

- Stig Lindberg (1916–82) had a massive influence on post-war ceramic design.
- He worked for Gustavsberg in Sweden from 1937 to 1978, becoming head designer in 1949 (taking over from Wilhelm Kåge).
- Early designs are marked with 'G', an anchor and 'Stig L'.
- After 1948 he marked his pieces with a painted hand over Gustavsberg's 'G' and 'Stig L'.

► **A Gustavsberg Reptil vase,** by Stig Lindberg, Sweden, c1960, 13in (33cm) high.

$310–350 PI

◄ **A Gustavsberg Terma teapot,** by Stig Lindberg, Sweden, 1960s, 6in (15cm) diam.

$80–90 PI

◄ **A Gustavsberg candlestick,** by Berndt Friberg, Sweden, 1960s, 3in (7.5cm) high.

$110–125 MARK

◄ **A Rörstrand vase,** by Ilse Claesons, Sweden, 1939–42, 7in (18cm) high.

$95–105 MARK

A Rörstrand bowl, by Carl-Harry Stålhane, Sweden, 1950s, 6in (15cm) diam.

$120–135 MARK

A Rörstrand Chamotte vase, by Gunnar Nylund, Sweden, 1950s, 6in (15cm) high.

$120–135 MARK

A Rörstrand stoneware dish, by Carl-Harry, Stålhane, Sweden, 1950s, 7in (18cm) diam.

$60–70 MARK

A Rörstrand Granada tureen and cover, Sweden, 1950s, 6in (15cm) wide.

$5–10 UD

A Royal Copenhagen Faïence stoneware vase, by Nils Thorsson, impressed and painted marks, Denmark, 1960s, 6¾in (17cm) high.

$120–140 WAD

A Royal Copenhagen Tenera vase, by Nils Thorsson, Denmark, c1960, 8in (20.5cm) high.

$130–145 PI

A Royal Copenhagen pillow vase, by Nils Thorsson, Denmark, 1967, 9in (23cm) wide.

$110–125 FRD

◄ **Two Royal Copenhagen models of bear cubs,** by Knud Kyhn, Denmark, 1960s, 3in (7.5cm) wide.

$110–125 each MARK

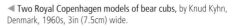

► **A Royal Copenhagen model of a rabbit,** Denmark, c1970, 3in (7.5cm) wide.

$60–70 RUSK

An Upsala Ekeby Paprika footed bowl, by Anna-Lisa Thompson, Sweden, c1950, 9in (23cm) wide.

$110–125 MARK

Anna-Lisa Thompson worked at Upsala Ekeby from 1935 to 1952.

SHELLEY

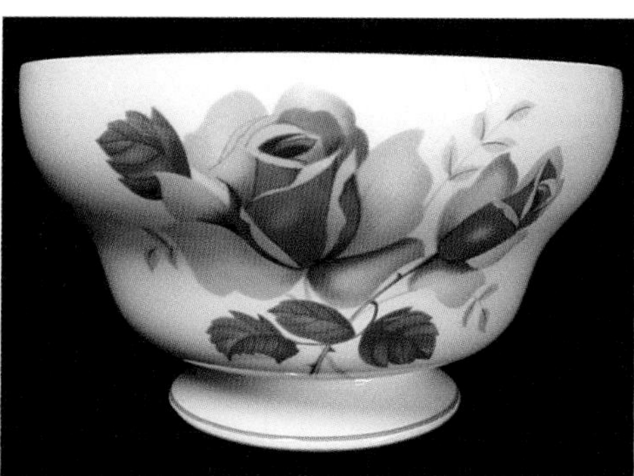

A Shelley sugar bowl, decorated with Mayfair Autumn Rose pattern, 1963, 2¾in (7cm) high.

$20–25 R2G

A Shelley powder bowl and cover, decorated with Tulip pattern, c1935, 7in (18cm) high.

$240–270 HEW

A Shelley chamberstick, decorated with Harmony pattern, c1933, 6¼in (16cm) wide.

$45–50 TOP

► **A Shelley ginger jar and cover,** decorated with Harmony pattern, c1935, 10in (25.5cm) high.

$380–420 BEV

A Shelley Regent teapot, decorated with Syringa pattern, 1934, 6in (15cm) high.

$230–260 BEV

A pair of Shelley napkin rings, 1930s, 2¾in (7cm) diam.

$120–135 BEV

SHELLEY

A Shelley trio, decorated with Melody pattern, c1928, 7in (18cm) diam.

$60–70 WAC

A Shelley cream jug, decorated with Patches pattern, 1930s, 3½in (9cm) high.

$90–100 SAT

A Shelley Vogue trio, with hand-painted decoration, 1930–33, plate 6in (15cm) wide.

$470–520 BEV

- Originally known as Wileman & Co, the firm changed its name to Shelley in 1925.
- Collectors associate this pottery with the angular 'moderne' china designed by Eric Slater (1902–84) from 1930.
- Slater's first shape was Vogue, quickly followed by Mode.
- Shelley china was firmly aimed at the younger middle classes.
- The angular sets were somewhat impractical, meaning fewer have survived.
- Highly prized by collectors are the angular shaped wares with abstract designs, often highlighted in platinum.

A Shelley Eve trio, with transfer-printed decoration, 1932, plate 6in (15cm) wide.

$230–260 BEV

A Shelley Mode trio, 1932–38, plate 6in (15cm) wide.

$380–420 BEV

A Shelley vase, decorated with Harmony pattern, c1933, 5in (12.5cm) high.

$60–70 TOP

◄ A Shelley vase, decorated with Swirls pattern, c1934, 8½in (21.5cm) high.

$60–70 WAC

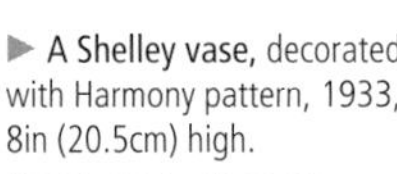

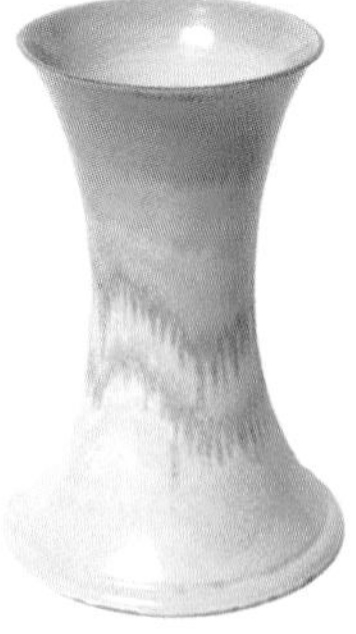

► A Shelley vase, decorated with Harmony pattern, 1933, 8in (20.5cm) high.

$260–290 HEW

STUDIO POTTERY

STUDIO POTTERY has held a long appeal to collectors as they represent – in the purest sense of the term – individual items hand made by potters. The top of the market is dominated by Lucie Rie, Hans Coper and Bernard Leach, whose work can fetch four-figure sums.

Lower down the scale there is still much to be found. Good post-war examples from the Celtic Pottery or those by Jo Lester on the Isle of Wight can still be found relatively inexpensively. Although they will never reach the prices of Lucie Rie's work, they will increase in value.

CELTIC POTTERY

A Celtic Pottery mug, decorated with Folk pattern, c1970, 3in (7.5cm) high.

$10–15 ⊞ **MARK**

A Celtic Pottery tray, decorated with Folk pattern, c1970, 6in (15cm) wide.

$25–30 ⊞ **PrB**

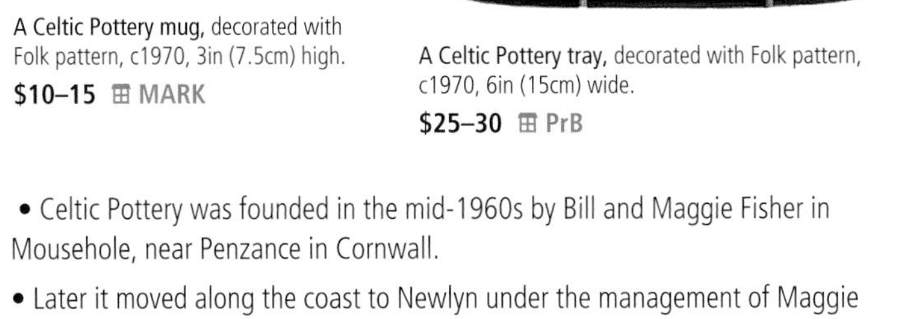

- Celtic Pottery was founded in the mid-1960s by Bill and Maggie Fisher in Mousehole, near Penzance in Cornwall.

- Later it moved along the coast to Newlyn under the management of Maggie Fisher, later joined by Ev (Everidge) Stevens.

- Celtic became famous for two main designs: 'Folk' which shows aggressive cockerels in dark green on a green/white ground and the later geometric 'Medallion'.
- Look for items marked with paper labels: early pieces mention 'Mousehole' and 'William Fisher', later gold labels mention 'Celtic' and 'Newlyn'.

A Celtic Pottery vase, decorated with Folk pattern, c1970, 6in (15cm) high.

$25–30 ⊞ **PrB**

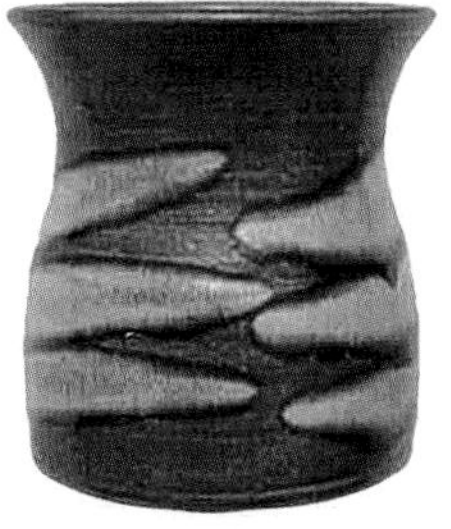

A Culloden Pottery mug, Scotland, 1970s, 3¼in (8.5cm) high.

$10–15 ⊞ **SSS**

◀ **A Ewenny Pottery tankard,** inscribed 'Buller Love Luck Iechyd Da', Wales, c1930, 5in (12.5cm) high.

$80–90 ⊞ **IW**

Dating back as far as 1427, the Ewenny Pottery has been run by generations of the Jenkins family since 1610. This item is a typical piece of Ewenny pottery.

A Ewenny Pottery jug, Wales, 1970s, 4¾in (12cm) high.

$85–95 ⊞ **OACC**

A Wiliam Fishley Holland Pottery jug, c1930, 5in (12.5cm) high.

$85–95 IW

William Fishley Holland was the grandson of Edwin Beer Fishley and taught the art of potting to Michael Cardew. Fishley worked at his family pottery at Fremington from 1902 until it closed in 1912. He then set up at Braunton until 1921, finally establishing his own pottery at Clevedon in north Somerset.

A William Fishley Holland Pottery bowl, c1930, 11in (28cm) diam.

$120–135 IW

◀ **A Geoffrey Luff Palissy-style bowl,** decorated with snakes and a dragonfly, c2000, 23in (58.5cm) wide.

$2,400–2,650 BRT

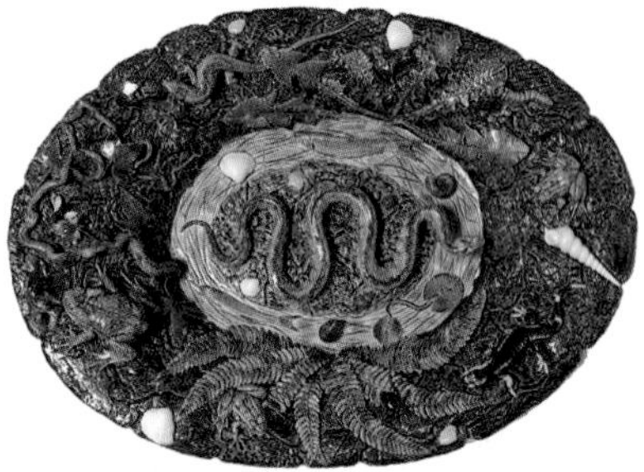

A Geoffrey Luff Palissy-style dish, decorated with lizards, snakes and a frog, c2001, 22in (56cm) wide.

$2,400–2,650 BRT

Born in 1948 in Berlin and educated in the UK and France, Geoffrey Luff began working as a furniture restorer. In 1993 he began producing pottery inspired by Bernard Palissy.

A Bernard Leach earthenware jug, c1930, 7in (18cm) high.

$180–200 OD

A Bernard Leach stoneware vase, with three lug handles, impressed marks, c1947, 8¾in (22cm) high.

$2,150–2,550 BEA

▶ **A Lucie Rie bowl,** c1955, 4½in (11.5cm) wide.

$2,250–2,650 JNic

SYLVAC

A SylvaC jug, mould No. 1195, the handle in the form of a squirrel, 1930s, 7½in (19cm) high.

$70–80 ⊞ KA

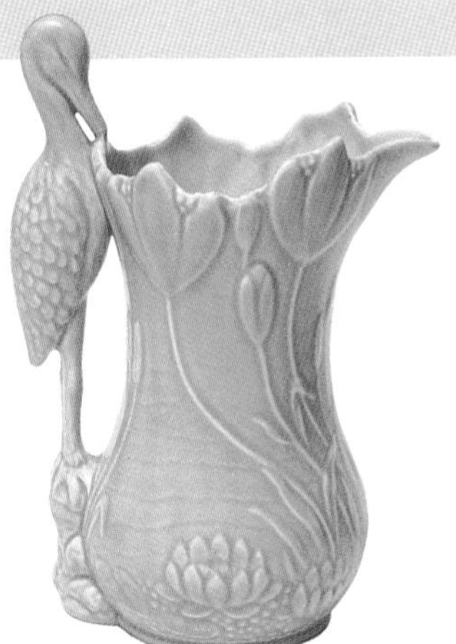

A SylvaC jug, the handle in the form of a stork, 1930s, 10in (25.5cm) high.

$60–70 ⊞ KA

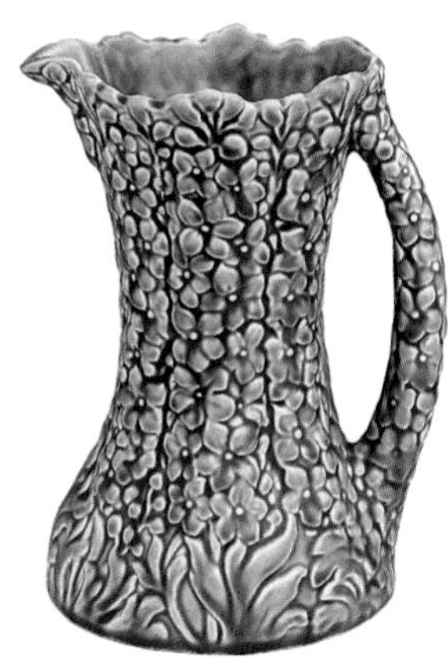

A SylvaC jug, 1930s, 9in (23cm) high.

$95–105 ⊞ BEV

A SylvaC Leaf vase, 1930s, 9in (23cm) high.

$70–80 ⊞ BEV

A SylvaC vase, mould No. 1484, in the form of a top hat with a cat and dog, impressed mark, 1930s, 4in (10cm) high.

$50–55 ⊞ KA

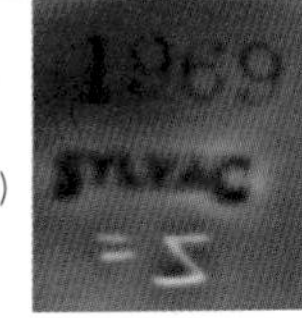

A SylvaC jug, the handle in the form of two elves, late 1930s, 8½in (21.5cm) high.

$105–120 ⊞ KA

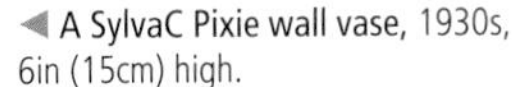

◀ **A SylvaC Pixie wall vase,** 1930s, 6in (15cm) high.

$110–125 ⊞ BEV

A SylvaC posy holder, late 1930s, 7in (18cm) wide.

$60–70 ⊞ BEV

◀ **A SylvaC basketweave vase,** mould No. 2817, 1940s, 4in (10cm) high.

$10–15 ⊞ KA

▶ **A SylvaC jug,** 1940s, 5½in (14cm) high.

$45–50 ⊞ OACC

A SylvaC onion face pot, mould No. 4750, 1950s, 4in (10cm) high.

$10–15 ⊞ KA

A SylvaC beetroot face pot, mould No. 4553, 1950s, 5½in (12.5cm) high.

$10–15 ⊞ KA

A SylvaC model of a dog, 1930s, 5in (12.5cm) high.

$35–40 ⊞ KA

◀ **A SylvaC model of a dog,** 1932, 5¼in (13.5cm) high.

$45–50 ⊞ OACC

A SylvaC model of a rabbit, 1930s, 4½in (11.5cm) high.

$50–55 ⊞ KA

TROIKA

TROIKA IS A PHENOMENON – once practically unheard of, it underwent a dramatic increase in popularity in the 1990s. Pots costing a few pounds or less when new have gone on to achieve three-figure sums and, for some top pieces, four-figure prices.

Established in 1963 by Benny Sirota and Lesley Illsley at St Ives, Cornwall, the pottery moved to Newlyn in 1970 and closed in 1983. Many of the early products were small, the sort of items that were perfect for bringing home from a Cornish holiday – perfume bottle, plates, mugs and double eggcups.

Later, more sculptural pieces were made, along with stunning smooth-glazed white architectural pieces designed for an exhibition at Heals in 1968. These exhibition pieces are highly prized today as with an original price tag of $45, few were sold. Much of what is seen today is the so-called 'rough texture wares' introduced in 1967 but despite its handcrafted appearance, Troika is moulded, with hand-finished painting and decoration.

Today the price of Troika has fallen a little behind its peak. Collectors are now more choosey and often go for bigger and more unusual piece. Plaques, large Wheel vases, Anvils and Doublebased vases all remain popular.

Buyers should be aware that a number of clumsy fakes exist and many original moulds survive which increases the chance of modern pieces being sold as an originals.

A Troika marmalade pot, 1967–70, 3½in (9cm) high.

$120–140 G(B)

A Troika marmalade pot, decorated by Alison Brigden, painted mark, 1967–83 , 3½in (9cm) high.

$60–70 ROS

A Troika vase, monogrammed mark possibly for Marilyn Pascoe, c1973, 5in (12.5cm) high.

$540–640 FLDA

A Troika Chimney vase, painted mark, artist's monogram, 1970s, 8in (20.5cm) high.

$310–370 BWL

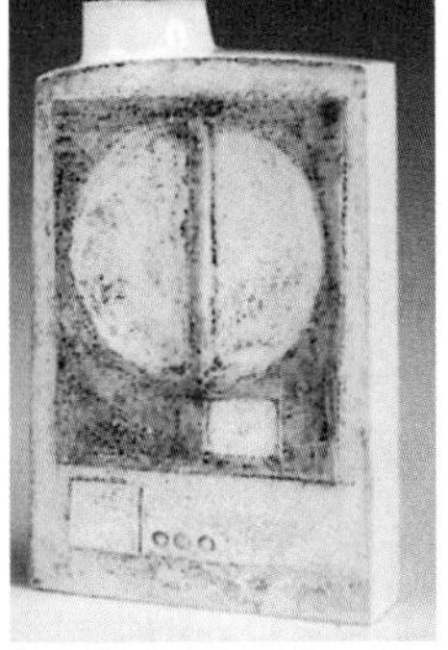

A Troika Chimney vase, decorated by Ann Lewis, painted mark, artist's monogram, 1970–72, 7¾in (19.5cm) high.

$310–370 RTo

◄ **A Troika Coffin vase,** c1970, 6¾in (17cm) high.

$140–165 DA

Introduced at Newlyn, the so-called Coffin vase was very popular and is often found on the market. It was designed as a 'kiln filler', its shape designed to fill spaces in between other pieces in the kiln. Unlike most Troika shapes, this was not designed by Lesley Illsley but contracted out to Phil Read, a mould maker.

A Troika **Coffin vase,** c1970, 16½in (42cm) high.

$190–220 HAD

Two Troika **Coffin vases,** one by Annette Walters, the other probably by Shirley Warf, 1970s, 17½in (44.5cm) high.

$290–340 CGC

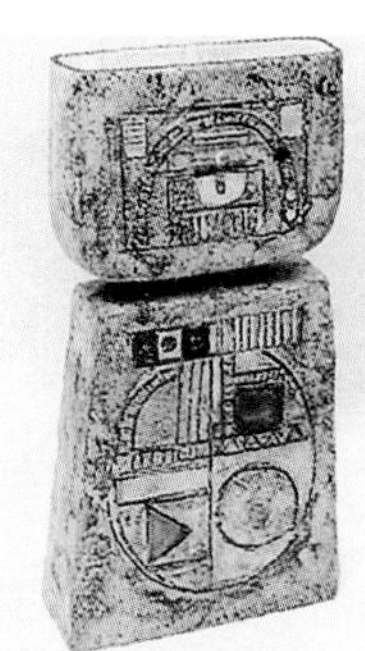

A Troika **Doublebased vase,** by Holly Jackson, marked, artist's monogram, mid-1970s, 14¼in (36cm) high.

$760–910 DD

A Troika **Doublebased vase,** by Avril Bennett, painted mark, artist's initials, 1973–79, 13½in (34.5cm) high.

$900–1,050 BAM

A Troika **dish,** by Avril Bennett, marked, 1973–79, 6¼in (16cm) square.

$280–330 G(L)

A Troika **Wheel vase,** by Penny Black, 1970–76, 4½in (11.5cm) high.

$140–165 PFK

A Troika **Wheel vase,** artist's initial 'V', mid-1970s, 6¼in (16cm) high.

$480–570 GTH

A Troika **Wheel lamp base,** 1970s, 11in (28cm) high.

$1,550–1,850 G(L)

A Troika **Anvil vase,** by Avril Bennett, painted mark, artist's initials 'AB', 1973–79, 9in (23cm) high.

$850–950 ROS

A Troika **vase,** by Avril Bennett, artist's initials 'AB', 1976–83, 8in (20.5cm) high.

$200–220 BWL

► A Troika **Love Plaque,** moulded with stylized figures, painted marks, artist's cypher, 1967, 14½in (37cm) wide.

$2,400–2,800 WW

SALLY TUFFIN

A Moorcroft tea-for-two set, by Sally Tuffin, painted marks, 1990s, teapot 4¼in (11cm) high, with presentation case.

$700–840 WW

► **A Sally Tuffin vase,** decorated with Rainforest pattern, impressed and painted marks, 1992, 12½in (32cm) high, with presentation case.

$700–840 SWO

A Dennis Chinaworks Primrose box and cover, by Sally Tuffin, dated 2001, 4½in (11.5cm) high.

$410–460 NP

A Dennis Chinaworks Artichoke vase, by Sally Tuffin, 2002, 7¾in (19.5cm) high.

$470–520 PASC

A Dennis Chinaworks Crab box and cover, by Sally Tuffin, dated 2003, 6in (15cm) high.

$550–660 NP

A Dennis Chinaworks Willow and Bee box and cover, by Sally Tuffin, dated 2005, 5in (12.5cm) high.

$550–660 NP

A Dennis Chinaworks Polar Bear vase, by Sally Tuffin and Heidi Warr, dated 2000, 15in (38cm) high.

$1,550–1,750 NP

DENNIS CHINAWORKS

- Sally Tuffin and her husband, Richard Dennis, started the Dennis Chinaworks in 1985.
- Production was postponed between 1986 and 1993 while Sally was partner and director of the Moorcroft Pottery.
- Dennis Chinaworks is still in production today, with Sally taking inspiration from nature, abstract art and the Arts & Crafts movement.

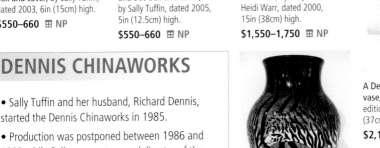

A Dennis Chinaworks Minstrel vase, by Sally Tuffin, limited edition, dated 2002, 14½in (37cm) high.

$2,150–2,400 NP

The decoration on this vase was adapted by Sally Tuffin from a William Morris design.

◄ **A Dennis Chinaworks Tiger vase,** by Sally Tuffin, dated 2002, 14½in (37cm) high.

$1,000–1,100 NP

A Dennis Chinaworks Strawberry vase, by Sally Tuffin, dated 2003, 7in (18cm) high.

$410–460 ⊞ NP

A Dennis Chinaworks Chaucer vase, by Sally Tuffin, inscribed 'The Notable Rhetor, Poet of Britaine', limited edition, 2003, 9½in (24cm) high.

$600–660 ⊞ NP

A Dennis Chinaworks Sunflower vase, by Sally Tuffin, edition of 25, 2003, 19in (48.5cm) high.

$1,750–1,950 ⊞ PASC

A Dennis Chinaworks Lion vase, by Sally Tuffin, No. 12 of edition of 25, 2003, 14½in (37cm) high.

$2,400–2,650 ⊞ PASC

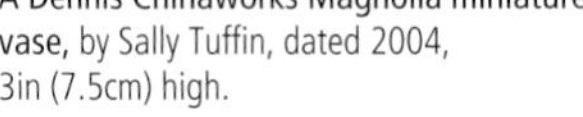

A Dennis Chinaworks Magnolia miniature vase, by Sally Tuffin, dated 2004, 3in (7.5cm) high.

$280–310 ⊞ NP

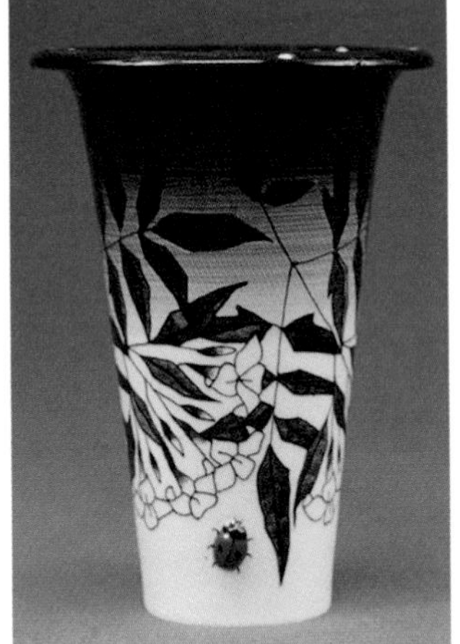

A Dennis Chinaworks Jasmine and Ladybird vase, by Sally Tuffin, 2004, 6in (15cm) high.

$220–250 ⊞ PASC

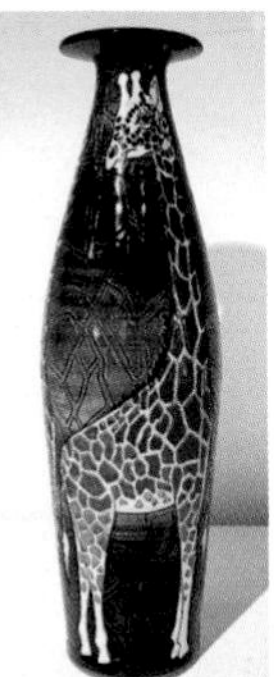

◄ A Dennis Chinaworks Giraffe vase, by Sally Tuffin, edition, of 30, dated 2005, 15in (38cm) high.

$1,000–1,100 ⊞ NP

► A Dennis Chinaworks Tulip Tree jug, by Sally Tuffin, dated 2003, 9in (23cm) high.

$550–660 ⊞ NP

A Dennis Chinaworks Jasmine teapot, by Sally Tuffin, 2003, 5½in (14cm) high.

$670–740 ⊞ PASC

UNITED STATES

A Sascha Brastoff Gold Boomerang bowl, with three legs, 1950s, 9in (23cm) wide.

$70–80 H&LM

A Sascha Brastoff Star Stud vase, signed, 1950s, 5½in (14cm) wide.

$70–80 H&LM

A pair of Sascha Brastoff Rooster bowls, signed, 1950s, 5½in (14m) wide.

$220–250 H&LM

◀ **A Castleton China coffee service,** by Eva Zeisel, 1946, cups 5½in (14cm) high.

$350–390 H&LM

The Castleton porcelain service was commissioned by the Museum of Modern Art and shown there in 1947.

A Franciscan cup and saucer, decorated with Starburst pattern, 1954–57.

$10–15 H&LM

▶ **A Franciscan plate,** decorated with Starburst pattern, 1954–57.

$20–25 H&LM

A Franciscan teapot, decorated with Starburst pattern, 1954–57.

$240–270 H&LM

Franciscan Ware's Starburst pattern was firmly in tune with the fascination for space that ran through the 1950s. It was made in 50 different shapes from 1954 to 1957. Look out for good condition large serving pieces as these were not made in the same quantity as the smaller tablewares.

A Franciscan vegetable dish, decorated with Starburst pattern, 1954–57, 8in (20.5cm) wide.

$45–50 H&LM

▶ **A Homer Laughlin China Co Fiesta mixing bowl,** slight damage, 1930s–1940s, 5¼in (13.5cm) diam.

$250–280 ATT

An Iroquois China Co cheese plate, designed by Michael Lax, from the Primaries range, with a wooden cover, 1968.

$110–125 H&LM

An Iroquois China Co Casual bowl, designed by Russel Wright, 1946–59.

$80–90 H&LM

A Marblehead vase, by Arthur Baggs, slight damaged, restored, marked, 1926, 6¾in (17cm) high.

$500–600 DRO(C)

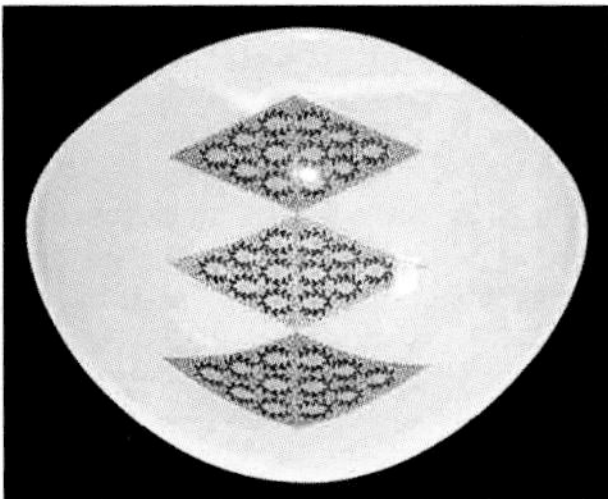

An Iroquois China Co Informal vegetable dish, designed by Ben Seibel, decorated with Blue Diamonds pattern, 1958, 10½in (26.5cm) wide.

$10–15 SSS

An Iroquois China Co coffee pot, designed by Ben Seibel, decorated with Vision pattern, c1966.

$110–125 H&LM

An Iroquois China Co Casual coffee pot, designed by Russel Wright, cover missing, 1946–59.

$80–90 H&LM

► **An Iroquois China Co Informal jug,** designed by Ben Seibel, decorated with Harvest Time pattern, c1955.

$40–45 H&LM

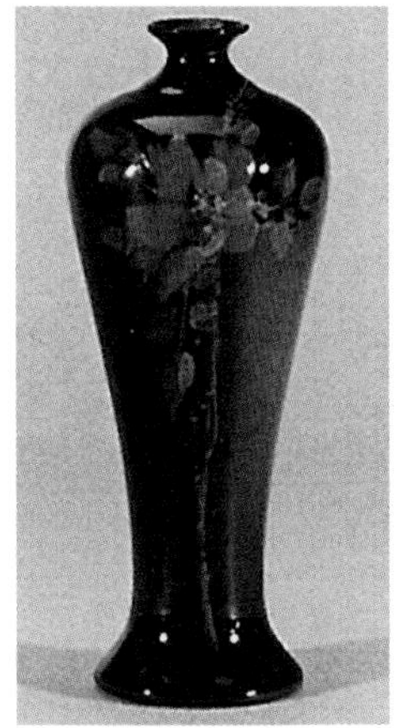

An Owens Utopian vase, early 20thC, 11in (28cm) high.

$175–210 WAD

A Pfaltzgraff Country Time jug, designed by Ben Seibel, decorated in Aztec Blue colourway, slight damage, c1956, 10½in (26.5cm) high.

$140–155 H&LM

◄ **Four Red Wing China Town and Country hors d'oeuvre bowls,** by Eva Zeisel, 1950s, 7in (18cm) long.

$105–120 H&LM

A Red Wing China gravy boat, decorated with Bob White pattern, cover missing, marked, 1955–67, 4in (10cm) high.

$25–30 R2G

► **A Red Wing China vase,** embossed mark and No. 900, 1960s, 10½in (26.5cm) high.

$155–175 H&LM

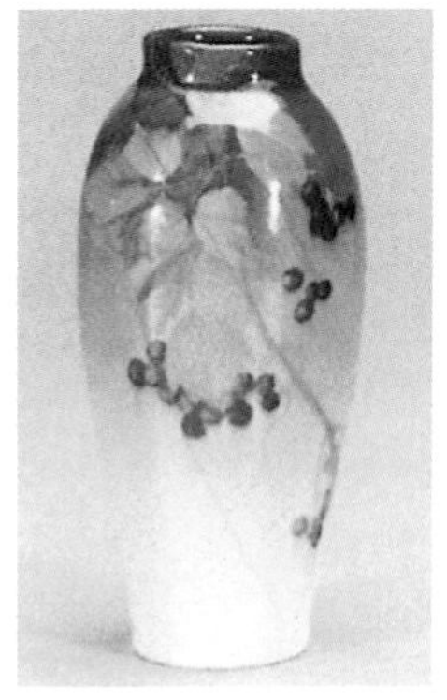

A Rookwood Iris vase, by Lenore Asbury, slight damage, incised and impressed marks, 1904, 8½in (21.5cm) high.

$300–360 WAD

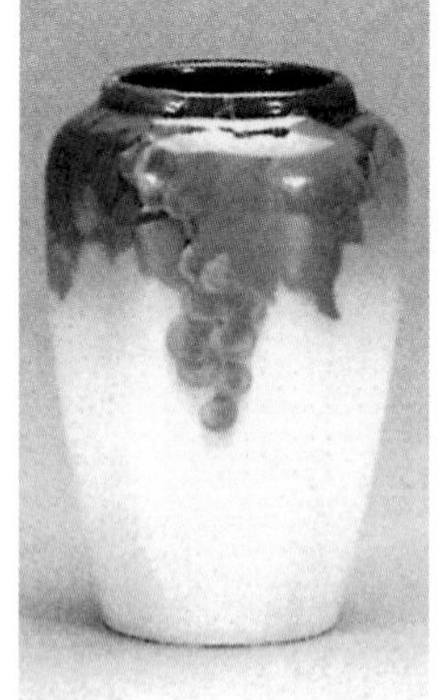

A Rookwood Iris vase, by Irene Bishop, incised and impressed marks, 1908, 6in (15cm) high.

$240–280 WAD

A Rookwood vase, impressed marks, 1922, 7½in (19cm) high.

$300–360 WAD

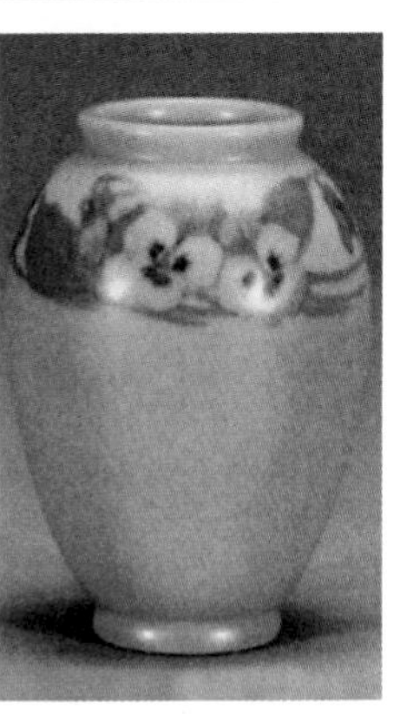

A Rookwood Vellum vase, by Edward Diers, 1928, 5¼in (13.5cm) high.

$700–840 WAD

Two Salem China dinner plates, decorated with Carrousel pattern, 1963, 10in (25.5cm) diam.

$10–15 R2G

► **Four Salem China Free Form dinner plates,** designed by Viktor Schreckengost, decorated with Daybreak-Turquoise pattern, 10in (25.5cm) diam.

$45–50 R2G

The Salem China Company was founded in 1898 in Salem, Ohio. Salem produced many types of tableware including porcelain, ironstone and earthenware but china production was discontinued in 1967.

KATHIE WINKLE

A Kathie Winkle Broadhurst serving bowl, Riviera shape, decorated with Renaissance pattern, 1960s, 9in 923cm) diam.

$10–20 ⊞ R2G

▶ **A Kathie Winkle Broadhurst oatmeal bowl,** Delta shape, decorated with Calypso pattern, 1963, 6in (15cm) diam.

$10–20 ⊞ HIGG

Calypso was supposed to evoke the palm-fringed beaches of the West Indies. This design is very much an all-over affair, which means that thanks to day-to-day use many plates are knife-scratched and dishwasher-worn. Search for unblemished examples if you can. Also look out for the range of co-ordinating enamelled ovenware.

BEAUTY ON A BUDGET

A Kathie Winkle Broadhurst plate, Delta shape, decorated with Calypso pattern, 1963, 9½in (24cm) diam.

$10–20 ⊞ HIGG

Four Kathy Winkle Broadhurst coffee pot, Riviera shape, decorated with San Tropez pattern, 1967, 9in (23cm) high.

$25–30 ⊞ SSS

A Kathie Winkle Broadhurst plate, decorated with Romany pattern, 1975, 9in (23cm) diam.

$10–20 ⊞ R2G

- Kathie Winkle (b1932) is known for her stylish mass-market designs of the 1960s and '70s.
- She was first asked to design for James Broadhurst & Sons in the 1950s and her launch pattern was Pedro in 1958.
- Items were sold in boxed sets via mail order as well as through shops.
- Rushstone, (1965), Barbeque (1968), Eclipse (1971), Safari and Mikado (1963) are all popular designs.
- The wares are still cheap to buy, which makes them popular with collectors.

◀ **Four Kathie Winkle Broadhurst cups and saucers,** decorated with Romany pattern, 1975, cup 2¾in (7cm) high.

$25–30 ⊞ R2G

▶ **A Kathie Winkle Broadhurst gravy boat,** decorated with Newlyn pattern, 1963, 8½in (21.5cm) wide.

$10–20 ⊞ R2G

CHRISTMAS

A chromolithograph postcard, depicting children, c1900, 5in (12.5cm) high.

$20–25 M&C

A Steiff Santa Claus, Germany, 1950s, 5in (12.5cm) high.

$310–350 NAW

► **A set of six Tom Smith Christmas Time crackers,** each containing a Wade porcelain bear, 1996, boxed, 12in (30.5cm) wide.

$80–90 MTB

A Mackintosh's Christmas Carnival Assortment biscuit tin, c1925, 10in (25.5cm) diam.

$105–120 HUX

A box of eight Tom Smith Animates Crackers, containing Wade porcelain miniatures, 1973, boxed, 16in (40.5cm) wide.

$80–90 MTB

A Huntley & Palmer's biscuit tin, decorated with images of Father Christmas, 1950, 7in (18cm) diam.

$70–80 Do

A Royal Copenhagen porcelain plate, entitled 'Bringing Home the Christmas Tree', 1980, 7in (18cm) diam.

$20–25 OACC

A Royal Doulton snowman character jug, designed by Robert Tabbenor, edition of 500, 2005, 7in (18cm) high.

$200–220 PASC

CIGARETTE & TRADE CARDS

CIGARETTE CARDS

Allen & Ginter, Great Generals, set of 50, America, 1886.

$2,340–2,600 ⊞ **MURR**

Allen & Ginter was formed by John Allen and Lewis Ginter in Richmond, Virginia in 1875. The company was known for creating and marketing the first cigarette cards for collecting and trading. Their brands of cigarettes included Richmond Gems, Virginia Brights, Perfection, Dandies and Little Beauties.

Allen & Ginter, City Flags, set of 50, America, 1888.

$970–1,100 ⊞ **MURR**

W. A. & A. C. Churchman, Flags and Funnels of Leading Steamship Lines, set of 50, 1912.

$500–550 ⊞ **MURR**

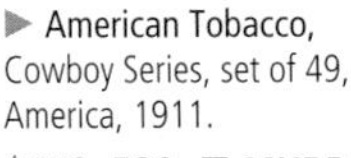

▶ **American Tobacco,** Cowboy Series, set of 49, America, 1911.

$470–520 ⊞ **MURR**

American Tobacco, Lighthouse Series, set of 50, America, 1912.

$540–600 ⊞ **MURR**

W. A. & A. C. Churchman, Association Footballers, Series A, set of 50, 1938.

$50–55 ⊞ **MURR**

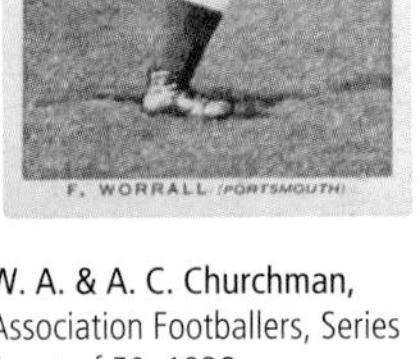

◀ **Edwards, Ringer & Bigg,** Portraits of His Majesty the King, set of 10, 1902.

$590–650 ⊞ **MURR**

W. Duke & Sons, Fishers and Fishing, set of 50, America, 1888.

$1,150–1,300 ⊞ **MURR**

Washington Duke began his tobacco manufacturing career at the end of the American Civil War in 1865. The business expanded from mule and cart and mail order to being one of four US firms manufacturing 90 per cent of America's cigarettes during the 1880s. W. Duke & Sons, Allen & Ginter, F. S. Kinney Co and Goodwin Co merged in 1890 to form the American Tobacco Company. The age and rarity of this set contributes to its high value.

W. & F. Faulkner, Prominent Racehorses of the Present Day, Second Series, set of 25, 1923.

$190–210 ⊞ MURR

W. & F. Faulkner, Angling, set of 25, 1929.

$270–300 ⊞ MURR

Gallaher, Woodland Trees, set of 100, 1912.

$700–770 ⊞ MURR

Gallaher, Signed Portraits of Famous Stars, set of 48, 1935.

$165–195 ⊞ MURR

Richard Lloyd & Sons, Cinema Stars, Second Series, set of 27, 1935.

$85–95 ⊞ CWD

Ogden's, Leaders of Men, set of 50, 1924.

$85–95 ⊞ CWD

Ogden's, ABC of Sport, set of 25, 1927.

$85–95 ⊞ CWD

Ogden's, A. F. C. Nicknames, set of 50, 1933.

$310–350 ⊞ CWD

John Player & Sons, Military Series, set of 50, 1900.

$20–25 per card ⊞ CWD

John Player & Sons, Dogs from Paintings by Arthur Wardle, set of 50, 1931.

$60–70 ⊞ SOR

John Player & Sons, Film Stars, set of 50, 1934.

$85–95 ⊞ MURR

◀ John Player & Sons, Cats, set of 24, 1936.

$260–290 ⊞ MURR

John Player & Sons, Types of Horses, set of 27, 1939.

$110–125 ⊞ CWD

Taddy & Co, Autographs, set of 25, 1912.

$780–860 ⊞ MURR

Taddy & Co, Clowns & Circus Artistes, Reprint, set of 20, 1939.

$10–15 ⊞ MURR

James Taddy & Co began in 1740 as a purveyor of tea, snuff and tobacco. In the 1890s they became known for their trading cards and the most famous of the sets is Clowns & Circus Artistes. A small set of 20, it only reached proof stage before the factory was closed down. It is reputed that there are 20 sets of these original cards in existence and a complete set can be expected to achieve $22,500.

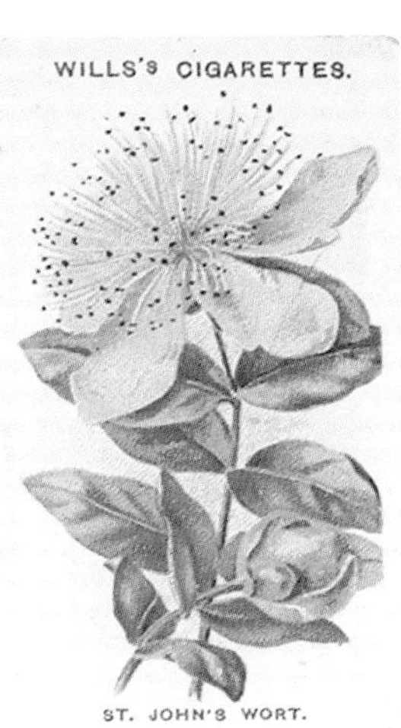

W. D. & H. O. Wills, Old English Garden Flowers, Second Series, set of 50, 1913.

$60–70 ⊞ SOR

W. D. & H. O. Wills, Physical Culture, set of 50, 1914.

$60–70 ⊞ MURR

◀ W. D. & H. O. Wills, Railway Engines, set of 50, 1924.

$85–95 ⊞ MURR

W. D. & H. O. Wills, Racehorses and Jockeys, set of 40, 1939.

$85–95 ⊞ MURR

TRADE CARDS

Calvert & Co, Dan Dare, set of 25, 1954.

$5–10 ⊞ CWD

Dan Dare was the main character of the Eagle comic, first published in 1950. Created by artist Frank Hampson, the English hero is the solar system's most accomplished spy. At the height of his popularity in the 1950s, a large amount of Dan Dare merchandise was produced, including jigsaws, models, guns, walkie-talkies, stamps, toothpowder and even trade cards like this.

Collect-A-Card Corporation, Vette Set, set of 109, 1991.

$40–45 ⊞ MURR

J. Fry & Sons, With Captain Scott at the South Pole, set of 25, 1913.

$430–480 ⊞ MURR

Captain Robert Falcon Scott reached the South Pole in January 1912, one month after his rival, Roald Amundsen. Tragically, Scott and his four companions died on the return journey. This set of cards, depicting activities during the trip, were published only one year later by Fry's Chocolate, probably in acknowledgement of the fact that Scott took some Fry's Cocoa with him on the expedition.

Como Confectionery, Sooty's Latest Adventures, Third Series, set of 50, 1960.

$140–155 ⊞ MURR

Kellogg's, Motor Cars, set of 40, America, 1949.

$360–400 ⊞ MURR

Robertson's, Sporting Gollies, shaped, set of 10, 1962.

$60–70 ⊞ MURR

Weetabix, British Cars, set of 25, 1963.

$120–135 ⊞ MURR

◀ Typhoo Tea, Robin Hood & His Merry Men, set of 30, 1928.

$310–350 ⊞ MURR

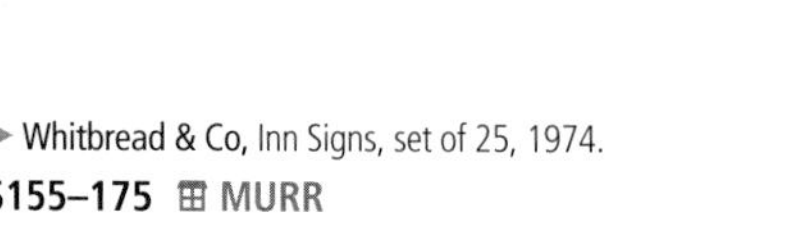

▶ Whitbread & Co, Inn Signs, set of 25, 1974.

$155–175 ⊞ MURR

COMICS & ANNUALS

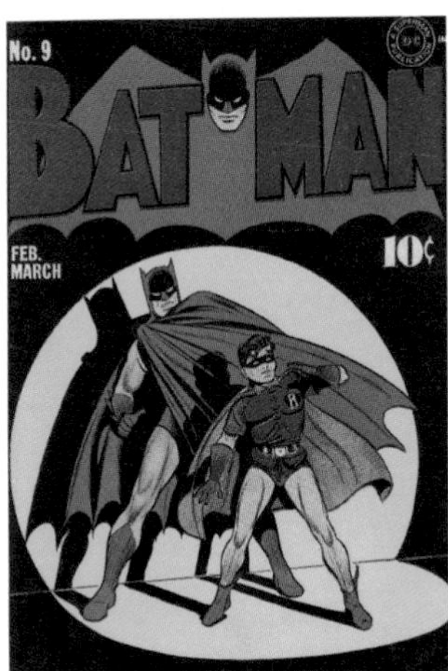

Batman comic, No. 9, published by DC Comics, cover by Jack Burnley, first Christmas story, restored, America 1942.

$1,500–1,800 VAU

Batman comic, No. 306, published by DC Comics, America, 1978.

$10–15 CoC

Batman comic, No. 429, published by DC Comics, A Death in the Family, America, 1988.

$5–10 CoC

Vault of Horror comic, published by M. C. Gaines, file copy, America, 1952.

$1,400–1,650 VAU

The publisher, M. C. Gaines kept up to 12 copies of each issue he published. This is one example.

The Amazing Spider-Man comic, No.1, published by Marvel Comics, The Chameleon Strikes, 1963.

$4,950–5,900 VAU

Giant-Size X-Men comic, No.1, published by Marvel, America, 1974.

$2,000–2,200 VAU

MARVEL COMICS

- Created in 1939 in New York City, Marvel Comics has developed a huge list of publications and characters. The creation of the Fantastic Four in the 1960s led to increased merchandise previously only available by mail order in the comics.
- Marvel went on to produce animated television shows and, in more recent years, full-length feature films. This has allowed them to capitalize on the many new readers and merchandise buyers who were not familiar with their comics but are now familiar with the characters through their films.

◄ **A Fantastic Four cotton T-shirt,** by Marvel Comics, illustrated by Jack Kirkby, 1966, original bag.

$500–600 VAU

This and other Marvel Comics T-shirts were advertised in the comics in the mid-1960s and were available via mail order only.

A set of six Marvel mini books, *Captain America, The Amazing Spider-Man, The Incredible Hulk, The Mighty Thor, Sgt Nick Fury, Millie the Model*, 1966, 1 x ¾in (2.5 x 1.5cm).

$120–140 VAU

► **A set of 40 Marvel Super Heroes stickers with nine puzzle cards,** featuring Conan No. 1 cover, published by Topps Chewing Gum, America, 1976.

$120–140 VAU

***The Beano* comic,** No. 74, Christmas Number, 1939.

$570–680 CBP

***The Beano* comic,** No. 76, 1940.

$155–175 PSH

Big Eggo appeared on the Beano comic cover from 1938 to 1948, being surpassed by Biffo the Bear. Early strips included Pansy Potter and Lord Snooty and His Pals, which was the longest running Beano strip.

***The Beano* comic,** No. 200, 1943.

$60–70 PSH

Paper shortages during WWII meant that comics were produced on poorer quality paper and in lower print runs. Consequently, war time comics rarely appear on the market and attract significant interest from collectors.

***The Beano* comic,** No. 300, Christmas number, 1946.

$50–55 PSH

Themed issues such as this Christmas issue usually had very attractive covers. They are therefore more collectable than regular issues and command higher prices.

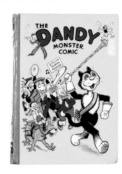

Dennis the Menace annual, 1964.

$45–50 PSH

Arguably the most popular character and an institution in himself, Dennis the Menace was created in 1951 by Davey Law and is still around in today's Beano comic. In 1956 he had an annual dedicated to himself which ran bi-annually with Beryl the Peril annuals which started in 1959. Books from the 1960s are hard to find due to low distribution and the cover and spine lamination being prone to splitting.

The Beano Summer Special comic, No. 300, 1965.

$50–55 PSH

A joint Dandy-Beano *Summer Special comic only appeared in 1963. Every year after that separate* Dandy *and* Beano *editions were published. They are collectable but due to their large size often turn up with a centrefold.*

The Dandy comic, No. 6, slight damage, 1937.

$220–260 CBP

The Dandy Monster comic, No. 6, boards, slight damage, 1941.

$1,650–1,950 CBP

For more Children's books, please see the Books section on pages 34–44.

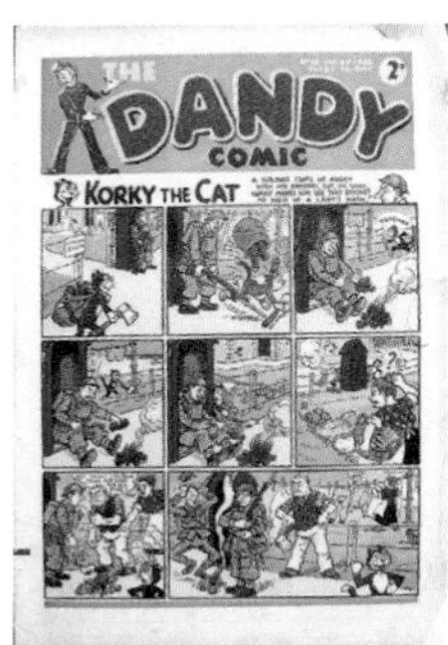

The Dandy comic, No. 110, artwork by James Crichton, boards, slight damage, 1946.

$80–90 PSH

The Dandy *bravely poked fun at the Allied enemies as early as 1940 with Sam Fair's comic strip creation of Addie and Hermy the Nasty Nazis, who were usually up to no good but came unstuck at the end.*

Black Bob **annual,** published by D. C. Thomson & Co, 1951.

$50–55 PSH

Created in 1944 by Jack Prout, one of the artists at D. C. Thomson & Co, Black Bob's adventures as the Dandy Wonder Dog with his master Andrew Glenn appeared for nearly four decades in the Dandy *comic. He was the first character to have his or her own annual. Eight were produced from 1950 to 1965 and this second annual of 1951 is rare.*

The Topper **comic,** published by D. C. Thomson & Co, 1953.

$35–40 PSH

The Topper *comic was launched in February 1953 and was an instant success with its larger tabloid-sized pages. Dudley Watkins created the cover star Mickey the Monkey. Inside were factual pages and adventure stories lasting many issues.*

▶ *The Beezer* comic, published by D. C. Thomson & Co, with Baby Crockett's Rocket fee gift, 1958.

$25–30 PSH

This comic was the fourth title in the D. C. Thomson & Co 'stable four', comprising Beano, Dandy, Topper *and* Beezer. *Two free gifts were issued each year and these are now hard to find.*

Original *Eagle* comic artwork, by Keith Watson, Vol 17, No. 40, page 1, featuring Dan Dare, watercolour on board, 1966.

$750–900 VAU

COMMEMORATIVES

A Booths British Empire Exhibition 'Palace of Industry' commemorative dish, 1924, 5in (12.5cm) wide.

$60–70 ⊞ OIA

A Poole Pottery earthenware plate, commemorating the Festival of Britain, dated 1951, 10in (25.5cm) diam.

$230–260 ⊞ H&G

The Festival of Britain opened in London in May 1951. As well as celebrating the centenary of the 1851 Great Exhibition, the festival was an attempt to raise the spirits of the nation after WWII. The promotion of art, design and industry led to the creation of the South Bank Exhibition and the Festival Pleasure Gardens in Battersea, along with many travelling exhibitions around the UK.

The Times, commemorating the lunar expedition, June 1969.

$155–175 ⊞ HaR

A Carlton model of Felix the Cat, the base printed with the Wembley British Empire Exhibition crest, c1924, 3¼in (8.5cm) long.

$760–910 ⚒ AH

A Paragon bone china mug, commemorating the Festival of Britain, 1951, 4in (10cm) high.

$350–390 ⊞ H&G

A teapot, 'The Eagle Has Landed', commemorating the 30th anniversary of the lunar landing, No. 1 of edition of 50, 1999, 9in (23cm) wide.

$350–390 ⊞ TEA

Neil Armstrong, commander of the US Apollo 13 mission, was the first human to step foot on the moon on 20 July 1969. He was accompanied by his colleague Buzz Aldrin and they used the Eagle lunar module to explore the moon's surface.

A Bakelite powder compact, commemorating the New York World's Fair, showing the Trylon and Perisphere landmarks, 1939, 2½in (6.5cm) wide.

$180–200 ⊞ SUW

Daily Mirror

The time: 9.18 pm, July 20, AD 1969

MAN ON THE MOON

AND THE MESSAGE FROM EARTH: WE'RE BREATHING AGAIN!

Man has landed on the Moon. A new era in his history began at 9.18 last night when the lunar module Eagle settled gently on the dusty surface of the Sea of Tranquillity. Inside it—astronauts Armstrong and Aldrin, destined now for a permanent place in history. They immediately began to prepare for their Moon walk. There are still great perils ahead. But these are truly great achievements. America, the land of frontierence, has opened up a new frontier.

The last practice run

The *Daily Mirror*, commemorating the lunar landing, 21 July 1969.

$20–25 ⊞ COB

A teapot, 'Gunpowder, Treason and Pot' commemorating the 400th anniversary of the gundpowder plot, No. 1 of edition of 50, 2005, 14in (35.5cm) high.

$780–860 ⊞ TEA

MILITARY & NAVAL

A Royal Doulton glazed stoneware loving cup, commemorating the life of Lord Nelson, with three rope-effect handles, c1905, 6½in (16.5cm) high.

$950–1,100 G(L)

A Dutch Delft plate, commemorating the end of WWII, depicting William of Orange on horseback, Holland, Maastricht, 1945, 9in (23cm) diam.

$90–100 COMM

A Kendal bone china plate, commemorating the liberation of Kuwait, 1991, 8in (20.5cm) diam.

$60–70 H&G

A Royal Doulton salt-glazed jug, commemorating the life of Lord Nelson, circle mark, lion and crown, c1905, 7in (18cm) high.

$280–330 BBR

A studio pottery plaque, commemorating the 350th anniversary of the Mayflower and the Pilgrim Fathers sailing to America, 1970, 10in (25.5cm) diam.

$60–70 COMM

A Wilkinson Toby jug, designed by Sir Francis Carruthers Gould, in the form of Admiral John Jellicoe, inscribed 'Hell Fire Jack', 1920, 10in (25.5cm) high.

$870–960 BRT

Admiral Jellicoe (1859–1935) led the British Navy to victory at the Battle of Jutland in 1916. The British sustained heavier losses than the German fleet and Jellicoe was subsequently criticized for his tactics, which some thought were too cautious.

A Panorama Studios bone china commemorative mug, commemorating the Falklands Campaign, No. 41 of edition of 500, 1982, 3in (7.5cm) high.

$90–100 H&G

◀ **A teapot,** 'Trafalgar', commemorating the 200th anniversary of the Battle of Trafalgar, No. 1 of edition of 50, 2005, 9in (23cm) high.

$280–310 TEA

POLITICAL

A pottery plate, commemorating W. E. Gladstone MP, late 19thC, 9in (23cm) diam.

$70–80 COMM

An Ashstead Pottery character jug, by Percy Metcalfe, in the form of Stanley Baldwin MP, No. 715 of edition of 1,000, signed, printed mark, 1926–36, 7½in (19cm) high.

$240–280 PFK

NOW SHOW YOURSELVES MEN, 'TIS FOR LIBERTY.

WITH GREETINGS

FROM

THE PRIME MINISTER AND MRS. CHAMBERLAIN

FOR

CHRISTMAS AND THE NEW YEAR.

10, DOWNING STREET, S.W.

A Christmas card, from the Prime Minister and Mrs Chamberlain, 1939, 4½ x 7in (11.5 x 18cm).

$70–80 AEL

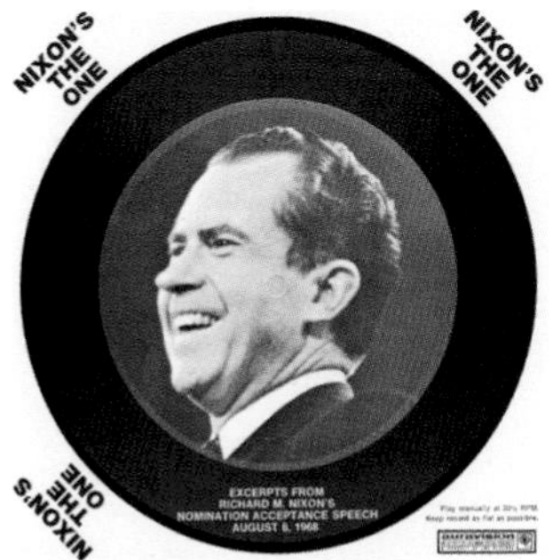

A Richard Nixon presidential campaign record/postcard, the reverse printed with quotes, c1968.

$25–30 KBE

► An earthenware mug, commemorating Harold Wilson's devaluation of the pound, 1968, 3½in (9cm) high.

$70–80 H&G

A Portmeirion mug, commemorating the Liberal Party General Election results, with printed signatures of 14 elected Liberal MPs, 1974, 4in (10cm) high.

$50–55 COMM

► A Paragon plate, commemorating the centenary of Sir Winston Churchill, No. 137 of edition of 1,000, 1974, 10in (25.5cm) diam.

$130–145 COMM

A Paragon presentation cigar box, commemorating the centenary of Sir Winston Churchill, 1974, 10¼in (26cm) wide.

$270–300 BuA

A Panorama Studios bone china plate, commemorating the election of Margaret Thatcher, with election results printed on reverse, No. 13 of edition of 500, 1979, 8in (20.5cm) diam.

$70–80 ⊞ H&G

A pottery plate, commemorating the formation of Britain's Social Democratic Party, dated 26 March 1981, 9in (23cm) diam.

$50–55 ⊞ COMM

The Social Democrats merged with the Liberal Party in 1988, becoming the Liberal Democrats.

◀ **A Christmas card,** from The President, George H. W. Bush and Mrs Barbara Bush, 1990, 8 x 5in (20.5 x 12.5cm).

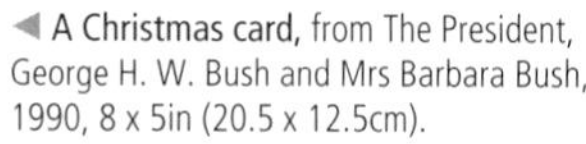

$110–125 ⊞ AEL

Franklin D. Roosevelt was the first US president to send a Christmas card rather than a signed photograph or letter. The last presidential Christmas card that mentioned the word 'Christmas' was sent by George W. H. Bush in 1992. Now, the presidential cards wish receivers a 'Happy Holiday Season' to encompass people of different faiths.

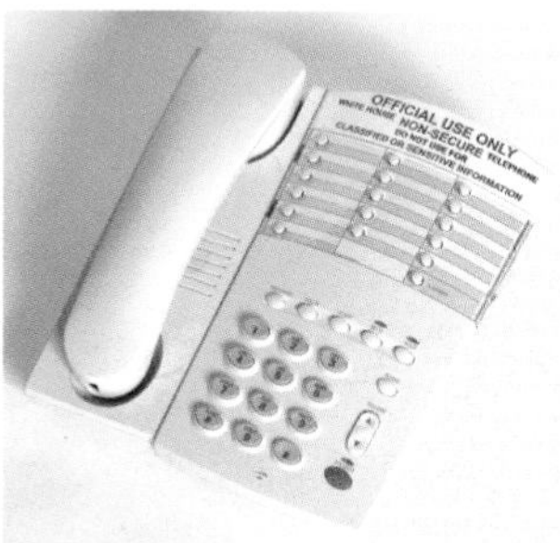

▶ **An AT&T White House non-secure telephone,** replaced during Hillary Clinton's redecoration, America, 1990s.

$1,150–1,250 ⊞ FRa

A teapot, 'Liarbillytea', inscribed 'Behind Every Great Man Lies a Harmonica', No. 1 of edition of 40, 2003, 9in (23cm) high.

$300–330 ⊞ TEA

A Chown bone china mug, commemorating the 80th birthday of Margaret Thatcher, No. 9 of edition of 20, 2005, 3in (7.5cm) high.

$60–70 ⊞ H&G

◀ **A teapot,** 'For Fox Sake', issued to mark the ban on foxhunting, 2005, 9½in (24cm) high.

$340–380 ⊞ TEA

ROYAL

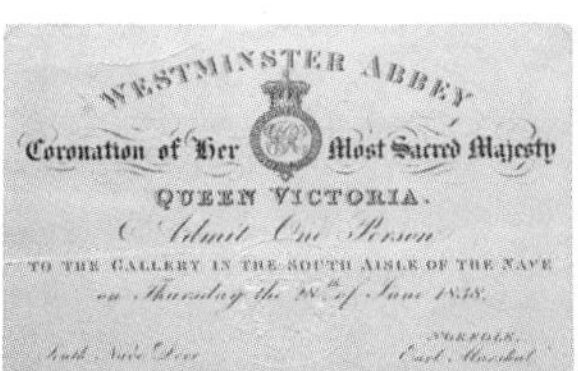
WESTMINSTER ABBEY
Coronation of Her Most Sacred Majesty
QUEEN VICTORIA.
Admit One Person
TO THE GALLERY IN THE SOUTH AISLE OF THE NAVE
on Thursday the 28th of June 1838.
NORFOLK,
Earl Marshal

A printed ticket, for the coronation of Queen Victoria, held at Westminster Abbey on 28th June 1838, 4½ x 6¾in (11.5 x 17cm).

$430–480 ⊞ CFSD

A bone china cup and saucer, commemorating the Golden Jubilee of Queen Victoria, 1887, cup 3in (7.5cm) high.

$120–135 ⊞ COMM

A Mauchline ware box, commemorating the Golden Jubilee of Queen Victoria, 1887, 7in (18cm) wide.

$120–135 ⊞ LSA

Daily Mail.

The *Daily Mail*, reporting the Diamond Jubilee of Queen Victoria, 23 June 1897.

$155–175 ⊞ HaR

A Copeland pottery mug, commemorating the Diamond Jubilee of Queen Victoria, made for Thomas Goode, London, with Royal arms and inscription, 1897, 3in (7.5cm) high.

$95–105 ⊞ COMM

A pottery plaque, commemorating the Diamond Jubilee of Queen Victoria, 1897, 7in (18cm) diam.

$85–95 ⊞ COMM

A Carr's biscuit tin, commemorating the Diamond Jubilee of Queen Victoria, c1897, 10in (25.5cm) wide.

$380–420 ⊞ SAFF

A Fry's Chocolate souvenir tin, commemorating the opening of the Royal Edward Dock, Bristol, 1908, 5in (12.5cm) wide.

$25–30 ⊞ SAFF

► **A Buckingham Palace dinner menu,** 1900, 9 x 5½in (23 x 14cm).

$380–420 ⊞ Qua

◄ **A pair of photographs of King George V and Queen Mary,** in original frames, c1910, 9in (23cm) high.

$1,150–1,350 ⊞ SHa

A Thorne's Super Creme Toffee tin, depicting the Prince of Wales, 1920, 5in (12.5cm) wide.

$35–40 ⊞ SAFF

The Sphere, George V Silver Jubilee Record edition, 1935.

$5–10 ⊞ J&S

The Illustrated London News, Coronation Record Number, 1937.

$10–15 ⊞ J&S

A signed photograph of Queen Mary, by Downey, dated 1924, 11 x 7in (28 x 18cm).

$780–860 ⊞ CFSD

An Edward VIII Oxo tin chest, c1936, 4in (10cm) wide.

$60–70 ⊞ M&C

A Paragon loving cup, commemorating the coronation of King George IV, No. 16 of edition of 1,000, 1937, 4in (10cm) high.

$380–420 ⊞ SAAC

► A signed photograph of the Duke and Duchess of Windsor, dated 1941, 14 x 11in (35.5 x 28cm), framed.

$3,400–3,800 ⊞ CFSD

A pottery egg cup, commemorating the Silver Jubilee of King George V and Queen Mary, 1935, 2½in (6.5cm) high.

$35–40 ⊞ COMM

A signed coronation photograph of King George VI and Queen Elizabeth with Princesses Margaret and Elizabeth, by Dorothy Wilding, dated 1937, 11 x 9in (28 x 23cm).

$8,650–9,550 ⊞ CFSD

A Burleigh Ware jug, commemorating the coronation of Queen Elizabeth II, with inscription, 1953, 7in (18cm) high.

$300–330 ⊞ H&G

An Aynsley bone china cup and saucer, commemorating the coronation of Queen Elizabeth II, 1953, saucer 4in (10cm) diam.

$150–165 ⊞ H&G

A Tuscan bone china loving cup, limited edition, No. 213, 1953, 5in (12.5cm) diam.

$350–390 ⊞ H&G

A Burleigh Ware earthenware plate, commemorating the coronation of Queen Elizabeth II, 1953, 10in (25.5cm) diam.

$100–110 ⊞ H&G

An Arthur Bowker bone china mug, commemorating the coronation of Queen Elizabeth II, with coat-of-arms and gilt lion handle, 1953, 2½in (6.5cm) high.

$60–70 ⊞ H&G

A set of 58 photographs, taken on the Royal yacht, 1970s, 5 x 7in (12.5 x 18cm).

$260–290 ⊞ COB

◄ A Greenock tin money box, commemorating the coronation of Queen Elizabeth II, 1953, 4½in (11.5cm) high.

$50–55 ⊞ M&C

► A British Railways and London Transport map, commemorating the coronation of Queen Elizabeth II, 1953.

$20–25 ⊞ KBE

A Post Office plastic telephone, commemorating the Silver Jubilee of Queen Elizabeth II, 1977, 10in (25.5cm) wide.

$105–120 ⊞ TL

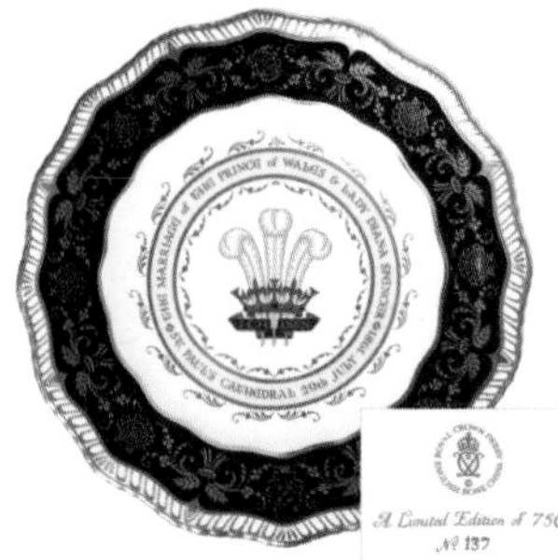

A Royal Crown Derby bone china plate, commemorating the wedding of Prince Charles and Lady Diana Spencer, No. 137 of edition 750, 1981, 9in (23cm) diam.

$220–250 ⊞ H&G

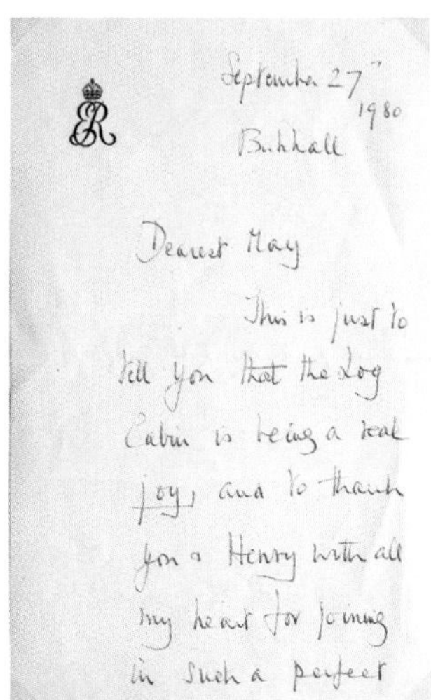

September 27th
1980
Birkhall

Dearest May

This is just to tell you that the Log Cabin is being a real joy, and to thank you & Henry with all my heart for joining in such a perfect

A hand-written letter, by Queen Elizabeth II from Birkhall, to Mary, Marchioness of Cambridge, 1980, 8 x 5in (20.5 x 12.5cm).

$700–770 ⊞ AEL

A tin money box, commemorating the wedding of Prince Charles and Lady Diana Spencer, 1981, 4½in (11.5cm) high.

$5–10 ⊞ M&C

◄ **Two Carlton Ware earthenware mugs,** commemorating the wedding of Prince Charles and Lady Diana Spencer, the overlapping handles forming a heart, dated 1981, 5in (12.5cm) high.

$200–220 ⊞ H&G

◄ **An earthenware mug,** commemorating the wedding of Prince Charles and Lady Diana Spencer, with transfer-printed design, 1981, 3½in (9cm) high.

$5–10 ⊞ H&G

An Aynsley bone china loving cup, commemorating the birth of Prince William, 1982, 2½in (6.5cm) high.

$95–105 ⊞ H&G

An Ansley bone china loving cup, commemorating the birth of Prince Henry, 1984, 2½in (6.5cm) high.

$85–95 ⊞ H&G

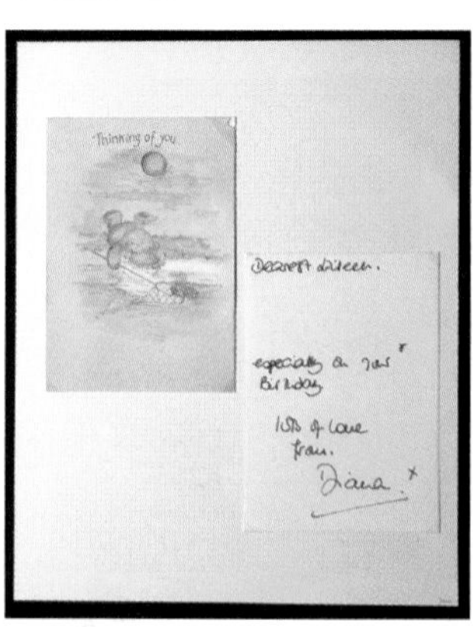

A birthday card from Diana, Princess of Wales, to Eileen Malone, c1990, 7 x 5in (18 x 12.5cm).

$3,900–4,300 ⊞ AEL

A Queen's China **mug,** made for Ringtons Ltd, commemorating the 90th birthday of HM Queen Elizabeth, the Queen Mother, 1990, 3½in (9cm) high.

$10–15 KA

A teapot, '20th Century Queens', depicting Queen Elizabeth II and Queen Victoria, No. 1 of edition of 99, 1999 edition, 9in (23cm) high.

$360–400 TEA

◀ **A bone china plate,** issued to mark the divorce of the Prince and Princess of Wales, 1996, 10½in (26.5cm) diam.

$70–80 COMM

A silk first day cover, commemorating the life of Diana, Princess of Wales, a full set of stamps issued to mark her death, postmarked Althorp, 1998, 9in (23cm) long.

$20–25 COMM

◀ **A Cash's of Coventry silk bookmark,** commemorating the 100th birthday of HM Queen Elizabeth, the Queen Mother, 2000, 11in (28cm) long.

$10–15 COMM

A Royal Doulton bone china tankard, commemorating the 21st birthday of Prince William, limited edition, 164 of 500, 2003, 5in (12.5cm) high.

$110–125 H&G

An Aynsley bone china mug, commemorating the 21st birthday of Prince Harry, limited edition of 950, 2005, 3½in (9cm) high.

$60–70 H&G

A Chown bone china teapot, commemorating the wedding of the Prince of Wales and Camilla Parker-Bowles, No. 13 of edition of 20, 2005, 5in (12.5cm) high.

$85–95 H&G

CORKSCREWS

A steel and enamel folding corkscrew, Germany, c1900, 2¾in (7cm) long.

$380–450 DN

◀ A corkscrew, the turned wood handle with Codd bottle marble ejector, c1900, 5in (12.5cm) long.

$25–30 CS

◀ A steel concertina-style corkscrew, 8in (20.5cm) wide.

$70–80 CS

This corkscrew is of the type patented by H. D. Armstrong in 1902 called 'The Pullezi'.

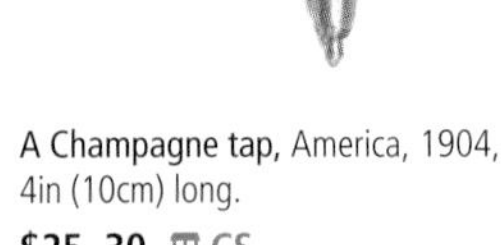

A Champagne tap, America, 1904, 4in (10cm) long.

$25–30 CS

A steel Monopol continuous action corkscrew, Germany, c1910, 5in (12.5cm) long.

$25–30 CS

A cast-brass Peter Pan corkscrew, c1920, 6in (15cm) long.

$20–25 CS

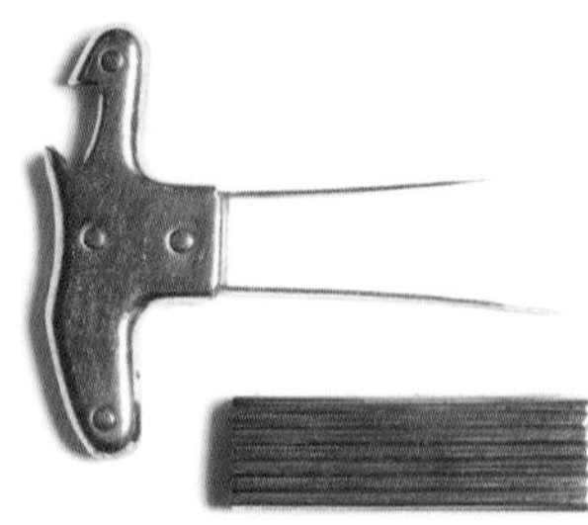

A tin-cased cork extractor, 'Le Pratique Paris', France, c1920, 4in (10cm) long.

$20–25 CS

CORKSCREW FACTS

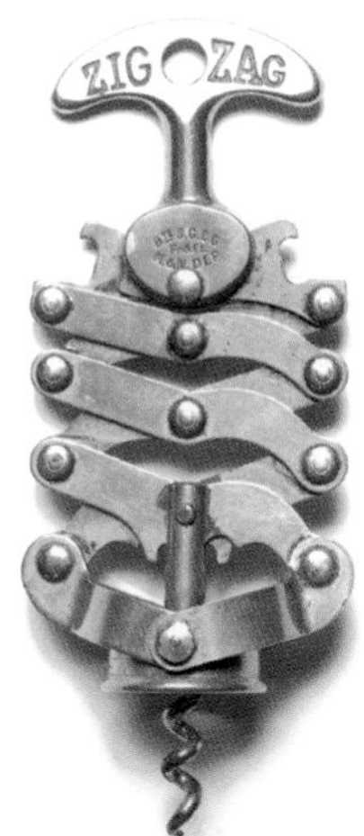

A nickel-plated Zig Zag corkscrew, France, c1930, 6in (15cm) long.

$70–80 ⊞ CS

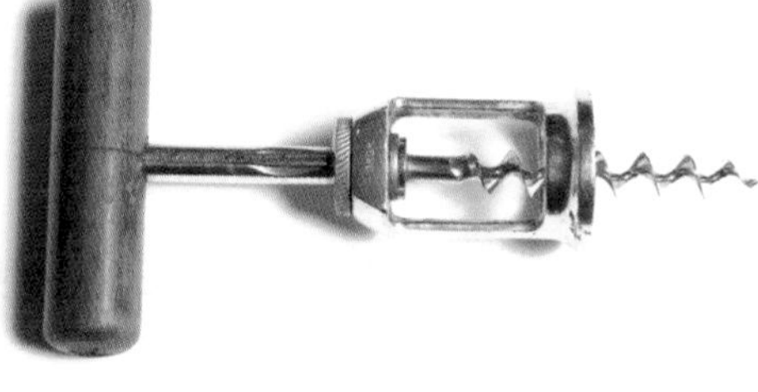

A nickel-plated corkscrew, with a turned wood handle, Germany, c1935, 6in (15cm) long.

$45–50 ⊞ CS

▶ **A Syracuse Ornamental Co 'Syroco wood' corkscrew,** in the form of a Scottie dog's head, America, New York, c1950, 5in (12.5cm) long.

$20–25 ⊞ CS

Syroco wood is a composition of moulded wood and resin made by the Syracuse Ornamental Co. It is a very hard material that does not warp.

- The first corkscrew patent was registered to Samuel Henshall in 1795.
- Between 1795 and the early 20th century over 300 corkscrew patents have been registered.
- Wine experts have estimated that pulling a cork from a bottle requires the same force as lifting 100lbs (45kgs).
- Many improvements have been made to the traditional design: some provide leverage for pulling out the cork, others emphasize more torque during twisting.
- Common designs include the single-lever or waiter's corkscrew, patented in the UK in 1883, the double-winged lever corkscrew, patented in the UK in 1888 and the bell-shaped corkscrew, patented in the US in 1893.
- The Screwpull is one of the more significant designs of 20th century, patented by Texan Herbert Allen in 1978.
- Steel is the preferred material for the worm; steel or cast-zinc alloy is used for the levers and gears.
- Handles can be made from many materials, including common or exotic woods, bone, plastic or various metals.
- Popular corkscrew worms did not work well with the synthetic corks introduced by some wineries at the end of the 20th century – an additional turn provided by an elongated worm may have solved this problem.
- As improvements are made to synthetic cork composition, additional corkscrew modifications may be needed.

A cast-brass corkscrew, in the form of a key, the handle incorporating a crown cap lifter, Germany, c1950, 5in (12.5cm) high.

$20–25 ⊞ CS

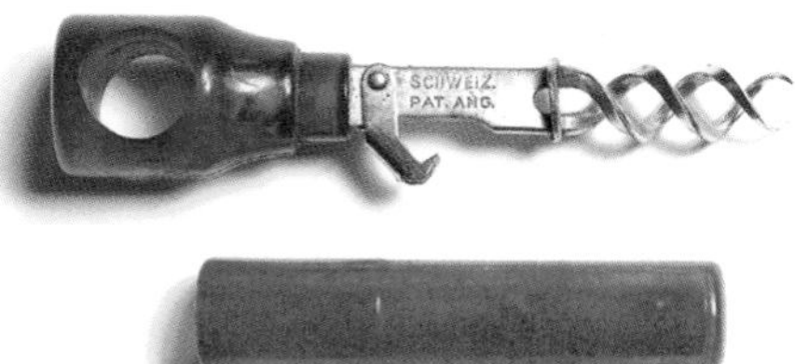

A plastic pocket corkscrew, with double helix, incorporating a cap lifter, marked 'Maxram', Switzerland, c1950, 4in (10cm) long.

$10–15 ⊞ CS

DOLLS

CLOTH

◀ A Chad Valley cloth *Queen Elizabeth* sailor doll, 1960, 8in (20.5cm) high.

$70–80 ⊞ COB

A cloth Ida Lupino doll, 1930s, 10in (25.5cm) high.

$70–80 ⊞ COB

Ida Lupino (c1918–95) starred in many films in the 1930s and '40s; she also wrote and directed six feature films.

A Nora Wellings cloth sailor doll, 1920s–30s, 12in (30.5cm) high.

$150–165 ⊞ SAAC

A Deans cloth Betty doll, with Oxo label, 1930, 17in (43cm) high.

$200–210 ⊞ UD

◀ A Nora Wellings cloth doll, 1920s–30s, 16in (40.5cm) high.

$130–145 ⊞ SAAC

A Coleco Industries Inc cloth and vinyl Cabbage Patch baby doll, with freckled face and wool hair, 1980s, 16in (40.5cm) high.

$35–40 ⊞ POLL

A Coleco Industries Inc cloth and vinyl Cabbage Patch doll, with wool hair and original dress, 1980s, 16in (40.5cm) high.

$35–40 ⊞ POLL

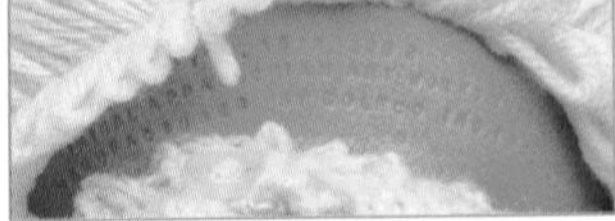

A Coleco Industries Inc cloth and vinyl Cabbage Patch doll, with wool hair and knitted dress, 1983, 16in (40.5cm) high.

$35–40 ⊞ POLL

The Cabbage Patch kids were manufactured by Coleco from 1983–88.

HARD PLASTIC, COMPOSITION & VINYL

An E. I. Horsman composition Rosebud doll, with swivel head, shoulder plate, soft body and articulated arms and legs, late 1940s, 22in (56cm) high.

$200–220 ⊞ BWH

► **A doll,** possibly by Diamond Doll Co, with original hair, 1940, 23in (58.5cm) high.

$180–200 ⊞ POLL

An E. I. Horsman composition Bright Star doll, America, mid 1930s, 13in (33cm) high.

$130–145 ⊞ BWH

A Pedigree composition doll, 1930–40, 18½in (47cm) high.

$120–135 ⊞ BWH

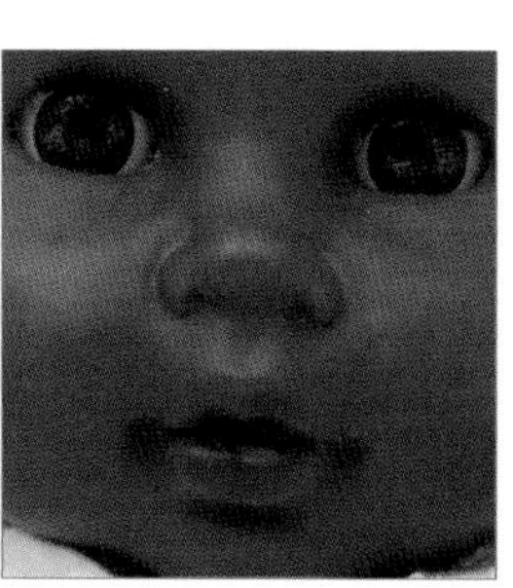

A Zapff plastic doll, with soft body, Germany, 1970s–80s, 6in (40.5cm) high.

$45–50 ⊞ POLL

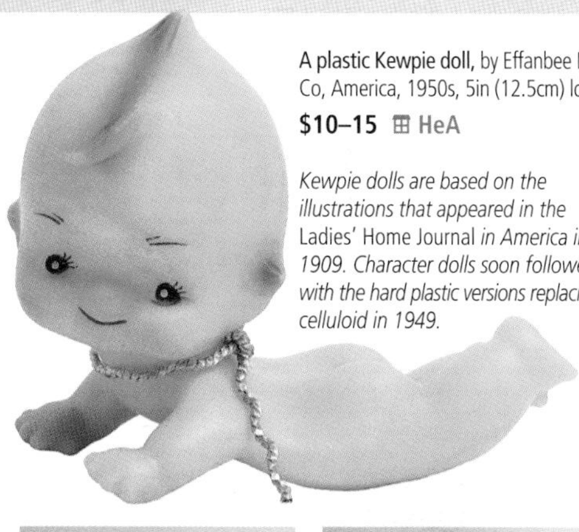

A plastic Kewpie doll, by Effanbee Doll Co, America, 1950s, 5in (12.5cm) long.

$10–15 ⊞ HeA

Kewpie dolls are based on the illustrations that appeared in the Ladies' Home Journal *in America in 1909. Character dolls soon followed, with the hard plastic versions replacing celluloid in 1949.*

A Madame Alexander plastic Nina Ballerina doll, with original clothes, 1949–51, 14in (35.5cm) high.

$80–90 ⊞ BWH

An Arranbee composition Nancy doll, marked, America, 1930s, 17½in (44.5cm) high.

$150–165 ⊞ BWH

A Palitoy Tiny Tears doll, with original dress, 1970, 15in (38cm) high.

$50–55 ⊞ POLL

◀ **A Roddy vinyl doll,** 1960s, 21in (53.5cm) high.

$80–90 ⊞ POLL

A Pedigree walker doll, with original wig, c1957, 22in (60cm) high.

$200–220 ⊞ BWH

A Pedigree First Love doll, with moveable waist, 1970, 16in (40.5cm) high.

$60–70 ⊞ POLL

A Roddy vinyl doll, with fixed eyes and moulded head, c1960, 9in (23cm) high.

$50–55 ⊞ POLL

A Pedigree vinyl doll, with fixed eyes and moulded head, 1950s–60s, 10in (25.5cm) high.

$50–55 ⊞ POLL

A pair of Rosebud twin dolls, with sleep eyes, 1950s, 7in (18cm) high.

$105–120 ⊞ POLL

◀ **A Palitoy Carrie doll,** with sleep eyes, 1970, 6in (15cm) high.

$50–55 ⊞ POLL

▶ **A Remco Sweet April doll,** with original outfit, America, 1970s, 5in (12.5cm) high.

$35–40 ⊞ POLL

A Kadar doll, with moveable hands, sleep eyes, 1940s–50s, 6in (40.5cm) high.

$60–70 ⊞ POLL

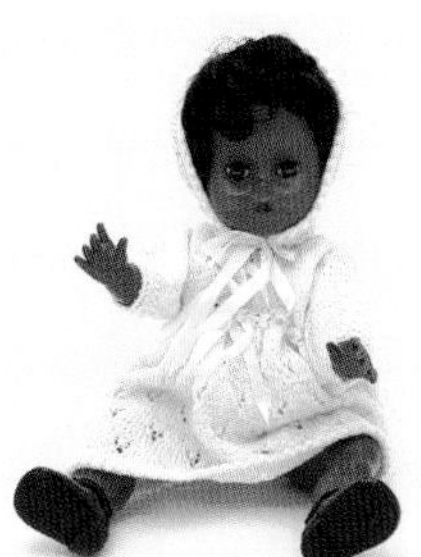

A Palitoy doll, 1950s–60s, 9in (23cm) high.

$60–70 ⊞ POLL

A Palitoy doll, with original outfit, 1950s–60s, 15in (38cm) high.

$50–55 ⊞ POLL

► **A Pedigree Delite walker doll,** with original wig, 1950s, 17in (43cm) high.

$220–250 ⊞ POLL

An Amanda Jane doll, with sleep eyes and original dress, 1960, 7½in (19cm) high.

$105–120 ⊞ POLL

A Roddy walker doll, 1950, 15in (38cm) high.

$130–145 ⊞ POLL

A Magic Roundabout Florence doll, with semi-moveable arms and legs, head moves, 1968, 7½in (19cm) high.

$95–105 ⊞ MTB

A Kadar baby doll, with moveable wrists, 1940s–50s, 15in (38cm) high.

$50–55 ⊞ POLL

These dolls were often used for modelling baby clothes.

A vinyl doll, with fixed eyes, moulded head and moveable hands, 1950s, 20in (51cm) high.

$60–70 ⊞ POLL

A Sasha vinyl doll, c1970, 11in (28cm) high.

$250–280 ⊞ POLL

A Pedigree walker doll, with original mohair wig, 1950s, 21in (53.5cm) high.

$220–250 ⊞ POLL

A plastic doll, with sleep eyes, Hong Kong, 1950s–60s, 20in (51cm) high.

$95–105 ⊞ POLL

BARBIE

A Mattel Barbie doll, wearing American Airlines Stewardess outfit, America, 1963, 11¾in (30cm) high, with box.

$180–200 BWH

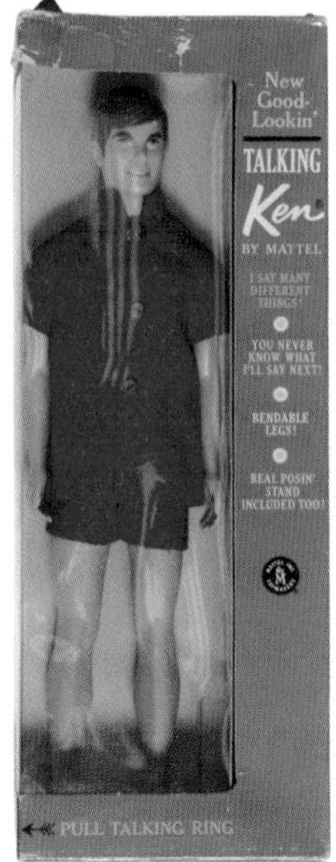

A Mattel talking Ken doll, America, 1971, 13in (33cm) high, with box.

$155–175 MTB

Ken was Barbie's boyfriend – he arrived in 1961.

A Mattel talking Stacey doll, America, 1967, 13in (33cm) high, with box.

$590–650 MTB

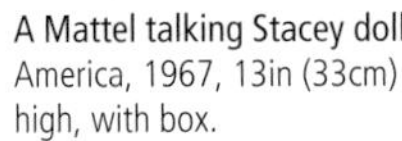

A Mattel Twist'n' Turn Christie doll, America, 1969, 12½in (32cm) high, with box.

$430–480 MTB

► A Mattel Lifelike Bendable Legs Midge doll, America, 1964, 12in (30.5cm) high, with box.

$780–860 MTB

► A Mattel 30th Anniversary Francie doll, America, 1996, 14in (35.5cm) high, with clothes and box.

$90–100 MTB

Francie was Barbie's 'modern cousin'.

- Barbie appeared in America in 1959 and in the UK in 1961. Her creator, Ruth Handler, wanted to make a doll that her daughter could play with. Little Barbara Handler (whose name was the inspiration for 'Barbie') loved paper dolls that came with a choice of outfits.
- When she was released, Barbie was noticably different. She was glamorous, with an accentuated 'hour glass' figure, long legs and side-glancing eyes.
- For a matter of months Barbie came on a pronged stand – these first dolls have locating holes in their feet and are very valuable today, worth over $1,750.
- Original boxes add to her value.
- One of the most sought-after items of clothing are Barbie's stilettoes as many fell off and were lost.

SINDY

A Pedigree Sindy vinyl doll, with her Weekenders outfit designed by Foale & Tuffin, 1963, 12in (30.5cm) high, with box.

$280–310 ⊞ MTB

◄ A Pedigree Mary Poppins vinyl doll, 1964, 12in (30.5cm) high, with box.

$1,000–1,100 ⊞ MTB

Pedigree was commissioned in New Zealand only to make this very rare doll that resembled the film's leading character, Mary Poppins, played by Julie Andrews.

A Pedigree Sweet Dreams Sindy doll, with twist neck and body, sleeping eyes and bending knees, 1978, 12in (30.5cm) high, with box.

$200–220 ⊞ MTB

A Pedigree Sindy's Air Hostess/BOAC outfit, 1968, 9½in (24cm) wide, in original packaging.

$280–310 ⊞ MTB

A Pedigree Sindy Sunshine Girl outfit, 1977, with packaging, 10in (25.5cm) wide.

$80–90 ⊞ MTB

A Louis Marx & Co Sindy Go Anywhere outfit, 1978, with packaging, 10in (25.5cm) wide.

$45–50 ⊞ MTB

Between 1978 and 1981 Louis Marx was licensed to distribute Sindy in America.

- Sindy, 'the doll you love to dress' was Britain's upbeat answer to Barbie.
- She made her debut in 1963 when a TV commercial showed her wearing a snazzy 'Weekenders' outfit designed by Carnaby Street's Foale & Tuffin (see p180).
- The accessories are of great interest to colelctors. Outfits were tied to cards overseas and assembled into protective cases in the UK.

VINYL DOLLS

An Ideal vinyl Tammy doll, with Strawberry blonde hair, 1963, 13in (33cm) high, with box.

$220–250 ⊞ MTB

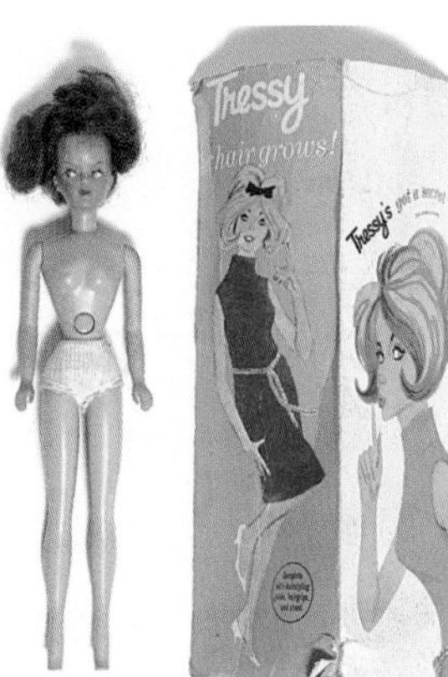

A Palitoy vinyl Tressy doll, with growing hair, c1962, with box.

$190–210 ⊞ MTB

Boxed examples of this Tressy are rare as the cardboard was of poor quality. This also came with a hair styling booklet which showed very complicated hair styles.

A Palitoy vinyl Toots doll, with growing hair and bendable legs, c1970, 10½in (26.5cm) high, with box.

$165–185 ⊞ MTB

Toots was Tressy's little sister, and also came with a hair style booklet. These dolls were made by Palitoy under licence from American Character Inc.

◄ **A Palitoy vinyl Tressy doll,** with growing hair, c1970, 15in (38cm) high, with box.

$35–40 ⊞ MTB

A Palitoy Toots Kitchen Cutie outfit, 1968, with packaging, 10in (25.5cm) wide.

$105–120 ⊞ MTB

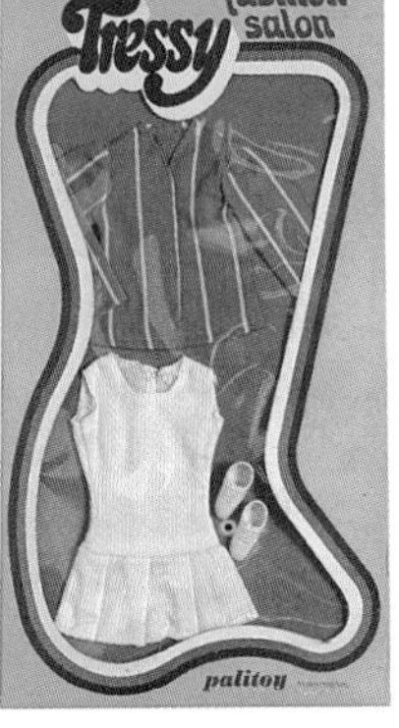

A Palitoy Tressy fashion salon sports outfit, c1970, 12in (30.5cm) high, with packaging.

$20–25 ⊞ MTB

A Palitoy Pippa the Holiday Girl outfit, c1970, with packaging, 9in (23cm) wide.

$220–250 ⊞ MTB

This is a rare outfit.

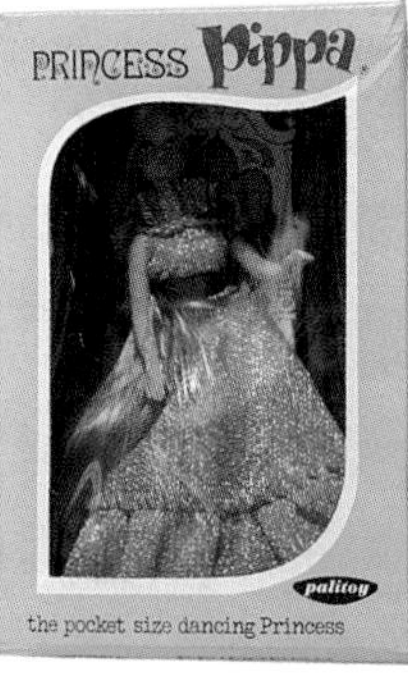

A Palitoy vinyl Princess Pippa doll, c1970, 7in (18cm) high, with packaging.

$480–530 ⊞ MTB

◄ **A Palitoy vinyl Mandy doll,** c1970, 7in (18cm), with packaging.

$250–280 ⊞ MTB

Mandy is Pippa's friend.

► **A Palitoy Pippa Fashion in Your Pocket Monaco Collection outfit,** c1970, with packaging, 8in (20.5cm) wide.

$35–40 ⊞ MTB

A Palitoy vinyl Pippa doll, 1972–80, 7in (18cm) high.

$25–30 UD

▶ **An Otto Simon vinyl Fleur doll,** Holland, 1980s, 14in (35.5cm) high, with box.

$45–50 MTB

An Otto Simon vinyl Mount Everest Fleur doll, Holland, 1980s, 14in (35.5cm) high, with box.

$45–50 MTB

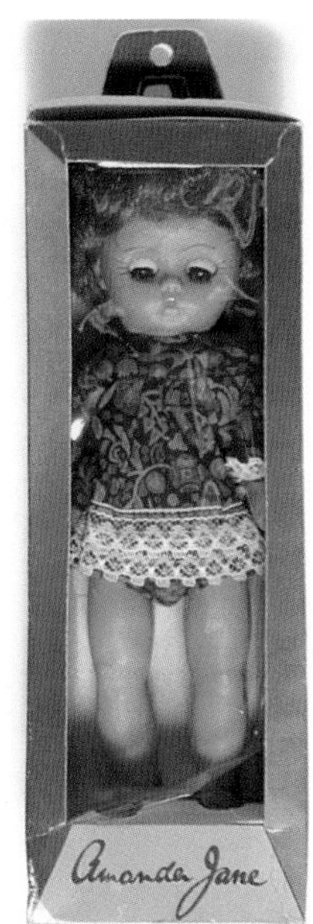

An Amanda Jane vinyl Party Dress doll, c1960, 8in (20.5cm) high.

$90–100 MTB

An Amanda Jane doll and bed set, doll with painted eyes, with teddy bear, 8in (20.5cm) long.

$85–95 POLL

Three Amanda Jane vinyl dolls, one with carry cot and hot water bottle, c1970, 6in (15cm) high.

$10–15 each UD

A Faerie Glen vinyl Gigi doll, c1980, with box, 15in (38cm) high.

$80–90 MTB

◀ **A Mary Quant Dizzy Daisy vinyl doll,** by Flair Toys, c1970, with box, 9½in (24cm) high.

$200–220 MTB

▶ **A Mary Quant vinyl Dizzy Daisy doll,** by Flair Toys, c1970, with box, 9½in (24cm) high.

$230–260 MTB

This doll is wearing a leotard with a pale blue stripe, which is a rarer version than the orginal.

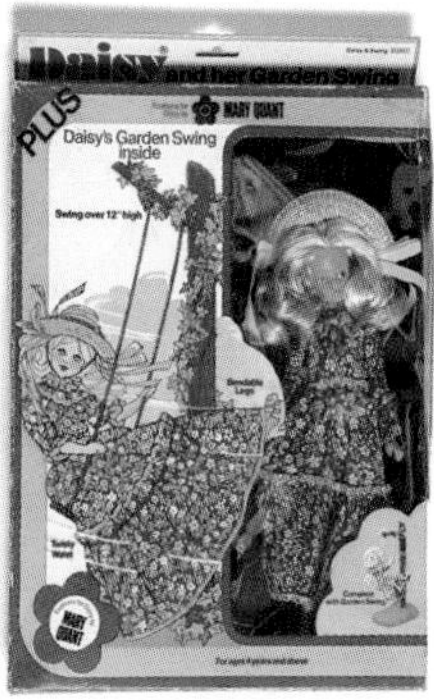

◀ **A Mary Quant Daisy vinyl doll with Garden Swing,** doll with twisting waist and bendable legs, c1970, with original box, 12in (30.5cm) high.

$280–310 MTB

A Mary Quant Bubbles vinyl doll, c1972, 8½in (21.5cm) high, with original packaging.

$130–145 MTB

A Palitoy vinyl Dolly Darlings Strawberry Fair doll, c1970, with box, 5½in (14cm) high.

$150–165 MTB

A Palitoy vinyl Dolly Darlings Tea Time doll, c1970, with box, 5½in (14cm) high.

$120–135 MTB

A Hornby Flower Fairies vinyl Garden Ballet doll, c1980, with box, 12in (30.5cm) wide.

$90–100 MTB

An American Topper vinyl Dawn Head to Toe doll, with three additional wigs, c1970, with original box, 8in (20.5cm) high.

$150–165 MTB

This is a UK issue Dolly Darlings, made under licence from the American firm Hassenfeld Bros. The reverse of the box is printed with the other dolls in the series, which vary from the US issues.

► A Hornby Cassy doll, wearing Getting Ready outfit, 1991, 10in (25.5cm high), with original plastic box.

$45–50 MTB

The box becomes part of Cassy's home.

A Kenner plastic Blythe doll, with eyes that change colour, 1970s, 11in (28cm) high.

$710–790 BWH

This doll was made for one year only and her eyes had four colour changes.

BOY DOLLS

◄ A Pedigree Paul doll, wearing Casuals outfit, 1966, 12in (30.5cm) high, with box.

$220–250 MTB

When Sindy's boyfriend Paul was introduced in 1965 he had moulded hair. This second version, introduced in 1966, has rooted hair.

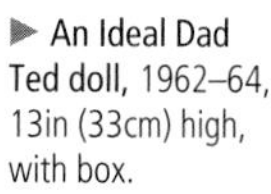

► An Ideal Dad Ted doll, 1962–64, 13in (33cm) high, with box.

$155–175 MTB

This is Tammy's dad, Ted. Of Tammy's family, Mom is the hardest to find.

A Palitoy Action Man doll, with original Royal Canadian Mounted Police outfit and dog, 1970s, 12in (30.5cm) high.

$90–100 STBL

A Palitoy Action Man doll, with original Australian Jungle Fighter outfit, 1960s, 12in (30.5cm) high, with box.

$175–195 STBL

A Palitoy Action Man doll, with original Life Guard outfit, doll 1960s, outfit 1980s, 12in (30.5cm) high, with box.

$470–520 ⊞ STBL

A Palitoy Action Man doll, with original British Army Officer outfit, 1980, 12in (930.5cm) high, with box.

$175–195 ⊞ STBL

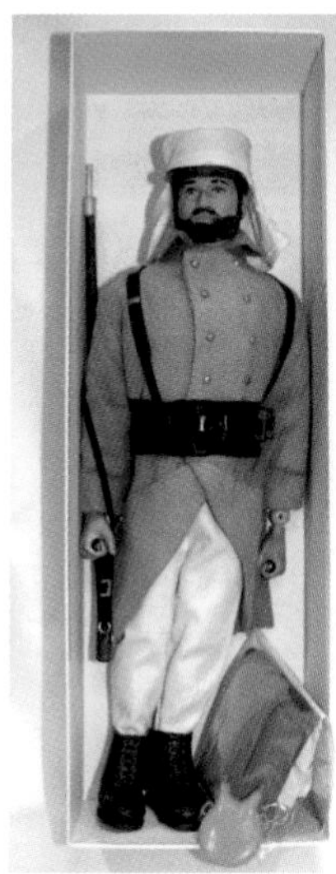

A Palitoy Action Man doll, with French Foreign Legion outfit, 1970s, 12in (30.5cm) high, with box.

$70–80 ⊞ STBL

A Palitoy Action Man doll, with Green Berets outfit, 1960, 12in (30.5cm) high, with box.

$250–280 ⊞ STBL

DOLLS' ACCESSORIES

A Coats knitting pattern for Sindy, 1960s, 10 x 7in (25.5 x 18cm).

$5–10 ⊞ UD

A Brimtoy My Dolly's tinplate kitchen unit, 1950s–60s, 4in (10cm) wide, with box.

$35–40 ⊞ HOB

◀ **A paper cut-out figure of Shirley Temple,** with clothes, c1938.

$70–80 ⊞ BGe

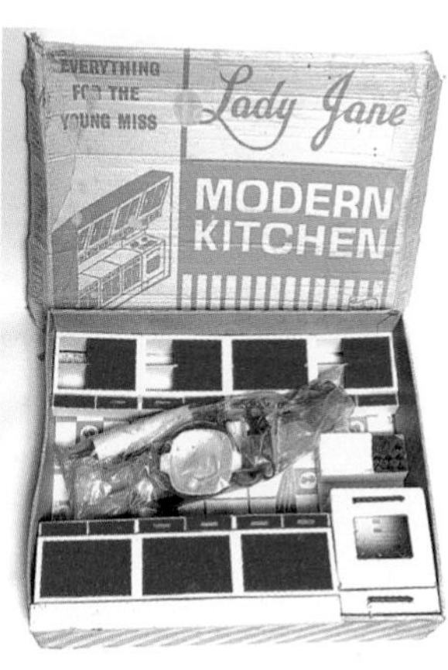

A Lady Jane plastic Modern Kitchen, c1970, boxed, 21 x 17in (53.5 x 43cm).

$10–15 ⊞ UD

A Brimtoy My Dolly's tinplate washing machine, 1950s–60s, 3½in (9cm) wide, with box.

$25–30 ⊞ HOB

A dolls' tea set, possibly French, 1890–1900, with original box, 15in (38cm) wide.

$300–330 ⊞ POLL

EPHEMERA

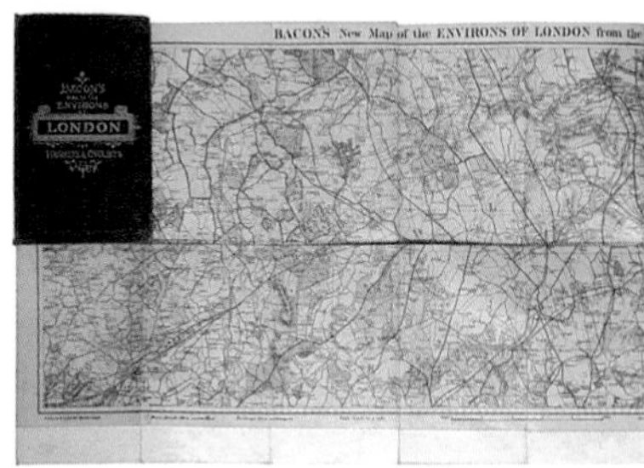

A Bacon's map of London, c1898, 8 x 4in (20.5 x 4cm).
$20–25 ⊞ COB

A 1955 calendar, with over 40 photographs of Scotland, 11¼ x 12½in (28.5 x 32cm).
$20–25 ⊞ RTT

▶ *Manual of Protection Against Gas and Air Raids*, issued by the Ministry of Defence, 3 vols, 1939, 8 x 5in (20.5 x 12.5cm)
$35–40 ⊞ J&S

A paper doily, 1950s, 8½in (21.5cm) diam.
$5–10 ⊞ MSB

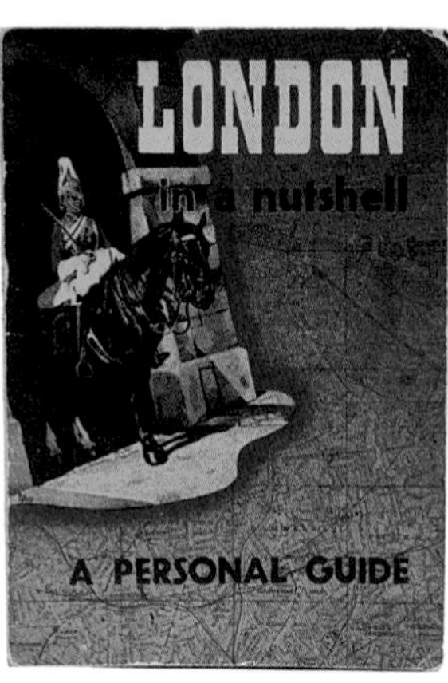

London in a Nutshell – A Personal Guide, 1930s, 6½ x 4¾in (16.5 x 12cm).
$20–25 ⊞ RTT

LICENCE AR 0423
FOR
ONE MALE SERVANT, 15s. 0d.

T. Sutton Timmis Esq
of Cleveley in the
Civil Parish or Township of Allerton within the
Administrative County* Lanc
is hereby authorized to employ ONE MALE SERVANT from the day of the date hereof until the 31st day of December next following; the sum of FIFTEEN SHILLINGS having been paid for this Licence.

Granted at Mossley Hill
this Sixth day of Jany 1910
by

*If the residence is within a County Borough strike out "Administrative" and insert "Borough" after "County".
S.D. 1909.

A tourist map of California, 1950s, 9 x 4in (23 x 10cm).
$10–15 ⊞ RTT

A Queensland brochure, 1920s, 8 x 5in (20.5 x 12.5cm).
$10–15 ⊞ COB

In a bid to attract more female domestic servants to Queensland, authorities in Australia offered free or assisted passage in the inter-war years.

◀ A licence for one male servant, 1910, 6in (15cm) wide.
$20–25 ⊞ COB

EROTICA

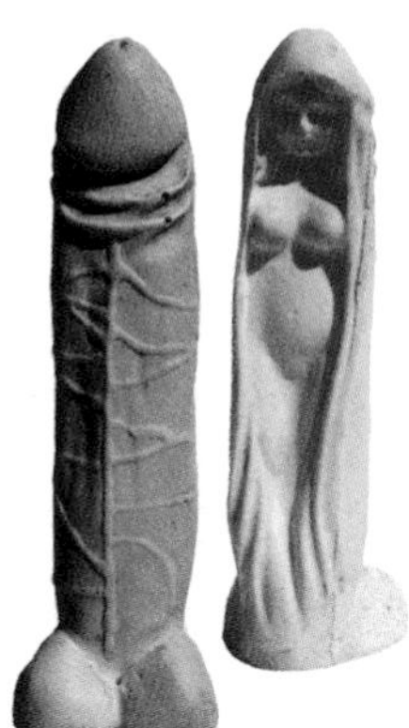

An earthenware phallus, an erotic figure of a nude woman to one side, the reverse with detailed penis, late 19thC, 5in (12.5cm) long.

$170–200 BBR

Two ceramic salt and pepper shakers, with naked girls, 1930, 2in (5cm) high.

$190–220 SpM

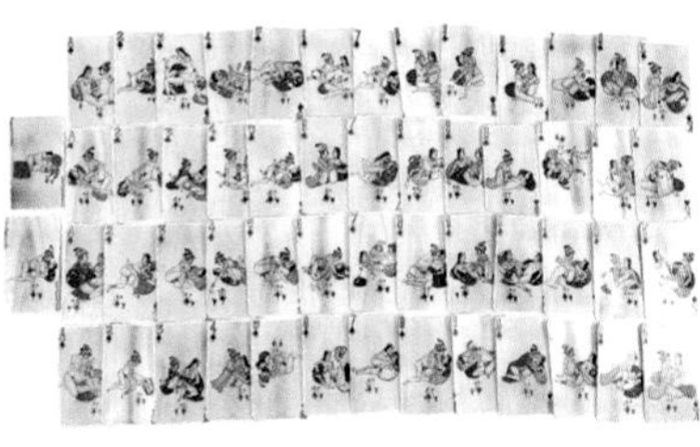

A pack of hand-painted Kama Sutra playing cards, plus two jokers, c1930.

$3,200–3,800 G(L)

A drinking glass, hand-painted with an image of an ice-skater, with erotic view on reverse, 1940, 4½in (11.5cm) high.

$45–50 SpM

A Heritage Films home movie of Jayne Mansfield, 1950, in a box 5½in (14cm) wide.

$270–300 SpM

Born Vera Jayne Palmer on 19 April 1933, Jayne Mansfield set her sights on Hollywood at the age of 13, following a tour of the 20th Century Fox Studios. Her career began in 1954 with a modelling shoot for General Electric, but she was cut from the final picture as she was considered too sexy. Under the guidance of the Hollywood publicity agent, Jim Byron, her career flourished as she starred in films including The Girl Can't Help It *and* Kiss Them For Me, *and made a number of television appearances. Her career was tragically cut short when she was killed in a car crash at the age of 34.*

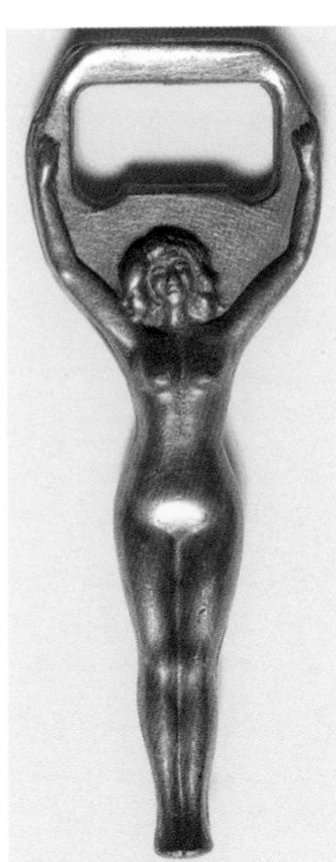

A metal bottle opener, in the form of a naked lady, 1930, 4in (10cm) long.

$10–15 CS

A pair of bronzed-metal cufflinks, each with a raised nude, 1950, 1¼in (3cm) long.

$190–220 SpM

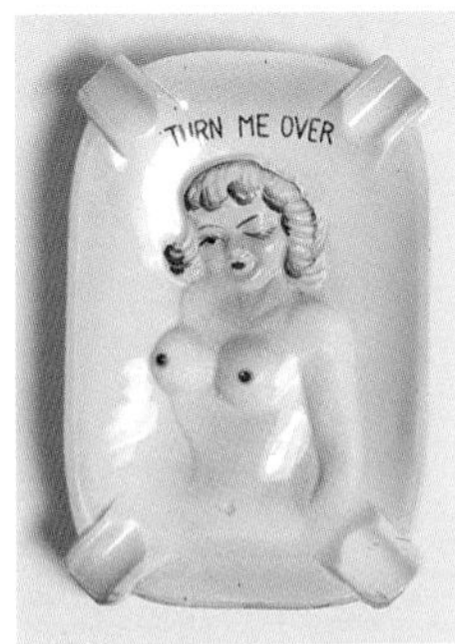

► **A hand-painted ceramic double-sided ashtray,** 1950, 6½in (16.5cm) long.

$130–155 SpM

► **A ceramic teapot,** 'Armour Suitra', No. 1 of edition of 50, 2005, 10in (25.5cm) high.

$320–360 TEA

FASHION

DRESSES & SUITS

A beaded dress, 1920s.

$1,700–2,000 ⊞ WARD

Beaded dresses are synonymous with the style of the 1920s. The most desirable, like this, mix tiny glass beads with sequins. Everything was hand-stitched, representing hours of work for a seamstress. Over the years the weight of these beads can cause the silk beneath to stress, wear and eventually tear, so do spend some time looking carefully at the condition.

◀ A silk day suit, 1930.

$600–670 ⊞ TIN

Unlabelled fashion like this is still extremely desirable, especially if it conveys the 'look' of the age. The fine linen fabric, silk revere and superb cut all point to this suit being made by an established couturier. To date it remains a mystery as to who this might be. The only history we do know is that it was once part of the mammoth Castle Howard Costume Collection, which was sold at Sotheby's in 2003.

A crepe utility dress, 1940s.

$130–155 ⊞ CLOB

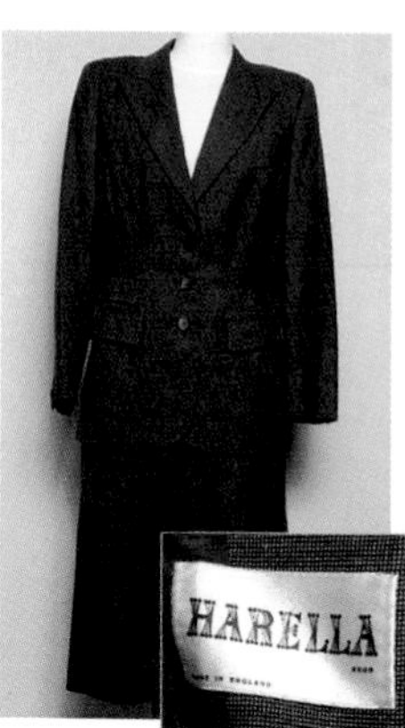

◀ A Harella Utility wool suit, 1940s.

$110–130 ⊞ CLOB

UTILITY FASHION

A Charles Butter Utility suit, with circus print and original CC41 label, 1940s.

$200–230 ⊞ FC

- Britain's Utility Scheme ran from 1941 to 1952.
- Adults received 66 clothing coupons every year, which was enough for roughly one new outfit.
- The Board of Trade designated manufacturers, specified cloth and restricted style. Men's trousers appeared without turn-ups. For women, the number of pleats, seams, buttons and buttonholes were limited.
- All garments had to carry the CC41 mark (called the 'two cheeses'). Sometimes these labels are hard to find, hidden in the side seams.
- Square padded shoulders, shorter straighter skirts, compared with those of the 1930s, and an economic use of fabric denote Utility style.
- Utility clothing was made to last. It's often in great condition and remains remarkably affordable.

HORROCKSES

A Horrockses floral print cotton day dress, with matching jacket, and partially-boned bodice, 1950s.

$145–165 ⊞ WARD

A Horrockses printed cotton day dress, with button front, 1950s.

$130–150 ⊞ WARD

- Founded in 1791 in Preston, Lancashire, Horrockses gained a name for its fine quality cotton cloth.
- In April 1946, it launched a read-to-wear label – Horrockses Fashions Ltd. The line of mass-produced dresses that followed were worn by the Queen and '50s housewives alike.
- Designs like these cost the equivalent of an average week's wage in 1950, between $7 and $12.
- Colour-fast dyes and an exclusive 'Quintafix' finish meant these brightly-printed florals and stripes retained their crispness and colour.
- Look for the quality and for the vivid printed fabrics, then you've found Horrockses.

A Norman Harntell printed silk dress, late 1950s.

$230–260 ⊞ WARD

If, in the 1950s, you wore an outfit by the British-born couturier Norman Hartnell (1901–79) you were at the cutting edge of fashion. Only a few years before he designed this, Hartnell was tailoring the Queen's Coronation gown.

A Leannie nylon ball gown, 1950s.

$120–140 ⊞ CLOB

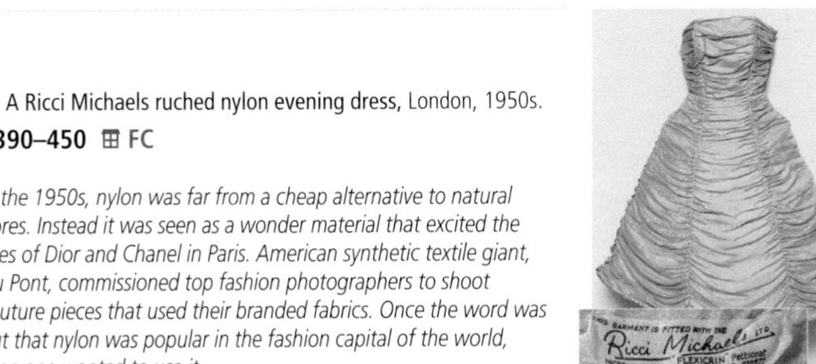

▶ **A Ricci Michaels ruched nylon evening dress,** London, 1950s.

$390–450 ⊞ FC

In the 1950s, nylon was far from a cheap alternative to natural fibres. Instead it was seen as a wonder material that excited the likes of Dior and Chanel in Paris. American synthetic textile giant, Du Pont, commissioned top fashion photographers to shoot couture pieces that used their branded fabrics. Once the word was out that nylon was popular in the fashion capital of the world, everyone wanted to use it.

A rose print cotton day dress, with YKK zip, 1950s.

$130–150 ⊞ WARD

It would have been a pricey finishing touch to use a YKK zipper from Japan, so this dress was probably more expensive than the average. Coupled with its great condition, it's likely it was kept for 'best'.

A lady's woollen suit, with a pencil skirt and tailored jacket with hand-painted buttons, 1950s.

$170–200 ⊞ FC

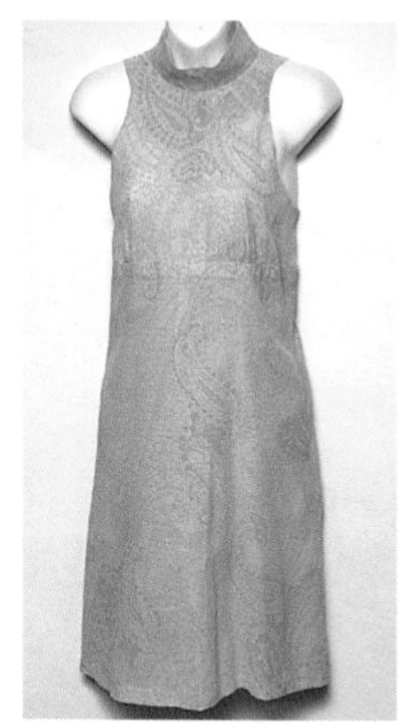

A Paisley print polyester summer dress, 1960s.

$80–90 FC

Polyester first made its appearance in the 1940s. Two decades later, thanks to aggressive marketing by its manufacturers (Du Pont in America and ICI in Britain) polyester was a High Street favourite. Cheap to make up, it was the ideal material for the short-lived fun fashions of the '60s.

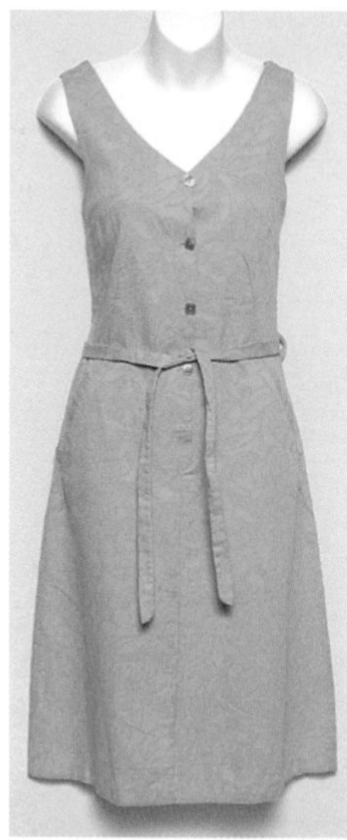

An Atlantic psychedelic print cotton summer dress, 1960s.

$80–90 FC

A rose print stretch nylon dress with matching jacket, with Lightning zip, 1960s.

$70–80 FC

An acetate summer dress, with Cort zip, 1960s.

$80–90 FC

A Foale & Tuffin Liberty Varuna wool tunic and culottes, late 1960s.

$480–560 EG

Twiggy wore their dresses and so did Sindy! Marion Foale (b1939) and Sally Tuffin (b1938) launched their 'Foale & Tuffin' label in 1961. The look was all about being part of the scene – youthful fashion for a young market. The brand was licensed in America and sold under the Paraphernalia label.

KNOW YOUR FABRICS – TRICEL

- If you know a bit of history about fabrics then it's hugely helpful with dating.
- British Celanese and Courtauld developed triacetate yarns independently, but it was after their merger in 1957 that the Tricel brand was born.
- Manufacturers found it easy to print and make up. Customers loved the fact that Tricel garments could drip dry, were shrink resistant and needed little or no ironing.
- Frank Usher was one of a number of British designers who were sponsored to work with synthetics like Tricel. His creations were unveiled at well-publicized fashion shows.
- Tricel was a quality fibre and garments made from it are well made and worth collecting.

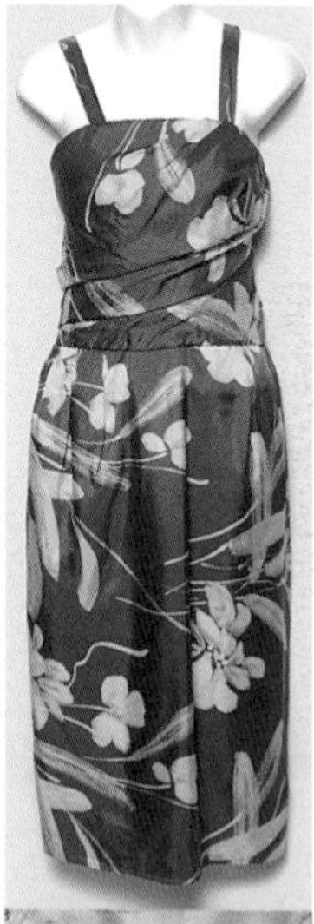

A Frank Usher floral print Tricel cocktail dress, London, with Lightning zip, 1960s.

$125–150 FC

A Pucci-style psychedelic print Tricel trouser suit, with Lightning zip, 1960s.

$90–100 FC

A Wallis printed cotton mini dress, with Opti zip, early 1970s.

$40–45 ⊞ FC

Wallis opened their first store in Britain in 1923. By the 1970s, they were a high street favourite and business was booming so much that they expanded into Europe. The first years of the 1970s saw mix-and-match hemlines with mini dresses like this running alongside flowing maxi dresses.

A John Charles triacetate and nylon maxi dress, with batwing sleeves, 1970s.

$85–95 ⊞ FC

A stretch polyester maxi dress, with gathered cuffs, 1970s.

$70–80 ⊞ WARD

Nova *magazine described this style as 'The droopy romantic look'. Maxi dresses were a big part of fashion in the '70s and took their inspiration from the Pre-Raphaelite style of the late 19th century.*

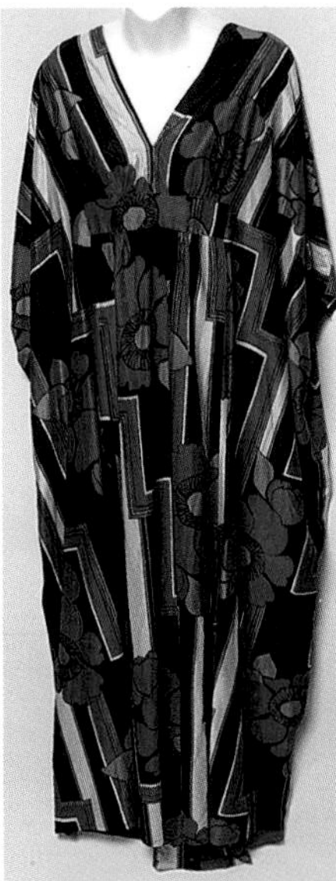

A poppy print stretch-polyester kaftan dress, 1970s.

$85–95 ⊞ FC

A stretch polyester pleated maxi dress, 1970s.

$90–100 ⊞ FC

A Joseph Bancroft nylon and polyamide dress and jacket set, designed by Anne Tyrrell for the John Marks label, Ban-Lon trademark, America, 1970s.

$95–110 ⊞ WARD

◀ *The flowing Kaftan shape worked for women of any size. It was based on a Turkish man's tunic. The mass of fabric lent itself to big bold prints and vivid colour.*

A Carnegie stretch polyester jersey maxi dress and cape, 1970s.

$130–150 ⊞ FC

A sequinned and ruched evening dress, designed by Ronald Joyce for the After Six range, late 1970s.

$150–170 ⊞ FC

Designers in the 1970s experimented with different support combinations from strapless to halterneck. Here the dress is held in place with a single shoulder strap, very reminiscent of classical styling.

A polyester handmade kaftan dress, 1970s.

$70–80 FC

A Mathilde linen double-fronted suit, by J. Rondinaud, Paris, with softly padded shoulders, France, 1980s.

$70–80 FC

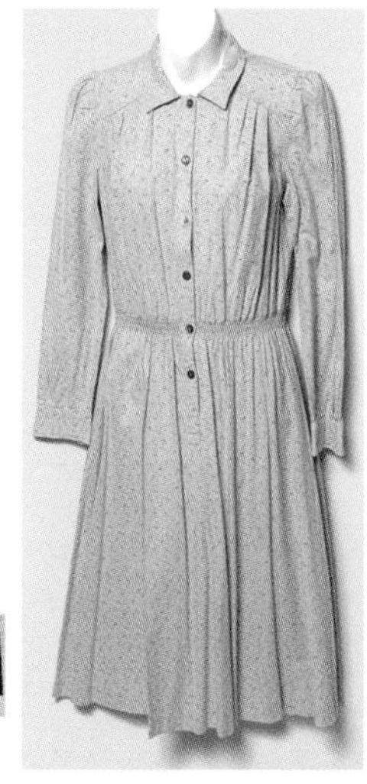

A Laura Ashley cotton dress, in a floral pattern, early 1980s.

$60–70 FC

A Laura Ashley Dior-style ruched acetate evening dress, with off-the-shoulder neckline, 1980s.

$85–95 WARD

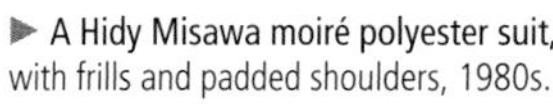

▶ **A Hidy Misawa moiré polyester suit,** with frills and padded shoulders, 1980s.

$110–130 FC

A Frank Usher polyester short evening dress, with softly padded shoulders, 1980s.

$110–130 FC

A leather-look dress, 1980s.

$85–95 WARD

◀ **A Roots acetate and polyester strapless short evening dress,** 1980s.

$85–95 FC

JACKETS, JUMPERS & BLOUSES

A beaded and sequinned **chiffon evening jacket,** 1920s.

$580–660 ⊞ Ech

A **Mary Quant lady's corduroy jacket,** late 1960s.

$70–80 ⊞ CLOB

In the swinging sixties, youth fashions came from the street rather than the couture houses. Mary Quant's 'Bizarre' boutiques in London were at the heart of modern style, largely driven by her trademark minidresses and skirts that finished 7in (18cm), or even 8in (20.5cm) above the knee. By 1966, Quant clothes were exported with great success to a captive audience in America. This Mod jacket carries Quant's classic daisy label, which was used across her range from make-up and tights to boots.

► An **Arkay Tricel blouse,** with frilled collar and cuffs, 1970s.

$30–35 ⊞ FC

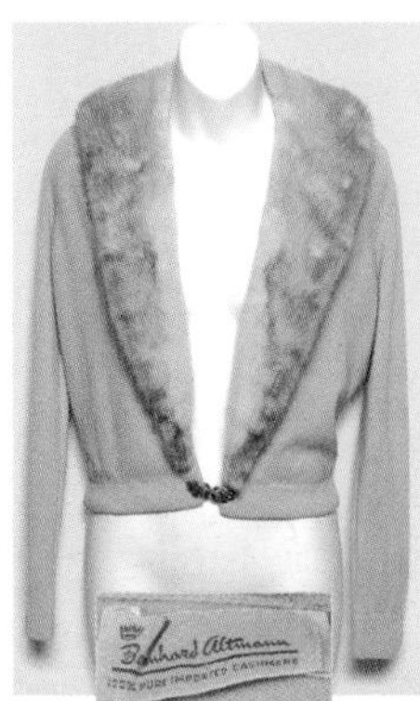

A **Bernard Altmann cashmere cardigan,** with paste clasp and fur collar, 1950s.

$160–190 ⊞ FC

Fur accents, whether real or faux, were a recurrent feature of 1950s style. Film stars, including Marilyn Monroe, sported Bernard Altmann's fabulously soft cashmere creations.

A **Jean Muir kid leather top,** 1970s.

$160–190 ⊞ FC

A **cotton velvet tailored jacket,** 1940s.

$20–25 ⊞ WARD

► An **Alice Pollock jacket,** the calico ground with a print depicting Ancient Egyptian wings, labelled 'Alice Pollock, size 10, made in London', c1970.

$950–1,100 KTA

Alice Pollock designed in partnership with Ossie Clark for Quorum, the London-based wholesale and boutique business.

A **hand-knitted lady's jumper,** with Fairisle-inspired pattern, 1950s.

$70–80 ⊞ WARD

Hollywood actresses Jane Russell and Lana Turner popularized the 'sweater girl' look in the 1950s. This figure-hugging style emphasized the bust line. Beneath the soft wool there would have been an elaborately-structured padded bra to give support and shape where it was needed.

A **lady's hand-knitted wool jumper,** with Lightning zip, 1950s.

$70–80 ⊞ FC

A **Biba corduroy jacket and hat,** late 1960s.

$270–310 ⊞ CLOB

An angel wing blouse, with cotton lace detailing, 1970s.

$50–60 FC

Loose-fitting sleeves grew out of a revived interest in ethnic clothes. The angel-wing style of this top was popularized by Agnetha Fältskog, the blonde-haired singer in ABBA. She wore hers with white flared trousers.

A Lady Di polyester blouse, with *faux* pearl buttons, 1980s.

$30–35 FC

PUNK STYLE

A screenprinted cotton punk T-shirt, 'Voodoo Dolly', early 1980s.

$60–70 FC

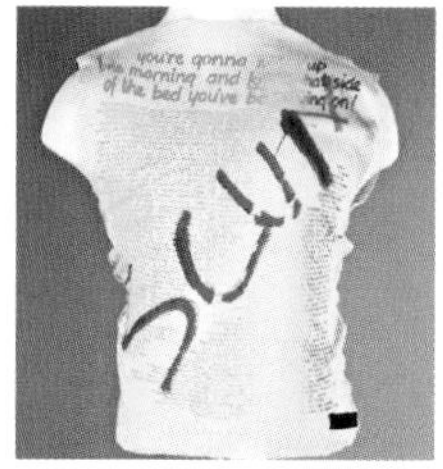

A Westwood/McLaren cotton T-shirt, 'Scum', with 'SEX Original' and 'Seditionaries' labels, 1977.

$1,600–1,800 KTA

◄ **A glazed rayon parachute-style top,** with ruched detailing, late 1970s.

$85–100 FC

- Punk emerged in the mid-1970s as a youth-led anti-establishment movement that demanded social change.
- Bands such as The Damned, The Clash and The Sex Pistols became the voice of punk.
- Music fans were quick to adopt the look of the bands they supported. Johnny Rotten of The Sex Pistols made a punk statement when he wore torn and safety-pinned clothes designed by Vivienne Westwood and Malcolm McLaren.
- Shops like 'Seditionaries' (run by Westwood and McLaren) and 'Boy' in London's King's Road became a Mecca for teenagers with dyed and spiked hair.
- The look was anti-fashion. At its crudest, charity shop garments were cut up and resewn or pinned together. Zips and stitching appeared on the outside.
- Sex/Seditionaries originals can command four-figure sums. A better bet in terms of price are punk-influenced styles like this ruched fashion top. Although punk had fizzled out by the early 1980s, the style did run on. This Voodoo Dolly T-shirt was inspired by the Siouxsie and the Banshees single of the same name from 1981.

◄ **A Janice Wainwright printed silk jacket,** in the style of a man's smoking jacket, with cord edging, padded shoulders and belt, 1980s.

$80–90 FC

◄ **A Marks & Spencer viscose and cotton printed jacket,** with original St Michael stock control label, 1980s.

$100–115 FC

SKIRTS & TROUSERS

A cotton rock and roll skirt, 1950s.

$280–320 SpM

A leather miniskirt, with YKK zip, 1960s.

$80–95 FC

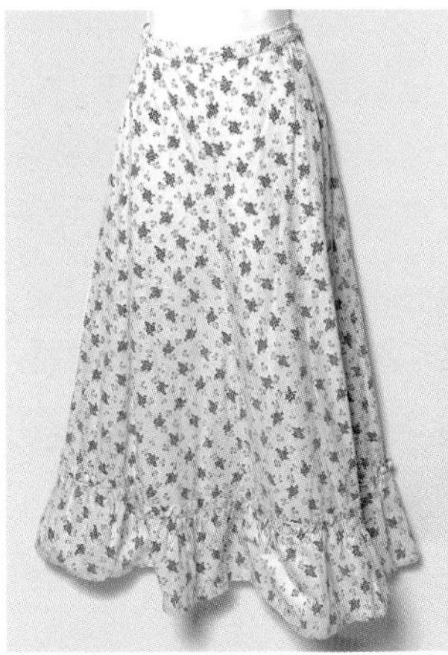

A Laura Ashley printed cotton maxi skirt, 1970s.

$70–80 FC

By the end of the 1970s there were 25 Laura Ashley stores in Britain plus a host more in Europe and America. This skirt is a perfect example of her revivalist patterns based on Victorian and Edwardian floral prints. Flower designs and natural cottons turned grown women into country maids.

A cotton printed skirt, with Swift zip, 1950s.

$80–95 FC

Printed with everything from garlic to coffee grinders, the pattern on this fabric was very much in tune with the times. French-style cooking as promoted by Elizabeth David and Fanny Craddock dominated British menus in the 1950s.

A Deréta textured cotton-mix skirt, early 1960s.

$80–95 FC

A printed cotton skirt, 1950s.

$70–80 FC

A pair of Emilio Pucci printed silk trousers, with Rulon zip, Italy, 1960s.

$230–260 FC

The 1960s jet-set who could afford transatlantic air travel needed clothing that was chic but easy to pack. Italian designer Emilio Pucci (1914–92) was at hand with the answer – brightly-printed luxuriously silky garments that were as light as a feather. His early pieces are simply labelled but he swiftly moved on to incorporate his distinctive 'Emilio' signature into the fabric's pattern.

◀ **A leather hotpant/pinafore combination,** with TEX zip, 1970s.

$85–100 FC

A denim all-in-one suit, 1970s.

$105–120 ⊞ ROK(B)

◀ **A cotton patchwork maxi skirt**, with Prym zip, 1970s.

$50–60 ⊞ FC

▶ **A hand-made bedspread skirt**, 1970s.

$15–25 ⊞ FC

This is very much a home-made affair, stitched together from two coverlets.

A pair of Peter Golding stretch trousers, 1977.

$30–35 ⊞ FC

British designer Peter Golding is credited with bringing us the world's first stretch jeans in 1978. These trousers, made from 100% spandex Lycra, give us a sense of what was to come a year later. Golding's style, defined as 'Glam Hollywood meets King's Road aristocracy', made women feel supremely sexy, chic and beautiful. The high waistline gave an unrivalled fit. No wonder celebrities like Jerry Hall and Marianne Faithful flocked to Ace, Golding's Chelsea shop, to buy them.

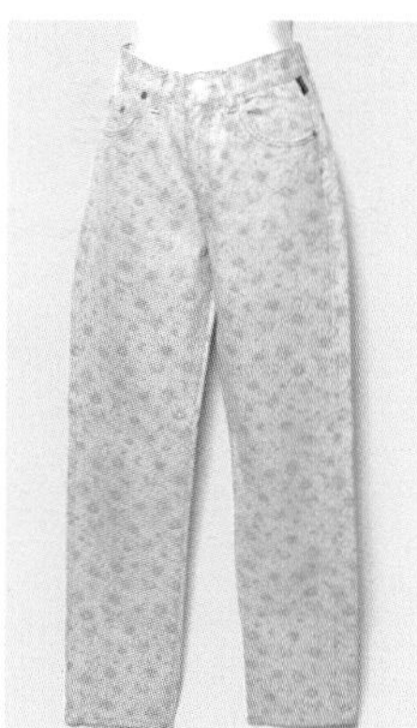

A pair of Versace Sport cotton trousers, Italy, 1980s.

$155–170 ⊞ FC

ZIP TIPS

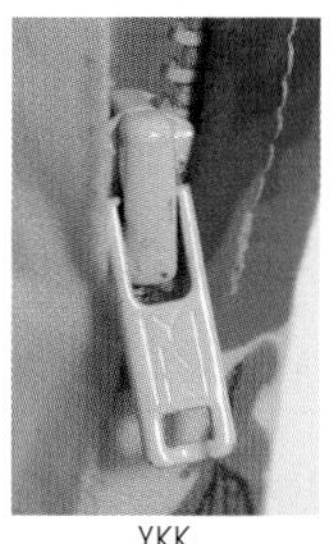

YKK

YKK

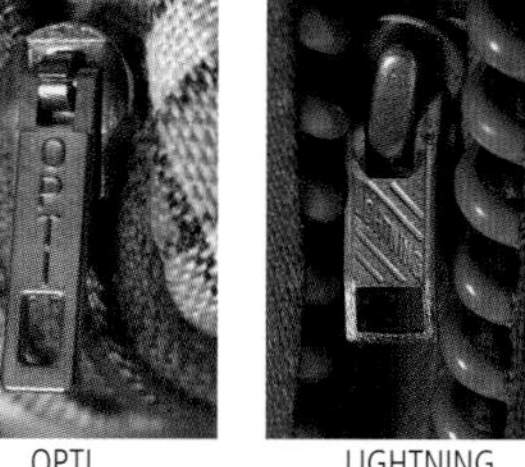

OPTI

LIGHTNING

- Looking at the zip can tell you a lot about the quality and age of a garment.
- The 'clasp locker' of the 1890s with hooks and eyes, which was used to seal mailbags, was the precursor of today's zipper. The first metal teeth fastener to see practical use was patented in 1917 by the Swedish-born engineer, Gideon Sundback. Its use in rubber boots by B. F. Goodrich & Co spawned the name 'zipper', which was linked to the sound the fastener made and the fact that it could be operated with one hand.
- Zips were used briefly in the 1910s for corsets and again in the 1930s by a few couturiers, but not on a mainstream basis until WWII when they were key to fastening flying jackets and boots.
- From the 1950s their use was widespread. Brand names to look for are Lightning (a Canadian firm), Opti (British), and increasingly in the post-war years, YKK (Japanese).
- Metal zips gradually gave way to synthetic and coil zips from the 1960s.
- YKK zips gained a stronghold in the post-war decades. Founded in 1934 as San-es-Shokai in Japan, the YKK trademark was registered in 1946. They started to manufacture zips overseas in 1959.

SWIMWEAR

A wool swimsuit, with inset net chest support and button detailing, 1930s.

$95–110 FC

A strapless swimsuit, the front panel cut to resemble a skirt, 1950s.

$60–70 FC

A rayon ruched swimsuit, 1950s.

$65–75 FC

A Jantzen stretch cotton swimsuit, 1950s.

$75–85 FC

A nylon swimsuit, America, 1960s.

$50–60 FC

A stretch nylon and Lycra swimsuit, by Marks & Spencer, with original St Michael label,1960s.

$50–60 FC

A polyester and cotton bikini, retailed by Marks & Spencer, with original St Michael label, 1960s.

$40–50 FC

A pair of Huber striped nylon swimming trunks, Austria, 1960s.

$30–40 FC

◀ **A pair of nylon and polyamide swimming trunks,** retailed by Marks & Spencer, 1975.

$25–30 FC

SHIRTS & JUMPERS

A Howe Street Hawaiian shirt, 1950s.

$95–110 ⊞ ROK(B)

A Mr Chips printed polyester shirt, 1970s.

$50–60 ⊞ FC

A Ramrod short-sleeved shirt, c1980.

$30–40 ⊞ CLOB

A knitted wool Cowichan-style cardigan, with Lightning zip, 1960s.

$60–70 ⊞ FC

Traditional Cowichan sweaters, which originate from the Cowichan Valley on Vancouver Island, Canada, are knitted from natural, undyed wool. Hunting motifs are popular and this garment is very much aligned with that style. This Native American look was popularized by the Mary Maxim and Northland labels in the 1950s and '60s. Comedian Bob Hope and Canada's 13th Prime Minister, John Diefenbaker (in office 1957–63), helped to spread the word after they were seen relaxing in something very similar.

A Country Road cotton work shirt, Australia, 1980s.

$10–15 ⊞ FC

Striped shirts were essential office wear in the 1980s. They were usually teamed with vivid spotted, Paisley or animal print ties.

A Foster Brothers Courtelle button cardigan, 1960s.

$25–30 ⊞ FC

A Burton polyester shirt, with appliqué check, 1970s.

$65–75 ⊞ FC

A Paul Smith cotton shirt, 1990s.

$75–85 ⊞ FC

MEN'S JACKETS

A Ralphs Pugh B15-style parker jacket, with fake fur collar, America, San Francisco, 1940s.

$180–200 ⊞ ROK(B)

An Adidas track suit top, with matching trousers, West Germany, late 1970s.

$60–70 ⊞ CLOB

A John Collier striped wool teddy boy jacket, with cotton velvet trim, retailed by L. & H. Nathan, London, 1950s.

$310–340 ⊞ FC

◀ **A Lord John leather jacket,** 1960s.

$230–250 ⊞ CLOB

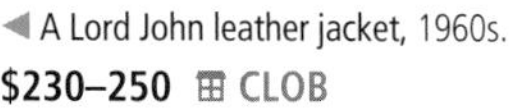

The Lord John boutique opened in London's Carnaby Street in 1963 and quickly became a Mecca for Mod fashion. Soon Brian Jones from The Rolling Stones and Micky Dolenz from The Monkeys were seen shopping there.

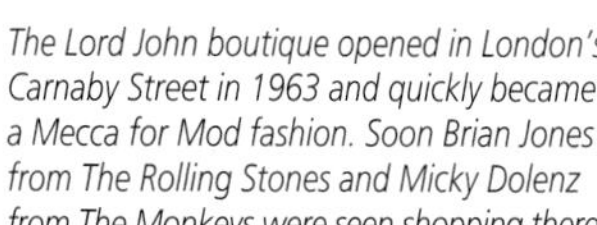

A Val Cassi cotton, polyester and nylon seersucker jacket, 1970s.

$105–120 ⊞ FC

1970s fashion magazines advised men to wear a plain polo-neck jersey beneath their 'window-pane' check jackets.

▶ **An Adidas windcheater,** France, 1980s.

$85–95 ⊞ CLOB

A Take 6 man's floral satin jacket, c1960.

$380–430 ⊞ CLOB

A John Weitz polyester/cotton safari-style jacket, retailed by Burton, 1970s.

$50–60 ⊞ FC

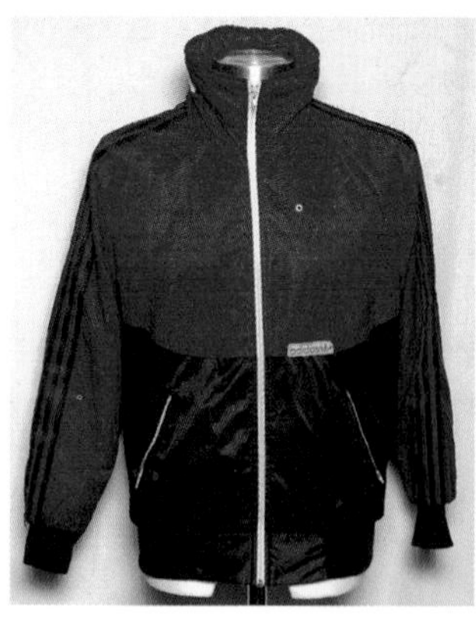

MEN'S TROUSERS

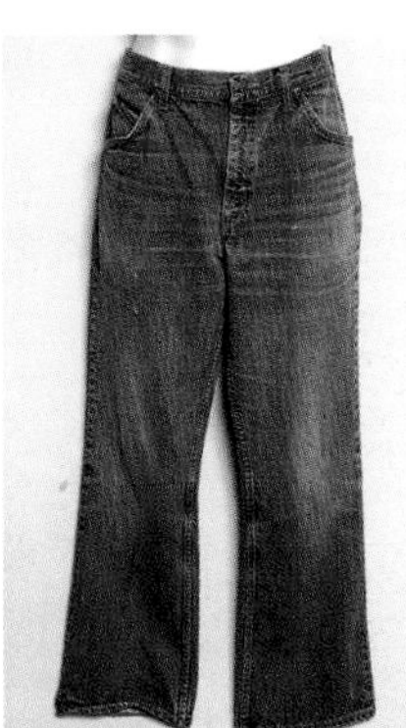

A pair of vintage Lee Cooper blue jeans, 1970s.

$95–110 ⊞ ROK(B)

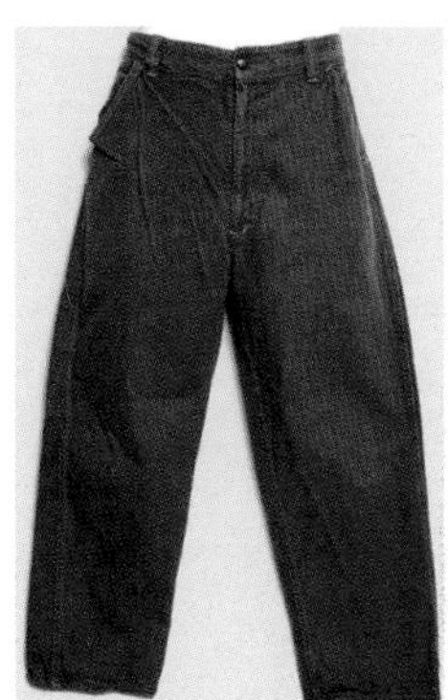

A pair of vintage GWG Red Strap blue jeans, Canada, 1950s.

$95–110 ⊞ ROK(B)

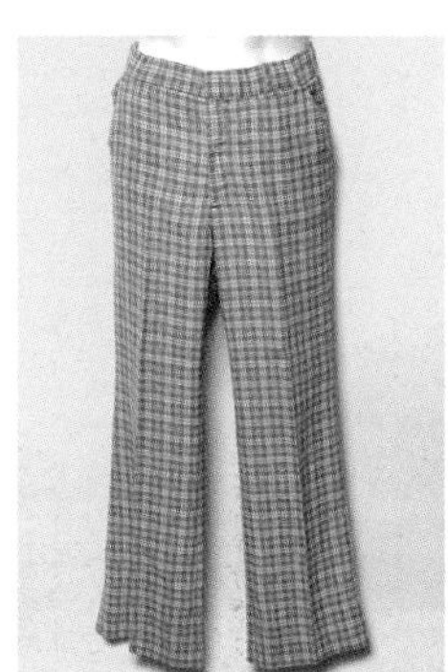

A pair of Johnny Miller Collection leisure trousers, with Opti zip, 1970s.

$50–60 ⊞ FC

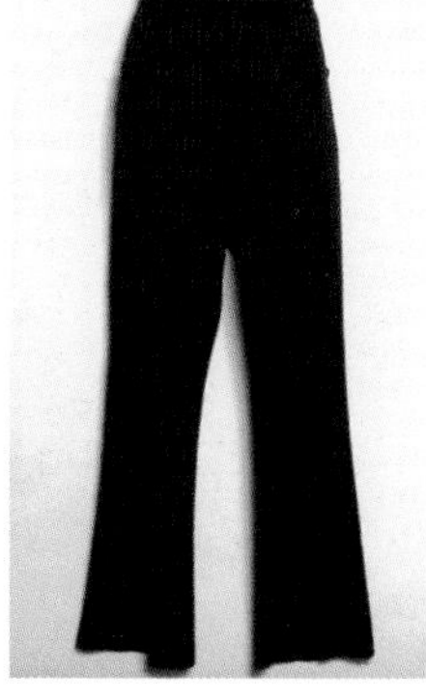

A pair of Haggar double-knit trousers, America, 1980s.

$30–40 ⊞ ROK(B)

VINTAGE LEVI 501S

A pair of Levi 501 jeans, with offset back loop, 1950s.

$690–770 ⊞ DeJ

A pair of Levi 501 red line jeans, button marked 524, 1970s.

$170–200 ⊞ DeJ

◄ A pair of vintage Levi 501 jeans.

$510–600 ⊞ ROK(B)

- American-based Levi Strauss made their first jeans in 1873.
- Levi 501 jeans are the original shrink-to-fit, button-fly blue jeans first created in the 1800s. The 501 number appeared around 1890.
- The red tab ran from 1936 to help identify the jeans from a distance. Until 1971, the Levi name appeared in capitals. After this date the 'e' appeared in lower case, so look out for big 'E' pairs.
- Up until the late 1950s, the label says 'Lot 501 XX', after this period simply '501 XX 501' is used to denote the style. The XX refers to the weight and quality of the denim.
- Red line jeans are considered vintage and therefore collectable. Levi 501s traditionally used a narrow-loom XX denim made by Cone Mills in North Carolina. In the early 20th century, they added a coloured line to their fabric's selvage to identify different grades of denim. Red identified the top grade as used for the 501s.
In 1983, Levi switched to wide-loom XXX denim for the 501s and the selvage disappeared.

BAGS

A W. Whiteley bag, with Moroccan leather interior, c1900, 9½in (24cm) wide.

$85–100 ⊞ CCO

A leather handbag, with Lucite and brass catch, 1940s.

$85–100 ⊞ FC

A fabric and leatherette bucket bag, 1950s, 12in (30.5cm) wide.

$50–60 ⊞ FC

A Bakelite clutch bag, with stainless-steel detail, 1920s, 8in (20.5cm) wide.

$340–410 ⊞ FC

A crocodile handbag, with brass bracelet-style frame, 1940s, 9in (23cm) wide.

$390–480 ⊞ FC

A basketweave handbag, with felt appliqué decoration, 1950s.

$40–50 ⊞ WARD

▶ **A wicker bag,** with a plastic and Lucite frame and plastic interior, America, 1950s, 12in (30.5cm) wide.

$120–135 ⊞ PAST

A beaded bag, with paste and filigree metal clasp and frame, France or Belgium, c1930, 9in (23cm) wide.

$210–240 ⊞ WARD

A leopard print handbag, with Bakelite handle, 1940, 17in (43cm) high.

$280–320 ⊞ SpM

A Wilardy Lucite bag, America, 1950s, 10½in (26.5cm) wide.

$280–320 ⊞ PAST

A National fabric handbag, Canada, 1950s, 8in (20.5cm) wide.

$40–50 FC

► A plastic 'telephone coil' clutch bag, with Lightning zip, early 1960s, 10in (25.5cm) wide.

$125–145 FC

A Union Jack handbag, 'made in Britain' to zip, 1960s, 11in (28cm) wide.

$85–100 FC

This bag evokes the strongly nationalistic feel that swept British style during the 1960s. The British brand was carried worldwide by Twiggy, Carnaby Street and The Beatles. Teenage youth culture proudly incorporated elements of British design into their everyday look and this handbag is just one example of how they achieved it.

A Freedex 'Caressa' vinyl handbag, Ireland, 1960s, 10in (25.5cm) wide.

$65–75 FC

An Enid Collins canvas tote bag, with wooden base, hand decorated with rhinestones, copyright to interior, America, 1960s, 12in (30.5cm) wide.

$120–135 PAST

A Hermès crocodile-skin handbag, 1960s, 10in (25.5cm) wide.

$2,350–2,550 TIN

A patent leather telephone bag, with working push-button telephone, plug-in adaptor, cotton lining and zip pocket, America, 1960s–70s, 12in (30.5cm) wide.

$270–310 ROS

A bamboo basket bag, 1970s, 12½in (32cm) wide.

$85–100 PAST

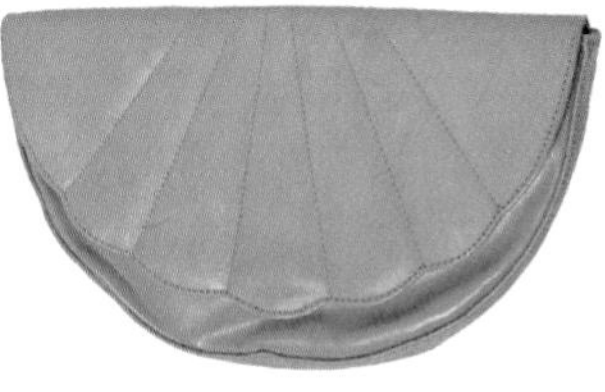

A vinyl clutch bag, 1980s, 10in (25.5cm) wide.

$25–30 FC

A Suzy Smith Chanel-style padded leatherette handbag, 1980s, 14in (35.5cm) wide.

$40–50 FC

BUTTONS

A set of 12 cameo buttons, on onyx, with cut steel edges, early 19thC, 1in (2.5cm) diam.

$740–830 ⊞ JBB

A wooden button, applied with a stamped and tinted brass motif of Little Bo-Peep, from a Kate Greenaway illustration, late 19thC, 1¼in (3cm) diam.

$270–300 ⊞ TB

A *Shibayama* ivory button, inlaid with a carved mother-of-pearl heron with incised and pigmented legs, c1875, 1¼in (3cm) diam.

$1,050–1,200 ⊞ TB

A Wedgwood jasper ware button, depicting a classical scene, in a cut-steel setting by Matthew Boulton, 1770–80, 1½in (4cm) diam.

$2,150–2,400 ⊞ TB

British steel manufacturer and engineer Matthew Boulton collaborated with Josiah Wedgwood in the 1770s. He was known for his fine cut steel buttons and buckles. The facets on this button are meant to imitate precious stones.

A porcelain button, with Royal Copenhagen Factory mark, Denmark, late 18thC, 1¼in (3cm) diam.

$1,350–1,500 ⊞ TB

A Satsuma pottery button, depicting flowers and bamboo, the crackle glaze encrusted with gold, Japan, 1875–1925, 1in (2.5cm) diam.

$170–195 ⊞ TB

▶ **An Arita glazed and gilded porcelain button,** in the form of a leaf, Japan, mid-20thC, ¾in (2cm) wide.

$170–195 ⊞ TB

A set of four ceramic buttons, depicting scenes from the 'Hey Diddle Diddle' nursery rhyme, c1950, 1in (2.5cm) diam.

$25–30 ⊞ JBB

A set of six coconut shell buttons, modelled as flying birds, Hawaii, c1940, 1½in (4cm) diam.

$40–50 ⊞ JBB

◀ **A set of four ceramic buttons,** designed by Piero Fornasetti, Italy, 1950s, 1in (2.5cm) diam.

$75–85 ⊞ MARK

A paste and opaline glass button, in a silver setting, 1780–99, 1½in (4cm) diam.

$1,350–1,500 ⊞ TB

A reverse-painted glass button, with copper border, 1720–50, 1½in (4cm) diam.

$1,600–1,800 ⊞ TB

A set of chased gilt gentlemen's buttons, 1830–50, largest 1in (2.5cm) diam.

$15–25 each ⊞ EV

A set of four silver paste and peridot buttons, copies of 1780 buttons, France, 1880, 1¼in (3cm) diam, boxed.

$1,150–1,250 ⊞ JBB

The products of Parisian fashion workshops, especially from the St Honoré area, have long been the yardstick for fashion. The value of this set of buttons has been increased by having the A. Risler & Carré silversmiths' original case.

A set of six brass buttons, with photographs of beautiful ladies, c1900, ¼in (0.5cm) diam.

$95–110 ⊞ JBB

A stamped brass button, with faceted steel on a pearl ground, within a steel border, late 19thC, 1½in (4cm) diam.

$75–85 ⊞ TB

A stamped brass button, depicting 'The Wounded Cuirassier', after a painting by Théodore Géricault, early 20thC, 1¼in (3cm) diam.

$75–85 ⊞ TB

A carved and hand-painted plastic button, in the form of a donkey's head, c1930, 1¼in (3cm) diam.

$195–220 ⊞ TB

A carved celluloid button, depicting a sleeping owl, 1930s, 1¾in (4.5cm) diam.

$160–190 ⊞ TB

A set of six plastic buttons, 1930, 1¾in (4.5cm) diam.

$10–15 ⊞ 299

A carved and tinted Bakelite button, in the form of a horse's head, late 1930s, 1in (2.5cm) diam.

$220–250 ⊞ TB

COSTUME JEWELLERY

A Bakelite hinged bracelet, with carved decoration, 1930s.

$440–500 WARD

A Bakelite bangle, 1930s.

$195–220 WARD

A gold-plated flower bracelet, 1940s, 8in (20.5cm) long.

$105–120 DUR

A glass bead, *faux* pearl, paste and seed pearl bracelet, by Miriam Haskell, c1950, 2in (5cm) wide.

$500–570 ADV

American jewellery-maker, Miriam Haskell (1899–1981), opened her first shop in New York in 1926. In the early days it is believed that she made the pieces herself, but as business boomed Haskell relied on the skills of her chief designer, Frank Hess – a former window-dresser at Macy's. Haskell jewellery is always finely detailed, often with minute filigree work and a bevy of tiny beads and crystals. Much of the firm's early work is unsigned and only from the late 1940s was the 'Miriam Haskell' signature widely used. Haskell retired from the firm in the 1950s and in 1960 Robert F. Clark was appointed chief designer. He was replaced in the 1970s by Larry Vrba. Popularity bred copies, so study the detail – Frank Hess was a perfectionist and poor wirework is a sure sign that it is not a piece by Haskell.

A *faux* topaz and gilt-metal bangle, by Hollycraft, America, c1950, 1in (2.5cm) wide.

$190–210 ADV

Hollycraft (not to be confused with Joseff of Hollywood) began life as The Hollywood Jewellery Manufacturing Company in the 1930s but simplified its name in the late 1940s. From the 1950s they dated most of their jewellery. Look out for the firm's distinctive antique-gold plated settings and array of colourful crystal rhinestones.

A gilt-metal and glass bangle, c1960, 2in 5cm) wide.

$190–210 ADV

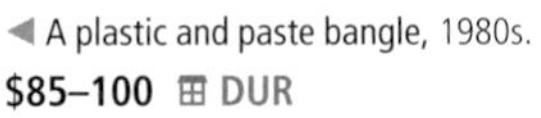

◄ A plastic and paste bangle, 1980s.

$85–100 DUR

A Bakelite bangle, 1960s, 2½in (6.5cm) wide.

$145–160 WARD

BROOCHES

A Bakelite brooch, in the form of a dagger, America, 1930s, 4in (10cm) long.

$430–480 WARD

This rare piece is one of several designs in the Crusader series.

A Royal Worcester porcelain brooch, in the form of lily of the valley, 1931, 3in (7.5cm) wide.

$50–60 WAC

A metal and glass dress clip, Czechoslovakia, c1930, 2in (5cm) long.

$10–15 CCO

► **A Lucite floral brooch,** c1950, 1½in (4cm) square.

$15–25 CCO

The rose design was created by carving and painting the reverse of this brooch. This version in Lucite takes its inspiration from the carved apple juice Bakelite bangles of the 1930s.

MILLER'S COMPARES

(L) A Bakelite brooch, in the form of a bunch of cherries, 1930s, 2in (5cm) diam.

$190–210 WARD

(R) A plastic brooch, in the form of two bunches of cherries, 2006.

$120–135 WARD

Prices for genuine Bakelite jewellery have risen in the past few years and this has inspired many reproductions. The brooch on the left is solid and weighty and has coated strings, while the reproduction on the right is of a lighter colour, has crudely knotted leather strings and has a light-weight plastic chain that is at odds with the naturalistic theme. Some quick tests can help to spot genuine Bakelite items: when Bakelite is tapped it makes a solid 'clunk' that goes with its weight and that light-weight cast plastic cannot replicate; when rubbed Bakelite gives off a distinct chemical odour.

◄ **A gunmetal and paste brooch,** in the form of a bird, c1940, 2½in (6.5cm) long.

$60–70 JBB

A silver-gilt and rhinestone brooch, 1940s, 3in (7.5cm) long.

$95–110 DUR

A gilt-metal and paste brooch, by Trifari, in the form of a butterfly, America, c1955, 2¼in (5.5cm) wide.

$260–300 ⊞ ADV

Italian-born Gustavo Trifari settled in the US in 1902 and started his own jewellery business with his uncle in 1910. When Leo Krussman and Carl Fishel came on board the firm was re-named Trifari, Krussman and Fishel in 1925 and the 'TKF' mark was used. With great foresight, the trio snapped up a young French designer, Alfred Philippe, who had been working with jewellery giants like Cartier and Van Cleef & Arpels. They persuaded him to turn his attention to fantasy costume jewellery and he designed some of Trifari's finest pieces, including the famous Trifari crown brooch/pin patented in 1944. Look out for the firm's distinctive crown over 'T' signature.

A gilt-metal and paste 'day and night' brooch, by Kenneth Jay Lane, the rotating rays revealing paste stones, c1960, 2½in (6.5cm) diam.

$240–260 ⊞ ADV

A *faux* pearl and paste brooch, by Christian Dior, in the from of an elephant's head, 1966, 3in (7.5cm) high.

$770–860 ⊞ DUR

◀ **An enamel and paste brooch,** in the form of an ostrich, c1950, 3in (7.5cm) high.

$110–125 ⊞ JBB

▶ **A brass and glass brooch,** in the form of a mouse, 1950, 1¾in (4.5cm) high.

$25–30 ⊞ SpM

LEA STEIN

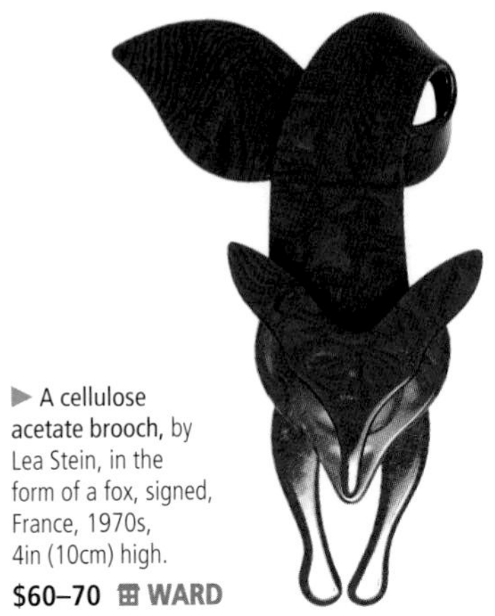

▶ **A cellulose acetate brooch,** by Lea Stein, in the form of a fox, signed, France, 1970s, 4in (10cm) high.

$60–70 ⊞ WARD

A cellulose acetate brooch, by Lea Stein, in the form of a cat, signed, France, 1970s, 3in (7.5cm) high.

$60–70 ⊞ WARD

- French artist Lea Stein was born in Paris in 1931. She started designing her famous animal jewellery in 1969 after her husband, Fernand Steinberger, discovered that by laminating cellulose acetate sheets (rhodoid) he could create a fantastic array of colours and patterns.
- Sometimes as many as 20 layers of rhodoid were used to give her designs a real 3-D feel. Look at the side of an item and see how it is bonded.
- The true 'vintage period' covers the years up to 1981 when the company ceased trading. In the late 1980s, Stein returned to making jewellery and now issues new designs on an annual basis.
- The fox brooch was one of her most popular creations. Often lace or metal layers were incorporated into the celluloid, which means that it appears in a wide variety of textures. The tail is made from a single piece of cellulose carefully looped into place.
- Outright fakes don't really exist as the technique is hugely complicated but there are lookalikes. Be guided by the 'V' shaped pin on the back, which is heat-mounted onto the reverse and signed 'Lea Stein Paris'.

EARRINGS

A pair of celluloid earrings, in the form of gardenias, signed, 1920s, 2in (5cm) long.

$95–110 ⊞ **DUR**

A pair of Indian-style papier-mâché earrings, by Trifari, 1937, 6in (15cm) long.

$770–860 ⊞ **DUR**

A pair of straw earrings, in the form of baskets of fruit, 1940, 1½in (4cm) high.

$60–70 ⊞ **SpM**

A pair of Bakelite and diamanté earrings, 1940s, 1in (2.5cm) diam.

$60–70 ⊞ **WARD**

► **A brass and paste brooch and earrings set,** by Joseff of Hollywood, signed, America, 1940s, brooch 2in (5cm) wide.

$620–690 ⊞ **WARD**

A pair of mother-of-pearl earrings, in the form of artists' pallets and brushes, 1950, 1½in (4cm) wide.

$85–100 ⊞ **SpM**

A pair of plastic and metal earrings, 1960s, 3in (7.5cm) long.

$30–30 ⊞ **DUR**

A pair of Bakelite hoop earrings, France, 1960s, 1½in (4cm) diam, on original card.

$60–70 ⊞ **WARD**

A pair of plastic earrings, 1960, 4in (10cm) long.

$85–100 ⊞ **SpM**

NECKLACES

A Bakelite necklace, with carved decoration, 1930s, 16in (40.5cm) long.

$240–260 WARD

A Bakelite necklace, 1930s, 16in (40.5cm) long.

$160–190 WARD

A Bakelite and silvered-metal necklace, 1930s, 18in (45.5cm) long.

$110–125 WARD

► A beaded necklace, with a paste clasp, Italy, 1950s, 18in (45.5cm) long.

$330–380 DUR

◄ A gilt-metal and plastic necklace, 1950s, 14in (35.5cm) long.

$85–100 WARD

A paste choker and earrings, by Christian Dior, 1950s, necklace 1in (2.5cm) wide.

$460–510 TDG

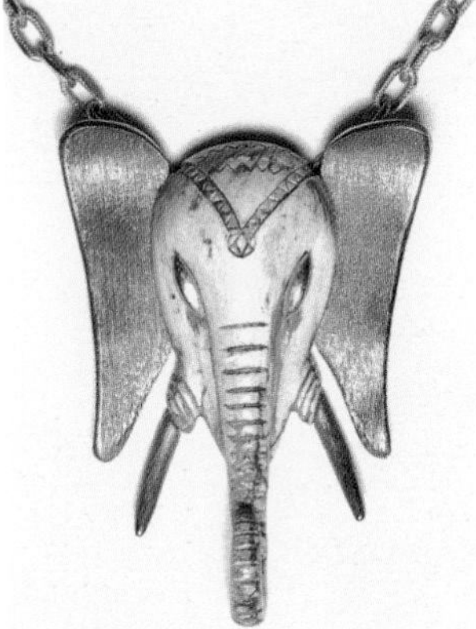

A gilt-metal and plastic necklace, by Luca Razza, in the form of an elephant's head, America, late 1960s, 4in (10cm) high.

$530–600 ADV

◄ A filigree metal and diamanté necklace, by Miriam Haskell, signed, America, 1960s, 16in (40.5cm) long.

$930–1,000 WARD

A gilt-metal and plastic necklace, by Luca Razza, in the form of an owl, America, late 1960s, owl 4in (10cm) high.

$530–600 ADV

Luca Razza began working in the jewellery business in America in the 1950s. He formed Raz-Mer Castings with Lionel Mercier and gained a name for making raw cast pieces for well-known jewellery brands. Probably his greatest achievement was to develop a method of casting from liquid plastic, which became his signature style when he designed jewellery for the Certified Corporation until the mid-1970s.

HATS

A straw cloche hat, with ribbon detail, 1920s.

$180–200 ⊞ **FC**

► **A straw hat,** with feathers within the crown, 1920s.

$75–85 ⊞ **DE**

A straw boater, 'The York Hat', retailed by Bruno Crosby, New Malden, Surrey, 1930s.

$65–75 ⊞ **FC**

A straw hat, with ribbon detail, 1930s.

$75–95 ⊞ **FC**

A Margaret Miller straw and jersey sunhat, 1930s–40s.

$105–120 ⊞ **SpM**

A Huckel wool felt trilby hat, 1940s.

$85–95 ⊞ **FC**

◄ **A cocktail hat,** with applied velvet flowers and diamantés, 1950s.

$75–85 ⊞ **FC**

► **A *faux* straw and net hat,** 1950s.

$95–110 ⊞ **FC**

A *faux* straw hat, with bow decoration, 1950s.
$105–120 FC

An Edward Mann 'Edma' cocktail hat, with applied *faux* cherry blossom, 1950s.
$95–110 FC

A Paquita Fuster cap-back straw hat, Spain, 1950s.
$85–95 FC

▶ A cotton sun hat, 1960s.
$10–15 DE

A gingham hat, 1960s.
$40–50 FC

A Coors Beer hat, the body made from pressed aluminium beer cans, America, 1970s.
$65–75 FC

A sequinned disco hat, 1970s.
$65–75 FC

A leopard print beret, 1960s.
$25–30 FC

▶ A Charo hat, 1980s.
$65–75 FC

SHOES

A pair of leather and canvas boots, marked 'La Belle', 1920s.

$125–145 ⊞ BGe

A pair of two-tone lace-up shoes, 1930s.

$110–125 ⊞ FC

A pair of De Belder satin evening shoes, France, 1920s.

$75–95 ⊞ Ech

A pair of leather and suede shoes, made and retailed by P. Beeson, France, Paris, 1940s.

$125–145 ⊞ FC

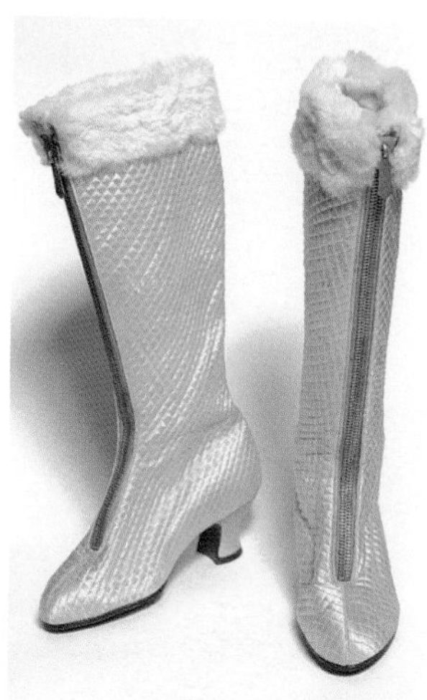

A pair of quilted satin boots, with fur lining, 1930s.

$135–150 ⊞ CLOB

► A pair of Bective Chiquita shoes, with diamanté decoration, retailed by McDonald's of Glasgow, 1950s.

$250–270 ⊞ FC

A pair of hand-carved wood and canvas pagoda mules, 'Jeanette', Phillipines, 1940s, 2½in (6.5cm) heel.

$240–260 ⊞ SpM

Mules such as these were made during WWII as souvenirs for the American troops.

A pair of patent leather shoes, 1960s.

$65–75 ⊞ FC

A pair of Shoefayre Paris Girl suede shoes, kitten heels, 1960s.

$95–110 ⊞ FC

► A pair of Biba suede shoes, with printed logo, 1970s.

$30–40 ⊞ KA

◀ A pair of Fashion Daisies leather Mary-Jane-style platform shoes, 1970s.

$85–100 ⊞ FC

▶ A pair of A. R. Sons leather platform boots, America, Los Angeles, 1970s.

$210–240 ⊞ CLOB

A pair of Fraporr platform sandals, Italy, 1970s.

$135–150 ⊞ FC

◀ A pair of Clarks Profile fabric shoes, 1980s.

$65–75 ⊞ FC

A pair of glitter shoes, 1980s.

$65–75 ⊞ FC

A pair of Katherine Hamnett leather platform shoes, retailed by Shelly's, London, 1980s.

$85–100 ⊞ FC

A pair of Pied à Terre shoes, late 1980s.

$50–60 ⊞ WARD

WEDGE SHOES

◀ A pair of leather wedge shoes, resprayed, 1930s.

$110–125 ⊞ FC

▶ A pair of denim wedge shoes, with rope detailing, 1970s.

$50–60 ⊞ FC

- Wedge shoes have been used throughout history to make women look taller and elongate their leg length. In ancient Greece raised shoes were used to increase the height of theatrical performers.
- Italian shoe designer Salvatore Ferragamo revived the wedge in the 1930s and most famously designed a pair of wedge shoes for Judy Garland in 1938. The heels were made from layers of Sardinian cork.
- Stiletto heels replaced wedges in the 1950s and they were not revived again until the 1970s, when they appeared in soft denims and cotton with rope inserts. They matched '70s relaxed style of fashion and the decade's preference for natural materials.

SUNGLASSES

THE CHINESE ARE SAID to have developed the process of darkening eyeglasses around 1430 as a means of keeping secret the eye expressions of their judges. However, it was not until the 20th century that tinted glasses were worn specifically to protect the wearer from the sun's rays. In 1929, Sam Foster, founder of Foster Grant, began retailing his first sunglasses.

Advances in tinting and light-absorption were rapid once the military became involved. In the 1930s, the US Army Air Corps was delighted when the American optical giant, Bausch & Lomb, unveiled a special dark-green tinted glass that would protect their pilots from high-altitude glare. This ultimately led to the Ray-Ban brand, which Bausch & Lomb went public with in 1937 in the form of their 'Aviator'-style sunglasses. These took advantage of the Polaroid Corporation's new polarized lenses.

Until the 1950s, frame shapes were unisex, but in the post-war decades women were treated to styles of their own. One of the most popular 1950s outlines was the browliner frame, which at its most exaggerated became the 'cat's-eye' shape. Trends in successive decades were largely set by the rich and famous – the 'Jackie O' style cover-ups dominated the 1960s along with the space age/Op Art look. Today there is much demand for vintage sunglasses, but remember to take a close look at the frame and avoid anything that is cracked.

A pair of Astro-Matic plastic sunglasses, 1950, 6½in (16.5cm) wide, with instructions and original box.

$155–170 ⊞ SpM

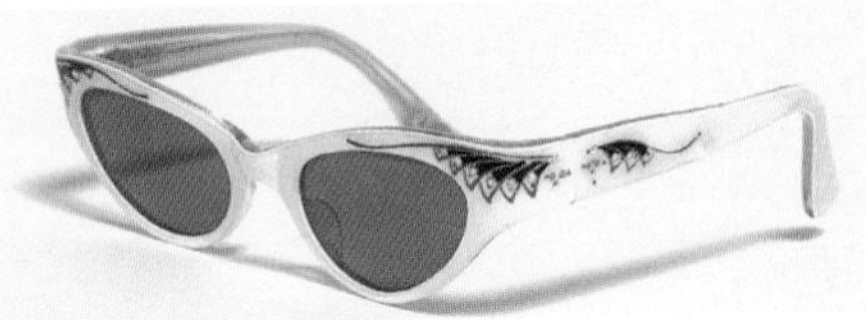

A pair of plastic sunglasses, with diamanté decoration, 1950s, 14in (35.5cm) wide.

$50–60 ⊞ CLOB

A pair of Helmeke plastic sunglasses, 1960s, 14in (35.5cm) long.

$50–60 ⊞ CLOB

A pair of sunglasses, France, c1960, 14in (35.5cm) wide.

$40–50 ⊞ CLOB

A pair of plastic Mod sunglasses, 1960.

$105–120 ⊞ SpM

▶ **A pair of Margery Proops-style sunglasses,** with paste rim, late 1960s, 6in (15cm) wide.

$75–85 ⊞ DUR

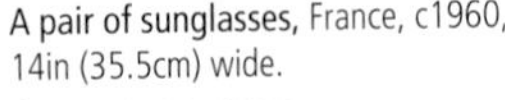

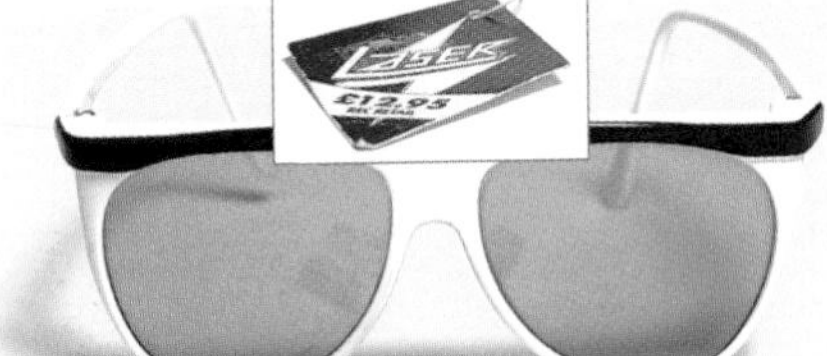

A pair of Laser plastic sunglasses, with original label, 1980s, 14in (35.5cm) wide.

$15–25 ⊞ CLOB

A pair of Carrera metal-rimmed sunglasses, with graduated lenses, 1980s.

$210–240 ⊞ ROK(B)

MEN'S TIES & SCARVES

An Arrow synthetic clip-on bow tie.

$10–15 FC

A Supreme Tie printed polyester tie, 1960s, 3in (7.5cm) wide.

$15–25 FC

A synthetic tie, 1950s, 2½in (6.5cm) wide.

$15–25 FC

A printed silk tie, Thailand, 1970s, 4¼in (11cm) wide.

$10–15 FC

A Liberty printed silk tie, 1980s, 3½in (9cm) wide.

$25–30 FC

A Ralph Marlin & Co silk tie, printed with a portrait of Marilyn Monroe, America, 1990s, 3in (7.5cm) wide.

$15–25 WARD

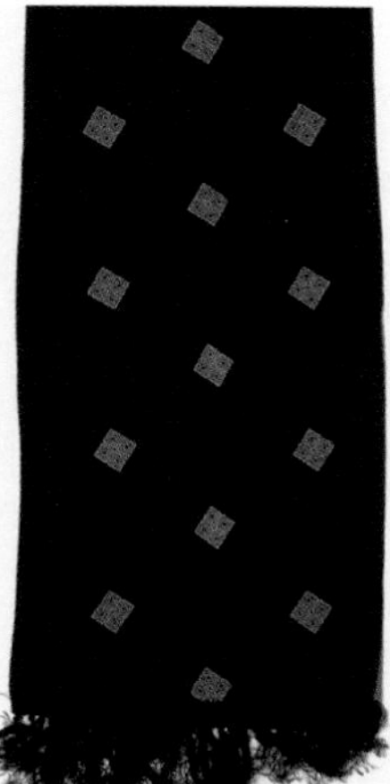

A Tootal printed rayon scarf, 1960s.

$30–40 FC

A Tootal printed rayon scarf, 1950s, 48in (122cm) long.

$15–25 CCO

A Tootal rayon Paisley-print cravat, c1950, 44in (112cm) long.

$10–15 CLOB

FILM & ENTERTAINMENT

PROPS AND COSTUMES have been collected in the US since the golden age of Hollywood. In the UK this hobby is much younger, and really began with Bonham's 1987 sale where an *Aliens* Colonial Marine costume sold for $480 – it would now command $26,000.

Science fiction and action are the most popular genres for collecting and accordingly command the highest prices. Some collectors concentrate on pre-production paperwork, which is cheap to buy and rarely goes up in value but it does provide a fascinating insight into the movie-making process.

If investment is crucial to your decision to buy, go for movies with a blue-chip history such as Star Wars or Indiana Jones, but expect to pay a premium. For example, a Stormtrooper helmet from Star Wars A New Hope will cost $17,300–20,700, about three times what it would have fetched five years ago. Values of film collectables should steadily increase if the film remains popular.

There are not really any props to avoid, if you love the film and the piece, go for it. Do your research – watch the movie and make sure your supplier is reputable, there should be a money-back guarantee and a certificate of authenticity.

Stephen Lane

◄ **A Paragon Charlie Chaplin nursery ware saucer,** 1920s, 5in (12.5cm) diam.

$40–50 ⊞ OIA

Sheet music, for *I Was Lucky*, starring Maurice Chevalier and Merle Oberon, 1930s, 13 x 9in (33 x 23cm).

$10–15 ⊞ POS

A collection of 26 *Motion Picture* magazines, America, 1925–28.

$155–170 ⚒ Her

In the early days of Hollywood film-making, even before the 'talkies', there was Motion Picture *– a magazine filled with photographs and features about movies and their stars. The colour cover portrait enticed fans to part with 25c per copy. Today, copies in good condition are hard to find.*

A pair of cuff links, once owned by Stan Laurel, 1932, America, together with a letter of authenticity.

$880–1,050 ⚒ Her

Laurel bought these in Mexico City in 1932 and wore them on a number of occasions. They were later given by Laurel's widow to his biographer, Tom McCabe, after the actor's death in 1965.

► **A silk parasol,** from *Gone with the Wind*, 1939.

$760–890 ⚒ Her

This parasol belonged to Sarah Jane 'Pittypat' Hamilton (played by Laura Hope Crews) in the epic Gone with the Wind*.*

A photographic postcard of Fred Astaire, c1940.

$10–15 MCS

A photographic postcard of Ginger Rogers, c1940.

$10–15 MCS

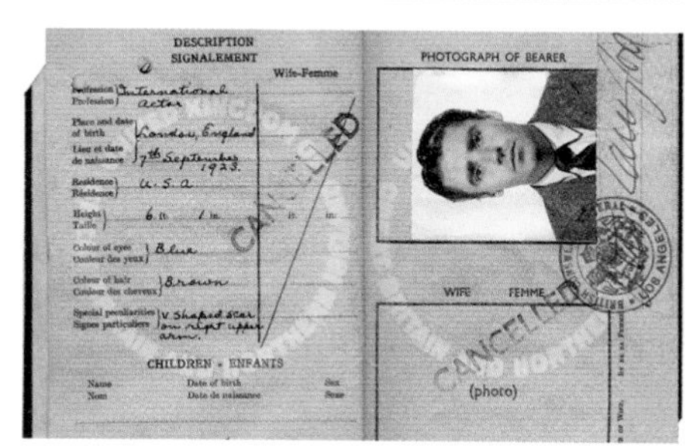

A British passport, owned by Peter Lawford, 1940s–50s, 6 x 4in (15 x 10cm).

$830–980 Her

Lawford was known as 'the man who kept secrets' – be they for 'the Rat Pack', Marilyn Monroe or the Kennedy family.

A *Film Fun* annual, published by Amalgamated Press, 1952, 11 x 8in (28 x 20.5cm).

$25–30 UD

Film Fun ran from 1938 to 1961. Filled with Hollywood trivia, cartoons and photographs, it made popular reading.

A pair of jeans and a scarf, worn by Marlon Brando in *One-Eyed Jack's*, with Western Costume Company label, 1961.

$1,900–2,200 Her

Bert Stern, a photograph entitled 'Marilyn with Veil', stamped 'rough print', 1962, 14 x 11in (35.5 x 28cm).

$3,100–3,700 S

A Colgate James Bond 007 shaving kit, 1967, box 7in (18cm) wide.

$95–110 JB7

The British commercial that accompanied the launch of the 007 range of toiletries promoted the brand as 'the licence to kill...women'...'When you use 007, be kind.'

A pair of denim jeans, worn by Steve McQueen in *The Sand Pebbles*, with Western Costume Company label, 1966.

$4,550–5,100 FRa

Hugo Montenegro, 'The Good, the Bad and the Ugly', EP record, by RCA Victor, France, 1970.

$10–15 TOT

◄ **An election badge display,** from *The Candidate*, starring Robert Redford, 1972, 16½ x 19¼in (42 x 49cm).

$530–600 PROP

SUPERMAN

The New York Times
BLUE BOMB BUZZES METROPOLIS

A copy of the *New York Times*, used in *Superman*, 1978, 24 x 16in (61 x 40.5cm).

$380–430 ⊞ **PROP**

Two make-up charts, used by Christopher Reeve in *Superman*, 1978, framed with a photograph of Reeve in costume and the movie logo, 21 x 33in (53.5 x 84cm).

$1,400–1,550 ⊞ **PROP**

- Superman was created by Canadian artist Joe Shuster and American writer Jerry Siegal in 1932. He first appeared in Action Comics in 1938, and subsequently in radio serials, television programmes, newspaper strips, films and video games.
- Superman props and costumes are once again highly sought after following the release of *Superman Returns* in 2006.
- One of Christopher Reeve's Superman costumes sold for $3,450–5,200 approximately 10 –15 years ago. A complete suit would now command $44,000–61,000.

◄ **An acrylic and wood Fortress of Solitude crystals miniature model,** used in *Superman*, 1978, 21in (53.5cm) high.

$1,200–1,350 ⊞ **PROP**

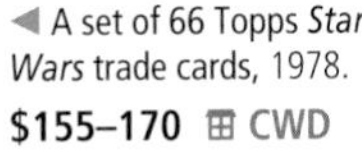

◄ A set of 66 Topps *Star Wars* trade cards, 1978.

$155–170 ⊞ **CWD**

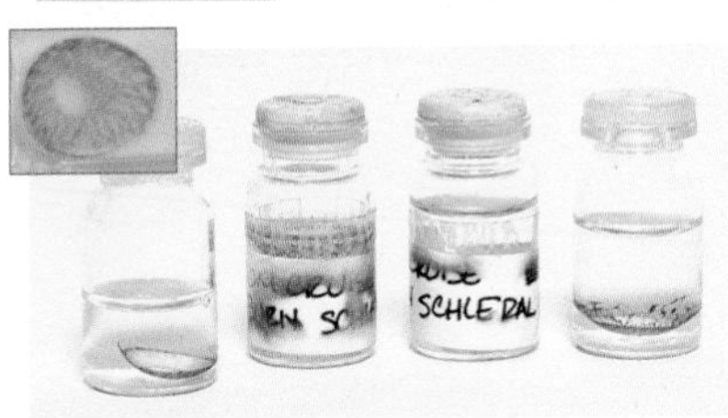

Two pairs of contact lenses, from *Interview with the Vampire*, worn by Brad Pitt and Tom Cruise, together with an editing schedule, 1994.

$1,050–1,200 ⊞ **PROP**

A glass snow globe, used by Arnold Schwarzenegger as Harry Renquist in *True Lies*, 1994, 7½in (19cm) high, with box.

$380–430 ⊞ **PROP**

A script and production paperwork set, from the British TV series *The Bill*, comprising a 67-page shooting script from an episode, three production schedules and 12 photographs of cast members, 1989.

$30–40 ⊞ **PROP**

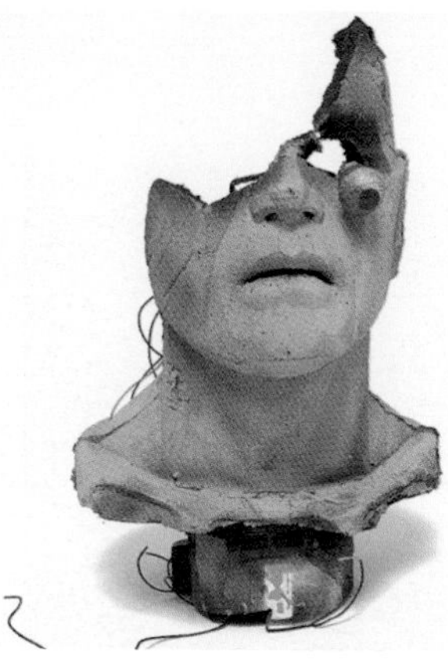

A Kryten blown-up foam head, from the British TV series *Red Dwarf*, 1996.

$1,550–1,700 PROP

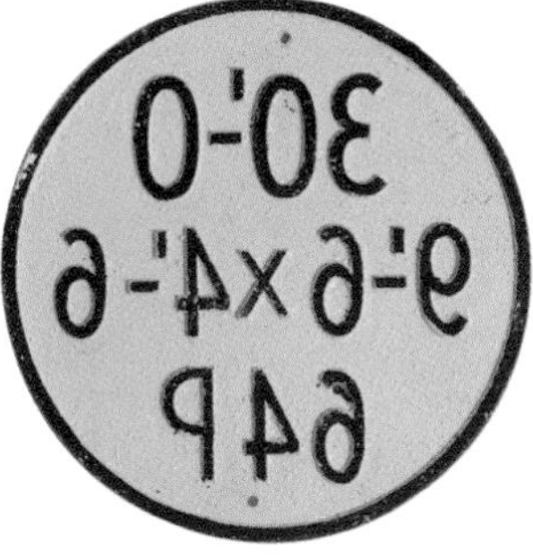

A plastic lifeboat sign, from *Titanic*, 1997, 7in (18cm) diam.

$220–250 PROP

This plastic sign has the lifeboat's number on it, but it has been written backwards. This is because when they made the giant Titanic model they only made one side of it, so when they wanted to show the other side, they just swapped all the signs for backwards signs and reversed the image.

A back pack, worn by Tom Cruise in *Mission Impossible 2*, 2000.

$1,400–1,550 PROP

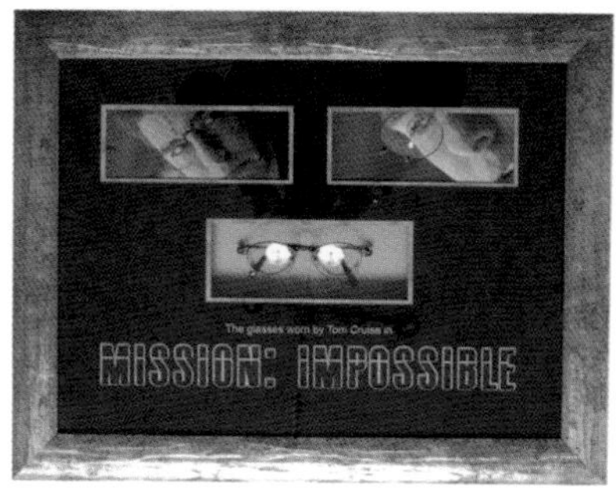

A pair of glasses, used by Tom Cruise in *Mission Impossible*, 1996, framed, 19 x 25in (48.5 x 63.5cm).

$3,100–3,700 PROP

In the film Mission Impossible *Ethan Hunt, played by Tom Cruise, wears glasses in the famous CIA vault scene where he is seen hanging from the roof in a harness.*

Two blood-stained pieces of wood with nails, props used by Brendan Fraser in the hospital-based TV comedy *Scrubs*, together with a 30-page script, 2002.

$600–670 PROP

A wooden stake, from *Buffy the Vampire Slayer*, 1997, 8in (20.5cm) long.

$600–720 Her

Writer-director Joss Whedon's cult TV series made a star out of Sarah Michelle Gellar by casting her as a typical high school girl with a not-so-typical knack for fighting evil. Buffy referred to her 8in (20.5cm) stake that was ideal for vanquishing the forces of darkness as 'Mr Pointy'.

◄ **A plastic chicken pie dish and vegetables, a Plasticine chicken mouth and rubber chicken legs,** by Aardman Studios, used in *Chicken Run*, 2000, dish 11in (28cm) diam.

$890–1,000 FRa

A prop magazine, from *I, Robot*, entitled *Household Robot Management*, 2004, 10½ x 8in (26.5 x 20.5cm).

$50–60 PROP

A rubber sword, from *Troy*, starring Brad Pitt, Orlando Bloom and Eric Bana, 2004, 29in (73.5cm) long.

$380–420 PROP

WALT DISNEY

A set of Chad Valley Snow White and the Seven Dwarfs figures, c1930, Snow White 16in (40.5cm) high.

$1,000–1,100 ⊞ DOAN

A Snow White and the Seven Dwarfs celluloid brooch, c1932, 2in (5cm) wide.

$180–200 ⊞ CWO

A collection of Disneyland memorabilia, comprising two Disneyland opening day passes, two windscreen cards, a $1 Disneyland money order, a map of the park and six Disneyland postcards and a letter from Disneyland Inc, 1955.

$500–580 Her

In 1954, Walt Disney set about building his Magic Kingdom. Initially the plans called for a 45-acre park costing $9 million, but by the opening day, 17 July 1955, 160 acres of orange groves had been turned into Disneyland's California Adventure, at a cost of $17 million.

► A plaster promotional figure of Minnie Mouse, from *Fantasia*, 1950s, 17in (43cm) high.

$310–340 ⊞ COB

A Donald Duck celluloid plastic egg cup, 1930s–50s, 6½in (16.5cm) high.

$95–110 ⊞ CWO

Donald Duck, created by Dick Lundy, first appeared in Silly Symphonies, The Wise Little Hen *in 1934. Donald's easily identifiable voice was first performed by voice actor Clarence 'Ducky' Nash until 1985, when Tony Anselmo took over the role.*

A Dean's Rag Book Company velveteen Mickey Mouse, c1930, 12in (30.5cm) high.

$300–330 ⊞ DOAN

A Mickey Mouse tin post box money box, c1960, 6in (15cm) high.

$110–125 ⊞ M&C

A Disneyland postcard, c1999, 6 x 4in (15 x 10cm).

$5–10 ⊞ POS

LOBBY CARDS

A lobby card, *A Dog's Life*, starring Charlie Chaplin, 1916, 11 x 14in (28 x 35.5cm).

$1,200–1,350 ⊞ CINE

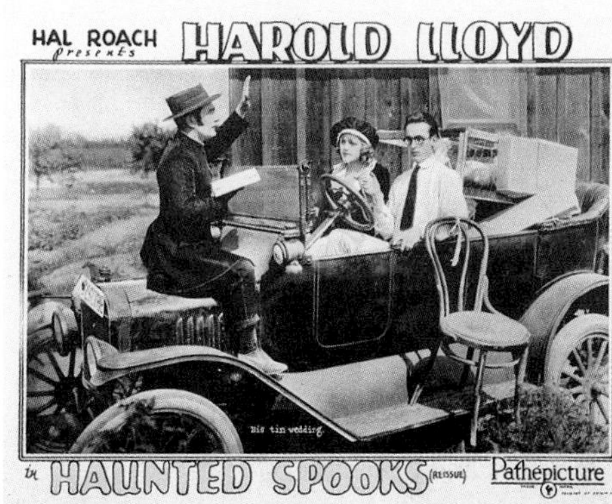

A lobby card, *Haunted Spooks*, starring Harold Lloyd, reissue, 1922, 11 x 14in (28 x 35.5cm).

$620–690 ⊞ CINE

A lobby card, *Pack up your Troubles*, starring Laurel and Hardy, 1932, 11 x 14in (28 x 35.5cm).

$1,450–1,600 ⊞ CINE

A lobby card, *A Streetcar Named Desire*, starring Marlon Brando and Vivien Leigh, 1951, 11 x 14in (28 x 35.5cm).

$1,000–1,100 ⊞ CINE

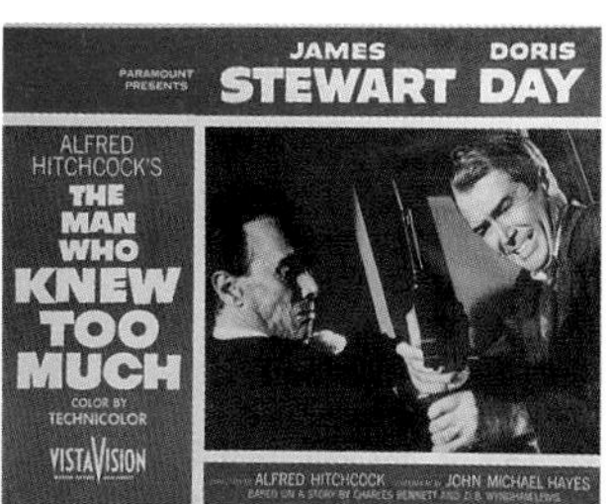

A lobby card, *The Man Who Knew Too Much*, starring James Stewart and Doris Day, 1956, 11 x 14in (28 x 35.5cm).

$190–210 ⊞ Lim

► A lobby card, *Let's Make Love*, starring Marilyn Monroe, 1960, 11 x 14in (28 x 35.5cm).

$340–390 ⊞ Lim

A lobby card, *The Errand Boy*, starring Jerry Lewis, 1961, 11 x 14in (28 x 35.5cm).

$85–95 ⊞ Lim

A lobby card, *Oceans 11*, starring Frank Sinatra, Dean Martin, Sammy Davis Jr, Peter Lawford and Angie Dickinson, 1960, 11 x 14in (28 x 35.5cm).

$840–950 ⊞ CINE

◄ A lobby card, *Le Mans*, starring Steve McQueen, 1971, 11 x 14in (28 x 35.5cm).

$190–210 ⊞ Lim

THEATRE

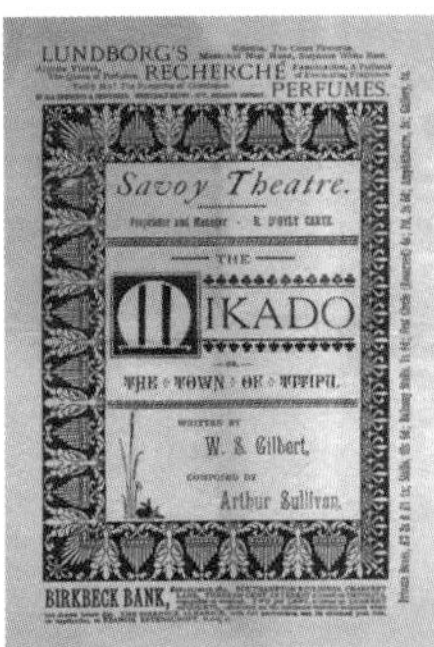

A programme, *The Mikado*, by Gilbert and Sullivan, 1885, 9 x 5½in (23 x 14cm).

$40–50 c20th

The Mikado, with music by Arthur Sullivan and libretto by W. S. Gilbert, is a comic opera in two acts. It was first performed in London in 1885 where it ran for 672 performances. The ninth operatic collaboration between Gilbert and Sullivan, The Mikado *is possibly the most frequently played piece of musical theatre in history.*

A programme, *Veronique*, starring George Edwards, 1905, 9in (23cm) high.

$15–25 J&S

George Edwards was born Harold Parks in Kent Town, South Australia, in 1886. He changed his name when he moved to England and became an actor and producer. In 1938, he took part in a radio serial based on the novel Frankenstein.

A theatre magazine, *The Play*, 1905, 12in (30.5cm) high.

$10–15 J&S

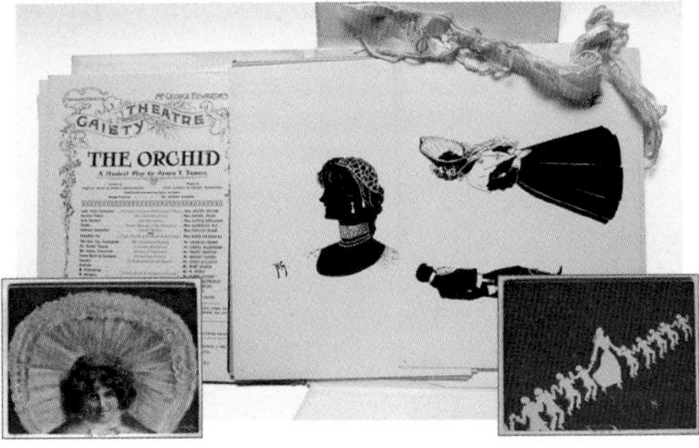

◄ A programme, *The Orchid*, starring George Edwards and Marie Studholme, including silhouettes of the cast, c1910, 14in (35.5cm) wide.

$40–50 J&S

A costume design *pochoir* print, by Leon Bakst, *The Firebird*, signed, c1910, 12½ x 9½in (32 x 24cm).

$1,550–1,800 CAG

Leon Nikolayevich Bakst (1866–1924) was a Russian painter and scene and costume designer. Based on his grandmother's family name of Baxter, he took the name Bakst for his first exhibition. In 1899 he and Sergei Diaghilev co-founded the influential periodical World of Art. *In 1910 Igor Stravinsky commissioned from Diaghilev a musical score for the new ballet* The Firebird.

A programme, *Beau Geste*, 1930s, 8¼ x 5in (21 x 12.5cm).

$10–15 c20th

A programme, *Hamlet*, starring John Geilgud and Ralph Richardson, 1930s, 8¼ x 5½in (21 x 14cm).

$5–10 c20th

A programme, *The Millionairess*, starring Katherine Hepburn, 1952, 8¾ x 4¼in (22 x 11cm).

$10–15 c20th

GARDENING

BOOKS & MAGAZINES

My Garden Diary for 1897, 7in (18cm) wide.

$10–15 ⊞ HOP

The Single Handed Gardener, published by Temple Press, c1910, 8in (20.5cm) high.

$10–15 ⊞ HOP

T. W. Sanders, *The Amateur's Greenhouse*, published by W. H. & I. Collingridge, 1922, 8in (20.5cm) high.

$10–15 ⊞ HOP

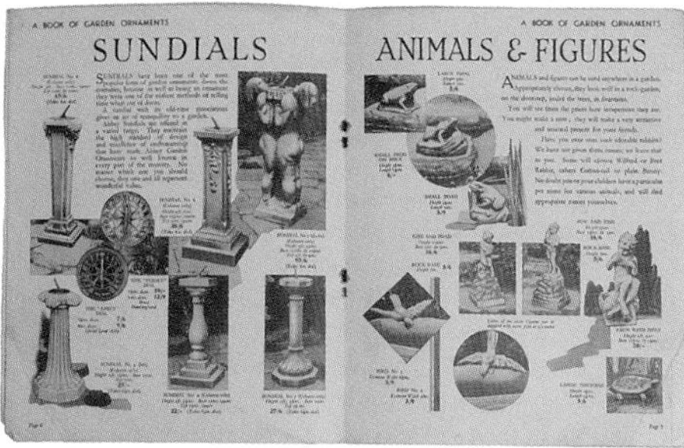

The Book of Garden Ornaments, Abbey Catalogue, 1930s, 11in (28cm) high.

$10–15 ⊞ HOP

▶ *Popular Gardening*, January 1946, 11in (28cm) high.

$5–10 ⊞ HOP

Gardening Illustrated, published by *Country Life*, October 1949, 11in (28cm) high.

$5–10 ⊞ HOP

◀ *Garden and Estate Guide 1957*, John Hodgkinson tool catalogue, 9in (23cm) high.

$10–15 ⊞ HOP

▶ *Your Garden in 1965*, Woodman's of Pinner catalogue, 9in (23cm) high.

$5–10 ⊞ HOP

Alastair Forsyth, *Yesterday's Gardens*, published by Her Majesty's Stationery office, 10in (25.5cm) high.

$10–15 ⊞ BIB

PLANTING

A selection of terracotta flowerpots, by Ward Bardlaston, Staffordshire, c1930, 6in (15cm) high.

$5–10 each ⊞ HOP

A Sankeys terracotta rhubarb forcing pot, 1920s, 17in (43cm) high.

$280–320 ⊞ HOP

▶ A selection of painted, galvanized plant labels, c1920, 11in (28cm) high.

$10–15 each ⊞ HOP

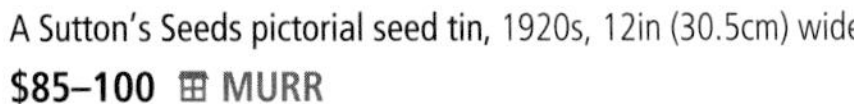

A Sutton's Seeds pictorial seed tin, 1920s, 12in (30.5cm) wide.

$85–100 ⊞ MURR

A Carters seed box, 1940s, 8in (20.5cm) wide.

$10–15 ⊞ HOP

A selection of seed packets, America, c1950, 5in (12.5cm) wide.

$5–10 each ⊞ HOP

A Plastigon Bakelite 'So-Easy' seed sower, c1950, 2in (5cm) diam.

$25–30 ⊞ HOP

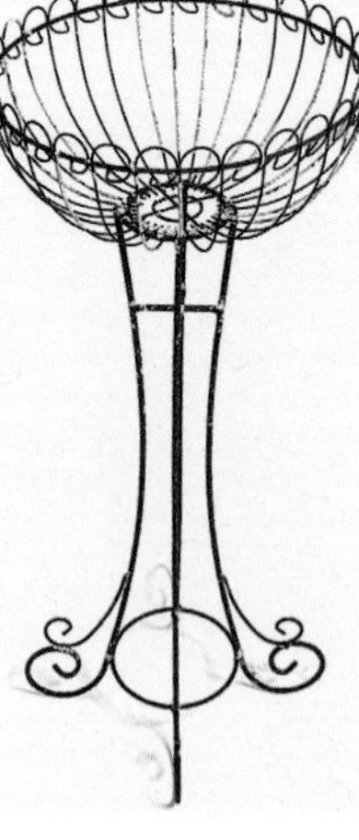

▶ A pair of wirework plant holders, 1950s, 31in (78.5cm) high.

$120–135 ⊞ HOP

TOOLS

◀ **A cast-iron lawn aerator,** with wooden handle, late 19thC, 63in (160cm) long.

$75–85 ⊞ HOP

▶ **A wooden dibber,** c1890, 47in (119.5cm) long.

$50–60 ⊞ TOP

A steel dock rooter, with ash handle, c1900, 47in (119.5cm) long.

$145–160 ⊞ HOP

A spud weeder, c1910, 48in (122cm) long.

$25–30 ⊞ HOP

This type of implement, which consisted of a tiny spade head on a long shaft, would have been used by ladies for light weeding.

An Atco cast-iron mechanical edge trimmer, 1920s, 44in (112cm) long.

$50–60 ⊞ HOP

A clay digging fork, c1920, 43in (109cm) long.

$60–75 ⊞ TOP

A Hercules Co brass plant sprayer, 1920–50, 19in (48.5cm) long.

$50–60 ⊞ HOP

A brass pump action plant spray, c1920, 17in (43cm) high.

$65–75 ⊞ HOP

A brass sprayer, c1920, 26in (66cm) long.

$50–60 ⊞ TOP

An Acme garden powder blower, c1920, 12in (35.5cm) high.

$25–30 ⊞ OIA

LAWN SPRINKLERS

A Cooper Stewart cast-iron Rain King lawn sprinkler, 1930s–50s, 8in (20.5cm) diam.

$60–70 HOP

A Mysto lawn sprinkler, with brass top, 1950s, 7in (18cm) diam.

$25–30 HOP

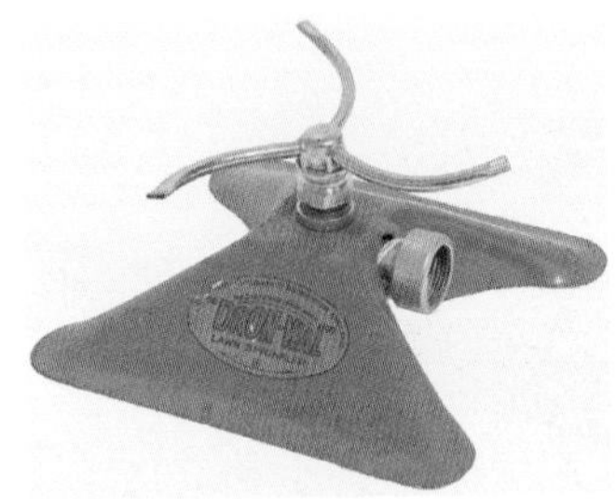

A Dron-Wal tin and brass lawn sprinkler, 1930s–50s, 7in (18cm) wide.

$50–60 HOP

- Gentrified homeowners who employed the services of a gardener during the inter-war and early post-war years were certain to have used a lawn sprinkler.
- Increasingly they appealed to a new breed of house-proud suburban families who prided themselves on good garden care.
- In the heat of summer a lawn sprinkler was an essential time-saver. It was designed to be connected to a ribbed rubber hose.
- Collectors like good examples that are solidly made and proudly display the maker's brand, either in transfer print or casting. Larger examples that pre-date these are rarely seen and tend to command higher prices.

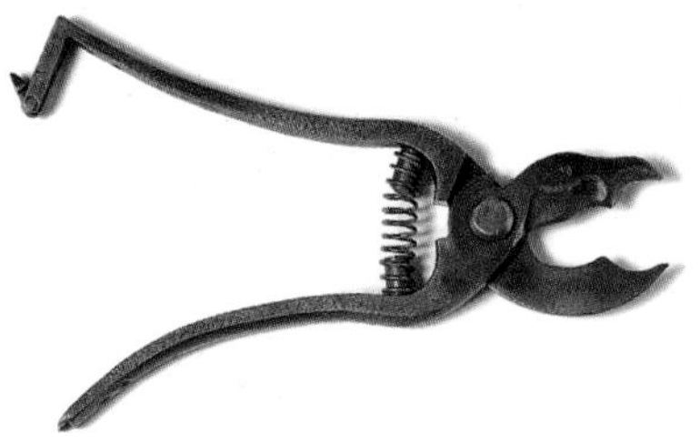

A pair of steel secateurs, c1920, 7in (18cm) long.

$10–15 TOP

A pair of wooden-handled secateurs, c1930, 7in (18cm) long.

$25–30 HOP

Two wooden-handled pruning knives, 1930s, 8in (20.5cm) long.

$10–15 each HOP

A Haws galvanized ¾-gallon watering can, c1930, 29in (73.5cm) long.

$85–95 HOP

► A willow trug, c1930, 18in (45.5cm) long.

$30–40 LA&I

GLASS

AMERICAN

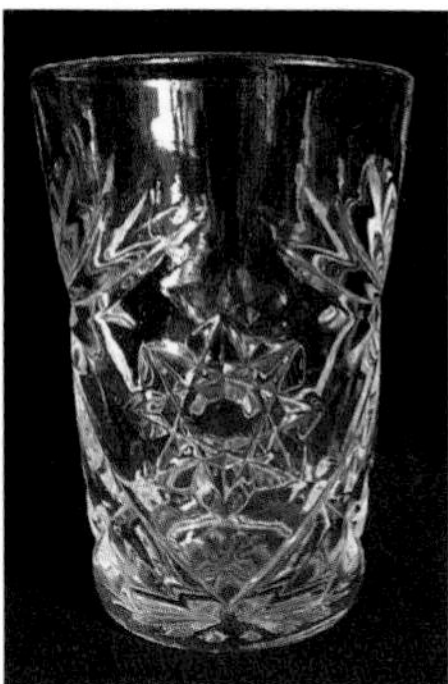

A set of eight Anchor Hocking Glass Co glasses, EAPC/Star of David pattern, Ohio, 1960s, 4½in (11.5cm) high.

$30–35 R2G

The Anchor Hocking Glass Co was one of the most prolific mass-producers of glass in the USA. After the 1929 Wall Street crash they were able to make inexpensive glass in good designs, often in the style of expensive cut glass, which became known as Depression glass. They produced good ranges of textured and colourful machine-printed tablewares in the 1960s.

STEUBEN GLASS

A Steuben Gold Aurene glass vase, engraved mark, early 20thC, 8in (20.5cm) high.

$690–830 WAD

A Steuben Gold Aurene glass Fan vase, engraved mark, c1920, 8½in (21.5cm) high.

$4,600–5,500 WAD

A Steuben Gold Aurene glass vase, engraved mark, c1920, 13½in (34.5cm) high.

$1,450–1,700 WAD

- Steuben was formed in 1903 by Thomas Hawkes and Englishman Frederick Carder, who had previously worked with the Stourbridge glassmakers.
- Throughout the 20th century, Steuben kept up with the trends and designs required by its discerning customers.
- Steuben began by experimenting with various types of coloured and iridescent glass. One, Gold Aurene, so upset Tiffany that a lawsuit was threatened. Over the years they produced all manner of blown, cut and engraved glass which is now highly collected. Prices are quite low for small items, but larger pieces fetch three-figure sums.
- Over the years they commissioned many famous artists to produce crystal designs, notably Jean Cocteau, Salvador Dali, Eric Gill and Henry Matisse, who featured in the Twenty-Seven Artists exhibition in 1940.

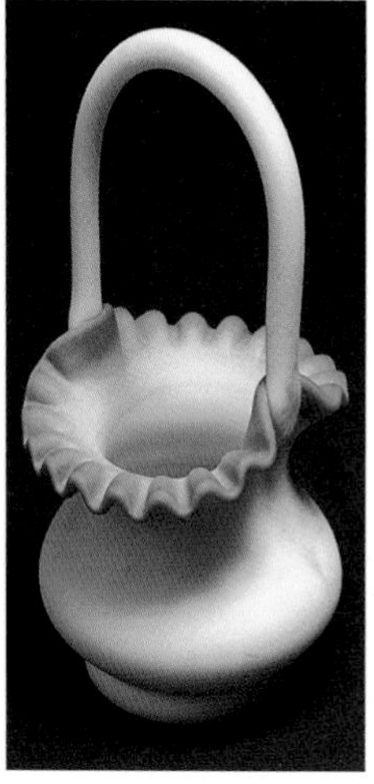

◄ **A Fenton glass basket,** c1960, 8in (20.5cm) high.

$70–80 DEB

Founded in Ohio in 1905 by brothers Frank and John Fenton, Fenton Art Glass is now the largest manufacturer of hand-made coloured glass in the US. Originally known for its carnival glass, the firm switched production to coloured tablewares and practical items during the Depression and war years – a tactic that enabled it to survive. In the 1940s they made opaque coloured glass and from 1952 produced huge quantities of milk glass, a top-selling line. Today Fenton is known worldwide for its beautiful coloured and patterned glass.

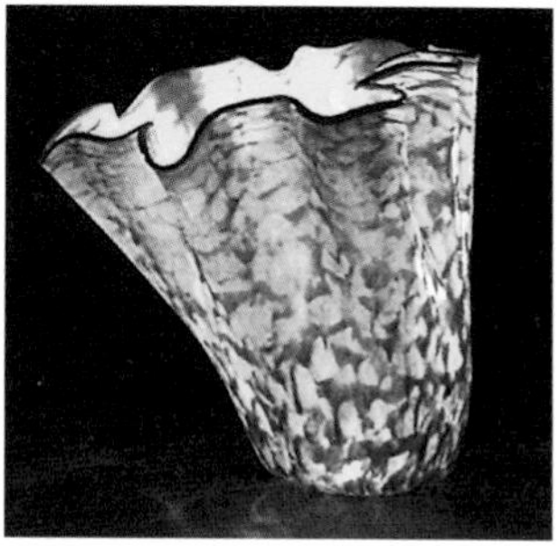

A Dale Chihuly Yellow Macchia glass vase, signed, 2000, 10in (25.5cm) high.

$3,800–4,500 WAD

BLENKO

WILLIAM J. BLENKO founded the Eureka Art Glass Company, producers of speciality sheet glass with thousands of trademark colours, in Milton, West Virginia in 1921. In 1929, the Depression sharply reduced demand for sheet glass and the company began producing decorative wares, interpretations of classical Italian forms.

The most significant development in the company's history was the hiring of Winslow Anderson as design director, responsible for Blenko's new designs from 1947 to 1953. Trained as a ceramicist and without glass knowledge, Blenko gave him free reign to innovate, and thus began Blenko's remarkable transformation into one of America's most recognized glass producers.

Blenko's second designer, Wayne Husted, was responsible for new designs from 1954 to 1963. Husted's unprecedented sculptural designs took the company to a new level of sophistication; his legacy is his architectural scale design work, several feet tall and suited to being displayed as freestanding sculptures.

Joel Myers was Blenko's third resident designer, responsible for new designs from 1964 to 1971. As a craftsman and designer, the development of studio glass and the 1960s psychedelic re-interpretation of the Art Nouveau aesthetic proved to be crucial influences on Myers. Today he ranks as one of the most exhibited and recognized glass artists in the world, thanks largely to his beginnings at Blenko.

The company is still operating today, having had seven designers and produced thousands of original designs. Collectors focus on the works of Anderson, Husted, Myers and John Nickerson (1971–74). While the vast majority of Blenko designs sell for \$50–200, the truly sought-after items range from \$300–3,000. Particularly popular are sculptural non-utilitarian forms and oversized items. Although size is not a reliable indicator of value, colour is and this can double a design's value. Rare colours made for one or two years, such as Plum, are desirable, but vibrant and unusual colours such as Jonquil or Persian Blue are also in demand. Rarity and oddity drives value to the extreme.

Identification is difficult without knowing production catalogues, although colour is always a good indicator. Blenko had many competitors in West Virginia, all of whom emulated the designs to some degree. They share similar characteristics such as bright colours, simple forms, thick walls and pontils. The vast majority of rims on Blenko items are fire-polished and most bases have rough pontils. Italian copies of Blenko and comparable Italian products are more easily distinguished; lacking pontils they also have thinner glass, mould lines and less vibrant colours.

Damon Crain

A Blenko Sea Green glass Cobweb vase, c1936, 6½in (16.5cm) high.

\$220–250 ⊞ GLH

A Blenko Sky Blue glass amphora, No. 438, 1930s, 10¾in (27.5cm) high.

\$200–230 ⊞ GLH

A Blenko Sea Green glass ewer, by Winslow Anderson, No. 905LH, c1947, 13¼in (33.5cm) high.

\$180–200 ⊞ GLH

A Blenko Amethyst glass Aquarium vase, by Winslow Anderson, No. 949L, 1947–53, 13½in (34.5cm) high.

$360–400 ⊞ GLH

This large, modern piece is particularly noteworthy for its freeform design, of which Anderson was a major proponent. Influenced by the Bauhaus 'form follows function' mantra, Anderson's designs were on the cutting edge of the plastic and organic design sensibilities of the time.

A Blenko Chartreuse glass chalice, by Winslow Anderson, No. 986, 1947–53, 11in (28cm) high.

$360–400 ⊞ GLH

A Blenko Tangerine glass vase, by Wayne Husted, No. 597, with applied glass blobs, signed, 1959, 7in (18cm) high.

$450–500 ⊞ GLH

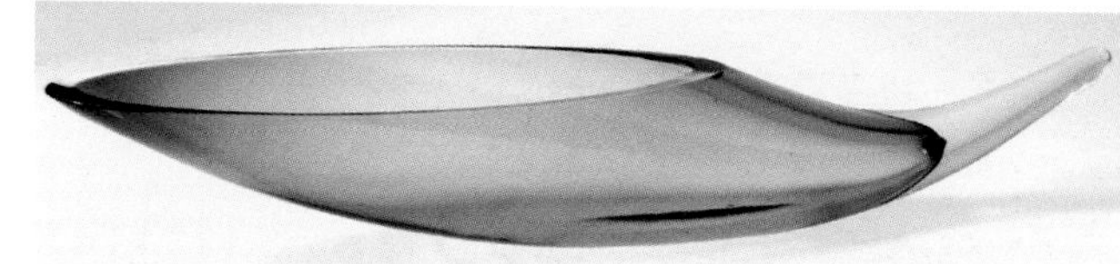

A Blenko Lilac glass horn vase, by Winslow Anderson, No. 964L, encased in crystal, 1947–53, 3¼in (8.5cm) high.

$250–280 ⊞ GLH

A Blenko Persian Blue glass floor decanter, by Wayne Husted, No. 587L, signed, 1958, 36½in (92.5cm) high.

$2,250–2,500 ⊞ GLH

This form of decanter is officially called the 'Spool Decanter' and was produced in three sizes, the largest of which is shown here. It is indebted to Constantine Brancusi's 'Endless Column' sculpture and reflects Husted's knowledge of contemporary art and design.

A Blenko Gold glass epergne, by Wayne Husted, No. 5833, signed, 1958, 17¾in (45cm) high.

$810–900 ⊞ GLH

The form of this decanter is technically an epergne, with a central vase for flowers and a rim for foodstuffs, yet in classic Husted mode the historic form has been contorted and reduced to a sculpture unlike any epergne seen before. Blenko's signature appeared only between 1958 and 1961. The first ones were hand etched in script 'Blenko ©', replaced in 1958 by a sand-blasted logo, and the Blenko 'hand' symbol. The signature was not reintroduced until after 2000. Signatures can be useful for identifying the years of production.

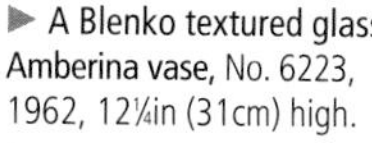

► **A Blenko textured glass Amberina vase,** No. 6223, 1962, 12¼in (31cm) high.

$60–70 ⊞ COO

A Blenko Lilac glass decanter, by Wayne Husted, No. 5929S, signed, 1959, 22in (56cm) high.

$1,050–1,200 ⊞ GLH

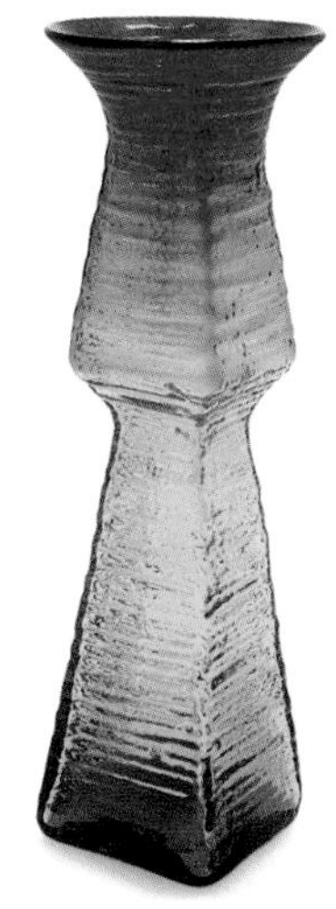

A Blenko glass Rialto decanter, by Wayne Husted, No. 4-T0, 1960, 15in (38cm) high.

$1,350–1,500 GLH

Produced with Raindrop and Regal, the Rialto line was Blenko's first official attempt to market a speciality line of similarly-styled and coloured designs. In addition, it was the first application of lattimo *or opalescent glass at Blenko. However, the lines proved costly and only lasted one year for Rialto and Raindrop and two for Regal.*

◄ A Blenko glass decanter, by Joel Philip Myers, No. 6527, 1965, 22¼in (56.5cm) high.

$900–1,000 GLH

This decanter depicts three butterflies in raised relief on a textured surface, a theme played out in Myers' work for Blenko and in his later studio work. The form of the container is a canvas for his compositions, both abstract and inspired by nature. It not only evokes his training as a graphic designer keenly aware of the emerging Pop aesthetic of the time, but also the elaborate carved and cameo glass designs of Emile Gallé, with their flying insects and plant life.

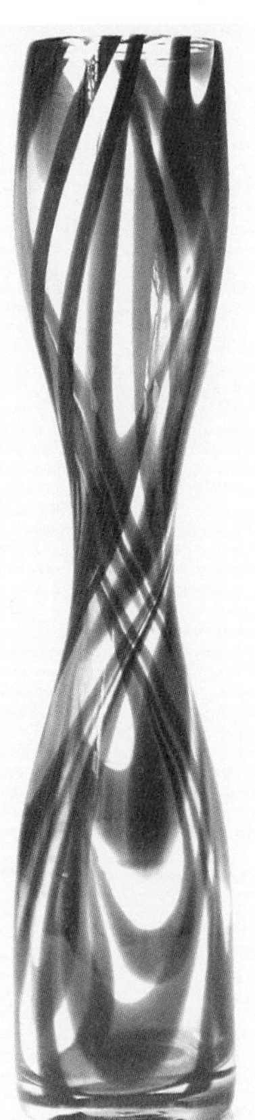

► A Blenko glass Charisma vase, by John Nickerson, No. 7221X, 1972, 17¼in (44cm) high.

$1,050–1,200 GLH

The Charisma line, executed in crystal with a garland pattern and Ruby internal colourway, represented a major step towards more technical and elaborate work. Charisma was the first internal colourway to be produced at Blenko as well as the revival of the concept of the speciality line and its purpose was to hold ground against the encroaching competition represented by studio glass. Charisma was a revival of a technique used in the mid-Atlantic region of America from 1860 to 1880.

A Blenko Turquoise glass decanter, by Joel Philip Myers, No. 6732L, 1967, 12in (30.5cm) high.

$1,350–1,500 GLH

This dramatically extenuated, sinuous decanter is a superb example of the psychedelic Art Nouveau aesthetic so popular at the time. Myers' methodology, of which he said 'I permit the glass to sag, flop, flow, stop, start, stretch; I control and yet am being dictated by the glass' was common to all emerging studio glass artists of the time, perhaps most literally seen in the freeflowing sculptures of Harvey Littleton and his followers.

A Blenko bias-cut Olive Green glass vase, by John Nickerson, No. 7220S, 1972, 12½in (32cm) high.

$450–500 GLH

Nickerson was the first designer to arrive at Blenko after the onset of the Studio Glass movement and this vase is a prime example of the design of the time. Not only is it Nickerson's best design, it anticipates his future indepen-dent studio glasswork, for which he has since achieved much fame. The vase began life as a bottle form and was then cut on the bias. Such cold work was rare for Blenko products due to the significant expense and, accordingly, this design was only produced for one year. By way of comparison, freeblown forms with dramatically cold-worked areas can be seen in the work of Marvin Lipofsky during the same period.

CUT-GLASS

UNTIL RECENTLY, cut-glass has been out of fashion, as it seemed to conjure up a picture of granny's sherry glasses. Today, thanks to the popularity of Art Deco, this is no longer the case. The simple designs from the 1930s to the 1960s from the UK, France, Belgium, Austria, and Czechoslovakia, especially by manufacturers such as Val St Lambert, Baccarat, Stuart, Webb and Webb & Corbett are all gaining ground. Look for items with deep cutting which reflects and refracts the light, giving it luminescence. An example of this is the 1,000 Windows vase by Simon Gate (similar to the vase on p232). If you are buying an item by a known designer make sure that it is an original piece rather than a later reissue, as this should be reflected in the price. With the exception of most Czechoslovakian designs, cut-glass from this period was generally marked, so check that the item you are buying carries the relevant maker's mark. Make sure also that the item is cut and not pressed; this can be seen by looking at the sharp edge of the cuts which, if pressed, will be soft and rounded.

Prices in this group range from a few dollars for small mass-produced items through to three- or four-figure sums for rare or unique works of art. As always, buy what you like at a price you can afford and, remember, the pain of the price is always outweighed by the pleasure of the purchase.

Three wheel-cut dessert glasses, by Stevens & Williams, with overlaid decoration, c1920, 4in (10cm) diam.

$270–310 ⊞ TOP

A cut-glass decanter and stopper, c1930, 8in (20.5cm) high.

$80–90 ⊞ CHAC

A Hawkes cut-glass jar, with a silver cover, America, early 20thC, 4¾in (12cm) diam.

$240–280 ⚒ JAA

A crystal vase, 1940s, 9½in (24cm) high.

$100–120 ⊞ HEM

A cut-glass claret jug and stopper, with a silver spout, Birmingham 1920, 9in (23cm) high.

$230–260 ⊞ JG

A cut-glass vase, c1960, 7in (18cm) high.

$150–170 ⊞ RUSK

ITALIAN GLASS

A *latticinio* glass bowl, Italy, 1920s, 5in (12.5cm) wide.

$170–200 BET

This 20th-century latticinio *glass, which has coloured canes and what is known as a wavy rim, was inspired by 17th-century pieces. It was made by laying thin canes of prepared patterns on the metal marver, which were picked up by rolling them into a gather of clear glass which was then blown into the desired shape. It is difficult to date some* latticinio *items as this centuries-old technique is still used today.*

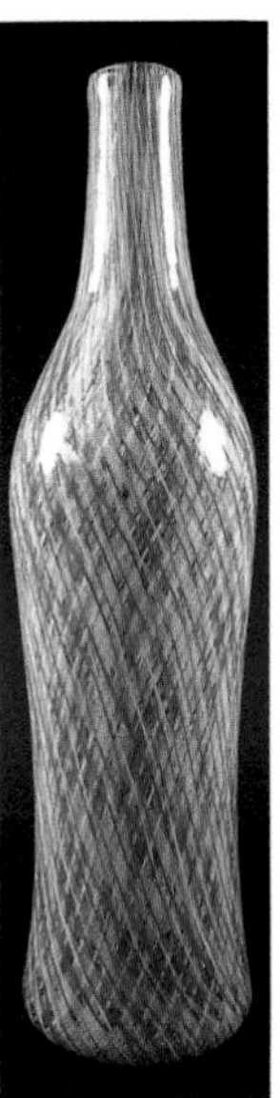

◀ A *zanfirico* glass vase, by Paolo Venini, three-line acid-etched mark, Italy, 1954, 5in (38cm) high.

$950–1,100 ROS

The term zanfirico *refers to the technique of incorporating canes between layers of glass. This example is marked with the early Venini mark. However, do not assume all* zanfirico *glass was made by Venini as the same technique has been used by all glassmakers.*

▶ An Arnolfi di Cambio Smoke glass, by Joe Columbo, Italy, 1964, 13¾in (35cm) high.

$80–90 MARK

Joe Colombo (1930–71) designed the Smoke glass to enable its user to smoke at the same time by clutching the glass with the thumb, leaving the fingers free to hold a cigarette. A completely new concept, this design was a departure from conventional symmetrical shapes.

MURANO GLASS

A Murano cased glass model of a fish, Italy, 1950s, 10in (25.5cm) high.

$45–55 HEM

A Murano sommerso glass vase, Italy, 1950s, 9in (23cm) high.

$60–70 HEM

Sommerso glass is coloured glass with a clear outer layer.

A Murano glass jug, possibly by Ercole Barovier or Giorgio Ferro, Italy, 1950s, 11in (28cm) high.

$130–150 FD

- Murano glass demonstrates the best in terms of variety of shape, form and techniques of hot glass.
- Murano is not just an island of major factories such as Venini, Barovier, Tosso, Salviati and Avm, it is also the home of many small family glass-blowing workshops.
- The versatility of Murano is illustrated by the diversity of the items shown above, none of which are attributable to a major maker, but would have originally been sold with a paper label, now long lost.
- When buying, be aware that modern copies are available on the market that have been inspired by these original pieces.

A Murano cased glass vase, Italy, 1950s, 15in (38cm) high.

$40–45 HEM

MDINA

A Mdina glass vase, Malta, 1970s–90s, 4in (10cm) high.

$60–70 ⊞ **BrL**

A Mdina glass vase, Malta, 1970s–90s, 6½in (16.5cm) high.

$90–100 ⊞ **COO**

A Mdina glass vase, Malta, No. 55, 1970s–90s, 7in (18cm) high.

$90–100 ⊞ **COO**

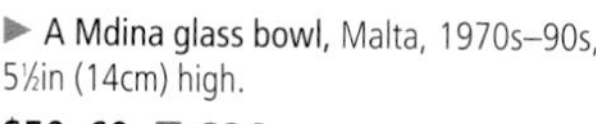

► **A Mdina glass bowl,** Malta, 1970s–90s, 5½in (14cm) high.

$50–60 ⊞ **COO**

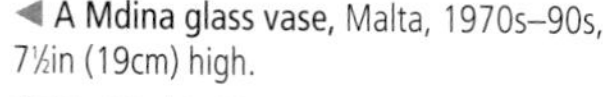

◄ **A Mdina glass vase,** Malta, 1970s–90s, 7½in (19cm) high.

$70–80 ⊞ **COO**

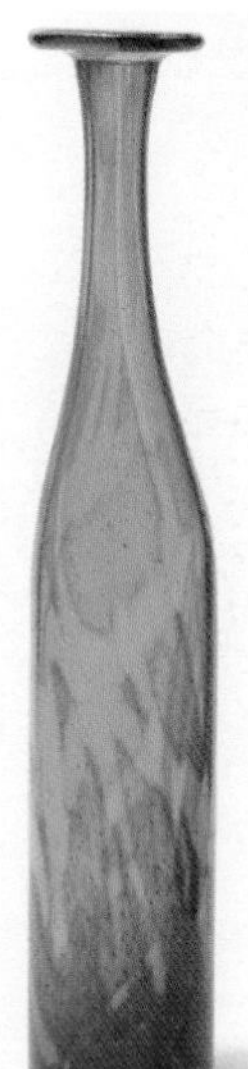

◄ **A Mdina glass bottle,** Malta, 1970s–90s, 16in (40.5cm) high.

$150–165 ⊞ **COO**

► **A Mdina glass bottle,** Malta, 1970s–90s, 10in (25.5cm) high.

$150–165 ⊞ **COO**

► **A Mdina glass bottle,** signed, Malta, 1970s, 10in (25.5cm) high.

$80–90 ⊞ **RETC**

This bottle-shaped vase was made by randomly trailing colour on the bubble and then covering it with clear glass. The vase was then applied with a different colour of random trailing. No two examples of this technique can be the same due to the nature of production. The early pieces are now avidly collected, but note that Mdina is still operating today.

MODERN

A Peill & Pützler glass Rondella vase, by Horst Tuselmann, stamped mark, Germany, Duren, c1965, 8¼in (21cm) high.

$360–400 FREE

◀ An Exbor glass vase, in the manner of Pavel Hlava, stamped mark, Czechoslovakia, 1960s, 8¼in (21cm) high.

$190–200 FREE

▶ A Dillon Clarke glass bottle vase, engraved mark, 1970, 13in (33cm) high.

$190–200 FREE

A Columbia Glass Works/Factory J glass ornament, 1980s, 6¼in (16cm) high.

$70–80 MARK

A Siddy Langley vase, with trailed glass decoration, 2001–02, 7in (18cm) high.

$150–170 RW

Siddy Langley was an apprentice to Peter Layton at the London Glassblowing Workshop between 1979 and 1981; she remained there until 1987, when she set up Alchemy Glass. Initially, her iridescent designs were similar to her previous work, but she soon developed her own styles and colours of iridescent decoration. Look for her early pieces which are often signed with her initials only and a date, or for her exhibition designs.

A Jonathan Harris Studio glass bowl, 2001–02, 5½in (14cm) high.

$170–190 RW

An Okra Studio reheat cameo glass vase, by Richard P. Golding, signed, 2005, 3½in (9cm) high.

$540–620 CBi

Okra was one the earliest studios producing well-defined iridescent decoration, and are continuously developing their technqiue. Look for limited editions from the 1980s and early 1990s.

An Okra Studio trial glass vase, 2005, 9in (23cm) long.

$1,800–2,100 CBi

◀ An Okra Studio glass Humming Bird vase, limited edition of 50, 2005, 7in (18cm) high.

$580–660 CBi

PAPERWEIGHTS

PAUL YSART

A Paul Ysart paperweight, signed, 1930s, 3in (7.5cm) diam.

$720–820 ⊞ SWB

A Paul Ysart sulphide, 1930s, 3in (7.5cm) diam.

$2,000–2,250 ⊞ SWB

A Paul Ysart paperweight, 1960, 3in (7.5cm) diam.

$850–950 ⊞ SWB

- Paul Ysart was the eldest son of Salvador Ysart. They both joined John Moncrieff Ltd in Perth, Scotland, in 1921, where they principally made Monart Art Glass (the name derived from the 'Mon' of Moncrieff and the 'art' of Ysart).
- During the 1930s Paul developed an interest in making paperweights. Both he and his father made weights during this period, many of which carried the Monart label.
- Pre-WWII weights were made with a dark tinted glass, post-war examples have clearer glass.
- In 1963 Paul left Moncrieffs to become Training Officer at Caithness Glass, although he continued to make paperweights, producing around 20 types.
- In 1970 he left Caithness to form his own company, Paul Ysart Glass, based in Harland, Wick, Scotland.
- Paul Ysart paperweights are highly collectable; they are usually signed or include a PY or H cane. Weights with H canes are definitely by Ysart – the H stands for Harland; weights with a PY cane can be more difficult to identify as the PY was often faked.

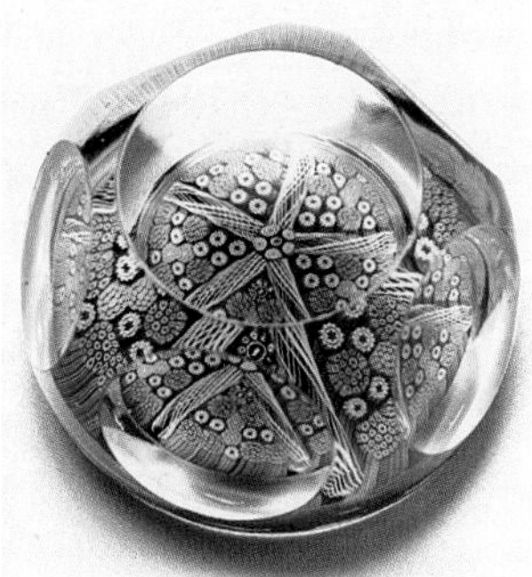

A Whitefriars Starfish paperweight, 1976, 3in (7.5cm) diam.

$360–400 ⊞ RW

This pattern can be found in a variety of colour combinations.

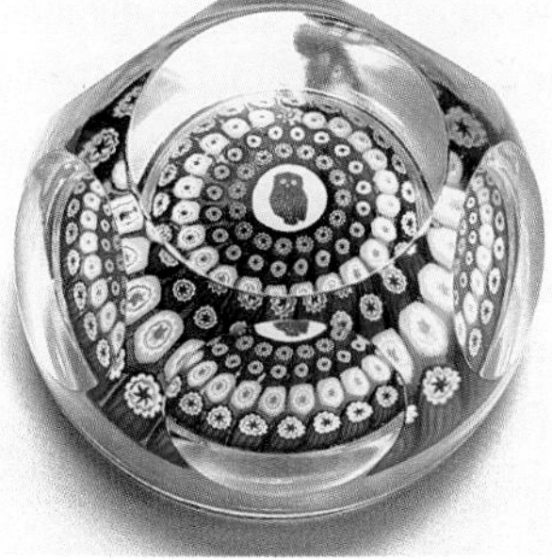

A Whitefriars paperweight, with date cane for 1976, 3in (7.5cm) diam.

$690–780 ⊞ RW

Although this is an unlimited edition, it is quite rare and very desirable because of the owl picture cane in the middle.

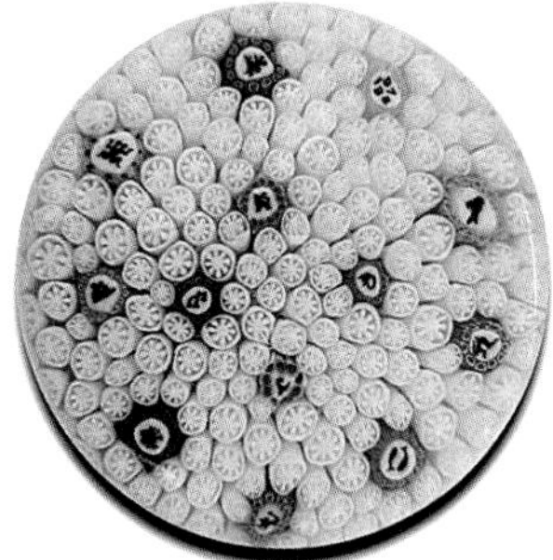

A Baccarat Zodiac paperweight, edition of 250, 1978, 3in (7.5cm) diam.

$620–690 ⊞ SWB

A St Louis millefiori paperweight, edition of 250, France, 1980, 3in (7.5cm) diam.

$690–780 SWB

A Perthshire Marmalade Cat paperweight, Scotland, 1987–89, 2¾in (7cm) diam.

$180–210 SWB

A Perthshire Scrambled paperweight, Scotland, 1987–97, 2¾in (7cm) diam.

$310–350 SWB

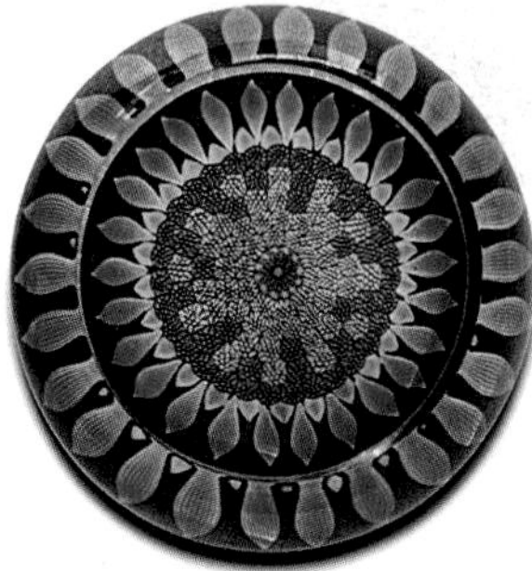

A Perthshire Sunflower paperweight, edition of 350, Scotland, 1992, 3in (7.5cm) diam.

$430–480 SWB

A Lundberg Studios White Crane paperweight, America, 2001, 2¾in (7cm) diam.

$380–430 SWB

A Lundberg Studios Columbine paperweight, America, 2004, 3in (7.5cm) diam.

$320–360 SWB

► A Victor Trabucco Bee and Flowers paperweight, America, 2004, 3in (7.5cm) diam.

$850–950 SWB

A Victor Trabucco Flowers paperweight, America, 2004, 3in (7.5cm) diam.

$850–950 SWB

Victor Trabucco is one of the most creative studio glass artists working today. He has the distinction of being one of only a handful of American glass artists who have developed new techniques that have led to changes in traditional glassmaking.

A Caithness Glass Mystic Mountain paperweight, Scotland, 2005, 5in (12.5cm) high.

$150–170 Cai

◄ A Caithness Glass Evening Primrose paperweight, Scotland, 2005, 5in (12.5cm) high.

$190–220 Cai

SCANDINAVIAN

A Holmegaard glass Aqua vase, by Per Lütken, Denmark, 1952, 7¾in (19.5cm) high.

$120–140 ⊞ Getc

A Holmegaard glass Beak vase vase, by Per Lütken, with bubble inclusions, Denmark, 1955, 7¾in (19.5cm) high.

$70–80 ⊞ Getc

▶ **A Holmegaard glass ashtray,** Denmark, 1960s, 5¼in (13.5cm) wide.

$40–45 ⊞ MARK

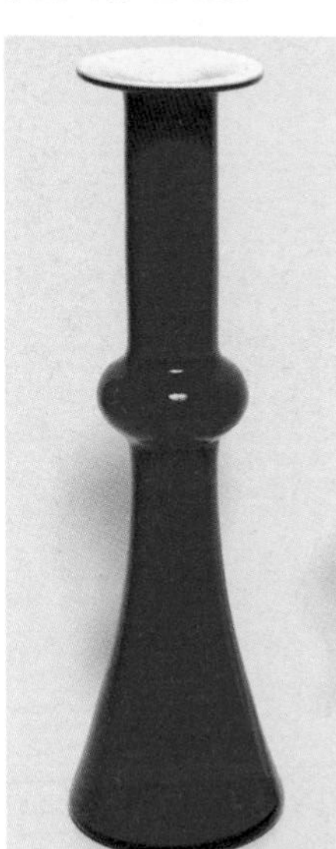

◀ **A Holmegaard glass candlestick,** Denmark, c1960, 12in (30.5cm) high.

$190–220 ⊞ RUSK

A Holmegaard glass dish, Denmark, 1960s, 5½in (14cm) wide.

$60–70 ⊞ MARK

A Holmegaard glass bowl, with hole handles, Denmark, 1955, 4½in (11cm) high.

$180–200 ⊞ FREE

A Holmegaard glass bowl, Denmark, 1950s, 7in (18cm) wide.

$50–60 ⊞ MARK

A pair of Holmegaard Carnaby glass salt and pepper pots, Denmark, c1960, 3in (7.5cm) high.

$40–45 each ⊞ PI

These pots were also available in five other colours.

◀ **A Kosta glass vase,** by Vicke Lindstrand, Sweden, c1950, 10in (25.5cm) high.

$310–350 ⊞ RETC

Formerly one of the chief designers at Orrefors, Vicke Lindstrand was appointed chief designer at Kosta in 1950, a post he held until 1973. His designs were not just for hot glass forms but include many beautiful abstract engraved vases, as well as domestic table glass. It is possible to identify his designs from the complicated set of letters and numbers and the Kosta signature on the base of the items, as well as from the factory catalogues.

◀ **A Kosta glass bowl,** Sweden, 1950s, 4¼in (11cm) wide.

$60–70 ⊞ MARK

A Kosta sommerso glass vase, by Vicke Lindstrand, engraved mark, Sweden, 1950s, 4¾in (12cm) high.

$140–160 ⊞ FREE

A Kosta glass bowl, by Vicke Lindstrand, engraved marks, Sweden, 1950s, 7½in (19cm) high.

$140–160 ⊞ FREE

A Kosta glass Colora vase, by Vicke Lindstrand, engraved mark, Sweden, 1955–56, 9in (23cm) high.

$790–900 ⊞ FREE

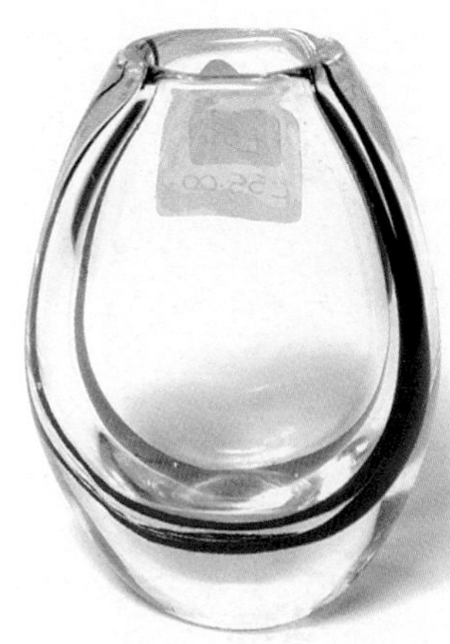

A Kosta glass vase, by Vicke Lindstrand, Sweden, c1958, 3½in (9cm) high.

$85–95 ⊞ MARK

A Kosta Mona Morales glass bowl, Sweden, 1960s, 4in (10cm) diam.

$110–130 ⊞ MARK

▶ **A Kosta glass bowl,** Sweden, 1960s, 8in (20.5cm) wide.

$95–110 ⊞ MARK

A Kosta glass bowl, Sweden, 1960s, 4¼in (11cm) wide.

$10–15 ⊞ MARK

An Orrefors glass jug, by Simon Gate, Sweden, 1933, 3¼in (8.5cm) high.

$80–90 ⊞ MARK

Slice-cut vessels with black bases were very popular in the 1930s. All Orrefors pieces will be marked with a factory signature. Other examples, which were sometimes left unmarked, were made in most countries, including the UK. Simon Gate joined Orrefors in 1916 and Evard Hald in 1917. Together they designed some of the most beautiful engraved, cut or coloured glass in various innovative techniques of the period.

An Orrefors glass Kraka vase, by Sven Palmqvist, internally decorated with bubbles, engraved mark, Sweden, 1959, 8in (20.5cm) high.

$720–820 ⊞ FREE

An Orrefors glass Ariel vase, by Ingeborg Lundin, No. 146H, internally decorated with bubbles, engraved mark, Sweden, 1959, 6¾in (17cm) diam.

$1,250–1,400 ⊞ FREE

An Orrefors glass Graal bowl, by Edward Hald, No. 557, engraved mark, Sweden, 1939, 6¾in (17cm) diam.

$900–1,000 ⊞ FREE

An Orrefors cut-glass 1,000 Windows vase, Sweden, 1950s, 9in (23cm) high.

$430–480 ⊞ MARK

Designed in the mid-1930s, the 1,000 Windows were created by making deep, half-circle cuts between vertical flutes, which acted as lenses, visually producing 1,000 windows. The vases and bowls were either in clear glass or with a black foot and marked with GA and the pattern number.

► **An Orrefors glass vase,** by Sven Palmqvist, Sweden, 1960, 9in (23cm) high.

$120–140 ⊞ MARK

Sven Palmqvist was trained as an engraver. He began working for Orrefors under Simon Gate in 1928 and was a designer from 1936 to 1971. During that time he developed the Kraka technique which encases tiny bubbles in Graal glass, Ravenna designs in which patterns were sandlbasted onto a cased blank and the pocket-like cavities filled with crushed glass of another colour, as well as simple pure forms for everyday life.

An Orrefors glass vase, by Edvin Ohrström, engraved mark, Sweden, 1954, 5in (12.5cm) high.

$170–200 ⊞ FREE

An Orrefors glass Cyrano vase, by Gunnar Cyrén, engraved mark, Sweden, 1950s, 10¾in (27.5cm) high.

$710–800 ⊞ FREE

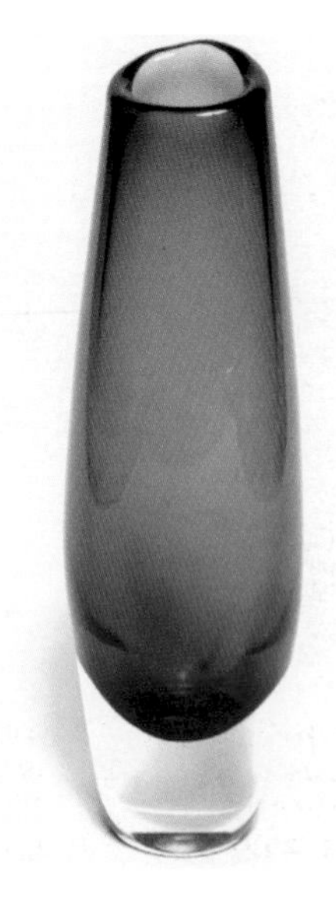

An Orrefors glass Ariel vase, by Edvin Ohrström, engraved mark, Sweden, 1962, 7½in (19cm) high.

$1,450–1,650 ⊞ FREE

A pair of Orrefors glass candle holders, 1960s, 2¾in (7cm) high.

$40–45 ⊞ MARK

An Orrefors soda glass vase, by Eric Hoglund, Sweden, 1970s, 5½in (14cm) high.

$60–70 ⊞ MARK

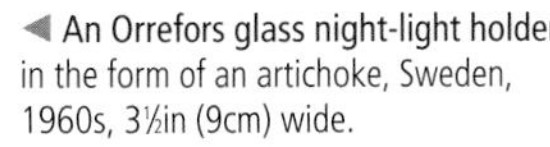

◀ **An Orrefors glass night-light holder,** in the form of an artichoke, Sweden, 1960s, 3½in (9cm) wide.

$30–35 ⊞ MARK

An Orrefors glass Graal vase, by Ingeborg Lundin, engraved mark, Sweden, 1966, 5in (12.5cm) high.

$1,350–1,500 ⊞ FREE

An Orrefors glass Graal vase, by Edward Hald, engraved mark, Sweden, 1985, 8in (20.5cm) diam.

$350–400 ⊞ FREE

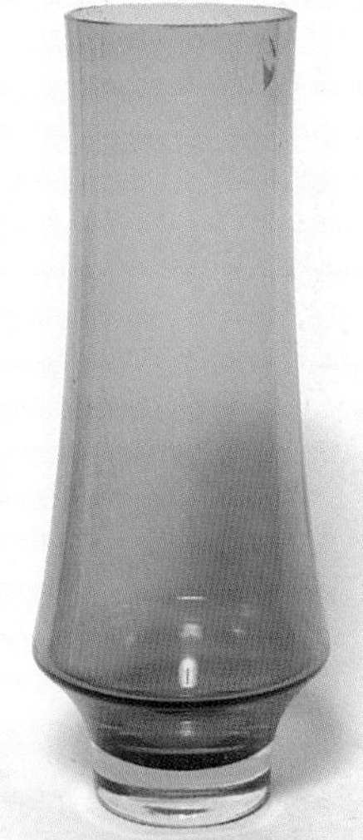

A Riihimaki glass vase, by Tamara Aladin, Finland, 1960s, 10in (25.5cm) high.

$40–45 ⊞ UD

A Riihimaki glass Taalari vase, by Tamara Aladin, Finland, 1970, 8in (20.5cm) high.

$30–35 ⊞ UD

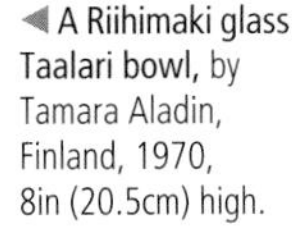

◀ **A Riihimaki glass Taalari bowl,** by Tamara Aladin, Finland, 1970, 8in (20.5cm) high.

$80–90 ⊞ RETC

Three Riihimaki glass vases, Finland, 1970, 7in (18cm) high.

$85–95 each ⊞ COO

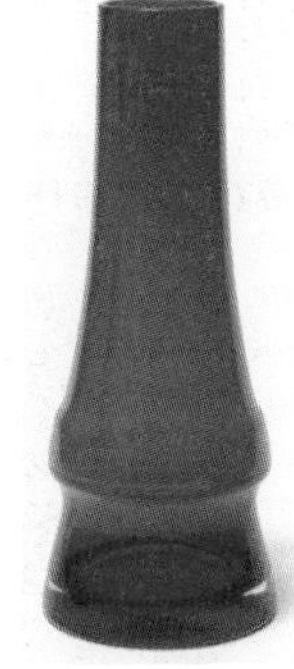

A Riihimaki glass vase, Finland, 1970–74, 10in (25.5cm) high.

$70–80 ⊞ COO

An Ekenas glass vase, incised mark L931, Sweden, 1950–76, 9½in (24cm) high.

$60–70 ⊞ **MARK**

A Benny Motzfeldt glass bowl, internally decorated with aventurine, engraved mark, Norway, 1975, 6in (15cm) high.

$350–400 ⊞ **FREE**

A Nuutajärvi-Notsjö cased-glass vase, by Jaako Niemi, marked, Finland, 1964, 6½in (16.5cm) diam.

$220–250 ⊞ **FREE**

An Ekenas glass decanter, by John Orwar Lake, Sweden, 1950–76, 10in (25.5cm) high.

$45–50 ⊞ **UD**

Ekenas was founded in 1917 by two former Orrefors employees making traditional Swedish art glass. John Orwar Lake, a sculptor who had worked for the ceramics department of Arabia in Finland, became chief designer from 1953 to 1976. This green decanter has the applied band of impressed circles which is the typical hallmark of one of his designs.

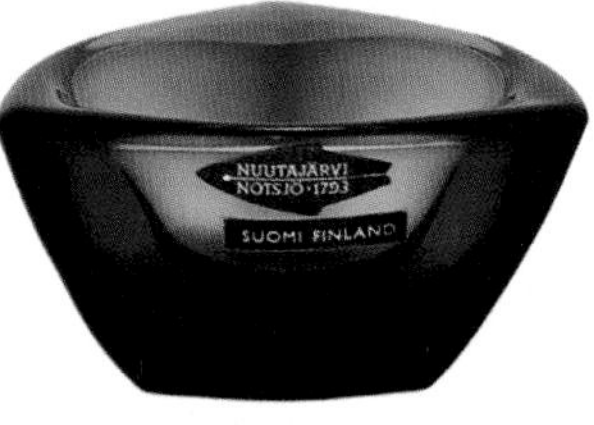

A Nuutajärvi-Notsjö glass ashtray, by Kaj Franck, Finland, 1956, 1½in (4cm) high.

$30–35 ⊞ **Getc**

A Flygsfors glass basket, by Paul Kedelv, Sweden, 1950s, 7in (18cm) high.

$100–120 ⊞ **MARK**

Paul Kedelv, a former employee of Orrefors, was appointed as a designer for Flygsfors from 1949 until 1956. His Coquille range, which appeared in 1952, remained very popular into the 1960s. He designed many freeform vases, bowls and baskets, mostly in a cased colour with an opaque thread.

A Pukeberg cast-glass eggcup, by Eva Englund, Sweden, c1970, 3in (7.5cm) square.

$30–35 ⊞ **Getc**

Until the 1950s Pukeberg was mainly a domestic factory when, in 1957, they employed architect Uno Westerberg and the young and enthusiastic Goren Warff, who was joined by his wife Ann in 1960. Together they produced a series of spontaneous new freeform textured designs for domestic items as well as stylized figural sculptures and individual pieces of art glass; they also employed Eva Englund and Eric Hoglund. Pukeberg is an underrated glass manufacturer, especially when one considers that they employed great designers. Do look out for their glass – even a commercial eggcup such as this – is a great reflection of the period.

◄ **A Strömbergshyttan glass vase,** Sweden, 1950s, 6¼in (16cm) high.

$100–115 ⊞ **MARK**

UK GLASS

A Caithness glass vase, 1970s, 5½in (14cm) high.

$20–25 ⊞ COO

A Caithness lamp base, 1970s, 11in (28cm) high.

$130–150 ⊞ COO

◄ A Caithness glass vase, 1970s, 9in (23cm) high.

$805–95 ⊞ COO

► A Caithness glass vase, 1970s, 11in (28cm) high.

$115–130 ⊞ COO

A Chance Brothers glass handkerchief vase, c1960, 5½in (14cm) high.

$50–60 ⊞ Getc

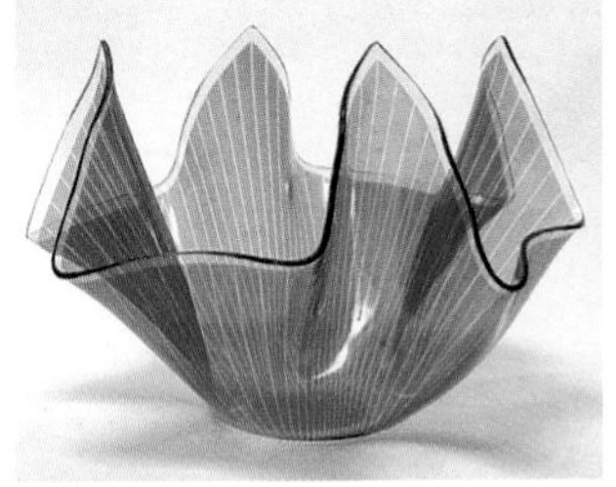

A Chance Brothers glass handkerchief vase, 1964, 9in (23cm) wide.

$30–35 ⊞ COO

A Dartington Crystal glass vase, by Frank Thrower, 1969, 4in (10cm) high.

$40–45 ⊞ COO

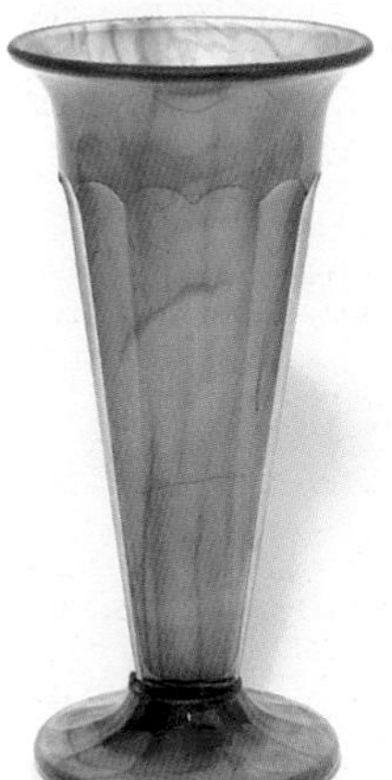

A George Davidson glass vase, c1925, 7in (18cm) wide.

$50–60 ⊞ TOP

A George Davidson glass tray and candlestick set, 1920–30, tray 13in (33cm) wide.

$80–90 ⊞ UD

A Vasart glass bowl, 1930s, 5in (12.5cm) diam.

$50–60 ⊞ TOP

◄ A set of two Nailsea glass marbles, mid-19thC, 1¼in (3cm) diam.

$10–20 each ⊞ HUM

ALEXANDER HARDIE WILLIAMSON

A Sherdley Conical glass, by Alexander Hardie Williamson, decorated with Festival pattern, 1950s, 4½in (11.5cm) high.

$30–35 ⊞ COO

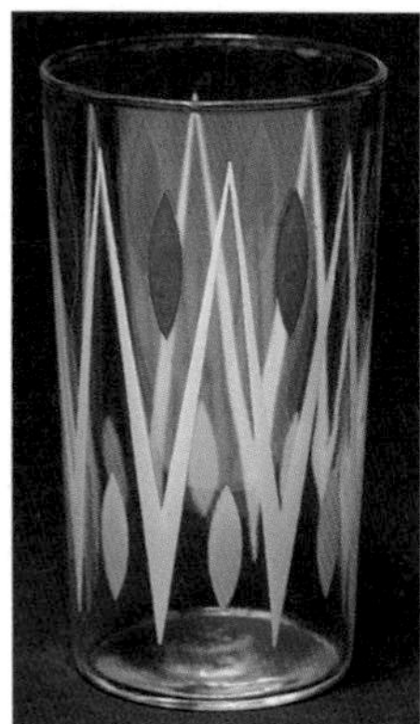

A Conical glass, by Alexander Hardie Williamson, decorated with Lotus pattern, 1950s, 4½in (11.5cm) high.

$20–25 ⊞ COO

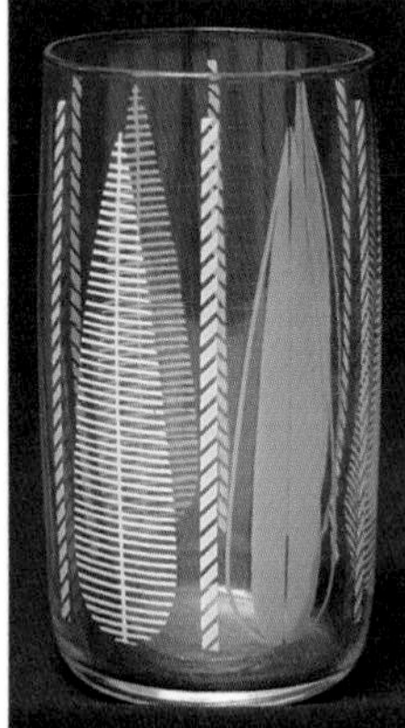

A Chubbie glass, by Alexander Hardie Williamson, 1950s, 5in (12.5cm) high.

$10–20 ⊞ COO

A Gaytime glass, by Alexander Hardie Williamson, 1960s, 5in (12.5cm) high.

$10–20 ⊞ COO

◀ **A Ravenhead Conical glass,** by Alexander Hardie Williamson, with screen-printed decoration, c1965, 5¼in (13.5cm) high.

$5–10 ⊞ Getc

▶ **A glass,** by Alexander Hardie Williamson, 1960s, 4½in (11.5cm) high.

$10–20 ⊞ COO

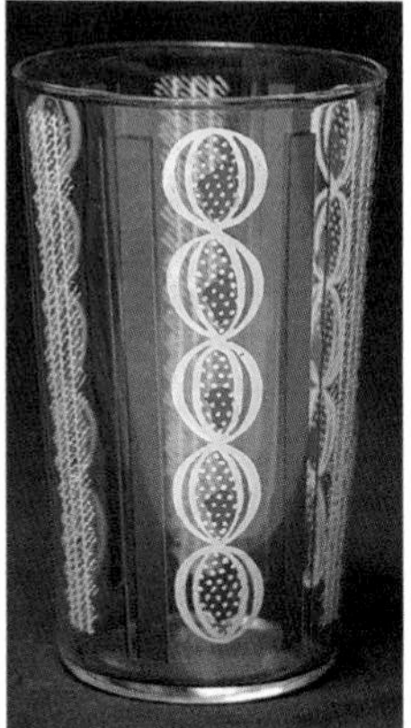

▶ **A Slim Jim glass,** by Alexander Hardie Williamson, decorated with Bamboo pattern, 1960s, 5½in (14cm) high.

$10–20 ⊞ COO

- Trained textile designer, Alexander Hardie Williamson (1907–94) was appointed consultant designer for United Glass Bottle Manufacturers (UGBM) in 1947. UGBM manufactured glasswares under the Sherdley and Ravenhead tradenames.
- His mission was to create glass that was 'pleasant to handle and look at.'
- There are over 1,700 glassware designs attributed to Williamson and, aside from undecorated press-moulded glass, he is best remembered for his brightly-coloured, enamel-printed tumbler sets made by Sherdley.
- Fully automatic screen-printing directly onto glass was made possible in the 1950s. Initially only two enamel colours were used. In 1967 new machines were installed to overprint three enamel colours in one run.
- Williamson's patterns echo contemporary architecture, fabrics and interiors, which makes dating fairly straightforward. The range of tumbler shapes (from `Conical' and `Slim Jims' to `Gaytime') were said to 'provide style to suit every taste.'
- Single glasses are still reasonably cheap and easy to find (they were originally sold in six-piece carry packs).

WEDGWOOD

A Wedgwood Midnight wine glass, by Frank Thrower, 1982, 8in (20.5cm) high.

$30–35 COO

A Wedgwood glass vase, by Ronald Stennett-Wilson, signed, 1969–80, 6in (18cm) high.

$45–50 UD

A Wedgwood Midnight glass vase, by Frank Thrower, 1982, 7in (18cm) high.

$20–25 COO

A Wedgwood Midnight glass vase, by Frank Thrower, 1982, 7in (18cm) high.

$20–25 COO

► A Wedgwood Midnight glass vase, by Frank Thrower, 1982, 5in (12.5cm) high.

$20–25 COO

A Wedgwood Midnight glass vase, by Frank Thrower, 1982, 7in (18cm) high.

$20–25 COO

A pair of Wedgwood glass candle holders, by Frank Thrower, 1982, larger 10in (25.5cm) high.

$50–60 each COO

WHITEFRIARS

A Whitefriars wave-ribbed glass vase, by Marriott Powell, c1930, 10in (25.5cm) high.

$230–260 POI

A Whitefriars threaded glass lamp base, by Harry Powell, c1930, 10½in (26.5cm) high.

$600–690 HUN

This lamp base was made by trailing ruby glass around a clear glass body, which was then blown into a ribbed mould. The size was increased by further blowing which created the uneven threading.

A pair of Whitefriars amber claret glasses, by Barnaby Powell, c1930, 4in (10cm) high.

$130–150 HUN

A Whitefriars ribbon-trailed glass lamp base, Barnaby Powell, c1933, 8in (20.5cm) high.

$310–350 HUN

A Whitefriars amethyst glass lotus bowl, by Barnaby Powell, c1935, 11in (28cm) diam.

$250–290 HUN

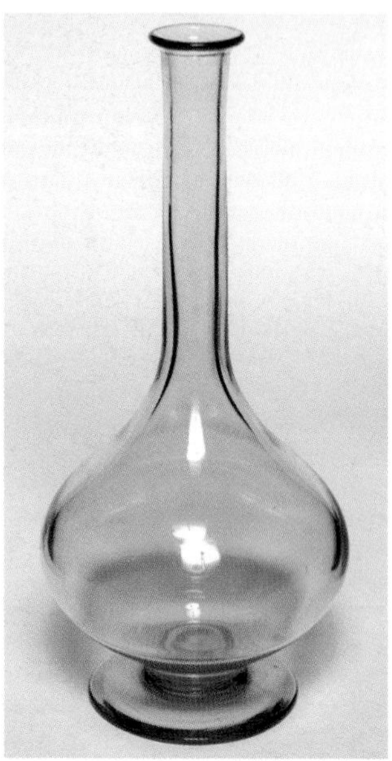

A Whitefriars amber glass carafe, c1936, 8in (20.5cm) high.

$100–120 HUN

► A Whitefriars amber glass ribbed optic vase, by James Hogan, c1938, 10in (25.5cm) high.

$310–350 HUN

◄ A Whitefriars lobed glass bowl, by James Hogan, c1945, 11in (28cm) wide.

$130–150 HUN

A Whitefriars cased bubble-glass bowl, with bubble inclusions, 1950s, 8in (20.5cm) diam.

$60–70 HEM

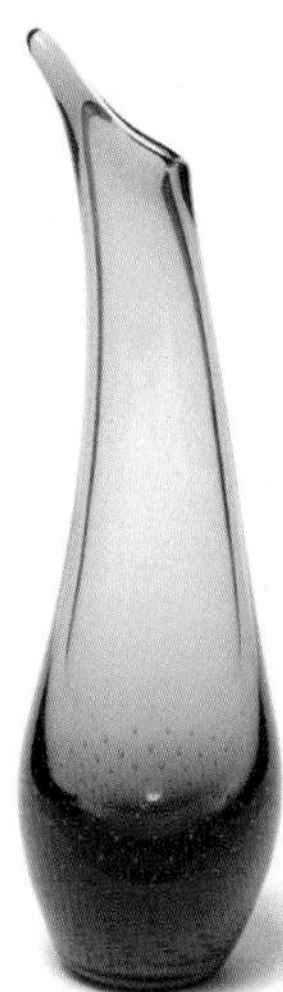

► A Whitefriars Twilight glass Beak vase, by Geoffrey Baxter, 1957, 8in (20.5cm) high.

$210–240 COO

A Whitefriars freeblown arctic blue glass vase, by Geoffrey Baxter, c1960, 6in (15cm) high.

$60–70 HUN

A Whitefriars ruby glass Barrel vase, by Geoffrey Baxter, c1962, 9½in (24cm) high.

$130–150 HUN

A Whitefriars streaky glass vase, by William Wilson and Harry Dyer, c1964, 9½in (24cm) high.

$70–80 HUN

A Whitefriars Knobbly glass ashtray, 1964, 9¾in (25cm) diam.

$40–45 MARK

The Knobbly range was designed by William Wilson and Harry Dyer in 1963 and produced until 1972. Items were either made in a single colour or in streaky browns or greens or, as the example shown, inside-cased. The knobbly effect was obtained by pinching the thick molten glass into random shapes with an S-shaped tool – the equivalent of glassmaker's tweezers.

A Whitefriars cinnamon glass Basket Weave vase, by Geoffrey Baxter, c1967, 10½in (26.5cm) high.

$600–670 HUN

A Whitefriars glass Banjo vase, by Geoffrey Baxter, 1960s, 12½in (32cm) high.

$2,150–2,400 MARK

◄ A Whitefriars tangerine glass Totem Pole vase, by Geoffrey Baxter, c1969, 10in (25.5cm) high.

$310–350 HUN

► A Whitefriars tangerine glass Cello vase, by Geoffrey Baxter, c1972, 7in (18cm) high.

$270–310 FRD

A Whitefriars gold glass vase, by Geoffrey Baxter, c1979, 7½in (19cm) high.

$95–110 HUN

GRAMOPHONES

A Decca Junior portable gramophone, in a Rexine case, c1920, 11in (28cm) wide.

$150–170 ⊞ OTA

An HMV gramophone, model No. 110, in an oak case, c1924, 18in (45.5cm) wide.

$230–260 ⊞ OTA

A Bon Marché table gramophone, the walnut case with transfers simulating inlay, France, 1922, 16in (40.5cm) wide.

$230–260 ⊞ GM

An HMV gramophone, model No. 250, in a mahogany cabinet, c1924, 29in (73.5cm) wide.

$380–430 ⊞ OTA

◀ **An Antoria portable gramophone,** c1930, 15in (38cm) long.

$120–140 ⊞ JUN

▶ **A Decca portable gramophone,** model No. 50, c1956, 12in (30.5cm) wide.

$150–170 ⊞ OTA

An HMV portable gramophone, model No. 101, c1920, 11in (28cm) wide.

$150–170 ⊞ OIA

An Amplion speaker, c1925, 10in (25.5cm) diam.

$120–140 ⊞ OTA

A Victor Talking Machine catalogue, c1903, 6in (15cm) high.

$150–170 ⊞ OTA

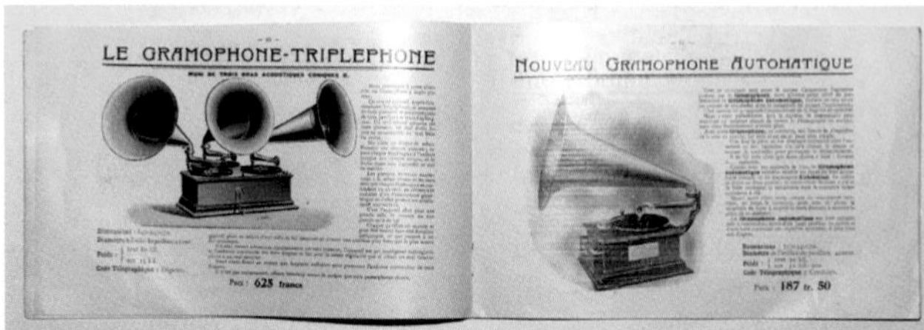

A catalogue of gramophones and accessories, France, 905, 9½in (24cm) wide.

$180–210 ⊞ ET

For more records, please see the Rock & Pop section on pages 328–343.

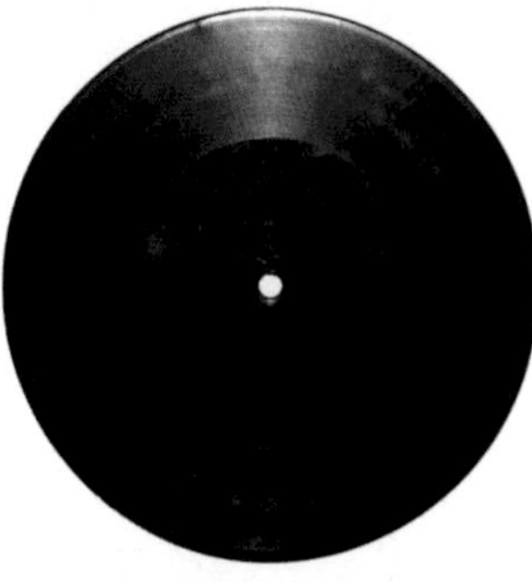

► **A Berliner gramophone record,** 'Street Faker', recorded by George Graham, America, dated 1896, 7in (18cm) diam.

$530–610 ⊞ ET

◄ **A Berliner gramophone record,** recorded in London, 1900, 7in (18cm) diam.

$50–60 ⊞ ET

Berliner Gramophone was the first company to produce disc gramophone records, and the earliest examples were used by toy companies. They were produced in Germany from 1890, and in the USA from 1892. Emile Berliner opened his first UK branch in London in 1898, which became His Master's Voice (HMV) in 1910.

A Gramophone Concert Record, 'Pagliacci' by Enrico Caruso, 1905.

$150–165 ⊞ ET

A Pathé gramophone record, 'Carmen', 1904–14, 20in (51cm) diam.

$230–260 ⊞ ET

Pathé gramophone records came in a variety of sizes – 10, 12, 14 and 20in. Consequently, some of the smaller ones can be purchased for less than $85.

A Gennett gramophone record, 'I'm Glad' and 'Flock O'Blues', by the Sioux City Six, featuring Bix Beiderbecke, 1924.

$180–210 ⊞ ET

CHRIS BAKER GRAMOPHONES

(CLPGS member)

Specialist dealer in high quality gramophones and phonographs. Cabinet, table-top, portable and horn style machines as well as phonographs. Usually over 30 in stock. All properly serviced and guaranteed. Also 78 records, cylinders, needles, accessories and gramophone collectables. Repairs undertaken. I also wish to purchase quality gramophones and phonographs.

Send for my free stock list!

At: All Our Yesterdays, 3 Cattle Market
Sandwich, Kent CT13 9AE
Tel: +44 (0)1304 614756
Email: cbgramophones@aol.com
Website: www.chrisbakergramophones.com

Philip Knighton

Established 1981

Tel: +44 (0)1823 661618
Email:
philip.knighton@btopenworld.com

Celebrating 26 years of trading in the world of Wireless, Gramophones and all Valve Equipment

Specialist Repairs

1c South Street,
Wellington,
Somerset TA21 8NR

Opening hours
Tuesday to Saturday
10.00am to 5.00pm

Skip & Janie Smithson Antiques

FRESH GATHERED RASPBERRIES OUR OWN GROWING

Specialist dealers in Kitchen, Laundry, Dairy and related Advertising items

THE BEST THAT MONEY CAN BUY

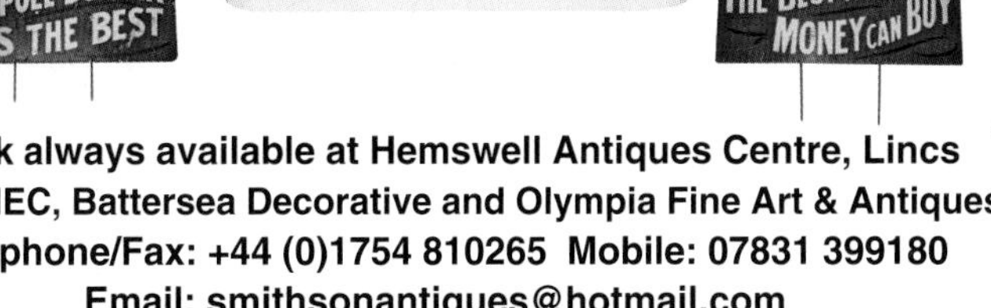

Stock always available at Hemswell Antiques Centre, Lincs
Fairs: NEC, Battersea Decorative and Olympia Fine Art & Antiques
Telephone/Fax: +44 (0)1754 810265 Mobile: 07831 399180
Email: smithsonantiques@hotmail.com

PURE MILK

PURE NEW MILK WELFORD & SONS

CONTACT BY APPOINTMENT SINGLE ITEMS OR COLLECTIONS BOUGHT

KITCHENWARE

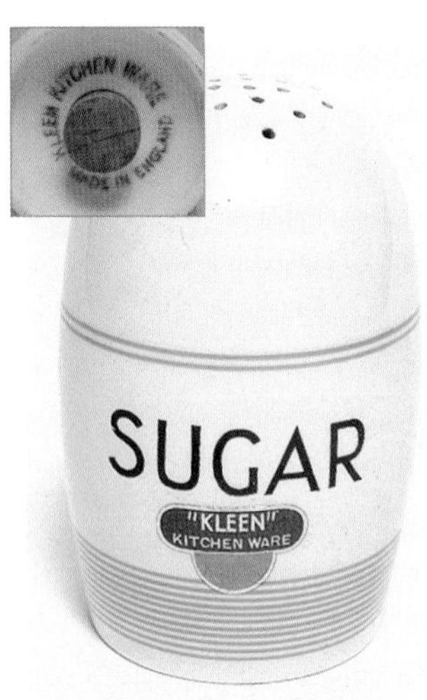

A Sadler ceramic Kleen Kitchen Ware sugar shaker, c1930, 5in (12.5cm) high.

$85–100 ⊞ LA&I

James Sadler & Sons was formed in 1882. During the 1930s the firm made a huge range of goods including kitchenware.

A Sotox aluminium pudding steamer, 1930s–50s, 6in (15cm) diam.

$40–50 ⊞ DaM

A kitchen apron, decorated with playing cards, 1950.

$45–50 ⊞ SpM

A Sadler ceramic Kleen Kitchen Ware Bi-Soda jar, c1930, 3½in (9cm) high.

$85–95 ⊞ LA&I

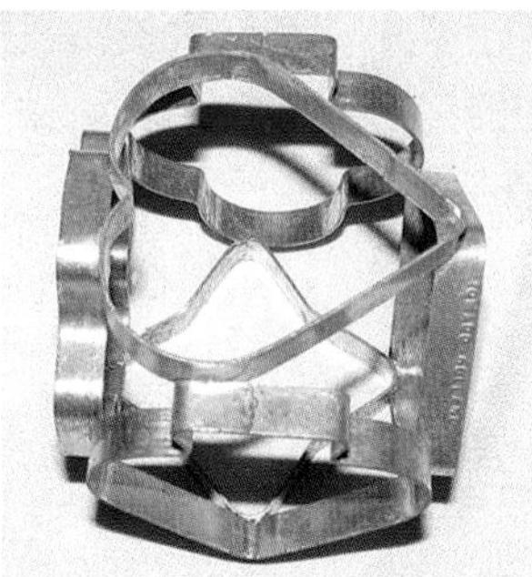

A Holland metal six-sided cookie cutter, comprising cross, star, diamond, heart, spade and club shapes, light wear, stamped, Holland, 1940s, 3in (7.5cm) square.

$20–25 ⊞ KKN

► A box of Kilner preserving jars, 1950–60, 9in (23cm) high.

$60–70 ⊞ JWK

A Sadler ceramic Kleen Kitchen Ware egg cup, c1930, 2in (5cm) high.

$25–35 ⊞ LA&I

A biscuit tin, c1950, 6in (15cm) high.

$40–45 ⊞ AL

A cotton seersucker tablecloth, 1950s, 47 x 70in (119.5 x 178cm).

$20–25 ⊞ JWK

A set of Tala meringue tubes, 1950s, 4in (10cm) high, boxed.

$30–35 ⊞ DaM

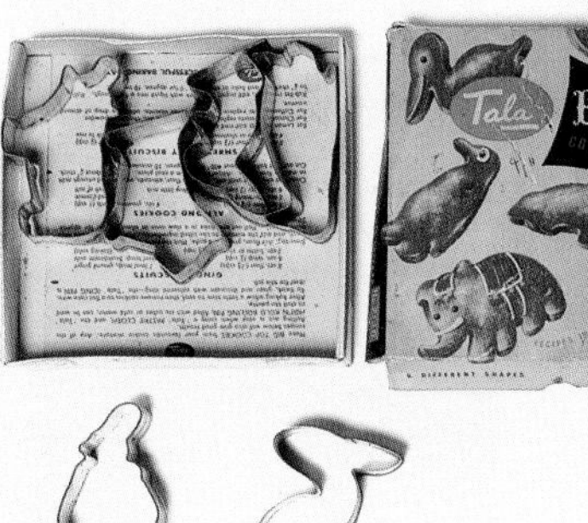

A set of six Tala Big Top cookie cutters, 1950s–60s, in original box, 7in (18cm) square.

$40–45 ⊞ DaM

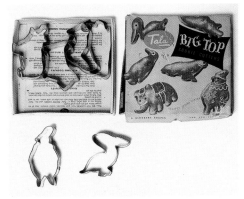

A Tala plastic icing turntable, 1950s, 9in (23cm) diam, boxed.

$20–25 ⊞ JWK

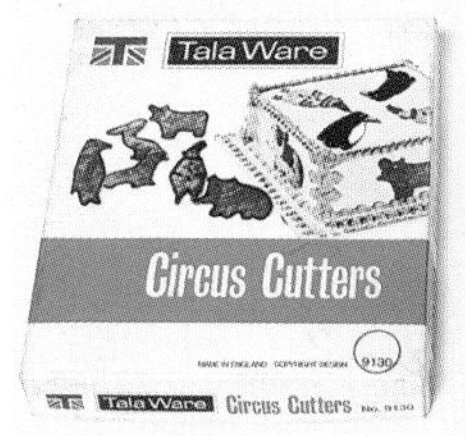

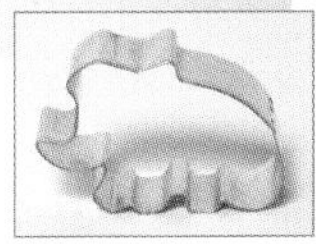

A set of Tala Ware Circus Cutters, 1970s, with box 7in (18cm) square.

$20–25 ⊞ JWK

◄ A Nutbrown De Luxe Icing Outfit, c1960, with box, 9 x 13in (23 x 33cm).

$30–35 ⊞ UD

► A glass and plastic sugar pourer, 1970s, 6in (15cm) high.

$10–20 ⊞ TWI

A roll of Crown vinyl kitchen wallpaper, 1970, 20½in (52cm) wide.

$60–70 ⊞ TWI

ENAMEL

◀ **An enamel teapot,** c1920, 6in (15cm) high.

$50–60 ⊞ LA&I

A set of six enamel storage jars, France, c1930, largest 5in (12.5cm) diam.

$190–210 ⊞ B&R

An enamel jug, c1930, 9½in (24cm) high.

$40–45 ⊞ AL

An enamel flour storage bin, Belgium, 1940s, 9in (23cm) high.

$30–35 ⊞ TWI

▶ **An enamel bowl,** Belgium, c1960, 6in (15cm) diam.

$10–20 ⊞ AL

An enamel pie dish, 1940s, 12in (30.5cm) wide.

$10–20 ⊞ JWK

JUDGE WARE

A Judge Ware enamel frying pan, c1940, 11in (28cm) diam.

$40–45 ⊞ JWK

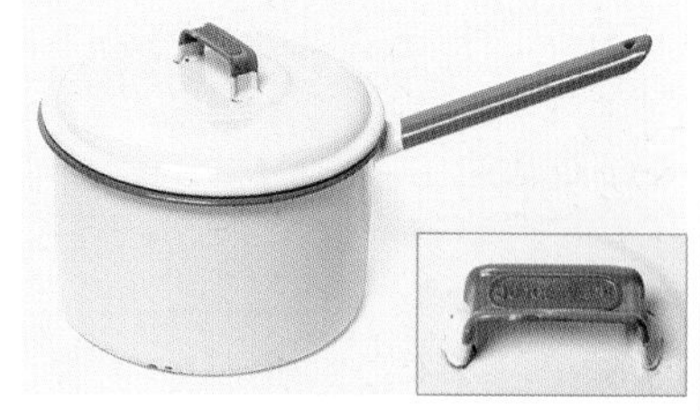

A Judge Ware enamel lidded saucepan, 1940s, 9in (23cm) diam.

$30–35 ⊞ JWK

- The Judge Ware brand was one of Britain's favourites from the 1930s through to the 1950s.
- Well made but light in weight, this range of enamel wares was easy to use, and co-ordinated with contemporary ceramics like T. G. Green's Streamline and Sadler's Kleen Kitchen Ware.
- The firm's owner, Mr Stevens, prospered along with his kitchenware and in the 1930s he purchased Walcot Hall in Shropshire with his saucepan fortune!

GADGETS

A cast-iron cherry stoner, US patent, c1900, 7in (18cm) long.

$280–320 ⊞ BS

A BEL glass and aluminium cream maker, c1930, 9in (23cm) high.

$60–70 ⊞ OIA

This is a pneumatic gadget that transformed melted unsalted butter and milk into cream. BEL was a market leader in the 1930s and its cream makers appeared in a variety of colours under a number of different names such as Jubilee and Empire.

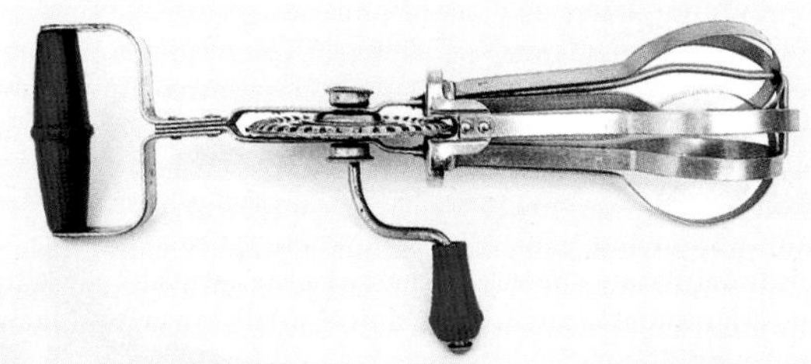

A Blue Whirl Rotary egg beater, 1940s, 12in (30.5cm) long.

$10–20 ⊞ R2G

The splayed blades gave superior whipping, incorporating more air with greater speed. These models were available in the US ahead of the UK.

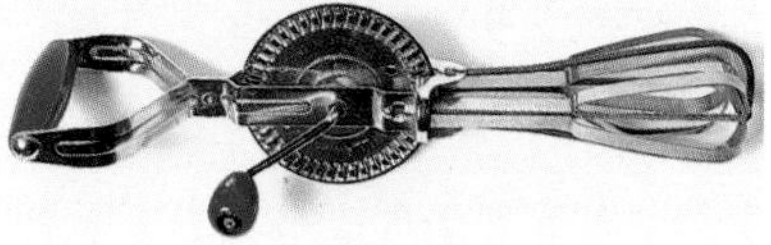

A rotary whisk, with wooden handle, 1950s, 13in (33cm) high.

$10–20 ⊞ JWK

A Tala tin flour sifter, 1950s, 6in (15cm) high.

$20–25 ⊞ JWK

A Juice-O-Mat chrome orange press, America, c1950, 7in (18cm) high.

$60–70 ⊞ UD

Vitamin C was isolated as an important vitamin in the 1940s and the rage for orange juice, which is high in vitamin C, resulted. The Juice-O-Mat was invented by Joseph M. Bajewski Jr from Kansas City, USA. His patent was granted on 3 January 1939 and the design has changed very little over the years.

A GEC chrome electric toaster, 1950s, 8in (20.5cm) high, boxed.

$85–95 ⊞ UD

Toasters were one of the most popular post-war wedding gifts. In real terms, quality brands were expensive, equivalent to two weeks' wages. This is a turn-over version rather than pop-up.

MOULDS

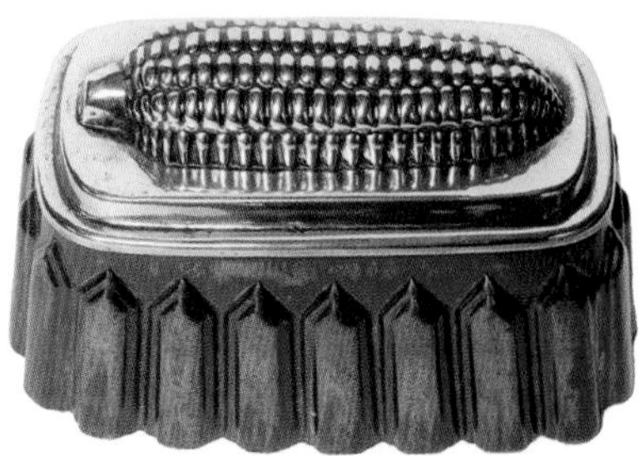

A copper and tin jelly mould, c1900, 7in (18cm) long.

$240–280 ⊞ **BS**

A tin-lined copper mould, c1910, 10in (25.5cm) high.

$50–60 ⊞ **LA&I**

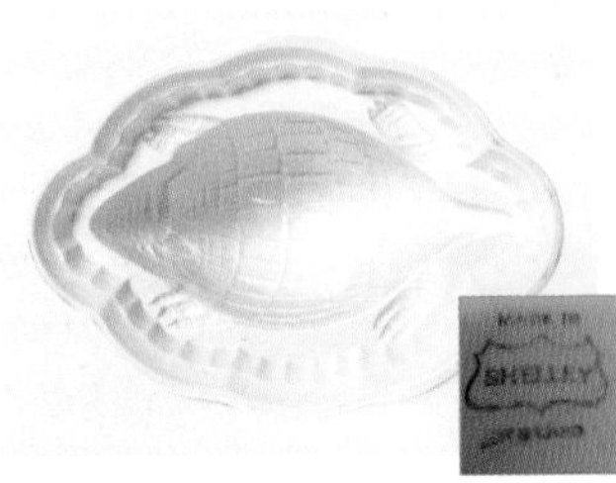

A Shelley ceramic jelly mould, impressed with an armadillo, 1912–25, 10in (25.5cm) wide.

$460–520 ⊞ **BS**

A stoneware jelly mould, impressed with a horse's head, c1920, 8in (20.5cm) wide.

$120–140 ⊞ **SMI**

A ceramic jelly mould, impressed with a dog on a cushion, registered 1929, 6in (15cm) wide.

$140–160 ⊞ **BS**

◀ **A glass one-pint jelly mould,** 1940s, 6in (15cm) diam.

$10–20 ⊞ **JWK**

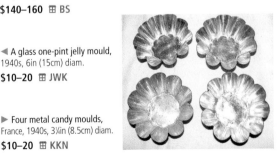

▶ **Four metal candy moulds,** France, 1940s, 3¼in (8.5cm) diam.

$10–20 ⊞ **KKN**

A plastic jelly mould, in the form of a house, 1950s, 5¼in (13.5cm) long.

$10–20 ⊞ **TWI**

◀ **A plastic jelly mould,** in the form of a racing car, 1940s, 5in (12.5cm) long.

$10–20 ⊞ **TWI**

PYREX

A Pyrex Flameware skillet, with detachable glass handle, marked 'E-U832B' to base, light wear, 1940s, 7in (18cm) diam.

$20–25 R2G

Corning, the makers of Pyrex, introduced Flameware in the US in 1936 for cooking on top of the stove. In 1938, James A. Jobling purchased the British Empire patent to make Flameware in Britain. Part of its success came with its guarantee: if a piece of Flameware broke from heat or degradation within its first year, it could be replaced. The 'cool glass' handle helps to date this skillet – it was used between 1943 and 1946, but proved too costly to manufacture. Flameware was a highly successful product that ran until the 1970s.

A Pyrex shallow baking and serving dish, light wear, marked, America, 1953, 9in (23cm) diam.

$10–20 JWK

This dish originally cost 60 cents in the US. Lime Green was a new 'decorator colour' that appeared in 1953 along with Flamingo Red to boost sales of Pyrex's tempered bakeware.

A Pyrex Cinderella divided serving dish, glass cover missing, 1957, 1½ quart.

$20–25 JWK

The daisy pattern first appeared in 1957, and this serving dish originally retailed at $2.95.

Three Pyrex glass ramekins, late 1950s, 3½in (9cm) diam.

$10–20 each JWK

▶ A Pyrex glass mixing/pouring bowl, late 1950s, 13in (33cm) wide.

$30–35 JWK

A Pyrex glass Gaiety casserole dish, with metal cradle, c1960, 14in (35.5cm) wide, boxed.

$35–45 JWK

A Pyrex glass dessert dishes and six serving bowls, c1960, serving bowl 8in (20.5cm) diam.

$35–45 JWK

A Pyrex glass casserole dish, decorated with Old Town or Brown Onion pattern, marked, early 1960s, 8in (20.5cm) wide.

$10–20 ⊞ R2G

Two Pyrex glass nesting bowls, Nos. 401 and 402, America, 1960s, larger 2½ quart.

$20–25 ⊞ R2G

There would have been three bowls in this nesting set, each sized to fit one inside the other for space-saving in the kitchen. In this case, the middle 1½-quart bowl is missing. 'Mix, bake and store all in the same bowl' said the advertisements. Complete boxed sets are particularly desirable among collectors.

◄ **A set of Pyrex glass serving dishes,** c1960, 6½in (16.5cm) diam.

$35–45 ⊞ JWK

A Pyrex glass instant coffee jug, No. 21, in metal stand, 1960s, 11in (28cm) high.

$20–25 ⊞ TWI

A Corning Ware skillet casserole dish, decorated with Cornflower pattern, marked, 1960s, 10in (25.5cm) wide.

$20–25 ⊞ R2G

Corning Ware (retailed as Pyrosil Ware in the UK) was an innovative aside for the glassware giant. Made from 'Pyroceram', a 'space-age ceramic' developed in 1953 that was heat-proof and completely non-porous, it allowed housewives to reduce their cooking temperatures and still get the same results. A lock-on handle fitted all casserole sizes.

► **A Pyrex glass oven dish,** 1970s, 9in (23cm) wide.

$10–20 ⊞ JWK

GLASS OVENWARE

PHOENIX GLASS

A Phoenix glass tureen and cover, marked, 1950, 10in (25.5cm) wide.

$30–35 JWK

A Phoenix glass sauce boat, 1950s, 8in (205cm) wide.

$30–35 JWK

A Phoenix glass mixing bowl, c1950, 10in (25.5cm) diam.

$30–35 JWK

- Phoenix is the brand name of the British Heat Resisting Glass Co, founded by Colonel P. V. W. Jell. Their headquarters were in Bilston, West Midlands and they made their first glass wares in 1934.
- The purpose of the company was to set up a patent for oven-proof glass.
- Many of their designs resembled those produced by the better-known American brand, Pyrex, with which they were in direct competition.
- A wide range of domestic ware was made, including clear and opalescent glass, some with decorative patterns that were very much of their time.
- As well as tableware and ovenware, the factory made glassware for laboratories.
- The firm closed in August 1970.

A set of six Phoenix glass plates, 1950s, 7in (1cm) diam.

$30–35 JWK

A Fire-King glass cup and saucer, marked, America, 1950s, cup 4in (10cm) diam.

$30–35 JWK

Produced by Anchor Hocking, Fire-King oven glass and heat-proof tables were produced during the 1940s, '50s and '60s. Hugely popular at the time, they are still a favourite with collectors today. The range included everything from pie plates and casseroles to bowls and refrigerator jars.

A milk glass mixing bowl, with pouring spout, 1960s, 4¾in (12cm) high.

$10–20 R2G

PLASTIC

A Bakelite egg stand, 1930s, 7in (18cm) diam.

$20–25 ⊞ UD

A set of four NB Ware plastic egg cups, 1950s, 2in (5cm) high.

$20–25 ⊞ JWK

NB Ware produced a wide range of moulded plastics for the home and were also specialists in the sewing field, making attractive cotton and wool holders.

◀ **Two Beetleware plastic flour scoops,** 1950s, 6in (15cm) long.

$10–20 each ⊞ JWK

Beetleware first appeared in the 1930s and the brand name was synonymous with quality mass-production. These two scoops show just how vibrant and varied the colour range was.

A plastic sugar shaker, 1950s, 4in (10cm) high.

$10–20 ⊞ JWK

The two-tone colour of this item fitted with contemporary kitchen design. Red and white was a popular colour combination that appeared again and again in the 1950s.

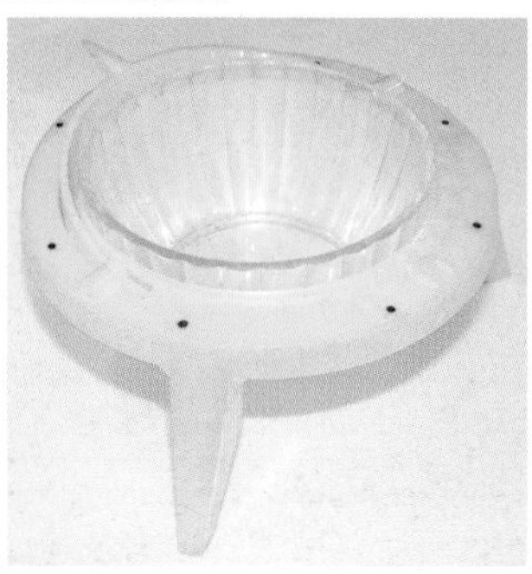

An Embee plastic butter dish, 1950s, 5in (12.5cm) diam.

$20–25 ⊞ TWI

A plastic lemon squeezer, 1950s, 7in (18cm) wide.

$20–25 ⊞ TWI

▶ **A plastic rolling pin,** 1950s, 16in (40.5cm) long.

$30–35 ⊞ TWI

◀ **A Melaware dinner service,** comprising 20 pieces, 1950s, largest plate 9½in (24cm) diam).

$85–100 ⊞ TWI

This set was available in four different colours. Melamine was an unbreakable and colourful plastic developed in the 1930s but not fully exploited in homes until the 1950s, and much tableware was produced in this material. The white liners had a habit of staining and getting scratched, so look out for quality survivors. 'Melaware', and Gaydon's 'Melmex' were brand names for melamine.

A set of Salter plastic scales, c1960, 7in (18cm) high.

$35–45 ⊞ JWK

A Melaware plastic butter dish, 1960s, 7¾in (19.5cm) wide.

$10–20 ⊞ TWI

An Embee plastic sugar shaker, 1960s, 5½in (14cm) high.

$5–10 ⊞ TWI

A pair of plastic containers, c1960, 6½in (16.5cm) high.

$30–35 ⊞ TWI

A plastic egg container, 1960s, 7in (18cm) wide.

$10–20 ⊞ TWI

A Jonas plastic jug, designed by Bjarne Bo Andersen, Denmark, 1960s, 7½in (19cm) high.

$35–45 ⊞ TWI

The bright colour of this jug is typical of Danish designer Bjarne Bo Andersen (more commonly known as Bjarne B). He is also known for his subtle curves and ergonomic design, something that is evident here. The gentle scoop on the lid makes it easy to open while the deep handle means this is a jug that is suitable for all sizes of hands.

Five Nally Ware plastic containers, America, c1970, largest 10in (20.5cm) high.

$100–115 ⊞ TWI

A plastic sugar shaker, early 1970s, 5in (12.5cm)high.

$5–10 ⊞ TWI

The circular 'thumb ring' handle not only matched the mood of 1970s tableware but also made this shaker easy to use.

A pair of plastic salad servers, Denmark, 1970s, 9in (213cm) long.

$10–20 ⊞ TWI

► Two Spillers Homepride plastic 'Fred' salts, 1970s, 4in (10cm) high.

$20–25 ⊞ KA

A plastic pepper grinder, 1970s, 7in (18cm) high.
$5–10 ⊞ MARK

An Albertini plastic hamburger press, with spring action, Italy, 1970s, 5in (12.5cm) high.
$10–20 ⊞ TWI

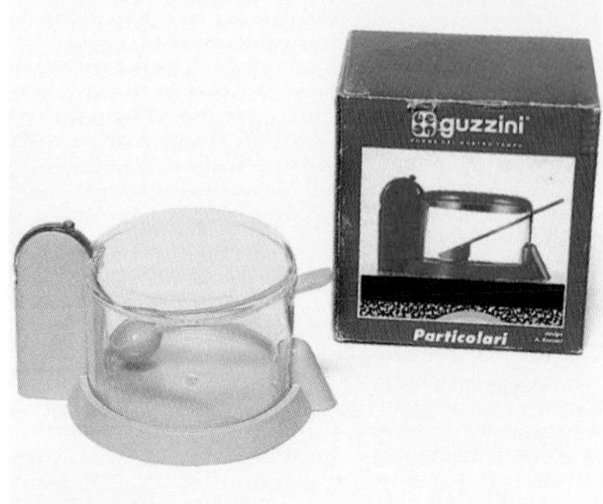

A Guzzini plastic jam pot, Italy, 1980s, 6in (15cm) wide, with box.
$30–35 ⊞ TWI

Established in 1912, Guzzini's designs combine technological innovation with creative expression to produce beautiful but functional household items.

TUPPERWARE

A Tupperware plastic colander, 1960s, 10in (25.5cm) diam.
$10–20 ⊞ JWK

A set of five Tupperware plastic stacking spice containers, 1970s, 10in (25.5cm) high.
$25–35 ⊞ TWI

- Tupperware was invented by American plastics chemist Earl S. Tupper (1907–83).
- Launched in 1946, one of the main selling points was the patented airtight seal which was so revolutionary that customers did not understand how to use it.
- Initially sales were slow until the company introduced home demonstrations under the direction of Bonnie Wise. The Tupperware party was born and the firm sold exclusively this way from 1951.
- Tupperware parties were an instant success in America and arrived in Britain in 1960. Hostesses were kept up-to-date with new product releases thanks to the in-house *Tupperware Sparks* magazine.
- In 2006 Tupperware celebrated its 60th anniversary.
- Although the company continues to introduce new ranges, collectors choose to focus on vintage products – the items that made Tupperware a household name.

LIGHTING

CEILING & FLOOR LIGHTS

A hammered-brass hall lantern, with original frosted glass, c1910, 15in (38cm) high.

$430–480 ⊞ **EAL**

A teardrop ceiling light, with top and bottom refractors, 1930s, 19in (48.5cm) diam.

$240–2260 ⊞ **SOU**

A Philips metal and plastic ceiling light, late 1960s, 7in (18cm) diam.

$85–100 ⊞ **SOU**

A spelter three-branch ceiling light, with frosted- and cut-glass lustres, c1910, 16in (40.5cm) wide.

$690–770 ⊞ **EAL**

A spun fibre and teak rocket lamp, 1960s, 44in (112cm) high.

$155–170 ⊞ **RETC**

A cast-brass ceiling light, with cut-glass shade, 1920s, 10in (25.5cm) high.

$1,150–1,250 ⊞ **TOL**

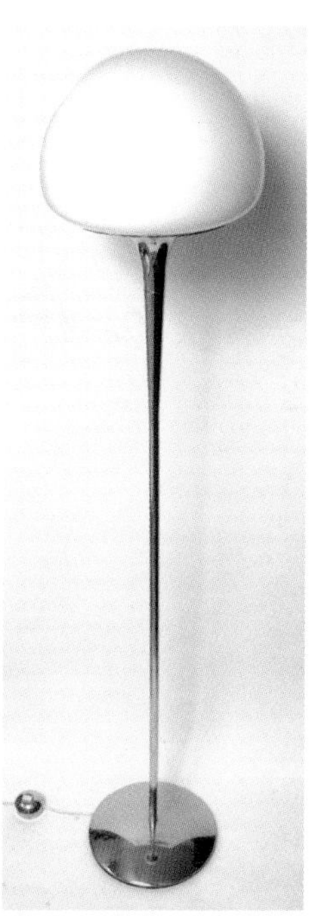

A Reggiani chrome and glass standard lamp, Italy, c1974, 58in (147.5cm) high.

$1,200–1,350 ⊞ **RETC**

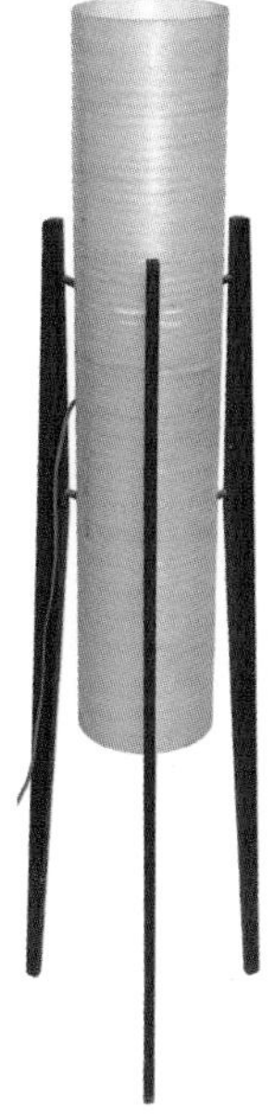

A spun fibre and teak rocket lamp, 1950s, 45in (114.5cm) high.

$250–260
⊞ **OCA**

TABLE & DESK LAMPS

A brass adjustable lamp, 1920–30, 17in (43cm) high.

$360–410 ⊞ **EAL**

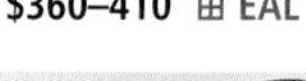

A table lamp, with a frosted and clear glass shade, 1920s, 24in (61cm) high.

$1,000–1,100 ⊞ **TOL**

A desk lamp, with a Wedgwood base, c1925, 15in (38cm) high.

$1,950–2,200 ⊞ **TOL**

A Bestlite crome desk lamp, 1930s, 19in (48.5cm) high.

$690–770 ⊞ **TOL**

◀ **A hollow cast-lead lamp,** surmounted by a hunter, c1930, 8in (20.5cm) high.

$65–85 ⊞ **SAAC**

▶ **A Perspex table lamp,** with a glass shade, c1935, 18in (45.5cm) high.

$690–770 ⊞ **TOL**

◀ **An Anglepoise chrome three-step desk lamp,** c1940, 40in (101.5cm) high.

$580–650 ⊞ **TDG**

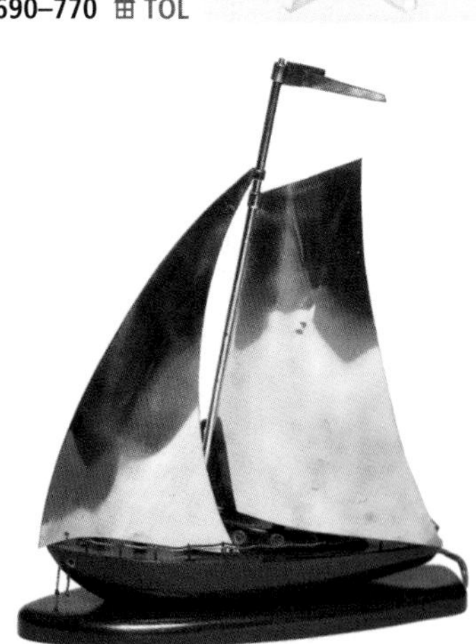

▶ **A mahogany and copper table lamp,** in the form of a boat, 1950s, 17in (43cm) high.

$110–125 ⊞ **OCA**

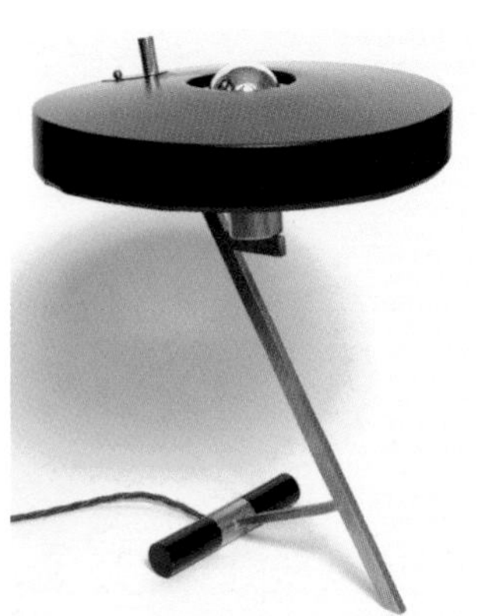

A pair of brass and enamelled table lamps, designed by Pierre Paulin for Philips, Holland, 1957, 16½in (42cm) high.

$1,250–1,450 ⊞ BOOM

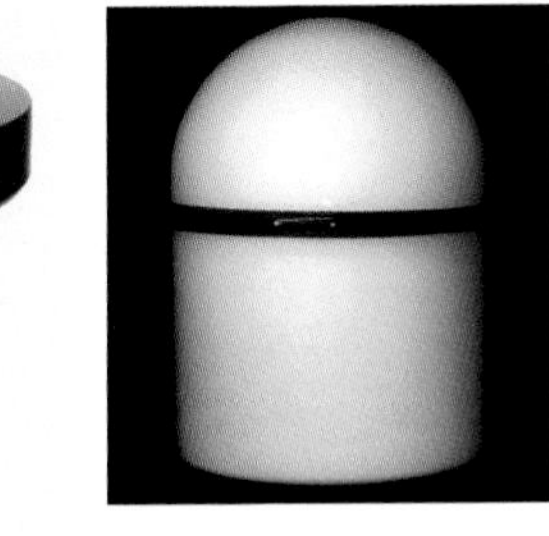

A pair of Murano glass table lamps, Italy, c1960, 12in (30.5cm) high.

$2,200–2,500 ⊞ CHAM

► A spun fibre and teak rocket table lamp, 1960s, 12in (30.5cm) high.

$65–75 ⊞ RETC

◄ A turned teak lamp base, 1960s, 18in (45.5cm) high.

$60–70 ⊞ OCA

◄ A Perspex lamp base, 1970s, 10in (25.5cm) high.

$85–100 ⊞ OCA

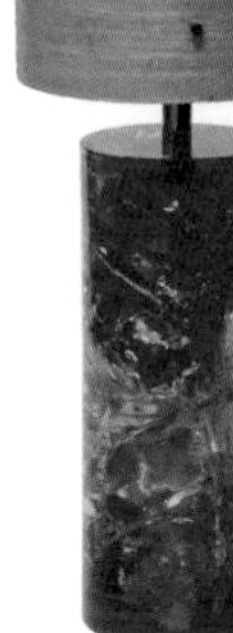

► A British Home Stores shatter line table lamp, with spun fibre glass shade, 1966–70, 18in (45.5cm) high.

$65–75 ⊞ RETC

A pair of carved teak table lamps, with hessian shades, America, c1960, 42in (106.5cm) high.

$1,800–2,050 ⊞ BOOM

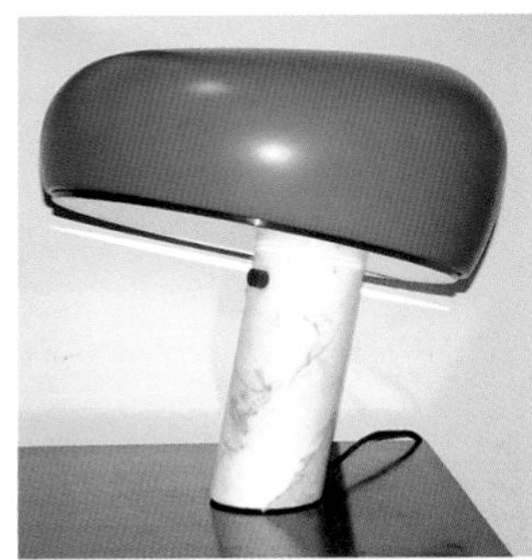

A Flos Snoopy table lamp, designed by Achille Castiglioni, Italy, 1967, 14in (35.5cm) high.

$1,150–1,250 ⊞ EMH

A pair of hand-blown Murano glass table lamps, Italy, c1970, 12in (30.5cm) high.

$600–680 ⊞ BOOM

Two Canedezi hand-blown glass table lamps, Italy, 1972, larger 10in (25.5cm) high.

$840–950 ⊞ BOOM

LUGGAGE

THOSE WHO COULD afford the luxury of travel on trains, cruise liners and motor vehicles in the early 20th century needed plenty of luggage and a bevy of servants to accompany them. Some aristocratic travellers would take as many as 40 cases, from wardrobes fitted with drawers, to hat and collar boxes. Cabin trunks made to slide under the berth became the norm for passengers on the Cunard and White Star liners. These early pieces of luggage are finely hand-crafted with polished leather, thick wear-resistant waterproof canvas and solid brass fittings.

As travel became more widely accessible luggage had to meet new criteria. Portability went with durability and cases shrunk in size to match smaller storage spaces. Finding leather suitcases from the post-war era is not difficult, but spotting quality pieces is harder. Serious collectors spend time looking at the overall patina of the leather – cracking is difficult and expensive to repair. Other hallmarks of quality are the fittings. The locks and hinges in well-made cases tend to be made from solid brass rather than pressed metal. A closer look at these will often reveal the maker, which should help with dating.

A Victorian leather hat box, by E. Goyard, France, Paris, 21in (53.5cm) wide.

$1,000–1,100 ⊞ MINN

Since 1853, La Maison Goyard has been making some of the finest luggage money can buy. The three chevrons, which cover the waterproof canvas and join to form the letter 'Y', are the firm's most obvious signature. They needed four successive applications by hand in ink before the design was complete. Goyard luggage was a favourite with the Rockefeller and Ritz families at the turn of the 20th century, and Arthur Conan Doyle, creator of Sherlock Holmes, even asked the firm to make his travel desk.

A tin hat box, c1900, 14in (35.5cm) wide.

$60–70 ⊞ JUN

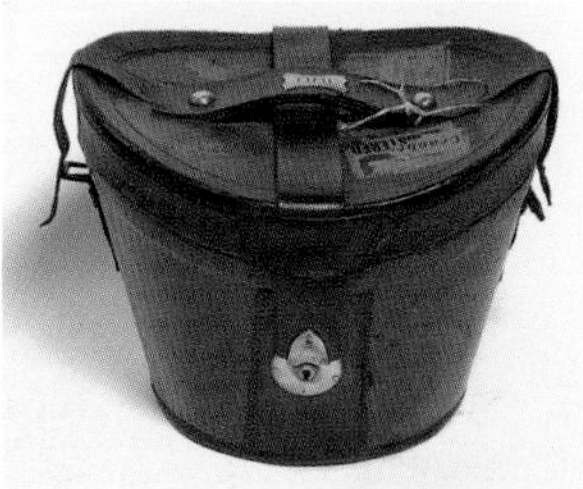

An Edwardian leather bucket hat box, 13½in (34.5cm) wide.

$210–240 ⊞ MINN

◀ **A canvas and leather hat box,** with brass fittings, c1910, 21in (53.5cm) wide.

$240–270 ⊞ PICA

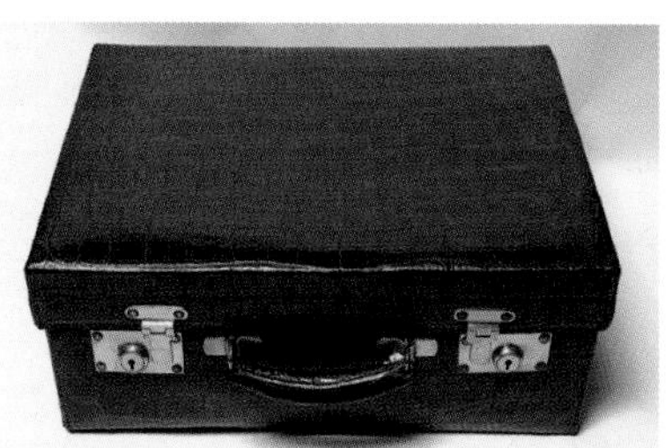

◀ **A crocodile-skin suitcase,** with brass fittings, c1910, 18in (45.5cm) wide.

$460–510 ⊞ MINN

▶ **A leather suitcase,** by John Pound, London, 1920, 18½in (47cm) wide.

$180–200 ⊞ MINN

A ribbed leather vanity case, with outer cover, 1920s, 14in (35.5cm) wide.

$95–110 ⊞ MINN

A tanned leather collar box, 1920s, 7in (18cm) diam.

$65–75 ⊞ MINN

A vacuum flask flask, with canvas and leather cover, 1930s, 14½in (37cm) high.

$30–40 ⊞ MINN

◀ **A leather writing case,** 1930s, 14in (35.5cm) wide.

$85–100 ⊞ MINN

A canvas, brass and leather case, by Louis Vuitton, 1930s, 18½in (47cm) wide.

$1,150–1,250 ⊞ MINN

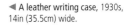

A leather attaché case, by Harrods, London, 1930s, 36in (91.5cm) wide.

$85–100 ⊞ MINN

◀ **A leather and canvas case,** 1930s, 18in (45.5cm) wide.

$85–100 ⊞ MINN

Two cowhide suitcases, 1950, larger 24in (61cm) wide.

$120–135 ⊞ ACAC

A leather document case, c1960, 32in (81.5cm) wide.
$95–110 ⊞ **HO**

A leather case, with leather corners and brass fittings, c1950, 24in (61cm) wide.
$75–95 ⊞ **HO**

▶ **A leather Keepall,** by Louis Vuitton, 1980s, 23½in (59.5cm) wide.
$690–830 **WAD**

BREXTON – A PICNIC DELIGHT

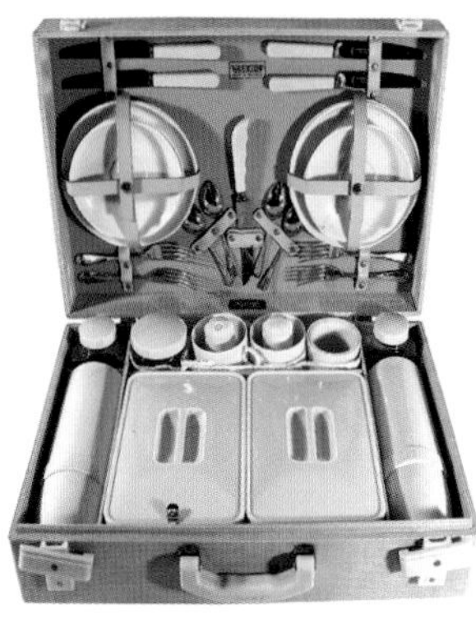

A drinks case, by Brexton, 1960s, 11in (28cm) wide.
$110–125 ⊞ **PPH**

◀ **A picnic case,** by Brexton, the fully fitted interior by Harrods, c1950, 16in (40.5cm) wide.
$85–100 **L&E**

A drinks case, by Brexton, late 1960s, 8in (20.5cm) wide.
$95–110 ⊞ **PPH**

- Picnic sets by the British firm Brexton were one of the most popular wedding gifts in the 1950s and 1960s. The company started life in the early days of motoring by making heavy leather trunks which were curved at the top to allow the rain to run off.
- In the 1920s Brexton began to produce wicker travelling hampers aimed specifically at first-time motorists who wanted to picnic. Many of these early designs were patented to ward off competition.
- Diversification saw Brexton make drinks cases like these and even car door trays.
- Everything is meticulously marked Brexton from the Bandalasta sandwich boxes to the cups and saucers made for them by Barker Bros.
- Value lies in a set being complete and original. Small items like the interlocking salt and pepper pot are sometimes lost, and often the vacuum flasks have been replaced.

MILITARY & NAVAL

BADGES

A Victorian Border Regiment 1st Volunteer Battalion helmet plate, with Guelphic crown.

$250–310 PFK

An Eton Volunteer Rifle Corps white metal badge, 1881–1908.

$145–160 PASM

A Gloucestershire Regiment helmet plate centre, 1900–14.

$50–60 PASM

◄ A Tank Corps other ranks' brass cap badge, 1914–18.

$25–30 PASM

► A Duke of Cornwall Light Infantry officer's silver-plated cap badge, c1914.

$25–30 PASM

A Norfolk Regiment other ranks' cap badge, c1914.

$15–25 PASM

A Comrades of the Great War brass and enamel lapel badge, c1920.

$25–30 OIA

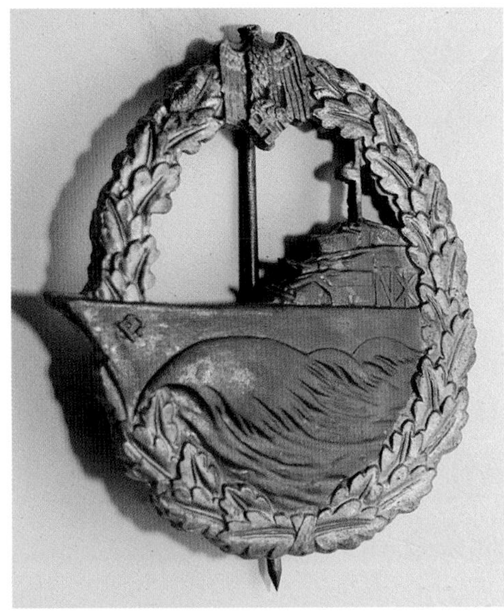

A Nazi Destroyer service badge, Germany, c1940.

$170–200 PASM

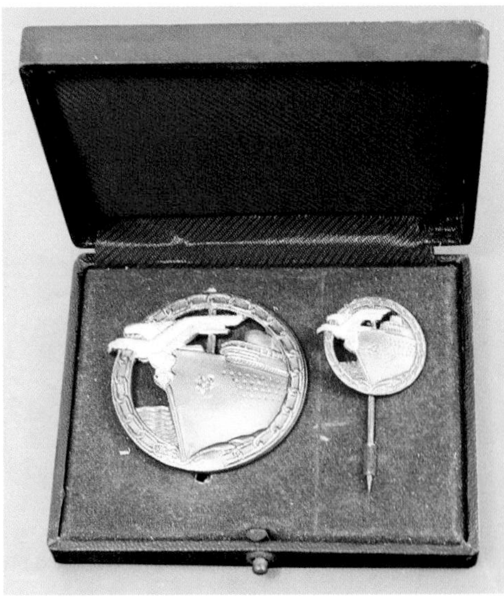

A white metal Nazi Blockade Breaker badge and lapel pin, each with a burnished eagle, Germany, 1941–45.

$480–570 G(L)

An Artillery Regiment brass cap badge, Italy, c1940.

$15–25 PASM

An Alpine Artillery other ranks' brass helmet badge, Italy, c1940.

$40–50 PASM

A Colonial Fascist Militia brass cap badge, Italy, c1940.

$40–50 PASM

A Home Guard cloth badge, 1940s.

$40–50 KA

CAPS & HELMETS

A US Navy cap, marked 'Jack Harrison', 1939–45.

$40–50 ⊞ MYS

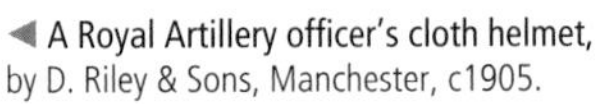

◀ **A Royal Artillery officer's cloth helmet,** by D. Riley & Sons, Manchester, c1905.

$630–690 ⊞ GMI

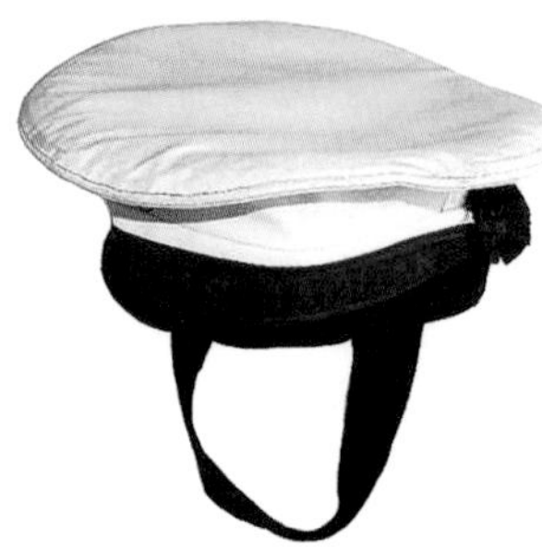

A Royal Navy cap, from HMS *Jaguar*, 1939–45.

$25–30 ⊞ MYS

HMS Jaguar *was sunk during WWII by a German U-boat in 1942.*

A steel M35 German helmet, with Norwegian Army decals, c1944.

$210–240 ⊞ Tus

A Royal Fusiliers officer's bearskin helmet, pre-1950.

$1,050–1,200 ⊞ Q&C

A Welsh Guards other ranks' bearskin helmet, c1950.

$580–650 ⊞ Q&C

A 7th Gurkhas Rifles pillbox cap, 1952–94.

$60–70 ⊞ Q&C

A USS *Enterprise* cap, 1970s.

$15–25 ⊞ COB

A French Foreign Legion kepi, c1990.

$40–50 ⊞ Q&C

MEDALS & PLAQUES

◀ **A group of four medals,** awarded to Private J. Sullivan, Grenadier Guards; Queen's South Africa 1901 with six bars; King's South Africa 1902 with two bars; Victory Medal; British War Medal.

$390–490 Mal(O)

A pair of silver medals, awarded to Private H. McKenzie, BlackWatch; Queen's South Africa 1901 with two bars; King's South Africa 1902 with two bars.

$390–470 BuA

A group of five medals, awarded to Stoker J. P. Welch of HMS *Swiftsure,* 1914–15 Star, British War Medal, Victory Medal, Naval General Service Medal with one bar and Royal Naval Long Service and Good Conduct Medal, 1914–15.

$740–830 Q&C

HMS Swiftsure *was the lead ship of the Swiftsure class battleships built c1871. It was the last battleship to spread sail while travelling in company with a fleet in 1893.*

A King's Royal Rifle Corps 9ct gold fob medal, 1914–18.

$120–135 FOF

An Iron Cross, 2nd Class, Germany, 1914–18.

$50–65 Q&C

A group of three medals, awarded to Private William Hogsflesh, Middlesex Regiment; Military Medal and British War and Victory Medals, with two discharge certificates, 1914–18.

$720–860 DN

The Military Medal is listed in the London Gazette *of 12 March 1918 for bravery in the field.*

▶ **A pair of medals,** Victory medal and Medal of the Revolution, Czechoslovakia, 1914–18.

$120–135 Q&C

A group of five medals, awarded to Sergeant Samuel Brock, Royal Irish Rifles; Military Medal first type Aug/Nov star; War Medal; Victory and Elizabeth II Medals; Imperial Service Medal, 1914–18.

$1,550–1,750 G(L)

► **A pair of medals,** British War Medal and Victory Medal, from the Army Veterinary Corps, 1914–18.

$50–65 Q&C

A group of three medals, awarded to Private H. Gayton, Royal Army Medical Corps; Star War Medal 1914–15; British War Medal; Victory Medal.

$95–110 Q&C

A pair of medals, Victory Medal and World War Service Medal, issued by the State of Oregon, America, 1917–19.

$155–170 Q&C

A bronze death plaque, 1920.

$105–120 Tus

During WWI, all next-of-kin of service personnel who lost their lives during the conflict were presented with a memorial scroll and a bronze memorial plaque. The plaque was designed by Edward Carter Preston, who won a competition with 800 entries. Names, but no ranks, were included on the plaque in order to show equality in death. Troops nicknamed the plaque 'the Dead Man's Penny'. A tragic 1,350,000 plaques were made for men, but only 600 for women. A Dead Woman's Penny could be worth as much as $3,450.

A group of five medals, awarded to Flight Sergeant W. T. Briggs, Royal Air Force; 1939–45 and Africa Stars; Defence and War Medal with M.I.D. emblem; Royal Air Force Long Service and Good Conduct Medal; George VI.

$190–220 DN

A group of four medals, awarded to Sergeant Gurang, 2nd Gurkha Rifles; War Medal 1939–45; General Service Medal with Malaya clasp (Geo VI); Army Long Service and Good Conduct Medal; India Independence Medal.

$600–690 Q&C

A Nazi Iron Cross, 2nd class, Germany, 1939.

$95–110 PASM

► **A War Merit cross,** Germany, 1939.

$40–50 SOR

A pair of medals, Korea Medal; United Nations Korea Medal,1950–53.

$260–300 ⊞ Q&C

An Imperial Service Medal, post-1955, in a fitted case.

$25–30 ⊞ Q&C

A General Service Medal, with two bars: Malay Peninsula and Borneo, 1962.

$155–170 ⊞ ABCM

► **A Kuwati Liberation Medal,** 1991, with fitted case.

$15–25 ⊞ Q&C

A US Army Bronze Star group for Korea, 1950–53.

$250–260 ⊞ Q&C

A group of three medals, awarded to Sergeant Sherwin, Royal Air Force; General Service Medal, Cyprus 1955–59; General Service Medal 1962, Malay Peninsula; Royal Air Force Long Service and Good Conduct Medal 1968.

$340–400 ⊞ Q&C

A pair of US Army Korean War medals, Korean War Service Medal and United Nations Korea Medal, 1950–53.

$120–145 ⊞ Q&C

A group of three American Legion National Convention delegate pins, Miami 1955, Los Angeles 1956 and Denver 1961, pin missing from Denver.

$10–15 ⊞ MYS

Founded in 1919, the American Legion consists of veterans who served in the US Armed Forces during WWI and WWII. The legion campaigns for veteran's rights, organizes commemorative events and is involved in American political issues.

◄ **A group of three medals,** awarded to W. Littler, REMI; Campaign Medal for Northern Ireland, UN Cyprus Medal and Medal for Long Service & Good Conduct, 1963–86.

$340–400 ⊞ Q&C

A NATO Service Medal, with Kosovo clasp, 1994, boxed.

$25–30 ⊞ Q&C

MILITARY EQUIPMENT & ACCESSORIES

A US Cavalry sabre, by the Ames Sword Company, dated 1906, blade 35in (89cm) long.

$480–550 ⊞ FAC

A George V infantry officer's 1897 pattern sword, 1910–36, 40in (101.5cm) long.

$430–480 ⊞ ARB

A Barker patent prismatic marching compass, with jewelled bearing, metal dial and patent oil-filled damping using vegetable oil, 1910, 2¼in (5.5cm) diam, with original leather case.

$250-300 ⊞ FOF

A US Army Signal Corps field telephone, 1914–18, in original canvas case.

$40–50 ⊞ MYS

A Verner's Pattern Mark VI prismatic marching compass, by Short & Mason, with jewelled bearing, transit and temporary lock, dial with mother-of-pearl chapter ring, dated 1910, 2¼in (5.5cm) diam, with original leather case.

$250–270 ⊞ FOF

◀ **A telescope,** by Siemens Brothers & Co, No. 2551, with four-drawer brass and leather-bound barrel, Germany, 1914–18, 35in (89cm) extended, on a wooden tripod, with hide case.

$430–510 ⚒ L&E

A George V army officer's 1821 pattern sword, c1914, 40in (101.5cm) long.

$650–750 ⊞ ARB

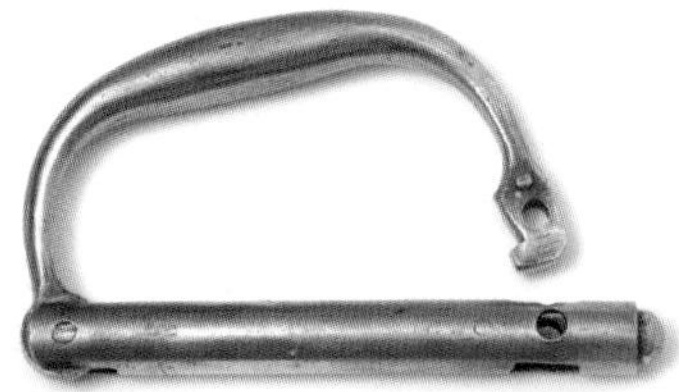

A brass self-fastening kit bag lock, 1914–18, 5in (12.5cm) wide.

$40–50 ⊞ FST

A brass trench periscope, by R. J. Beck, No. 13687, model IX, with wooden handle, dated 1917, 23in (58.5cm) long.

$510–570 ⊞ HOM

A Royal Worcester figure of a WWI soldier, shape No. 2646, marked, date code for 1917, 5½in (14cm) high.

$600–720 BAM

A steel officer's trench periscope, 1918, 26½in (67.5cm) long, with leather case.

$250–270 Tus

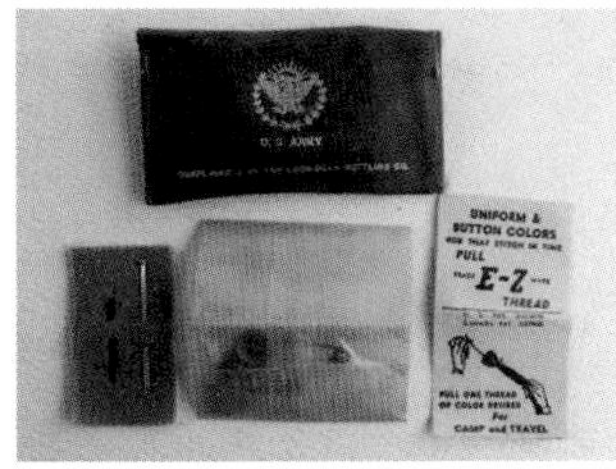

A US Army sewing kit, 1939–45.

$25–30 MYS

This complimentary sewing kit was given out by the Coca-Cola Bottling Co.

A Grimwades Bruce Bairnsfather wall plate, the centre printed with a cartoon by Bruce Bairnsfather, 'What time do they feed the sea-lions, Alf?', printed mark, inscribed, 'Made by the girls of Staffordshire during the winter of 1917 when the boys were in the trenches fighting for liberty and civilisation', 10in (25.5cm) diam.

$50–60 DN

◀ **A Waltham paratrooper's wrist compass,** R88-C-890, 1939–44, dial 1in (2.5cm) diam.

$145–160 FOF

A steel blackout coal shovel, 1942, 18½in (47cm) long.

$40–50 Tus

▶ **A chrome desk set,** 1940, 9½in (24cm) wide.

$75–85 Tus

This is a one-off Home Guard presentation piece.

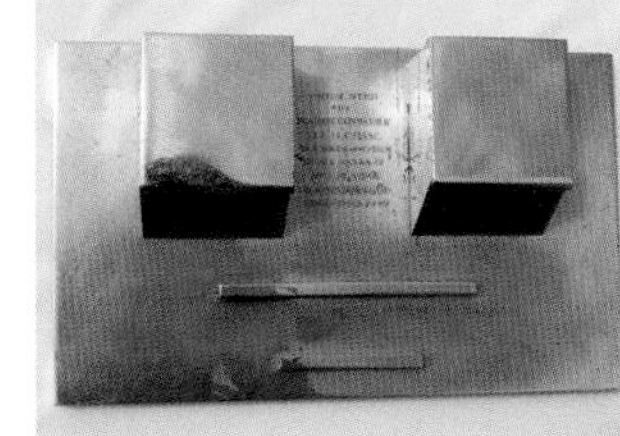

A linen table napkin and a knife and fork, made for Adolf Hitler, knife marked 'rostfrei' and stamped 'A.H.' beneath the Nazi eagle carrying a swastika, c1945, napkin 10in (25.5cm) square.

$9,300–10,300 FRa

These items were among a number of personal possessions recovered by an American GI from Hitler's underground bunker at the time of the defeat of Nazi Germany.

◀ **An East German Army leather belt,** with white-metal buckle, c1970, 2in (5cm) wide.

$25–30 PASM

NAVAL EQUIPMENT & MISCELLANEOUS

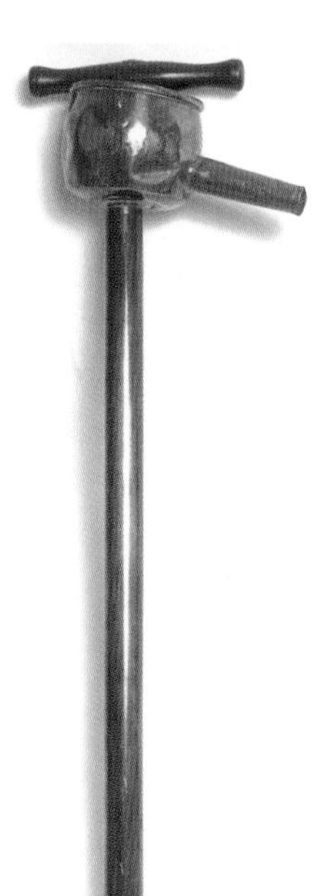

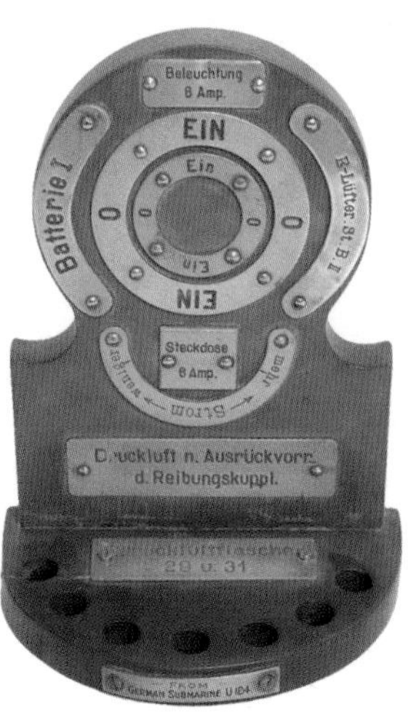

A pipe rack, constructed from engine plates taken from German U-boat U124, 1914–18, 10in (25.5cm) high.

$290–320 ⊞ OLD

◀ **A Royal Navy copper-barrelled rum pump,** c1900, 41in (104cm) long.

$290–320 ⊞ OLD

A chrome-on-brass model torpedo, 1914–18, 10in (25.5cm) long, on a slate base.

$190–210 ⊞ OLD

A Royal Navy mahogany sweetheart trinket box, with King's crown and naval motif, 1914.

$220–250 ⊞ OLD

A painted glass plaque, commemorating the loss of SS *Braemer Castle*, 1916, 7in (18cm) square.

$105–120 ⊞ CGA

The Union Castle Line Braemer Castle *was lost while serving as a hospital ship.*

◀ **A brass ashtray,** from HMS *Vendetta*, with crest, 1920s, 6in (15cm) diam.

$65–75 ⊞ OLD

In 1920, HMS Vendetta *played an important part in escorting the vessel carrying the coffin of The Unknown Warrior, which was interred at Westminster Abbey. She was sold for scrap in 1947.*

▶ **Two silver-plated and enamel napkin rings,** from the Royal Navy light cruiser HMS *Neptune*, 1933–41, 2in (5cm) wide.

$30–40 ⊞ CGA

HMS Neptune *was sunk by enemy mines in 1941.*

An Australian Merchant Navy felt flag, 1940s, 26in (66cm) wide.

$30–40 COB

A torpedo sight, dated 1940, 20in (51cm) long.

$380–440 ET

◀ **A Bofors Guns and Wheelhouse copper, brass and aluminium speaking tube and pipe,** c1940, 19in (48.5cm) long.

$110–125 OLD

A Kriegsmarine chrome-on-brass and leather spirit flask, with Kriegsmarine motif, Germany, 1914–18, 6in (15cm) high.

$290–320 OLD

A pair of German Naval or U-boat binoculars, by Zeiss, Germany, 1942, 6in (15cm) long.

$1,200–1,350 OLD

A silver-plated bowl and tray, with US Navy engraving, c1942, bowl 8in (20.5cm) diam.

$145–160 OLD

A US Navy military wool blanket, marked 'USN Medical', 1940s, 46 x 70in (117 x 178cm).

$40–50 MYS

A brass rolling rule, from SS *President Coolidge*, 1942, 18in (45.5cm) long.

$210–240 CGA

The US merchant ship SS President Coolidge *was sunk by friendly mines in 1942, while serving as a troop ship.*

A silk pillow, commemorating the Japanese attack on Pearl Harbour, 1940s, 11¾in (30cm) square.

$40–50 ⊞ MYS

A Kriegsmarine brass ship's clock, No. 9886N, with eagle and marine stamp, c1943, 8in (20.5cm) diam.

$1,800–2,050 ⊞ OLD

Clocks such as this were carried on U-boats.

A Kriegsmarine anemometer, c1944, 9in (23cm) long, in original deck box.

$530–600 ⊞ OLD

This would have been used on a ship or U-boat to measure wind strength.

A brass U-boat souvenir compass holder, with compass, No. U4120, 1944, 2½in (6.5cm) diam.

$250–280 ⊞ Tus

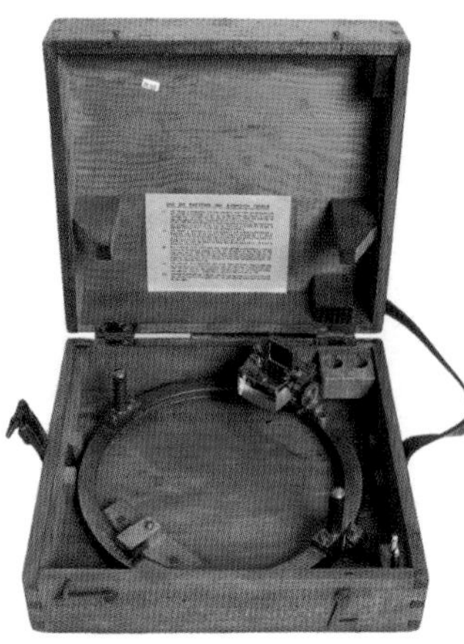

▶ **A Royal Navy brass azimuth circle,** c1944, 12in (30.5cm) diam.

$95–110 ⊞ OLD

This instrument would have been used to take bearings from the bridge.

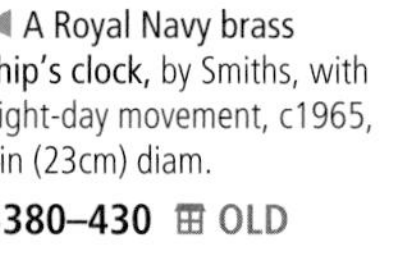

◀ **A Royal Navy brass ship's clock,** by Smiths, with eight-day movement, c1965, 9in (23cm) diam.

$380–430 ⊞ OLD

▶ **A Russian Navy communist leather belt,** with brass buckle, c1970, 2in (5cm) wide.

$15–25 ⊞ PASM

A US Naval Academy coffee mug, mid-1980s, 4in (10cm) high.

$25–30 ⊞ CWO

Commonly referred to as 'the Academy', 'the Fund' or 'the Boat School', the United States Naval Academy has trained officers of the US Navy and Marine Corps since 1845.

PUBLICATIONS

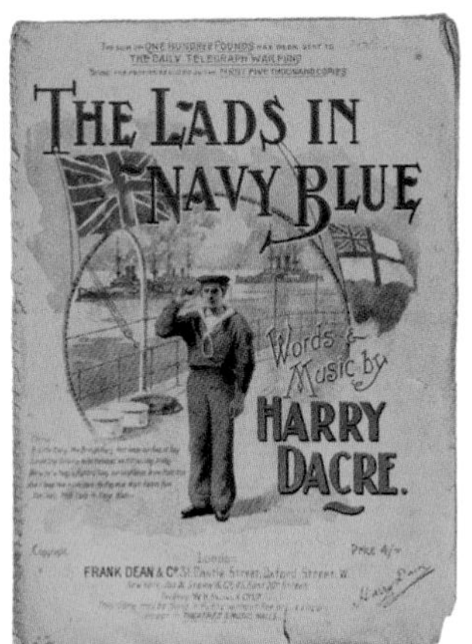

A song sheet, 'The Lads in Navy Blue', published by Frank Dean & Co, 1890s, 14in (35.5cm) high.

$10–15 ⊞ **COB**

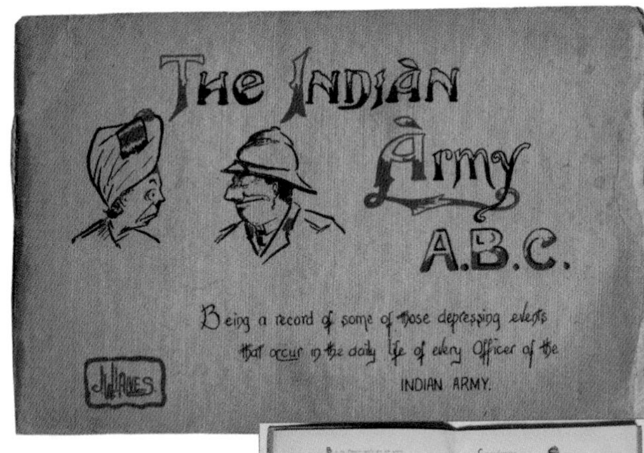

The Indian Army A. B. C., a military humour booklet, 1910, 7in (18cm) wide.

$10–15 ⊞ **J&S**

◀ *Daily Sketch*, reporting on the price of war, September 1914, 15in (38cm) high.

$10–15 ⊞ **J&S**

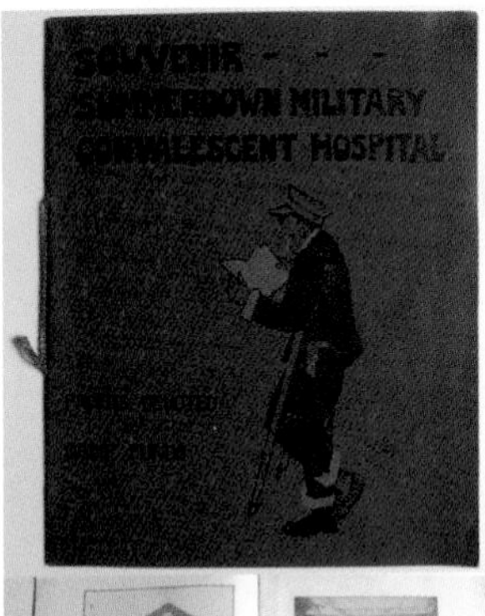

Souvenir...Summerdown Military Convalescent Hospital, a fundraising magazine, 1914–18, 12in (30.5cm) high.

$15–25 ⊞ **J&S**

Daily Mail Bird's-Eye Map of The Front, Section 2, 1914–18, 12in (30.5cm) high.

$30–40 ⊞ **J&S**

◀ An Official Guide and Souvenir to Portsmouth Navy Week, 10in (25.5cm) high.

$25–30 ⊞ **COB**

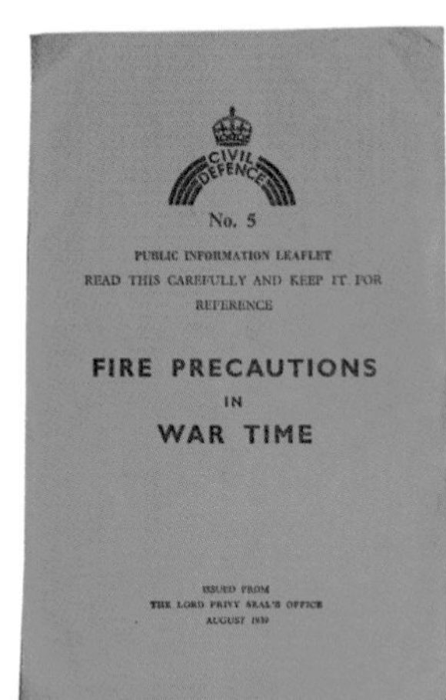

◀ *Fire Precautions in War Time*, a public information leaflet, No. 5, issued by the Lord Privy Seal's Office, 1939, 9in (23cm) high.

$10–15 ⊞ J&S

A set of three *Newsmap* industrial editions, published by the War Department, 1939–45.

$40–50 ⊞ MYS

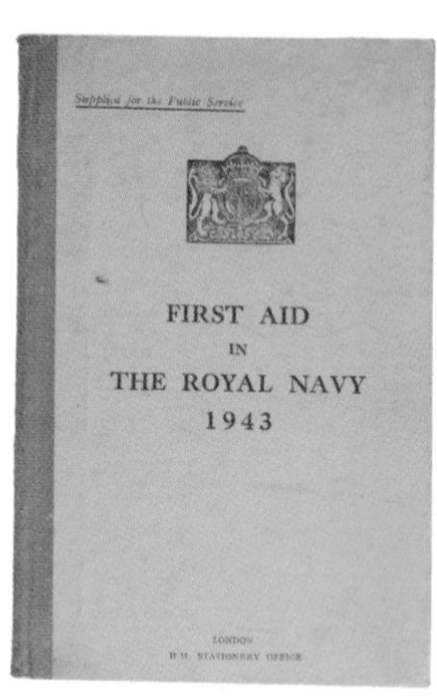

First Aid in The Royal Navy 1943, published by HMSO, 7in (18cm) high.

$10–15 ⊞ J&S

Daily Mail

5,000 PLANES SMASH REICH NON-STOP

German Blows Fail at Stanislavov

NIGHT HAWKS WIPE OUT 4 JUNCTIONS

Daily Mail, 20 April 1944, 24 x 18in (61 x 45.5cm).

$10–15 ⊞ J&S

Daily Mail

'THIS IS YOUR VICTORY'

Princesses mix with crowd: PM leads songs

And this is VE-Day for the Russians

Thanksgiving

Daily Mail, 9 May 1945, 24 x 18in (61 x 45.5cm).

$10–15 ⊞ COB

A set of four US Navy training books, 1945–52.

$40–50 ⊞ MYS

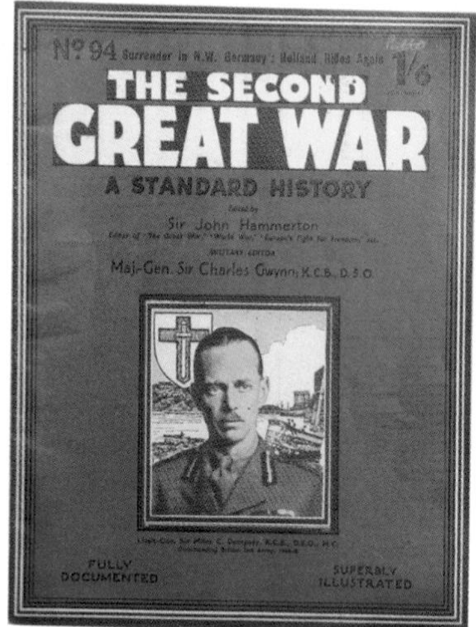

◀ *The Second Great War A Standard History*, No. 94, edited by Sir John Hammerton, 1946, 11 x 9in (28 x 23cm).

$5–10 ⊞ HOM

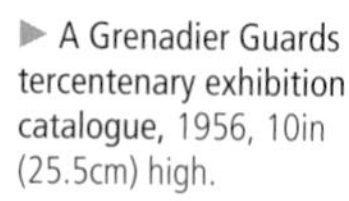

▶ A Grenadier Guards tercentenary exhibition catalogue, 1956, 10in (25.5cm) high.

$15–25 ⊞ J&S

MODERN TECHNOLOGY

DID YOU KNOW the old calculator in your loft is worth money? Do you remember life before the home computer? The technology of the last 30 years is rapidly becoming collectable and will be tomorrow's antiques. Today the world moves fast and it is increasingly difficult to spot what is collectable now and what will be in the future. Five years ago Sinclair and other old home computers were very hot but today the market is less liquid, probably because of internet trading. However, the old factors of quality and exclusivity apply as much to technology collectables as they do antique furniture. Technology items that have designer heritage or are of historical importance have grown in value and will continue to do so.

Look for items like the Sinclair Executive calculator. It is scarce because it was very expensive when new, it is a first because it was the smallest calculator of its time and is of great interest to collectors of modern design. Other sought-after items include LED watches (the ones with a red digital display) from the best manufacturers such as Omega or Pulsar. These are commanding ever-increasing prices because of their rarity and the fact that they are still useable today. Quality and function are vital – make sure you buy the best you can afford and acquire examples with the original box and paperwork. Avoid broken or damaged examples even if the price is tempting.

Pepe Tozzo

CALCULATORS

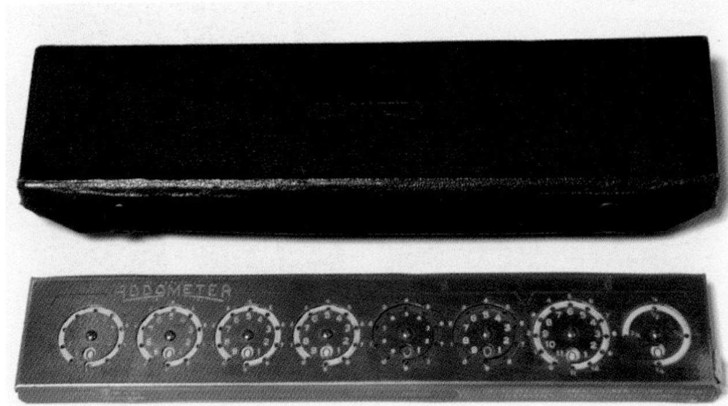

A Reliable Typewriter and Adding Machine Co brass Addometer, with stylus, marked 'Taylor's', America, Illinois, c1920, 12in (30.5cm) long.

$95–110 FST

Various versions of the American-made Addometer exist. As well as a decimal model, denoted by two white wheels at the end for cents, there was a model for working in feet and inches. This example was made for use in countries with sterling currency. The four white dials on the left are for pounds, the two red dials for shillings, the second dial from the right for pennies and the last for farthings. Users operated it with a stylus that was placed in the appropriate holes of the dial. In the UK they were distributed by Taylor's, London.

A tinplate Jacko The Calculating Monkey, patent No. 17778, c1916, 6 x 5½in (15 x 14cm).

$135–155 ROS

This patented metal teaching toy was used for additions, subtractions, multiplication and division. The monkey's feet point to the numbers to be multiplied and the hands point to the result. A version of this device was sold in the US by the Educational Manufacturing Co under the brand name of 'Consul The Educated Monkey'.

An Otis King calculator, by Carbic Ltd, 1930, with instructions and case, 6in (15cm) long.

$270–300 ⊞ WAC

▶ **A brass Bri-Cal British Calculator,** patented by H. & N. D. Dickinson, in original leatherette case, c1950, 6in (15cm) square.

$200–230 ⊞ WAC

A Sinclair Executive calculator, 1972.

$330–380 ⊞ PEPE

The Sinclair Executive is classed as the first truly pocket-sized calculator . It was exhibited at the Museum of Modern Art in New York. The display used a Light Emitting Diode array which was bright but needed a lot of power and this led to a technical problem of a short battery life. The Executive is probably the scarcest of the Sinclair calculators and market prices reflect this.

A Sinclair Executive Memory calculator, 1973.

$310–350 ⊞ PEPE

◀ **A Sharp LC EL-805 calculator,** c1973.

$120–140 ⊞ PEPE

This is a very scarce example of one of the first liquid crystal calculators. These early models had lids to protect the light-sensitive liquid crystal from damaging UV. The display on these early machines showed the digits in light relief against a dark background. Nowadays the reverse is the case on most LCD displays.

SINCLAIR CAMBRIDGE RANGE

A Sinclair Cambridge Memory calculator, 1974.

$85–100 ⊞ PEPE

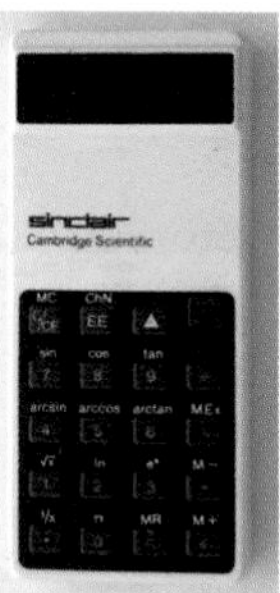

A Sinclair Cambridge Scientific calculator, 1975.

$100–120 ⊞ PEPE

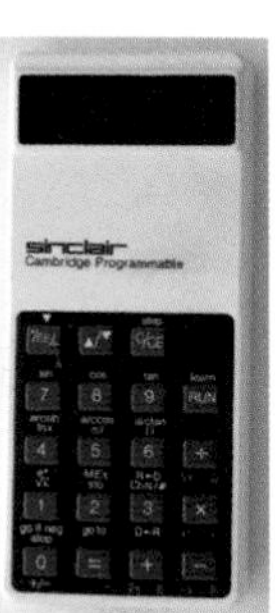

A Sinclair Cambridge Programmable calculator, 1975.

$100–120 ⊞ PEPE

A Sinclair Cambridge % calculator, with percentage key, 1974.

$85–100 ⊞ PEPE

A Sinclair Cambridge Memory calculator, with 9v battery and 'pregnant' back, 1974.

$100–120 ⊞ PEPE

A Sinclair Cambridge calculator, with brown case and red display, 1974.

$100–120 ⊞ PEPE

- Clive Sinclair developed the Cambridge range of calculators in 1973 in response to the success of the Executive model.
- The Sinclair Cambridge was thicker, smaller and heavier than the Executive.
- It was sold in a kit form that took three hours to assemble.
- More models were added in following years which included different colours and Scientific and Programmable versions.

A Commodore 899 calculator, 1975.

$20–25 ⊞ **PEPE**

▶ A Sharp EL-120 calculator, c1975.

$45–50 ⊞ **PEPE**

Note the unusual format of this calculator with the keypad at the side of the fluorescent display.

A Sinclair Sovereign calculator, 1977.

$470–520 ⊞ **PEPE**

Possibly the most beautiful calculator ever made, the Sinclair Sovereign was inspired by the Queen's Silver Jubilee in 1977. The high-quality instrument was housed in a metal case and had an LED display. Many versions were made including a silver-plated one with an engraved crest and chrome, black and gold-plated examples. There were even rumours that some were made in solid gold.

A Casio FX-31 calculator, 1976.

$10–15 ⊞ **PEPE**

The high quality of the range of Casio FX calculators means that, while many examples are around today, values are buoyant because of an enthusiastic following of collectors.

A Sinclair Enterprise calculator, 1978.

$120–140 ⊞ **PEPE**

A programmable version of the Sinclair Enterprise was also available but it could not compete with Japanese LCD calculators. Despite its compact design the battery was hard to change and required the removal of the top of the case.

A Sinclair President calculator, 1977.

$150–170 ⊞ **PEPE**

The Sinclair President was manufactured in Hong Kong and had a power-zapping fluorescent display and poor-quality case. Sales were not good, which has resulted in them being rare today. Some examples have been seen bearing corporate logos, suggesting that they were given away as marketing gifts.

A Harvard Teaching Computer calculator, 1978

$10–15 ⊞ **PEPE**

This was a direct competitor to the Texas Instruments Little Professor which was also aimed at children.

A Texas Instruments TI-30 LCD calculator, c1978.

$10–15 ⊞ **PEPE**

▶ A Texas Instruments Little Professor calculator, 1978.

$20–25 ⊞ **PEPE**

COMPUTER GAMES

An Atari 2600 Video Computer System, 1977.
$120–140 ⊞ ASP

The Atari 2600 was a cartridge-based video game machine for use on a home television. It came with two joysticks and a pair of paddles that were used with tennis games. Nine games were developed by Atari during the first year but they soon allowed other developers to create more games for the console. The original wood-effect console is more sought after by collectors than the later silver version.

◄ An MB Milton electronic game, 1980.
$30–35 ⊞ PEPE

The Milton game involves players trying to complete phrases by listening to one half of a sentence and finding the other half by pressing the correct button.

MILLER'S COMPARES

(L) A Sinclair ZX81, 1980.
$75–85 ⊞ PEPE

(R) A Sinclair ZX80, 1980.
$620–690 ⊞ PEPE

The item on the right, a Sinclair ZX80 home computer, was viewed on a television screen and was very successful in both kit form and fully assembled. Only 70,000 were made, making it a rare machine, and mint boxed examples trade for large sums. The item on the left, a Sinclair ZX81, was made in far greater numbers and being more easily found, it attracts much lower values.

A Milton Bradley Simon game, 1978.
$75–85 ⊞ PEPE

The Simon game was a very simple idea that proved popular. Four buttons lit up in a sequence and played a tone; the player had to memorize the sequence and repeat it. As the sequence became longer the game sped up. Milton Bradley also made a pocket version but it is the full-sized original that collectors want most and boxed examples command the highest prices.

A Grandstand Astro Wars game, 1981.
$50–60 ⊞ PEPE

Astro Wars was a Space Invaders-style game on a fluorescent screen. The unusual round screen had a magnifying lens which gave a big-screen feel. It is often found on the collectors market today.

A pair of Nintendo Game & Watch Multi Screen hand-held games, Pinball and Black Jack, 1983.
$100–120 ⊞ PEPE

A Tomytronic Shark Attack 3-D game, 1983.

$40–45 ⊞ **PEPE**

A Namco Pac-Land hand-held game, 1984, with box.

$20–25 ⊞ **PEPE**

◀ A Sega Mega Drive II, 1989.

$40–45 ⊞ **PEPE**

The Sega Mega Drive, also known as Genesis, was the first 16-bit console to be launched in America. It could be attached to a CD drive and had the added boost of Disney-manufactured games.

A Super Nintendo Entertainment System, 1989.

$50–60 ⊞ **PEPE**

A Nintendo Game Boy, 1989.

$20–25 ⊞ **PEPE**

This small machine, with its monochrome LCD screen and cartridge games, was a very successful hand-held game that sold in millions. It is easy to find examples today that are still playable and it would be a worthwhile addition to a technology collection.

◀ A Sega Game Gear portable video game, 1992.

$60–70 ⊞ **PEPE**

▶ A Bandai Tamagotch virtual pet, Japan, 1996.

$20–25 ⊞ **PEPE**

The Tamagotchi phenomena, started by the Japanese toy manufacturer Bandai, swept the globe during the 1990s and other manufacturers copied the format. The game required an owner to feed, play with, teach and nurse a tiny electronic pet which grew bigger the longer it was kept alive. Many versions have been produced and new models are on the market today which can interact with others. The first Japanese version was called 'Tamagotch' but the name was soon changed to 'Tamagotchi'.

HAND-HELD DEVICES

A US Robotics Palm Pilot Personal, America, 1996.

$45–50 ⊞ PEPE

An Amstrad Pen Pad, 1993.

$10–15 ⊞ PEPE

This was one of the first personal digital assistants (PDAs) to offer handwriting recognition.

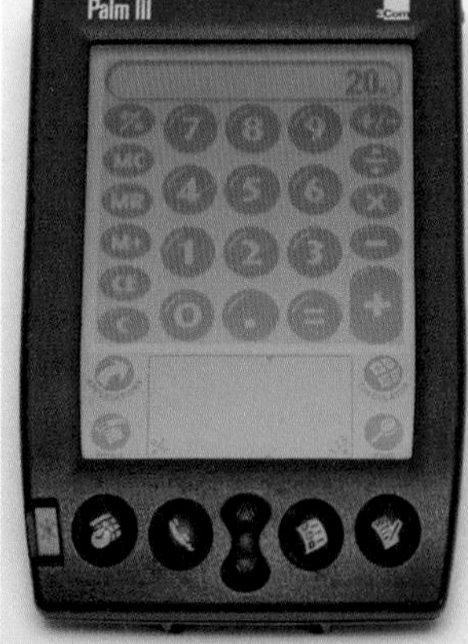

A 3Com Palm III, c1997.

$30–35 ⊞ PEPE

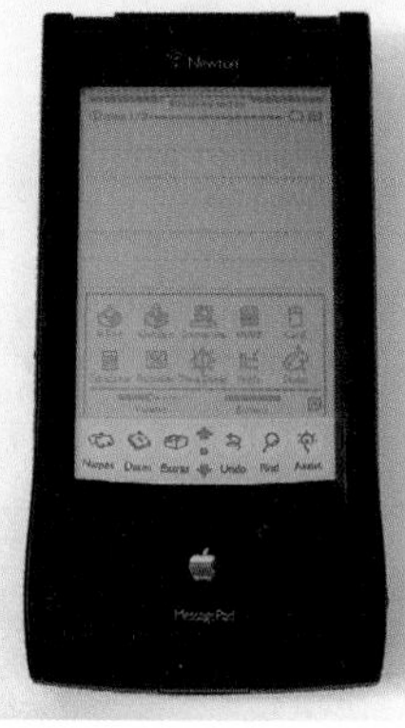

An Apple Message Pad, 1993–98.

$230–260 ⊞ PEPE

The Message Pad was born in 1993 and Apple's John Sculley coined the term personal digital assistant to describe it. However, it was ahead of its time and suffered from bugs and problems with reliability. The large screen, easy expansion and wireless capability were popular with users

An Agenda organizer, c1988.

$60–70 ⊞ PEPE

The most striking feature of the Agenda is its microwriter keyboard. The microwriter is a descendent of the first chord keyboards, pioneered by Doug Engelbart, inventor of the mouse. The Agenda enjoyed extended battery life, and when new could last weeks on a single charge.

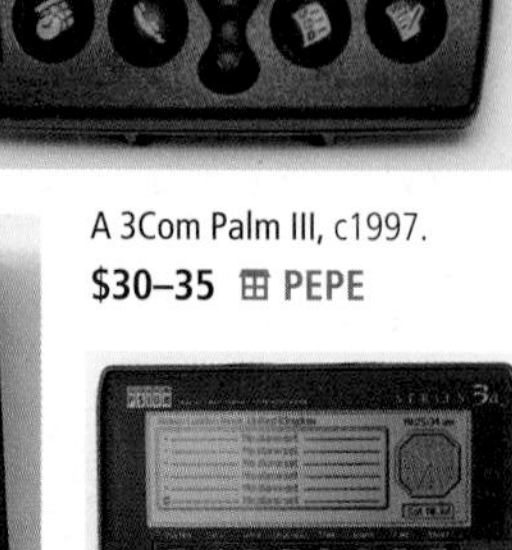

A Psion 3a, 1991.

$195–220 ⊞ PEPE

► A Voice Powered Technology Voice Organizer, America, 1993.

$30–35 ⊞ PEPE

The Voice Organizer featured a 512K memory, date clock, appointment book, telephone directory, time reminder, voice recorder and recognition.

A Cybiko organizer and game, 2000.

$30–35 ⊞ PEPE

The Cybiko was a hand-held wireless computer. Aimed at teenagers, it allowed them to send and receive emails and chat to other Cybiko users. It was also a personal organizer.

A Philips Pocket Memo Mini 596, 2003.

$10–15 ⊞ PEPE

HI-FI

A Pye black box record player, with four-watt push-pull audio amplifier, in a walnut case with twin speakers mounted on end panels, 1957, 17in (43cm) wide.

$75–85 ⊞ **GM**

A Ferguson reel-to-reel tape deck, 1960s.

$40–45 ⊞ **PEPE**

A Panasonic RQ-210S portable compact cassette recorder, RQ-210S, Japan, 1968.

$20–25 ⊞ **PEPE**

◄ A Garrard/Sinclair record deck, 1969.

$230–260 ⊞ **PEPE**

A Sony portable stereo cassette system, 1968.

$60–70 ⊞ **PEPE**

A JVC tape deck, Japan, c1974.

$75–85 ⊞ **PEPE**

The top-loading cassette player was popular during the 1970s.

A Sony Walkman Professional cassette recorder, Japan, 1983, 7in (18cm) wide, with original box.

$75–85 ⊞ **IQ**

◄ A Philips plastic 603 portable battery and mains record player, c1970.

$180–200 ⊞ **TWI**

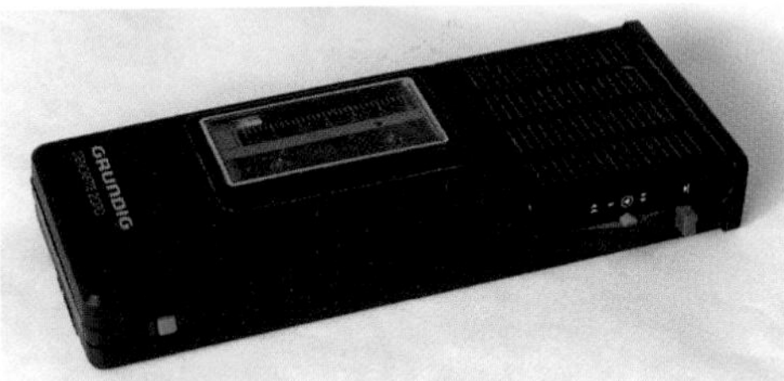

A Grundig Stenorette 2070, Germany, 1989.

$20–25 ⊞ **PEPE**

A Marantz PMD430 cassette recorder, Japan, 1994.

$120–140 ⊞ **PEPE**

RADIOS

◄ **A Stewart-Warner R452S radio,** in a Bakelite case, 1930s, 13in (33cm) high.

$95–110 WAD

In 1912, the Stewart-Warner Instrument Co was founded in Chicago, USA. The factory manufactured instruments, hourmeters and senders for the automotive industry and also produced radios and refrigerators. Now under the name of Maxima Technologies, it is a global supplier of vehicle instrumentation and control systems.

A GEC Wartime Civilian Receiver, 1940s, 14in (35.5cm) high.

$135–155 DECO

The Wartime Civilian Receiver was popularly known as the 'Utility' set. Due to the importance of the public being informed of the latest news, the RMA came up with a standardized government approved design that avoided competition and enabled parts to be reused across the board. They were produced with a label that stated 'In the interests of wartime economy, switch off when not in use'. Makers included Marconi, Murphy and the General Electric Co.

► **A Bush DAC10 radio,** in a Bakelite case, three presets, restored, 1950s, 13in (33cm) wide.

$170–200 DECO

ROBERTS RADIO

A Roberts Radio P4D radio, in a Rexine-covered plywood case, 1949, 11in (28cm) high.

$75–85 OTA

A Roberts Radio R55 Valve portable radio, 1955, 9in (23cm) wide, with case.

$75–85 OTA

A Roberts Radio R66 Valve portable radio, 1956, 10in (25.5cm) wide.

$60–70 GM

- In 1932 Harry Roberts and Leslie Bidmead founded the Roberts Radio Co in London.
- By 1935 the company was producing an average of eight radios a week. These were of the 'suitcase' design with a loudspeaker and frame arial in the lid.
- In 1937 Roberts Radio introduced the M4Q – similar to the P4D shown above – a design that took up less table space than the 'suitcase' model.
- In 1941 the company moved to East Molesey, Surrey due to the wartime bombing raids on London.
- In 1955 the company was granted a Royal Warrant, with two more being granted in 1982 and 1985.
- Now based in Mexborough, South Yorkshire, the Roberts range has been expanded to include high-quality short-wave radios, pocket radios, radio/CD players and digital radios.

An Ekco A147 Festival radio, in a walnut-veneered case, restored, 1951, 17in (43cm) wide.

$170–200 ⊞ DECO

This radio was designed for the Festival of Britain.

A Fidelity radio, in a teak case, 1960s, 9in (23cm) wide.

$30–35 ⊞ COB

A Hacker Herald VHF radio, 1969, 11in (28cm) wide.

$75–85 ⊞ PEPE

This set has 13 transistors and is essentially an RP25 without the AM components.

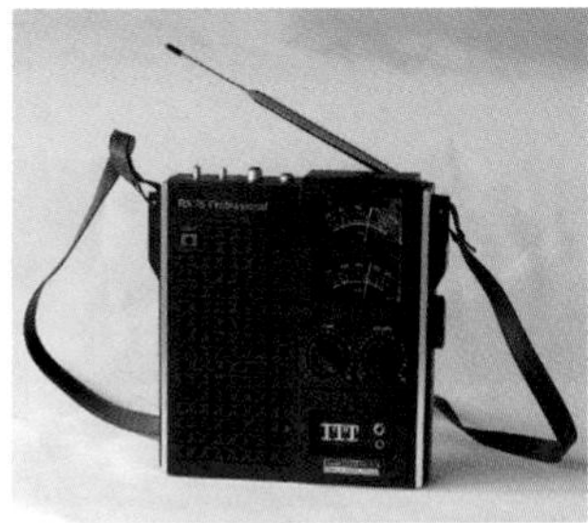

A Grundig 3028GB radio, 1958, 23in (58.5cm) wide.

$85–100 ⊞ GM

A Hacker Herald radio, c1965, 11in (28cm) wide.

$20–25 ⊞ PEPE

Hacker, makers of high-class radio equipment, were trading until the late 1970s. Their main competitors were Roberts and Dynatron. The Herald is a long- and medium-wave design, and benefits from a large loudspeaker.

A Heathkit GR-98 Airband Receiver, 1970, 10¼in (26cm) wide.

$60–70 ⊞ PEPE

◀ **An ITT RX75 Professional radio,** c1979, 7in (18cm) wide.

$20–25 ⊞ PEPE

▶ **A Ministry of Sound DAB radio,** c2003, 3½in (9cm) high.

$20–25 ⊞ PEPE

A Ferguson portable radio, in a Bakelite case, restored, 1950s, 12in (30.5cm) wide.

$60–70 ⊞ DECO

A Sinclair Radionics Micromatic radio, 1967, 1¾in (4.5cm) long.

$150–170 ⊞ PEPE

A President CB radio, America, 1979, 7¼in (18.5cm) wide.

$60–70 ⊞ PEPE

TELEPHONES

An Ericsson wall-mounted telephone, Sweden, 1895, 15in (38cm) high.

$6,200–6,900 ⊞ TL

A Bakelite 200 Series 232L model telephone, with bell set, 1932–60, 9in (23cm) wide.

$530–600 ⊞ SSPP

► A metal and Bakelite wall-mounted telephone, 1940–50, 10in (25.5cm) wide.

$140–155 ⊞ TL

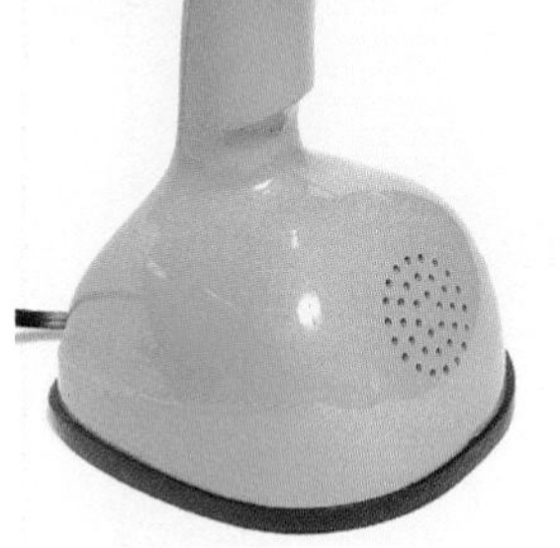

An Ericsson Ericofon telephone, Sweden, c1960, 10in (25.5cm) high.

$170–200 ⊞ TL

This model was available in many colours including red, orange and pink, which is the most sought after.

A Bakelite telephone, 1920s, 13in (33cm) high.

$380–430 ⊞ TL

An ABS plastic 700 Series 8746 model telephone, 1975, 8in (20.5cm) wide.

$75–85 ⊞ SSPP

The 700 Series, also known as the Modern Telephone, was available to customers in the early 1960s. It came in a variety of colours, the most popular being ivory. Each telephone was rented from the GPO and there was substantial cost if the phone was changed when the room was redecorated. The ABC lettering was changed on the dial during the late 1960s when numbers were more commonly used. The design was changed slightly around 1967 when the dial was replaced by a transparent one and the ABC-style lettering was dropped as all figure numbering became more common. This version, known as the 8746 continued into the 1970s.

A Bakelite 200 Series telephone, with cheese drawer, bell set missing, 1930, 10in (25.5cm) wide.

$380–430 ⊞ TL

The Bakelite 200 Series telephone was designed in 1929 and became Britain's GPO (General Post Office) standard during the 1930s. Early 200 Series telephones did not have an internal bell attached but needed an external bell set. Pyramidal in shape, the 200 Series phones were usually in black Bakelite although other colours were available.

An acrylic Diacon 300 Series 328 model telephone, with bell on/off switch, 1954, 9in (23cm) wide.

$1,300–1,500 ⊞ SSPP

An ACL plastic telephone, in the form of Snoopy, inscribed 'Joe Cool', 1990, 7in (18cm) high.

$40–45 ⊞ TL

THE WORLD'S FIRST commercial handheld cellular phone was the Motorola Dyna TAC 8000X in 1983. Early phones used the analogue network, which was switched off in the UK in 2001 after the development of GSM digital networks (Global System for Mobile Communications). This service is now used by over 2 billion people in more than 210 countries and territories.

Although mobile phones have been with us for less than 25 years, the early models have achieved cult status and are prized by collectors. The icons, firsts and unusual models are the most collectable, followed by early analogue phones, which were hugely expensive new and therefore now scarce.

Later GSM phones are increasing in popularity – especially the classic handset designs, such as the top of the range Nokia and Motorola models.

Mobile phones can be identified by the manufacturer's name and most have a model number or can be traced from serial numbers. Nokia and Motorola are the most widespread and collectable phones as they were the main product developers and market leaders. Boxes and original accessories are very scarce and will add to value, as do original instruction manuals. A boxed phone in mint condition can be worth up to 10 times as much as a single well-used example with no box or accessories. 'New old stock' phones, unused and boxed are a great investment as they are extremely rare. The top 10 Collectable handsets are: Motorola 8000x; Motorola 4500x Transportable; Nokia Mobira Cityman; Nokia 2110; Motorola MicroTAC; Sony 'Mars Bar' CM-H333; Motorola StarTAC; Nokia 8110 (as used in the Matrix movie); Nokia 8850 and Motorola V70.

Tom Cable

A Motorola 8000X Dyna TAC mobile **telephone,** AMPS system, America, 1983, 8in (20.5cm) long, boxed.

$460–520 RB

A Motorola 4500X transportable telephone, analogue, c1985, 10in (25.5cm) wide, boxed.

$230–260 RB

A Motorola Pulsar mobile **telephone,** AMPS system, America, 1979–83, 8in (20.5cm) long.

$460–520 RB

► A Nokia Mobria Cityman 1320 **mobile telephone,** analogue, 1987, 7½in (19cm) high.

$310–350 RB

◄ A Maxon EPC 590E **mobile telephone,** analogue, c1989, 8in (20.5cm) high, boxed.

$150–170 RB

► A Motorola Micro TAC 950 mobile **telephone,** with flip mouthpiece, LED display, 1989, 7in (18cm) long, boxed.

$230–260 RB

A Nokia Cityman 190 mobile **telephone,** analogue, 1989, 7in (18cm) long, boxed.

$120–140 RB

A Swatch mobile telephone, analogue, c1991, 7in (18cm) long.

$75–85 RB

An NEC PT100 **mobile telephone,** analogue, 1991, 6½in (16.5cm) long, boxed.

$50–60 RB

A Panasonic EB-KJ3650 J-Series mobile **telephone,** analogue, c1992, 5½in (14cm) long, boxed.

$75–85 RB

A Sony CM-HH333 mobile **telephone,** analogue, 1994, 6in (15cm) high, boxed.

$75–85 RB

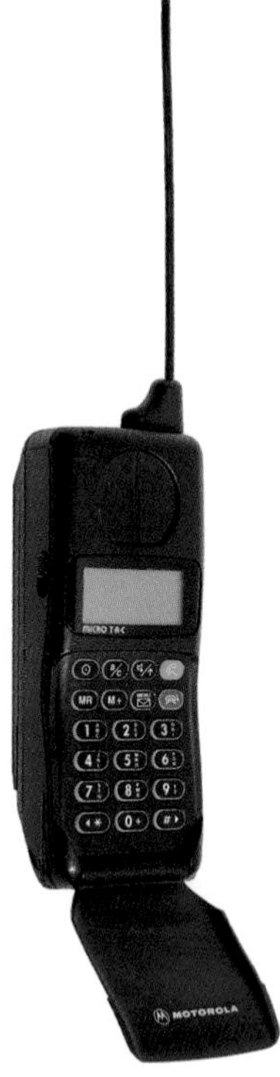

A Nokia 2140 mobile **telephone,** GSM, 1996, 6in (15cm) high, boxed.

$45–50 RB

◀ A Motorola Micro TAC International 7200 mobile **telephone,** with flip mouthpiece, 1994, 6in (15cm) long, boxed.

$75–85 RB

A Nokia 8110 mobile **telephone,** GSM, 1996, 5½in (14cm) long, boxed.

$85–100 RB

This telephone became popular after it was featured in the film the Matrix, and is known as the banana phone.

TELEVISIONS

An HMV television catalogue, 1938, 10in (25.5cm) high.

$115–130 ⊞ ET

An HMV 1803 television, in a walnut case, c1949, 14in (35.5cm) wide.

$120–140 ⊞ OTA

A Bush TV43 television, in a walnut-veneered case, 1954, 16in (40.5cm) wide.

$85–100 ⊞ OTA

◄ A Bush TV62 radio television, in a Bakelite case, 1956, 16in (40.5cm) wide.

$310–350 ⊞ OTA

► A Sylvania Dualette television, on original stand, America, c1960, 24in (61cm) wide.

$230–260 ⊞ OTA

Until 1953 television was only available in black and white. The RCA 'Compatible-Color' system was recognized as the standard but by 1965 Sylvania was ranked as one of America's largest manufacturers of colour television sets.

An HMV 1830 television, in a lacquered wood case, c1960, 20in (51cm) wide.

$45–50 ⊞ OTA

A KB television, on chrome legs, c1965, 25in (63.5cm) wide.

$45–50 ⊞ OTA

A Sony TV110 portable television, c1970, 11in (28cm) wide.

$10–15 ⊞ OTA

MONEY BOXES

An owl mechanical money box, by J. & E. Stevens, minor damage, America, patented 1880, 7½in (19cm) high.

$450–520 JDJ

A clown mechanical money box, by J. & E. Stevens, with wind-up spring mechanism, America, patented 1890, 9¼in (23.5cm) high.

$1,250–1,500 JDJ

A Punch and Judy mechanical money box, minor wear, America, patented 1884, 7¼in (18.5cm) high.

$780–940 JDJ

► **A cast-iron mechanical money box,** in the form of a lion attacking two monkeys, America, c1890, 9in (23cm) high.

$770–870 HAL

A Rothwell's Chocolates tin money box, c1900, 4in (10cm) high.

$85–100 M&C

► **A Post Office tin money box,** c1900, 2½in (6.5cm) high.

$85–100 M&C

A Trick Pony mechanical money box, by Shepherd Hardware, America, patented in 1885, 8in (20.5cm) long.

$620–750 JDJ

A cast-iron mechanical money box, 1910, 7in (18cm) high.

$180–210 ⊞ JUN

A Spillers Nephews biscuit tin/money box, c1910, 8in (20.5cm) high.

$220–260 ⊞ MURR

To ensure memories of their products lasted well beyond the last mouthful, biscuit manufacturers cleverly issued tins that doubled as money boxes.

A Royal Arsenal Co-operative Society tin money box, c1910, 4½in (11.5cm) high.

$85–100 ⊞ M&C

A painted wood money box, 1930s, 4½in (11.5cm) wide.

$30–35 ⊞ TOP

A Chad Valley tin money box, in the form of a book, c1950, 5½in (14cm) long.

$35–45 ⊞ M&C

A *Robin* comic tin money box, c1950, 3in (7.5cm) high.

$30–35 ⊞ M&C

A Rye Pottery hedgehog money box, by David Sharp, c1970, 6in (15cm) long.

$75–85 ⊞ MARK

◄ A Happy Nak tin money box, 1950, 4in (10cm) high.

$20–25 ⊞ M&C

Pam West

Buying/selling bank notes

White Fivers
Bank Notes old and new
Postal Orders
Bank of England related items
material as featured!

Pam West
British Notes
PO Box 257
Sutton
Surrey SM3 9WW

Tel/Fax: +44 0208 641 3224
Email: pamwestbritnotes@aol.com
Website: www.britishnotes.co.uk

Colin Narbeth & Son Ltd.

20 CECIL COURT,
LONDON WC2N 4HE
TEL: 0207 379 6975
FAX: 01727 811244

e-mail: colin.narbeth@btinternet.com
Web: www.colin-narbeth.com

BUYING & SELLING
OLD PAPER MONEY

FOR LARGE STOCKLIST
SEE WEBSITE

DIX • NOONAN • WEBB

Auctioneers and Valuers of all types of Banknotes and Paper Money

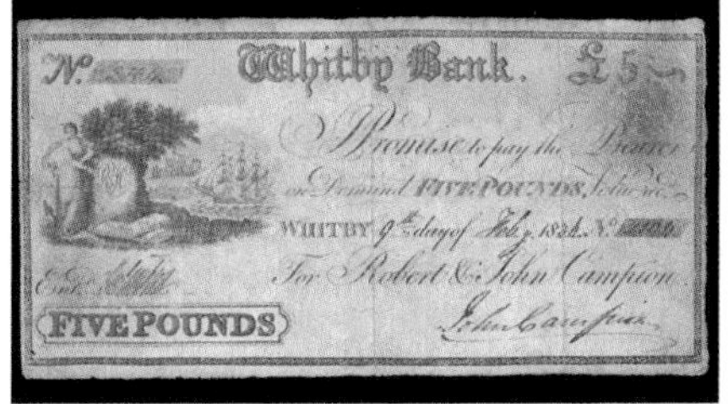

Call us for free confidential sale advice and valuations and check out our website for the latest auction information

16 BOLTON STREET LONDON W1J 8BQ
TELEPHONE 44 (0) 20 7016 1700 FAX 44 (0) 20 7016 1799
EMAIL **coins@dnw.co.uk** WEB **www.dnw.co.uk**

Collectors Old Toy Shop Halifax

(SHOP OPEN 10.30–4.30 TUES, WEDS, FRIDAY & SAT)

Unusual old money boxes are my speciality

The more weird and wonderful the better with or without moving mechanical actions. Cast-iron, tin and soft metal buildings, animals and figures. Consider offering me any money box. My offers are without obligation and you really must contact me before guessing a price and selling.

I BUY ALL KINDS OF OLD TOYS TOO!

JOHN AND SIMON HALEY
89 Northgate, Halifax, Yorkshire HX1 1XF
Tel: 01422 822148/360434
Email: toysandbanks@aol.com

PAPER MONEY

ENGLAND

A Bank of England £5 note, signed by J. G. Nairne, 1907.

$1,200–1,400 NAR

White notes were issued soon after the Bank of England opened in 1694. The £5 note was the most common in later years and finally ceased being issued in 1956.

A Bank of England £100 note, 1938.

$1,800–2,100 CWD

One of the last high denomination notes issued by the Bank of England, a £100 note would only have been handled by a privileged few. These notes, which are scarce and sought after, are not prohibitively expensive and in real terms are good value for money.

A Bank of England 10 shilling note, emergency issue, No. 1000000, 1940.

$150–170 CWD

This seven-digit 'million' note was numbered by hand, a feature that boosts a collection, as well as adding to its value.

Two Bank of England £1 notes, consecutive numbers, signed by K. O. Peppiatt, 1948.

$45–50 CWD

These £1 notes were in issued from 1928 until 1960, when they were replaced with notes featuring Queen Elizabeth II. Condition is all-important as collectors prefer mint notes, and two uncirculated consecutive notes are desirable but getting harder to find. If sold individually each would probably carry a price tag of $15–20.

A Bank of England £1 note, signed by J.B. Page, 1978.

$5–10 NAR

A Bank of England 10 shilling note, 1955.

$20–25 NAR

A Bank of England £5 error note, signature missing, 1970s.

$150–170 CWD

An error note is a piece of currency that has a manufacturing mistake or misprint. With a signature this note would be worth $10–15.

A Bank of England £1 note, signed by Hollom, 1960s.

$5–10 NAR

This note is in mint condition which is critical to value. With several folds or creases the condition is termed as 'very fine', one fold as 'extremely rare' and uncirculated as 'mint'.

A Bank of England £50 note, first issue, A01 prefix, 1981.

$150–170 CWD

IRELAND

A Provincial Bank of Ireland £1 note, 1919.

$380–430 ⊞ WP

A Currency Commission £1 note, 1941.

$60–70 ⊞ WP

A Central Bank of Ireland £5 note, 1975.

$40–45 ⊞ NAR

A Central Bank of Ireland £10 note, 1975 replacement.

$210–240 ⊞ WP

► **A Central Bank of Ireland £100 note,** depicting Lady Lavery, 1977.

$310–350 ⊞ NAR

Central Bank of Ireland £100 notes are scarce as there was little demand for notes of such high value.

SCOTLAND

A British Linen Bank £1 note, 1917.

$170–210 ⊞ NAR

The British Linen Company was set up in 1746 to promote the linen industry, with banking as a secondary side of the business. It was not until 1849 that it was recognized as a banking corporation and in 1906 it changed its name to the British Linen Bank. It merged with the Bank of Scotland in 1970.

► **A Bank of Scotland £20 note,** 1960.

$85–100 ⊞ CWD

Scottish £20 notes can usually be found in good condition. Prior to 1970s inflation and decimalization, £20 was a tidy sum.

► **A Commercial Bank of Scotland £1 note,** depicting John Pitcairn, 1924.

$150–170 ⊞ NAR

This very desirable note is known among collectors as the Square note, due to its unusual shape.

A Clydesdale Bank £1 note, 1925.

$310–350 ⊞ NAR

A National Bank of Scotland £5 note, 1951.

$85–100 ⊞ CWD

This colourful and impressive note circulated at the same time as the English white £5 notes, and is the same size. This example , which is classed as Very Fine, has been circulated but is still presentable and, with no faults, is not expensive. An uncirculated example might cost three or four times as much, but should prove a good investment.

WORLD

A United States $5 note, Pioneer Family series, 1907.

$230–260 CWD

This is a classic American note with President Andrew Jackson's portrait and a vignette depicting a pioneer family. Originally issued in 1869, it was designed to promote a sense of community and pride, the illustration of the pioneer family is one of a number of powerful images that grace these early issues.

A 100 rouble note, depicting Catherine the Great, Russia, 1910.

$5–10 CWD

This is a super note for the aspiring collector: it is printed with an image of Catherine the Great, is full of Russian symbolism and at 10 x 4¾in (25.5 x 12cm) is an impressive size. Fortunately these notes became worthless after the Russian revolution, so there are plenty for the collectors' market – every collection should have one.

◀ A Commonwealth of Australia £1 note, 1927.

$150–170 NAR

A States of Jersey sixpence note, occupation issue, 1941.

$30–35 CWD

During WWII, occupied Jersey suffered a shortage of small change, so permission was given for small change notes to be issued from 6d to £1. They were designed by a local artist and printed locally. They were in circulation from April 1942 until liberation in 1945.

A Japanese Government 1,000 dollar note, 1944.

$5–10 CWD

These notes were not US, but Malayan Dollars, issued by the Japanese during their WWII occupation of the area. When occupation ended these notes lost all their value, and many found their way home with liberated allied forces, to be kept as souvenirs. The letter 'M' indicates Malaya.

▶ A Bank of France 100 new francs note, depicting Napoleon, 1962.

$40–45 CWD

This is a superb item for collectors, featuring Napoleon Bonaparte on both sides, as well as the Arc de Triomphe. If you come across one it would be worth putting it carefully to one side – they are becoming scarce and expensive in top condition.

A 50 million mark note, Germany, 1923.

$5–10 CWD

Rampant inflation in Germany in 1923 was the cause of banknotes being issued with increasingly higher denominations. As a result of this there are many banknotes of unbelievably high values available for collectors, most of them costing just a pound or two.

A Palestine Currency Board £1 note, 1939.

$230–260 NAR

Palestine Currency Board notes are among the most expensive notes to collect. Low denominations are obtainable but fetch three-figure sums in perfect condition. The notes were backed by the Bank of England and when Israel took over they sent them back by ship to England. To avoid heavy insurance costs they tore the notes in half and sent half in one ship and half in another; consequently the few high value £100 notes in existence fetch four-figure sums.

A Reserve Bank of India 1,000 rupees note, Bombay, 1975.

$85–100 CWD

All early colonial period Indian notes have a good following, but this later note still maintains the air of quality and value in a higher denomination than usually seen. The item shown is a good example of this large note. Again, a strictly uncirculated example might be worth much more.

PENS

A bottle of Webster's Blue-Black Diamine Writing Fluid, c1900, 7in (18cm) high.

$10–15 OIA

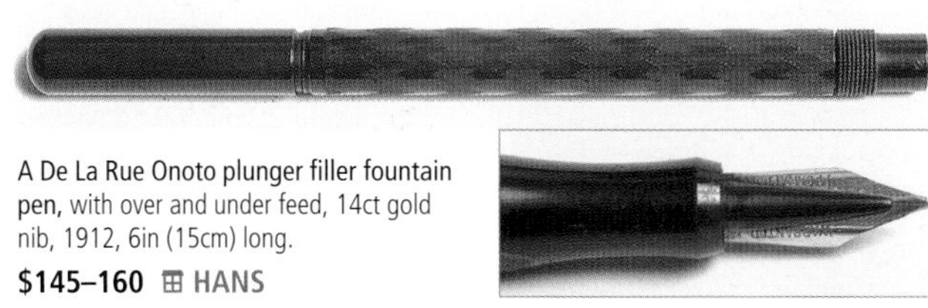

A De La Rue Onoto plunger filler fountain pen, with over and under feed, 14ct gold nib, 1912, 6in (15cm) long.

$145–160 HANS

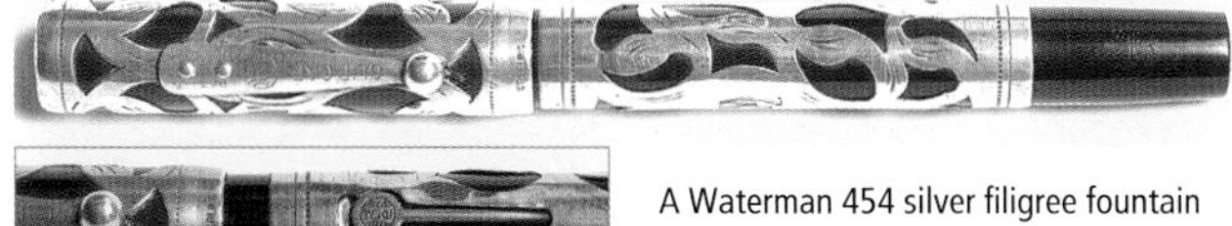

A Waterman 454 silver filigree fountain pen, America, 1920s, 5½in (14cm) long.

$430–490 HANS

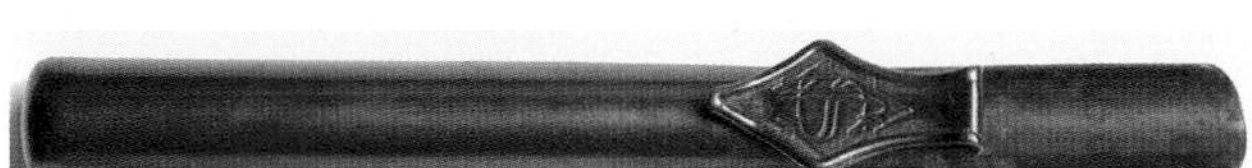

A Conway Stewart metal pocket pen holder, c1920, 4¾in (12cm) long.

$15–25  HANS

A Parker Lucky Curve fountain pen, with an M Canadian Duofold nib, America, c1926, 5¼in (13.5cm) long.

$270–310 HANS

A Conway Stewart 476 Universal fountain pen, with a 14ct gold M Conway Stewart nib, 1930s, 5in (12.5cm) long.

$85–100 HANS

A Mabie Todd Swan Visofil fountain pen, clipless model, with a No. 1 flexible 14ct gold Swan nib, America, c1935, 4¾in (12cm) long.

$155–170 HANS

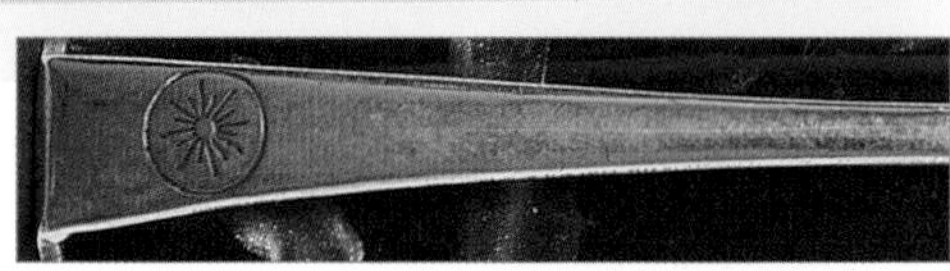

A De La Rue Onoto 4701 plunger filler fountain pen, with a 14ct gold Onoto 3 nib, c1948, 5¾in (14.5cm) long.

$110–125 HANS

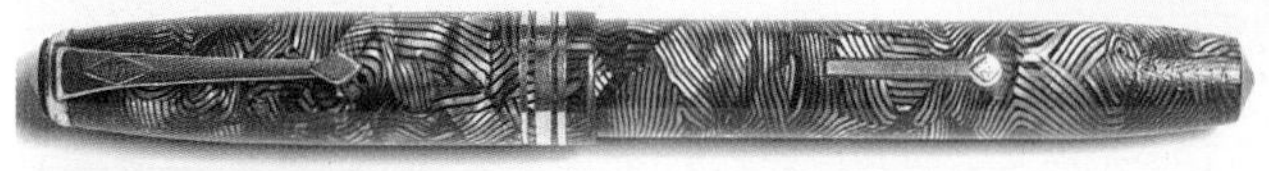

A Conway Stewart 58 fountain pen, with a Duro M 58 nib, c1951, 5in (12.5cm) long.

$160–180 HANS

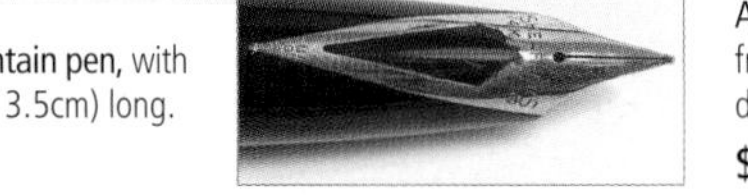

A Sheaffer PFM III plastic snorkel filler fountain pen, with a 14ct gold F nib, America, c1960, 5¼in (13.5cm) long.

$240–270 HANS

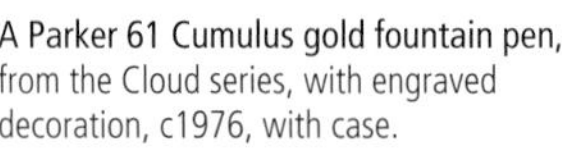

A Parker 61 Cumulus gold fountain pen, from the Cloud series, with engraved decoration, c1976, with case.

$250–300 G(L)

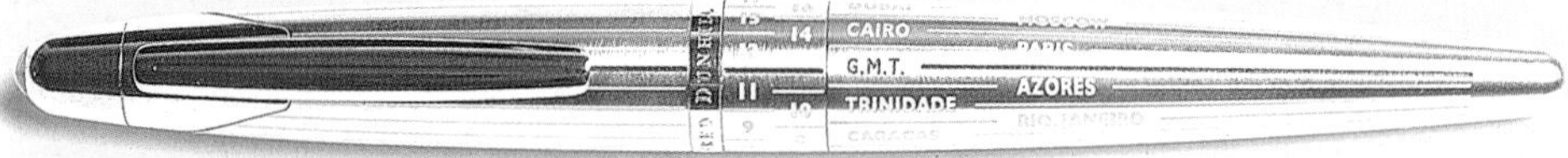

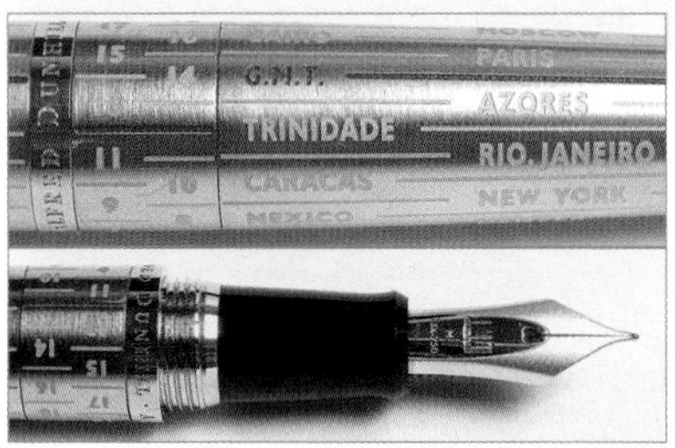

A Dunhill 0003 GMT stainless steel fountain pen, engraved 'Alfred Dunhill', 18ct gold M nib, edition of 1,884, 1996, 6in (15cm) long.

$340–400 HANS

This pen was developed to commemorate the creation of Greenwich Mean Time in 1884. A red line is engraved down the centre of the pen to signify GMT. A bezel is fitted which, when turned to the relevant marked city, identifies its time zone compared with GMT. The top of the pen has a blue and white cabochon which represents the earth viewed from space.

A Montblanc Nicolaus Copernicus fountain pen, edition of 4,810, with 18ct gold M nib engraved with Nicolaus Copernicus historic sketch of the orbit of the planets, 2003, 5½in (14cm) long, with case and paperwork.

$1,900–2,100 HANS

This limited edition pen was available worldwide and sold out very quickly. The design incorporates eight sterling silver rings representing the orbits of planets circling the sun.

PERFUME BOTTLES

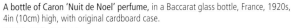

A J. Grossmith of London crystal perfume **bottle,** c1908, 3in (7.5cm) high, with original label and leather case.

$260–300 LaF

A bottle of Caron 'Nuit de Noel' perfume, in a Baccarat glass bottle, France, 1920s, 4in (10cm) high, with original cardboard case.

$340–370 LaF

'Nuit de Noel' was created in 1922 by Ernest Daltroff, founder of the House of Caron, for his lover Félicie Vanpouille, who loved Christmas Eve and the scents associated with it.

A bottle of J. Grossmith & Son 'Phul-Nana' **perfume,** c1920, 4in (10cm) high.

$30–40 LaF

This scent was said to be as refreshing as 'a summer breeze in a garden full of fresh flowers'.

A bottle of Lucien Lelong 'Indiscreet' **perfume,** in a glass bottle, France, 1924, 6in (15cm) high.

$480–530 LaF

A bottle of Guerlain 'Mitsouko' perfume, France, 1920s, 3in (7.5cm) high, with original box.

$145–160 LeB

Japanese-inspired 'Mitsouko' was launched by Jacques Guerlain in 1919. It fitted with the vogue for the Far East that swept Europe in the Art Deco era. Translated, 'Mitsouko' means 'mystery' in Japanese.

► A bottle of Caron 'Les Pois de Senteur de Chez Moi' **perfume,** in a Baccarat glass bottle, France, 1927, 6½in (16.5cm) high, with original box.

$340–400 LeB

Baccarat designed a number of bottles for the French perfume house, Caron. Parfums Caron was founded in 1904.

Three bottles of Cardinal perfume, 'Bouquet', 'Chypre' and 'Gardenia', contained in a tantalus, 1930s, 4in (10cm) long.

$320–360 LaF

A bottle of Caron 'Fleur de Rocaille' perfume, France, c1933, 3in (7.5cm) high, with original box.

$220–2505 LeB

A bottle of Elizabeth Arden 'Blue Grass' perfume, America, c1935, 3in (7.5cm) high, with orginal box.

$240–270 LeB

The 'Blue Grass' fragrance, the first from Arden, was created to commemorate Elizabeth Arden's passion for horse racing. The name referred to the horse breeding region of Kentucky and Tennessee.

A bottle of Worth 'Je Reviens' eau-de-cologne, in a Lalique glass bottle, France, 1950s, 4in (10cm) high.

$10–15 KA

'Je Reviens' was commercially launched by the House of Worth in 1932, although Charles Frederick Worth had given the perfume to his customers from 1858. The name was based on a letter sent by Napoleon to Josephine saying 'Je reviens en trois jours, ne te laves pas' meaning 'I will return in three days, do not wash until then'.

A Nina Ricci 'Nina' shop display glass perfume bottle, 1987, 6in (15cm) high.

$250–270 LaF

This scent was launched by Robert Ricci in homage to his late mother, Nina, who founded the fashion house in 1932.

A bottle of Schiaparelli 'Shocking' perfume, France, c1936, 7in (18cm) high, with original box.

$260–300 LBr

'Shocking' was launched in 1936 and the design of the perfume bottle was as cutting-edge as the scent inside. Elsa Schiaparelli chose to represent female glamour with a seamstress's mannequin bust based on the curvaceous body of one her clients, Mae West.

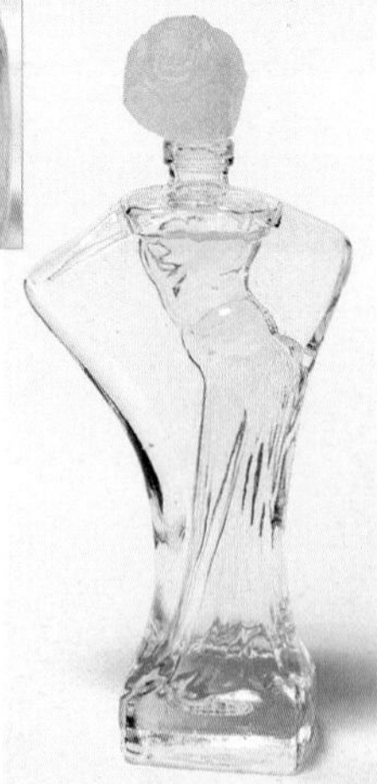

► **A bottle of Salvador Dali 'Daliflor' perfume,** 2000, 3in (7.5cm) high.

$10–15 KA

The inspiration for this perfume and bottle design was Dali's painting Woman with a Head of Roses.

POSTCARDS

GLAMOUR

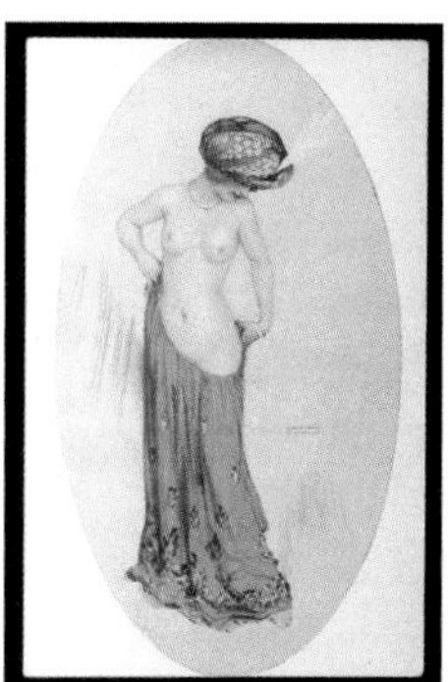

A glamour postcard, by Raphael Kirchner, entitled 'Princess Riquette', France, c1900, 6 x 4in (15 x 10cm).

$110–125 S&D

A glamour postcard, by Raphael Kirchner, France, c1900.

$105–120 MCS

A glamour postcard, by Philip Boileau, entitled 'Rings on her Fingers', America, c1910.

$10–15 MCS

A glamour postcard, by Harrison Fisher, entitled 'Alert', America, c1914.

$10–15 MCS

A glamour postcard, by F. Fabiano, France, c1914.

$15–25 MCS

COLLECTING TIPS

A glamour postcard, by Raphael Kirchner, entitled 'Lulu', France, c1900, 6 x 4in (15 x 10cm).

$110–125 S&D

A glamour postcard, by Raphael Kirchner, entitled 'Salome', France, c1900, 6 x 4in (15 x 10cm).

$110–125 S&D

A glamour postcard, by Charles Dana Gibson, entitled 'Irene', America, c1905.

$5–10 MCS

- Glamour postcards have an international appeal. Many have superb artwork and collectors are particularly attracted by Art Nouveau and Art Deco cards.
- French artists tended to produce work that was more risqué than that of American artists.
- Works by Austrian artist, Raphael Kirchner (1876–1917), are sought after. Cards produced between c1900 and the outbreak of WWI, when he was living in France, are the most desirable; they have a strong Art Nouveau style and chromolithographic printing.
- Prices for Kirchner postcards can exceed $170 for examples in good condition.
- American artist Charles Dana Gibson (1867–1944) is credited with creating the first pin-up postcard, the Gibson Girl. This was soon followed by a series featuring glamorous women, including Irene.
- When collecting glamour postcards, buy what appeals to you, but condition always affects value.

VIEWS

A photographic postcard of Croydon, by Raphael Tuck & Sons, c1900, 4 x 6in (10 x 15cm).

$5–10 POS

A souvenir postcard of Atlantic City, by Raphael Tuck & Sons, 1900–05.

$10–15 JMC

A photographic postcard, depicting keddle net fishing near Rye, 1905, 5in (12.5cm) wide.

$25–30 M&C

A photographic postcard, depicting Wimbledon Common windmill, 1910, 5in (12.5cm) wide.

$15–25 M&C

A photographic postcard, depicting the new Post Office, Cinderford, 1910, 5in (12.5cm) wide.

$25–30 M&C

A photographic postcard, depicting salt workers at Droitwich, Cheshire, c1910, 5in (12.5cm) wide.

$25–30 M&C

A photographic postcard, depicting South Shields docks, 1915, 5in (12.5cm) wide.

$25–30 M&C

◄ A postcard, depicting the Royal York Hotel, Brighton, 1917.

$10–15 MCS

A photographic postcard, depicting a horse-drawn bus, London, 1920, 5in (12.5cm) wide.

$15–25 M&C

POSTERS

ADVERTISING

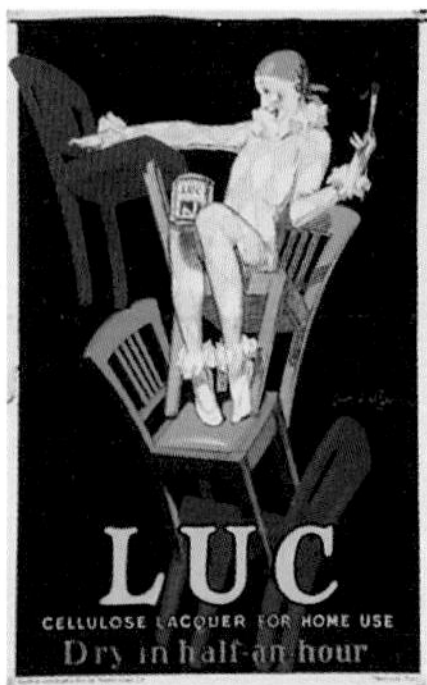

A LUC cellulose lacquer poster, by Jean d'Ylen, printed for Louis Berger & Sons by Vercasson, France, 1927, 30 x 20in (76 x 51cm).

$1,050–1,250 ONS

A Samson Kina poster, printed by J. L. Goffart, Belgium, Brussels, c1930, 13½ x 13in (34.5 x 33cm).

$175–200 VSP

◀ **A New Zealand Apples poster,** 1920, 30 x 20in (76 x 51cm).

$620–690 Do

A Blaupunkt Radio poster, on linen, Germany, c1940, 46¾ x 33½in (119 x 85cm).

$460–550 VSP

An RCA Radiotron poster, signed 'Viale 1933', America, New Jersey, 42½ x 27½in (108 x 70cm).

$1,750–2,100 JDJ

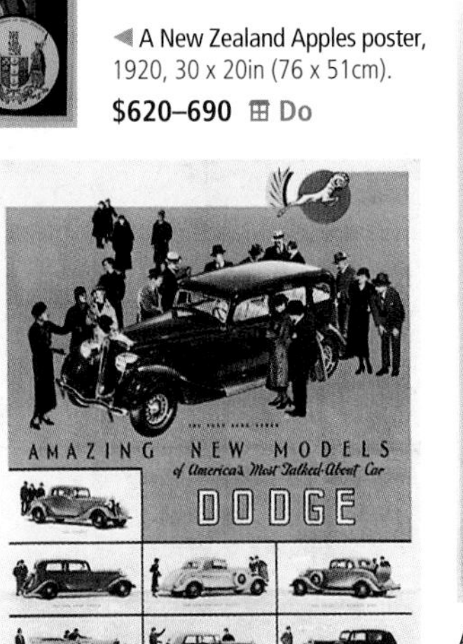

A Dodge poster, 'Amazing New Models of America's Most Talked-About Car', America, 1934, 50 x 38¼in (127 x 97cm).

$830–980 VSP

▶ **An Imperial Airways poster,** after Adam Dacres, 'Imperial Airways Use Shell Petrol Exclusively', c1940, 20 x 28in (51 x 71cm).

$155–175 ROS

A Daimler poster, c1940, 29½ x 20in (75 x 51cm).

$340–410 VSP

An Olivetti Lexikon poster, by Marcello Nizoli, printed by Officine Grafiche Ricordi, Milan, 1953, 40 x 27½in (100.5 x 70cm).

$310–360 VSP

A Grolsch Pilsner poster, by Jacob Jansma, printed by A. Van der Weerd, Holland, c1950, 38½ x 26¾in (98 x 68cm).

$340–410 VSP

A Heineken poster, by Frans Mettes, c1957, 45¾ x 32½in (116 x 82.5cm).

$530–640 VSP

◀ A Vespa poster, by B. Ambroise, featuring Gilbert Bécaud, on japan paper, France, 1960, 47 x 31½in (119.5 x 80cm).

$700–840 VSP

▶ A Levi's poster, by Ida van Bladel, 1971, 33 x 22in (84 x 56cm).

$640–760 VSP

A Billy Smart's Circus poster, 1950, 30 x 20in (76 x 51cm).

$230–260 Do

An Amstel poster, c1959, 45 x 32in (114.5 x 81.5cm).

$300–350 VSP

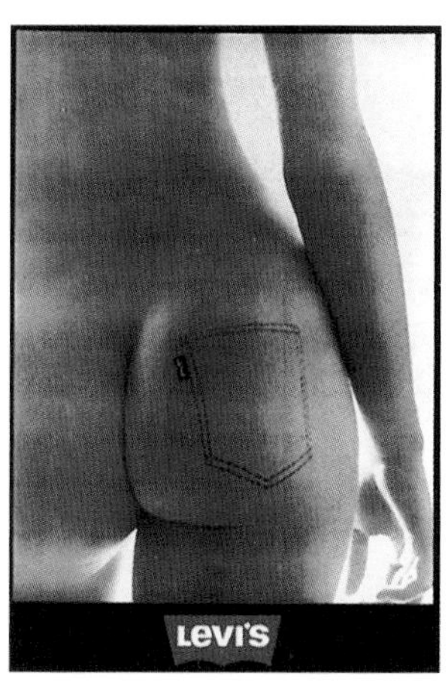

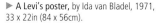

EXHIBITIONS

A Galerie Louis Carré poster, 'Dufy', 1953, framed, 25¾ x 18¾in (65.5 x 47.5cm).

$200–240 SK

A Galerie Maeght poster, 'Chagall', printed by Mourlot, 1962, 27½ x 21in (70 x 53.5cm).

$340–410 VSP

A Haags Gemeentemuseum poster, by Wim van/Aart Verhoeven, 'Kandinsky', printed by de Jong & Co, Holland, 1963, 39½ x 27½in (100.5 x 70cm).

$175–200 VSP

A promotional poster, 'Picasso', printed by Mourlot, 1973, 28 x 18½in (71 x 47cm).

$250–300 VSP

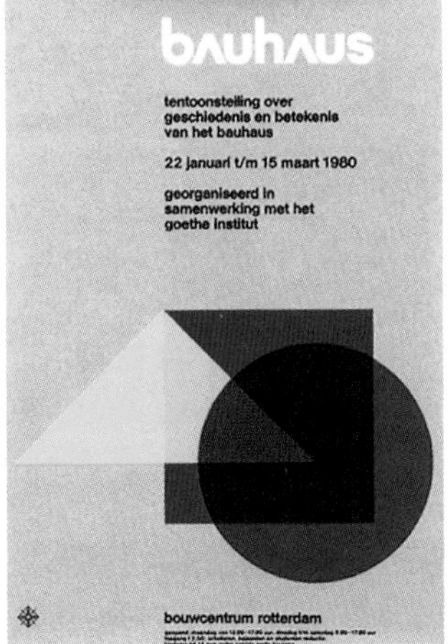

A promotional poster, 'Bauhaus', 1979, 33¼ x 23½in (84.5 x 59.5cm).

$135–160 VSP

A Galerie Jofa Kim poster, 'Joan Miró', 1983, 29¾ x 21¼in (75.5 x 54cm).

$200–240 VSP

LOCATE THE SOURCE

The source of each illustration in Miller's can be found by checking the code letters below each caption with the Key to Illustrations, pages 444–452.

▶ A promotional poster, 'Max Ernst, Koln', Germany, 1980, 23 x 33in (58.5 x 84cm).

$155–175 MARK

FILM

KING KONG

A BFI film poster, *King Kong*, 2005, 11¾ x 15¾in (30 x 40cm).

$70–80 JCos

◄ A film poster, *King Kong*, on japan paper, printed by Nornotrik, 1948, 33½ x 24¼in (85 x 61.5cm).

$1,250–1,500 VSP

- King Kong is the name of a fictional giant gorilla immortalized in the 1933 film and by subsequent remakes, sequels, comics and even a cartoon show.
- The original *King Kong* film is remembered for its pioneering special effects, courtesy of Willis O'Brien, who gained a name for himself in 1925 with the screen version of Sir Arthur Conan Doyle's *Lost World*.
- The 2005 Universal Pictures film, the longest at three hours and eight minutes, won three Academy Awards.
- Paper collectables from 1933 are super rare – an original RKO poster sold at auction for a record $62,000.

A film poster, *In Society*, starring Bud Abbott & Lou Costello, on linen, America, 1953, 41 x 27in (104 x 68.5cm).

$410–480 Lim

A film poster, *A Matter of Who*, starring Terry Thomas, 1961, 41 x 27in (104 x 68.5cm).

$190–210 Lim

A film poster, *It! The Terror from Beyond Space*, c1958, 41½ x 27½in (105.5 x 70cm).

$175–200 G(L)

A foyer poster, *Roman Holiday*, starring Audrey Hepburn and Gregory Peck, 1960, 14 x 11in (35.5 x 28cm).

$210–230 Lim

► A film poster, *A Very Private Affair*, starring Brigitte Bardot and Marcello Mastroianni, 1962, 22 x 28in (56 x 11in).

$190–210 Lim

► A film poster, *The Nutty Professor*, starring Jerry Lewis, on linen, 1963, 41 x 27in (104 x 68.5cm).

$340–400 ⊞ Lim

A film poster, *Kill or Cure*, starring Terry Thomas and Eric Sykes, 1962, 41 x 27in (104 x 68.5cm).

$155–175 ⊞ Lim

A film poster, *Love with the Proper Stranger*, starring Steve McQueen and Natalie Wood, 1964, 41 x 27in (104 x 68.5cm).

$340–400 ⊞ Lim

► A film poster, *Once Upon a Time in the West*, starring Henry Fonda, Charles Bronson, Jason Robards and Claudia Cardinale, 1968, 36 x 14in (91.5 x 35.5cm).

$1,000–1,100 ⊞ CINE

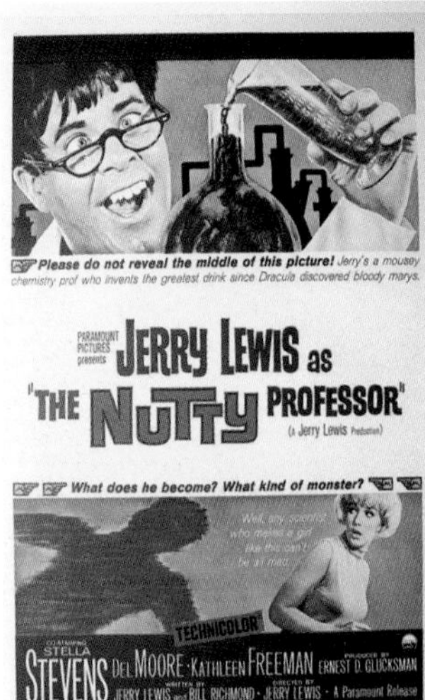

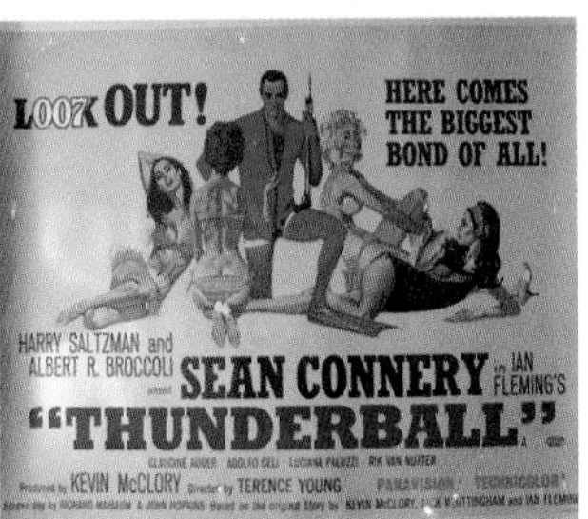

A UK film poster, *Thunderball*, starring Sean Connery, 1965, 30 x 40in (76 x 101.5cm).

$3,350–3,800 ⊞ CINE

A film poster, *Charade*, starring Audrey Hepburn and Cary Grant, 1963, 22 x 28in (56 x 71cm).

$520–590 ⊞ Lim

A film poster, *Point Blank*, starring Lee Marvin and Angie Dickinson, 1967, 41 x 27in (104 x 68.5cm).

$1,050–1,200 ⊞ Lim

A film poster, *Le Renard*, on linen, France, 1968, 30 x 27in (76 x 68.5cm).

$270–300 ⊞ Lim

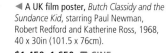

◀ A UK film poster, *Butch Cassidy and the Sundance Kid*, starring Paul Newman, Robert Redford and Katherine Ross, 1968, 40 x 30in (101.5 x 76cm).

$1,450–1,650 ⊞ CINE

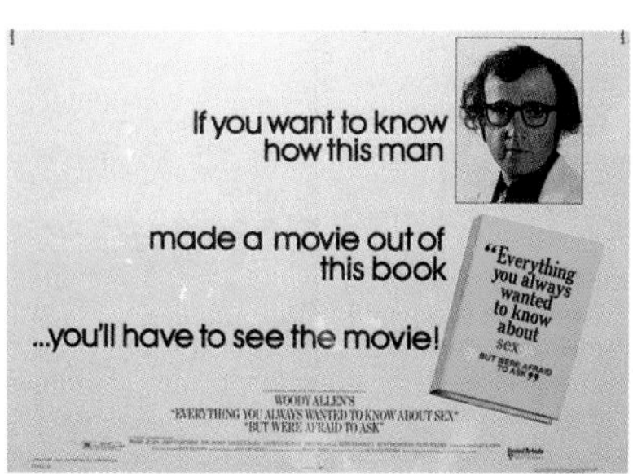

A film poster, *Everything You Always Wanted to Know About Sex But Were Too Afraid to Ask*, starring Woody Allen, 1972, 22 x 28in (56 x 71cm).

$155–175 ⊞ Lim

A film poster, *Carry on Loving*, 1970, 41 x 27in (104 x 68.5cm).

$200–230 ⊞ Lim

A film poster, *The 24 Hours of Le Mans*, starring Steve McQueen, Japan, 1971, 58 x 20in (147.5 x 51cm).

$2,300–2,600 ⊞ CINE

◀ A foyer poster, *The Pink Panther Strikes Again*, starring Peter Sellers, 1976, 11 x 14in (28 x 35.5cm).

$60–70 ⊞ Lim

A film poster, *The Shootist*, starring John Wayne and Lauren Bacall, 1976, 30 x 40in (76 x 101.5cm).

$850–950 ⊞ CINE

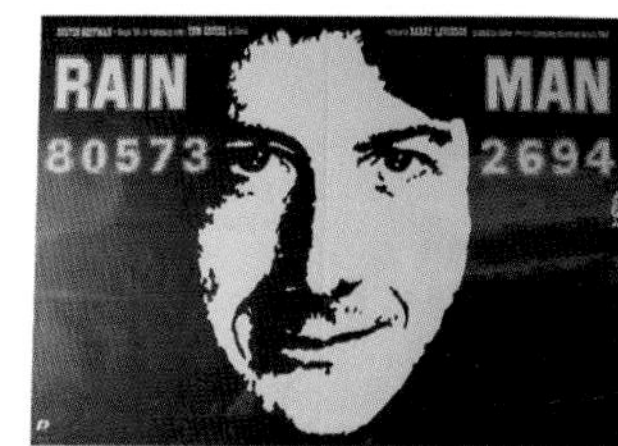

A film poster, *Rain Man*, starring Dustin Hoffman and Tom Cruise, 1988, 26 x 37in (66 x 94cm).

$190–210 ⊞ Lim

◀ A film poster, *Silence of the Lambs*, 1990, 39 x 27in (99 x 68.5cm).

$190–210
⊞ CINE

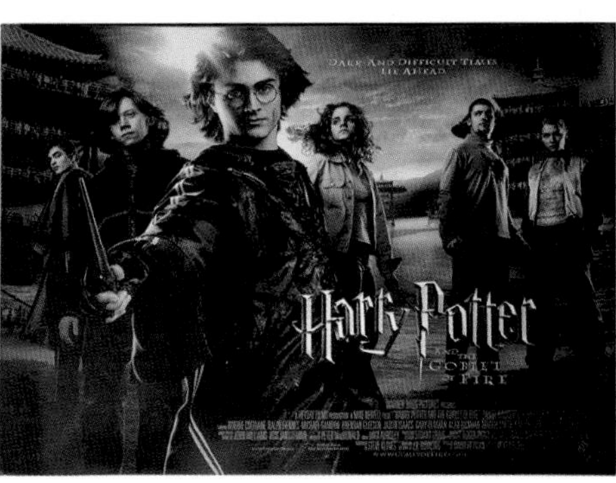

▶ A British Film Institute film poster, *Harry Potter and the Goblet of Fire*, 2005, 11¾ x 15¾in (30 x 40cm).

$25–30 ⊞ JCos

HEALTH

A St John Ambulance poster, by Doris Zinkeisen, 1920, 30 x 20in (76 x 51cm).

$460–520 Do

Doris Zinkeisen (1898–1991) was a painter, stage set and costume designer who was also the official war artist for the St John Ambulance Brigade.

▶ A Ministry of Health poster, 'They need orange juice every day', printed by Fosh & Cross, London, c1943, 30¼ x 20in (77 x 51cm).

$135–160 VSP

HEALTH IS PRECIOUS
Start early!
BUILD AN A1 NATION
CONSULT THE NATIONAL ADVISORY COUNCIL FOR PHYSICAL EDUCATION • NEW STANDARD BANK BUILDING • PRETORIA

A National Advisory Council poster, 'Health is Precious, Start Early!', printed by Cape Times Ltd, South Africa, 1943, 40¼ x 26in (102 x 66cm).

$400–480 VSP

NEW HEALTH
for Convalescents
SANATOGEN
renews the blood
strengthens the nerves

A Sanatogen New Health poster, c1935, 27¼ x 19¼in (69 x 49cm).

$175–200 VSP

▶ A public health poster, 'Eat More Oranges and Keep Away "Flu"', 1935, 32in (81.5cm) high.

$500–570 Do

They need
orange juice
every day
The concentrated juice of
12 FRESH ORANGES
ASK AT THE WELFARE CENTRE OR FOOD OFFICE

A Dental Council poster, 'Cleaning Foods for Good Sound Teeth', 1950, 30 x 20in (76 x 51cm).

$85–95 Do

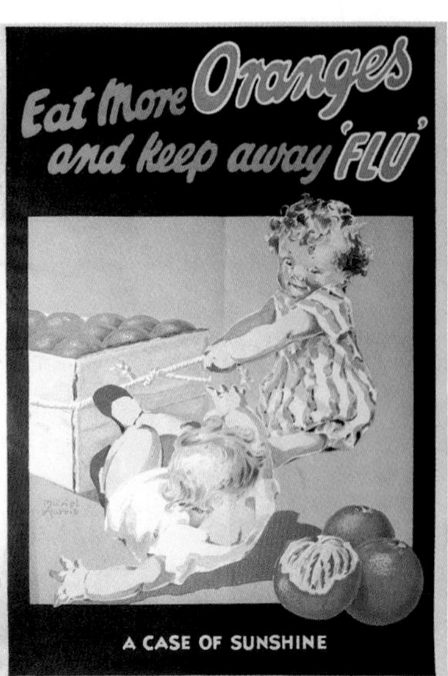

A health and safety poster, 'Lift the Safe Way', 1950, 30 x 20in (76 x 51cm).

$460–520 Do

▶ A public health poster, 'Malaria', printed by Fosh & Cross, London, 1951, 19 x 14¼in (48.5 x 36cm).

$135–160 VSP

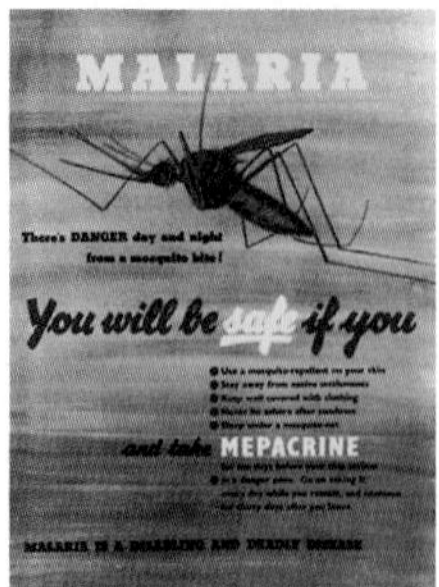

MALARIA
You will be safe if you
and take MEPACRINE

ROCK & POP

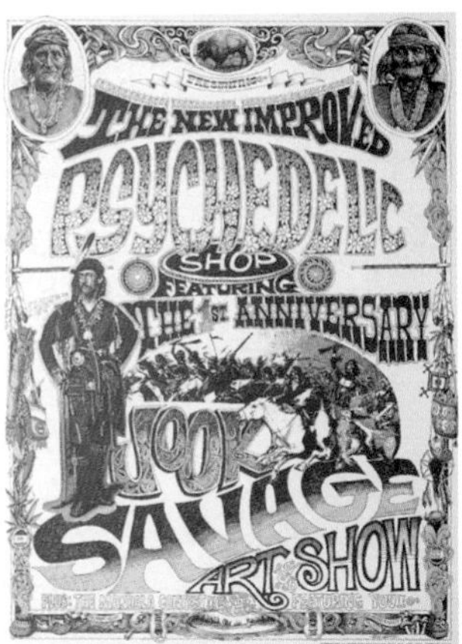

A promotional poster, by Rick Griffin, 'New Improved Psychedelic Shop and Jook Savage Show', printed by Berkeley Bonaparte, 1966, 19 x 14¼in (48.5 x 36cm).

$85–95 ⊞ ASC

Californian artist Rick Griffin (1944–91) created posters, record sleeves and comic art. His inspiration came from many sources such as Native American culture, surfing, beetles, skulls, vivid colours and lettering. In 1964 he became part of the Jook Savages group of artists and musicians and his first San Francisco rock poster was for the Jook Savages Art Show.

A Filmore Auditorium concert poster, for The Jimi Hendrix Experience, printed by Osiris Visions, 1967, 29½ x 19¼in (75 x 49.5cm).

$410–490 VSP

An Apple Boutique poster, 'A is for Apple', 1967, 29 x 22in (73.5 x 56cm).

$85–100 Her

► **A concert poster,** by Nigel Waymouth, advertising The Who, printed by T.S.R, 1967, 29¾ x 19¾in (75.5 x 50cm).

$310–360 VSP

A Tyrone Guthrie Theatre poster, by Robert Indiana, 'The Mother of Us All', printed by Johnson Printing Co, America, 1967, 36¾ x 24in (93.5 x 61cm).

$530–640 VSP

► **An American Folk Blues Festival poster,** by Günther Kieser, 1968, 46¾ x 33in (119.5 x 84cm).

$250–290 VSP

An Avalon Concert poster, for The Doors, Country Joe and the Fish, and Sparrow, 1967, 20 x 14in (51 x 35.5cm).

$220–260 Her

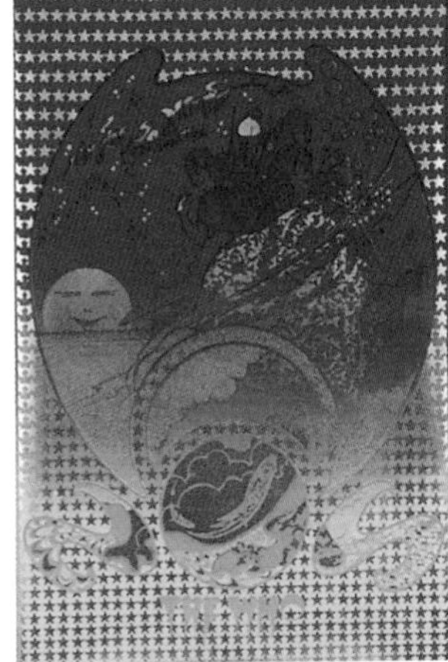

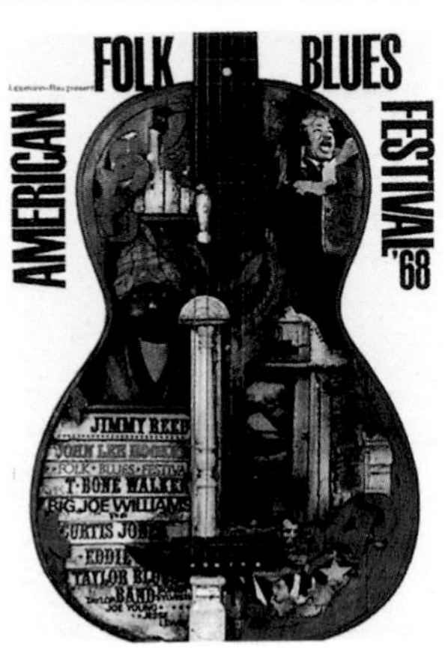

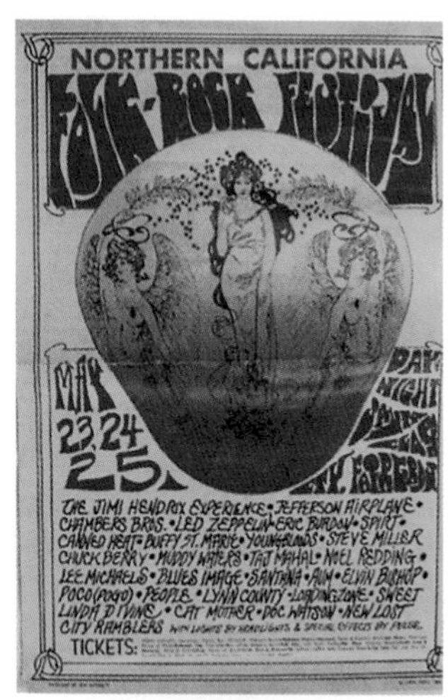

◄ **A concert poster,** for Jimi Hendrix and Led Zeppelin at the Northern California Rock Festival, 1969, 21 x 14in (53.5 x 35.5cm).

$290–340 CO

► **A poster,** by Edward D. Byrd, 'Jesus Christ Superstar', America, 1971, 30¼ x 15¾in (77 x 40.5cm).

$280–330 VSP

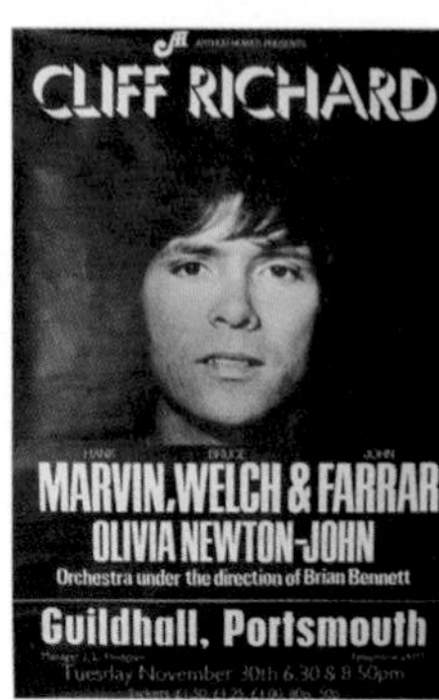

A concert poster, for Cliff Richard, c1971, 30 x 20in (76 x 51cm).

$85–95 CTO

An American Folk Blues Festival poster, by Günther Kieser, 1972, 33½ x 23¾in (85 x 60.5cm).

$250–300 VSP

A concert poster, for the Electric Light Orchestra, America, 1973, 22 x 14in (56 x 35.5cm).

$110–130 HER

A concert poster, for Count Basie at the Pablo Jazz Festival, slight damage, 1978, 24 x 17in (61 x 43cm).

$50–60 Her

For more rock and pop, please see the Rock & Pop section on pages 328–343.

A concert poster, for Charles Mingus, slight damage, 1970s, 24 x 17in (61 x 43cm).

$110–130 Her

◄ **A concert poster,** by Dennis Larkins and Ron Larson, for The Rolling Stones at Oakland Stadium, America, 1989, 28½ x 19½in (72.5 x 49.5cm).

$95–110 Her

► **A concert poster,** for The Who at Madison Square Gardens, New York, America, 2000, 23 x 12in (58.5 x 30.5cm).

$145–165 Lim

SPORTING

A London Tramways poster, 'Football Grounds, Tramway Services', after Bestall, designed at the L. C. C. Central School of Arts & Crafts, printed by Vincent Brooks, 1920s, 27½ x 12in (70 x 30.5cm), framed and glazed.

$520–620 DW

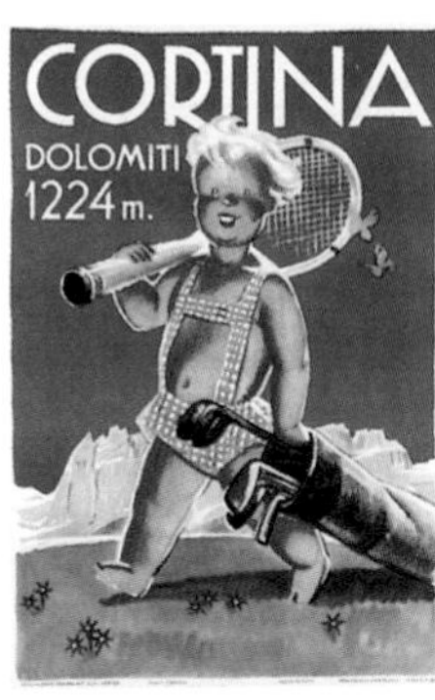

A poster, by Franz Lenhart, 'Cortina Dolomiti', printed by Ennio Travagliati, Italy, Verona, c1950, 39½ x 27½in (100.5 x 70cm).

$1,250–1,450 VSP

▶ A poster, by F. Schneider, 'Championnats du monde de foot-ball La Suisse', Switzerland, 1954, 40¼ x 25in (102 x 63.5cm).

$250–300 VSP

A K.N.A.U. poster, 'Athletiek maakt fit', printed by Plandruk Gräfe-Delft, Holland, 1935, 28¾ x 19¼in (73 x 49cm).

$340–410 VSP

A World Cup poster, 'IV Campeonato Mundial de Futebol', published by Maua, Rio de Janeiro, signed, restored, Brazil, 1950, 35½ x 23¾in (90 x 60.5cm).

$6,200–7,400 BUDD

A poster, by Franz Würbel, 'Olympische Spiele Berlin', on japan paper, Germany, 1936, 39¾ x 24½in (101 x 62cm).

$2,050–2,450 VSP

A Sportpaleis poster, advertising Ray Sugar Robinson, 1951, 43¼ x 28¾in (110 x 73cm).

$175–200 VSP

A poster, 'Jeux Olympiques d'Hiver', printed by Bimospa-Roma, Italy, 1956, 39½ x 24¾in (100.5 x 63cm).

$1,050–1,250 VSP

A FIFA World Cup poster, 'Coupe du Monde', published by Desme, Paris, signed, 1938, 61 x 45in (155 x 114.5cm).

$11,000–13,100 BUDD

A poster, by Ilmari Sysimtsa, 'Olympic Games, Helsinki', printed by Oy Tilgmann, Finland, 1952, 39½ x 24½in (100.5 x 62cm).

$590–690 VSP

A poster, 'Olympische Spiele München', Germany, 1972, 40 x 25in (101.5 x 63.5cm).

$270–300 MARK

TRAVEL

A travel poster, by Anthony Hansen, 'New England', printed by Latham Litho, Long Island City, America, c1920, 41 x 27¼in (104 x 69cm).

$1,000–1,200 VSP

A Royal Mail travel poster, by Padden, 'Mediterranean by RMSP Arcardian', printed by the Baynard Press, 1929, 39¾ x 25in (101 x 63.5cm).

$480–570 VSP

An LNER poster, by E. Ryatt, 'North East Dales', printed by Waterlow & Sons, c1930, 39¾ x 50in (101 x 127cm).

$570–670 VSP

A United State Lines poster, by Y. Delfo, 'Europe – America', c1950, 20 x 15in (51 x 38cm).

$200–240 VSP

A travel poster, by Paul Erkelens, 'Holland', on japan paper, c1945, 40 x 24in (101.5 x 61cm).

$135–160 VSP

A French National Railways poster, by Herve Baille, 'All the year round the French Riviera calls you', No. 41, printed by Hubert Baille & Cie, 1949, 39¾ x 24½in (101 x 62cm).

$520–620 ONS

◀ **A travel poster,** by Thomas Train, 'The Cairngorm Mountains', printed by Jordison & Co, c1950, 39¾ x 50in (101 x 127cm).

$830–980 VSP

▶ **A travel poster,** by Edouard Collin, 'Cie Gile Transatlantique Paris Marseille', on linen, France, c1950, 22¾ x 15½in (58 x 39.5cm).

$175–200 VSP

A KLM poster, by Kees van Roemburg, 'Australia', on japan paper, printed by Kühn & Zoon, Holland, 1951, 40¼ x 25in (102 x 63.5cm).

$480–570 VSP

A Holland-America Line, by Frank H. Mason, cardboard on tin, c1955, 11 x 15¼in (28 x 39cm).

$200–240 VSP

A Holland-America Cruises poster, by David Klein, 'Caribbean South America', America, 1974, 38 x 25in (96.5 x 63.5cm).

$190–220 VSP

A travel poster, by Cervin-A. Perren/Barberini, 'Zermatt', printed by Orell Füssli, Switzerland, 1953, 40¼ x 25¼in (102 x 64cm).

$220–260 VSP

A travel poster, by Abram Games, 'Holiday in Israel', printed by Lewin-Epstein, Tel Aviv, Israel, 1956, 38½ x 25½in (98 x 65cm).

$240–280 VSP

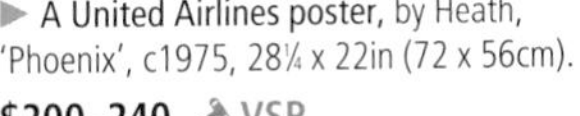

► **A United Airlines poster,** by Heath, 'Phoenix', c1975, 28¼ x 22in (72 x 56cm).

$200–240 VSP

A travel poster, 'Norway', c1955, 39 x 24in (99 x 61cm).

$430–480 Do

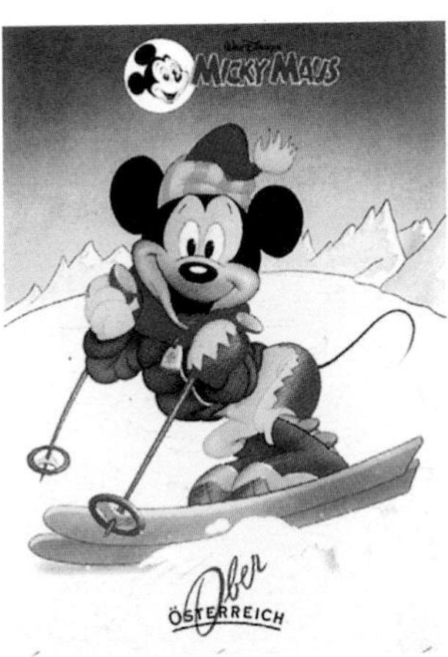

A travel poster, by Walt Disney, 'Ober Osterreich', c1960, 33¼ x 23½in (84.5 x 59.5cm).

$250–300 VSP

WARTIME

A poster, by Hans Friedrich, 'Das freie Meer!', printed by Wezel & Naumann, Germany, c1915, 35¼ x 23¾in (89.5 x 60.5cm).

$410–490 VSP

A poster, 'Seeleute Alle Mannen an Bord!', printed by Dinse & Eckert, Germany, 1916, 37½ x 23¾in (95.5 x 60.5cm).

$400–480 VSP

A poster, by Egon Tschirch, 'Was England will!', printed by Selmar Bayer, Germany, 1918, 38¼ x 26½in (97 x 67.5cm).

$500–590 VSP

A National Savings Group poster, by Rowland Hilder, 'Convoy your Country to Victory', 1939–45, 30 x 19¾in (76 x 50cm).

$270–320 SWO

◄ An Office for Emergency Management poster, by Jean Carlu, 'Give 'em Both Barrels', America, 1941, 15 x 20in (38 x 51cm).

$480–570 VSP

An HMSO poster, by Terence Cuneo, 'Back Them Up!', c1942, 30 x 20in (76 x 51cm).

$270–320 VSP

An HMSO poster, 'Telling a Friend May Mean Telling the Enemy', c1942, 21¼ x 11in (54 x 28cm).

$60–70 DW

◄ A poster, by Studio Arend Meijer, 'Driekamp Kampioenschap de W.A.', Holland, 1943, 30¾ x 21in (78 x 53.5cm).

$410–490 VSP

WEERSPORT KAMPEN
DENEN · DUITSCHERS · NEDERLANDERS
NOREN · VLAMINGEN · WALEN
ÉÉN IN WEERSPORTKAMPEN

A poster, 'Weersport Kampen', Holland, c1943, 31½ x 21¾in (80 x 55.5cm).

$400–480 VSP

◄ A poster, 'De Motor WA', c1943, 30¾ x 20¾in (78 x 52.5cm).

$200–240 VSP

A poster, by Frank Wootton, 'Help Britain Finish the Job!', printed by Fosh & Cross, c1945, 30 x 19¾in (76 x 50.5cm).

$410–490 VSP

A poster, by Ronay, 'Help Holland', c1945, 19¼ x 13½in (49 x 34.5cm).

$85–100 VSP

POWDER COMPACTS

A paper box of Coty Airspun loose powder, 1913, 1¾in (4.5cm) wide.

$10–15 KKN

A celluloid and tin powder compact, worn, 1920s, 2½in (6.5cm) diam.

$260–290 SUW

A gilt-metal powder compact, the lid set with moulded glass, signed 'R. Robert', France, 1920s, 4½in (11.5cm) diam.

$310–350 SUW

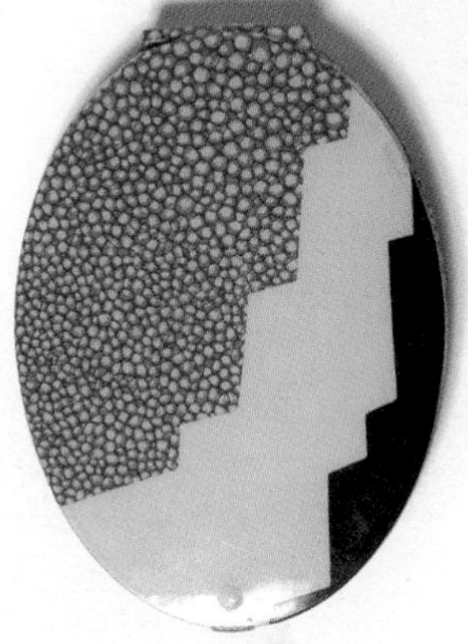

A celluloid powder compact, 1925–30, 3½in (9cm) wide.

$140–160 SUW

An enamelled metal rouge and powder compact, with patent number, America, 1930s, 3¼in (8.5cm) long.

$140–160 SUW

A machined metal rouge and powder compact, with chain and finger ring, the lid set with an enamel rose plaque, 1930s, 2½in (6.5cm) long.

$140–160 PAST

An Amita damascene gold and silver powder compact, inlaid with a chinoiserie scene, 1930s, 4in (10cm) wide.

$100–115 SUW

► A base metal powder compact, set with paste stones and pearls, 1940, 3¼in (8.5cm) wide.

$50–60 299

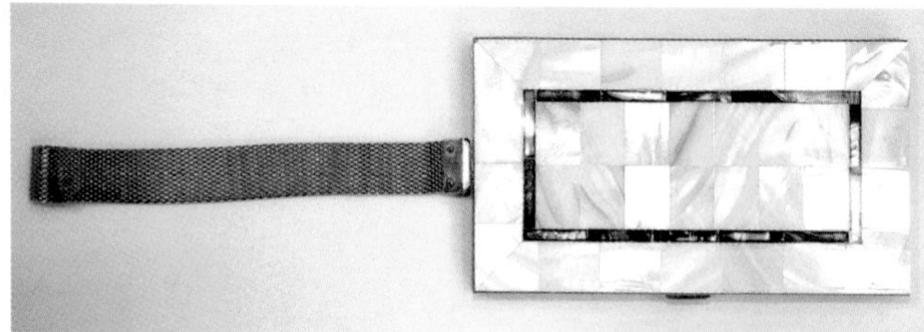

An abalone and mother-of-pearl carry-all, with secret compartment and wrist strap, containing a cigarette, powder, rouge, comb and mirror, America, 1940s, 5¼in (13.5cm) long.

$150–160 ⊞ PAST

A Mondaine celluloid make-up compact, with rouge, powder, mirror, mascara, eye pencil, lipstick and eye shadow, the lid set with an enamel plaque, America, 1940s, 3in (7.5cm) wide.

$150–160 ⊞ PAST

An enamel powder compact, set with paste stones, America, late 1940s, 5in (12.5cm) wide.

$330–380 ⊞ DUR

► **A Bourgois metal and enamel compact,** 'Evening in Paris', containing powder, rouge and lipstick, America, 1940s–50s, 3in (7.5cm) long.

$150–170 ⊞ PAST

A sterling silver and Lucite powder compact, 1940s–50s, 3in (7.5cm) diam.

$150–170 ⊞ SUW

◄ **A metal make-up compact,** with chinoiserie decoration, Austria, 1940–50, 5in (12.5cm) wide.

$150–160 ⊞ SUW

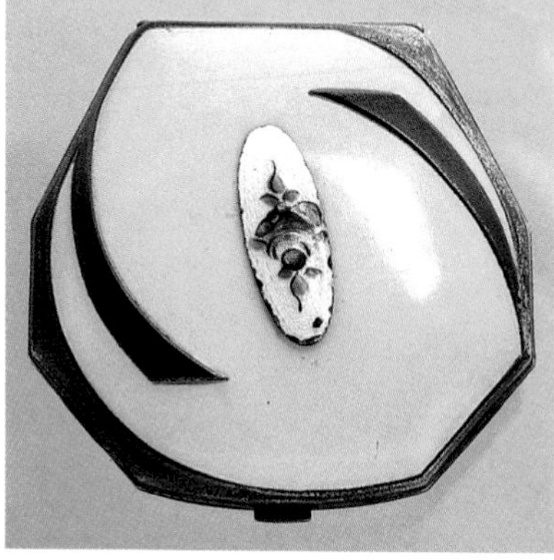

◄ **An Elgin brass and enamel compact,** in the shape of saddle bag, the guilloche medallion hand-painted with a rose, contains powder puff, mirror and rouge compartment, America, New York, 1950s, 2½in (6.5cm) wide.

$60–70 ⊞ KKN

A Kigu metal powder compact, the lid set with diamanté and *faux* pearl decoration, signed 'KG', 1950s, 3in (7.5cm) diam.

$50–60 ⊞ KA

A Rex Fifth Avenue *faux* guilloche and enamel compact, decorated with stylized leaves, with powder puff, America, 1950s, 3in (7.5 cm) wide.

$10–15 ⊞ KKN

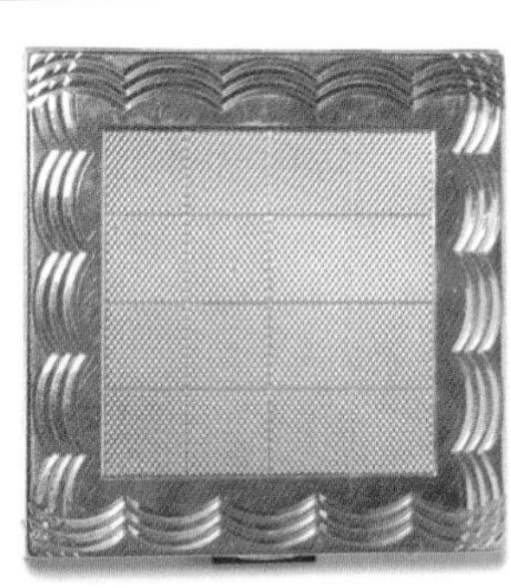

► **A Corona metal powder compact,** containing a swan's-down puff, France, 1950s, 3in (7.5cm) wide.

$40–45 ⊞ KA

► **A Henriette lipstick and powder compact,** on a stand, America, 1950s, 3½in (9cm) wide.

$220–250 ⊞ SUW

◄ **A base metal and plastic powder compact,** in the form of a ball, 1950s, 3½in (9cm) diam.

$50–60 ⊞ 299

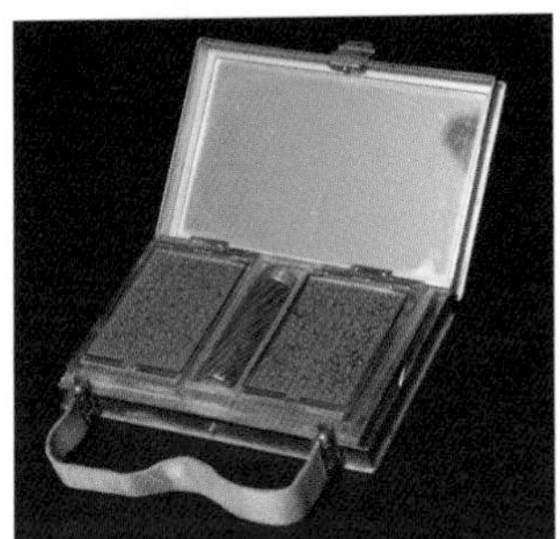

A metal powder compact, in the form of a party bag, with rouge, powder and lipstick, c1960, 5in (12.5cm) wide.

$120–120 ⊞ SBL

A Japanese-style metal powder compact, signed 'Olfa', France, Paris, 1950s, 3½in (9cm) wide.

$40–45 ⊞ KA

◄ **An Elgin enamelled powder compact,** in the shape of a saddle bag, contains powder puff and loose powder, with original 'sock' sheath, America, 1960s, 3¼in (8.5cm) wide.

$20–25 ⊞ KKN

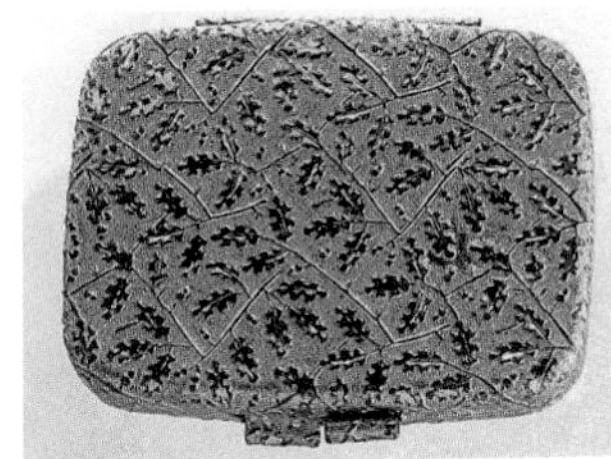

A powder compact, decorated in relief with oak leaves, contains removable solid powder insert and Revlon powder puff, 1970s, 2½in (6.5cm) wide.

$10–15 ⊞ KKN

PUPPETS

STRING PUPPETS

A Pelham Goofy string puppet, 1950, 10in (25.5cm) high, with box.

$360–400 MTB

From 1956 this puppet's hands and head were reduced in size. Most of these early puppets suffered from felt mite damage.

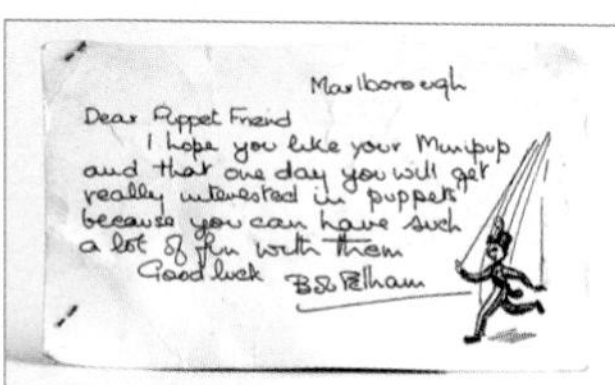

Marlborough

Dear Puppet Friend

I hope you like your Minipup and that one day you will get really interested in puppets because you can have such a lot of fun with them

Good luck BS Pelham

A Pelham Minipup Poodle string puppet, 1952–53, 5in (12.5cm) high, with header card.

$80–95 MTB

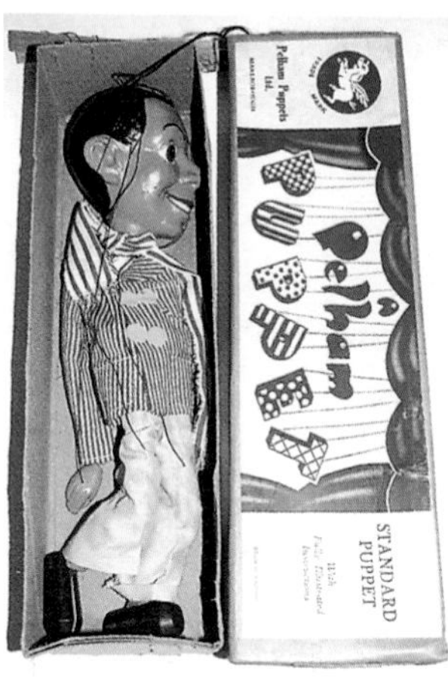

A Pelham Archie Andrews string puppet, 1950s–early 1960s, 12in (30.5cm) high, with box.

$250–300 GTH

In the summer of 1950, the BBC produced Educating Archie *and although not the first ventriloquist act to perform on the radio it was by far the most successful, with a combined audience of more than 16 million for its Thursday and Sunday afternoon slots. It captured the imagination of British radio audiences, its success largely due to the quality of its other performers such as Harry Secombe, Dick Emery, Bruce Forsyth, Hattie Jacques and Max Bygraves, with Beryl Reid taking the part of Archie's girlfriend.*

A Pelham Minipup Caesar string puppet, 1952–53, 5in (12.5cm) high, with header card.

$145–165 MTB

A Pelham Minipup Horse string puppet, 1952–53, 5in (12.5cm) high, with header card.

$100–115 MTB

It is rare to find Minipup puppets with header cards. Without these cards value would be around $20–25.

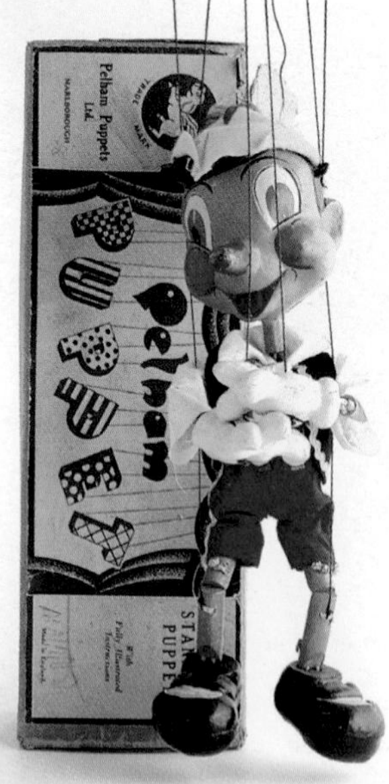

A Pelham Pinocchio string puppet, second issue, 1952–55, 12in (30.5cm) high, with third issue box.

$165–190 MTB

A Pelham Noddy string **puppet,** with solid head, 1953, 12in (30.5cm) high, in original box with copyright label.

$220–250 ⊞ MTB

The inclusion of the copyright label on the box adds to value.

A Pelham Dutch Girl string **puppet,** 1953–55, 12in (30.5cm) high, with original box.

$110–130 ⊞ MTB

► A Pelham Noddy string **puppet,** 1956, 10in (25.5cm) high, with box.

$220–250 ⊞ MTB

A Pelham Mr Turnip string **puppet,** 1953, 12in (30.5cm) high, in original box with copyright label.

$130–150 ⊞ MTB

To retain its value, Mr Turnip must have the original hair coil on his head.

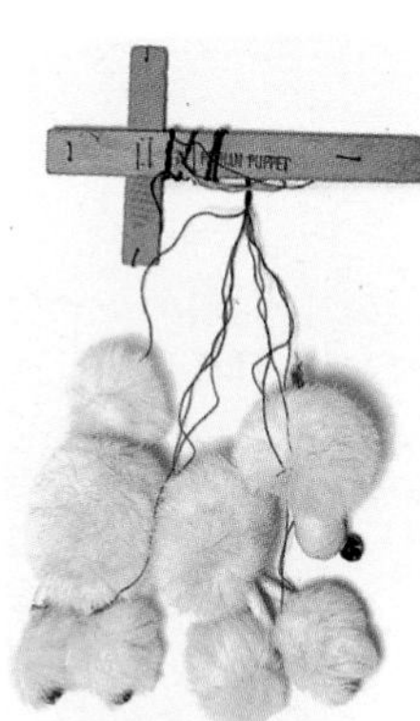

A Pelham Big Ears string **puppet,** large head, 1953, 13in (33cm) high, in original box with copyright label.

$270–300 ⊞ MTB

A Pelham Noddy string **puppet,** large head, 1953–54, 12in (30.5cm) high, with original third type box.

$250–290 ⊞ MTB

Large head Noddy puppets are more sought after.

◄ A Pelham **poodle string puppet,** early 1950s, 7in (18cm) wide, with box.

$70–80 ⊞ J&J

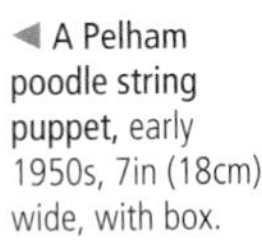

► A Pelham Big **Ears string puppet,** 1956, 13in (33cm) high, with fourth-type box.

$220–250 ⊞ MTB

Two Pelham Jumpetts Ostrich Iz and Oz string puppets, 1958–70, 5½in (14cm) high, with original boxes.

$85–100 each ⊞ MTB

A Pelham **Frog string puppet,** 1963, 12in (30.5cm) high, with box.

$145–165 ⊞ MTB

The round toes on this Frog puppet cracked easily and so from c1970 they were altered to square toes and made of fabric.

A Pelham **Girl in Green Dress string puppet,** c1965, 12in (30.5cm) high, with original box.

$130–150 ⊞ MTB

A **Linda Big Ears string puppet,** 1963, 8in (20.5cm) high, with original box.

$100–115 ⊞ MTB

Linda puppets are very hard to find.

A **Pelham Owl string puppet,** from the animal range, with tag on clothing dated 1965, 8in (20.5cm) high.

$460–520 ⊞ MTB

The range of animals was only produced for five years due to poor sales. Owl, Pig, Tiger, Hedgehog, Tortoise, Katy Caterpillar, Mother Bear, Father Bear, Baby Bear, Rabbit and Crow were soon discontinued, but King, Witch, Old Man, Elephant, Queen, Frog, Fox, Giant, Baby Dragon and Mother Dragon were more popular. Wheny buying it is important to find a puppet with the yellow tag that denotes it is a genuine Pelham puppet, as lesser quality copies were imported from Hong Kong in the early 1960s.

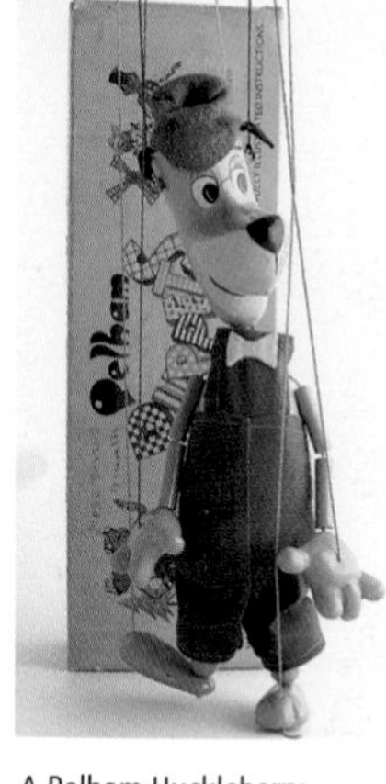

A Pelham **Huckleberry Hound string puppet,** 1963, 9in (23cm) high, in original box with copyright label.

$280–320 ⊞ MTB

◄ A Pelham **King string puppet,** 1963, 12in (30.5cm) high, with original box.

$380–430 ⊞ MTB

As with the toes of the Frog puppet, the moulded crown on the King cracked easily, and from 1964 the crown was made of fabric.

A **Pelham Ermintrude string puppet,** first issue, 1968–75, 8in (20.5cm) long, with box.

$100–115 ⊞ MTB

Ermintrude is a character in The Magic Roundabout, *a children's televsion programme created by Serge Danot. First shown in France in 1964, it has subsequently been broadcast in over 98 countries and translated into 28 languages. It was made into a film in 1995. Other characters in the story are Dougal, Dylan, Florence, Brian, Mr McHenry and Zebedee.*

A Lady Rosemary of Bayleaf **string puppet,** c1970, 7½in (19cm) high.

$85–95 ⊞ MTB

Lady Rosemary was a character in BBC television's The Herbs, *which was first shown in 1968. Created by Michael Bond – of* Paddington Bear *fame – it was designed for pre-school children and ran for only 13 episodes. Other characters included Sir Basil, Parsley the Lion, Dill the dog, Bayleaf the gardner and Constable Knapweed.*

A Pelham Pop Star Guitarist **string puppet,** first version with grey check weave suit, 1970, 12in (30.5cm) high, with original box.

$190–210 ⊞ MTB

Other members of the four-man group included a drummer (and separate drum kit), singer with microphone and saxophonist. The complete set, in grey suits, would sell for $1,000. In 1967, the year the Beatles' Sgt Pepper's Lonely Hearts Club Band *was released, a set was made with psychedelic clothing which is now worth $860.*

A Bluebell of Bayleaf **string puppet,** c1970, 8½in (21.5cm) high, with original box.

$145–165 ⊞ MTB

Bluebell was also a character in The Herbs.

A Pelham Baby Dragon **string puppet,** c1970, 9in (23cm) high, with original box.

$130–150 ⊞ MTB

A Pelham Cat **string puppet,** c1970, 5in (12.5cm) high, with box.

$45–50 ⊞ MTB

► A Pelham Dopey **display puppet,** 1970s, 24in (61cm) high.

$460–520 ⊞ ARo

A Pelham *The Wombles* Madame Cholet **string puppet,** 1974, 8in (20.5cm) high, with original box.

$75–85 ⊞ MTB

◄ A Pelham Snake Charmer **string puppet,** with flute and snake, c1979, 13in (33cm) high, with box.

$165–190 ⊞ MTB

Cellophane window boxes were first used c1979.

A Pelham Devil **string puppet,** c1980, 12in (30.5cm) high, with box.

$220–250 ⊞ MTB

After the death of Bob Pelham in 1980, the puppets were repackaged into larger boxes and labelled 'De Luxe'.

ROD PUPPETS

A Pelham Zebedee rod **puppet**, 1966, 11in (28cm) high, with original box.

$165–190 ⊞ MTB

Wooden rod puppets are sought after and therefore more valuable.

A Pelham Florence rod **puppet**, 1966, 12in (30.5cm) high, with original box.

$165–190 ⊞ MTB

A Pelham Dougal rod puppet, c1966, 12in (30.5cm) long, with original box.

$100–115 ⊞ MTB

► A Pelham Mr Rusty rod **puppet**, 1966, 12in (30.5cm) high, with original box.

$180–200 ⊞ MTB

GLOVE PUPPETS

A Mr Punch hand **puppet**, possibly papier-mâché, with a velvet coat, 1930s, 19¾in (50cm) high.

$60–70 ⊞ KLH

► A Pelham Crow **glove puppet**, with moulded head and felt body, 1976, 7in (18cm) high, with box.

$60–70 ⊞ MTB

◄ A Chad Valley **Parsley glove puppet**, 1970s, 10in (25.5cm) high.

$75–85 ⊞ MTB

◄ Four SAPRO ***Magic Roundabout* glove puppets,** Florence, Zebedee, Ermintrude and Dougal, with rubber heads and fabric bodies, France, 1992, 10in (25.5cm) high.

$30–35 each ⊞ MTB

Six ***Magic Roundabout* glove puppets,** Mr Rusty, Paul, Florence, Mr McHenry, Margot and Mr McHenry, France, 1996, 9in (23cm) high.

$40–45 each ⊞ MTB

RAILWAYANA

UNION PACIFIC RAIL ROAD

A Union Pacific Old Timers Club cloth badge, America, 4in (10cm) long.

$10–15 ⊞ MYS

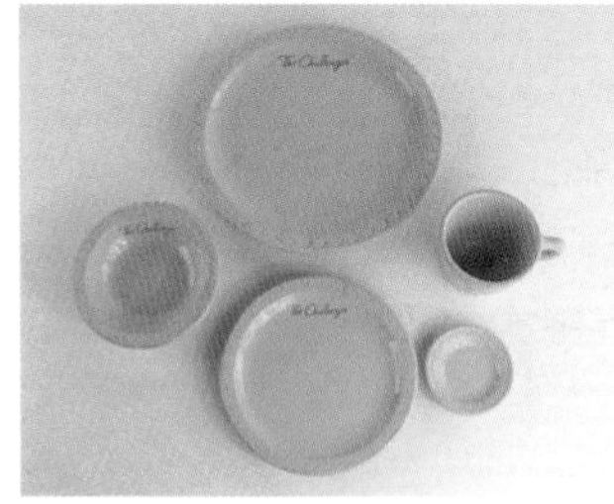

Five pieces of The Challenger dining car china, marked 'Syracuse China', America, c1930s.

$130–150 ⊞ MYS

A Union Pacific set of four match boxes, with box car, America, 4in (10cm) long.

$20–25 ⊞ MYS

- The first rails of the American Union Pacific Rail Road were laid in 1862.
- The railroad took six years and an army of 20,000 men, most of them immigrants from China and Europe.
- The railroad initially stretched from Omaha to Salt Lake City.
- Union Pacific ran its passenger service in July 1866.
- Owned by the Union Pacific Corporation today, the railroad has expanded across 23 US states.

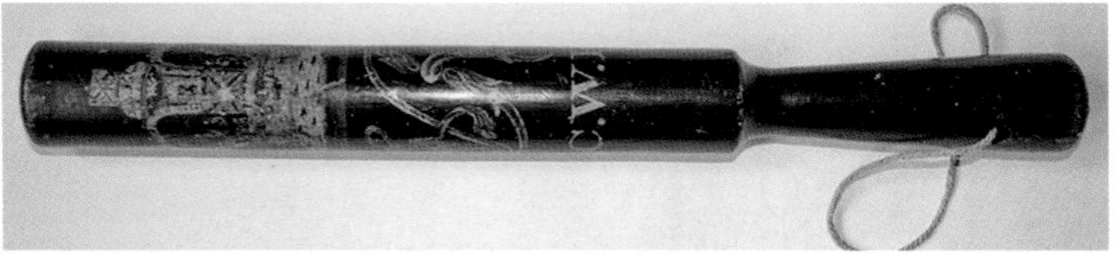

◄ **A Canterbury & Whitstable Railway police truncheon,** with crown and company initials, 1837–53, 14in (35.5cm) long.

$5,200–6,200 GWRA

A British Railways steel and enamel totem, early 1950s, 36in (91.5cm) wide.

$7,100–8,500 GWRA

The station at the small fishing and seaside town of Musselburgh, just outside Edinburgh, was opened in 1847 as a link from the East Coast main line. It closed in September 1964, when this totem, believed to be the only surviving example, was obtained.

A steel bunkering lamp, c1900, 9in (23cm) wide.

$60–70 ⊞ FST

This lamp would have been used when inspecting the underside of locomotives.

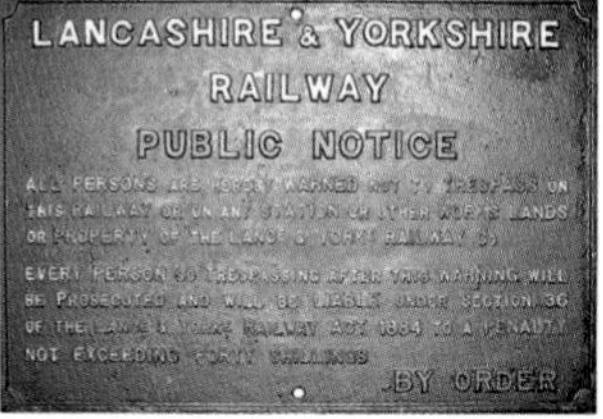

◄ **A Lancashire & Yorkshire Railway cast-iron public notice,** early 20thC, 22in (56cm) wide.

$30–35 ⊞ CGA

A London & North Eastern Railway steel and wood locomotive fireman's shovel, shaft inscribed, c1900, 35in (89cm) high.

$75–85 ⊞ CGA

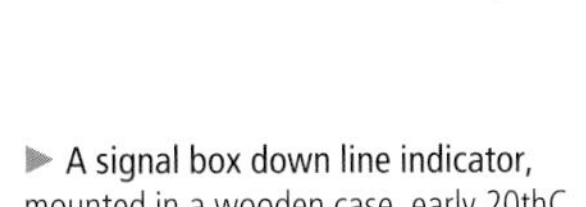

► **A signal box down line indicator,** mounted in a wooden case, early 20thC, 12in (30.5cm) high.

$210–240 VEC

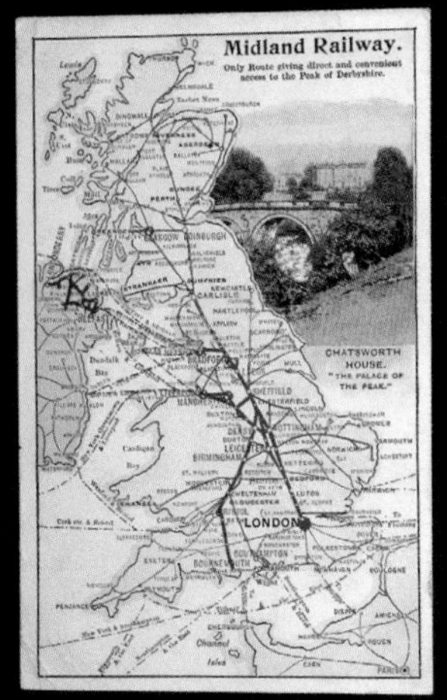

A Midland Railway advertising postcard, 1905.

$45–50 ⊞ MCS

A Queen Adelaide's Railway Saloon photographic postcard, 1908, 4 x 6in (10 x 15cm).

$5–10 ⊞ S&D

Princess Adelaide of Saxe-Meiningen became Queen Consort of King William IV in 1918.

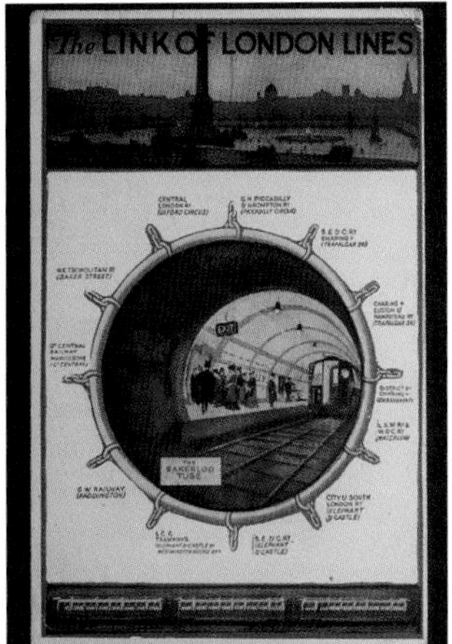

A London Underground postcard, advertising the Bakerloo line, 1911.

$85–100 ⊞ MCS

◄ **A set of six Burlington Route telegrapher's books,** including rules, rates of pay and constitution, 1918–60, 7 x 4in (18 x 10cm).

$5–10 each ⊞ MYS

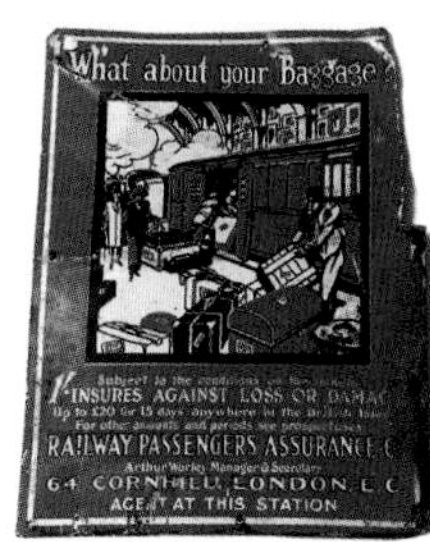

► **A Railway Passengers Assurance Co metal advertisement,** 1920s, 12 x 10in (30.5 x 25.5cm).

$50–60 ⊞ COB

A London & North Western Railway salt-glazed inkwell, with four quill holes, 1910–20, 4¾in (12cm) diam.

$40–45 BBR

A Zenith presentation railway pocket watch, engraved with symbol and initials of the Turkish State Railway, the enamelled dial with Arabic numerals, in a nickel-silver case, 1920s, 2in (5cm) diam.

$720–810 ⊞ WAC

A London & North Eastern Railway seatback, 1920s, 25¾in (65.5cm) long.

$1,000–1,200 GWRA

Coxwold is a former North Eastern Railway station between Malton and Thirsk in north Yorkshire.

► **A London & North Eastern Railway steel and copper oil lamp,** c1925, 12in (30.5cm) high.

$120–140 ⊞ CGA

◄ **A Burlington Route railroad instruction booklet,** America, 1937, 7½in (19cm) high.

$20–25 ⊞ MYS

A Salmon Series Manchester & Blackpool Express postcard, 1938, 5½in (14cm) wide.

$5–10 ⊞ SOR

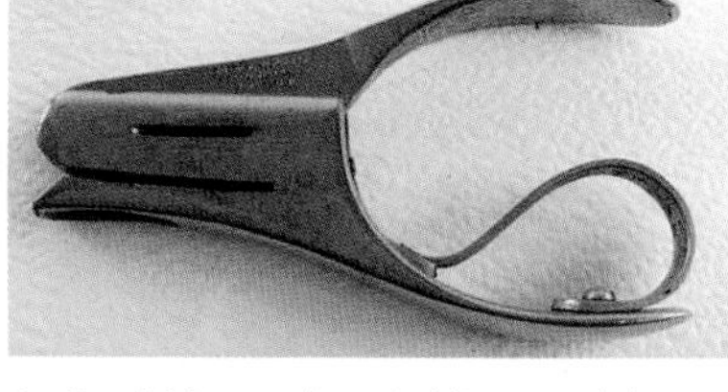

A railroad ticket punch, marked 'Bonney-Vehslage Tool Co, New York', America.

$20–25 ⊞ MYS

This would have been used on the Union Pacific passenger train lines.

An aluminium railway carriage emblem, Russia, 1940s, 14in (35.5cm) high.

$360–430 ⊞ COB

***On Dress Parade*, by The Pullman** Company, featuring passenger car designs, America, 1948, 7½in (19cm) high.

$45–50 ⊞ MYS

A smokebox numberplate, from 'Earl Baldwin', dated 1948.

$2,600–3,100 GWRA

A collection of *Railroad* magazines, published by Frank A. Munsey Co, America, 1940s.

$20–25 each ⊞ MYS

A Pennsylvania Rail Road **lighter,** America, 1940s–50s, 2in (5cm) high.

$30–35 MYS

A brass switch lock key, stamped 'Adlake P.R.R.' for the Pennsylvania Rail Road, America, 1950s.

$20–25 MYS

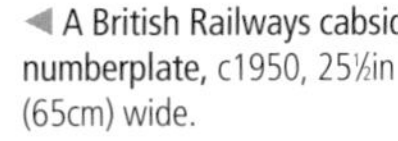

◄ A British Railways cabside numberplate, c1950, 25½in (65cm) wide.

$3,800–4,450 GWRA

This plate was allocated new to Tyseley and later Worcester, before being withdrawn in June 1965.

A brakeman's cloth hat band, used during the passenger service days of the Union Pacific Railroad, America, 26in (66cm) long.

$10–15 MYS

A British Railways station direction sign, early 1950s, 28in (71cm) wide.

$1,000–1,200 GWRA

Sutton Park is a former Midland Railway station situated between Walsall and Water Orton.

A Colorado Rail Road cast-iron trivet, marked 'The Iron Horse', 1954, 7in (18cm) long.

$30–35 MYS

A British Railways Southern Region enamel sign, with hanging loops, refurbished, 1950s, 18 x 24in (45.5 x 61cm).

$100–120 VEC

A British Railways engine driver's cap, stamped, 1965.

$20–25 VEC

A Seaboard Railroad timetable, America, 1966–67.

$10–15 MYS

◄ **A print of the London & North Eastern Railway 4468 'Mallard',** signed 'Cuneo', dated October 1967, 35 x 30in (89 x 76cm).

$85–100 VEC

A Long Island Railroad trainman's hat, worn, America, size 7, 1971–78.

$70–80 MYS

ROCK & POP

WHEN I STARTED selling records and rock memorabilia in 1973 it was once a month at an open air record fair in the US. Formalized auctions didn't exist and items changed hands on the collectors' circuit or appeared tucked away in general sales. The music that everyone wanted was The Beatles and British invasion, '50s and '60s Rock 'n' Roll, Surf, Soul, Psychedelic and Blues. I opened my first shop in 1976 just before Punk and New Wave hit, followed by Metal a few years later. The same groups and artists remain at the top, but today's collectors look for classic and obscure artists and original vinyl pressings in mint condition, as well as autographs, concert posters and ultra-rare pieces of music memorabilia.

Over the past year the big movers have been posters, vinyl and memorabilia. There is very strong demand for psychedelic posters from the 1960s promoting artists such as Jimi Hendrix and The Doors. The famous Hendrix Flying Eye Fillmore concert poster from 1968 can sell for $4,000–6,000 and a very rare Hendrix/ Doors Festival poster from New York in the same year went for an unbelievable $23,165 at auction.

In the world of vinyl it's the closing days mono that fuels collecting interest. From the mid-1960s record companies re-channelled many of their mono best-sellers, adding extra echo to create a false stereo sound that captivates today's fans. This year I was lucky enough to handle Bob Dylan's 'Freewheelin' album (1963) – not unusual in itself, only this version was a stereo copy with four songs that were deleted in later pressings. The fact that it's one of only two known means it could be worth over $75,000 or more at a forthcoming auction.

Here at Heritage Auction Galleries I've seen more vinyl rarities than I did durig the 30 years in my shop, including Buddy Holly's personal record and acetate collection selling for over $70,000 and a still sealed Beatle's `Yesterday and Today' Butcher cover that sold for almost $39,000. Now is the time to buy vinyl because mint condition copies are disappearing fast and prices will continue to rise.

Condition is the main factor that separates seemingly identical albums. Covers run from mint to bad and there is a big price difference between the two. Then there's the albums you can only dream of, the truly rare still sealed copies. When it comes to bands like The Beatles, it's astonishing how much difference a piece of plastic wrapping can make!

Garry Shrum

Dean Martin, first recording contract with Capitol Records, signed, 1948, 13 x 8½in (33 x 21.5cm).

$3,550–4,250 Her

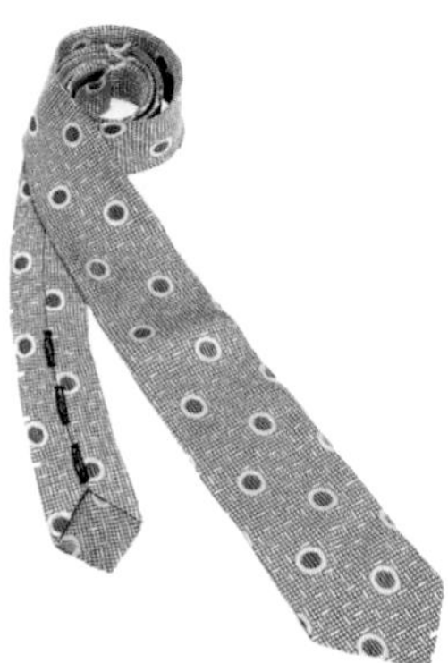

A Buddy Holly stage tie, with authentication certificate from Maria Elena Holly, c1958.

$950–1,100 Her

Elvis Presley, a postcard promoting the film *Flaming Star*, 1961, 5 x 3in (12.5 x 7.5cm).

$10–15 CTO

Elvis Presley, a personality postcard promoting the film *Blue Hawaii*, 1961, 5 x 3in (12.5 x 7.5cm).

$10–15 CTO

The Ronettes, sheet music for 'Do I Love You?', 1964.

$100–120 Her

A brass ring, engraved 'Jai Guru Dev', formerly owned by George Harrison and Magic Alex, 1968.

$1,000–1,200 CO

This ring was given to George Harrison during the Beatles' visit to the Maharishi Mahesh Yogi's transcendental meditation academy, 16 February –12 April 1968.

A Diana Dors wax portrait bust, used on the cover of 'Sgt. Pepper's Lonely Hearts Club Band', make-up retouched, 1967, 24in (61cm) high with stand.

$20,700–24,900 CO

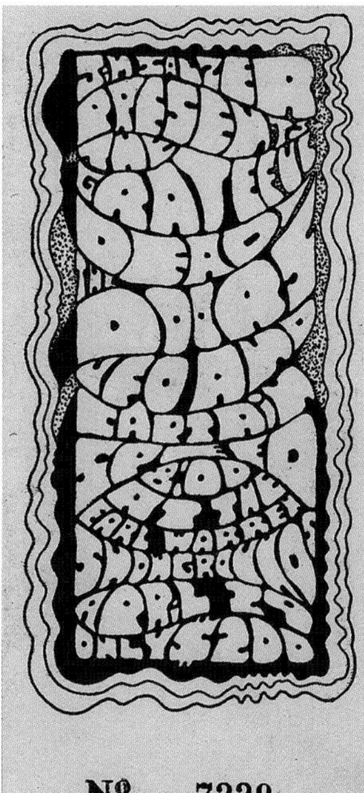

A Grateful Dead concert ticket, with The Doors, UFO and Captain Speed, Earl Warren Showground, 29 April 1968.

$430–510 Her

◄ ***Pop Weekly Annual,*** edited by Albert Hand, published by World Distributors, 1970, 10in (25.5cm) high.

$10–15 NGL

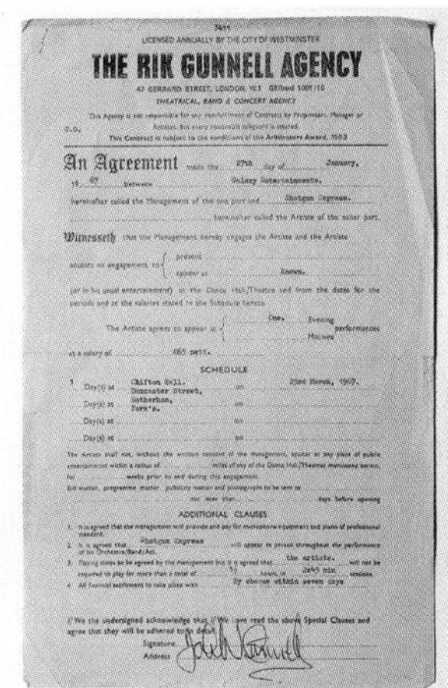

LICENSED ANNUALLY BY THE CITY OF WESTMINSTER

THE RIK GUNNELL AGENCY

47 GERRARD STREET, LONDON, W.1

THEATRICAL, BAND & CONCERT AGENCY

This Contract is subject to the conditions of the Arbitrators Award, 1963

An Agreement made the 27th day of January, 19 67 between Galaxy Entertainments, hereinafter called the Management of the one part and Shotgun Express, hereinafter called the Artiste of the other part.

Witnesseth that the Management hereby engage the Artiste and the Artiste accepts an engagement to present / appear as Known.

The Artiste agrees to appear at One Evening performances at a salary of £65 nett.

SCHEDULE

1 Day(s) at Chifton Hall, Doncaster Street, Rotherham, York's. on 23rd March, 1967.

ADDITIONAL CLAUSES

Signature

Address

A signed contract for a Shotgun Express concert, between the Rik Gunnell Agency and the Chifton Hall, Rotherham, dated 27 January 1967, 13in (33cm) high.

$60–70 CTO

Rod Stewart joined the blues-based group Shotgun Express as joint vocalist in 1965. The line-up included Peter Green and Mick Fleetwood.

Two Small Faces fan club newsletters, with original mailing envelopes, 1967–68, 7 x 5in (18 x 12.5cm).

$20–25 each CTO

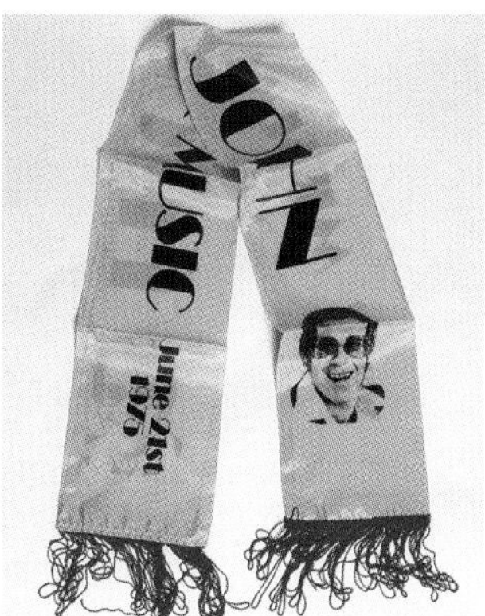

An Elton John nylon tour scarf, 1975, 36in (91.5cm) long.

$20–25 CLOB

A Mattel Donny & Marie Osmond dolls gift set, 1976, 13in (33cm) high.

$165–180 ⊞ MTB

A Matchbox ABBA doll, 'Frida', 1978, 10in (25.5cm) high.

$190–220 ⊞ MTB

Ten Frank Sinatra concert tickets, unused, for Alpine Valley Music Theatre, East Troy, Wisconsin, 17 August 1977.

$260–310 Her

Three Frank Sinatra backstage passes, 1980s.

$410–480 Her

A Pink Floyd The Wall tour T-shirt, 1980–81.

$60–70 ⊞ CLOB

'The Wall' was released in the UK on 30 November 1979. The tour began in Nassau Coliseum, New York, in 1980, travelling through America, Europe and the UK before finishing in September 1981.

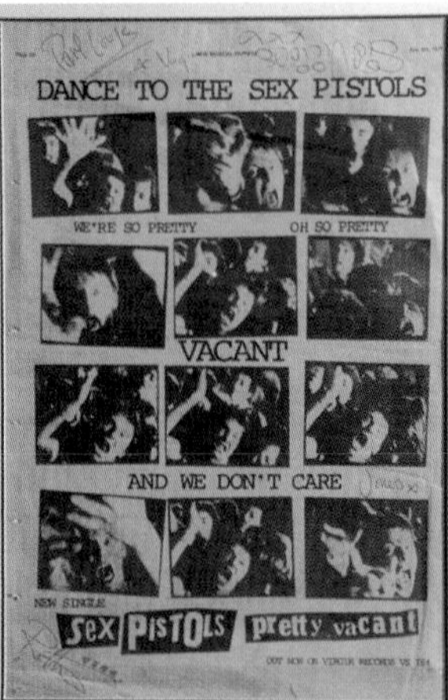

New Musical Express, a page featuring the release of the Sex Pistols' single 'Pretty Vacant', signed by Sid Vicious, Paul Cook, Johnny Rotten and Steve Jones, 9 July 1977.

$4,500–5,100 ⊞ FRa

A Genesis tour jacket, 1982.

$155–180 CO

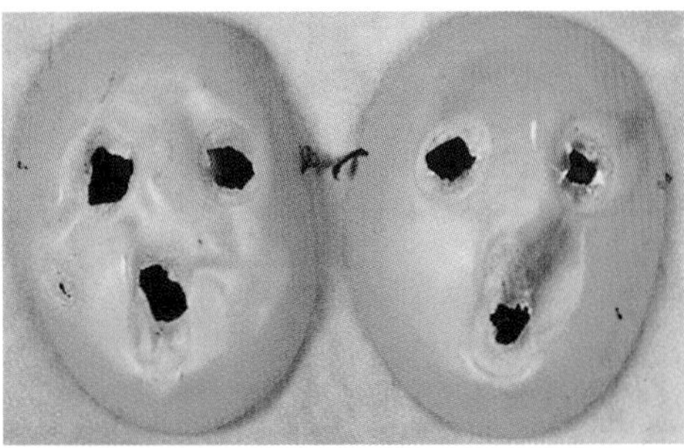

Four Pink Floyd face masks, used in the film *The Wall*, 1982.

$510–610 CO

▶ An Oasis signed newspaper headline, reporting Noel Gallagher's illegal walk along a Cornish railway line, signed by Liam Gallagher, Gem Archer and Andy Bell, cropped, 2004, 9in (23cm) high.

$170–200 ⊞ IQ

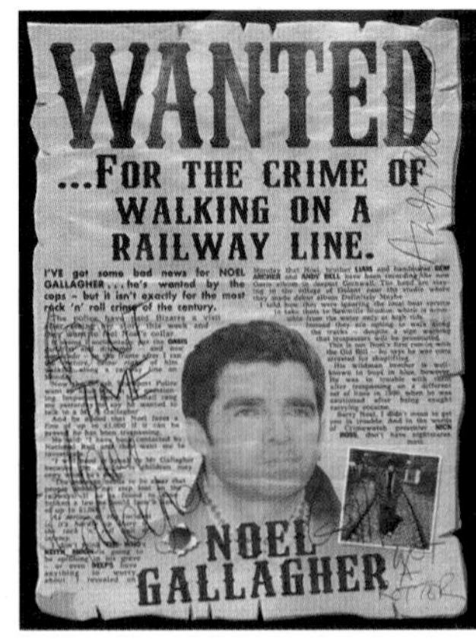

BEATLES
& Pop Memorabilia
WANTED
UP TO £2000 PAID PER SET OF BEATLES AUTOGRAPHS ON ONE PAGE
UP TO £5000 PAID FOR BEATLES CONCERT POSTERS
Any Pop Memorabilia Considered - Free Quotations
Beatles, Stones, Who, Zeppelin, Hendrix, Floyd, 60's, 70's.
Posters, Handbills, Autographs, Tickets, Photos, Lyrics, Personal Effects.
Only Rare Records Considered
TRACKS
PO BOX 117, Chorley, Lancashire, PR6 0UU
TEL: 01257 269726 - FAX: 01257 231340
e-mail: sales@tracks.co.uk

THE BEATLES

The Beatles, a postcard, 1960s, 5¾ x 4in (14.5 x 10cm).

$10–15 RTT

A Washington Pottery earthenware plate, transfer-printed with a picture of the Beatles and their facsmilie signatures, 1960s, 7in (18cm) diam.

$60–70 KA

Four Emirober plastic figures of The Beatles, 1960s, pack 6½in (16.5cm) high.

$70–80 KA

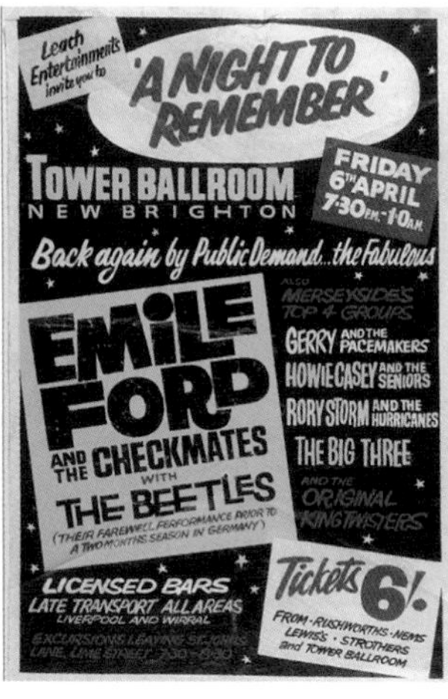

A Beatles concert poster, 1962, 29 x 20in (73.5 x 51cm).

$12,100–14,500 CO

This is a rare early concert poster in which the Beatles are quite low down in the order of appearance. Note also the mis-spelling of their name.

A set of Beatles Christmas flexi discs, in original sleeves, with fan club newsletters, 1960s.

$1,150–1,350 CO

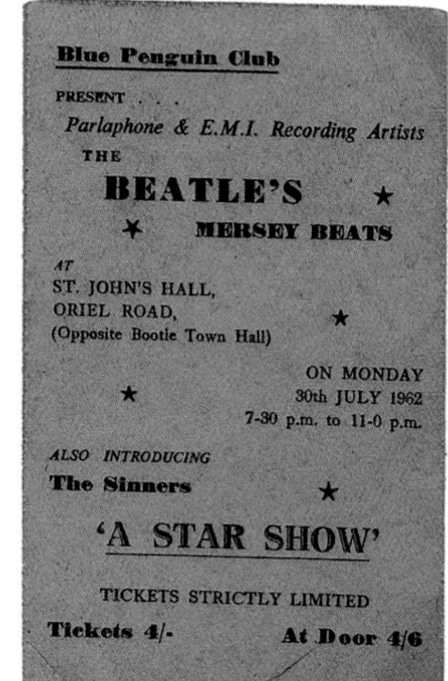

Blue Penguin Club
PRESENT . . .
Parlaphone & E.M.I. Recording Artists
THE
BEATLE'S
MERSEY BEATS
AT
ST. JOHN'S HALL,
ORIEL ROAD,
(Opposite Bootle Town Hall)
ON MONDAY
30th JULY 1962
7-30 p.m. to 11-0 p.m.
ALSO INTRODUCING
The Sinners
'A STAR SHOW'
TICKETS STRICTLY LIMITED
Tickets 4/- At Door 4/6

A Beatles concert ticket, St John's Hall, Bootle, 30 July 1962.

$1,200–1,400 Her

The Beatles, 'She Loves You/I'll Get You', single record, by Swan, white label version with 'Don't Drop Out' message, 1963.

$340–410 Her

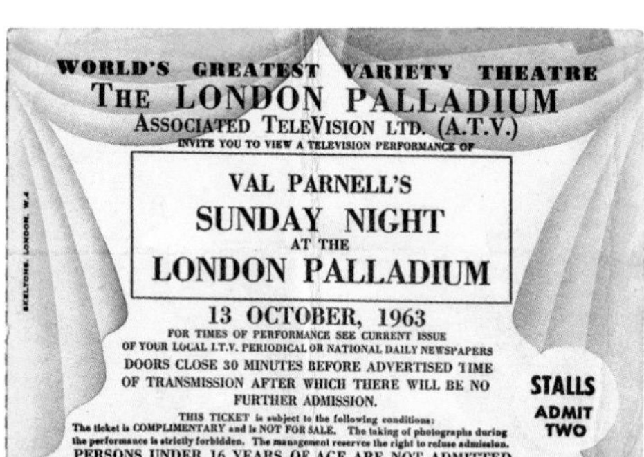

WORLD'S GREATEST VARIETY THEATRE
THE LONDON PALLADIUM
ASSOCIATED TELEVISION LTD. (A.T.V.)
INVITE YOU TO VIEW A TELEVISION PERFORMANCE OF
VAL PARNELL'S
SUNDAY NIGHT
AT THE
LONDON PALLADIUM
13 OCTOBER, 1963
FOR TIMES OF PERFORMANCE SEE CURRENT ISSUE
OF YOUR LOCAL I.T.V. PERIODICAL OR NATIONAL DAILY NEWSPAPERS
DOORS CLOSE 30 MINUTES BEFORE ADVERTISED TIME
OF TRANSMISSION AFTER WHICH THERE WILL BE NO
FURTHER ADMISSION.
THIS TICKET is subject to the following conditions:
The ticket is COMPLIMENTARY and is NOT FOR SALE. The taking of photographs during the performance is strictly forbidden. The management reserves the right to refuse admission.
PERSONS UNDER 16 YEARS OF AGE ARE NOT ADMITTED
STALLS
ADMIT TWO

◄ **A Beatles concert ticket,** for the London Palladium, 13 October 1963.

$1,300–1,550 Her

The Beatles, 'A Hard Day's Night', signed LP record, by Parlophone, 1964, framed with a photograph of the band.

$45,000–50,000 ⊞ FRa

It is extremely rare to find signed copies of LP records by the Beatles, and this particular record has a full set of four signatures, all of which are in excellent condition.

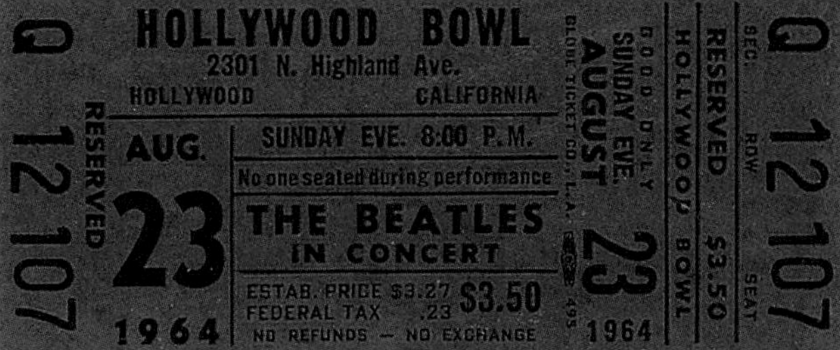

A Beatles concert ticket, for the Hollywood Bowl, California, 23 August 1964.

$1,300–1,500 Her

A Selcol Beatles New Beat Guitar, with four strings, the case with sticker and facsimile signatures, c1964, in original box with instructions and song chart, 23in (58.5cm) long.

$510–610 G(L)

For more signatures, please see the Autographs section on pages 26–28.

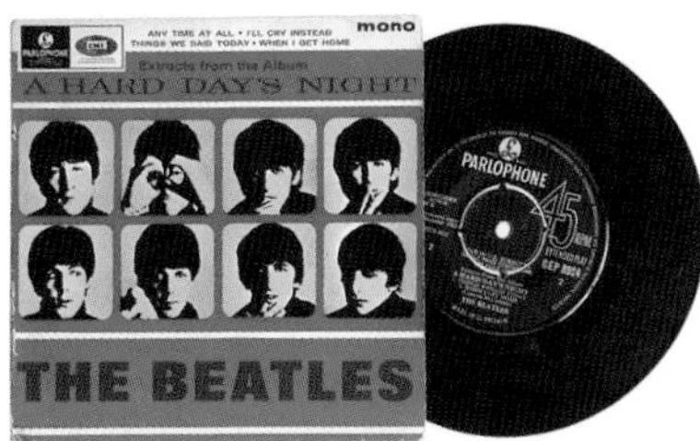

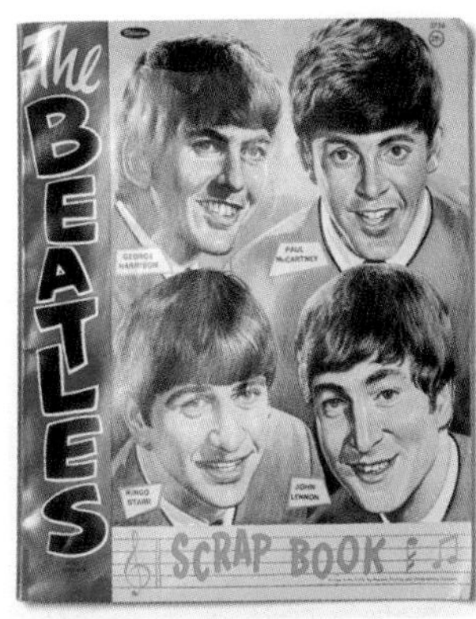

The Beatles Scrap Book, published by Whitman, America, 1964, 13½in (34.5cm) high.

$110–120 ⊞ KA

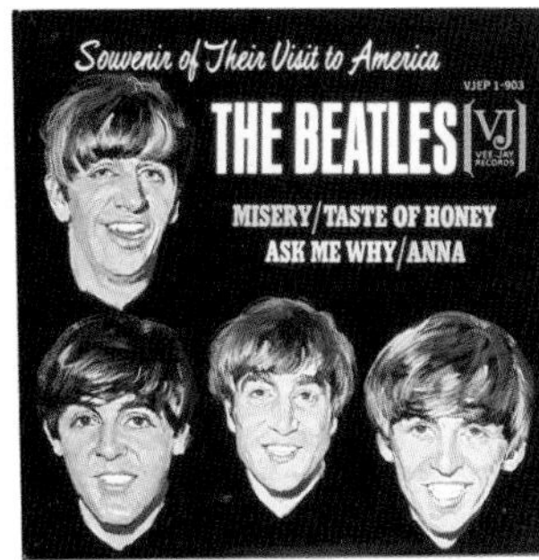

The Beatles, 'Misery/Taste of Honey/Ask Me Why/Anna' souvenir of their visit to America, EP record, by Vee-Jay, 1964.

$500–580 Her

The Beatles, 'A Hard Day's Night', EP record, German test pressing, 1964.

$160–310 Her

◄ The Beatles, 'A Hard Day's Night', EP record, by Parlophone, 1964.

$50–60 ⊞ SDR

MILLER'S COMPARES

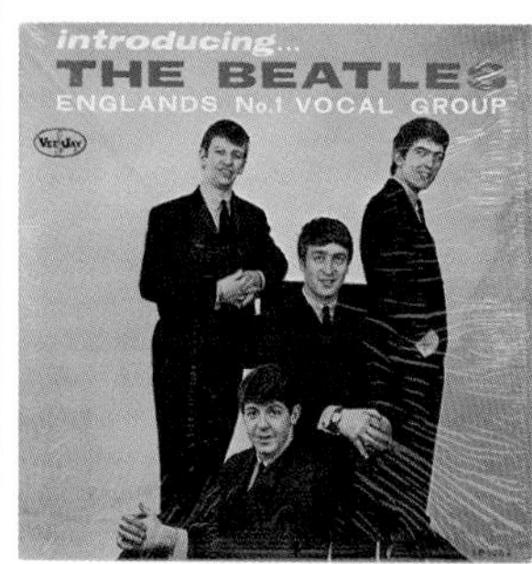

(L) The Beatles, 'Introducing The Beatles', mono LP record, by Vee-Jay, 1964.

$1,000–1,200 Her

(R) The Beatles, 'Introducing The Beatles', mono LP record, by Vee-Jay, 'titles back' copy, 1964.

$7,700–9,100 Her

One of the most sought-after Beatles records, this was their first album to be released in the US and both these copies are on the sought-after Vee-Jay label. The tracks 'Please, Please Me' and 'Ask Me Why', which appear on the album on the right, were replaced with 'Love Me Do' and 'P.S I Love You' on the album on the left. The item on the left has been opened, whereas the item on the right sold for a very high price because it is a rare early issue, has never been opened and the plastic wrapper shows its original selling price.

The Beatles, 'Introducing the Beatles', promotional mono LP record, by Vee-Jay, 1964.

$1,000–1,200 Her

A Beatles cushion, 1964, 12in (30.5cm) square.

$165–190 Her

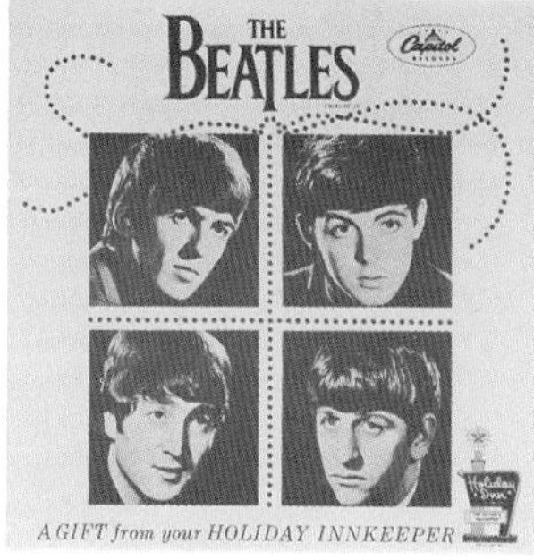

A Holiday Inn Beatles flyer, 1964.

$410–480 Her

▶ A Beat Productions Beatles diary, unused, 1965, 4in (10cm) high.

$85–100 KA

A military-style cotton twill jacket, owned by John Lennon, c1965.

$14,700–17,600 CO

This jacket was the inspiration for those worn by The Beatles at Shea Stadium, New York.

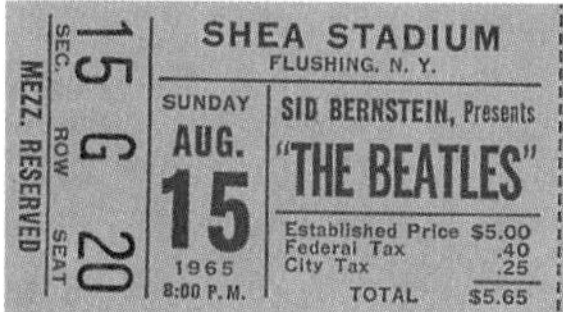

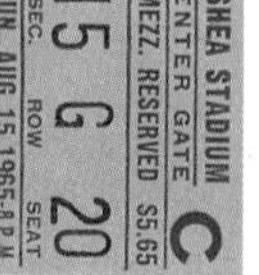

◀ A Beatles concert ticket, unused, Shea Stadium, New York, 15 August 1965.

$3,550–4,250 Her

The Beatles, 'The Beatles' Hottest Hits', mono LP record, by Parlophone, 1965.

$1,250–1,450 Her

This LP was only issued in Denmark.

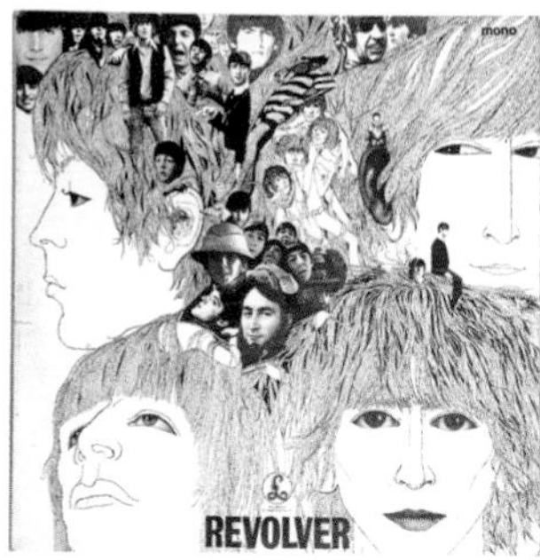

The Beatles, 'Revolver', mono LP record, by Parlophone, 1966.

$85–95 SDR

The Beatles, 'Revolver', sealed stereo LP, by Capitol, 1966.

$340–410 Her

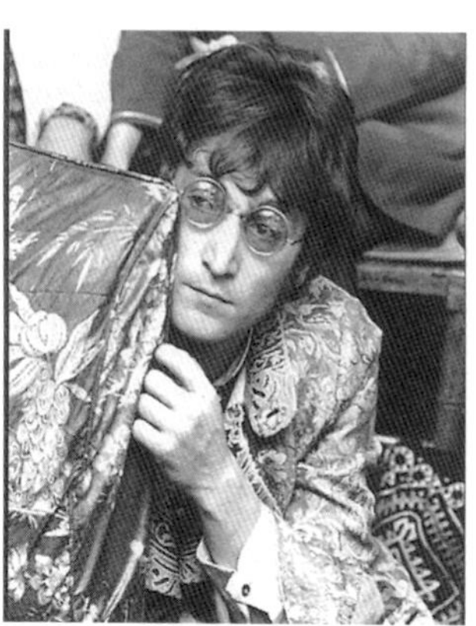

◄ **John Lennon,** a photograph taken in Bangor, North Wales, August 1967.

$270–320 CO

► **John Lennon,** a signed registered postage card to 'Mrs John Lennon Kentwood...Surrey', America, 1969.

$1,000–1,200 CO

Registered article — ONE REGISTERED LETTER
Parcel insured for — NO VALUE
Mailed at the post office of — STATION "A" HICKSVILLE, NY
on SEPTEMBER 3 1965 under No. 10555
MRS JOHN LENNON
KENTWOOD CAVENDISH RD ST. GEORGES HILL
(Street and number)
WEYBRIDGE, SURREY, ENGLAND
(Place of destination) (Country of destination)

The undersigned declares that the article mentioned above was duly delivered

Signature of the addressee: [signature]

Postmark of the office — WEYBRIDGE 6 SEP 65

The Beatles, 'Yellow Submarine', LP record, original film soundtrack, 1969.

$85–95 SDR

Warus Cards, set of 10,'Beatles for Sale' series, late 1980s.

$10–15 SOR

The Beatles, 'I Feel Fine', single record, picture disc, limited edition, by Parlophone, 1984.

$20–25 MTM

► A set of four **Royal Doulton Beatles character jugs,** 1984–91, 5½in (14cm) high.

$720–860 LT

GUITARS

A Gibson L30 acoustic guitar, America, 1936.

$1,900–2,200 VRG

A Martin 000.18 acoustic guitar, America, 1943.

$8,500–9,500 VRG

A Gibson L4-E acoustic guitar, 1949.

$6,900–7,800 VRG

A Martin 000.21 acoustic guitar, America, 1953, with original *faux* crocodile case.

$10,000–11,200 VRG

An Epiphone Frontier acoustic guitar, 1964.

$2,650–3,000 VRG

A Gibson mahogany B15 guitar, with six strings, America, 1964, 40in (101.5cm) high.

$1,300–1,500 ACOU

A Gibson Hummingbird acoustic guitar, 1964.

$8,500–9,500 VRG

A Gibson J45 acoustic guitar, in factory black, America, 1965.

$4,650–5,200 VRG

A Gibson J45 acoustic guitar, America, 1967.

$2,400–2,800 VRG

A Gibson Everly Brothers acoustic guitar, 1984.

$3,100–3,500 VRG

A Martin spruce and laminate mahogany Shenandoah semi-acoustic guitar, with 12 strings, fitted with Martin 332 thin-line pick up, America, 1985, 41in (104cm) high.

$1,150–1,300 ACOU

A Guild D4 mahogany and spruce guitar, with six strings, signed by George Strait, America, c1993, 41in (104cm) high.

$950–1,100 ACOU

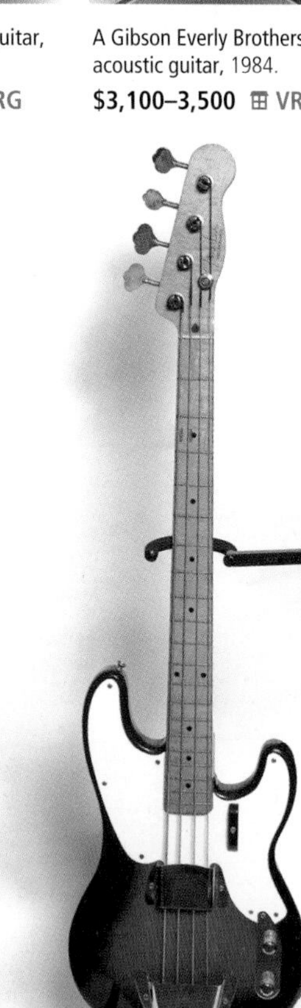

A Fender precision electric bass guitar, America, 1956.

$13,100–14,700 VRG

A Fender Bass VI electric bass guitar, America, 1962.

$10,000–11,200 VRG

A Gibson E5125 electric guitar, America, 1964.
$2,900–3,300 ⊞ VRG

► A Gibson Firebird electric guitar, America, 1964.
$6,100–6,800 ⊞ VRG

A Fender electric jazz bass guitar, America, 1966.
$10,000–11,300 ⊞ VRG

A Fender Telecaster thin line electric guitar, America, 1969.
$9,300–10,300 ⊞ VRG

A Gretsch super chet electric guitar, 1973.
$2,900–3,300 ⊞ VRG

A Dan Armstrong sliding pick-up guitar, 1975.
$1,550–1,750 ⊞ VRG

A Gibson Explorer Camouflage guitar, America, 1984.
$1,550–1,750 ⊞ VRG

A Gibson '54 Historic Les Paul Classic electric guitar, c1999.
$6,900–7,800 ⊞ VRG

RECORDS

The Beach Boys, 'Surfin' Safari', American import mono LP record, by Capitol Records, 1962.

$45–50 SDR

The Beach Boys, 'All Summer Long', test pressing mono LP record, by Capitol Records, 1964.

$380–450 Her

James Brown, 'Please Please Please', EP record, by King, 1959.

$530–640 Her

◄ Black Sabbath, 'Black Sabbath' stereo LP record, by Vertigo, 1970.

$60–70 SDR

► Johnny Cash, 'The Songs that Made Him Famous', mono LP record, by London, 1957.

$20–45 SDR

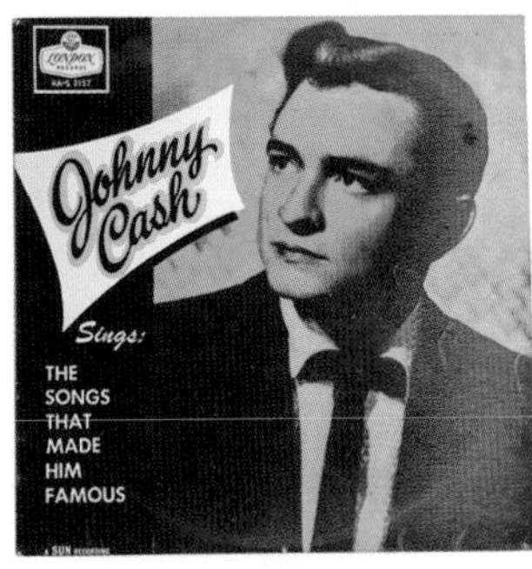

The Chameleons UK, 'Strange Times', stereo LP record, double album, by Griffin Records, 1988.

$20–25 SDR

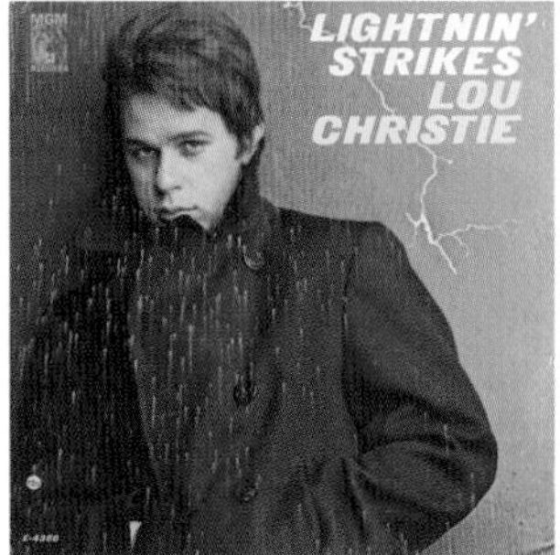

► Lou Christie, 'Lightning Strikes', US import LP record, by MGM, 1963.

$40–45 SDR

Ray Charles and Betty Carter, mono LP record, by HMV, 1961.

$20–25 SDR

► The Crests, 'The Angels Listened In', EP record, by Coed Records, 1959.

$1,300–1,550 Her

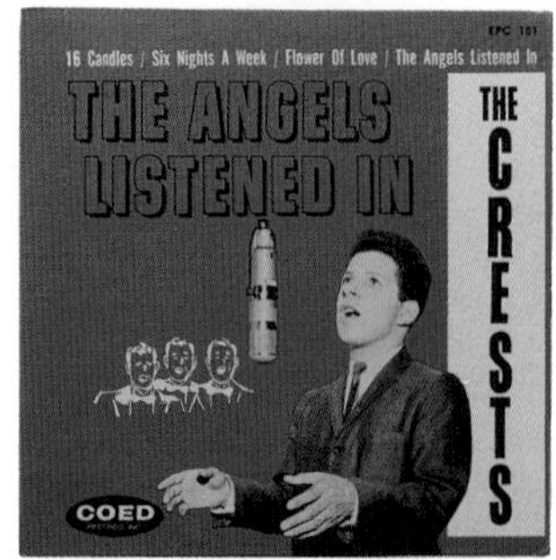

◀ **Hawkwind**, 'In Search of Space', stereo LP record, by United Artists, 1973.

$40–45 SDR

▶ **Bill Haley and His Comets**, 'Rock'N'Roll', EP record, by Decca Records, 1957.

$40–45 SDR

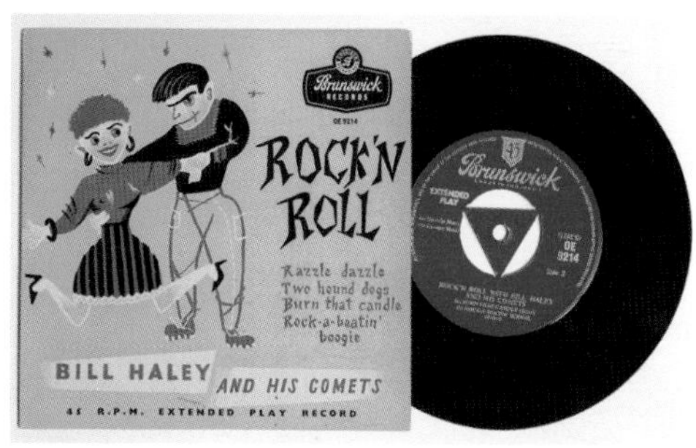

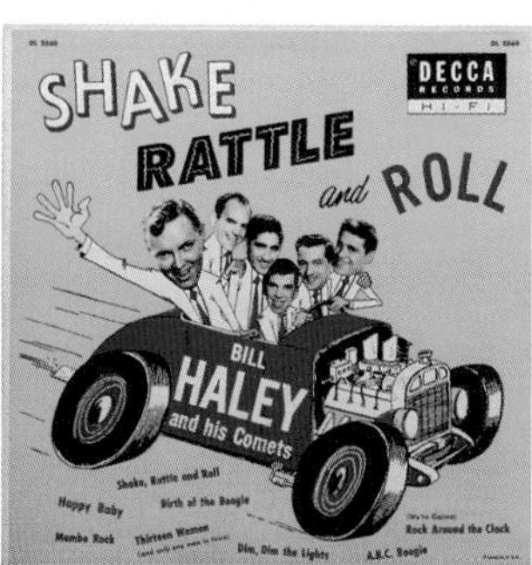

Bill Haley and His Comets, 'Shake Rattle and Roll', mono LP record, by Decca Records, 1955.

$790–950 Her

Buddy Holly, 'The Buddy Holly Story', mono LP record, by Coral, 1958.

$95–110 SDR

Buddy Holly and The Crickets, 'The "Chirping" Crickets', EP record, blank back cover, by Brunswick Records, 1957.

$550–660 Her

'The "Chirping" Crickets' was the group's first EP, taken from the classic first album of the same name. The version with the blank back cover is much rarer than the later version with the printed back, hence it commands a high price.

Buddy Holly and The Crickets, 'The "Chirping" Crickets', LP record, by Coral, 1959.

$80–90 SDR

◀ **The Jazz Couriers**, 'The Jazz Couriers in Concert with Ronnie Scott and Tubby Hayes', LP record, by EMI, 1958.

$110–130 SDR

▶ **Mary Hopkin**, 'Those Were The Days', stereo LP record, by Apple, 1971.

$90–100 SDR

◀ **The Kinks**, 'Kinksize Session', mono EP record, by Pye, 1966.

$40–45 SDR

The Kinks, 'Face to Face', mono LP record, by Pye, 1966.

$90–100 SDR

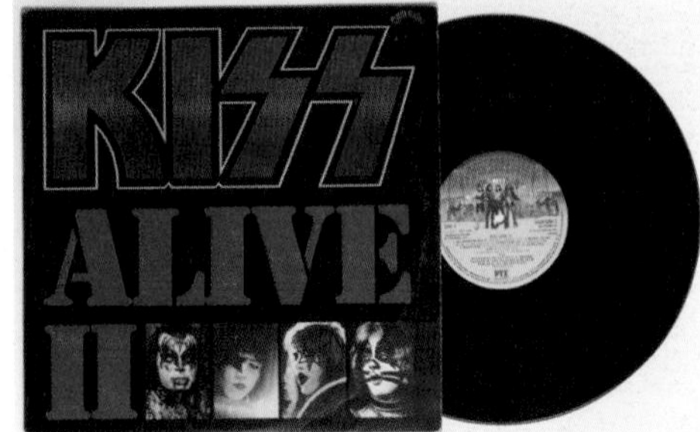

Kiss, 'Alive II', LP record, double album, by Casablanca, 1977.

$40–45 SDR

Led Zeppelin, 'Led Zeppelin II', import stereo LP record, by Atlantic, Turkey, 1970s.

$690–830 Her

Manic Street Preachers, 'You Love Us', stereo LP record, 1991.

$40–45 SDR

Nirvana, 'Smells Like Teen Spirit', stereo LP record, by DGC, 1991.

$40–50 SDR

◄ The Pixies, 'Doolittle', stereo LP, by 4AD, 1991.

$20–25 SDR

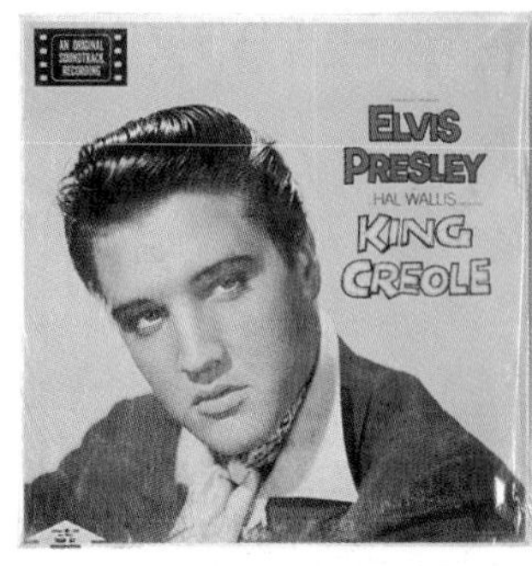

► Elvis Presley, 'King Creole', sealed mono LP record, RCA Victor, 1958.

$890–1,050 Her

Elvis Presley, 'Jailhouse Rock', imported EP record, by Victor Co, Japan, c1960.

$150–165 SDR

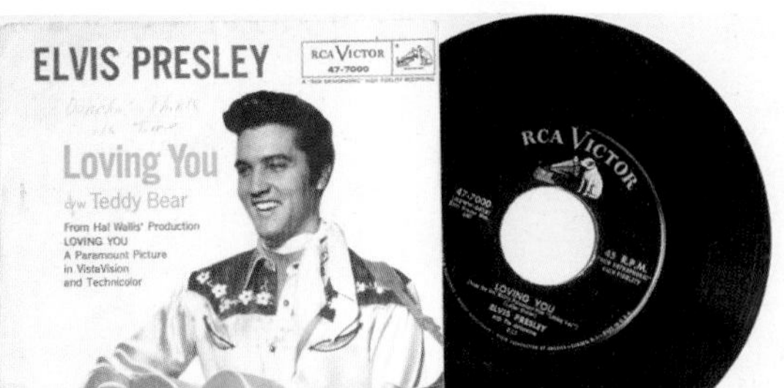

◄ Elvis presley, 'Loving You', import single record, by RCA Victor, America, 1959.

$70–80 SDR

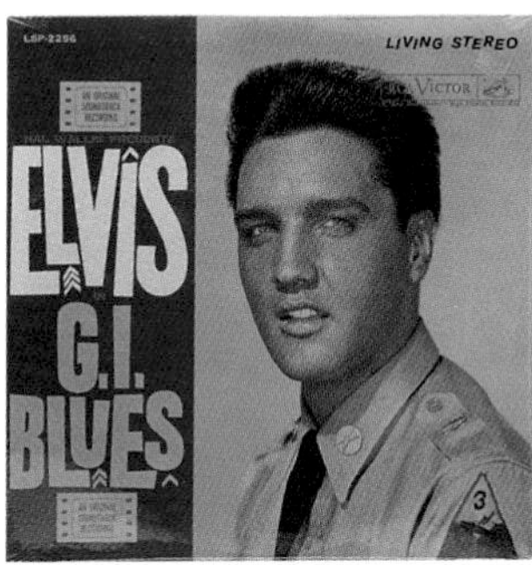

Elvis Presley, 'GI Blues', sealed stereo LP record, by RCA, 1960.

$170–200 Her

▶ Prince, 'Kiss', shaped picture disc, by Paisley Park, 1988.

$30–35 SDR

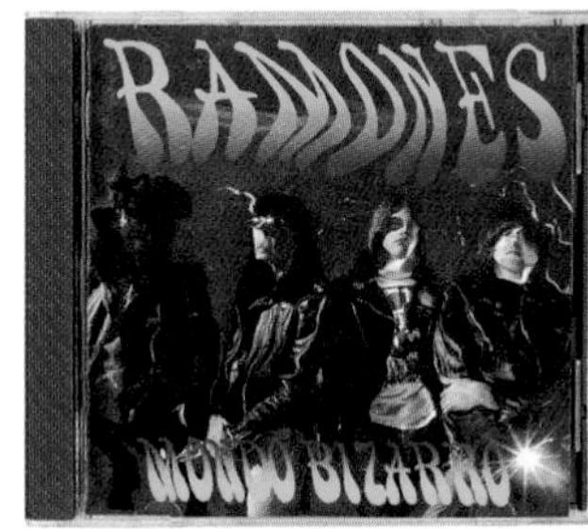

The Ramones, 'Mondo Bizarro', autographed CD, signed by Joey, Johnny, C. J. and Marky, 1992.

$220–260 Her

Edwin Starr & Blinky, 'Just We Two', stereo LP record, by Tamla Motown, 1969.

$40–45 SDR

◀ Cliff Richard, 'Cliff in Japan', mono LP record, by Columbia, 1967.

$40–50 SDR

◀ The Rolling Stones, 'It's All Over Now', single record, by London, 1964.

$280–330 Her

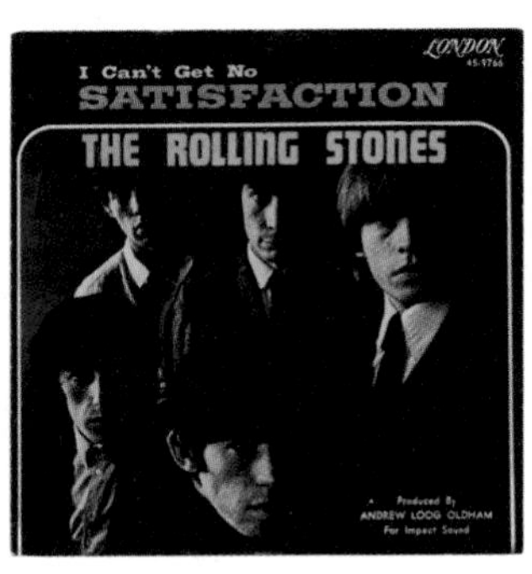

The Rolling Stones, 'I Can't Get No Satisfaction', single record, by London, 1965.

$570–670 Her

Zeebrugge Ferry Aid, 'Let It Be', EP record, March 1987.

$20–25 COB

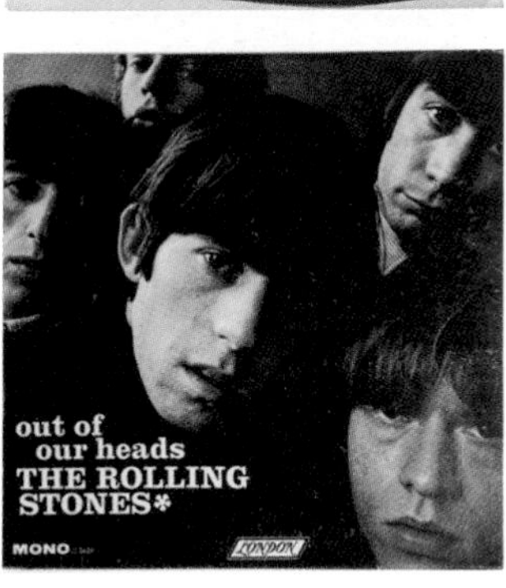

◀ Rolling Stones, 'Out Of Our Heads', mono LP record, by London, 1967.

$120–140 SDR

SCIENTIFIC & MEDICAL

SCIENTIFIC INSTRUMENTS

◀ **A Campbell-Stoke pattern Sunshine recorder,** by Short & Mason, London, the 4in (10cm) glass ball mounted on a polished slate plate, c1935, base 8in (20.5cm) square.

$1,700–2,250 RTW

The glass sphere focuses the sun's rays to an intense spot, which leaves a mark on a card marked with hourly intervals. At the end of the day, the total length of the trace is proportional to the duration of the sunshine. The idea was the brainchild of Scotsman John Francis Campbell (1822–85).

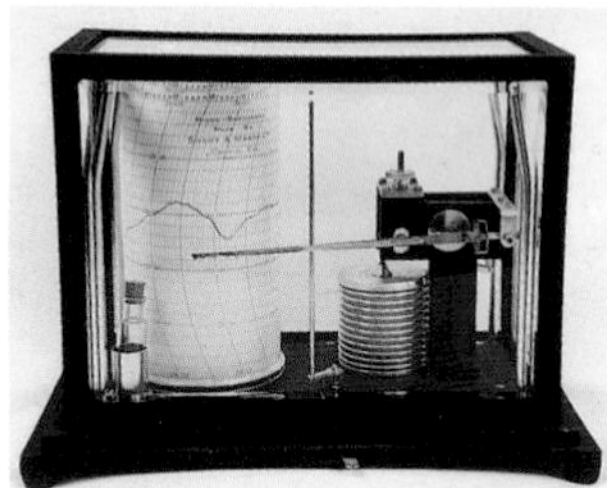

A micro barograph, by Short & Mason, London, in a black japanned case with bevelled glass, 1950s, 13in (33cm) wide.

$1,000–1,100 RTW

SHORT & MASON

A barograph, by Short & Mason, London, in an oak case, early 20thC, 21¾in (55.5cm) wide.

$590–650 SWO

A patent Stormoguide aneroid barometer, by Short & Mason, London, the dial with Copes working, in an ebonized walnut desk stand, patented 1932, dial 5½in (14cm) diam.

$340–400 FOF

An electroplated aneroid altimeter, by Short & Mason, London, reads to 4,000ft, 1930s, 3in (7.5cm) diam.

$230–260 RTW

- The UK firm Short & Mason were established scientific instrument makers who supplied equipment for the Scott and Shackleton polar expeditions of the early 20th century.
- Their popular single-bellows barograph, produced under the 'Tycos' trade name, was a classic retirement gift during the 1930s.
- Short & Mason exhibited a multitude of scientific devices at the 1924 British Empire Exhibition at Wembley, London.
- Their Stormoguide was also incorporated into their barograph designs and wall-hung barometer cases.

A brass anemometer, by Negretti & Zambra, 1920s, 4in (10cm) high.

$380–430 ET

This model has a vertical axis for measuring wind velocity. Mechanical anemometers like this were commonly used in collieries to measure mine ventilation.

A McCormick Star Globe, by Heath & Co, with instructions, in a mahogany case with leather carrying handle, 1930s–50s, globe 8¼in (21cm) diam.

$720–860 DA

Public interest in astronomy boomed in the late 1920s and 1930s thanks to the newly-opened planetarium. From beginnings in Germany in 1923, sky shows spread throughout Europe, then America in 1930, and Japan in 1938. Heath & Co were established instrument makers known for their quality sextants.

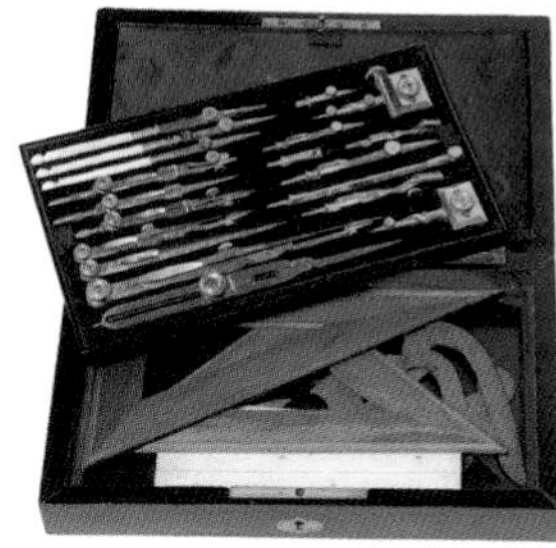

A drawing instrument set, in a rosewood box with brass inlay and banding, c1920, 10in (25.5cm) wide.

$460–510 WAC

An oxidized brass surveyor's level, by W. F. Stanley, c1920, in original box with trade label, 11in (28cm) wide.

$250–280 WAC

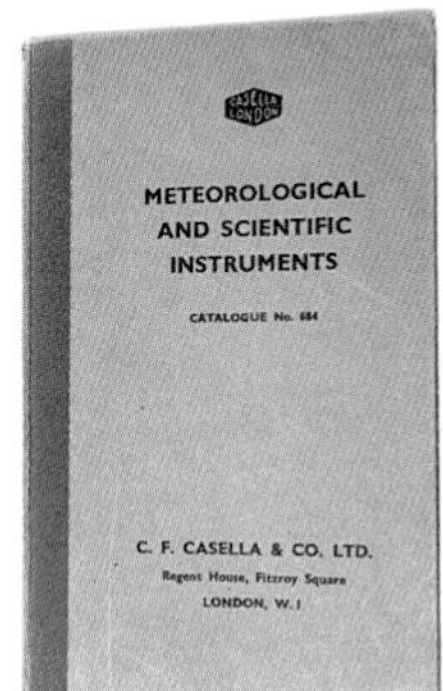

CASELLA LONDON

METEOROLOGICAL AND SCIENTIFIC INSTRUMENTS

CATALOGUE No. 684

C. F. CASELLA & CO. LTD.
Regent House, Fitzroy Square
LONDON, W.1

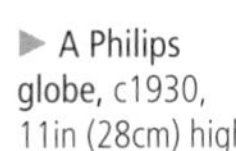

▶ **A Philips globe,** c1930, 11in (28cm) high.

$290–330 GSA

◀ **A Meteorological and Scientific Instruments Catalogue,** No. 648, by C. F. Casella & Co, c1930, 10 x 6in (25.5 x 15cm).

$240–270 RTW

A lacquered brass and painted compound microscope binocular, by W. Watson & Sons, No. 68371, with rack-and-pinion focusing, mid-20thC, 14½in (37cm) high.

$260–310 G(B)

A presentation baro-thermograph, by J. Lizars, Edinburgh, with eight-day movement and chart drawer, 1956, 15in (38cm) wide.

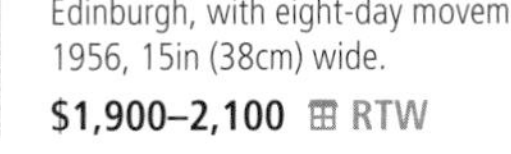

$1,900–2,100 RTW

John Lizars founded the firm in 1830, primarily to make and repair optical instruments. In the 1880s Lizars diversified into photographic apparatus and in the 1890s launched a range of Challenge cameras. The manufacture of precise instruments like the baro-thermograph was a natural extension for the firm to make.

◀ **A valve oscilloscope,** by A. C. Cossor, 1952, 11in (28cm) long.

$45–50 GM

This basic instrument was aimed specifically at TV engineers. Cossor promoted their oscilloscope as being 'fairly portable', weighing 'only 9¼lbs' (4.2kg). Despite its small size, this was still an expensive gadget – priced at £29 10s in 1954 – equivalent to roughly one month's salary.

MEDICAL

An H. Gilbertson & Sons glass wedge-shaped poison bottle, embossed 'regd. 30th Octr 1861', 3¾in (9.5cm) long.

$1,250–1,500 BBR

This is a rare and early dated poison bottle. The majority of examples are found in South Africa.

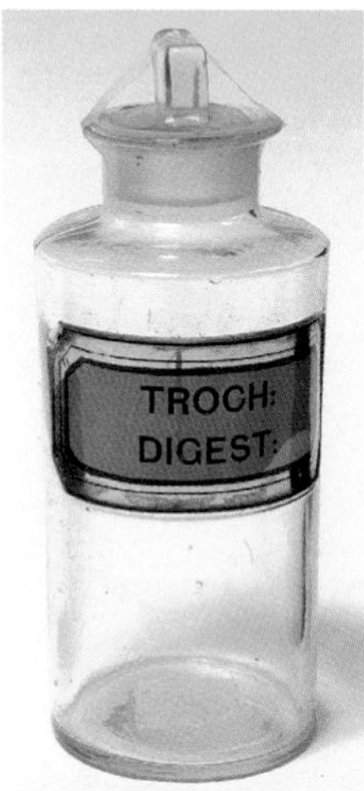

A glass apothecary's jar, 19thC, 8in (20.5cm) high.

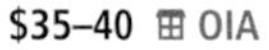

$35–40 OIA

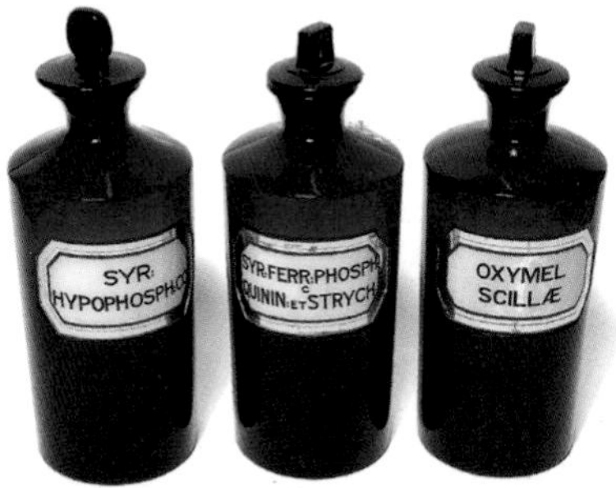

Three glass chemist's bottles, c1900, 10in (25.5cm) high.

$220–260 JUN

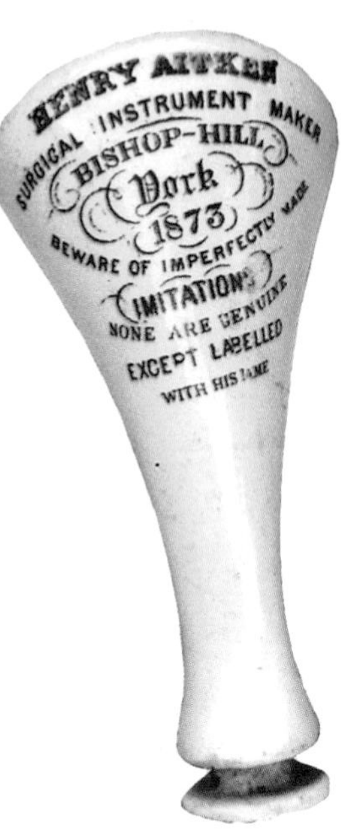

An Aitken's Improved Porcelain Pessary, with transfer-printed label, 1848, 3¾in (9.5cm) long.

$145–1700 BBR

A tin hearing trumpet, 1900, 5in (12.5cm) long.

$175–210 ET

A chrome dentist's mouth rinse, 1910, 34in (86.5cm) high.

$1,300–1,450 CuS

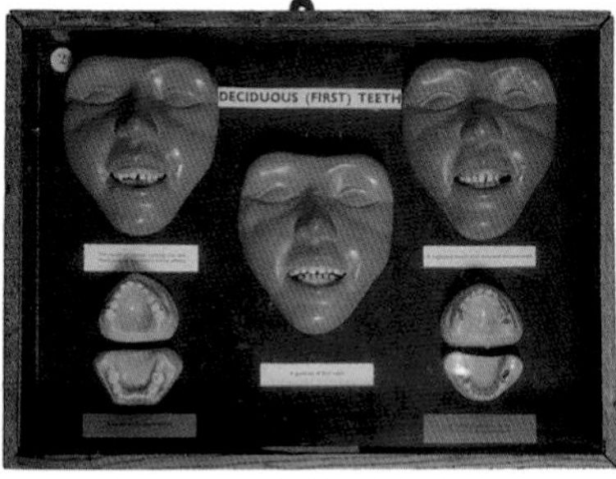

A set of wax dental models, showing tooth development, 1910, in a case 13 x 18in (33 x 45.5cm).

$1,900–2,150 CuS

A Dr. Kern's headache remedy vending machine, in an oak cabinet, America, early 1900s, 15in (38cm) high.

$12,000–13,000 JDJ

The value reflects dual interest to both vending machine and medical collectors.

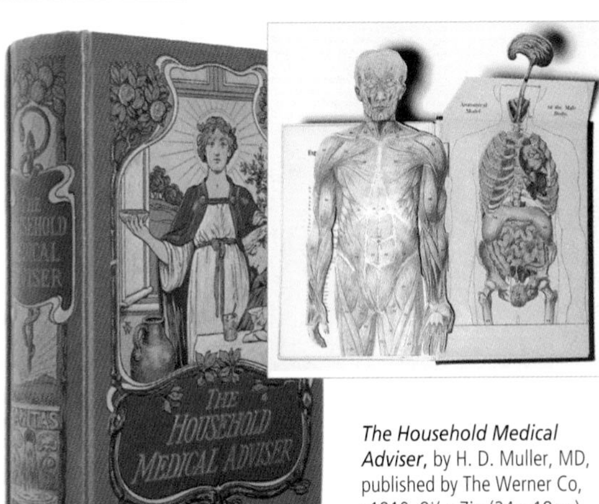

The Household Medical Adviser, by H. D. Muller, MD, published by The Werner Co, c1910, 9½ x 7in (24 x 18cm).

$60–70 BAY

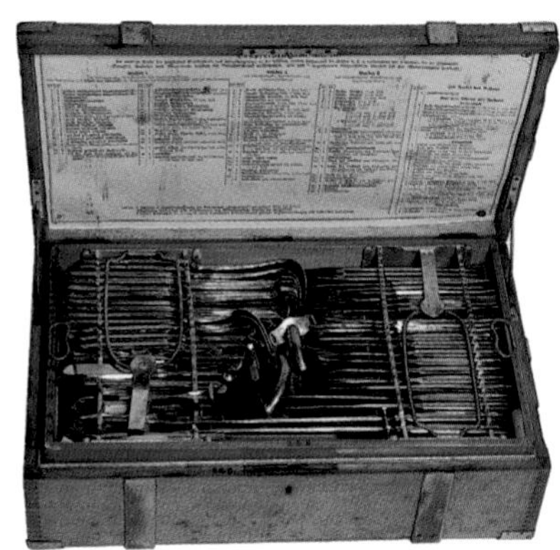

A set of nickel-plated operating tools, Germany, 1920, in a wooden case, 20in (51cm) wide.

$3,450–3,900 CuS

A glass eyebath, with finger indents, embossed 'Erin/C & Cie', France, 1920–30, 1½in (4cm) high.

$135–155 BBR

A glass eyebath, embossed 'Optalmol', 1920–30, 1½in (4cm) high.

$50–60 BBR

A pot lid for 'Doctor Shower's Radium Salve', 1920s, 2in (5cm) diam.

$110–130 BBR

Radium was isolated in 1898 and used to treat cancer until the 1940s, before it was recognized as being hazardous. By-products from radium extraction were turned into 'cure-alls' for the general public. Radium salve was sold alongside 'radon water' which was impregnated with radium.

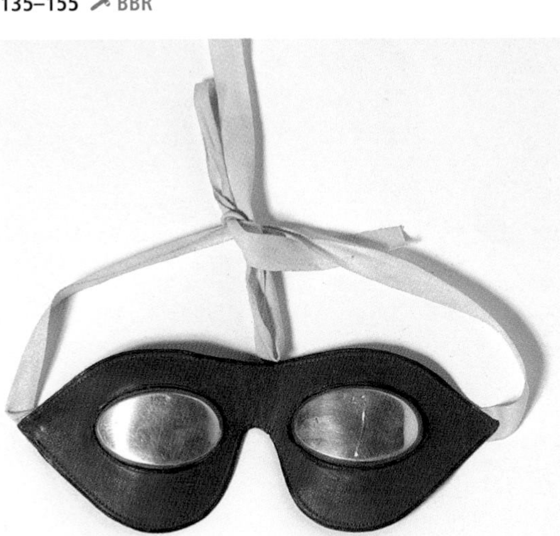

A leather X-ray protection mask, 1920s, 8in (20.5cm) wide.

$850–950 CuS

These leather goggles were designed to protect the eyes from the harmful effects of X-ray induction. Similar tinted lead glass versions were used by physicians during fluoroscoping procedures.

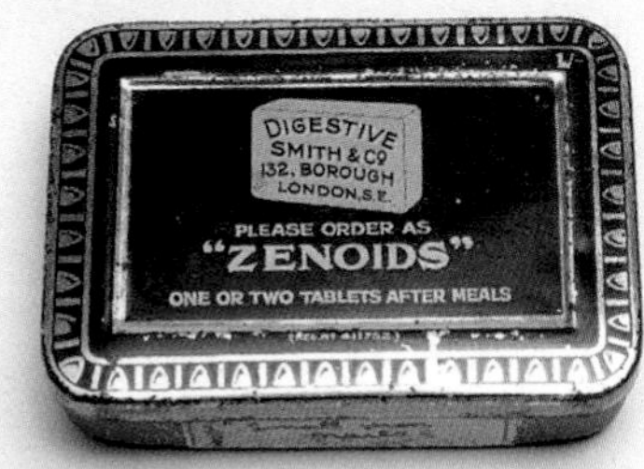

A Zenoids Digestive Tablets tin, 1930s, 2¼ x 3¼in (5.5 x 8.5cm).

$10–15 RTT

A corrugated boxwood mouth wedge, 1940s, 5½in (14cm) long.

$85–100 ⊞ ET

This would have been used as part of the anaesthetic procedure and to maintain an open airway in patients who had difficulty breathing.

◄ A chemist's glass display bottle, c1930, 31in (78.5cm) high.

$350–400 ⊞ JUN

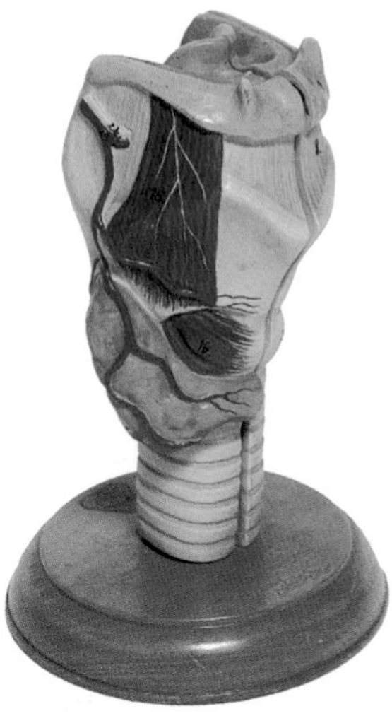

A plaster model of the throat, 1950, 7in (18cm) high.

$230–260 ⊞ CuS

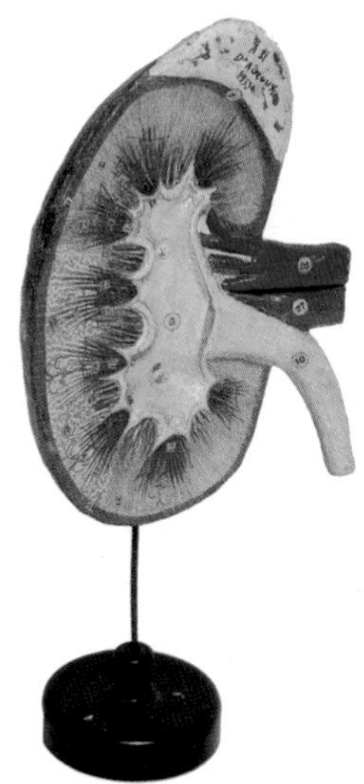

A papier-mâché model of the kidney, by Auzoux, France, 1950, 6in (15cm) high.

$690–780 ⊞ CuS

The French physician Louis Auzoux (1797–1880), improved and popularized papier-mâché anatomical models. As a student he was frustrated with the lack of human corpses for studying anatomy, so he embarked on making models.

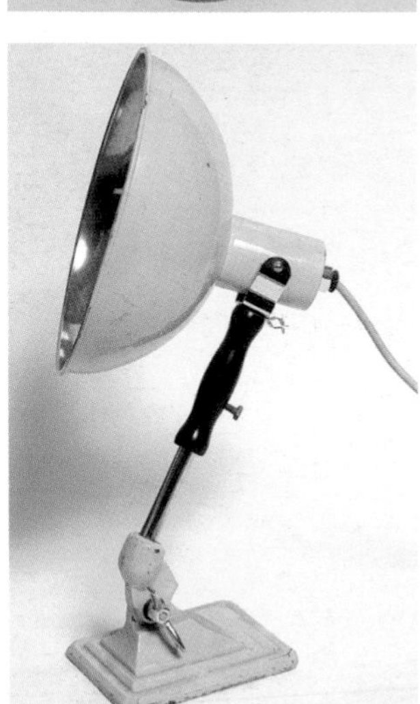

A Soltan medical lamp, c1950, 21in (53.5cm) high.

$95–110 ⊞ SOU

Light therapy was popular for its health-giving properties during the 1920s and '30s. 'Bask in the health-protecting UV rays while you read', said advertisements for lamps similar to this. By the 1950s, concerns about the harmful effects of UV rays meant that lamps were used primarily for other medical purposes, such as a means of preventing rickets.

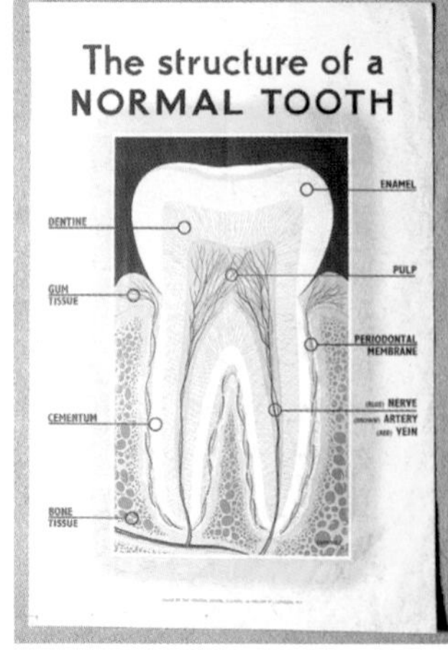

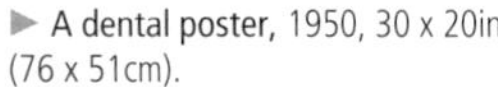

► A dental poster, 1950, 30 x 20in (76 x 51cm).

$85–95 ⊞ Do

SHIPPING

FITTINGS & INSTRUMENTS

A brass ship's clock, with a silvered dial, c1950, 7in (18cm) diam.

$230–260 OLD

A Shipwrecked Fishermen & Mariners Royal Benevolent Society marine barometer, by Dollond, c1930, 7in (18cm) diam.

$460–510 RTW

► **A japanned Sestrel sextant,** by Henry Brown & Son, 1960s, 6in (15cm) radius, in original mahogany box.

$190–230 DMC

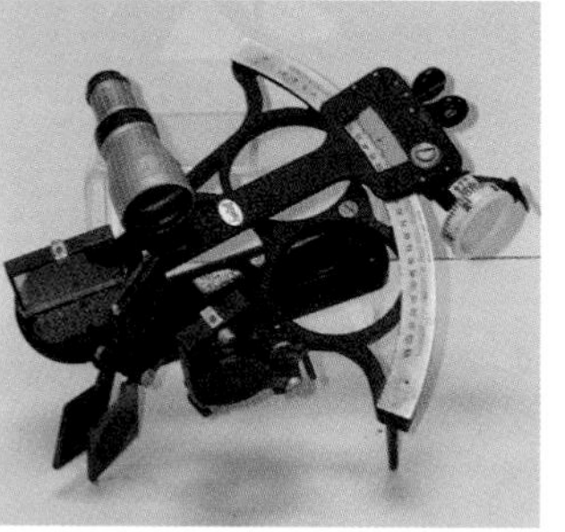

A souvenir bell, from the Safmarine liner *SA Oranje*, South Africa, 1948–72, 5in (12.5cm) high.

$35–40 OLD

Safmarine (South African Marine Corporation) is a well-known and respected name in international shipping. The company has grown significantly since its formation in 1946 and is today one of the leading north/south operators offering container and breakbulk shipping services to many parts of the world.

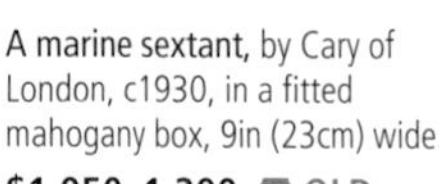

A marine sextant, by Cary of London, c1930, in a fitted mahogany box, 9in (23cm) wide.

$1,050–1,200 OLD

► **A ship's flag,** Russia, 1996, 18in (45.5cm) wide.

$60–70 COB

LINERS

◀ A copy of an original photograph of the *Titanic* leaving Belfast in 1912, 9in (23cm) wide.

$20–25 COB

An original photograph of the Titanic *could fetch upwards of $850 if in good condition.*

▶ A *Titanic* memorial song card, 1912, 5in (12.5cm) high.

$25–35 M&C

CANADIAN PACIFIC OCEAN SERVICES

A Canadian Pacific passenger list, 1920, 7in (18cm) high.

$20–25 COB

Two Canadian Pacific baggage labels, 1930s, 6in (15cm) wide.

$10–15 COB

A Canadian Pacific brochure, 1935, 9in (23cm) high.

$20–25 COB

- The Canadian Pacific Railway Co entered the shipping business in 1884 when they commissioned three steamers to operate services for the Great Lakes.
- Passenger services were started between Port Moody and Montreal in 1886 and in 1887 a service between Vancouver and the Orient began using chartered vessels.
- By 1891 the company was using its own Empress ships and transatlantic passenger services began in 1913.
- In 1914 most of the fleet was requisitioned for war service.
- In 1915 Canadian Pacific Ocean Services was formed, combining the Canadian Pacific Railway and Allan Line fleets.
- The title Canadian Pacific Steamships was adopted in 1921.

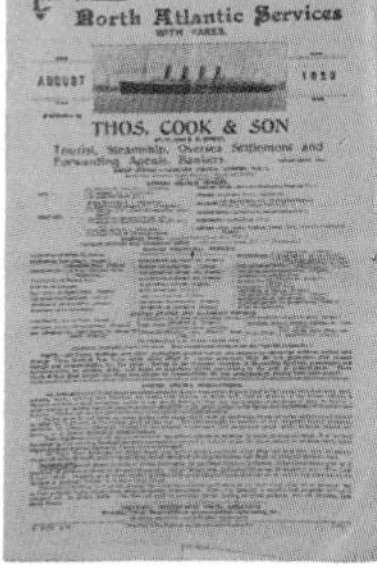

A Thomas Cook list of North Atlantic Services, August 1923, 14in (35.5cm) high.

$10–15 COB

Thomas Cook, the founder of the modern tourist industry, was just 20 when he became a Bible reader and a missionary with the Baptists. When organizing transportation and entertainment for a temperance rally he hired a special train, printed flyers and sold shilling tickets. By 1845 Cook was running similar tours as a business. He negotiated a deal with the railway and received a commission for every ticket he sold. Five shilling package tours of travel, hotel and board to the Great Exhibition in London in 1851 followed. Similar tours to the Paris Exhibition included help getting passports, language guides, transportation, food, lodging and travellers' cheques, and thus the modern tourist industry was founded.

◀ A suede leather RMS *Almanzora* photograph album, 1930s, 11in (28cm) wide.

$35–40 COB

◀ A White Star Line silver plated sugar bowl, by The Goldsmiths & Silversmiths Co, c1930, 3in (7.5cm) high.

$310–350 OLD

UNION-CASTLE LINE

A Union-Castle Line South & East Africa Christmas lunch menu, 1930, 8in (20.5cm) high.

$20–25 ⊞ COB

A Union-Castle Line *Cape Town Castle* souvenir tea strainer, 1938–67, 6in (15cm) long.

$30–35 ⊞ CGA

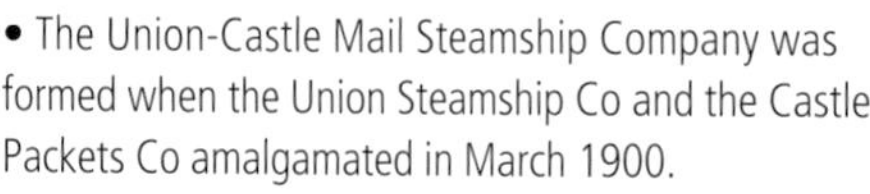

- The Union-Castle Mail Steamship Company was formed when the Union Steamship Co and the Castle Packets Co amalgamated in March 1900.
- The famous lavender-hulled liners of the Union-Castle Line ran a clockwork timetable between Southampton and South Africa. The mail ships carried very few passengers.
- In 1964 the Reina del Mar was purchased and the company became involved in holiday cruising.
- Due to increased competition from the growing airline industry, the last mail run was in 1977 and the Union-Castle Steamship Company ceased to operate.

◀ A Cunard White Star Line *Queen Mary* menu, 1937, 14in (35.5cm) high.

$5–10 ⊞ J&S

By 1937 RMS Queen Mary *had completed one year's service and carried over 56,000 passengers. Earlier in the year the luxurious Cunard liner had graced the covers of* Life *magazine.*

◀ A tin, decorated with the SS *Normandie*, France, c1930, 7in (18cm) wide.

$45–50 ⊞ SAFF

A butterfly wing picture of RMS *Mauretania*, c1932, 4in (10cm) wide.

$70–80 ⊞ COB

The RMS Mauretania *made her maiden voyage in 1907 from Liverpool to New York. The technique used on this picture compares with that used in brooches of the time and is very 1930s.*

◀ A Transatlantic Merry-Go-Round music sheet, by Sterling Music Publishing Co, 1934, 12in (30.5cm) high.

$10–15 ⊞ COB

The Wonder Book of Ships, published by Ward Lock & Co, 1936, 10in (25.5cm) high.

$20–25 ⊞ COB

◀ A Cunard White Star Line RMS *Coronia* passenger list, 1949, 8in (20.5cm) high.

$10–15 ⊞ J&S

SS UNITED STATES

An SS *United States* souvenir sailor's cap, America, 1950s, 8in (20.5cm) diam.

$60–70 COB

◄ An SS *United States* blotter, America, 1950s, 11in (28cm) high.

$10–15 COB

An SS *United States* dinner menu, October 1958, 11in (28cm) high.

$10–15 COB

- Built between 1949 and 1952, the SS *United States* was the fastest ocean liner ever and the largest passenger liner to be built in the US.
- The ship had accommodation for 2,000 passengers and 1,000 crew.
- Her maiden voyage was on 3 July 1952, bound for Le Havre and Southampton – she completed the crossing in three days, ten hours and 40 minutes at an average speed of 35.59 knots.
- Her 726th and final crossing took place on 25 October 1969.

QUEEN MARY II

A *Queen Mary II* maiden voyage postal cover, April 2004, 7½in (19cm) wide.

$20–25 COB

A *Queen Mary II* maiden voyage souvenir key ring, 2004, 1½in (4cm) diam.

$30–35 COB

A *Queen Mary II* transatlantic maiden voyage badge, limited edition of 250, 2004, 6in (15cm) high.

$110–130 COB

- At the time of her construction in 2003 *Queen Mary II* was the world's largest and most luxurious ocean liner.
- She set sail from Southampton on her maiden voyage to Florida on 12 January 2004.
- At 1,132ft (345m) long she carries 2,620 passengers, 1,253 crew and has five swimming pools, ten restaurants and a planetarium.
- Collectors view her merchandising as a future collectable and pieces for limited-edition maiden voyage material have already appreciated in value.

SMOKING

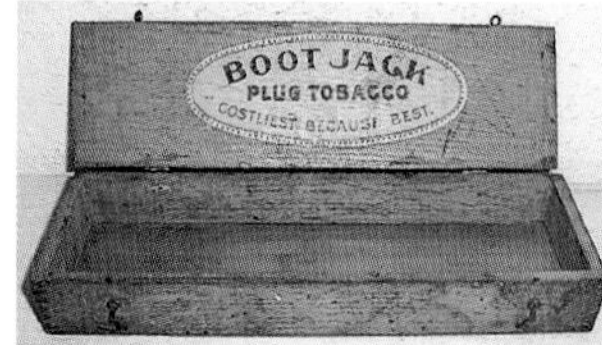

An oak Boot Jack Plug Tobacco box, 1910–20, 11in (28cm) wide.

$45–50 MYS

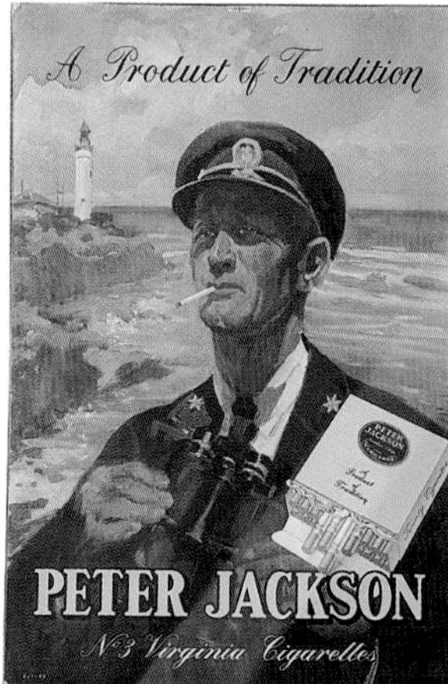

A Peter Jackson Cigarettes showcard, 1940s, 14½ x 10in (37 x 25.5cm).

$60–70 LeB

A Berneval Cigarettes showcard, 1930s, 19½in (49.5cm) high.

$190–220 BBR

A wooden cigarette case, possibly walnut, with a chrome-plated frame, 1940s–50s, 3½in (9cm) wide.

$100–115 SUW

◄ **An advertising poster for City Club cigarettes,** 1950s, 30 x 20in (76 x 51cm).

$160–190 Do

► **A W. D. & H. O. Wills Capstan Cigarettes advertising mirror,** 1950s, in an oak frame, 10 x 8 in (25.5 x 20.5cm).

$70–80 RTT

A Bakelite pipe stand, 1930s, 5in (12.5cm) high.

$20–25 UD

A silver cigarette case, with engine-turned decoration, inscribed with initials and dated 1943, 3¾in (9.5cm) wide.

$70–80 Tus

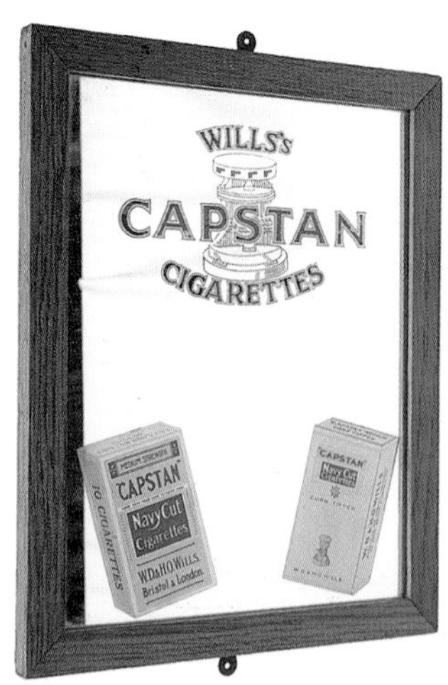

CIGARETTE PACKETS

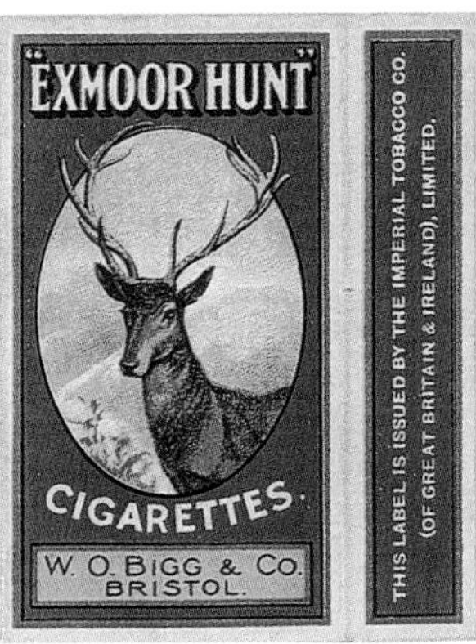

A W. O. Bigg & Co Exmoor Hunt Cigarettes packet, c1920.

$45–50 ⊞ CPCC

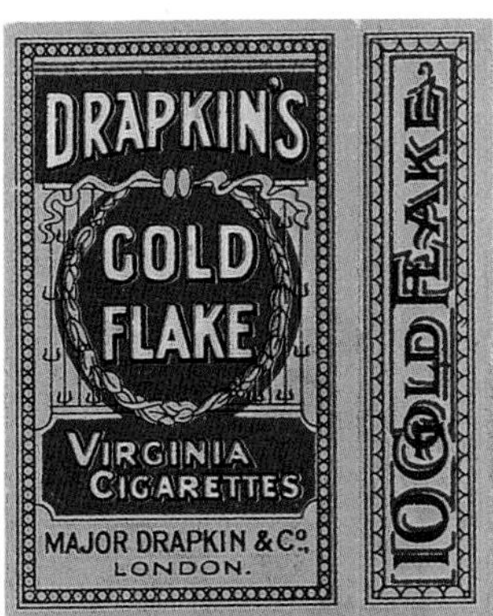

A Drapkin's Gold Flake Virginia Cigarettes packet, c1925.

$20–25 ⊞ CPCC

A United Kingdom Tobacco Co Lion Virginia Cigarettes packet, c1930.

$30–35 ⊞ CPCC

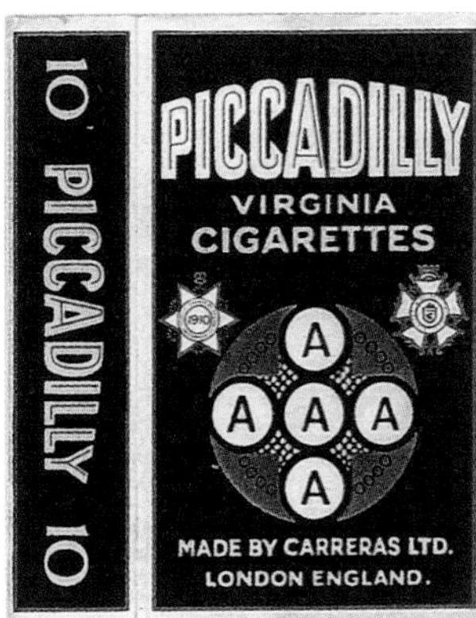

A Carreras Piccadilly Virginia Cigarettes packet, c1935.

$20–25 ⊞ CPCC

A Carreras Craven 'A' Virginia Cigarettes packet, pre-1939, 3in (7.5cm) high.

$5–10 ⊞ SOR

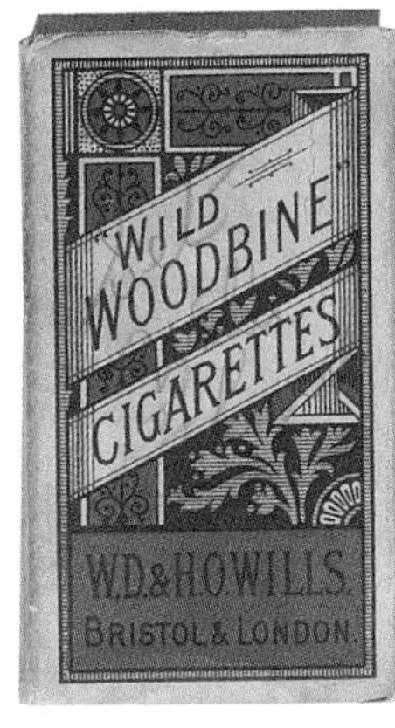

A W. D. & H. O. Wills Wild Woodbine Cigarettes packet, pre-1939, 3in (7.5cm) high.

$5–10 ⊞ SOR

A packet of Jubilaums cigarettes, Austria, 1939–45, 3½ (9cm) high.

$20–25 ⊞ MYS

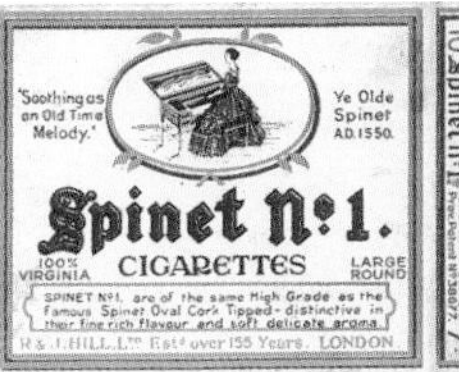

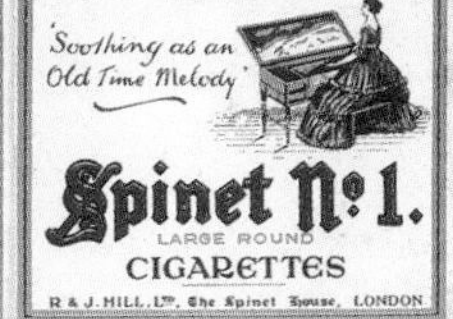

An R. & J. Hill Spinet No. 1 cigarettes packet, c1950, 3½in (9cm) wide.

$30–35 ⊞ CPCC

▶ A Lambert & Butler's Waverley Cigarettes packet, 1950s, 3¼in (8.5cm) high.

$5–10 ⊞ RTT

LIGHTERS

A silver-plated and lacquered table lighter, France, 1920s, 4in (10cm) high.

$310–350 ⊞ **DUR**

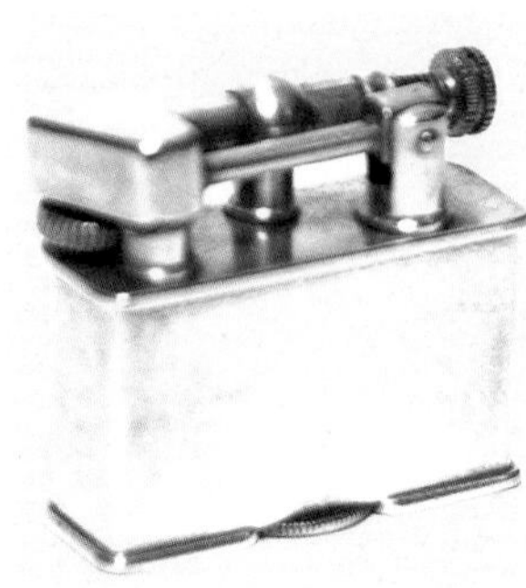

A Dunhill Parker Beacon lighter, 1930s, 1¼in (3cm) wide.

$380–430 ⊞ **OH**

A brass musical lighter, America, late 1930s, 3½in (9cm) high.

$100–120 ⊞ **DUR**

An Evans gilt-metal cigarette case/lighter, America, 1940s, 5in (12.5cm) high.

$85–100 ⊞ **DUR**

A K. K. M. lighter, in the form of a camera, Germany, 1950s, 3½in (9cm) high.

$120–140 ⊞ **DUR**

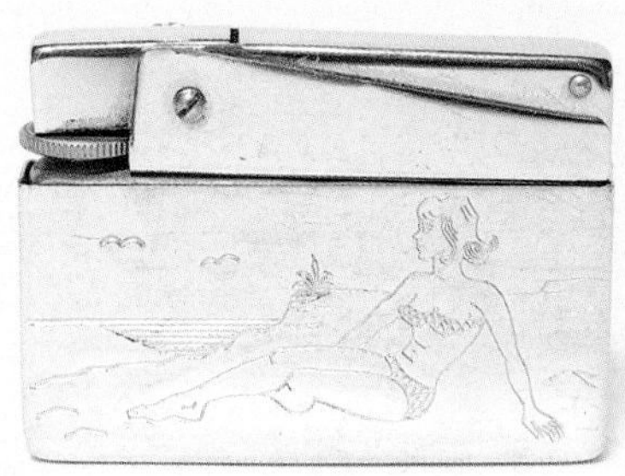

A chrome lighter, engraved with a seaside scene, Germany, 1950s, 3in (7.5cm) wide.

$60–70 ⊞ **DUR**

► **A Windmill brass and enamel table lighter musical box,** in the form a globe, decorated with paste stones, 1950s, 5in (12.5cm) high.

$110–130 ⊞ **DUR**

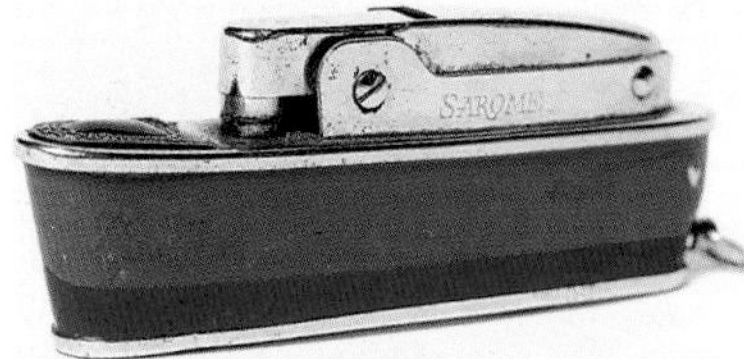

An enamelled Sarome Cruiser lighter, America, 1950s, 3in (7.5cm) wide.

$60–70 ⊞ **DUR**

◄ **A Perspex table lighter,** 1970s, 3in (75cm) high.

$5–10 ⊞ **MARK**

TOBACCO & CIGARETTE TINS

A Lea Egyptian cigarettes tin, 1905, 3¾in (9.5cm) wide.

$95–110 ⊞ HUX

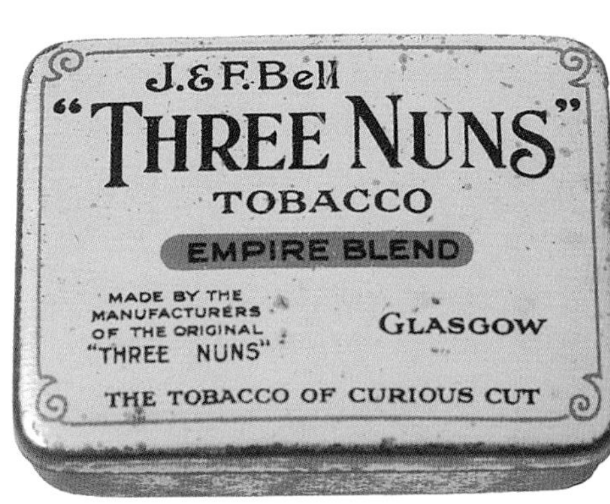

A J. & F. Bell Three Nuns Tobacco sample tin, 1920s, 2in (6.5cm) wide.

$40–45 ⊞ HUX

A US Marine cut plug tobacco tin, in the form of a lunch box, America, c1920s, 8in (20.5cm) wide.

$30–35 ⊞ MYS

A Nortag Kurs Tobacco tin, Germany, 1935, 5¾in (14.5cm) wide.

$170–200 ⊞ HUX

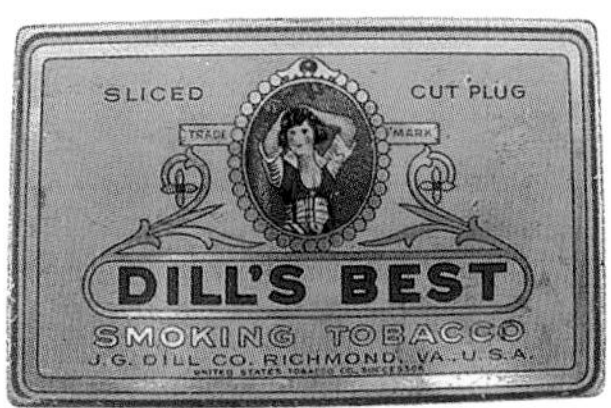

A J. G. Dill Co Dill's Best Cut Plug Tobacco tin, America, 1920s–30s, 4in (10cm) wide.

$30–35 ⊞ MYS

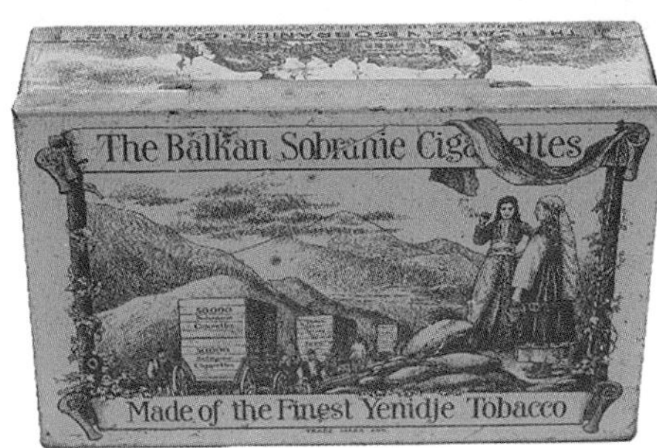

◄ **A Balkan Sobranie Cigarettes tin,** 1920s–30s, 5½in (14cm) wide.

$30–35 ⊞ RTT

◄ **Three American Tobacco Co Lucky Strike Cigarettes tins,** the interiors with Native American chief design, America, 1950s, 6in (15cm) wide.

$30–35 each ⊞ MYS

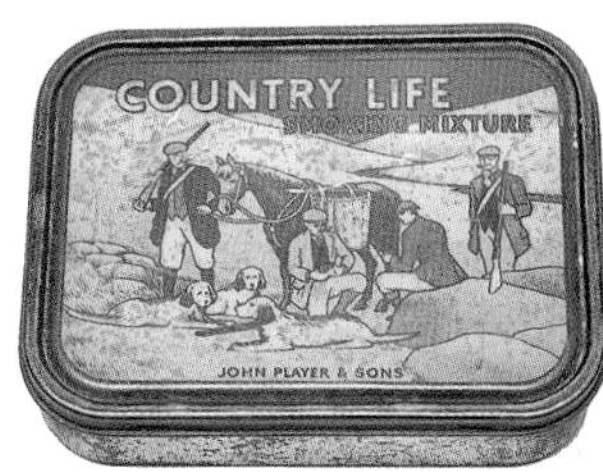

► **A John Player & Sons Country Life tobacco tin,** 1950s, 4½in (11.5cm) wide.

$10–15 ⊞ RTT

SPORT

ARTEFACTS FROM AMERICA'S favourite sport, baseball, are avidly collected. Game-used uniforms, equipment and autographed memorabilia are very hot at the moment, but the world record price is still $2.9m for the Mark McGwire record home run baseball in 1999. Baseball cards are also very popular and since the 1980s values have risen steeply.

In the UK football (soccer) has been the fastest growing market in the last ten years. Medals, shirts, caps and trophies of famous footballers always generate excitement. Paper collecting is also very popular with items such as vintage programmes, tickets, photographs, autographs and ephemera fetching high prices. Pre-1960 artefacts seem sought after, along with World Cup and FA Cup memorabilia.

Traditional sports such as cricket and golf are by comparison a little flatter, so perhaps now is a good time to buy, with potential opportunities for longer term growth. Antique and rare golf clubs and balls are very popular; the classic publication *Wisden Cricketers' Almanack* is still fetching premium prices for early issues and seems an extremely sound investment.

Sales of fishing reels, rods, equipment and angling memorabilia are patronized by an enthusiastic and loyal following. Horse racing, equestrian and country sports are also well received and sales are often punctuated by high-quality pictures, bronzes, trophies and other works of art. Other sports have their own dedicated collectors and there is plenty of sporting memorabilia from which they can choose.

Graham Budd

A Huntley & Palmers biscuit tin, depicting an athletics scene, c1892, 6in (15cm) wide.

$460–520 SAFF

A brass ashtray, depicting a runner, 1908, 4in (10cm) diam.

$140–160 BS

A Goudey Gum Co trade card, featuring Johnny Weismuller, No. 21, Sport Kings set, America, 1933.

$2,850–3,350 MN

A metal and enamel trophy, British Army of the Rhine Athletics Inter-unit team, 1946, 8in (20.5cm) high.

$30–35 Tus

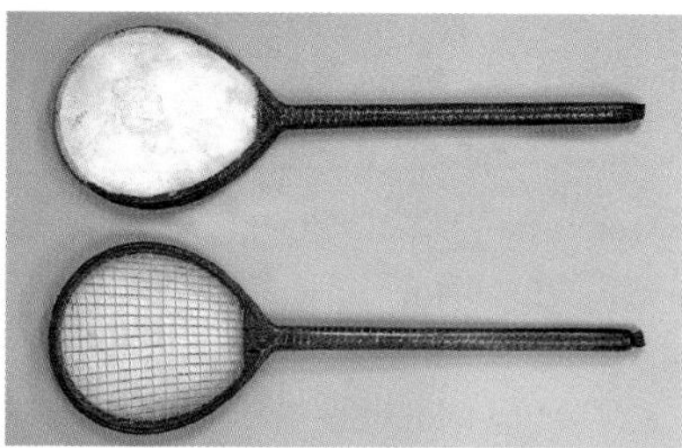

A pair of wood, leather and vellum battledores, by Payne, maker's stamp, late 19thC.

$510–620 BUDD

Battledore is an early game similar to badminton but the shuttlecock was kept up in the air for as long as possible.

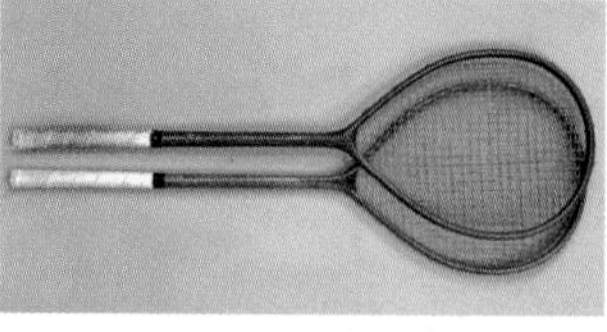

A pair of leather and wood badminton rackets, by M. Kane & Co, India, maker's stamp, c1880.

$430–510 BUDD

A Prosser shuttlecock container, c1920, 13in (33cm) high.

$50–60 SA

A BMS shuttlecock container, c1920, 16in (40.5cm) high.

$45–50 SA

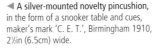

◀ Four cardboard cut-outs of North American sportsmen, by the Upper Deck Co, comprising Dan Marino, Michael Jordan, Wayne Gretzky and Ken Griffey Jr.

$190–220 BUDD

A Goudey Gum Co trade card, featuring Nat Holman, No. 3, Sport Kings set, America, 1933.

$13,6000–16,2000 MN

A Los Angeles Lakers jersey, worn by Jerry West, signed, 1973.

$8,100–9,600 MN

A Fleer trade card, featuring Michael Jordan, No. 57, 1986–87.

$5,900–7,000 MN

◀ A silver-mounted novelty pincushion, in the form of a snooker table and cues, maker's mark 'C. E. T.', Birmingham 1910, 2½in (6.5cm) wide.

$690–830 DN(HAM)

A brass billiard cue re-tipping tool, c1900, 4in (10cm) high.

$130–150 BS

A box of Crystalate billiard balls, 1920–30, 7in (18cm) long.

$85–100 BS

► Charles Roberts, *Roberts' Billiards Guide and Rules of Games*, with black and white illustrations, 1924, 8°.

$240–280 DW

A Mancho bowling jack, c1900, 2¾in (7cm) diam.

$60–70 BS

A pair of Taylor-Rolph lignum vitae bowls, c1900, 5in (12.5cm) diam, with box.

$140–160 BS

A pair of R. G. Lawrie lignum vitae carpet bowls, with ivory insets, 4in (10cm) diam.

$170–200 BS

A painted pine bowls score-board, 1920s, 30in (76cm) high.

$290–330 PICA

◄ A pair of bowls, c1930, in a carrying case, 10in (25cm) wide.

$45–50 SA

A set of four lignum vitae bowls, with ivory plaques, 1931, 5in (12.5cm) diam.

$250–290 BS

◄ A Clifton College velvet cap, c1920.

$110–130 BS

A Smiths Bowling Club silver trophy, 1949, 6in (15cm) high.

$130–150 LSA

A velvet cap, embroidered 'Y. H. A', with tassel and braid, 1927.

$190–220 MSh

A cap, with embroidered badge, 1950s.

$50–60 SA

A Winter Olympic Games bronze medal, by J. H. Coeffin, embossed with a Greek portrait, the reverse with aerial view of Grenoble, France, 1968, 2½in (7.5cm) diam.

$140–165 BBA

A velvet cap, embroidered 'B. V. G. S', with tassel and braid, 1927–28.

$110–130 MSh

OLYMPIC GAMES OF LONDON. 1908.

A Complete Record with photographs of winners of the Olympic Games held at the Stadium, Shepherd's Bush, London. July 13-25, 1908.

Along with Accounts of other Olympic Events.

1/- NET.

A London Olympic Games medal, by B. Mackennal, 1908, together with a complete record of photographs of the winners.

$430–510 BUDD

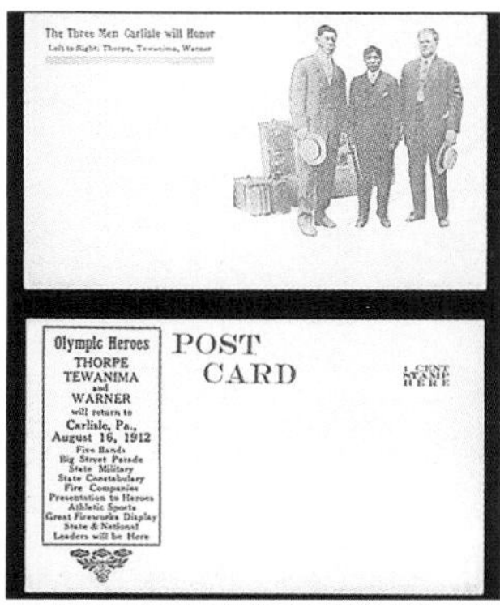
The Three Men Carlisle will Honor
Left to Right: Thorpe, Tewanima, Warner

Olympic Heroes
THORPE
TEWANIMA
and
WARNER
will return to
Carlisle, Pa.,
August 16, 1912
Five Bands
Big Street Parade
State Military
State Constabulary
Fire Companies
Presentation to Heroes
Athletic Sports
Great Fireworks Display
State & National
Leaders will be Here

POST CARD

A Stockholm Olympic Games homecoming postcard, depicting Jim Thorpe, Louis Tewanima and Pop Warner, America, 1912.

$550–650 MN

Jim Thorpe won the pentathlon and decathlon at the 1912 Olympics. This postcard was printed to advertise his jubilant homecoming to Pennsylvania.

◄ A Moscow Olympic Games plastic sports bag, 1980, 24in (61cm) wide.

$70–80 TWI

A cap, with embroidered decoration, 1947.

$85–100 SA

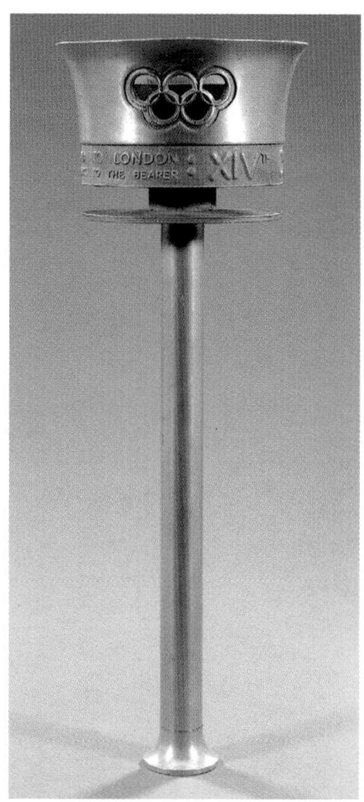

A 1948 Olympic bearer's aluminium torch, 1948, 16in (40.5cm) high.

$3,000–3,600 BUDD

A Moscow Olympic Games porcelain jar and cover, 1980, 5in (12.5cm) high.

$40–45 COB

BASEBALL

◄ **A Pennsylvania flannel baseball uniform,** embroidered 'Thompson', America, c1900, with letter of authentication.

$840–1,000 MN

► **A Pittsburgh Pirates wool team sweater,** worn by Elmer Steele, with original plastic buttons, America, 1911, with photograph, postcard and letter of authentication.

$15,200–18,100 MN

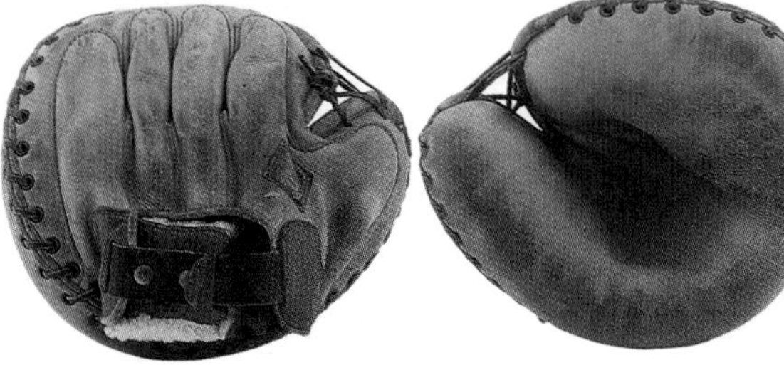

A catcher's leather mitt, worn by Al Lopez, with fur-lined wrist backing and Spalding label, signed, America, 1939, with letter of authentication.

$1,800–2,150 MN

A Cincinnati Reds satin warm-up jacket, worn by Jim Turner, embroidered 'Turner', with Spalding label, America, 1940, with letter of authentication.

$3,450–4,150 MN

◄ **A catcher's leather mitt,** worn by Gary Carter, with fur-lined wrist backing, signed and inscribed 'Best Wishes – God Bless always – Gary Carter "The Kid"', America, 1974–93, with letter of authentication.

$860–1,000 MN

A Philadelphia Phillies road uniform, worn by Pete Rose, with Wilson label, America, 1982, with letter of authentication.

$3,800–4,500 MN

A pair of Wade Boggs baseball boots, by Nike, signed, America, 1982–92, with letter of authentication.

$430–510 MN

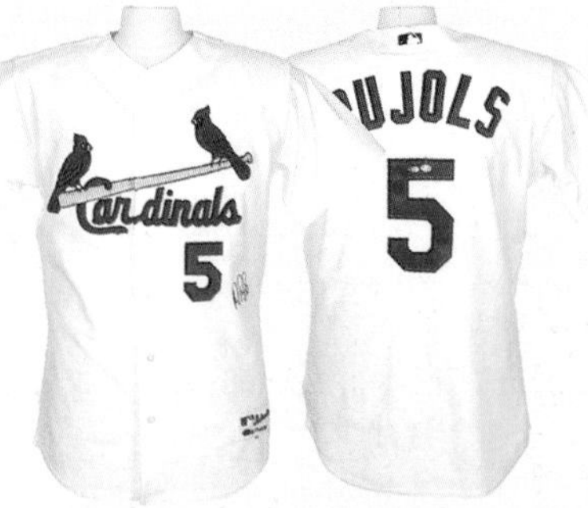

◄ **A St Louis Cardinals home jersey,** worn by Albert Pujols, with Majestic label, signed, America, 2003–04, with letter of authentication.

$2,900–3,450 MN

A collection of 69 Old Mill Tobacco cigarette cards, comprising 33 series No. 5 Carolina Association cards, 26 Series No. 6 Blue Grass League card, six Series No. 7 East Carolina League cards and four Series No. 8 Southern Association cards, America, 1910.

$3,100–3,700 MN

A T205 Gold Border Cy Young insert cigarette card, America, 1911.

$10,700–12,800 MN

A set of T205 Gold Border cigarette cards, America, 1911.

$15,200–18,100 MN

A Cleveland Indians yearbook, America, 1918, 4½ x 7½in (11.5 x 19cm).

$620–740 MN

A Boston Red Sox American Team Champions photograph, America, 1912, 13½ x 30¼in (34.5 x 77cm), framed.

$690–830 MN

A photograph of Grover Alexander, signed, America, late 1920s, 9 x 7in (23 x 18cm), with letters of authentication.

$1,400–1,650 MN

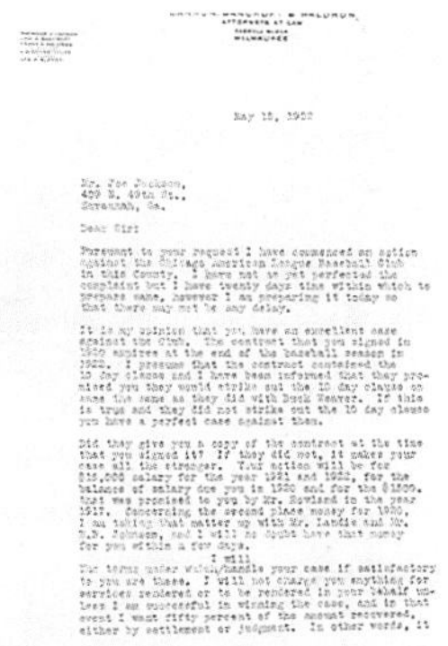

May [illegible], 1922

Mr. Joe Jackson,
[illegible] E. 49th St.,
Savannah, Ga.

Dear Sir:

Pursuant to your request I have commenced an action against the Chicago American League Baseball Club in this County. I have not as yet perfected the complaint but I have twenty days time within which to prepare same, however I am preparing it today so that there may not be any delay.

It is my opinion that you have an excellent case against the Club. The contract that you signed in [illegible] expires at the end of the baseball season in 1922. I presume that the contract contained the 10 day clause and I have been informed that they promised you they would strike out the 10 day clause on same the same as they did with Buck Weaver. If this is true and they did not strike out the 10 day clause you have a perfect case against them.

Did they give you a copy of the contract at the time that you signed it? If they did not, it makes your case all the stronger. Your action will be for $[illegible] salary for the year 1921 and 1922, for the balance of salary due you in 1920 and for the $[illegible] that was promised to you by Mr. Rowland in the year 1917. Concerning the second place money for 1920, I am taking that matter up with Mr. Landis and Mr. B.B. Johnson, and I will no doubt have that money for you within a few days.

The terms under which I will handle your case if satisfactory to you are these. I will not charge you anything for services rendered or to be rendered in your behalf unless I am successful in winning the case, and in that event I want fifty percent of the amount recovered, either by settlement or judgment. In other words, it

A legal letter to Joe Jackson, regarding the Chicago White Sox scandal, America, 1922.

$1,200–1,450 MN

Accused of taking a bribe from gamblers to lose the 1919 Fall Classic game, Joe Jackson was banned from baseball for ever. This two-page letter from an attorney informs Jackson that he has begun a long series of legal proceedings against the Chicago American League Baseball Club.

A photograph of Lou Gehrig, signed, America, 1930s, 10 x 8in (25.5 x 20.5cm), with letters of authentication.

$6,700–8,000 MN

▶ A Huskies Lou Gehrig cardboard counter display, America, 1930s, 25½ x 19¾in (65 x 50cm), framed.

$3,100–3,700 MN

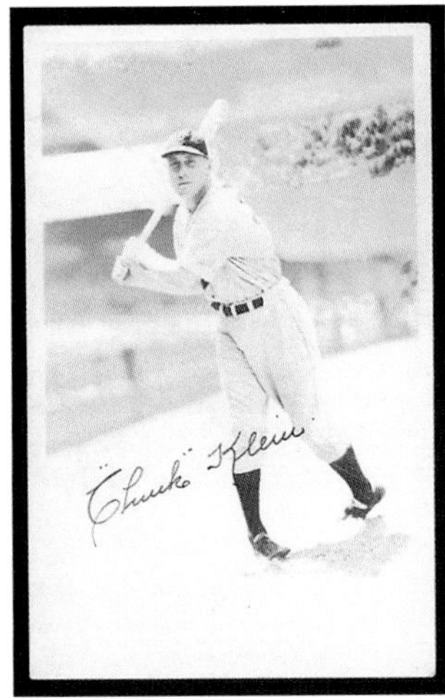

A signed photograph of Chuck Klein, by George Burke, America, 1930s, 6 x 4in (15 x 10cm), with letters of authentication.

$2,750–3,250 MN

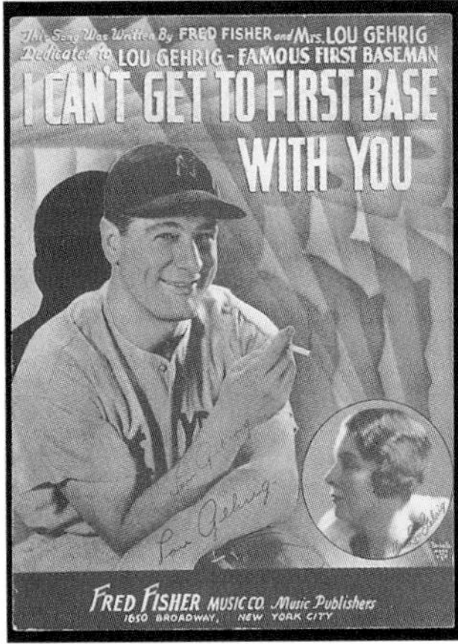

A Lou Gehrig pictorial music sheet, entitled 'I Can't Get to First Base with You', published by Fred Fisher Music Company, signed, America, 1935, 12¼ x 9½in (31 x 24cm), with letter of authentication.

$3,700–4,400 MN

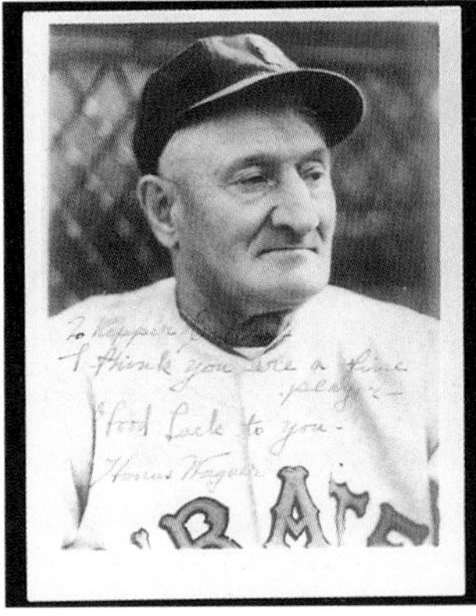

A photograph of Honus Wagner, by George Burke, signed and inscribed, America, 11 x 8½in (28 x 21.5cm), with letter of authentication.

$2,750–3,250 MN

A Nellie Fox Favorite Chewing Tobacco cardboard advertising sign, America, late 1950s, 15¼ x 21¼in (38.5 x 54cm), framed.

$1,000–1,200 MN

A World Series Game 1 Braves Field ticket, America, 1948, 2½ x 7½in (6.5 x 19cm).

$600–720 MN

A Hugh Jennings Cogan's Hiking Shoes celluloid advertising pin, America, 1910, 1¼in (3cm) diam.

$230–270 MN

The manufacturer pushed the bounds of tolerance with this advertising pin. The implied message was that Hughie Jennings endorsed the product, but nowhere is his name apparent.

A New York Giants World Series enamel lapel pin, possibly a press pin, maker's mark, America, 1917, ½in (1cm) wide.

$520–620 MN

A Brooklyn Dodger World Series enamel press pin, America, 1920, ¾in (2cm) diam.

$640–760 MN

A New York Yankees celluloid souvenir pin, America, 1953, 3½in (9cm) diam.

$1,000–1,200 MN

► A set of 24 R333 DeLong bubble gum cards, America, 1933.

$4,750–5,700 MN

A Joe Jackson Louisville Slugger mini decal bat, by Hillerich & Bradsby, depicting Joe Jackson, America, c1910, 14¼in (36cm) long.
$1,100–1,300 MN

A willow baseball bat, Wales, c1920, 32in (81.5cm) long.
$70–80 SA

A Joe Jackson-style ash barnstorming bat, by Hillerich & Bradsby, America, 1921–31, 35in (89cm) long.
$2,300–2,750 MN

After the scandal of the 1920 season, Jackson resorted to 'barnstorming' games with sparse crowds and limited publicity. The woodworkers at Hillerich & Bradsby ground the first name 'Joe' from the dies of his signature model bats in order to distinguish those that were used for his 'barnstorming' years.

◄ **An American League All-Star Team signed ball,** including the signatures of Lou Gehrig and Beau Bell, America, 1937, with letters of authentication.
$5,600–6,700 MN

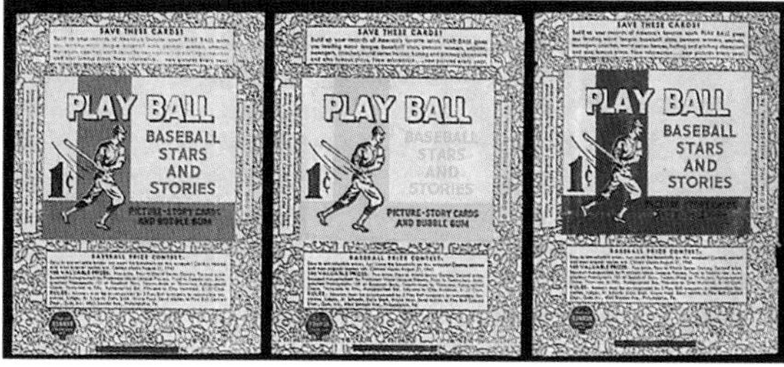

Three Play Ball R335 gum card wrappers, America, 1940, 6 x 4½in (15 x 11.5cm).
$2,600–3,100 MN

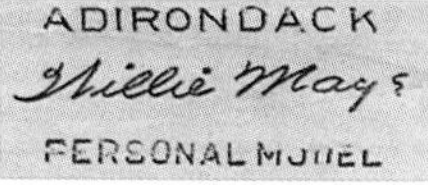

A Willie Mays ash game bat, by Adirondack, America, signed, 1961–67, 35in (89cm) long, with letters of authentication.
$3,700–4,400 MN

A Barry Bonds Home Run No. 533 maple Sam Bat, American, signed, 2001, 34in (86.5cm) long, with letters of authentication.
$6,700–8,000 MN

► **A Washington Nationals RFK Stadium Inaugural Season baseball,** inscribed 'Exclusive Stadium Collection Limited Edition', America, 2005, 3in (7.5cm) diam, with money box and original packaging.
$10–15 CWO

BOXING

A photograph of Tom Sayers, signed in ink, mounted above a handbill advertising a benefit bout, 1857, 12½ x 9¼in (32 x 23.5cm), framed and glazed.

$720–860 BUDD

Tom Sayers (1826–65) was a bare-knuckle fighter whose fighting career lasted from 1849 until 1860 when a fight against the American, John Heenan ended in disarray. Despite this, he was crowned World Boxing Champion and persuaded by his friends to retire. He died of TB and diabetes in 1865 and was elected to the Boxing Hall of Fame in 1954.

A pair of Benny Lynch's leather boxing gloves, the left glove with original stitching, 1930s.

$440–530 BUDD

Benny Lynch (1913–46) was born in Glasgow and won the Scottish flyweight boxing title in 1934. He subsequently lost the title as a result of a drinking habit that made him over the allocated weight. After a battle with alcohol he died of malnutrition at the age of 33. He was inducted into the International Boxing Hall of Fame in 1998 and a film about his life was made in 2003.

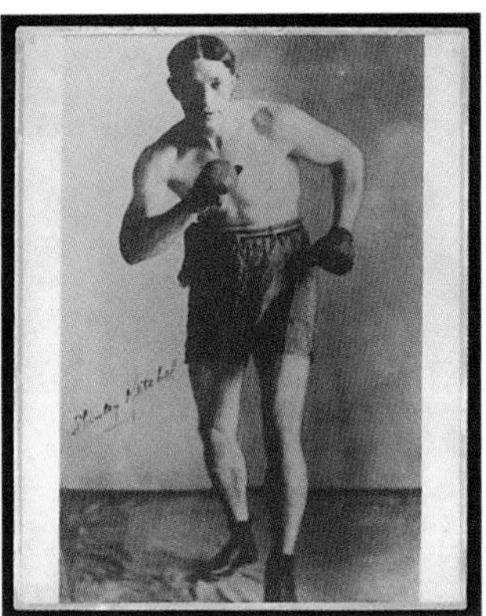

A signed photograph of Stanley Ketchel, America, c1910, 14 x 11in (35.5 x 28cm).

$720–860 MN

Stanley Ketchel (1886–1910) was an American boxer who became middleweight champion in 1908. Born in Grand Rapids, Michigan, he was nicknamed the Michigan Mauler or the Michigan Assasin. He attempted to win the World Heavyweight title against Jack Johnson in 1909 but lost to a blow that knocked out all his teeth and rendered him unconscious. He was shot dead in 1910 by farmhand Walter Dipley after a dispute.

A pair of leather boxing boots, 1950s.

$50–60 SA

A pair of Julio Cesar Chavez silk fight trunks, America, c1990.

$1,100–1,300 MN

A silver and enamel RACD boxing tournament medal, 1918, 3in (7.5cm) diam.

$220–250 LSA

W. A & A. C. Churchman, Boxing Personalities, set of 50, 1938.

$110–130 CWD

Issued as a sequel to the Boxing series in 1922. Boxing Personalities was issued at a time when sporting cards were very popular. The cards consist of black and white poses of boxing heros with a description on the back.

A leather medicine ball, 1960s, 10in (25.5cm) diam.

$100–110 MINN

Medicine balls were used to strengthen the upper body.

CRICKET

A group of four colour lithographs, by Jon Corbet Anderson, depicting cricketers at Lords, 1852, 8¼ x 5½in (21 x 14cm), framed and glazed, together with a framed reproduction photograph of England's 12 champion cricketers, 1859.

$1,400–1,650 BUDD

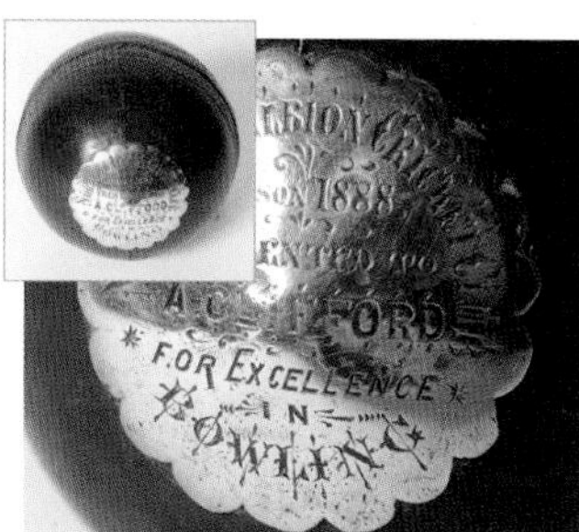

A presentation cricket ball, with silver plaque inscribed 'Presented to A. Clifford', 1888, 3in (7.5cm) diam.

$220–250 BS

A group of three bronze figures of cricketers, by Joseph Durham, signed and dated 1863, largest 15¾in (40cm) high.

$20,700–24,800 BUDD

A photograph of Victor Trumper, by George Beldam, published by the Swan Electric Engraving Co, London, signed, 1905, 19¼ x 21½in (49 x 54.5cm), framed and glazed.

$2,600–3,100 BUDD

A wooden cricket bat, by G. G. Hearne, signed by A. E. Stoddart, with embossed metal plaque, 1885–1915.

$3,800–4,500 BUDD

A. E. Stoddart (1863–1915) played 16 Test matches for the English cricket team between 1888 and 1898. He also played Rugby at an International level.

◀ **A commemorative mug,** depicting George Hirst and Wilfred Rose, 1905, 4in (10cm) high.

$1,450–1,650 RdV

A photograph of RMS *Orvieto*, signed by the returning MCC Ashes winners, with 16 ink signatures, 1911–12, framed and glazed, 12 x 20in (30.5 x 51cm), together with a photograph of an Australian tour match in England, 1911–12.

$2,900–3,450 BUDD

A silver salver, engraved with the signatures of the 1925 Yorkshire County Cricket champions, Sheffield 1924, 10in (25.5cm) diam.

$1,200–1,400 BUDD

A silver-mounted cricket ball, with presentation inscription, dated 1933, 2¾in (7cm) diam.

$500–580 G(L)

▶ A signed letter from Sir Don Bradman, 1948.

$450–530 BUDD

This letter was written two days after Don Bradman's final Test match at The Oval.

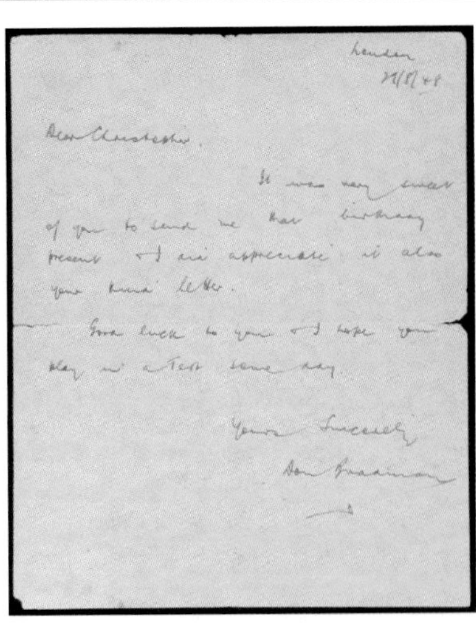

London
29/8/48

Dear Christopher,

It was very sweet of you to send me that birthday present and I appreciate it also your kind letter.

Good luck to you and I hope you play in a Test some day.

Yours sincerely
Don Bradman

◀ Jack O'Connor, *The Young Cricketer's Manual*, published by Thorsons Publishers, 1948, 7½ x 4¾in (19 x 12cm).

$30–35 BB

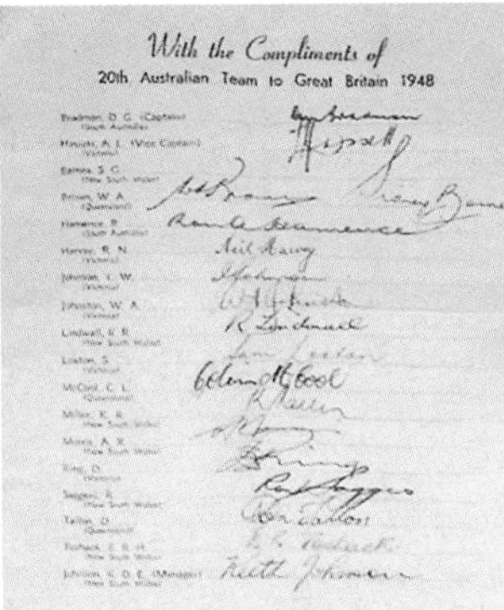

With the Compliments of
20th Australian Team to Great Britain 1948

A team sheet, for the 20th Australian Cricket Team's visit to England, with autographs, 1948.

$620–740 MAL(O)

A Royal Doulton figure of W. G. Grace, No. HN3640, 1995, 8in (20.5cm) high.

$150–170 BWL

◀ **An MCC blazer,** worn by Vic Wilson, 1954–55, together with a leather bag.

$170–200 BUDD

This blazer was worn during the 1954–55 MCC Tour of Australia.

▶ **An Australian Cricket Team woollen cap,** by Farmer's of Sydney, worn by Ray Lindwall, with embroidered emblem, 1954–55.

$6,200–7,400 BUDD

FISHING

A mahogany and brass star back fishing reel, with ebonized handles, c1900, 5in (12.5cm) diam.

$220–250 ⊞ MSh

A brass and aluminium big game reel, for tuna and shark fishing, 1930s, 6in (15cm) diam.

$190–210 ⊞ SA

A Hardy Uniqua alloy and brass trout fly reel, with telephone-shaped release catch, ridged brass foot and painted plate, slight wear, c1940, 4in (10cm) diam.

$60–70 ⊞ OTB

A brass trout/light salmon fly reel, with a raised Hercules-style face, engraved maker's name, horn handle and fixed check, c1920, 3½in (9cm) diam.

$75–85 ⊞ OTB

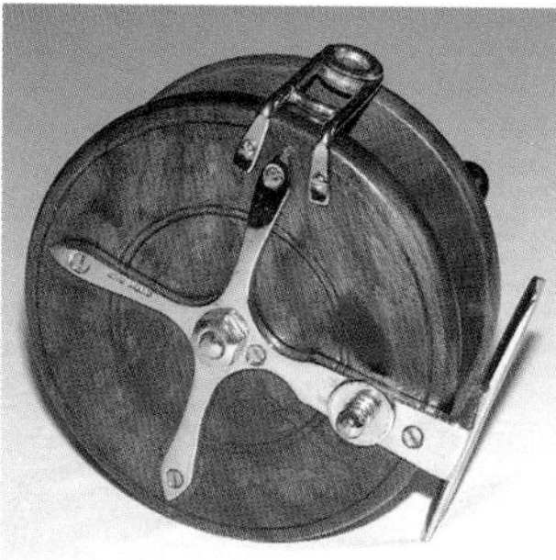

A wooden star back Nottingham reel, with chrome finish and drum rear flange, the rear engraved 'Eton Sun', c1930, 5in (12.5cm) diam.

$135–150 ⊞ OTB

A Hardy Sunbeam alloy fly reel, c1950, 2¾in (7cm) diam.

$155–170 ⊞ OTB

An Illingworth No. 3 gunmetal fixed spool reel, with exposed gears, alloy spool and roller-style line pick up, c1925, 4in (10cm) high, with a fitted wooden box.

$155–170 ⊞ OTB

A Dingley aluminium and brass big game reel, c1932, 7in (18cm) diam.

$230–250 ⊞ MINN

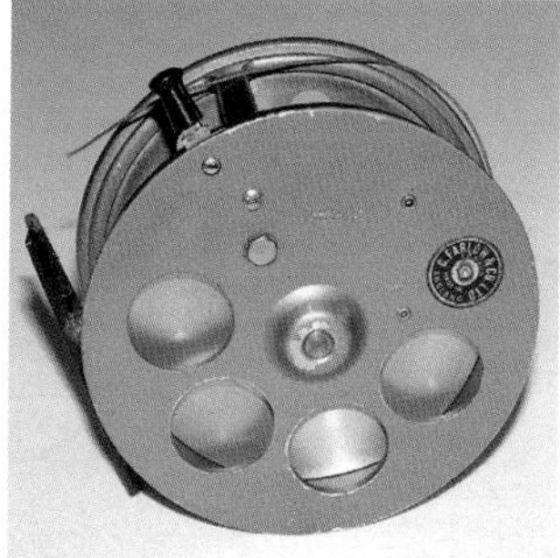

A Farlow & Co Barrett alloy casting reel, with manual brake control, c1950, 4¼in (11cm) diam.

$180–200 ⊞ OTB

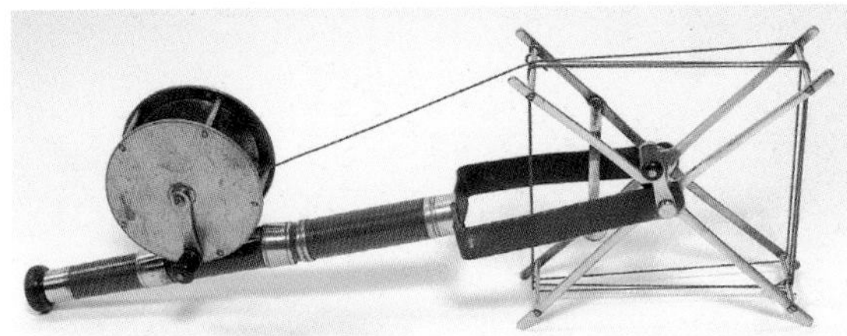

A Farlow & Co brass line dryer with reel, c1900, 22in (56cm) long.

$230–250 MINN

A Hardy pigskin fly wallet, 1920s, 6in (15cm) wide.

$250–260 MSh

An Allcock Schooling spoon, c1925, 2in (5cm) long.

$60–70 OTB

This Schooling spoon was named after the renowned angler John Holt Schooling.

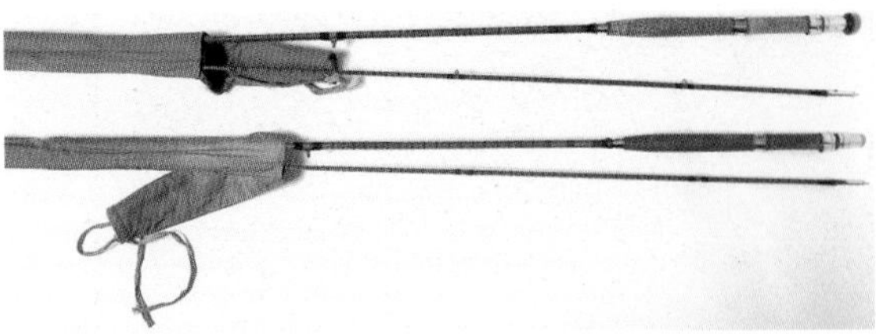

Two North Yorkshire trout fishing rods, c1930, largest 108in (274.5cm) long.

$50–60 each SA

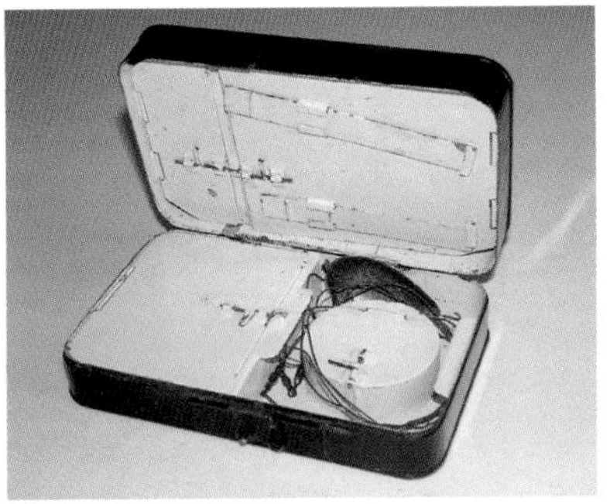

A Hardy Multum-in-Parvo tackle case, c1930, 1¾in (4.5cm) high.

$105–120 OTB

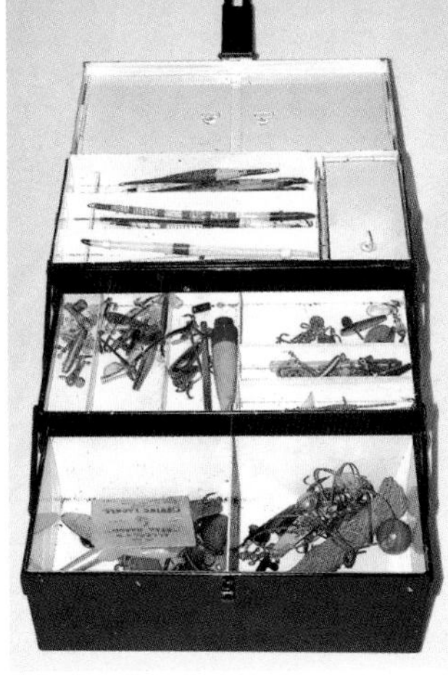

A japanned tackle case, 1930s, 7in (18cm) high.

$170–190 OTB

◄ An Allcocks hook packet, in the form of a fisherman's creel, 1930s, 3½in (9cm) wide.

$60–70 OTB

A Hardy chrome oil bottle, engraved mark, c1940, 4in (10cm) long.

$40–50 OTB

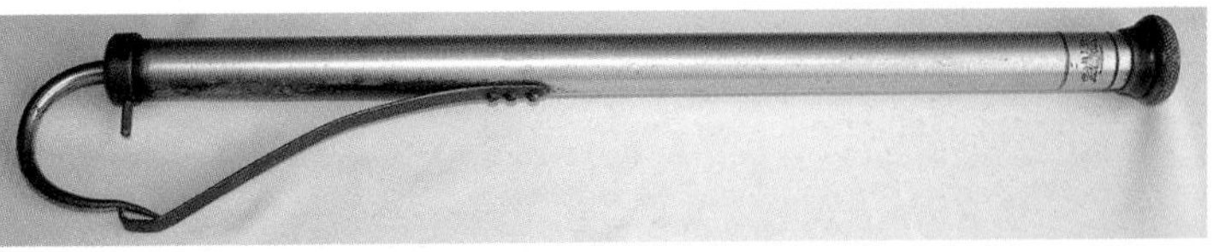

◄ A Hardy trout fisher's alloy gaff, 1930s, 13½in (34.5cm) long.

$40–50 OTB

AMERICAN FOOTBALL

An American football woollen jersey, by McMillan, with felt numbers to reverse, damaged and repaired, 1920s.

$1,200–1,450 MN

An American football woollen jersey, by Spalding, with felt numbers to reverse, damaged and repaired, 1930s.

$340–400 MN

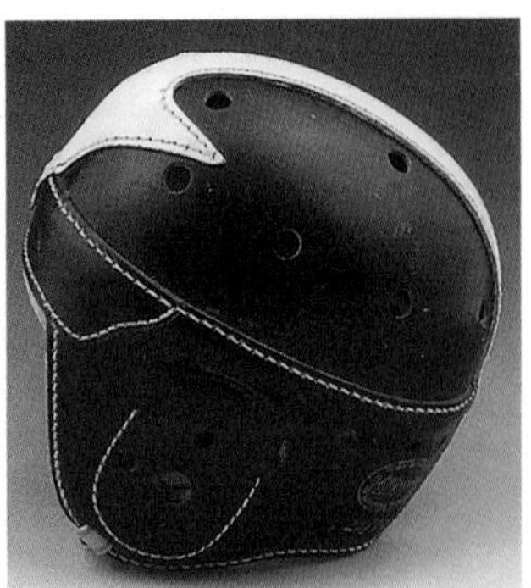

An American football leather helmet, by J. C. Higgins, stamped mark, 1930s.

$690–820 MN

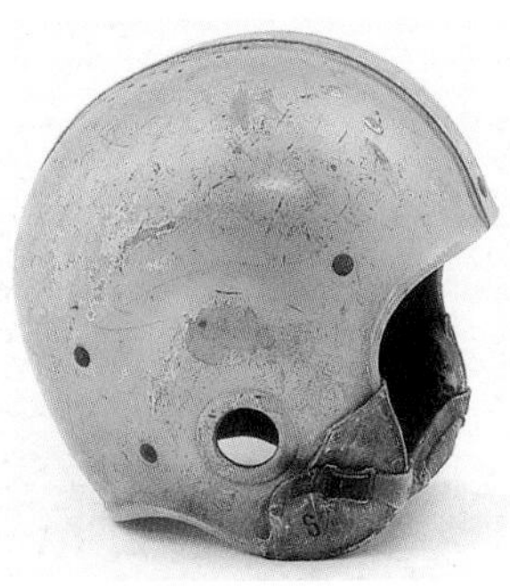

A Detroit Lions plastic helmet, worn by Doak Walker, America, 1950s.

$2,750–3,250 MN

Two American football helmets, Miami Dolphins helmet signed by Dan Marino, replica San Francisco 49ers helmet signed by Joe Montana, 1988, together with two footballs, an American Bowl programme and two posters.

$600–720 BUDD

A Washington Redskins helmet, signed by Joe Jacoby, with a four-bar cage mask, America, 1980s.

$1,100–1,350 MN

A San Francisco 49ers jersey, by Wilson, worn by Steve Young, America, 1990s.

$480–570 MN

A Detroit Lions jersey, by Wilson, worn by Barry Sanders, America, 1992.

$1,700–2,050 MN

The first initial on this jersey was necessary as fellow team-mate Eric Sanders was also playing that season.

▶ **A Miami Dolphins helmet,** worn and signed by Dan Marino, with a four-bar cage mask, America, 1990, together with a letter of authenticity.

$3,350–3,950 MN

A cardboard poster, 'Red Grange Chicago Bears vs Buck Bailey San Francisco Tigers', 1926, framed, 26½ x 15½in (67.5 x 39.5cm).

$510–610 MN

A Wilson shop display American football box, with Red Grange endorsement, 1930s, 13¼in (33.5) wide.

$1,950–2,300 MN

A cardboard counter display, advertising Cunningham Radio Tubes, 1930s, 19 x 16in (48.5 x 40.5cm) high.

$690–830 MN

A Goudey Gum Co trade card, featuring Jim Thorpe, No. 6, Sport Kings set, America, 1933.

$3,700–4,400 MN

A *Saturday Evening Post* advertising poster, America, 1938, 27½ x 21½in (70 x 54.5cm), framed.

$230–250 MN

An American Football League programme, for Dallas Texas v Oakland Raiders, America, 1960, 10½ x 7¾in (26.5 x 19.5cm).

$320–380 MN

A cardboard advertising sign, by Willard Mullin, advertising New York Jets home schedule, America, 1965, 20½ x 15½in (52 x 39.5cm).

$1,000–1,200 MN

A University of Chicago Maroons American football pennant, America, 1904–05, 35in (89cm) wide.

$320–360 MN

A New York Yankees American football, with 39 signatures including Frank 'Bruiser' Kinard, America, 1947.

$460–550 MN

Frank 'Bruiser' Kinard (1914–85) played American football for the Brooklyn Dodgers/Tigers and the New York Yankees during the 1930s and 1940s.

◄ **A 14ct gold and diamond Green Bay Packers chain bracelet,** c1996.

$530–640 MN

ASSOCIATION FOOTBALL

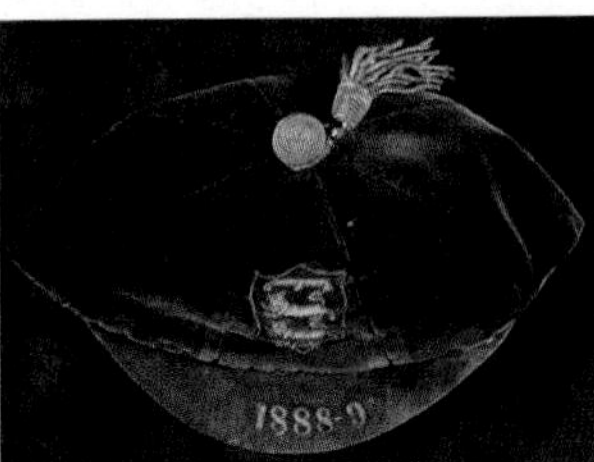

A velvet football cap, England v Ireland, worn by Jack Yates, 1888–89.

$6,200–7,400 BUDD

John 'Jack' Yates (1861–1917) was an instrumental figure in the formation of Blackburn Olympic, a team consisting of working men including spinners, cotton workers and blacksmiths.

A 14ct gold FA Cup Winner's medal, won by Ted Catlin, 1935.

$5,800–6,900 BUDD

In the 1935 FA Cup Final, Sheffield Wednesday defeated West Bromwich Albion by four goals to two.

A pair of leather football boots, 1950s.

$85–95 SA

An England International football cap, England v Hungary, embroidered '1936–37'.

$2,750–3,250 BUDD

This match was played at Highbury on 2 December 1936 and marked the Hungarian International team's first visit to England.

An International football shirt, worn by Stuart Williams, 1965–66.

$600–720 BUDD

This shirt was worn by Stuart Williams, Captain of Wales, during the World Cup qualifier between Wales and Denmark.

◄ **A leather football,** 1920, 11in (28cm) diam.

$85–95 DQ

An England International football shirt, worn by Fred Tilson, embroidered with Three Lions badge, 1934–35.

$1,550–1,850 BUDD

Samuel Frederick Tilson transferred from Barnsley to Manchester City in 1928 where he went on to win a Championship medal and an FA Cup winner's medal.

An England football shirt, worn by Nobby Stiles, embroidered with Three Lions badge, No. 4, 1966.

$4,300–5,100 BUDD

This shirt was worn by Nobby Stiles in one of the 1966 World Cup matches. Stiles played in all of England's games during the tournament and white shirts were worn on all five occasions. The Football Association (the FA) is the governing body of football in England and their logo is based on the English Royal Coat-of-Arms featuring three lions.

A photograph of Surbiton Rangers football team, 1899, 9 x 11in (23 x 28cm), framed and glazed.

$170–195 BS

A photograph of Higham Ferrers football team, 1907, 9 x 11in (23 x 28cm), framed and glazed.

$60–70 JUN

A photograph of Usworth Colliery football team, c1910, 14 x 19in (35.5 x 48.5cm), framed and glazed.

$60–70 SA

An Edwardian photograph of a football team, 8 x 11in (20.5 x 28cm).

$60–70 SA

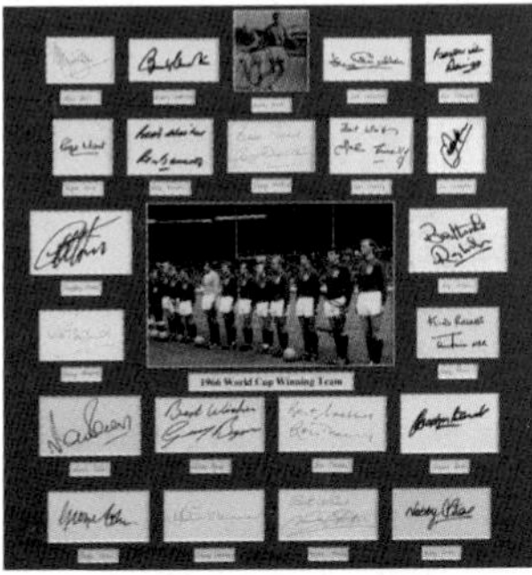

▶ A photograph of the England World Cup football team, together with 22 signatures, 1966, mounted, 31½ x 28¼in (80 x 72cm), framed and glazed.

$1,700–2,050 BUDD

A photograph of BHS School football team, 1914, 15 x 19in (38 x 48.5cm).

$125–145 BS

▶ A photograph of John Terry, Petr Cech and José Mourinho, at Chelsea Football Club, signed, 2005, 8 x 10in (20.5 x 25.5cm).

$380–430 FRa

The Athletic News Football Annual, four volumes, 1891, 1883, 1899–1900, 1900–01.

$1,350–1,600 BUDD

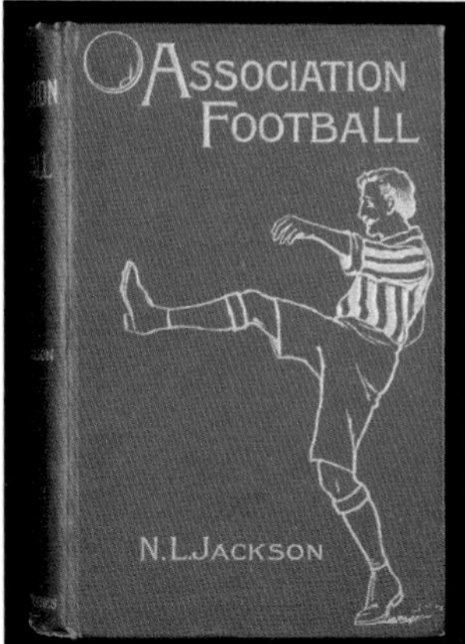

N. L. Jackson, *Association Football*, published by George Newnes, 1899.

$1,050–1,250 BUDD

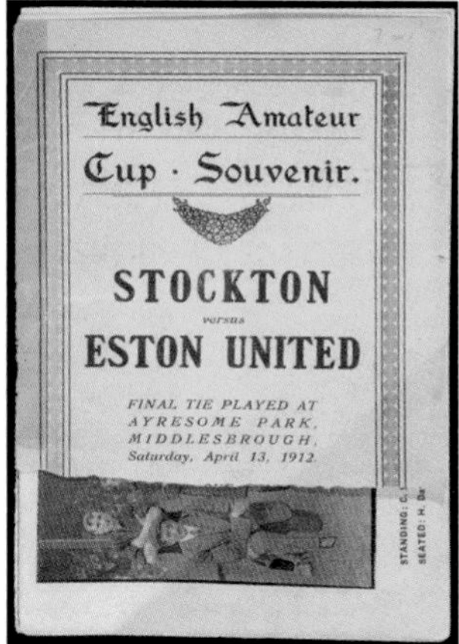

Three Bristol City Football Club/Bristol South End season ticket books, 1896–97.

$1,200–1,450 BUDD

Bristol South End changed their name to Bristol City Football Club in 1897. These books contain club details, rules, fixtures and advertisments.

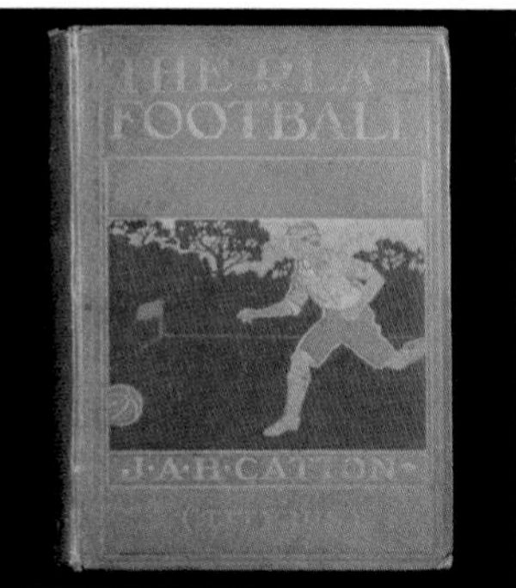

J. A. H. Catton, *The Real Football*, published by Sands & Co, 1900.

$1,100–1,300 BUDD

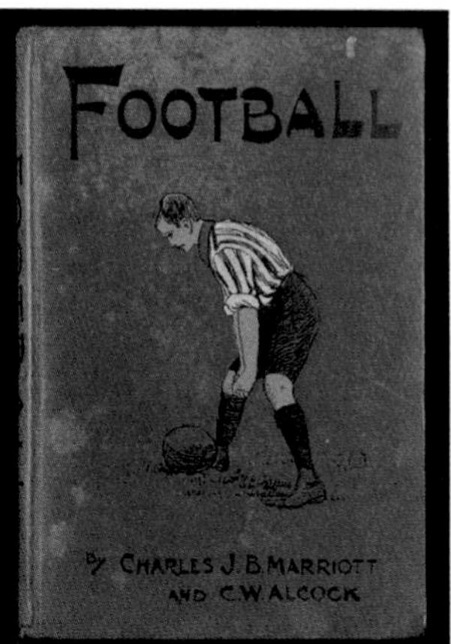

Charles J. B. Marriott and C. W. Alcock, *Football*, published by Sands & Co, 1900.

$1,350–1,600 BUDD

An FA Cup Final programme, Bolton Wanderers v West Ham, 1923.

$1,900–2,250 BUDD

◀ **A United English Amateur Cup programme,** Stockton v Eston United, published by Arthur Pickering, damaged, 1912.

$310–440 BUDD

An FA Cup Final programme, Aston Villa v Newcastle, covers replaced, interior restored, 1924.

$2,550–3,050 BUDD

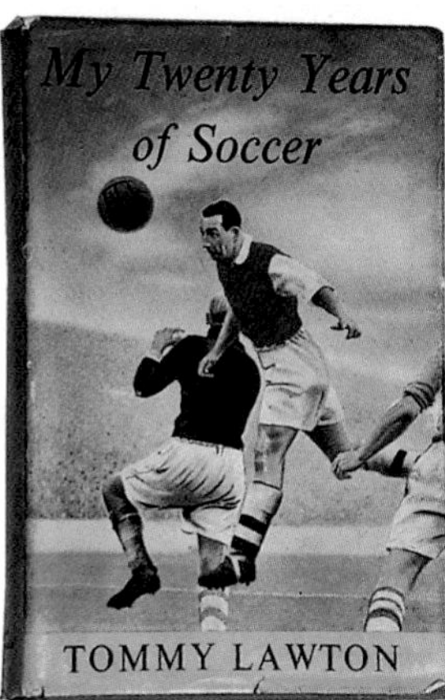

Tommy Lawton, *My Twenty Years of Soccer*, 1955, 8 x 6in (20.5 x 15cm).

$15–20 ⊞ EE

Football was commonly referred to as soccer in the UK until the 1960s. In 1963 the Football Association celebrated its centenary and published two commemorative volumes titled A Century of Soccer *and* 100 Years of Soccer in Pictures. *Tommy Lawton had an impressive start with Burnley FC, then Everton FC, but he is best remembered for playing centre forward for Nottinghamshire County FC between 1947 and 1952. His trademark skill was heading the ball.*

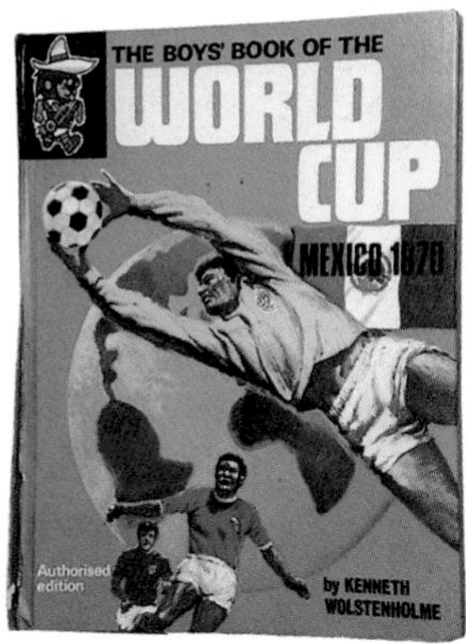

Kenneth Wolstenholme, *The Boy's Book of the World Cup Mexico 1970*, 11 x 8in (28 x 20.5cm).

$25–30 ⊞ EE

Kenneth Wolstenholme (1920–2002) was the original football commentator for BBC Television in the late 1950s and 1960s. He was also the commentator for the 1966 World Cup Final during which he shouted what is now the most famous phrase in English football, 'Some people are on the pitch...they think it's all over...it is now!'.

Three Chelsea Football Club programmes, one Chelsea v Sunderland and two Chelsea v Tottenham Hotspur, 1958, 9in (23cm) high.

$40–50 ⊞ MRW

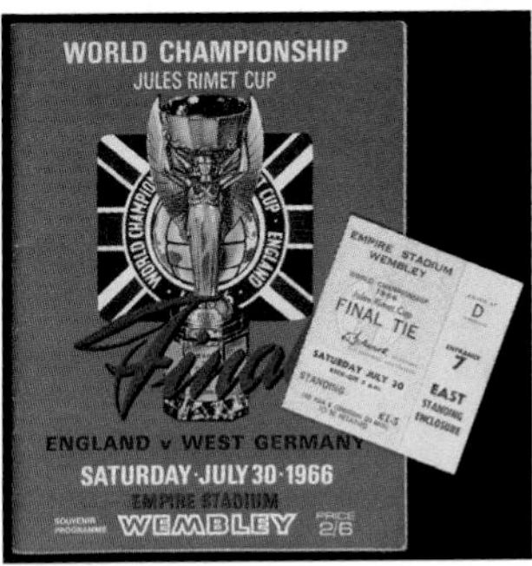

A World Cup Final programme and ticket stub, England v West Germany, 1966.

$410–480 ⚒ BUDD

A UEFA Cup Final programme, Tottenham v Wolverhampton, 1972, 8in (20.5cm) high.

$1–10 ⊞ MRW

► **A European Cup Winner's Cup Final ticket,** Chelsea v Madrid, Athens, 1971.

$620–740 ⚒ BUDD

George Best's Soccer Annual, No. 2, first edition, published by Pelham Books, 1969, 10in (25.5cm) high.

$15–20 ⊞ NGL

George Best (1946–2005) is often regarded as one of the best footballers of all time. Mainly known for his leading role at Manchester United, he also played for Northern Ireland at International level. He was named European Footballer of the Year and Football Writer's Association Player of the Year in 1968. His fun personality, good looks and talent won him many fans but he developed health problems which led to his retirement from football in 1984.

GOLF

An oak, steel and hickory putter, c1910, 37in (94cm) long.

$100–120 SHER

A wooden Auchterlone of St Andrews putter, c1920, 38in (96.5cm) long.

$300–340 SHER

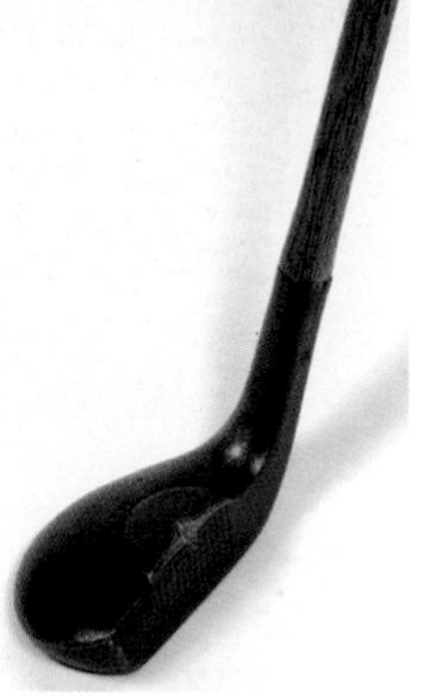

An aluminium Rodwell putter, c1910.

$165–190 MSh

A James Millar hickory and beech Brassie, c1920, 44in (112cm) long.

$120–140 SHER

During the 1890s, when golf became very popular in both the UK and America, many new club manufacturing techniques and designs were implemented. Brass plates were fitted to the bases of wooden drivers so they could be swung smoothly without wear on the fairway, and the new clubs became known as Brassies.

► A wood and brass Schenectady putter, c1930, 36in (91.5cm) long.

$300–340 SHER

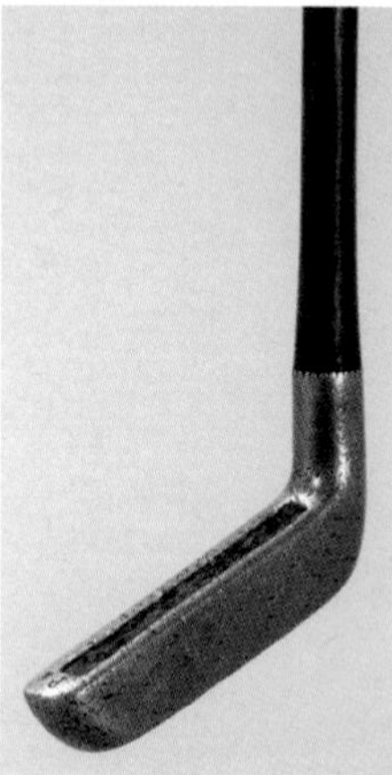

A James Ferguson of Sandy Lodge brass and hickory putter, filled with gutta percha, c1911.

$720–860 BUDD

A Spalding Gold Medal iron, 1920s, 40in (101.5cm) long.

$20–25 MSh

A Wright & Ditson steel and hickory Waterfall deep groove pitcher, America, c1920, 38in (96.5cm) long.

$300–340 SHER

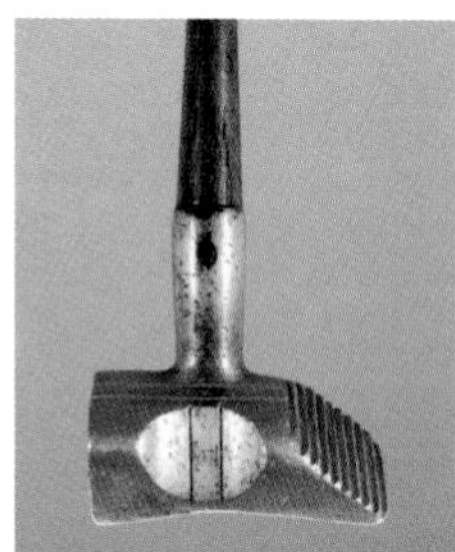

An aluminium and hickory pitcher/putter, 1920s.

$1,450–1,750 BUDD

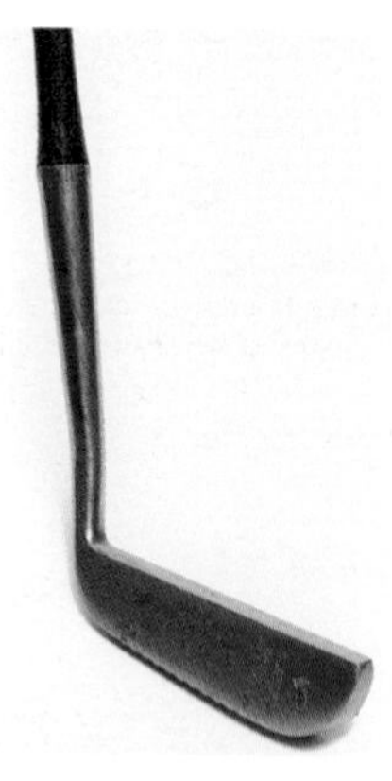

A wood and steel Benny putter, by Ben Sayers, c1930, 35in (89cm) long.

$75–85 SHER

A Copeland sugar bowl and cover, depicting a golfing scene, c1900, 5in (12.5cm) high.

$210–240 ⊞ OD

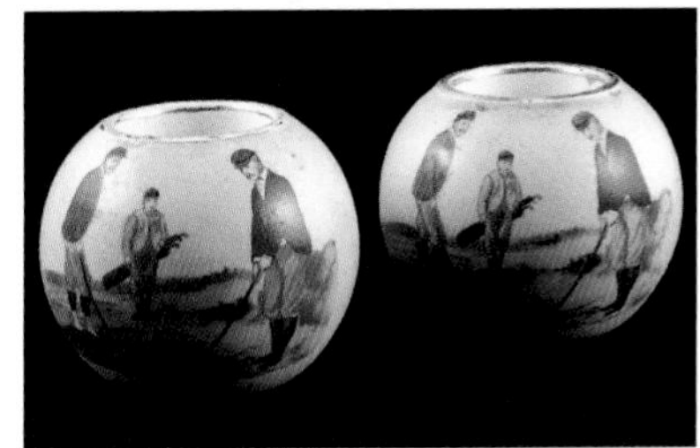

A pair of Carlton Ware match holders, printed with golfing scenes, printed marks, early 20thC, 3in (7.5cm) high.

$270–320 ⚒ WW

A ceramic figure of a caddy, Austria, c1910, 7in (18cm) high.

$270–310 ⊞ MSh

A porcelain teapot, decorated with a golfing scene, c1910, 5in (12.5cm) high.

$230–260 ⊞ BtoB

A Royal Doulton Series Ware plate, inscribed 'Every Dog Has His Day and Every Man His Hour', c1910, 10in (25.5cm) diam.

$240–290 ⊞ BtoB

A Royal Doulton tobacco jar, decorated with a golfing scene by Charles Crombie, 1911, 6in (15cm) high.

$1,050–1,200 ⊞ MSh

A Royal Doulton Series Ware dish, decorated with a golfing scene by Charles Crombie, c1910, 8½in (21.5cm) diam.

$630–700 ⊞ MSh

A Royal Doulton plate, inscribed 'The Nineteenth Hole', 1914, 10in (25.5cm) diam.

$630–700 ⊞ MSh

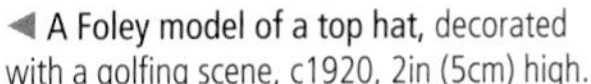

◄ **A Foley model of a top hat,** decorated with a golfing scene, c1920, 2in (5cm) high.

$155–175 ⊞ SHER

► **A Grimwades plate,** decorated with a golfing scene, c1920, 9in (23cm) diam.

$230–260 ⊞ SHER

The Glensaddell Gold Medal, North Berwick Golf Club, won outright by Sir David Baird of Newbyth, modelled with two golf clubs and three feather balls, engraved with Royal Burgh of North Berwick coat-of-arms, the reverse and hanging disc engraved with winning players, Edinburgh 1831, 2¼in (5.5cm) diam.

$38,000–45,000 BUDD

Sir David Baird of Newbyth (1796–1852) was a founding member of North Berwick Golf Club in 1832. He was also captain of the Royal & Ancient Golf Club in 1843. His hat trick of successive wins between 1847 and 1849 won him the Glensaddell medal outright.

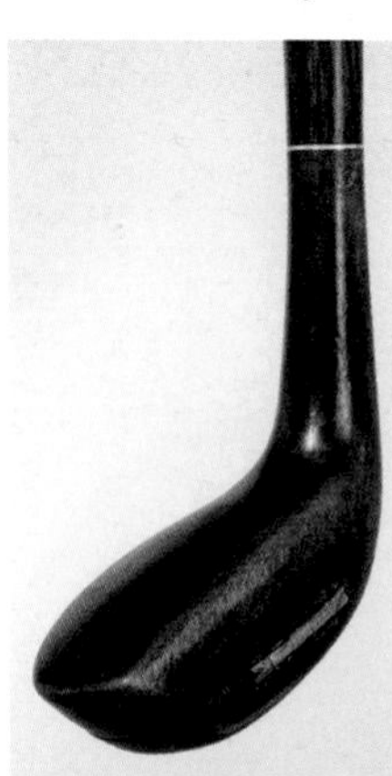

A silver-mounted walking stick/snuff box, in the form of a golf club, Birmingham 1920.

$450–530 BUDD

A set of six silver teaspoons, decorated with golf clubs, late 19thC, 4in (10cm) long, in a shagreen case.

$180–200 BS

A brass ashtray, decorated with a golfer, 1907, 4in (10cm) diam.

$100–120 BS

► **A Tavannes silvered and crocodile-skin golfer's belt watch,** with a 17 jewel movement, 1930s, 1½in (4cm) wide.

$460–520 WAC

A pair of silver and enamel pin trays, one depicting a male, the other a female golfer, 1901, 3in (7.5cm) diam.

$2,350–2,600 SHER

► **A silver-mounted leather book,** 1905, 4½ x 2¾in (11.5 x 7cm).

$1,300–1,500 MSh

◄ **A silver pill box,** decorated with a golfer, 1904, 2in (5cm) diam.

$310–350 SHER

A pair of silver cigarette cases, enamelled with golfers, 1930s, larger 3¾ x 3½in (9.5 x 9cm).

$280–330 MN

◄ **A pair of silver spoons,** decorated with golfers, Sheffield 1937, 5in (12.5cm) long.

$70–80 LSA

A Parker Bros Golf game, repaired, America, 1896, 14 x 21in (35.5 x 53.5cm).

$700–840 MN

► **Four mesh pattern golf balls,** 1920–30.

$50–60 each MSh

A Dunlop golf ball box, 1920s, 6in (15cm) wide.

$75–85 SHER

A Goudey Gum Co trade card, Bobby Jones, Golf, No. 38, Sport Kings set, 1933.

$7,350–8,800 MN

► **A metal and plastic model of a golf bag,** 1960s, 6½in (16.5cm) high.

$40–45 RTT

Harold Hilton and Gordon Grant Smith, *The Royal and Ancient Game of Golf*, 1912, 13in (33cm) high.

$3,550–4,000 MSh

► **A Wallasey golf club captain's ceremonial jacket,** by Joseph Brown, worn by Dr Frank Stableford, c1930s.

$2,750–3,300 BUDD

Dr Frank Stableford (1870–1959) invented the golf scoring system that bears his name. The first Stableford competition was held at Wallasey Golf Club on 16 May 1932.

A Joker mesh pattern rubber golf ball, c1920.

$20–25 SHER

Gameplan Leisure, Open Champions, set of 8, 1995, 3 x 2½in (7.5 x 6.5cm).

$10–15 MUR

HOCKEY, ICE HOCKEY & LACROSSE

An oak hockey stick, c1900, 37in (94cm) long.

$30–35 SA

A photograph of the Corinthian hockey team, 1910, 12 x 14in (30.5 x 35.5cm), framed.

$90–105 BS

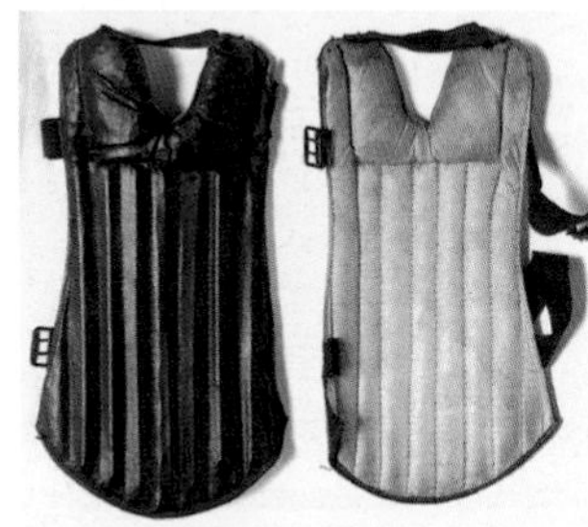

A pair of hockey shin guards, 1930s, 13in (33cm) high.

$50–55 SA

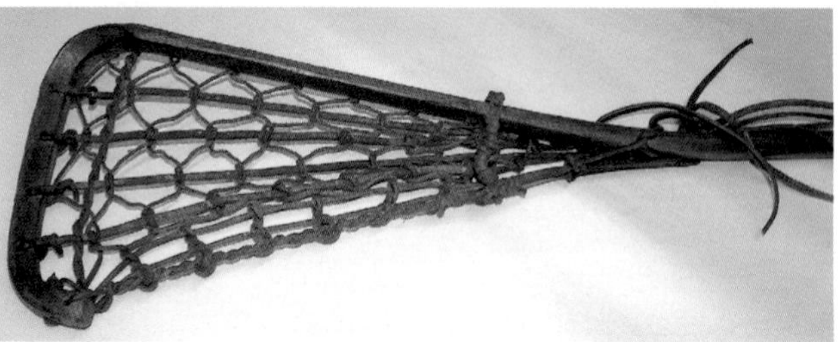

A wooden lacrosse stick, c1920, 46in (117cm) long.

$30–35 AL

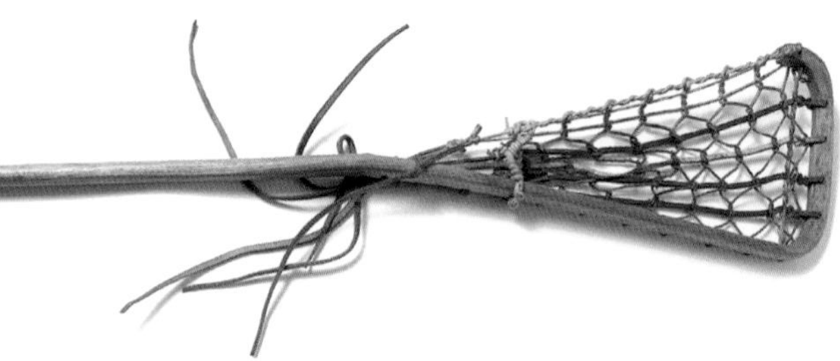

A wood and sinew lacrosse stick, c1930, 47in (119.5cm) long.

$50–55 SA

A pair of leather lacrosse/hockey boots, 1950s.

$50–60 SA

◄ **A New England Whalers jersey,** worn by Rick Ley, slight damage, America, mid-1970s.

$1,500–1,800 MN

O-Pee-Chee Gum, Rookie Card, Ken Dryden, No. 45, Canada, 1971–72,

$2,850–3,400 MN

HORSE RACING

DORLING'S LIST OF EPSOM RACES, 1851.

A **Derby Day race card,** Dorling's List of Epsom Races, 1851.

$430–520 BUDD

The 1951 Derby was won by Sir Joseph Hawley's 'Teddington'.

A **watercolour, *Mr Harnett's 'Gigante' by San Martin*,** by Basil Nightingale, inscribed with the horse's victories, signed, early 1900s, 16¼ x 21¾in (41.5 x 55.5cm), in an oak frame.

$1,450–1,750 L&E

A **spelter model of a horse,** c1920, 10in (25.5cm) long.

$710–820 MSh

A **Victorian lithograph of nine jockeys,** in a gilt frame.

$720–860 BUDD

This lithograph was exhibited at the Derby Day 200 Exhibition at the Royal Academy of Arts in London in 1979.

An **enamel stickpin,** illustrated with the racehorse 'Spearmint', c1906, ¾in (2cm) long.

$20–25 WAC

'Spearmint' was the winner of the 1906 Grand Prix de Paris, one of the most important horse races in France. Owned by Major Edmund Loder and trained by Peter Gilpin, 'Spearmint 'also won the prestigious Epsom Derby in 1906.

A **Goldscheider terracotta figure of a jockey,** signed, c1900, 21in (53.5cm) high.

$1,800–2,050 OAK

A **collection of 25 tin commemorative racing plates,** each painted and inscribed with the racehorse, race, year and prize money, on a mahogany backboard, 1914–64, 28½ x 33½in (72.5 x 85cm).

$2,400–2,850 BUDD

The plates dated 1914–16 relate to Sir Cecil Boyd-Rochfort's appointment as Sir Ernest Cassel's racing manager, while those dating from 1922 onwards relate directly to his training achievements at Freemason Lodge.

◄ A **silver and enamel cigarette case,** depicting three horses, Austria, c1920, 3½in (9cm) wide.

$850–950 SAT

A collection of 41 member's badges, comprising badges for Leopardstown, The Curragh and Naas racecourses, Ireland, 1924–68.

$1,000–1,200 BUDD

A silk scarf, commemorating the Derby, depicting the winner 'Trigo', 1929, 32 x 36in (81.5 x 91.5cm).

$200–240 BUDD

A Goebel pottery ashtray, in the form of a horse and rider, 1930s, 5in (12.5cm) wide.

$460–520 HEW

A silver and enamel cigarette case, by W. Wilkinson, depicting a polo match, Birmingham 1925, 3¼ x 4¼in (8.5 x 11cm).

$1,700–2,050 DN

A spelter model of a jockey on a racehorse, c1930, 7in (18cm) high.

$3100–350 BtoB

A jockey's silk jacket, by Boyce & Rogers, Newmarket, 1950s.

$860–1,000 BUDD

These colours were first registered in 1950 to Chesney Allen, a member of the Crazy Gang group of comedians. This distinctive and highly-coloured pattern, together with its association with the popular entertainer, made these colours instantly recognizable on British racecourses during the 1950s.

► **A Beswick model of Red Rum ridden by Brian Fletcher,** designed by Graham Tongue, model No. 2511, on a wooden plinth, 1975–82, 12¾in (32.5cm) wide.

$650–770 G(L)

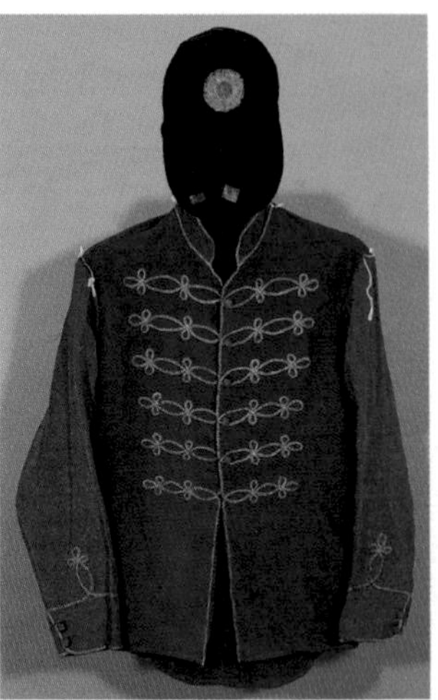

A set of King George V's royal racing silks, c1928.

$5,500–6,500 BUDD

These silks were kept at the Hon Aubrey Hasting's racing stables at Wroughton where the King had the horse 'St Sylvestre' in training in 1928.

A Royal Worcester model of Hyperion, by Doris Lindner, No. 197, on a wooden base, limited edition, 1968,

$950–$1,100 BUDD

RUGBY

A 15ct gold and enamel Rugby League Challenge Cup winner's medal, the reverse inscribed 'Widnes Football Club, Winners 1930, R. Topping', 1930.

$2,050–2,450 BUDD

A leather rugby ball, 1960s, 12in (30.5cm) long.

$90–105 TRA

A pair of rugby shirts, South Africa v British Lions, the Lions shirt worn by Tony Underwood, the other a South Africa spare player's shirt, signed by the squad, 1997.

$1,900–2,250 BUDD

A leather-covered ceramic butter dish, in the form of a rugby ball, 1930s, 5¾in (14.5cm) long.

$340–400 MSh

A Grand Slam winning rugby ball, Wales v Ireland Six Nations, Millennium Stadium, Cardiff, 19 March 2005, with match ticket and highlights video.

$3,500–4,150 BUDD

A British Lions blazer, worn by Phil Bennett on the New Zealand tour, 1977.

$1,000–1,200 BUDD

For more autographs, please see the Autographs section on pages 26–28.

► **A photograph of Johnny Wilkinson and Martin Johnson,** holding the Webb Ellis Cup, signed, 2003, 8 x 10in (20.5 x 25.5cm).

$520–600 FRa

A leather rugby ball, c1950, 13in (33cm) long.

$110–130 SA

A Bulldozers 15-a-side winner's wooden trophy, India, Bombay, 1944, 4in (10cm) wide.

$75–85 PEZ

A Royal Bradwell Sport Series earthenware mug, by Arthur Wood, 1945–54, 5in (12.5cm) high.

$70–80 BtoB

TENNIS

A wooden miniature tennis racket and ball, 1890s, 12in (30.5cm) long.

$430–520 MSh

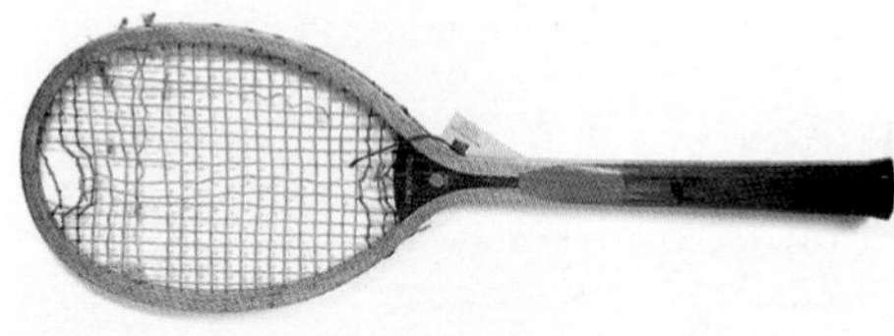

A wooden tennis racket, c1900, 27in (68.5cm) long.

$80–90 MSh

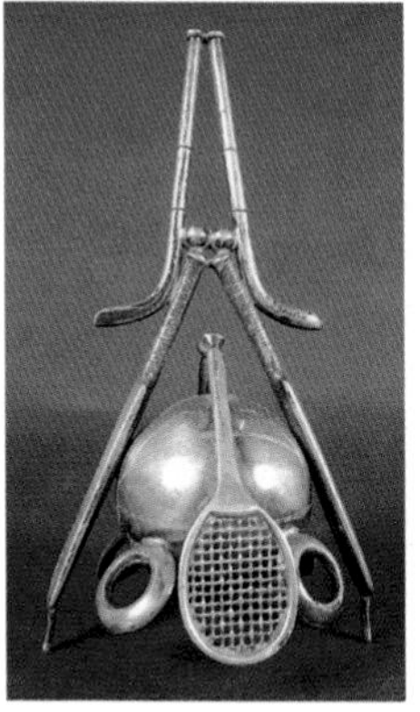

A silver sporting novelty stand, by W. Hutton, possibly for an epergne, in the form of hockey sticks, bats and tennis rackets around a football, London 1904.

$270–310 ROS

An Edwardian silver-plated figure of a female tennis player, on a white onyx base, 6¾in (17cm) high.

$75–90 ROS

A silver brooch, in the form of a tennis racket, 1920s, 2in (5cm) long.

$155–175 MSh

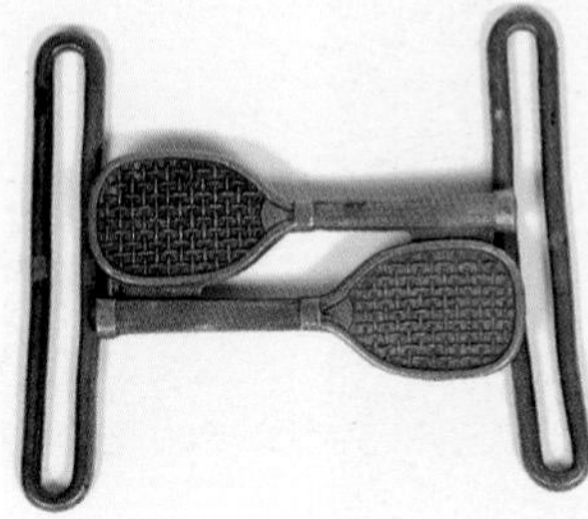

A brass belt buckle, in the form of two tennis rackets, c1900, 3½in (9cm) high.

$120–140 MSh

► **An Art Nouveau resin vanity case,** decorated with a picture of a female tennis player, the interior with satin fittings and vanity mirror, cord suspension and tassel, 5in (12.5cm) long.

$1,200–1,450 BUDD

► **A lithographic poster,** after Fernand Toussaint, published by De Rycker & Mendel, Belgium, Brussels, 1905, 39¼ x 28in (99.5 x 71cm).

$3,250–3,900 BUDD

A silver-plated tennis club trophy, 1930, 10in (25.5cm) high.

$360–420 MSh

This was presented to tennis player T. Abbott for Best Handicap and Scratch Singles Player.

A colour lithograph of the Davis Cup Challenge Round, Tilden v Cochet, July 1930, from *Les Joies du Sport* by Maurice and Jacques Goddet, France, Paris, 1932, 16½ x 12in (42 x 30.5cm).

$410–500 BUDD

A porcelain bottle and stopper, in the form of a tennis player, signed 'Margery', Paris mark to base, 1930s, 10½in (26.5cm) high.

$1,450–1,750 BUDD

◀ **A Davis Cup match picture disc record,** France v Great Britain, one side with a photographic match scene, the reverse with portraits of the players, 1933, 8in (20.5cm) diam.

$2,300–2,750 BUDD

A Wilson die-cut advertisement, featuring Jack Kramer, mid-1950s, 25½in (65cm) high.

$195–220 MN

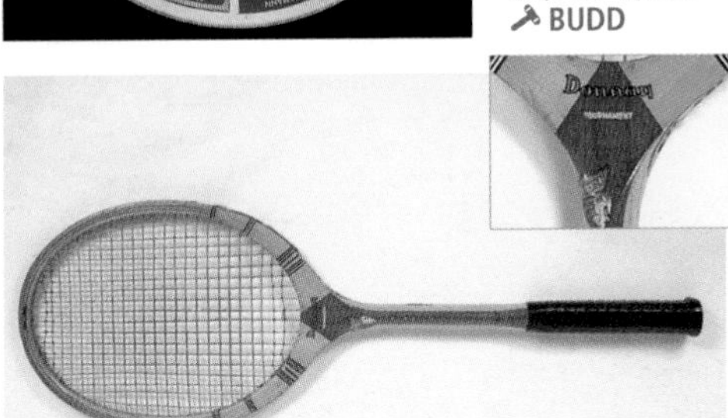

◀ **A Donnay tournament tennis racket,** 1950s, 27in (68.5cm) long.

$70–80 MSh

WINTER SPORTS

A pair of leather, wood and steel ice skates, c1880.

$170–190 CGA

A pair of curling stones, with brass and wood handles, Scotland, 1900, 10½in (26.5cm) diam.

$430–490 GAU

A pine sledge, Germany, c1920, 30in (76cm) long.

$100–120 HRQ

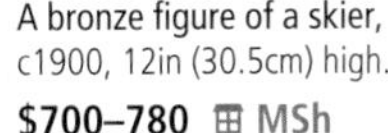

A bronze figure of a skier, c1900, 12in (30.5cm) high.

$700–780 MSh

▶ **An Ideal Dorothy Hamill vinyl doll,** 1977, 13in (33cm) high.

$100–120 MTB

Dorothy Hamill was a US Olympic figure skating champion. She won a gold medal in the 1976 Innsbruck Olympics.

TEDDY BEARS & SOFT TOYS

A Bing mohair teddy bear, with growler, Germany, 1915, 13in (33cm) high.

$1,800–2,100 ⊞ BaN

A Chad Valley teddy bear, with ear button, c1920, 26in (66cm) high.

$930–1,100 ⊞ BBe

A Chad Valley teddy bear, with growler, reinforced feet, c1930, 12in (30.5cm) high.

$380–430 ⊞ LSA

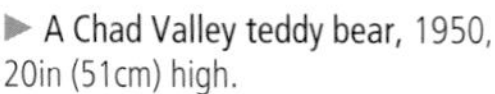

▶ **A Chad Valley teddy bear,** 1950, 20in (51cm) high.

$320–380 ⊞ WAC

A Chad Valley teddy bear, with original label, c1950, 14in (35.5cm) high.

$380–430 ⊞ BBe

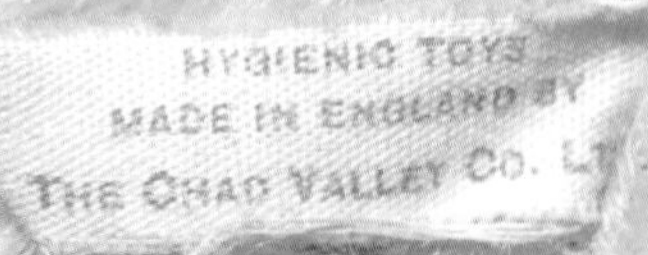

A Chad Valley mohair teddy bear, cardboard-reinforced feet, c1955, 14in (35.5cm) high.

$250–290 ⊞ LSA

CHILTERN HUGMEE

- Chiltern's Hugmee bears first appeared in the 1920s.
- The range took its name from the soft kapok used for stuffing, although the head was still filled with wood wool.
- Key identifiers are the cuddly softness of the bear, its quality mohair, and upturned stitching on the nose ends.
- The shape of the legs are said to resemble chicken drumsticks.

A Chiltern mohair Hugmee bear, with glass eyes, c1930, 12in (30.5cm) high.

$410–480 ⊞ LSA

A Chiltern Hugmee teddy bear, with glass eyes and Rexine pads, 1950s, 22in (56cm) high.

$690–780 ⊞ BBe

The post-war Hugmee style had shorter limbs and a flatter face to make the best use of plush fabrics which were scarce in the early 1950s. The nose stitching changes to a vertical shield shape and the pads are made from rexine.

A Chiltern Hugmee teddy bear, late 1950s, 20in (51cm) high.

$620–690 ⊞ BBe

Improved safety standards led to the introduction of plastic eyes at this time, and to keep up with the competition Chiltern added a plastic nose.

A Farnell mohair teddy bear, with label, c1930, 11in (28cm) high.

$930–1,100 ⊞ BBe

J. K. Farnell was established in London's Notting Hill in 1840. The first teddy bear was produced in 1908, and from 1921 they were produced from the Alpha works in collaboration with the designer Sybil Kemp. An Alpha bear was given to Christopher Robin Milne, and was believed to be the inspiration for the famous character, Winnie-the-Pooh, created by Christopher's father, Alan Alexander Milne. A number of books were written featuring the lovable bear with a taste for honey, the last of which, The House at Pooh Corner, *appeared in 1928.*

A Farnell mohair teddy bear, with original pads, c1920, 16in (40.5cm) high.

$2,100–2,400 ⊞ BBe

◄ **A Hermann teddy bear,** Germany, 1930s, 18in (45.5cm) high.

$50–60 ⊞ GLEN

◄ **A Jopi mohair musical teddy bear,** with glass eyes, Austria, 1920s, 12in (30.5cm) high.

$2,350–2,600 ⊞ BGe

PADDINGTON BEAR

• Paddington Bear was created in 1958 by the author Michael Bond and appeared in 11 books and two collections of short stories. He was given his own animated television series in 1975.

• The first Paddington soft toy was made by Gabrielle Designs in 1972. His relative Aunt Lucy soon followed. In the US Paddington was made by Eden Toys from 1975 – he was much softer than his UK equivalent and was sold without Wellington boots.

• Paddington has appeared on a wide variety of merchandise including clothes, bedding and kitchen items, but the bear remains the most collectable item.

A Gabrielle synthetic plush Aunt Lucy bear, with original tags and coins in knickers, 1970s, 20in (51cm) high.

$450–520 ⊞ BBe

Aunt Lucy (Paddington Bear's aunt) rarely comes complete with spectacles.

A Gabrielle Paddington Bear, 1970s, 19in (48.5cm) high.

$150–170 ⊞ BBe

A Gabrielle Paddington Bear glove puppet, with original label, 1970s, 8in (20.5cm) high.

$85–95 ⊞ BBe

A Pedigree mohair plush teddy bear, 1950s–60s, 22in (56cm) high.

$270–310 ⊞ BaN

An SAF mohair Zotty teddy bear, with glass eyes and ear tag, Austria, 1950s–60s, 24in (61cm) high.

$145–165 ⊞ BBe

A Steiff mohair teddy bear, with original pads, Germany, c1915, 12in (30.5cm) high.

$1,400–1,550 ⊞ BBe

A Steiff teddy bear, Germany, 1920s, 9in (23cm) high.

$640–730 ⊞ WAC

A Steiff teddy bear, with straw-stuffed body, glass eyes and felt paws, Germany, c1940, 13in (33cm) high.

$620–690 ⊞ DOAN

A Pedigree tiger, with label, 1950s, 12in (30.5cm) long.

$80–90 ⊞ GLEN

◀ A Schuco mohair Bigo Bello Tiger, with glass eyes and label, Germany, 1950s, 10in (25.5cm) long.

$80–90 ⊞ BWH

A Twyford hound pyjama case, 1965, 19in (48.5cm) long.

$85–100 ⊞ TIN

A Steiff Halloween cat, Germany, Germany, 1950s, 5in (12.5cm) high.

$75–85 ⊞ NAW

A plush Felix the Cat, with velvet eyes, 1930s, 15in (38cm) high.

$600–690 ⊞ DOAN

GOLLIES

A golly, with shoe-button eyes and original costume, c1900, 20in (51cm) high.

$450–520 ⊞ DOAN

A Pedigree cloth golly, with kapok stuffing, 1950s, 26in (66cm) high.

$250–290 ⊞ POLL

A Chiltern golly, with label, 1960s, 34in (86.5cm) high.

$150–165 ⊞ POLL

- The golly first appeared in a series of children's books written from 1895 by Florence and Bertha Upton.
- Commercial production began in the UK shortly before WWI, when one of James Robertson's sons returned from the USA with one of these fashionable toys.
- The golly was adopted by Robertson as a promotional image for the company's jams and marmalades, and labels could be exchanged for badges in what became one of the UK's longest-running collection schemes.
- The Robertson's golly was retired in 2002, but the wide range of memorabilia, which includes badges, soft toys, advertising figures and ceramics, is still popular with collectors today.

TOOLS

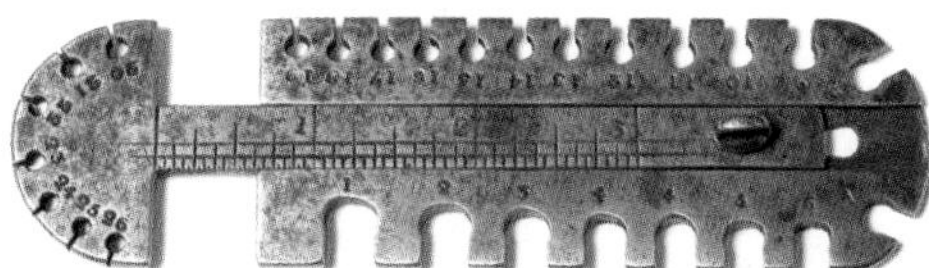

A steel wire gauge, by L. Partridge, early 20thC, 5in (25.5cm) long.

$45–50 ⊞ **FST**

A metal spanner, with a wood handle, America, early 20thC, 12in (30.5cm) long.

$20–25 ⊞ **FST**

A Preston's Patent spokeshave, by E. Preston & Sons, Birmingham, c1910, 9½in (24cm) long.

$40–45 ⊞ **ITB**

Edward Preston & Sons were established tool-makers who manufactured a variety of tools from planes and routers to rules. Originally made of wood and metal, a spokeshave is a tool used to straighten and smooth wooden rods and shafts used as wheel spokes, chair legs or arrows.

A cast-iron bevel gear drill, with bits, France, c1910, 11in (28cm) long.

$75–85 ⊞ **FST**

◀ **Three steel measuring tapes,** by Lufkin and Chesterman, America, 1950s, largest 60in (152.5cm) long.

$30–35 each ⊞ **WO**

▶ **A steel pocket knife,** with six tools, by J. Rodgers, Sheffield, 1930s–40s, 4in (10cm) long.

$130–150 ⊞ **BS**

A wood and steel paint scumbling/scraping tool, 1950s, 6in (15cm) long.

$5–10 ⊞ **HOP**

Two steel centre punches, 1950s, 4in (10cm) long.

$5–10 each ⊞ **HOP**

PLANES

A beech bead moulding plane, by Varvill, York, c1860, 9½in (24cm) long.

$10–20 ⊞ ITB

A beech and boxwood screw stem plough plane, by G. Eastwood, York, c1860, 9in (23cm) long.

$110–130 ⊞ ITB

◄ A beech hollow moulding plane, by G. Davis, c1870, 9½in (24cm) long.

$10–20 ⊞ ITB

A beech jack plane, by Mathieson & Son, Glasgow, c1880, 17½in (44.5cm) long.

$20–25 ⊞ ITB

A beech smoothing plane, c1890, 8in (20.5cm) long.

$10–20 ⊞ ITB

A mahogany spill plane, 19thC, 7½in (19cm) long.

$45–50 ⊞ ITB

A wooden drip mould plane, inscribed 'Burrell', 19thC, 7in (18cm) long.

$30–35 ⊞ WO

◄ An oak shoulder plane, possibly Continental, early 20thC, 9½in (24cm) long.

$60–70 ⊞ WO

A wood, brass and steel A31 thumb plane, by Karl Holtey, 1998, 6in (15cm) long.

$1,750–2,100 ⊞ WO

Contemporary British master craftsman, Karl Holtey, is credited with making some of the best British pattern planes. He is known for his meticulous attention to detail, which results in a fine modern-day collectable.

HAMMERS, MEASURES, SAWS & SCISSORS

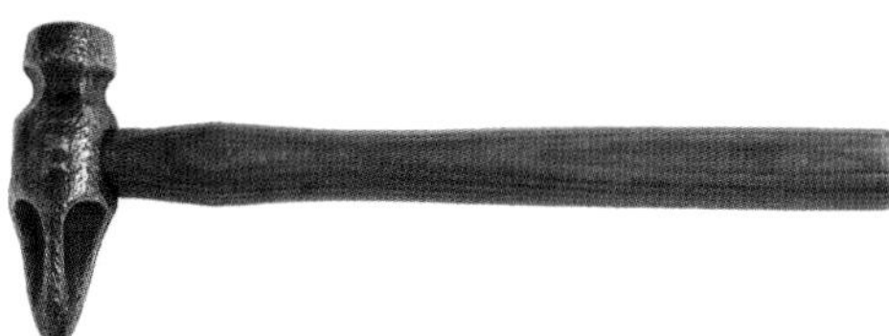

A cast-iron and wood coal hammer, 1930s, 12in (30.5cm) long.
$20–25 ⊞ **HOP**

A cast-iron and wood joiner's hammer, 1930s, 12in (30.5cm) long.
$30–35 ⊞ **HOP**

A boxwood measure, with brass trim, carved with owner's initials, c1920, 4in (10cm) long.
$30–35 ⊞ **LA&I**

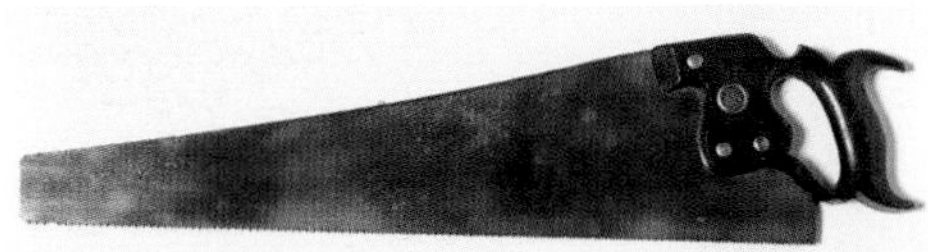

A Disston panel saw, with an applewood handle, America, c1860, 27in (68.5cm) long.
$40–45 ⊞ **ITB**

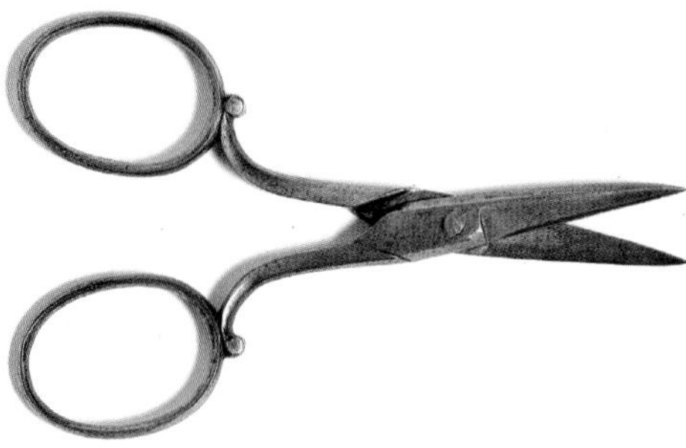

A pair of steel scissors, 19thC, 3½in (9cm) long.
$50–60 ⊞ **BS**

A cast-iron and wood brick hammer, 1930s, 10in (25.5cm) long.
$30–35 ⊞ **HOP**

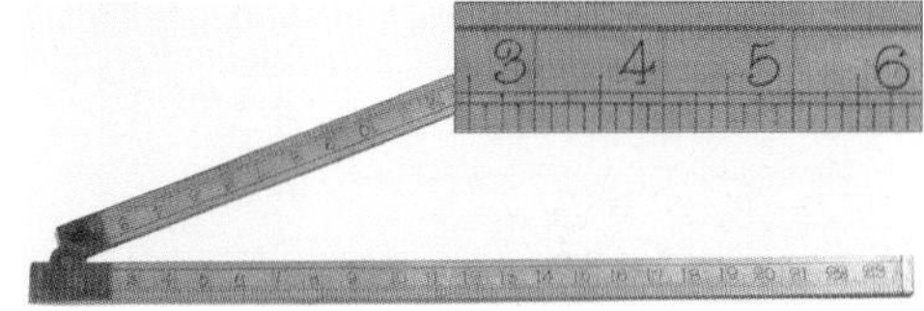

A boxwood measure, with a brass joint, c1920, 4in (10cm) long.
$30–35 ⊞ **LA&I**

A rip saw, by Toga, Sheffield, 1950s, 30in (76cm) long.
$60–70 ⊞ **ITB**

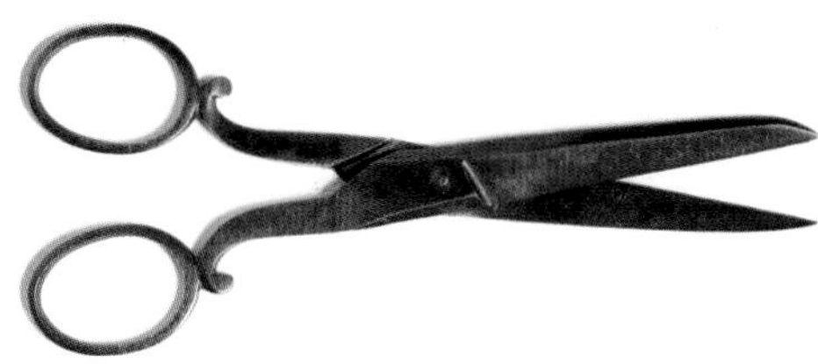

A pair of steel scissors, 19thC, 6in (15cm) long.
$85–100 ⊞ **BS**

► A pair of steel folding scissors, 1920s, 4in (9cm) long.
$50–60 ⊞ **BS**

TOYS & GAMES

A Meccano set, No. 1, containing nickel-plated parts, 1916–20, in a box, 13in (33cm) wide.

$85–95 DECO

Meccano was patented in 1901 by the Liverpool entrepreneur Frank Hornby. It was a perforated construction system with hundreds of parts that could be bolted together to make different models before being deconstructed and used again. Popular with both adults and children, booklets were published explaining how to make the most sophisticated and complex Meccano sconstructions. By the 1960s, a number of rival plastic kits were widely available, and the Liverpool Meccano factory closed its doors for the last time in 1979 after the company was purchased by a French corporation.

A Berwick Toy Post Office Set, 1950s, in a box, 16in (40.5cm) wide.

$45–50 NGL

◄ A Marx battery-operated Mr Mercury robot, mid-20thC, 13in (33cm) high.

$310–360 JAA

An Ideal plastic Robert the Robot, with talking voice box, mid-20thC, 14in (35.5cm) high.

$45–50 JAA

► An Ideal plastic Evil Knievel Gyro Powered Stunt Cycle, 1975, with box, 13½ x 9in (34.5 x 23cm).

$150–165 MTB

MY LITTLE PONY

A My Little Pony, Hop Scotch, 1985, 5in (12.5cm) high.

$5–10 KvW

A My Little Pony, Majesty, 1985, 5in (12.5cm) high.

$5–10 KvW

A My Little Pony, Candy Kisses, 1985, 5in (12.5cm) high.

$5–10 KvW

- Hasbro's My Little Pony (MLP), a restyled version of their My Pretty Pony from 1981, was officially registered in 1983. Twelve months on it was voted 'Best Girls' Toy of the Year and became one of the most successful toys of the 1980s, inspiring a TV series and a feature film. In 2003 the brand was relaunched.
- The pony's hooves help to identify early models and genuine examples. The first six ponies had flat hooves imprinted with circles. Later ponies have concave hooves. Authentic MPLs are printed 'Hasbro' on the hooves.
- The rarest MPL is 'Rapunzel' (1989–90) – a special mail order pony. Models have sold for $390.

CORGI

A Corgi Toys Plymouth Sports Suburban Station Wagon, No. 219, 1959–63, 5in (12.5cm) long, with box.

$110–130 ⊞ HAL

A Corgi Toys Neville Cement Tipper, No. 460, 1959–61, 4in (10cm) long, with box.

$80–90 ⊞ HAL

A Corgi Toys Fiat 2100, No. 252, 1961–65, 3½in (9cm) long, with box.

$60–70 ⊞ HAL

A Corgi Toys Mini Countryman, No. 485, complete with surfer, 1960, 3in (7.5cm) long, with box.

$200–220 ⊞ HAL

▶ A Corgi Toys Rover 200, No. 252, 1961–65, 3½in (9cm) long, with box.

$100–120 ⊞ HAL

A Corgi Toys Morris Mini Minor, No. 226, 1960–61, 3in (7.5cm) long, with box.

$100–120 ⊞ HAL

▶ A Corgi Toys Land Rover, No. 438, 1963–77, 4in (10cm) long, with box.

$85–100 ⊞ HAL

A Corgi Toys Citroën, No. 475, Olympic Winter Sports, 1964, 5in (12.5cm) long, with box.

$85–100 ⊞ HAL

This car is difficult to find complete with its accessories that comprise four skis, two poles and a skier.

A Corgi Toys Morris Mini-Cooper, with wickerwork detailing, 1965–69, 3in (7.5cm) long, with box.

$160–190 ⊞ PAST

A Corgi Toys Chevrolet Impala, No. 248, 1965, 5in (12.5cm) long, with box.

$100–115 ⊞ HAL

A Corgi Toys Lotus Elan S2, No. 318, 1965–67, 3½in (9cm) long, with box.

$120–140 ⊞ HAL

This car originally cost 5s 6d when new – about $6 at today's values.

► A Corgi Toys Monte Carlo Rally Hillman Imp, No. 340, 1967, 4in (10cm) long, with box.

$200–220 ⊞ HAL

A Corgi Toys ice cream van, No. 447, 1966, 3½in (9cm) long, with box.

$115–130 ⊞ DECO

This version of the Ford Anglia van was originally sold with a leaflet showing you where to put the self adhesive signs (also included). On the back of the leaflet was an invitation to join the Corgi Model Club.

◄ A Corgi Toys Iso Grifo 7 Litre, No. 301, with Whizzwheels, 1970–73, 4in (10cm) long, with box.

$50–60 ⊞ HAL

DINKY

A Dinky Toys 36F British Salmson Four-Seater sports car, with driver, 1937–41, 3½in (9cm) long.

$2,350–2,600 MILI

Other British Salmson models were available, some with two seats and others with drivers. Pre-WWII Dinky vehicles are sought after by collectors.

A Dinky Toys Austin A40 Shell BP Van, 1954–56, 3½in (9cm) long, with box.

$165–190 PAST

A Dinky Supertoys 10-ton Army Truck, No. 622, 1954–63, 6in (15cm) long, with box.

$85–100 HAL

This model cost 6s 10d when it first appeared on the market – about $10 at today's values .

A Dinky Toys Leyland Comet Lorry, No. 931, with Stake Body, with box, 1955, 6in (15cm) long.

$170–200 PAST

◄ A Dinky Toys Commer Fire Engine, No. 955, 1955, 6in (15cm) long, with box.

$150–170 PAST

This was a popular model due to the fact that it came with an extending ladder.

► A Dinky Toys Spratt's Guy Van, No. 917, 1954–56, 6in (15cm) long, with box.

$580–680 CBB

A Dinky Supertoys Wayne School Bus, 1961, 9in (23cm) long.

$140–160 DECO

A Dinky Toys Caravan, No. 190, 1974, 5in (12.5cm) long, with box.

$60–70 MILI

MATCHBOX

POCKET MONEY MATCHBOX

A Matchbox Regular Wheels Aveling Barford Diesel Road Roller, No. 1a, 1953–55.

$240–290 VEC

A Matchbox Regular Wheels Aveling Barford Diesel Road Roller, No. 1b, 1956–58, 2¼in (5.5cm) long, with box and tin Matchbox Collector badge.

$190–220 VEC

A Matchbox Regular Wheels Ford Prefect, No. 30a, 1956–58, 2½in (6.5cm) long, with box.

$45–50 HAL

Look out for the light blue coloured version as it is worth three times as much.

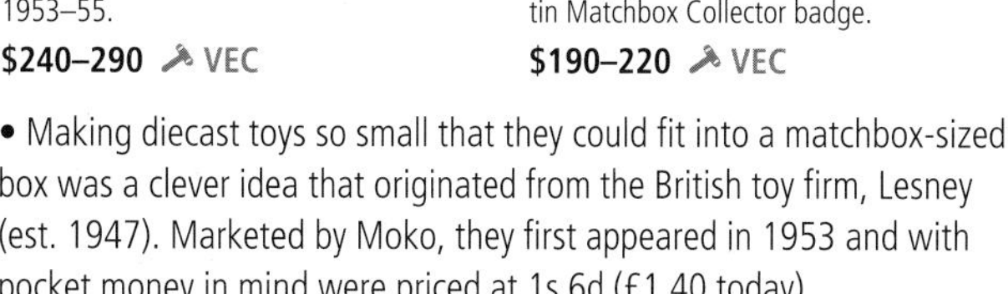

• Making diecast toys so small that they could fit into a matchbox-sized box was a clever idea that originated from the British toy firm, Lesney (est. 1947). Marketed by Moko, they first appeared in 1953 and with pocket money in mind were priced at 1s 6d (£1.40 today).

• Subtle changes in body design help with dating, For instance, glazed windows appeared after 1961 and suspension after 1965. Early wheels were made from cast metal which gradually gave way to grey, silver or black plastic. In the late '60s 'superfast' wheels were launched.

• Recently a Matchbox superfast Red Pontiac (MB22) set a new world record at £3,500 – it cost 2s 6d when new. Instead of the usual heavy black plastic wheels, this version had chrome and black superfast wheels thought to have been fitted when the factory ran out of the standard line.

A Matchbox Models of Yesteryear Ford Model T Tanker, No. Y3, pre-production issue with trial 'Unigate Dairies' decal, with 12-spoke plastic wheels, 1956–66.

$100–120 VEC

A Matchbox Regular Wheels ERF Esso Tanker, No. 11a, with metal wheels, 1955–58, 2¼in (5.5cm) long, with box.

$2,400–2,850 VEC

A Matchbox VW Delivery Van, No. 34, 1957, 2in (5cm) long, with box.

$45–50 HAL

A Matchbox Accessory Pack Bedford Articulated Car Transporter, No. A2, 1957.

$190–220 VEC

A Matchbox Regular Wheels Morris Minor, No. 46a, 1958, 2in (5cm) long, with box.

$140–165 VEC

MILLER'S COMPARES

(L) A Matchbox Regular Wheels London Trolleybus, No. 56a, one decal with factory location error, 1958–65, with box.

$100–120 VEC

(R) A Matchbox Regular Wheels London Routemaster Bus, No. 5c, 1961–65, 2½in (6.5cm) long, with box.

$1,300–1,550 VEC

The item on the left is a more commonly-found London Trolleybus but the item on the right is a more sought-after Routemaster. Matchbox produced two castings of the Routemaster, their first, the 5c (6.5cm long) and second, the 5d (7cm). The 5c is harder to find, especially in good condition and with the original box, and therefore commands very high prices.

A Matchbox King-Size Esso Scammell Wreck Truck, No. K2-3, 1960, 5in (12.5cm) long, with box.

$70–60 HAL

A Matchbox Regular Wheels Ford Zodiac, No. 53a, 1968–72, with box.

$5,000–6,000 VEC

This is a rare transitional model in a early type E box as opposed to a later type F box.

► A Matchbox Regular Wheels Ford Thunderbird, No. 75a, 1960–66, with box.

$240–270 VEC

A Matchbox King-Size Foden Dumper Truck, No. K5, 1961, 5in (12.5cm) long, with box.

$50–60 HAL

► A Matchbox Superfast Ford Mustang, No. 8e, with Superfast wheels, 1970, with box.

$260–310 VEC

A Matchbox Regular Wheels Vauxhall Victor Estate, No. 38b, pre-production model, 1963–67.

$4,300–5,200 VEC

◄ A Matchbox Superfast Mazda RX500, No. 66d, 1971–74, 2½in (6.5cm) long.

$10–20 HAL

A rarer version to look out for has an orange body with amber windows, this would be worth nearer $85.

FILM & TELEVISION TOYS

◀ Robert Tredinnick, *Archie Andrews Annual No. 2*, published by Preview Publications Ltd, early 1950s, 10¼in (26cm) high.

$20–25 NGL

Educating Archie was first broadcast on 6 June 1950 and Peter Brough and Archie were the first ventriloquist act on radio. The success of the show was surprising considering that ventriloquist acts are visual humour. Many famous comedians played Archie's tutors, among them Tony Hancock and Dick Emery. The series transferred to television in 1958.

A lead model of Prudence Kitten, by Luntoy UK, 1950s, 2¼in (5.5cm) high, with original box.

$90–100 MTB

MUFFIN THE MULE

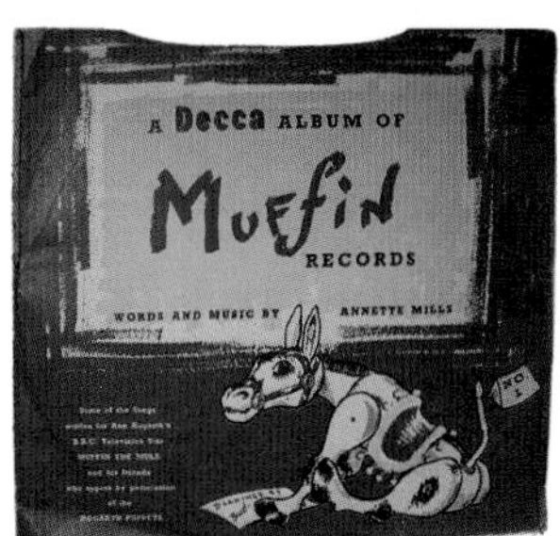

A Muffin the Mule LP record, by Decca, 1950.

$470–520 MTMC

A Muffin the Mule soap, 1950s, 3½in (9cm) high.

$20–25 MTB

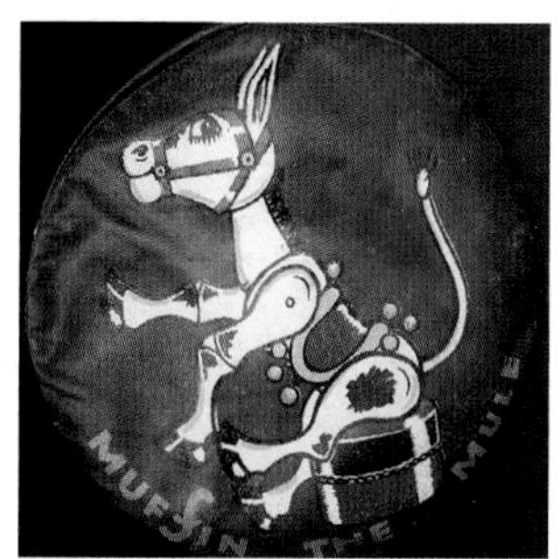

A Muffin the Mule leatherette pouffe, 1950s, 14½in (37cm) diam.

$380–430 MTMC

- *Muffin the Mule* was first televised in 1946, although he had been created by Fred Tickner and worked by puppeteer Ann Hogarth during the 1930s. He reappeared on BBC Television in 2005.
- Muffin sat on top of a piano and had 'conversations' with the presenter and piano player, Annette Mills.
- Various puppet friends appeared with Muffin including a bossy penguin called Mr Peregrine Esquire, Louise the Lamb, Oswald the Ostrich, Sally the Sealion and many more. Prudence and Primrose Kitten later had their own shows.
- Muffin made his final appearance in 1955, just days before Annette Mills died aged 61.
- Muffinabelia is remarkably diverse, ranginging from slippers as advertised in 1950 to enamel badges.

◀ An *Ozzie and Harriet – David and Ricky* Coloring Book, America, 1950s, slight damage.

$120–140 Her

Ozzie and Harriet - David and Ricky was first broadcast on radio in America in 1944 and featured the genial, bumbling Ozzie and the homemaker Harriet with their two sons, David and Ricky who, as a real-life family, played themselves. In 1952 the show transferred to television. When David and Ricky married, their wives joined the cast of the show. Ozzie and Harriet - David and Ricky was the most enduring family-based situation comedy on television.

▶ A Marx clockwork plastic walking *Mary Poppins* toy, c1964, 10½in (26.5cm) high, with original box.

$130–150 MTB

JAMES BOND

A Gilbert battery-operated tinplate James Bond's Aston-Martin DB5, 1965, 11in (28cm) long, with damaged box.

$530–600 MTB

Had its box been in mint condition this item could have achieved nearly three times this amount.

A Tri-Ang Scalextric 007 James Bond set, 1965, 27in (68.5cm) wide.

$3,100–3,450 JB7

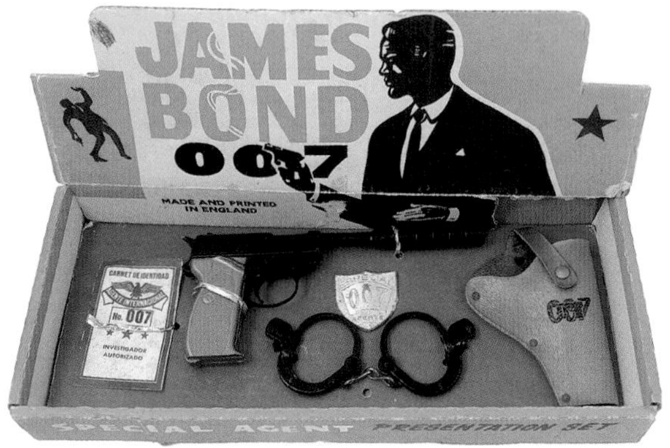

A Lonestar James Bond 007 Special Agent plastic and cardboard presentation kit, 1966, 17in (43cm) wide.

$540–610 JB7

- James Bond, British Secret Agent 007, was a fictional spy created by the writer Ian Fleming.
- He was first introduced in the novel *Casino Royale* (1953), which was published at the height of the Cold War.
- The first James Bond movie, *Dr No* (1962), brough Fleming's agent to life. A host of merchandise, both official and unofficial, followed.
- One of the best-known collectables is Corgi's Aston Martin DB5 (1965) from *Goldfinger*.

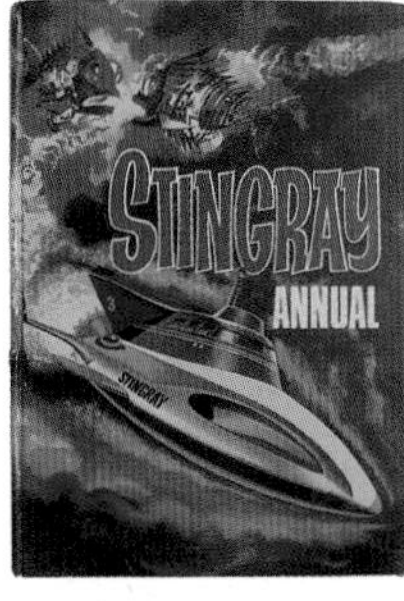

Gerry Anderson, *Stingray Annual*, published by City Magazines Ltd and A. P. Films Merchandising Ltd, 1966, 10½in (26.5cm) high.

$20–25 NGL

For more children's annuals, please see the Comics & Annuals section on pages 151–153.

An Airfix *Magic Roundabout* Train Set, 1967, 14½in (47cm) wide.

$200–230 MTB

A Codeg *Camberwick Green* plastic Windy Miller Roly Poly, 1967, 6in (15cm) high, with box.

$100–115 MTB

STAR TREK

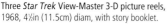

Three *Star Trek* View-Master 3-D picture reels, 1968, 4½in (11.5cm) diam, with story booklet.

$20–25 ⊞ MTB

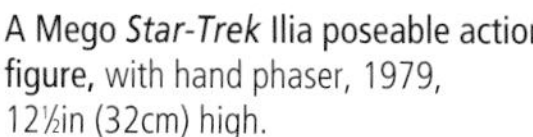

A Mego *Star-Trek* Ilia poseable action figure, with hand phaser, 1979, 12½in (32cm) high.

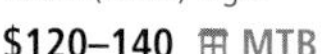

$120–140 ⊞ MTB

An Ertl *Star Trek V the Final Frontier* diecast model of a Klingon bird of prey, 1989, 3in (7.5cm) wide, on card.

$20–25 ⊞ MTB

- Star Trek was created by writer/producer Gene Roddenberry and first shown on America's NBC in 1966.
- Although it was terminated after just three years, 78 epsiodes of the original series were syndicated worldwide, spawning a vast array of merchandise.
- NASA named the first space shuttle *Enterprise* and the United States Postal Service produced a postage stamp depicting the *Enterprise* boldly going where no man has gone before.
- Star Trek items from the mid-1960s onwards are keenly collected by enthusiasts from all over the world.

A Mego *Planet of the Apes* rubber Bend 'n' Flex Soldier Ape, 1968, 5in (12.5cm) high, on card.

$100–115 ⊞ MTB

◀ A Mattel plastic model of *Chitty Chitty Bang Bang*, 1968, 5in (12.5cm) wide, with box.

$220–250 ⊞ MTB

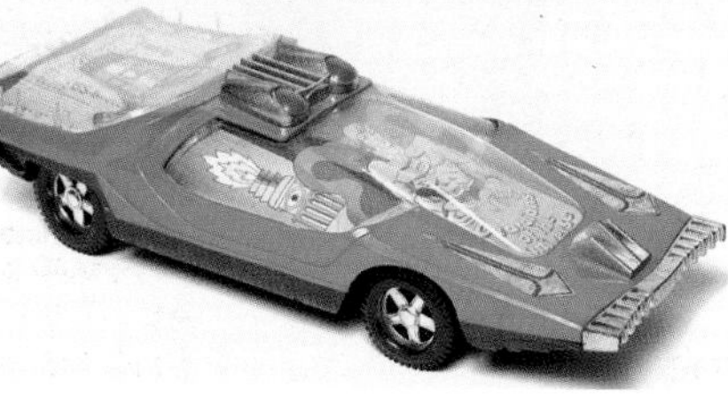

▶ A Guardians of the Universe Super Car, late 1960s, 17in (28cm) long.

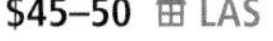

$45–50 ⊞ LAS

A Knickerbocker *Peanuts* Snoopy & Belle poseable plastic Belle, America, 1970s, boxed, 9in (23cm) high.

$50–60 ⊞ MTB

THE WOMBLES

A Marx Toys UK clockwork plastic walking Orinoco figure, 1974, 12in (30.5cm) high, with boxes.

$25–30 MTB

A Luma *Wombles* yoyo, 1974, 2¼in (5.5cm) diam.

$20–25 MTB

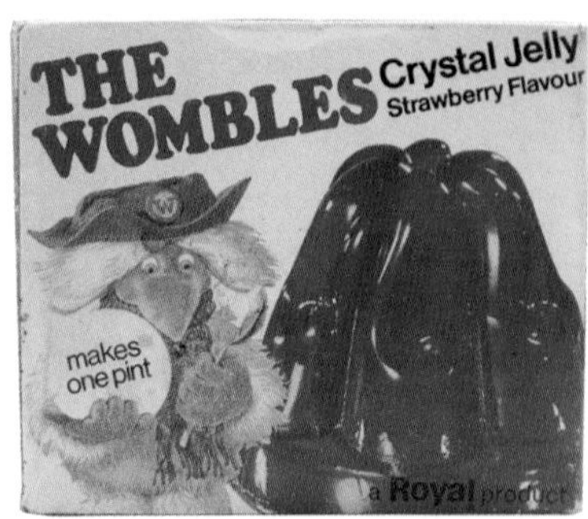

A Royal *The Wombles* packet of strawberry crystal jelly, 1974, 3¼in (8.5cm) wide, with box.

$35–40 MTB

- The Wombles were created by Elisabeth Beresford. She has written over 20 Wombles books, which have been translated into more than 40 languages. Also, a huge range of merchandise is available for the Womble collector.
- The characters of the Wombles of Wimbledon Common were all based on family and friends.
- The first book was published in 1968 and was made into an animated series after it was broadcast on the BBC TV children's programme *Jackanory*.
- The Wombles' passionate recycling habits were well ahead of their time and their slogan was 'Make good use of bad rubbish.'

A Marx Toys UK friction-drive plastic *Tom and Jerry* scooter, 1972, 5in (12.5cm) high, with box.

$130–150 MTB

◄ A Marx Toys *Lone Ranger*'s horse Silver, fully jointed, rearing action, 1973, with box, 15in (38cm) high.

$60–70 HeA

► A Marx Toys UK *Rupert the Bear* friction-drive plastic scooter, 1973, 4½in (11.5cm) high, with box.

$95–110 MTB

Two Mego *The Waltons* Mom and Pop poseable figures, America, 1974, boxed, 8in (20.5cm) high.

$70–80 MTB

A Mattel *Space 1999* Moon Base Alpha Doctor Russell character doll, 1975, boxed, 9in (23cm) high.

$110–130 MTB

A Mego *Starsky & Hutch* Starsky action figure, 1975, 7in (18cm) high, on card.

$75–85 MTB

◄ A Sub RTS Co rubber Noddy, with bell in hat, 1970s, 12in (30cm) high.

$45–50 BBE

A Denys Fisher *Six Million Dollar Man The Bionic Woman* Jaime Sommers action figure, 1976, 12in (30.5cm) high, with original sealed box.

$190–220 MTB

A Horsman Dolls *Police Woman* doll, America, 1976, boxed, 12in (30.5cm) high.

$130–150 MTB

Police Woman was an American police drama that ran from 1974 to 1978. Starring Angie Dickinson as Suzanne 'Pepper' Anderson, it was considered to be the first successful primetime drama to feature a female lead.

DOCTOR WHO

A Palitoy *Dr Who* plastic talking Dalek, 1975, 7in (18cm) high, with box.

$300–340 MTB

A Denys Fisher *Dr Who* plastic Tardis, with spinning interior, 1976, 13in (33cm) high, with box.

$150–165 MTB

A Denys Fisher *Dr Who* Doctor action figure, 1976, 9in (23cm) high, with box.

$180–210 MTB

- *Doctor Who* was first aired on BBC TV in 1963 and is the world's longest-running science fiction television programme. The first series ceased in 1989, but was rekindled and returned to television as a series in 2005.
- The Doctor is a Time Lord from the planet Gallifrey and is able to regenerate into a new body with a new personality. He travels through space and time with the help of his Tardis which is stuck, due to a malfunction, in the shape of a blue British police box.
- To date ten actors have played the part of the Doctor, starting with William Hartnell in 1963. The current Doctor is David Tennant, who took the role in 2005.

A Mego *Superman* action figure, with fly away action, 1977, boxed, 12½in (32cm) high.

$165–190 MTB

CHARLIE'S ANGELS

A Hasbro *Charlie's Angels* gift set, with three poseable dolls, Sabrina, Kris and Kelly, 1977, boxed, 12in (30.5cm) high.

$260–300 MTB

Two Hasbro *Charlie's Angels* Slalom Caper outfits, 1977, with packaging, 12in (30.5cm) high.

$75–85 MTB

• *Charlie's Angels* was a television series about three women who worked for a private intelligence agency. Their boss, Charlie, was rarely seen and only contacted the Angels by telephone.

• It was broadcast from 1976 to 1981 and starred John Forsythe, Kate Jackson, Farrah Fawcett-Majors and Jaclyn Smith.

◄ A Meccano plastic *Star Wars* Jawa figure, France, 1977, 7in (18cm) high, on card.

$90–100 POP

► A Mattel *Battlestar Galactica* plastic Cylon Raider, 1979, 7in (18cm) diam, with box.

$70–80 MTB

THE ARCHIES

A Marx Toys *The Archies* Veronica action figure, 1975, 9in (23cm) high, on card.

$70–80 MTB

A Mattel *The Archies* plastic Jalopy car, 1977, boxed, 10in (25.5cm) long.

$95–110 MTB

• *The Archies* was an animated TV series, a manufactured pop group and a comic strip of the same name.

• The five fictional characters had a series of top 40 songs, the most famous being 'Sugar Sugar' which went to No. 1 in 1969 and achieved Song of the Year.

A Mattel *Battlestar Galactica* Commander Adama poseable action figure, 1979, 4in (10cm) high, on card.

$45–50 MTB

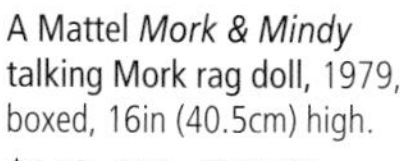

A Mattel *Mork & Mindy* talking Mork rag doll, 1979, boxed, 16in (40.5cm) high.

$140–155 ⊞ MTB

◄ An Aspen *M*A*S*H* Major 'Hotlips' Houlihan push-button action figure, 1979, 9in (23cm) high, on card.

$70–80 ⊞ MTB

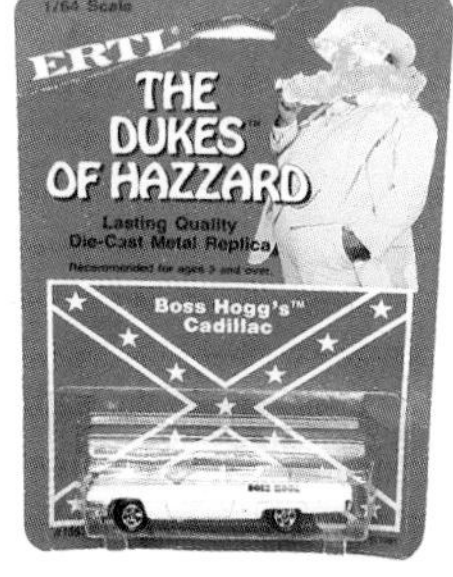

◄ An Ertl *The Dukes of Hazzard* Boss Hogg's diecast Cadillac, 1981, 3in (7.5cm) wide, on card.

$20–25 ⊞ MTB

A Mego *Buck Rogers in the 25th Century* plastic Laserscope Fighter, 1979, boxed, 11in (28cm) wide.

$75–85 ⊞ MTB

STAR WARS

A Kenner *Star Wars* action figure display stand for Star Wars figures, America, 1979, boxed, 20in (51cm) wide.

$1,050–1,200 ⊞ OW

• In 1977 *Star Wars – A New Hope* took space adventure into a new ultra-realistic realm. It was the first of six films written and directed by George Lucas.

• Officially licensed merchandising is desirable. Kenner made the bulk of the revolutionary figures which were fully moveable. Large action figures had limited runs and were launched before the film to promote a new character. Values for figures rests largely with their condition and completeness.

• If today's merchandising appeals look out for error figures with packaging or moulding mistakes. They can be worth far more than the average. Don't forget the mundane – a Death Star pencil sharpener made by Helix in 1978 cost pennies first time round – now it would be worth more than $70.

A Palitoy *Star Wars The Empire Strikes Back Millennium Falcon* Spaceship, with battle alert sound, boxed, 1980, 22in (56cm) wide.

$100–120 ⊞ POP

A Palitoy *Star Wars Return of the Jedi* Battle-Damaged Imperial Tie Fighter Vehicle, 1983, boxed, 11 x 12in (28 x 30.5cm).

$150–170 ⊞ OW

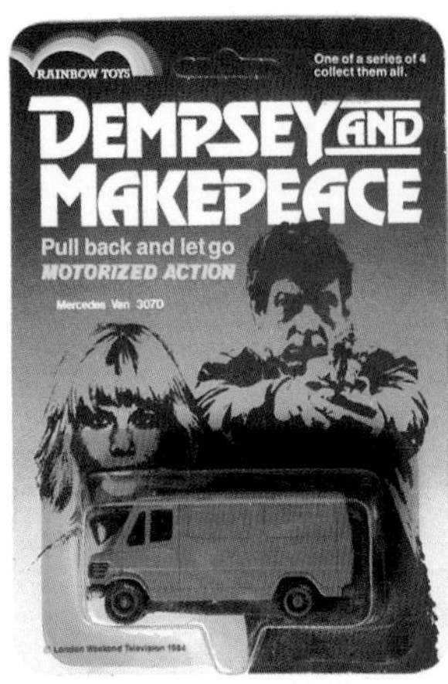

A Rainbow Toys *Dempsey and Makepeace* pull-back and go Mercedes van 307D, 1984, on card.

$30–35 ⊞ MTB

An Action GT *The Shoe People* Trampy, 1986, 4in (10cm) high, on card.

$20–25 ⊞ MTB

A Kenner *Robocop* Birdman Barnes poseable figure, 1988, 4in (10cm) high, on card.

$10–20 ⊞ MTB

A McDonald's *Back to the Future* plastic Doc's DeLorean car, 1991, 2in (5cm) wide, with original packaging.

$10–20 ⊞ STa

An Ljn *E.T. the Extra-Terrestrial* plastic talking figure, 1992, 10in (25.5cm) high, on card.

$50–60 ⊞ MTB

A Hasbro World Wrestling Foundation plastic Big Boss Man figure, 1992, 5in (12.5cm) high, on card.

$20–25 ⊞ STa

◀ A Kinnerton *Postman Pat* milk chocolate egg and ceramic egg cup and mug set, 1993, boxed, 8in (20.5cm) wide.

$20–25 ⊞ M&C

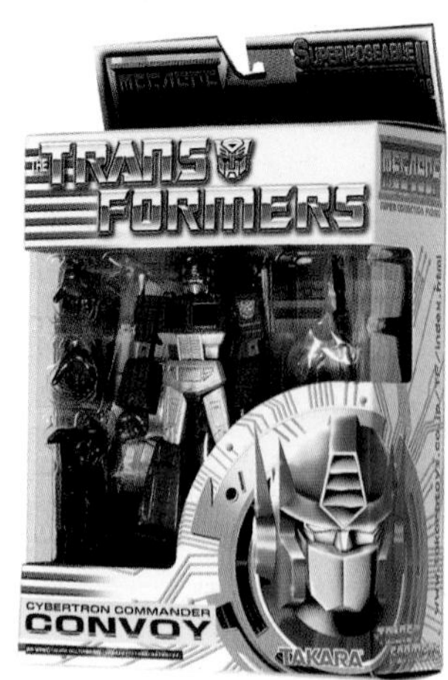

▶ A Takara *The Transformers* Cybertron Commander Convoy, Japan, 2002, boxed, 6in (15cm) wide.

$50–60 ⊞ NOS

PEDAL TOYS

An American National Co pressed steel pedal truck, America, early 1900s, 56in (142cm) long.

$1,800–2,150 JAA

A Lines Brothers Triumph pedal car, c1930, 35in (89cm) long.

$1,500–1,700 SPUR

A pressed steel pedal speedboat, restored, c1950, 46in (117cm) long.

$1,100–1,300 JAA

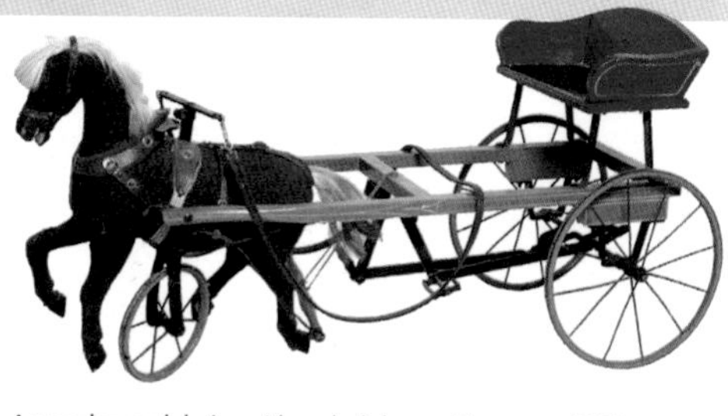

A wooden pedal gig, with a plush horse, Germany, c1920, 46in (117cm) long.

$1,500–1,700 SRH

An I. H. Farmall cast aluminium pedal tractor, c1949, 34in (86.5cm) long.

$320–380 JAA

A Leeway wooden pedal train, c1950, 45in (114.5cm) long.

$310–350 JUN

An Austin pedal car, 1950s, 59in (150cm) long.

$2,700–3,000 SPUR

An Austin Pathfinder metal pedal car, 1950s, 57in (145cm) long.

$4,300–4,800 SPUR

A John Deere cast aluminium pedal tractor, model No. 3010, America, c1962, 37in (94cm) long.

$250–290 JAA

ROCKING HORSES

An F. H. Ayres rocking horse, on a safety rocker, with side-saddle and original paint, c1890, 52in (132cm) long.

$17,000–19,000 ⊞ STE

An F. H. Ayres rocking horse, on a spring rocker, original paint, restored, c1910, 50in (127cm) long.

$23,400–26,000 ⊞ SRH

A G. & J. Lines rocking horse, on a safety rocker, original paint, tack and mane replaced, c1910, 50in (127cm) long.

$4,250–4,800 ⊞ SRH

A rocking horse, attributed to Swallow Toys, on a safety rocker, restored, 1940s, 64in (162cm) long.

$5,700–6,400 ⊞ SRH

A Stred straw and hessian rocking horse, on a bow rocker, Czechoslovakia, 1950–60, 42in (106.5cm) long.

$310–350 ⊞ SRH

A Thuriger plush rocking horse, on a bow rocker, Germany, c1960, 40in (101.5cm) long.

$620–690 ⊞ SRH

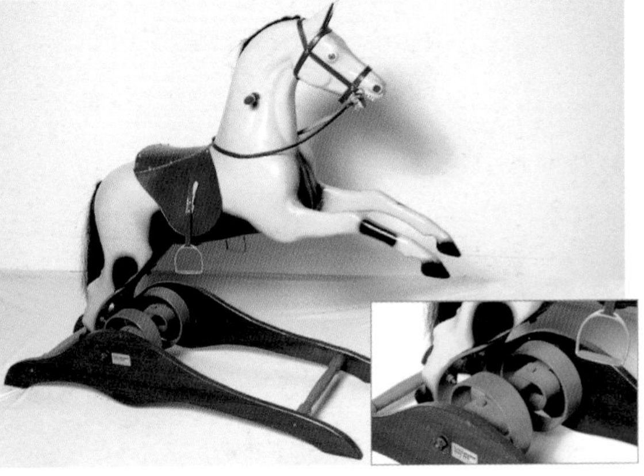

A Ragamuffin Toys fibreglass spring horse, on a mahogany base, edition of 200, Guernsey, c1970, 66in (167.5cm) long.

$2,350–2,600 ⊞ SRH

TINPLATE

A Schuco tinplate wind-up model car, 1930s, 5in (12.5cm) long.

$80–90 ⊞ **RTT**

A Günthermann tinplate model of Malcolm Campbell's *Blue Bird* car, Germany, 931, 20in (51cm) long.

$1,300–1,500 ⊞ **GEOH**

Sir Malcolm Campbell broke the speed record a total of nine times in various Blue Bird *cars, reaching 301.12mph at Bonneville Salt Flats, Utah, on 3rd September 1935.*

A tinplate clockwork tram, France, early 1950s, 11in (28cm) long.

$110–130 ⊞ **HIL**

A Bandai tinplate battery-operated Cadillac, one wing mirror missing, Japan, 1960, 13in (33cm) long.

$150–170 ⊞ **HAL**

Formed in Tokyo in 1950, the toys and games manufacturer Bandai is now a global force. The company's business philosophy is 'to provide timeless entertainment through endless creativity'.

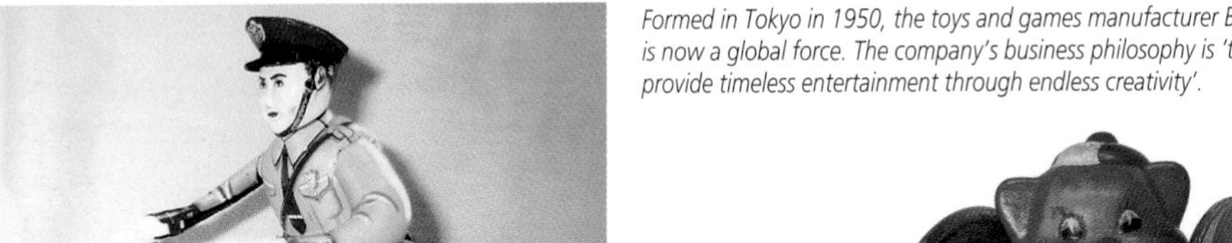

◄ A Masudaya tinplate battery-operated police rider motorcycle, with dismounting action, lights and sound, Japan, 1963, 11½in (29cm) long.

$1,200–1,400 ⊞ **TNS**

A tinplate clockwork toy, with key, 1960s–70s, 5in (12.5cm) high.

$40–45 ⊞ **TASV**

◄ A tinplate model of a Volkswagen Beetle, 1970s, 12in (30.5cm) long.

$95–110 ⊞ **GTM**

TRAINS

A Hull & Stafford tin Union Pacific locomotive and tender, hand-painted, with baggage car and coach, America, c1875, 25in (163.5cm) long overall.

$1,750–2,100 Bert

Three Bing clerestory roof bogie coaches, hand-painted, luggage van with sliding doors and fitted chair and table, 1905–10, 6½in (16.5cm) long.

$4,800–5,600 G(L)

A Bing gauge 1 0–4–0 LNWR clockwork locomotive and tender, No. 1942 'King Edward VII', pre-1914, 15in (38cm) long.

$790–950 VEC

A Lionel Electric passenger set, No. 347E, comprising locomotive and two Pullman coaches, America, 1920s,with instruction booklet and original box.

$450–520 JDJ

A Tri-Ang Railways R3VX Electric Model Railroad set, 1958, with box, 14 x 22in (35.5 x 56cm).

$140–165 VEC

In 1951 the three firms of Rovex Plastics, Zenith and Trackmaster were all purchased by Lines Brothers Group who launched the new combined company Tri-Ang at the British Industries Fair. In 1964 Meccano, makers of Hornby Dublo, was acquired by Tri-Ang, hence the Tri-ang-Hornby name which is often seen. Despite this merger, the Tri-Ang Group closed in 1969.

► A Chad Valley gauge 0 battery-operated train set, including 2–4–0 locomotive and tender, No. 60027 'Merlin', two four-wheel passenger coaches and tinplate two-rail track, 1950s, wth box, 14 x 16in (35.5. x 40.5cm).

$170–200 VEC

A Charles Rossignol gauge 0 0–4–0 double cab diesel locomotive, 1950s, 8in (20.5cm) long.

$170–200 VEC

The Charles Rossignol toy company was founded in Paris in 1868. They specialized in painted tin clockwork vehicles and manufactured the first automotive toy, a Renault taxi, in 1905. Their Parisian buses produced in the 1920s are highly sought after.

A Bassett-Lowke clockwork gauge 0 4-4-0 LMS locomotive and tender, No. 1108, 1950s, 16in (40.5cm) long.

$550–660 VEC

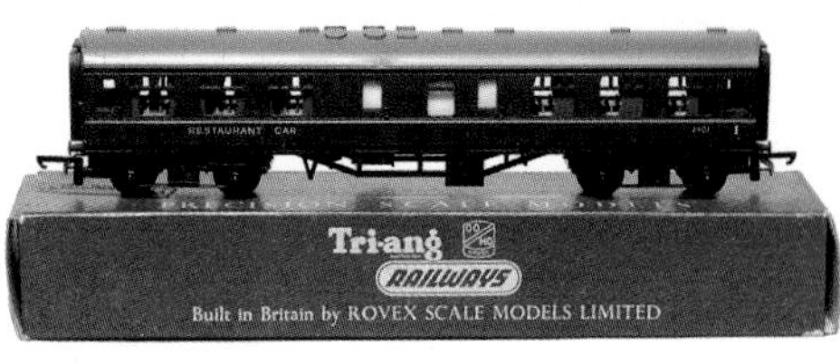

A Tri-Ang restaurant car, 1950–60, with box.

$20–25 JDJ

► A Tri-Ang Hornby R259S 4-6-2 Britannia Class locomotive, No. 70000 'Britannia', with smoke unit, dispenser and unused R521 smoke oil sachet, 1965–71, with box, 4 x 22in (10 x 56cm).

$85–100 VEC

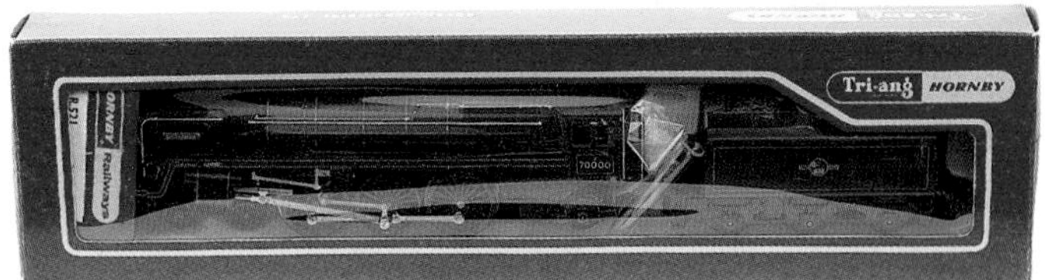

A Trix gauge 00 Footplateman Construction Kit, No. 2128, including AL1 overhead electric locomotive No. E3000 with twin pantographs, 1965–71, 10in (25.5cm) long, with box.

$200–240 VEC

A Wrenn W2229 4-6-2 Princess Coronation Class locomotive, No. 46242 'City of Glasgow', minor wear, 1973–81, 12in (30.5cm) long, with box.

$120–140 VEC

Brothers George and Richard founded G. & R. Wrenn in 1950 and began by manufacturing high quality track and points for 00 gauge model railways. By 1955 they were producing track suitable for Hornby, Tri-Ang, Trix, Märklin and Rivarossi stock. They were joined in the business by their brother, Cedric, in the late 1950s and in 1960 launched their famous Formula '152' Model Motor Racing System at the Brighton Toy Fair. From 1966 to 1972 Wrenn were part of the Lines Brothers Group and in 1973 adopted the now famous logo of a railway guard with a Union Jack flag. When the company ceased trading in 1992 the assets were bought by Dapol, but were again sold in 2001 to three Wrenn collectors whose intention was to preserve the company's original identity and prevent any other prospective purchaser from moving production overseas.

► Three Lima gauge 0 eight-wheeled bogie coaches, repainted, 1970s, 18in (45.5cm) long, with a Tri-Ang Big Train, D7011, and Lima four-wheeled closed van, boxed.

$140–165 VEC

◄ A Wrenn W2276/5P 4-6-2 SR West Country Class locomotive, No. 21C101 'Exeter', 1986–89, 11in (28cm) long, with box.

$1,000–1,200 VEC

HORNBY 0 GAUGE

- 0 Gauge was the standard model train track up to 1938. Crude tinplate clockwork early trains were quickly replaced with better made series that could be dismantled and rebuilt – like Meccano.
- Hornby's Metropolitan set from 1925 featured the firm's first electrically powered 0 gauge locomotive.

0 Gauge became second favourite to Hornby 00 in the post-war years although it continued to be made into the 1960s.

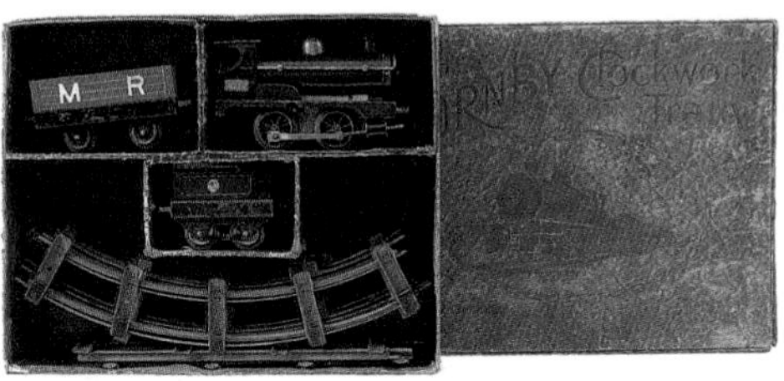

A Hornby No. 1 0 gauge clockwork locomotive and tender, No. 2710, with MR open wagon, tinplate track and key, 1920s, with box.

$280–320 VEC

A Hornby No. 2 0 gauge Timber wagon, 1930, 14in (28cm) long, with box.

$95–110 GTM

A Hornby 0 gauge 0-4-0 clockwork locomotive, 1930s, 8in (20.5cm) long.

$280–320 WOS

A Hornby 0 gauge 4–4–2 LNER electric tank locomotive, No. 5154, c1934, with box.

$860–1,000 VEC

This locomotive is extremely difficult to find, especially in the 20-volt electric version shown above.

A Hornby 0 gauge 4–6–2 LMS electric locomotive and tender, No. 6201 'Princess Elizabeth', replacement bogie and pony wheels, c1938, with box.

$2,600–3,100 VEC

The 'Princess Elizabeth' locomotive was a fine electric achievement for Hornby in 1936. Presented in a wooden box, it cost five guineas and in 1937 that proved to be way beyond the reach of most boys or their families, especially when the weekly wage was about $5.

A Hornby 0 gauge 0–4–0 LMS tank locomotive, No. 2270, 1947–54, with original box.

$85–100 VEC

A Hornby 0 gauge clockwork tank goods set, No. 40, 1950s.

$170–200 VEC

A Hornby Dublo three-rail LNER A4 class locomotive and tender, No. 7 'Sir Nigel Gresley', with horseshoe motor, 1948–49, with boxes.
$510–620 VEC

Without their boxes these items would be worth a third of this value.

HORNBY DUBLO

- Dublo Gauge was approximately half the size of 0 Gauge. It was available from 1938.
- Realistic cast metal bodies with accurately scaled figures and accessories meant Hornby Dublo was popular from the start. In the 1950s plastic was used for wagon bodies and buildings.
- In the 1960s Dublo was amalgamated with Tri-ang Railways to become Tri-ang Hornby.

A Hornby Dublo three-rail coach, 'Co-Co', 1950s, 9in (22cm) long.
$120–140 HAL

A Hornby Dublo three-rail SR meat van, 1950, with box.
$270–320 VEC

A Hornby Dublo D14 suburban coach, 1950s, 9in (22cm) long.
$20–25 HAL

A Hornby Dublo three-rail 2–6–4 Standard Class 4 tank locomotive, No. 80059, 1959, with instruction booklet and box.
$340–410 VEC

A Hornby Dublo two-rail A4 Class locomotive, No. 60030 'Golden Fleece', 1959, with instruction booklet and box.
$100–120 VEC

► A Hornby Dublo three-rail Deltic Class diesel-electric locomotive, No. D9001 'St. Paddy', 1961, with instruction booklet and box.
$450–540 VEC

A Hornby Dublo fold-out, 1939.

$200–240 VEC

A Hornby Dublo LMS electric train set, 1940s, with box, 14in (35.5cm) wide.

$150–170 HAL

A box of Hornby half straight rails, 1949, 5½in (14cm) long.

$10–15 HAL

► A Hornby Trains paper window flyer, minor wear, 1950s, framed, 14in (35.5cm) wide.

$45–50 VEC

◄ A Hornby Dublo Dinky Toys Land Rover and Horse Trailer, minor chips, c1957, with box.

$80–95 VEC

This range of smaller models (1/76 scale unlike regular Dinky Toys 1/43 or 1/35 scale) was introduced in 1957 to complement Hornby Dublo model railways. Production stopped in the mid-1960s.

A Hornby Dublo two-rail Terminal and Through Station Extension Kit, No. 5084, 1959–60, with box.

$580–690 VEC

This kit cost £1 2s in 1963.

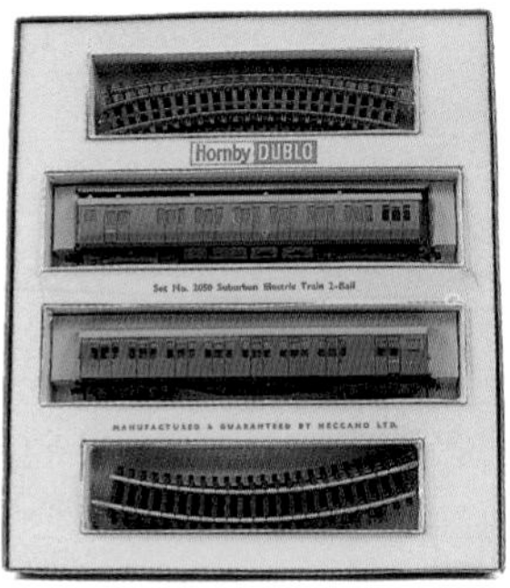

A Hornby Dublo two-rail SR electric motor unit set, comprising power and trailer cars and a circle of track, 1962, boxed, with instruction booklet and box.

$520–620 VEC

A Hornby Dublo two-rail breakdown crane set, including 0–6–2 N2 Class tank locomotive, No. 69550, with safety-valve dome, breakdown crane and brake coach, 1960–61, with instruction booklet and box.

$240–270 VEC

GAMES

A block puzzle, depicting an illustration by Ernest Aris, c1910, 6 x 8in (15 x 20.5cm), in original box.

$45–50 ⊞ **J&J**

A Chad Valley The Tailless Donkey game, 1920, in original box, 13½in (34.5cm) square.

$45–50 ⊞ **NGL**

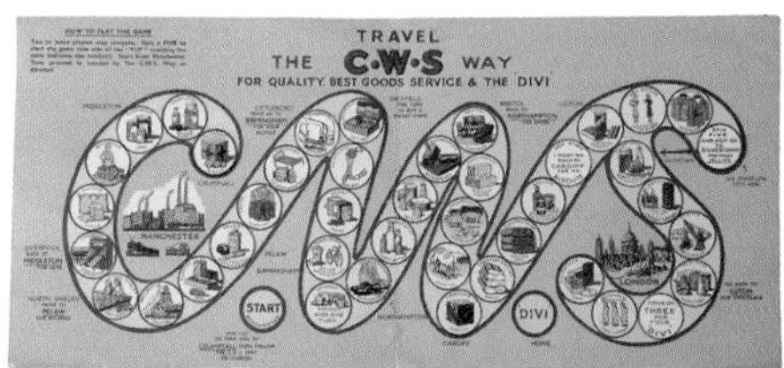

A Co-Op Travel the CWS Way advertising board game, 1920s, 8 x 18in (20.5 x 45.5cm).

$30–35 ⊞ **J&J**

The Co-operative Wholesale Society was formed from the merger of a number of independent retail societies. Its dividend stamps scheme revolutionized shopping and became part of the British way of life.

A Chad Valley Tidleywinks game, 1910s, 6½in (16.5cm) square.

$45–50 ⊞ **NGL**

A Glevum Series Railway Race game, 1920s, in original box 11in (28cm) wide.

$50–60 ⊞ **NGL**

A Chad Valley Escalado game, 1930s, in original box, 11in (28cm) wide.

$60–70 ⊞ **NGL**

◄ **The Victory Set table tennis game,** 1930s, in original box, 13½in (34.5cm) wide.

$40–45 ⊞ **NGL**

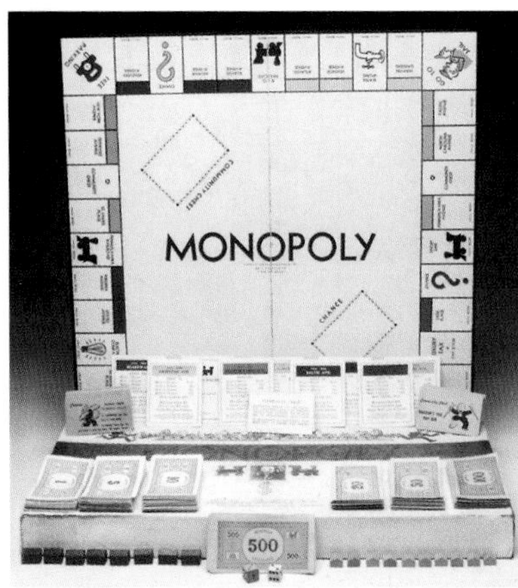

A Parker Bros Monopoly game, printed 'Chas. Darrow' in 'Just Visiting' square, copyright 1933, in original white box, 10¼ x 20in (26 x 51cm).

$85–100 JDJ

Darrow marketed an idea that had been around for decades. This version shows two figures running through the streets of Atlantic City, one with money in his hand.

A Merit Magic Robot game, third edition, 1953, with box, 10 x 15in (25.5 x 38cm).

$20–25 J&J

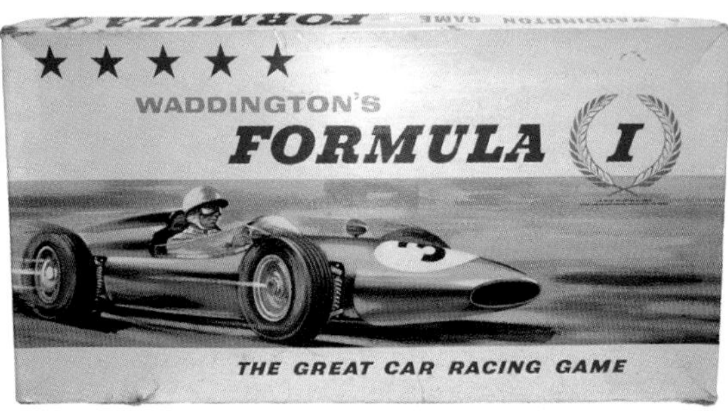

A Waddington's Formula I game, 1960, in original box 20in (51cm) wide.

$40–45 NGL

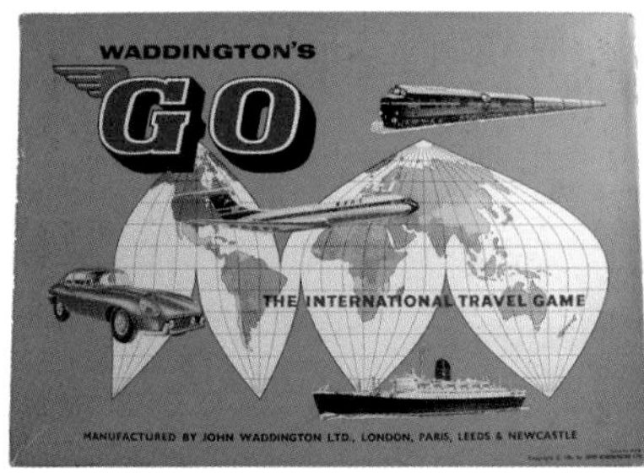

A Waddington's Go game, 1960s, with box, 20½in (52cm) wide.

$40–45 KLH

► An ASL Pastimes Chartbuster game, 1970, in original box, 17½in (44.5cm) wide.

$70–80 NGL

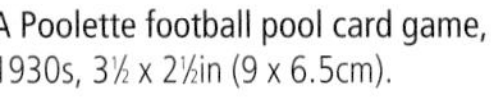

A Poolette football pool card game, 1930s, 3½ x 2½in (9 x 6.5cm).

$20–25 UD

◄ A Waddington's Bob's Yr Uncle card game, with three money cards, 1930, 3½ x 2½in (9 x 6.5cm).

$40–45 TAC

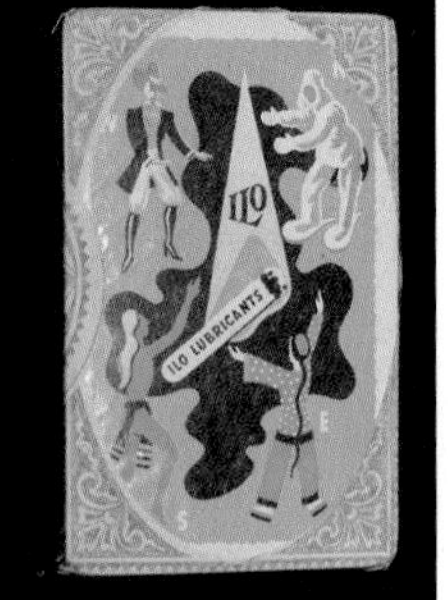

A pack of playing cards, in tax wrapper, 1940s, 3½ x 2½in (9 x 6.5cm).

$40–45 BOB

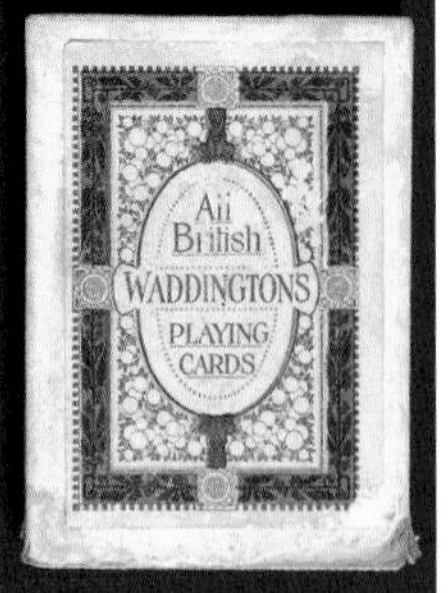

A pack of Waddington's advertising playing cards, 1950s, 4 x 3in (10 x 7.5cm).

$10–15 COB

UMBRELLAS & WALKING STICKS

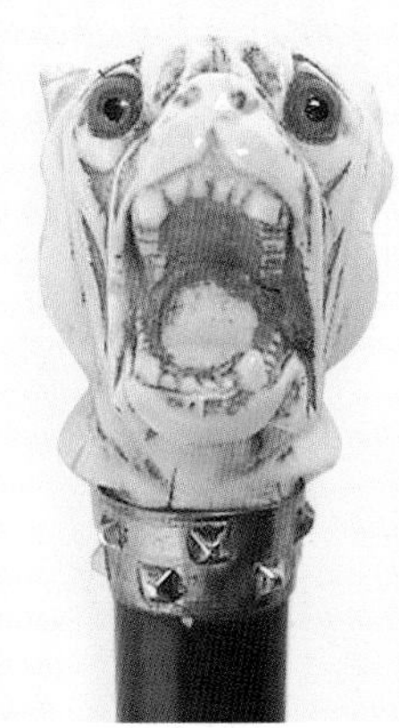

A silver-gilt-mounted snakewood walking stick, the ivory handle carved in the form of a dog's head, with glass eyes, horn tip, 19thC, 37in (94cm) long.

$930–1,050 ⊞ LSA

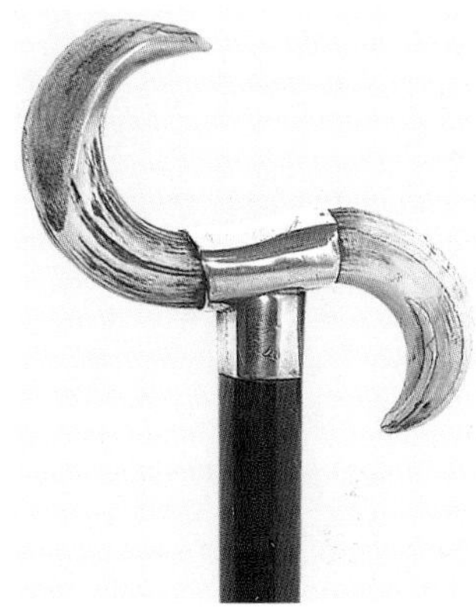

A silver-mounted malacca walking stick, with a warthog-tusk handle, London 1902, 34in (86.5cm) long.

$200–230 ⊞ GBr

A rosewood walking stick, with a cloisonné handle, 1910, 36in (91.5cm) long.

$330–370 ⊞ GBr

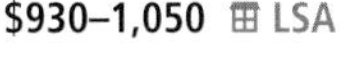

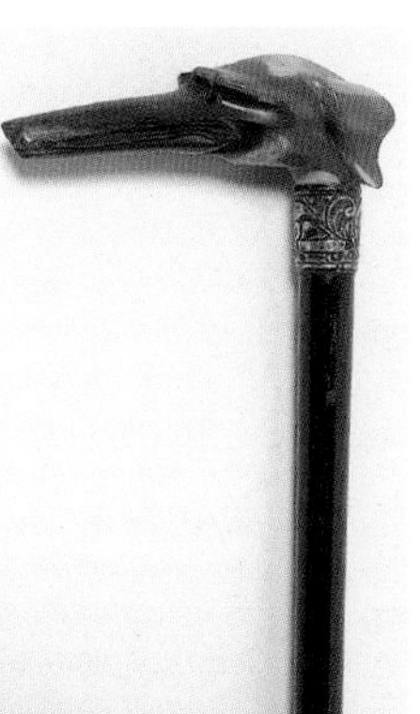

A malacca walking stick, the mother-of-pearl handle containing a powder compact, 1920, 33in (84cm) long.

$690–760 ⊞ GBr

◄ **An ebony walking stick,** with an embossed silver handle, London 1913, 35in (89cm) long.

$330–370 ⊞ GBr

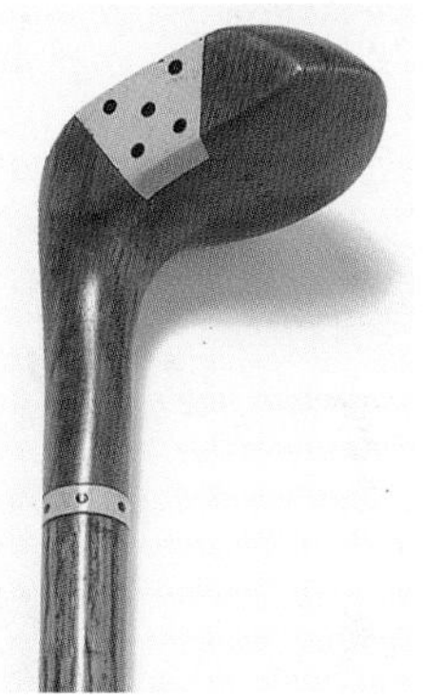

An ash Sabbath day golfing cane, 1920, 36in (91.5cm) long.

$290–320 ⊞ GBr

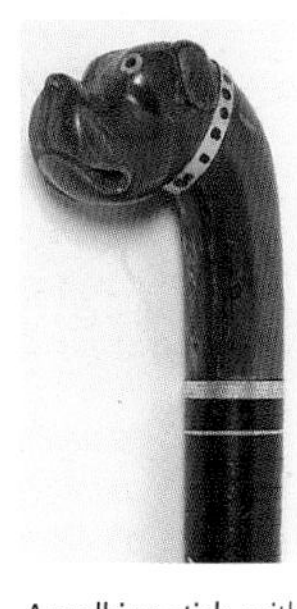

A walking stick, with leather shaft, the horn handle carved in the form of a bull-dog's head, 1920s, 36in (91.5cm) long.

$155–175 ⊞ GBr

A Fox & Co umbrella, with a Bakelite handle, c1920, 21in (53.5cm) long.

$10–15 ⊞ GBr

An umbrella, with a Bakelite and leather handle, c1920, 24in (61cm) long.

$35–40 ⊞ CCO

WATCHES & CLOCKS

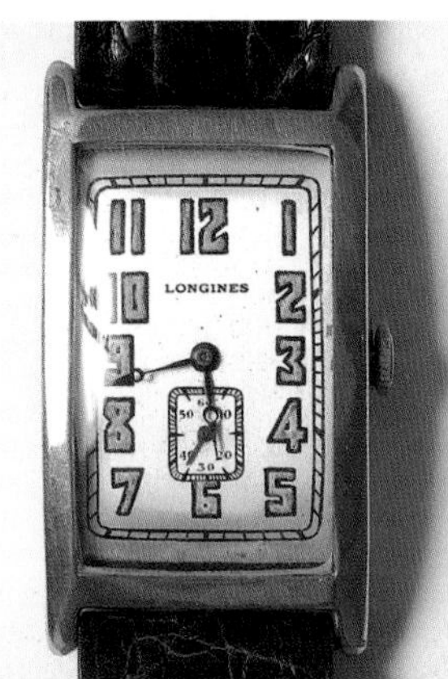

A Longines silver wristwatch, with a leather strap, c1924.

$1,250–1,400 ⊞ HARP

A Rolex gold and steel Oyster Perpetual wristwatch, with bubble back, with a leather strap, Switzerland, c1948.

$3,800–4,250 ⊞ HARP

A Bretling steel Top Time wristwatch, with a leather strap, c1960.

$920–1,050 ⊞ HARP

A mother-of-pearl wristwatch, 1930s.

$230–260 ⊞ LBe

A Hamilton gold wristwatch, 1950s.

$270–300 ⊞ OH

Hamilton produced its first watch in 1898 and swiftly gained a stronghold in the USA. In the 1930s Hamilton became the official timepiece of the booming aviation industry and was adopted by TWA, Eastern, United and Northwest airlines. The firm custom-made a number of watches for Tiffany. Hamilton are perhaps best known for bringing us the world's first digital watch, 'The Time Computer', unveiled on 6 May 1970.

A Bolaro Antimagnetique wristwatch, with a glass back, Switzerland, 1940s.

$270–300 ⊞ DUR

A Watra wristwatch, with unbreakable hairspring, 1950s.

$310–340 ⊞ DUR

A Longines Record wristwatch, with original tag, 1970.

$240–280 ⊞ WAC

◄ An Omega steel Constellation wristwatch, c1965.

$1,000–1,150 ⊞ HARP

A Heuer Autavia steel chronograph wristwatch, with date aperture and leather strap, 1970s.

$1,750–2,000 ⊞ HARP

An LED watch, c1974.

$45–50 ⊞ PEPE

LED displays used considerable power and the display was only visible for a few seconds when the button was pushed. They were superseded by LCD displays, which used much less power. Models from known manufacturers such as Omega and Girard Perregaux command considerable sums.

An Omega stainless steel Speedsonic electronic wristwatch, c1975.

$1,250–1,400 ⊞ Bns

Although this watch has a battery it is different to a quartz for a number of reasons. The hands have a continuous sweep and the tuning fork characteristic hum of the movement can be heard if the watch is placed to the ear.

A Citizen LCD digital watch, c1983.

$80–90 ⊞ PEPE

A Seiko RC-4000 digital watch, 1985.

$135–150 ⊞ PEPE

Also known as the PC Datagraph, this watch was dubbed the world's smallest computer terminal and had 2K of storage. A small port allowed it to be plugged into a home computer so that a variety of programmes could be uploaded.

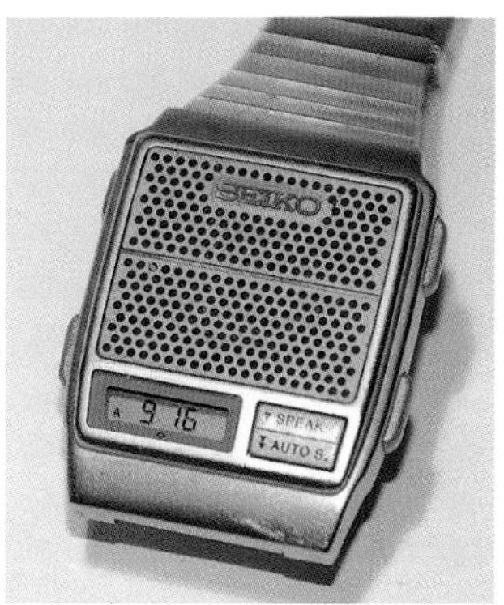

A Seiko speaking watch, c1988.

$230–260 ⊞ PEPE

A Swatch plastic Pop wristwatch, Switzerland, 1980s.

$85–95 ⊞ DUR

A Swatch Garden Turf watch, Switzerland, 1997.

$35–40 ⊞ PEPE

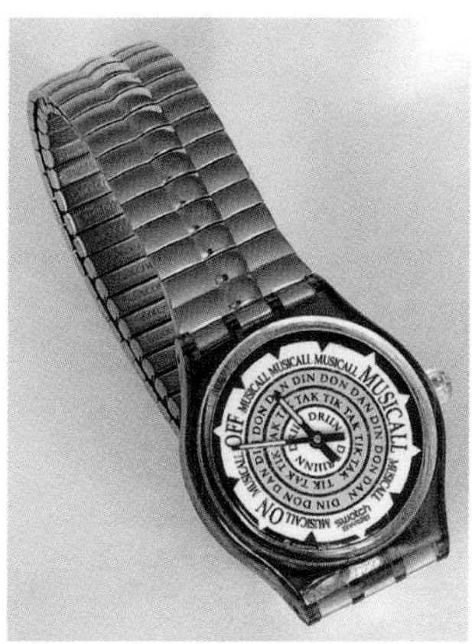

A Swatch musical watch, Switzerland, 1997.

$35–40 ⊞ PEPE

A Smiths Bakelite clock, 1930s, 8in (20.5cm) wide.

$40–45 ⊞ UD

A Jefferson Electric Manufacturing Co Golden Hour clock, America, 1950s, 9in (23cm) high.

$110–130 ⊞ MYS

The Illinois-based Jefferson Electric Manufacturing Co (founded in 1915) was named after American President Thomas Jefferson who was also an inventor. The Golden Hour was their first foray into clock manufacturing in 1949 and they used a production line method for assembly; it originally retailed for about $20. In 1953, the Philco Corporation ran an advertising campaign that offered a free Golden Hour clock with every Philco TV set purchased.

A Marksman plastic clock, 1970s, 10in (25.5cm) high.

$30–35 ⊞ MARK

An oak mantel clock, the eight-day movement striking the hours and half-hours, 1930s, 10in (25.5cm) wide.

$130–145 ⊞ HEM

A plastic clock, playing the 'River Kwai March', Japan, 1950s, 7in (18cm) high.

$20–25 ⊞ TWI

The film Bridge Over the River Kwai *(1957) featured prisoners-of-war whistling 'The Colonel Bogey March', originally written by Kenneth Alford. The tune is now widely associated with the film and it is sometimes referred to as the 'River Kwai March'.*

A Metamac battery-operated chrome Starburst wall clock, 1970s, 23in (58.5cm) diam.

$180–200 ⊞ RETC

An Electric Neon Clock Co clock, America, Ohio, 1940, 10¼in (26cm) diam.

$900–1,000 ⊞ MYS

From the 1930s, neon signs appeared above stores throughout America. To enliven their hoardings and capture attention, retailers would often incorporate clocks such as the example above.

A Westclock plastic Baby Ben wind-up alarm clock, Scotland, 1970s, 4in (10cm) diam.

$10–15 ⊞ MARK

A Rhythm chrome and plastic pedestal clockwork clock, Japan, 1970s.

$60–70 ⊞ RETC

COLLECTABLES OF THE FUTURE

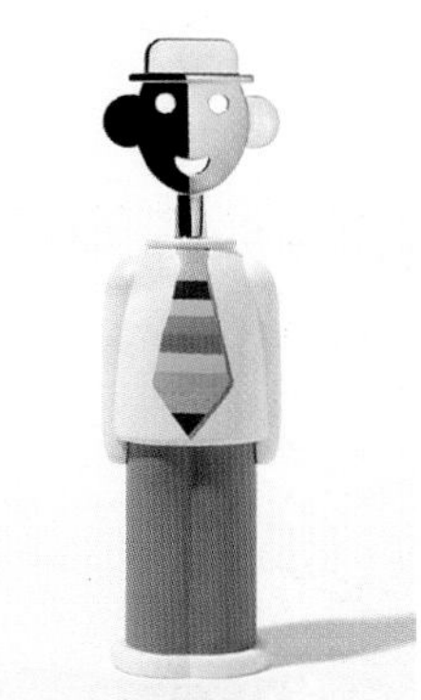

◀ **An Alessi Alessandro M. metal and plastic corkscrew,** entitled 'Country', limited edition, 2004, 8¼in (21cm) high.

$60–70 ⊞ DES

Alessi appeal is based on the way the Italian design giant (founded 1921) mass produces homewares with a strikingly different look. Already a fixture in museums around the world with an established collecting base, Alessi is still a hot bet for the future. Look out for their limited issues like this – one of a set of four.

A Sega Playstation 2 game, Spartan Total Warrior, 2005, 7½ x 5¼in.

$95–105 ⊞ MICH

Sony is a collectable brand for modern technology enthusiasts and the company's move into gaming, spearheaded by the Playstation 1 in 1995 brought another round of future collectables. The arrival of the next generation Sony console – the Playstation 3 in 2006 leaves room for collectors to snap up branded Playstation 2 games before they disappear – pristine, unopened condition will count years from now.

A glass jug, designed by Simon Stevens for Sainsbury's, 2005, 9¾in (25cm) high.

$10–15 ⊞ SAI

Supermarkets can yield unlikely future collectables. Taking Sainsbury's to a new level is their in-house design team – headed by British designer, Simon Stevens. The food aisles are quietly displaying thought-out contemporary ceramics and glasswares, which like Ikea's PS range in the 1990s, are sure to have plenty of followers. Stevens' credits include tableware that has been selected for the V&A's permanent collection.

An Emma Bridgewater Black Toast & Marmalade ceramic teapot, 2006, 8in (20.5cm) high.

$60–70 ⊞ WE

Emma Bridgewater's (b1960) decorative pottery captures the contemporary mood just as Clarice Cliff's wares did in the 1930s. The Black Toast & Marmalade series initially created in 1992 and inspired by Suffragette Movement china, is still her best-selling line. Much will get broken over time and damaged with knife scratches so preserve your pieces with care and watch out for a host of imitations.

▶ **A Star collection dress,** designed by Julien MacDonald for Debenhams, 2006.

$20–25 ⊞ DEBN

Presenting couture fashion at affordable prices is something the British retailer Debenhams have succeeded in doing with their Designers at Debenhams range. In 2004 the celebrated fashion designer, Julien MacDonald (b1972), joined the team and launched his glamorous Star collection. Second-hand trading of all the Designers at Debenhams range is rife on the internet with keen interest in accessories such as handbags and jewellery.

A Coca-Cola FIFA World Cup glass, by Pasabahce, limited edition, 2006, 6¼in (16cm) high, with box.

$10–15 ⊞ BRD

There is always a mass of merchandising with any World Cup and 2006 is no exception. The key to collecting is to build up a number of items rather than just one or two. Cross-over collectables like this Coca-Cola glass will always be of interest as they appeal to two groups.

COLLECTING BY STYLE

FIFTIES

A ceramic vase, in the form of a cat, 1950s, 8in (20.5cm) high.

$75–85 TOP

An enamel and silver pendant necklace, by Aksel Holmsen, Norway, c1950, pendant 2in (5cm) long.

$40–45 VDA

A wicker and straw handbag, with Lucite handle, 1950, 13in (33cm) wide.

$320–360 SpM

FIFTIES STYLE

- Shapes – asymmetrical with organic curves.
- Colours – two-tone primaries, 'gay' pastels and black, both matt and shiny.
- Materials – hard plastic, screen-printed cottons, Orlon, Tricel, moulded fiberglass.
- Motifs – starburst and orbit patterns; cats and dogs; polka dots everywhere.
- Influences – America, Scandinavia and France.

A coffee table, with printed formica top, 1950s, 44¾in (113.5cm) wide.

$135–160 SWO

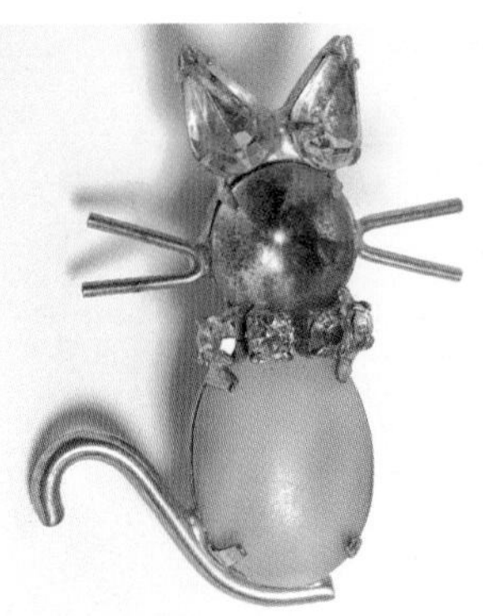

A brass, glass and diamanté brooch, in the form of a cat, 1950, 1½in (4cm) high.

$40–45 SpM

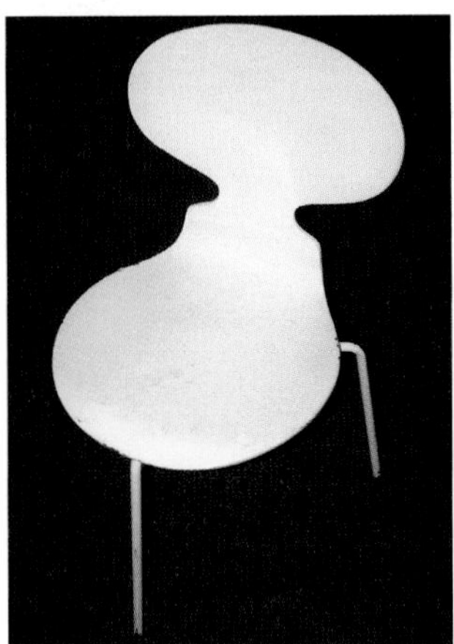

A pair of Arne Jacobsen painted plywood Ant chairs, with three legs, 1951–52.

$270–300 HSR

Originally designed for the Novo canteen, the Ant chair was the first stacking chair to be designed by Arne Jacobsen. It was manufactured simultaneously in both three-legged and four-legged versions with the latter becoming most common.

A Ridgway dinner plate, designed by Enid Seeney, decorated with Homemaker pattern, 1957, 9in (23cm) diam.

$20–25 ⊞ UD

Originally sold in Woolworth's for pennies, Homemaker is now avidly collected. Enid Seeney's distinctive printed design is scattered with recognizable symbols of contemporary furniture – from Robin Day's reclining chair for Hille to spindly-legged plant stands. Plates are fairly common, while coffee pots are harder to find.

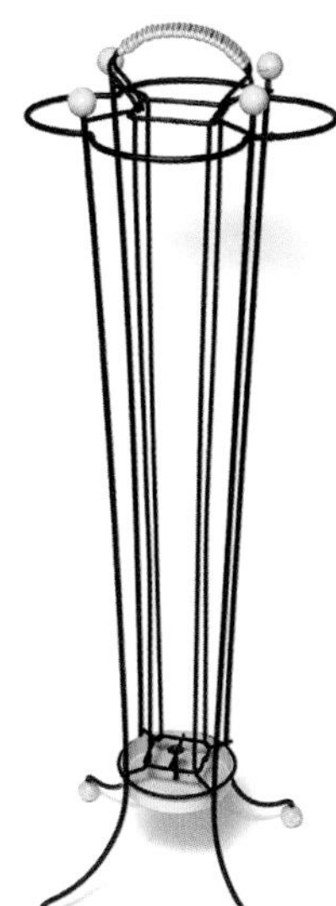

Three Foley Aurora candle holders, mid-late l950s.

$20–25 ⊞ RETRO

◄ **A wire umbrella stand,** 1950s, 29in (73.5cm) high.

$30–35 ⊞ UD

Wirework was popular inside 1950s homes. The skeletal structure of this umbrella stand was replicated in wallpaper and paint motifs throughout the decade. On ball feet with matching finials at the top, it was fashionably more space-shaped than umbrella stand!

A plastic wicker-effect bag, decorated with poodles on rhinestone leads, 1950s, 14in (35.5cm) wide.

$250–280 ⊞ PAST

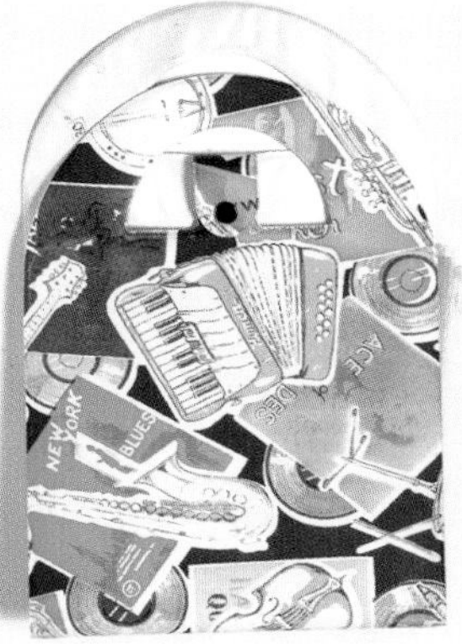

A 20-sleeve 7in record holder, made for Monica Plastics, 1950s, 13in (33cm) long.

$45–50 ⊞ TWI

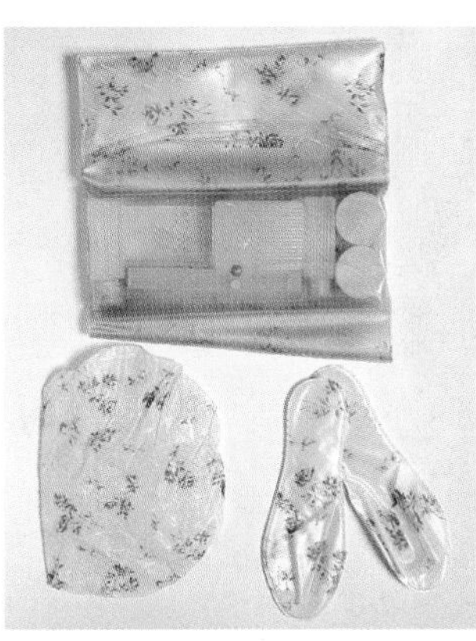

A lady's plastic washbag, 1950s, 12in (30.5cm) long.

$40–45 ⊞ TWI

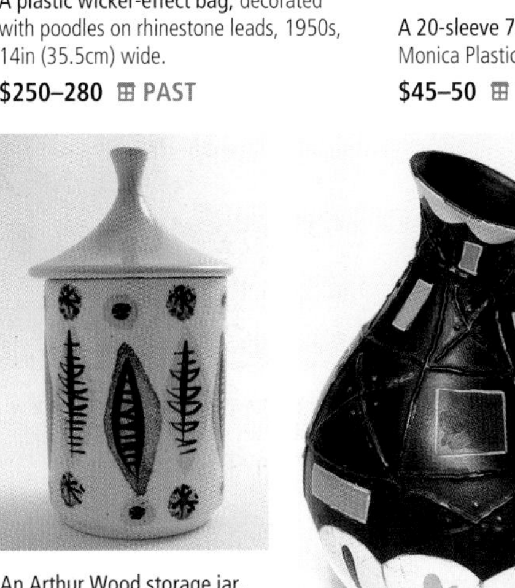

An Arthur Wood storage jar, 1950s, 7in (18cm) high.

$5–10 ⊞ MARK

A nylon and formica Fantastic cocktail tray, printed with recipes, 1950s, 16in (40.5cm) wide.

$30–35 ⊞ CWO

◄ **A Brentleigh ware vase,** in the form of a gourd 1950s, 7½in (19cm) high.

$100–115 ⊞ CWO

SIXTIES

A plastic drawstring handbag, 1960, 7in (18cm) high.

$45–50 SpM

Experimentation with plastics in fashion saw wet-look leatherette and PVC turned into coats, dresses and bags like this.

SIXTIES STYLE

- Shapes – symmetrical and cylindrical; hemlines became progressively shorter.
- Colours – oranges, browns, bright blues, white, yellow and red.
- Materials – moulded plastics, PVC, stainless steel.
- Motifs – Space Age & Sci-Fi.
- Influences – Scandinavia.

A Surrey Ceramics dish, 1960s, 6in (15cm) wide.

$10–15 MARK

◄ A pair of curtains, made from Bevis 'Apollo' pattern fabric, 1960, 90in (228.5cm) long.

$70–80 CLOB

A cardboard shoe box, for slippers, c1960, 8in (20.5cm) high.

$10–15 M&C

◄ A set of Barker Bros Royal Tudor Ware Springtime plates, comprising six salad plates and six dinner plates, marked, dinner plate 10in (25.5cm) diam.

$60–70 RETC

A Woolbro plastic Space Explorer Set, containing spacemen, spacecraft and a Titan rocket, Hong Kong, 1960s, 4½in (11.5cm) diam.

$20–25 CWO

On 13 June 1968, America's Titan rocket put eight military communication satellites into perfect orbit. They provided a vital communication link between Saigon and Washington. Space was formally on the agenda this decade and it is little wonder toys like these were popular. Only a few months later in 1968 the world would see the first TV pictures from space, transmitted by Apollo 8.

A G-Plan teak stool, with leatherette seat, 1960s, 20in (51cm) diam.

$125–140 NWE

A Kingston plastic storage jar, America, c1969, 4½in (11.5cm) diam.

$10–15 TWI

SEVENTIES

A Jan Ekselius chair, made for Etcetera, Denmark, c1970, 65in (165cm) wide.

$990–1,100 ⊞ MARK

A Rawlplastic tin, with original contents, contains asbestos, c1970, 3 x 5in (7.5 x 12.5cm).

$10–15 ⊞ Mo

A plastic picnic set, comprising six plates, six bowls, salt and pepper pots, tray and carrier, Italy, 1970s, 12in (30.5cm) diam.

$35–45 ⊞ MARK

SEVENTIES STYLE

• Shapes – in fashion everything flowed. Rustic solidity took over in ceramics.

• Colours – rustic brown, sludge green, purple, cream and white, natural hues.

• Materials – cork, hessian, vinyls, polyester, cotton.

•Motifs – all-over patterns, floral themes.

•Influences – America, Spain and Biba.

A pair of Lord Nelson Potteries oil and vinegar bottles, decorated with Rio pattern, 1971, 6in (15cm) high.

$20–25 ⊞ RETO

A Marks & Spencer Autumn Leaves teapot, manufactured by Johnson Bros, c1979, 8in (20.5cm) high.

$60–70 ⊞ CHI

◄ A Nenette dust-absorbing hand polisher, 1970s, 14in (35.5cm) wide.

$10–15 ⊞ TWI

A Crown Merton plastic Cass Bar cassette tape stand, 1970s, 7in (18cm) wide.

$15–20 ⊞ MARK

A Biba advertising card, 1970s, 13in (33cm) high.

$60–70 ⊞ CLOB

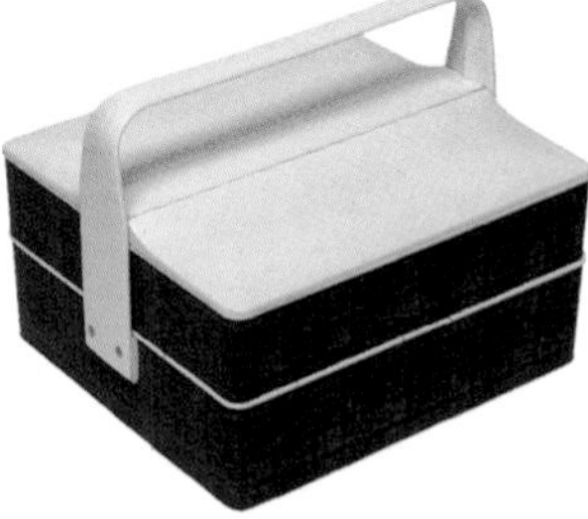

A plastic swivel sewing box, with tartan decoration, 1970s, 13in (33cm) wide.

$45–50 ⊞ TWI

The Bay City Rollers were the champions of tartan, and fans were quick to embrace Scottish clan history this decade. Tartan skirts, dresses and trouser suits were popular fashion items, so it is no wonder it crept into homestyle too.

DIRECTORY OF SPECIALISTS

If you wish to be included in next year's directory, or if you have a change of address or telephone number, please contact Miller's Advertising Department on +44 (0) 1580 766411 by May 2007. We advise readers to make contact by telephone before visiting a dealer, therefore avoiding a wasted journey.

UK & REPUBLIC OF IRELAND

Retroselect info@retroselect.com www.retroselect.com *Retro ceramics and glass from the 1950s–1980s.*

BEDFORDSHIRE

Sheffield Railwayana Auctions, 4 The Glebe, Clapham, Bedford, MK41 6GA Tel: 01234 325341 www.sheffieldrailwayana.co.uk *Railwayana, posters and models auctions.*

BERKSHIRE

Below Stairs, 103 High Street, Hungerford, RG17 0NB Tel: 01488 682317 hofgartner@belowstairs.co.uk www.belowstairs.co.uk *Collectables including kitchenware, textiles and lighting.*

Briggs, P.O. Box 3500, Wokingham, RG40 9BW Tel: 01344 466022 music@usebriggs.com www.usebriggs.com *Rock & pop memorabilia.*

Retro Centre Tel: 0118 950 7224 al@retro-centre.co.uk www.retro-centre.co.uk *20thC design, homewares, collectables.*

Special Auction Services, Kennetholme, Midgham, Reading, RG7 5UX Tel: 0118 971 2949 www.specialauctionservices.com *Commemoratives, pot lids & Prattware, Fairings, Goss & Crested, Baxter & Le Blond prints. Also toys for the collector.*

CAMBRIDGESHIRE

Fossack & Furkle, P.O. Box 733, Abington, CB1 6BF Tel: 01223 894296 or 07939078719 fossack@btopenworld.com www.fossackandfurkle. freeservers.com *Antique pocket watches, timepieces and scientific instruments.*

CHESHIRE

Collectors Corner, P.O. Box 8, Congleton, CW12 4GD Tel: 01260 270429 dave.popcorner@ukonline.co.uk *Beatles and pop memorabilia.*

M C Pottery Tel: 01244 301800 sales@moorcroftchester.co.uk www.moorcroftchester.co.uk *Moorcroft pottery.*

On The Air, The Vintage Technology Centre, The Highway, Hawarden, (Nr Chester), Deeside, CH5 3DN Tel: 01244 530300 or 07778 767734 www.vintageradio.co.uk *Vintage radios.*

Sweetbriar Gallery Ltd., 29 Beechview Road, Kingsley, Frodsham WA6 8DF Tel: 01928 788225 sales@sweetbriar.co.uk www.sweetbriar.co.uk *Paperweights.*

Charles Tomlinson, Chester Tel: 01244 318395 charlestomlinson@tiscali.co.uk *Scientific instruments.*

CLEVELAND

Vectis Auctions Ltd, Fleck Way, Thornaby, Stockton-on-Tees, TS17 9JZ Tel: 01642 750616 admin@vectis.co.uk www.vectis.co.uk *Toy auctions.*

DEVON

The Exeter Antique Lighting Co., Cellar 15, The Quay, Exeter, EX2 4AP Tel: 01392 490848 or 07702 969438 www.antiquelightingcompany.com *Antique lighting and stained glass specialists.*

DORSET

Murrays' Antiques & Collectables Tel: 01202 823870 *Shipping, motoring, railway, cycling items always required. Also advertising related items; showcards, enamel signs, tins & packaging and general quality collectables.*

Onslow Auctions Ltd, The Coach House, Manor Road, Stourpaine, Blandford Forum, DT8 8TQ Tel: 01258 488838 onslowauctions@btinternet.com *Vintage posters.*

ESSEX

20th Century Marks, 'The Office', Whitegates, Rectory Road, Little Burstead, CM12 9TR Tel: 01268 411 000 info@20thcenturymarks.co.uk www.20thcenturymarks.co.uk *Original 20th century design.*

GLOUCESTERSHIRE

Gloucester Toy Mart, Ground Floor, Antique Centre, Severn Road, Old Docks, Gloucester, GL1 2LE Tel: 07973 768452 *Buying and selling obsolete toys and collectables.*

Grimes House Antiques, High Street, Moreton-in-Marsh, GL56 0AT Tel: 01608 651029 grimes_house@cix.co.uk www.grimeshouse.co.uk www.cranberryglass.co.uk *Cranberry glass.*

GWR Auctions Tel: 01684 773487 or 01386 760109 master@gwra.co.uk www.gwra.co.uk *Specialist auctioneers of railway & transport memorabilia.*

Telephone Lines Ltd, 304 High Street, Cheltenham, GL50 3JF Tel: 01242 583699 info@telephonelines.net www.telephonelines.net *Antique telephones.*

Dominic Winter Book Auctions, Mallard House, Broadway Lane, South Cerney, GL7 5UQ Tel: 01285 860006 info@dominicwinter.co.uk www.dominicwinter.co.uk *Auctions of antiquarian and general printed books & maps, sports books and memorabilia, art reference & pictures, photography & ephemera (including toys, games and other collectables).*

HAMPSHIRE

Jim Bullock Militaria, P.O. Box 217, Romsey, SO51 5XL Tel: 01794 516455 jim@jimbullockmilitaria.com www.jimbullockmilitaria.com *War medals, decorations and militaria.*

Classic Amusements Tel: 01425 472164 pennyslot@aol.com www.classicamusements.net *Vintage slot machines.*

Cobwebs, 78 Northam Road, Southampton, SO14 0PB Tel: 023 8022 7458 www.cobwebs.uk.com *Ocean liner memorabilia. Also naval and aviation items.*

The Magic Toy Box, 210 Havant Road, Drayton, Portsmouth, PO6 2EH Tel: 02392 221307 magictoybox@btinternet.com www.sindy-dolls.co.uk *Mail order and retail business catering for the collectors of toys, dolls and china figurines, Pelham Puppets, plastic kits and models.*

Pepe Tozzo pepe@tozzo.co.uk *Collectable technology.*

Retrobrick www.retrobrick.com *Vintage and retro mobile phones.*

Spinna Disc Records, 2B Union Street, Aldershot, GU11 1EG Tel: 01252 327261 sales@spinnadiscrecords.com www.spinnadiscrecords.com *Specialists in rock, punk, heavy metal, progressive, folk, blues, pop, alternative, indie, also all other music genres. Everything from soul to sixties, jazz to dance, reggae to soundtracks.*

HERTFORDSHIRE

The Prop Store of London,
Great House Farm, Chenies,
Rickmansworth, WD3 6EP
Tel: 01494 766 485
steve.lane@propstore.co.uk
www.propstore.co.uk
Movie props and costumes.

ISLE OF WIGHT

Lisa & Andrew Dowden
Tel: 01983 867505
ilonatracey@hotmail.com
Authors of the Isle of Wight pottery book 'A Century of Ceramics'.

Nostalgia Toy Museum,
High Street, Godshill,
Ventnor, PO38 3HZ
Tel: 01983 522148
toyman@nostalgiatoys.com
www.nostalgiatoys.com
Diecast toys specialist and museum.

KENT

Chris Baker Gramophones,
All Our Yesterdays,
3 Cattle Market, Sandwich,
CT13 9AE Tel: 01304 614756
cbgramophones@aol.com
www.chrisbakergramophones.com
Specialist dealer in gramophones and phonographs.

Candlestick & Bakelite,
P.O. Box 308,
Orpington, BR5 1TB
Tel: 020 8467 3743
candlestick.bakelite@mac.com
www.candlestickandbakelite.co.uk
Telephones from the 1920s–70s.

Collected Works
Tel: 01732 452758
sa@collectedworks.co.uk
www.collectedworks.co.uk
Aviation & motoring photographs, books, historical documents & menus.

The Design Gallery 1850–1950,
5 The Green, Westerham,
TN16 1AS Tel: 01959 561234 or
07974 322858
sales@thedesigngalleryuk.com
www.thedesigngalleryuk.com
Original items 1850-1950.

J & M Collectables
Tel: 01580 891657 or
077135 23573
jandmcollectables@tinyonline.co.uk
Postcards, Crested china, Osborne (Ivorex) plaques and small collectables including Doulton, Wade.

Lambert & Foster,
102 High Street,
Tenterden, TN30 6HT
Tel: 01580 762083
saleroom@lambertandfoster.co.uk
www.lambertandfoster.co.uk
Regular monthly sales held at Tenterden Antique Auction Rooms.

The Old Tackle Box, P.O. Box 55,
High Street, Cranbrook,
TN17 3ZU Tel: 01580 713979 or
07729 278 293
tackle.box@virgin.net
Old fishing tackle.

Serendipity, 125 High Street, Deal,
CT14 6BB Tel: 01304 369165/
01304 366536
dipityantiques@aol.com
Staffordshire pottery.

Tussie Mussies, The Old Stables,
2b East Cross, Tenterden,
TN30 6AD Tel: 01580 766244
tussiemussies@btinternet.com
www.tussiemussies.co.uk
Handmade collectable bears. Arms & militaria, brocante antiques, collectables, glass & pottery, decorative items and local crafts.

LANCASHIRE

Decades, 20 Lord St West,
Blackburn, BB2 1JX
Tel: 01254 693320
Original Victorian to 1970s clothing, accessories, jewellery, decorative textiles, and more.

Tracks, P.O. Box 117, Chorley,
PR6 0UU Tel: 01257 269726
sales@tracks.co.uk
www.tracks.co.uk
Beatles and pop memorabilia.

LEICESTERSHIRE

Pooks Books, Fowke Street,
Rothley, LE7 7PJ
Tel: 0116 237 6222
pooks.motorbooks@virgin.net
Motoring books and automobilia.

LINCOLNSHIRE

Junktion, The Old Railway Station,
New Bolingbroke, Boston,
PE22 7LB Tel: 01205 480068 or
07836 345491
junktionantiques@hotmail.com
Advertising and packaging, automobilia, slot machines, pedal cars, etc.

Skip & Janie Smithson Antiques
Tel: 01754 810265 or
07831 399180
smithsonantiques@hotmail.com
Kitchen, laundry, dairy & related advertising items.

LONDON

299, 299 Lillie Road, SW6 7LL
Tel: 07860 223707
Period & vintage costume & accessories. Antique textiles & haberdashery.

Beth, GO 43-44, Alfies Antique
Market, 13-25 Church Street,
Marylebone, NW8 8DT
Tel: 020 7723 5613 or
0777 6136003
Glass & ceramics, porcelain, vases, bowls, jars, English china.

Beverley, 30 Church Street,
Marylebone, NW8 8EP
Tel: 020 7262 1576 or
0777 6136003
Art Deco furniture, glass, figures, metalware and pottery.

Bloomsbury, Bloomsbury House,
24 Maddox Street, W1S 1PP
Tel: 020 7495 9494
info@bloomsburyauctions.com
www.bloomsburyauctions.com
Books, manuscripts, art, prints, collectables auctions.

Comic Book Postal Auctions Ltd,
40-42 Osnaburgh Street,
NW1 3ND Tel: 020 7424 0007
comicbook@compalcomics.com
www.compalcomics.com
Comic book auctions.

Dix-Noonan-Webb, 16 Bolton
Street, W1J 8BQ
Tel: 020 7016 1700
coins@dnw.co.uk
medals@dnw.co.uk
www.dnw.co.uk
Specialist auctioneers and valuers of coins and medals. Also banknotes & paper money.

Tony Durante, Alfie's Antique
Market, G047/G048 Ground
Floor, 13–25 Church Street,
NW8 8DT Tel: 020 7723 0449 or
0789 446569
durantetony@hotmail.com
20th century accessories and collectables.

Fraser's, 399 Strand, WC2R OLX
Tel: 020 7836 9325/836 8444
sales@frasersautographs.co.uk
www.frasersautographs.com
Autographs, manuscripts and memorabilia from Henry VIII to the current day.

The Girl Can't Help It!, Sparkle
Moore & Cad Van Swankster,
Alfies Antique Market, G100 &
G116 Ground Floor, 13-25
Church Street, Marylebone,
NW8 8DT Tel: 020 7724 8984 or
07958 515614
sparkle.moore@virgin.net
www.sparklemoore.com
20th century pin-up & period clothing, accessories & collectables for sale and hire. Vintage men's clothing and top drawer accessories.

Hope & Glory, 131A Kensington
Church Street, W8 7LP
Tel: 020 7727 8424
Commemoratives.

Lucias Red Roses
Tel: 01793 790 607 or
07778 803 876
sallie_ead@lycos.com
19th & 20thC fashion, accessories and textiles.

Memories Collectors Shop,
130-132 Brent Street,
Hendon, NW4 2DR
Tel: 020 8203 1500
dave@ppv.uk.com
www.memoriespostcards.co.uk
Picture postcards.

Mimi Fifi, 27 Pembridge Road,
Notting Hill Gate,
W11 3HG
Tel: 020 7243 3154
info@mimififi.com
www.mimififi.com
Vintage and collectible toys.

Murray Cards (International) Ltd,
51 Watford Way,
Hendon Central, NW4 3JH
Tel: 020 8202 5688
murraycards@ukbusiness.com
www.murraycard.com/
Cigarette & trade cards.

Colin Narbeth & Son Ltd,
20 Cecil Court, Leicester Square,
WC2N 4HE
Tel: 020 7379 6975
Colin.Narbeth@btinternet.com
www.colin-narbeth.com
Old paper money.

Rokit Ltd,
101 & 107 Brick Lane,
E1 6SE Tel: 020 7375 3864
Vintage clothing and accessories.

Twinkled, 1.5 Kingly Court,
Carnaby Street, W1B 5PW
Tel: 020 7734 1978
info@twinkled.net
www.twinkled.net
Original furniture, homewares & vintage clothing from the 1940s through to the 1980s.

Vault Auctions Ltd,
P.O. Box 257,
South Norwood, SE25 6JN
Tel: 01342 300 900
contact@vaultauctions.com
www.vaultauctions.com
Vintage American and British comics, related artwork, toys & memorabilia auctions.

Vintage Modes,
Grays Antique Markets,
1-7 Davies Mews,
W1 Tel: 020 7409 0400
sallie_ead@licos.com
www.vintagemodes.co.uk
Vintage fashion.

NORFOLK

Cat Pottery,1 Grammar School
Road, North Walsham,
NR28 9JH Tel: 01692 402962
Winstanley cats.

NORTHAMPTONSHIRE

The Old Brigade,
10A Harborough Road,
Kingsthorpe, Northampton,
NN2 7AZ Tel: 01604 719389
theoldbrigade@btconnect.com

stewart@theoldbrigade.co.uk
www.theoldbrigade.co.uk
Military antiques.

NORTHUMBERLAND

Barter Books, Alnwick Station, Alnwick, NE66 2NP
Tel: 01665 604888
www.barterbooks.co.uk
One of the largest secondhand bookshops in Britain.

NOTTINGHAMSHIRE

The Autograph Collectors Gallery, 7 Jessops Lane, Gedling, Nottingham, NG4 4BQ
Tel: 0115 961 2956/987 6578
www.autograph-gallery.co.uk
Mail order dealers in autographs. Monthly catalogue published.

Collectors World, 188 Wollaton Road, Nottingham, NG8 1HJ
Tel: 0115 928 0347
markray@freeuk.com
Coins, banknotes, cigarette cards, bought & sold.

International Autograph Auctions Ltd., 10 Grosvenor Avenue, Mapperley Park, Nottingham, NG3 5DX Tel: 0115 844 0244
info@autographauctions.co.uk
www.autographauctions.co.uk
Specialist autograph auctioneers.

Luna, 23 George Street, Nottingham, NG1 3BH
Tel: 0115 924 3267
info@luna-online.co.uk
www.luna-online.co.uk
20th century objects for the home.

T. Vennett-Smith, 11 Nottingham Road, Gotham, NG11 0HE
Tel: 0115 983 0541
info@vennett-smith.com
www.vennett-smith.com
Ephemera and sporting memorabilia auctions.

OXFORDSHIRE

Alvin's Vintage Games & Toys
Tel: 01865 772409
alvin@vintage-games.co.uk
www.vintage-games.co.uk
Pelham puppets.

Avrick Antiques
Tel: 01295 738 318 or 07762 272846
avrick_antiques@tiscali.co.uk
www.avrick-antiques.co.uk
Antique firearms and edged weapons.

Comic Connections, 4a Parsons Street, Banbury, OX16 5LW
Tel: 01295 268989
Comicconnections@aol.com
www.american-comics.net/
Comics.

Mike Delaney
Tel: 01993 840064 or 07979 910760
mike@vintagehornby.co.uk
www.vintagehornby.co.uk
Vintage Hornby 0 gauge & other toy trains.

Manfred Schotten, 109 High Street, Burford, OX18 4RG
Tel: 01993 822302
sport@schotten.com
www.schotten.com
Specialist in high quality sporting antiques, memorabilia and collectibles.

Teddy Bears of Witney, 99 High Street, Witney, OX28 6HY
Tel: 01993 706616
www.teddybears.co.uk
Teddy bears.

SCOTLAND

Early Technology, Monkton House, Old Craighall, Musselburgh, Midlothian, EH21 8SF
Tel: 0131 665 5753
michael.bennett-levy@virgin.net
www.earlytech.com
www.rare78s.com
www.tvhistory.tv
Specialising in locating hard to find and rare items as well as the more common place.

Rhod McEwan - Golf Books, Glengarden, Ballater, Aberdeenshire, AB35 5UB
Tel: 013397 55429
www.rhodmcewan.com
Rare and out-of-print golfing books & memorabilia.

SHROPSHIRE

Mullock & Madeley, The Old Shippon, Wall-under-Heywood, Nr Church Stretton, SY6 7DS
Tel: 01694 771771
auctions@mullockmadeley.co.uk
www.mullockmadeley.co.uk
Sporting auctions.

SOMERSET

Philip Knighton, 1c South Street, Wellington, TA21 8NR
Tel: 01823 661618
philip.knighton@btopenworld.com
Wireless, gramophones and all valve equipment.

STAFFORDSHIRE

Peggy Davies Ceramics, Formerly St Luke's School Lower, Wellington Road, Hanley, Stoke-on-Trent, ST1 3QH
Tel: 01782 262002
rhys@peggydavies.com
www.peggydavies.com
Ceramics - Limited edition Toby jugs and figures.

Gordon Litherland, 25 Stapenhill Road, Burton on Trent, DE15 9AE
Tel: 01283 567213
gordon@jmp2000.com
Bottles, breweriana and pub jugs, advertising ephemera and commemoratives.

Potteries Specialist Auctions, 271 Waterloo Road, Cobridge, Stoke on Trent, ST6 3HR
Tel: 01782 286622
www.potteriesauctions.com
Regular sales in pottery and ceramics, and specialist sales in 20th century collectable ceramics.

SUFFOLK

W. L. Hoad, 9 St. Peter's Road, Kirkley, Lowestoft, NR33 0LH
Tel: 01502 587758
william@whoad.fsnet.co.uk
www.cigarettecardsplus.co.uk
Cigarette cards.

SURREY

British Notes, P.O. Box 257, Sutton, SM3 9WW
Tel: 020 8641 3224
pamwestbritnotes@aol.com
www.britishnotes.co.uk
Banking collectables.

Connoisseur Policies
Tel: 0870 241 0142
information@connoisseurpolicies.com
www.connoisseurpolicies.com
Insurance for collectors.

Cooper Owen, 74 Station Road, Egham, TW20 9LF
Tel: 01784 434 900
customerservice@cooperowen.com
www.cooperowen.com
Entertainment and musical collectables auctions.

West Street Antiques, 63 West Street, Dorking, RH4 1BS
Tel: 01306 883487
weststant@aol.com
www.antiquearmsandarmour.com
Specialist dealers in antique arms & armour.

EAST SUSSEX

First Call, Module B2, Enterprise Point, Melbourne Street, Brighton, BN2 3LH
Tel: 01273 202201
Vintage clothing and accessories.

Glass etc, 18–22 Rope Walk, Rye, TN31 7NA
decanterman@freezone.co.uk
www.decanterman.com
20thc glass.

Hans's Vintage Fountain Pens
Tel: 01323 765398 or 07850 771183 HSeiringer@aol.com
www.hanspens.com
Vintage and modern fountain pens.

Tony Horsley, P.O. Box 3127, Brighton, BN1 5SS
Tel: 01273 550770
Candle extinguishers, Royal Worcester and other porcelain.

phil-comics auctions, P.O. Box 3433, Brighton, BN50 9JA
Tel: 01273 673462 or 07739 844703
phil@phil-comics.com
www.phil-comics.com
Collector and trader/auctioneer specialising in Beano and Dandy children's annuals and comics. Also all types of children's books, annuals and comics, flyers, original artwork, ephemera, etc.

Soldiers of Rye, Mint Arcade, 71 The Mint, Rye, TN31 7EW Tel: 01797 225952
rameses@supanet.com
www.rameses.supanet.com
Military badges, collectors figurines, cigarette cards, trade cards & coins.

Wallis & Wallis, West Street Auction Galleries, Lewes, BN7 2NJ Tel: 01273 480208
auctions@wallisandwallis.co.uk
www.wallisandwallis.co.uk
Tinplate and diecast toys and arms & armour, militaria auctions.

Wardrobe, 51 Upper North Street, Brighton, BN1 3FH
Tel: 01273 202201
www.decoratif.co.uk
Vintage clothing and accessories.

Jane Wicks Kitchenalia, 'Country Ways', Strand Quay, Rye, TN31 7AY Tel: 01424 713635 or 07754 308269
janes_kitchen@hotmail.com
Specialising in kitchen, garden and textiles collectables.

WARWICKSHIRE

Bread & Roses
Tel: 01926 817342
Kitchen antiques 1800–1950s. Also at The Ark Angel, Long St, Tetbury, Glos. Tel: 01666 505820 & Zani Lady, Corfe St, Ludlow, Shropshire. Tel: 01584 877200.

Chinasearch, P.O. Box 1202, Kenilworth, CV8 2WW
Tel: 01926 512402
info@chinasearch.co.uk
www.chinasearch.co.uk
Discontinued dinner, tea and collectable ware bought and sold.

WEST MIDLANDS
Fragile Design,
8 The Custard Factory,
Digbeth, Birmingham,
B9 4AA Tel: 0121 693 1001
info@fragiledesign.com
www.fragiledesign.com
Dealers of original 20thC design.

WILTSHIRE
Books Illustrated,
P.O. Box 2052, Salisbury,
SP2 2AD Tel: 0777 1635 777
booksillustrated@aol.com
www.booksillustrated.com
Illustrated books and original artwork.

YORKSHIRE
Bears of Windy Hill,
P.O. Box 51, Shipley,
BD18 2YH
Tel: 01274 599175
info@bearsofwindyhill.co.uk
www.bearsofwindyhill.co.uk
Old and vintage bears. Specialists in 1920s–1950s composition & hard plastic American dolls.

BBR, Elsecar Heritage Centre,
Elsecar, Nr Barnsley, S74 8HJ
Tel: 01226 745156
sales@onlinebbr.com
www.onlinebbr.com
Advertising, breweriana, pot lids, bottles, Cornishware, Doulton and Beswick, etc.

The Crested China Co,
Highfield, Windmill Hill,
Driffield, YO25 5YP
Tel: 0870 300 1 300
dt@thecrestedchinacompany.com
www.thecrestedchinacompany.com
Goss and Crested china.

Echoes, 650a Halifax Road,
Eastwood, Todmorden,
OL14 6DW Tel: 01706 817505
Antique costume, textiles including linen, lace and jewellery.

Gerard Haley, Hippins Farm,
Black Shawhead, Nr Hebden
Bridge, HX7 7JG
Tel: 01422 842484
gedhaley@yahoo.co.uk
Toy soldiers.

John & Simon Haley,
89 Northgate, Halifax, HX1 1XF
Tel: 01422 822148/360434
toysandbanks@aol.com
Old toys and money boxes.

CANADA & U.S.A.

CANADA
Waddington's Auctions,
111 Bathurst Street, Toronto,
M5V 2R1 Tel: 416 504 9100
info@waddingtons.ca
www.waddingtons.ca
Weekly estate auctions, monthly art auctions, specialty and fine art auctions.

U.S.A.
Antique Mystique
Tel: 308 532 3404
www.antiquemystique.com
Antiques & collectibles from the 1870s to the 1970s.

Bertoia Auctions,
2141 DeMarco Drive,
Vineland, New Jersey 08360
Tel: 856 692 1881
bill@bertoiaauctions.com
www.bertoiaauctions.com
Mechanical bank and toy auctions.

Blenko Museum
info@BlenkoMuseum.com
www.BlenkoMuseum.com
The Blenko Museum of Seattle is the only museum devoted solely to Blenko Glass outside of the collection housed at the Blenko factory in Milton, WV.

Marilynn and Sheila Brass,
P.O. Box 380503, Cambridge,
MA 02238-0503
shelmardesign1@aol.com
Kitchenware.

British Collectibles,
917 Chicago Avenue,
Evanston, Illinois 60202
Tel: 800 634 0431
kevin@britishcollectibles.com
sheila@britishcollectibles.com
britcol@msn.com
David Winter cottages, Kevin Francis face pots and ceramic figurines and other British made gifts and collectibles.

Jim Call, Broomfield,
Colorado
tribalam@all2easy.net
www.3Gsmilkbottles.com
www.milkbottleworld.com
Collector of milk bottles.

Cara Antiques
cara_antiques@yahoo.com
www.caraantiques.com
Dealer in English and european pottery.

Chameleon Fine Lighting,
223 East 59th Street,
New York, NY 10022
Tel: 212 355 6300
mail@chameleon59.com
www.chameleon59.com
Antique and replica lighting.

Craftsman Auctions,
Rago Arts & Auction Center,
333 North Main Street,
Lambertville, New Jersey 08530
Tel: 609 397 9374
info@ragoarts.com
www.ragoarts.com
Auction house handling decorative arts and furnishings, fine art, jewelry, and property in a variety of other categories.

Du Mouchelles,
409 East Jefferson,
Detroit, Michigan 48226
Tel: 313 963 6255
www.dumouchelles.com
Fine arts auctioneers and appraisers.

The Dunlop Collection,
P.O. Box 6269, Statesville,
NC 28687
Tel: 704 871 2626 or Toll Free
Telephone (800) 227 1996
Paperweights.

Freeforms
nfo@freeformsusa.com
www.freeformsusa.com
20thC ceramics and glass.

Freeman's Fine Art Of
Philadelphia Inc.,
Samuel T. Freeman & Co.,
1808 Chestnut Street,
Philadelphia,
PA 19103
Tel: 215 563 9275
www.freemansauctions.com
Auctioneers.

Glasshouse
info@vmglasshouse.com
www.vmglasshouse.com
Specializing in free-blown vintage glass exclusively from the modernist period (1920s–1970s).

Karen Michelle Guido,
Karen Michelle Antique Tiles,
PMB 243,
1835 US 1 South #119,
St Augustine, FL 32084
Tel: 904 471 3226
karen@antiquetiles.com
www.antiquetiles.com
Antique and collectible tiles.

Heritage Auction Galleries,
3500 Maple Avenue,
17th Floor, Dallas,
Texas 75219-3941
Tel: 214 528 3500/
800 872 6467
bid@HeritageAuctions.com
www.HeritageAuctions.com
Collectibles auctions.

Jackson's International
Auctioneers & Appraisers of Fine
Art & Antiques,
2229 Lincoln Street,
Cedar Falls, IA 50613
Tel: 319 277 2256/
800 665 6743
sandim@jacksonsauctions.com
www.jacksonsauction.com
Antiques and collectibles auctions.

James D Julia, Inc.,
P. O. Box 830, Rte.201,
Skowhegan Road,
Fairfield, ME 04937
Tel: 207 453 7125
jjulia@juliaauctions.com
www.juliaauctions.com
Americana, firearms, lamps and glass, advertising, toys and dolls auctions.

Kit Barry Ephemera & Supplies,
74 Cotton Mill Hill,
#A252, Brattleboro,
VT 05301
Ephemera & supplies.

The Knick Knack Nook,
W. Pratt Boulevard,
Chicago, IL 60626
Tel: 773 274 9511
www.knickknacknook.com
Collectible and decorative items.

Mastro Auctions,
7900 South Madison Street,
Burr Ridge, Illinois 60527
Tel: 630 472 1200
jmarren@mastroauctions.com
www.mastroauctions.com
Classic collector auctions.

Melodies Memories,
2595 FM 275 S, Cumby,
TX 75433
Quality, classic, fun jewelry and collectables from Grandma's days.

New Orleans Auction Galleries,
Inc., 801 Magazine Street,
AT 510 Julia, New Orleans,
Louisiana 70130
Tel: 504 566 1849
www.neworleansauction.com
Auctioneers and valuers.

Pascoe & Company,
253 SW 22nd Avenue,
Miami, Florida 33135
Tel: 800 872 0195/
305 643 2550
mike@pascoeandcompany.com
www.pascoeandcompany.com
Hand-crafted porcelain collectibles and art pottery from Royal Doulton and other renowned european potteries.

Rachel's Attic,
P.O. Box 688, Dandridge,
TN 37725
General antiques and collectibles, art pottery, glassware, postcards & more.

Retro2Go,
P.O. Box 1171,
Sault Ste, Marie, MI 49783
Antiques and collectibles, including glass, pottery and vintage costume jewelry.

Skinner Inc.,
The Heritage On The Garden,
63 Park Plaza, Boston,
MA 02116
Tel: 617 350 5400
www.skinnerinc.com
Antiques, fine art and collectibles auctions.

DIRECTORY OF COLLECTORS' CLUBS

With new Collectors' Clubs emerging every day this directory is by no means complete. If you wish to be included in next year's directory or if you have a change of details, please inform us by May 2007.

A.C.O.G.B (Autograph Club of Great Britain), SAE to Mr R. Gregson, 47 Webb Crescent, Dawley, Telford, Shropshire, TF4 3DS Tel: 01952 410332 gregson@blueyonder.co.uk www.acogb.co.uk

The Action Soldier Collectors Club, 30 New Street, Deinolen, Gwynedd, North Wales, LL55 3LH

Alice in Wonderland Collectors Network, Joel Birenbaum, 2765 Shellingham Drive, Lisle, IL 60532-4245, U.S.A.

American Art Pottery Association, Patti Bourgeois, P.O. Box 834, Westport, MA 02790, U.S.A. Tel: 508 679 5910 patspots1997@aol.com www.amartpot.org

American Barb Wire Collector's Society, John Mantz, 1023 Baldwin Road, Bakersfield, CA 93304-4203, U.S.A.

American Breweriana Association, Inc., Stan Galloway, P.O. Box 11157, Pueblo, CO 81001, U.S.A. Tel: 719 544 9267 breweriana1@earthlink.net www.americanbreweriana.org

American Business Card Club UK, Robin Cleeter, 38 Abbotsbury Road, Morden, Surrey, SM4 5LQ

American Business Card Club US, Avery N. Pitzak, P.O. Box 460297, Aurora, CO 80046-0297, U.S.A.

American Ceramic Circle, Nancy K Lester, 520 16th St, Brooklyn, NY 11215, U.S.A. nlester@earthlink.net

American Credit Card Collectors Society, Bill Wieland, President, P.O. Box 2465, MI 48641, U.S.A. acccs1@charter.net

American Fish Decoy Collectors Association, P.O. Box 252, Boulder Junction, WI 54512, U.S.A.

American Hatpin Society, Virginia Woodbury, 20 Montecillo Drive, Rolling Hills Estates, CA 90274, U.S.A. www.americanhatpinsociety.com

American Lock Collectors Association, 36076 Grennada, Livonia, MI 48154, U.S.A.

American Matchcover Collecting Club, P.O. Box 18481, Asheville, NC 28814, U.S.A.

American Society of Camera Collectors, Inc., Sam Rosenfeld V.P., 6570 Kelvin Ave, Canoga Park, CA 91306-4021, U.S.A.

American Toy Emergency Vehicle (ATEV) Club, Jeff Hawkins, President, 11415 Colfax Road, Glen Allen, Virginia 23060, U.S.A.

Antiquarian Horological Society, New House, High Street, Ticehurst, East Sussex, TN5 7AL Tel: 01580 200 155 secretary@ahsoc.demon.co.uk www.ahsoc.demon.co.uk

Antique Bottles & Collectibles Club, Willy Young, P.O. Box 1061, Verdi, NV 89439, U.S.A.

Antique Comb Collectors Club International, Jen Cruse, European Coordinator, 75 Hall Drive, London, SE26 6XL www.antiquecombclub.com

Antique Comb Collectors Club International (US), Linda Shapiro, 8712 Pleasant View Road, Bangor, PA 18013, U.S.A.

Antique Wireless Association (AWA), Box E, Breesport, New York 14816, U.S.A.

Association for British Brewery Collectables, 28 Parklands, Kidsgrove, Stoke-on-Trent, ST7 4US Tel: 07952 141087 mike.breweriana@gmail.com www.breweriana.org.uk www.abbclist.info

Avon Magpies Club, Mrs W. A. Fowler, Le Bourg, St Quentin les Chardonnets, 61800 Orne, Normandie, France Tel: (0)2 33 96 36 29

B.E.A.R. Collector's Club, Linda Hartzfeld, 16901 Covello Street, Van Nuys, California 91406, U.S.A.

Badge Collectors' Circle, c/o Frank Setchfield, 57 Middleton Place, Loughborough, Leicestershire, LE11 2BY www.badgecollectorscircle.co.uk

Barbie Collectors Club of Great Britain, Elizabeth Lee, 17 Rosemont Road, Acton, London, W3 9LU

Barbie Lover's Club, Amy Reed, 399 Winfield Road, Rochester, New York 14622, U.S.A.

Battery-Operated Toy Collectors of America, Jack Smith, 410 Linden, P.O. Box 676, Tolono, IL 61880, U.S.A.

The Bead Society of Great Britain, Carole Morris (Dr), 1 Casburn Lane, Burwell, Cambridge, CB5 0ED Tel: 01638 742024 www.beadsociety.freeserve.co.uk

The Beano & Dandy Collectors' Club, phil-comics auctions, P.O. Box 3433, Brighton, East Sussex, BN50 9JA Tel: 01273 673462 phil@phil-comics.com www.phil-comics.com

Bearly Ours Teddy Club, Linda Harris, 54 Berkinshaw Crescent, Don Mills, Ontario, M3B 2T2, Canada

The Beatrix Potter Society, UK Registered Charity No. 281198, c/o Membership Secretary, The Lodge, Salisbury Avenue, Harpenden, Hertfordshire, AL5 2PS Tel: 01582 769755 beatrixpottersociety@tiscali.co.uk www.beatrixpottersociety.org.uk

Beer Can Collectors of America, Don Hicks, 747 Merus Court, Fenton, MO 63026-2092, U.S.A.

Belleek Collectors Group (UK), Chairman, Mr D. A. Reynolds, 7 Highfield Estate, Wilmslow, Cheshire, SK9 2JR Tel: 01625 537226 chairman@belleek.org.uk www.belleek.org.uk

The Belleek Collectors' International Society (USA), P.O. Box 1498, Great Falls, VA 2206, U.S.A. Tel: 800 235 5335 or 703 272 6270 info@belleek.ie www.belleek.ie/

Beswick Collectors Club, Barry Hill, P.O. Box 310, Richmond, Surrey, TW10 7FU barryjhill@hotmail.com www.collectingdoulton.com/

Black Memorabilia Collectors Association, Sharon Hart, 2482 Devoe Terrace, Bronx, NY 10468, U.S.A.

British Art Medal Society, Philip Attwood, c/o Dept of Coins and Medals, The British Museum, London, WC1B 3DG Tel: 020 7323 8260 membership@bams.org.uk www.bams.org.uk

The British Beermat Collectors' Society, Hon Sec, 69 Dunnington Avenue, Kidderminster, Worcestershire, DY10 2YT www.britishbeermats.org.uk

British Button Society, Membership Secretary, Rex Butler, 12 Middlefield, Gnosall, Stafford, ST20 0LS Tel: 01785 824426 rexbbs@tailend.fsnet.co.uk

The British Compact Collectors' Society, P.O. Box 131, Woking, Surrey, GU24 9YR www.compactcollectors.co.uk

British Equine Collectors Forum (Model Horses), SAE to Membership Secretary, Miss Helen Cooke, 24 Coleridge Close, Bletchley, Milton Keynes, Buckinghamshire, MK3 5AF www.worldofpaul.com/becf

British Model Soldier Society, Hon Secretary, Little Acorns, 12 Savay Lane, Denham Green, Denham, Bucks, UB9 5NH

British Novelty Salt & Pepper Collectors Club, Ray Dodd (Secretary), Coleshill, Clayton Road, Mold, Flintshire, CH7 1SX www.bnspcc.com Tel: 01352 759715 raydodd@ouvip.com

British Numismatic Society, Honorary Secretary, c/o Warburg Institute, Woburn Square, London, WC1H 0AB Tel: 01329 284661

British Postmark Society, General Secretary, John A. Strachan, 12 Dunavon Park, Strathaven, ML10 6LP Tel: 01357 522430 johlen@stracml10.freeserve.co.uk

The Brooklands Automobilia & Regalia Collectors' Club (B.A.R.C.C.), Hon Gen Sec, G. G. Weiner, P.O. Box No4, Chapel Terrace Mews, Kemp Town, Brighton, East Sussex, BN2 1HU Tel: 01273 622722 www.barcc.co.uk

Bubble Gum Charm Collectors, Maureen McCaffrey, 24 Seafoam Street, Staten Island, NY 10306, U.S.A.

The Buttonhook Society, (US contact), c/o Priscilla Stoffel, White Marsh, Box 287, MD 21162-0287, U.S.A. Tel: 410 256 5541 buttonhooksociety@tiscali.co.uk www.thebuttonhooksociety.com

The Buttonhook Society, c/o Paul Moorehead, Chairman, 2 Romney Place, Maidstone, Kent, ME15 6LE Tel: 01622 752949 buttonhooksociety@tiscali.co.uk www.thebuttonhooksociety.com

Cane Collectors Club of America, 2 Horizon Road, Suite G18, Fort Lee, NJ 07024, U.S.A.

Carlton Ware Collectors International, Carlton Factory Shop, Carlton Works, Copeland Street, Stoke on Trent, Staffordshire, ST4 1PU Tel: 01782 410504

Carltonware.com www.ckyk.com/carltonware

Carnival Glass Society (UK), P.O. Box 14, Hayes, Middlesex, UB3 5NU www.carnivalglasssociety.co.uk

Cash Register Collectors Club, P.O. Box 20534, Dayton, OH 45420-0534, U.S.A. Tel: 937 433 3529 www.crcci.org

Cigarette Case Collectors' Club, Colin Grey, 19 Woodhurst North, Raymead Road, Maidenhead, Berkshire, SL6 8PH Tel: 01628 781800

Cigarette Pack Collectors Association, Richard Elliot, 61 Searle St, Georgetown, MA 01833, U.S.A.

Cigarette Packet Collectors Club of GB, Barry Russell, Talisker, Vines Cross Road, Horam, Heathfield, East Sussex, TN21 0HF Tel: 01435 812453

Clarice Cliff Collectors' Club, P.O. Box 2706, Eccleshall, Stafford, ST21 6WY

Coalport Collectors Society, c/o Josiah Wedgwood & Sons, Freepost ST228, P.O. Box 2, Barlaston, Stoke on Trent, Staffs, ST12 9BR

The Coca-Cola Collectors Club, Membership Director, 4780 Ashford-Dunwoody Road, Suite. A, Atlanta, Georgia 30338, U.S.A. www.cocacolaclub.org

The Coleco Collectors Club, Ann Wilhite, 610 W 17th Freemont, NE 68025, U.S.A.

Collectors Penpal Club, Joan Charles, 15 Thetford Road, Great Sankey, Warrington, Cheshire, WA5 3EQ

The Comic Journal, C.J. Publications, c/o 6 Rotherham Road, Catcliffe, Rotherham, South Yorkshire, S60 5SW

Commemorative Collectors' Society and Commemoratives Museum, c/o Steven Jackson, Lumless House, 77 Gainsborough Road, Winthorpe, Newark, Nottinghamshire, NG24 2NR Tel: 01636 671377 commemorativecollectorssociety@hotmail.com

Compact Collectors Club International, Roselyn Gerson, P.O. Box 40, Lynbrook, NY 11563, U.S.A.

Cookie Cutters Collectors Club, Ruth Capper, 1167 Teal Road S. W., Dellroy, OH 44620-9704, U.S.A.

Corgi Collector Club, c/o Corgi Classics Ltd, Meridian East, Meridian Business Park, Leicester, LE19 1RL Tel: 0870 607 1204 susie@collectorsclubs.org.uk

Cornish Collectors Club, P.O. Box 58, Buxton, Derbyshire, SK17 0FH

The Costume Society, St Paul's House, Warwick Lane, London, EC4P 4BN www.costumesociety.org.uk

The Crested Circle, 42 Douglas Road, Tolworth, Surbiton, Surrey, KT6 7SA

Cricket Memorabilia Society, Steve Cashmore, 4 Stoke Park Court, Stoke Road, Bishop's Cleeve, Cheltenham, Gloucestershire, GL52 8US cms87@btinternet.com www.cms.cricketmemorabilia.org

Crunch Club (Breakfast Cereal Collectables), John Cahill, 9 Weald Rise, Tilehurst, Reading, Berkshire, RG30 6XB

Danesby Collectors Club, P.O. Box 2706, Eccleshall, Stafford, ST21 6WY

The Dean's Collectors Club, Euro Collectibles, P.O. Box 370565, 49 NE 39th Street, Miami FL33 137, U.S.A. Tel: US toll free 1 800 309 8336 www.deansbears.com

The Dean's Collectors Club, Pontypool, Gwent, NP4 6YY Tel: 01495 764881 www.deansbears.com

Dedham Pottery Collectors Society, Jim Kaufman, 248 Highland St, Dedham, MA 02026-5833, U.S.A. Tel: 800 283 8070 or 781 329 8070 dpcurator@aol.com www.dedhampottery.com/

Delftware Collectors Association, Ed Goldgehn, P.O. Box 670673, Marietta, GA 30066, U.S.A. Tel: 770 499 8515 comments@delftware.org www.delftware.org/

Derby Porcelain International Society, Box 6997, Coleshill, Warwickshire, B46 2LF Tel: 01675 481293 a.varnam@farming.co.uk

Devon Pottery Collectors' Group, Mrs Joyce Stonelake, 19 St Margarets Avenue, Torquay, Devon, TQ1 4LW

Die Cast Car Collectors Club, c/o Jay Olins (Chairman), P.O. Box 67226, Los Angeles, California 90067-0266, U.S.A. Tel: 310 629 7113 jay@diecast.org www.diecast.org

Dinky Toy Club of America, c/o Jerry Fralick, 7765-B Nelson Loop, Fort Meade, Maryland 20755, U.S.A. www.dinkytoyclub.net

Dinosaur Collectors Club, Mike Howgate, 71 Hoppers Road, Winchmore Hill, London, N21 3LP

Doll House & Miniature Collectors, P.O. Box 159, Bethlehem, CT 06751-0159, U.S.A.

E.T.B. Radford Collectors' Club, 27 Forest Mead, Denmead, Waterlooville, Hampshire, PO7 6UN www.radfordcollect.com

The Eagle Society, Membership Secretary, Keith Howard, 25a Station Road, Harrow, Middlesex, HA1 2UA

Embroiderers' Guild, Janet Jardine, Apartment 41, Hampton Court Palace, East Molesey, Surrey, KT8 9AU Tel: 020 8943 1229 administrator@embroiderersguild.com www.embroiderersguild.com

The English Playing Card Society, John Sings, Secretary, P.O. Box 29, North Walsham, Norfolk, NR28 9NQ Tel: 01692 650496 www.wopc.co.uk/epcs

Ephemera Society of America, Inc., P.O. Box 95, Cazenovia, NY 13035-0095, U.S.A.

The Ephemera Society, Membership Secretary, P.O. Box 112, Northwood, Middlesex, HA6 2WT Tel: 01923 829 079

The European Honeypot Collectors' Society, John Doyle, The Honeypot, 18 Victoria Road, Chislehurst, Kent, BR7 6DF Tel: 020 8289 7725 johnhoneypot@hotmail.com www.geocities.com/tehcsuk

Fan Circle International, Sec: Mrs Joan Milligan, Cronk-y-Voddy, Rectory Road, Coltishall, Norwich, NR12 7HF

Festival of Britain Society, c/o Martin Packer, 41 Lyall Gardens, Birmingham, West Midlands, B45 9YW Tel: 0121 453 8245 martin@packer34.freeserve.co.uk www.packer34.freeserve.co.uk

Fieldings Crown Devon Collectors' Club, P.O. Box 462, Manvers, Rotherham, S63 7WT Tel: 01709 874433 fcdcc@tiscali.co.uk www.fieldingscrowndevclub.com

Florence Ceramics Collectors Society, Marion White, 1000 E. Cordova St, #107, Pasadena, CA 91106, U.S.A. FCCSociety@aol.com

Florence Collectors Society, Christine Taylor, Society Secretary, Florence (UK) Ltd, 41 Evelyn Street, Beeston, Nottingham, NG9 2EU www.florence-sculptures.it

The Followers of Rupert, Mrs S. Reeves, The Membership Secretary, 31 Whiteley, Windsor, Berkshire, SL4 5PJ www.rupertthebear.org.uk

Friar Tuck Collectors Club, c/o Jim and Barbara Chilcutt, 903 Western Air Drive, Jefferson City, MO 65109-0617, U.S.A.

Friends of Blue Ceramic Society, Terry Sheppard, 45a Church Road, Bexley Heath, Kent, DA7 4DD www.fob.org.uk

The Furniture History Society, c/o Dr. Brian Austen, 1 Mercedes Cottages, St. John's Road, Haywards Heath, West Sussex, RH16 4EH Tel: 01444 413845 furniturehistorysociety@hotmail.com www.furniturehistorysociety.com

The Glass Gallery, L.H. Selman Ltd., 123 Locust Street, Santa Cruz, CA 95060-3907, U.S.A. Tel: 831 427 1177 www.glassgallery.com

The Glove Collector Club, Joe Phillips, 14057 Rolling Hills Lane, Dallas, TX 75240, U.S.A.

Goss Collectors' Club (est 1970), Brian Waller, 35 Felstead Way, Luton, LU2 7LH Tel: 01582 732063 commercialofficer@gosscollectorsclub.org

Hagen-Renaker Collectors Club (UK), Chris and Derek Evans, 97 Campbell Road, Burton, Christchurch, Dorset, BH23 7LY www.priorycollectables.co.uk

The Hagen-Renaker Collectors Club, Jenny Palmer, 3651 Polish Line Road, Cheboygan, Mitchigan 49721, U.S.A.

The Happy Pig Collectors Club, Gene Holt, P.O. Box 17, Oneida, IL 61467-0017, U.S.A.

Hat Pin Society of Great Britain, P.O. Box 625, Hull, East Yorkshire, HU5 3WJ www.hatpinsociety.org.uk

Honiton Pottery Collectors' Society, Ian McLellan (Chairman), 51 Cherryfields, Gillingham, Dorset, SP8 4TJ Tel: 01747 835299 www.hpcs.info

Hornby Collectors Club, P.O. Box 25, Melton Mowbray, Leicestershire, LE13 1ZG Tel: 0870 062 4001

The Hornby Railway Collectors' Association, David Embling, 77 Station Road, Rayleigh, Essex, SS6 8AR Tel: 01268 775072

Hummel Collector's Club, Inc., Dorothy Dous, 1261 University Drive, Yardley, PA 19067-2857, U.S.A. Tel: 215 493 6705 or 888 5 HUMMEL customerservice@hummels.com www.hummels.com/

Indian Military Historical Society, The Secretary/Editor, A N McClenaghan, 33 High Street, Tilbrook, Huntingdon, Cambridgeshire, PE28 0JP

Inner-Seal Collectors Club (National Biscuit Co and Nabisco Memorabilia), Charlie Brown, 6609 Billtown Road, Louisville, KY 40299, U.S.A.

International Association of Calculator Collectors, P.O. Box 345, Tustin, CA 92781-0345, U.S.A.

International Bank Note Society, c/o Milan Alusic, P.O. Box 1642, Racine, WI 53401, U.S.A.

International Bond & Share Society, American Branch, Ted Robinson, Vice President, P.O. Box 814, Richboro, PA, U.S.A. Tel: 1 215 357 6820 fandr@voicenet.com

International Bond and Share Society, c/o Peter Duppa-Miller, Beechcroft, Combe Hay, Bath, Somerset, BA2 7EG

International Map Collectors Society, (IMCoS), Secretary, Yasha Beresiner, 43 Templars Crescent, London, N3 3QR

The International Owl Collectors Club, 54 Tiverton Road, Edgware, Middlesex, HA8 6BE

International Perfume Bottle Association, Details from Lynda Brine, Assembly Antique Centre, 6 Saville Row, Bath, Somerset, BA1 2QP Tel: 01225 448488 lyndabrine@yahoo.co.uk www.scentbottlesandsmalls.co.uk

International Perfume Bottle Association, c/o Membership Secretary, P.O. Box 1299, Paradise, CA 95967, U.S.A.

International Philatelic Golf Society, Ron Spiers (Secretary), 8025 Saddle Run, Powell, OH 43065, U.S.A.

International Philatelic Golf Society, UK Secretary, Dr Eiron B.E. Morgan, 50 Pine Valley, Cwmavon, Port Talbot, Wales, SA12 9NF

The International Society of Meccanomen, Adrian Williams, Bell House, 72a Old High Street, Headington, Oxford, OX3 9HW Tel: 01865 741 057 www.internationalmeccanomen.org.uk

The James Bond Collectors Club, P. O. Box 1570, Christchurch, Dorset, BH23 4XS Tel: 0870 4423007 solopublishing@firenet.uk.com

James Sadler International Collectors Club, Customer Services, Churchill China PLC, High Street, Tunstall, Stoke on Trent, Staffordshire, ST6 5NZ Tel: 01782 577566 diningin@churchillchina.plc.uk www.james-sadler.co.uk

Jonathan Harris Studio Glass Ltd, Woodland House, 24 Peregrine Way, Apley Castle, Telford, Shropshire, TF1 6TH Tel: 01952 246381/588441 jonathan@jhstudioglass.com www.jhstudioglass.com

Kevin Francis Toby Jug Collectors Guild, 917 Chicago Avenue, Evanston, IL 60202, U.S.A. Tel: 800 634 0431 or 847 570 4867 Britcol@msn.com www.britishcollectibles.com/

Kewpie Traveler, Rose Morgan, P.O. Box 4032, Portland, OR 97208-4032, U.S.A.

King George VI Collectors' Society (Philately), Secretary, 17 Balcaskie Road, Eltham, London, SE9 1HQ www.kg6.info

The Lace Guild, Charity Reg No 274397, The Hollies, 53 Audnam, Stourbridge, West Midlands, DY8 4AE Tel: 01384 390739 hollies@laceguild.org www.laceguild.org

Lock & Key Collectors' Club, Mr Richard Phillips, Merlewood, The Loan, West Linton, Peebleshire, EH46 7HE Tel: 01968 661039 rphillips52@btinternet.com

M.I. Hummel Club, Goebel Plaza, Rte. 31, P.O. Box 11, Pennington, NJ 08534-0011, U.S.A. Tel: 609 737 8777 or 800 666 2582 memsrv@mihummel.com www.mihummel.com

The Maling Collectors' Society, Sec David Holmes, P.O. Box 1762, North Shields, NE30 4YJ www.maling-pottery.org.uk

Marble Collectors' Society of America, MCSA, P.O. Box 222, Trumball, CT 06611, U.S.A.

The Matchbox Toys International Collectors' Association, Editor, Kevin McGimpsey, P.O. Box 120, Deeside, Flintshire, CH5 3HE Tel: 01244 539414 kevin@matchboxclub.com www.matchboxclub.com

Mauchline Ware Collectors Club, Secretary, Mrs Christabelle Davey, P.O. Box 158, Leeds, LS16 5WZ www.mauchlineware.com

Memories UK Mabel Lucie Attwell Club, Abbey Antiques, 63 Great Whyte, Ramsey, Nr Huntingdon, Cambridgeshire, PE26 1HL www.mabellucieatwellclub.com

Merrythought International Collector's Club, Club Sec, Peter Andrews, Ironbridge, Telford, Shropshire, TF8 7NJ Tel: 01952 433116/Ext 21 contact@merrythought.co.uk www.merrythought.co.uk

Merrythought International Collector's Club, P.O. Box 577, Oakdale, California 95361, U.S.A.

Milk Bottle News, Paul & Lisa Luke, 60 Rose Valley Crescent, Stanford-le-Hope, Essex, SS17 8EF mbneditor@blueyonder.co.uk www.milkbottlenews.org.uk

Milk Bottle World, Jim Call, Broomfield, Colorado, U.S.A. www.3Gsmilkbottles.com www.milkbottleworld.com

The Model Railway Club, The Hon Sec, Keen House, 4 Calshot Street, London, N1 9DA www.themodelrailwayclub.org

Moorcroft Collectors' Club, W. Moorcroft PLC, Sandbach Road, Burslem, Stoke-on-Trent, Staffordshire, ST6 2DQ www.moorcroft.com

Muffin the Mule Collectors' Club, 12 Woodland Close, Woodford Green, Essex, IG8 0QH www.Muffin-the-Mule.com

Keith Murray Collectors Club, P.O. Box 2706, Eccleshall, Stafford, ST21 6WY

Musical Box Society of Great Britain, P.O. Box 373, Welwyn, AL6 0WY

National Association of Avon Collectors, Connie Clark, President, P.O. Box 7006, Kansas City, MO 64113, U.S.A.

National Button Society, Lois Poole, Secretary, 2733 Juno Pl., Apt 4, Akron, Ohio 44333-4137, U.S.A.

National Doll & Teddy Bear Collector, Rose Morgan, P.O. Box 4032, Portland, OR 97208-4032, U.S.A.

National Fishing Lure Collectors Club, Secretary-Treasurer, NFLCC, 197 Scottsdale Circle, Reeds Springs, MO 65737, U.S.A.

National Horse Brass Society, Steve Pink, Woodbine Cottage, Tarrington, Hereford, HR1 4HZ

National Shelley China Club, Rochelle Hart, 591 West 67th Ave, Anchorage, AK 99518-1555, U.S.A. Tel: 907 562 2124 imahart@alaska.net www.nationalshelleychinaclub.com/

National Toothpick Holder Collectors' Society, P.O. Box 852, Archer City, TX 76351, U.S.A.

New Baxter Society, Membership Secretary, 205 Marshalswick Lane, St Albans, Hertfordshire, AL1 4XA Tel: 01727 857945

NFFC - The Club for Disneyana Enthusiasts, P.O. Box 19212, Irvine, CA 92623-9212, U.S.A. Tel: 714 731 4705 www.nffc.org

Nutcracker Collectors' Club, Susan Otto, Editor, 12204 Fox Run Trail, Chesterland, OH 44026, U.S.A. Tel: 440 729 2686 nutsue@adelphia.net

Observer's Pocket Series Collectors Society (OPSCS), Alan Sledger, Secretary, 10 Villiers Road, Kenilworth, Warwickshire, CV8 2JB

The Official Betty Boop Fan Club, Ms Bobbie West, 10550 Western Avenue #133, Stanton, CA 90680-6909, U.S.A. BBOOPFANS@aol.com

Official Popeye Fan Club, 1001 State St, Chester, IL 62233, U.S.A.

Old Bottle Club of Great Britain, Alan Blakeman, c/o BBR, Elsecar Heritage Centre, Nr Barnsley, Yorkshire, S74 8HJ Tel: 01226 745156 sales@onlinebbr.com www.onlinebbr.com

The "Old Hall" Stainless Steel Tableware Collectors Club, Nigel Wiggin, Sandford House, Levedale, Stafford, ST18 9AH Tel: 01785 780376 oht@gnwiggin.freeserve.co.uk www.oldhallclub.co.uk

On the Lighter Side (OTLS), P.O. Box 1733, Quitman, TX 75783-1733, U.S.A. Tel: 903 763 2795 info@otls.com

Ophthalmic Antiques International Collectors' Club, Mr Frank Barraclough, Chairman, Beaulieu Lodge, 10 Beaulieu Road, Cooden, Bexhill-on-Sea, East Sussex, TN39 3AD Frankbarraclough@aol.com

Orders & Medals Research Society OMRS, P.O. Box 1904, Southam, CV47 2ZX Tel: 01295 690009 generalsecretary@omrs.org

The Oriental Ceramic Society, P.O. Box 517, Cambridge, CB1 0BF

Paperweight Collectors Circle, P.O. Box 941, Comberton, Cambridgeshire, CB3 7GQ

Peanuts Collector Club, Inc., 539 Sudden Valley, Bellingham, WA 98229-4811, U.S.A.

Pedal Car Collectors' Club (P.C.C.C.), Hon Sec, A. P. Gayler, P.O. Box No4, Chapel Terrace Mews, Kemp Town, Brighton, East Sussex, BN2 1HU Tel: 01273 622722 www.brmmbrmm.com/pedalcars

Pelham Puppets Collectors Club, Sue Valentine, 46 The Grove, Bedford, Buckinghamshire, MK40 3JN Tel: 01234 363336 sue.valentine@ntlworld.com

Pen Delfin Family Circle, P.O. Box 431, Burnley, Lancashire, BB10 2WT

The Pewter Society, Llananant Farm, Penallt, Monmouth, NP25 4AP secretary@pewtersociety.org www.pewtersociety.org

The Photographic Collector's Club of Great Britain, Membership Office, The Photographic Collector's Club International Ltd., 5 Buntingford Road, Puckeridge, Ware, Hertfordshire, SG11 1RT

Pilkington's Lancastrian Pottery Society, Wendy Stock, Sullom Side, Barnacre, Garstang, Preston, Lancashire, PR3 1GH

The Pipe Club of London, London www.pcol.freewire.co.uk

Postcard Club of Great Britain, c/o Mrs D. Brennan, 34 Harper House, St James Crescent, London, SW9 7LW Tel: 020 7771 9404 drenebrennan@yahoo.co.uk

The Pot Lid Circle, c/o Ian Johnson, Collins House, 32/38 Station Road, Gerrards Cross, Buckinghamshire, SL9 8EL Tel: 01753 279001 ian.johnson@bpcollins.co.uk

Potteries of Rye Society, Membership Secretary, Barry Buckton, 2 Redyear Cottages, Kennington Road, Ashford, Kent, TN24 0TF

Quimper Association, Odin, Benbow Way, Cowley, Uxbridge, Middlesex, UB8 2HD

Quimper Club International, Diane Robinson, 5316 Seascape Lane, Plano, TX 75093, U.S.A. Tel: 972 867 7839 dianerobinson@quimperclub.org/

Road Map Collectors Association, P.O. Box 158, Channelview, TX 77530-0158, U.S.A.

Royal Bayreuth Collectors' Club, Karen Church, 110 Blackwood St, Beaver Falls, PA 15010, U.S.A. Tel: 507 645 5382 tenebrous@aol.com www.royalbayreuth.com/

Royal Bayreuth International Collectors' Society, Howard & Sarah Wade, P.O. Box 325, Orrville, OH 44667 0325, U.S.A. Tel: 330 682 8551 RBCollectr@aol.com

The Russian Doll Collectors' Club, Gardener's Cottage, Hatchlands, East Clandon, Surrey, GU4 7RT

Silhouette Collectors' Club, c/o Miss Diana B. Joll, Flat 5, 13 Brunswick Square, Hove, East Sussex, BN3 1EH

Silver Spoon Club of Great Britain, 26 Burlington Arcade, Mayfair, London, W1J 0PU Tel: 020 7491 1720 silverspoonclub@bexfield.co.uk

Snuff Bottle Society, Elizabeth & Mike Kaynes, Swallows Rest, 3 Pitts Deep, Quay Road, Christchurch, Dorset, BH23 1BU Tel: 01202 469050 snuffbottles@onetel.com

The Soviet Collectors Club, P.O. Box 56, Saltburn by the Sea, TS12 1YD collect@sovietclub.com

Steiff Club - North America, Rebekah Kaufman, Steiff North America, Inc., 425 Paramount Drive, Raynham, MA 02767, U.S.A.

The SylvaC Collectors Circle, 174 Portsmouth Road, Horndean, Waterlooville, Hampshire, PO8 9HP Tel: 02392 591725 www.sylvacclub.com

TEAMS Club - The official club for Brooke Bond Card Collectors, P.O. Box 1672, Croydon, Surrey, CR9 4XW

Telecommunications Heritage Group, P.O. Box 561, South Croydon, Surrey, CR2 6YL www.thg.org.uk

The Thimble Society, c/o Bridget McConnel, 72 Admiral Vernon Arcade, 147 Portobello Road, London, W11 2DY Open Sat only www.thimblesociety.co.uk

Toaster Collector Association, P.O. Box 485, Redding Ridge, CT 06876, U.S.A.

Tobacco Jar Society, Colin Grey, 19 Woodhurst North, Raymead Road, Maidenhead, Berkshire, SL6 8PH

Torquay Pottery Collectors' Society, Membership Secretary, c/o Torquay Museum, 529 Babbacombe Road, Torquay, Devon, TQ1 1HG www.torquaypottery.com

Totally Teapots The Novelty Teapot Collectors Club, Vince McDonald Euxton, Chorley, Lancashire, PR7 6EY Tel: 01257 450366 vince@totallyteapots.com www.totallyteapots.com

Trade Card Collector's Association, P.O. Box 284, Marlton, NJ 08053, U.S.A.

Train Collectors Society, James Day, Membership Secretary, P.O. Box 20340, London, NW11 6ZE

Treasures for Little Children, c/o Gail Ryan, 6885 S. Mingus Drive, Chandler, AZ 85249, U.S.A. www.treasuresforlittlechildren.com

Treasury of Christmas Ornaments Collectors' Club, P.O. Box 277, Itasca, IL 60143-0277, U.S.A.

UK 1/6th Collectors Club, Adrian Pitman, 1 St Cadocs Rise, Barry, Vale of Glamorgan, CF63 2FG, South Wales

UK Football Programme Collectors Club, P.O. Box 3236, Norwich, NR7 7BE Tel: 01603 449237 progm@hotmail.com

UK McDonald's & Fast Food Collectors Club, c/o Lawrence Yap, 110 Tithelands, Harlow, Essex, CM19 5ND

United Kingdom Spoon Collectors Club, David Cross, General Secretary, 72 Edinburgh Road, Newmarket, Suffolk, CB8 0DQ Tel: 01638 665457 david.cross340@ntlworld.com

Universal Autograph Collectors Club, Michael Hecht, President UACC, P.O. Box 6181, Washington, DC 20044-6181, U.S.A. www.uacc.org

Vintage Fashion & Costume Jewelry Club, P.O. Box 265, Glen Oaks, NY 11004, U.S.A.

Vintage Model Yacht Group, Hon Membership Secretary, Alistair Roach, Windy Corner, Evercreech, Weston Town, Somerset, BA4 6JG www.vmyg.org.uk

Vintage Tupperware Collectors http://groups.yahoo.com/group/vintagetupperware/

Wade Attic, Carole Murdock, 8199 Pierson Ct, Arvada, CO 80005, U.S.A. carole@wadeattic.com www.wadeattic.com

The Washington Historical Autograph and Certificate Organization - Whaco!, P.O. Box 2428, Springfield, VA 22152-2428, U.S.A.

Zippo Click Collectors Club, Zippo Manufacturing Company, 33 Barbour Street, Bradford, PA 16701, U.S.A. Tel: 814 368 2725 kjones@zippo.com www.zippo.com www.zippoclick.com

DIRECTORY OF MARKETS & CENTRES

UK & REPUBLIC OF IRELAND

Berkshire

Great Grooms Antiques Centre, Riverside House, Charnham Street, Hungerford, RG17 0EP Tel: 01488 682314 www.greatgrooms.co.uk

Buckinghamshire

Jackdaw Antiques Centres Ltd, 25 West Street, Marlow, SL7 2LS Tel: 01628 898285 www.jackdaw-antiques.co.uk
Collectables, silver, china, specialist areas, books, Victorian glass, Quimper, coins, fishing tackle.

Marlow Antique Centre, 35 Station Road, Marlow, SL7 1NW Tel: 01628 473223
Wide range of antique and collectable items. Georgian, Victorian and Edwardian furniture, country pine, decorative furniture, silverware, glass, china, Art Deco, bedsteads, cameras, old tools, garden items, jewellery, pens, cufflinks, vintage toys. Also a secondhand book section.

Derbyshire

Alfreton Antique Centre, 11 King Street, Alfreton, DE55 7AF Tel: 01773 520781
Antiques, collectables, furniture, books, militaria, postcards, silverware.

Chappells Antiques Centre - Bakewell, King Street, Bakewell, DE45 1DZ Tel: 01629 812496 www.chappellsantiquescentre.com
Quality period furniture, ceramics, silver, plate, metals, treen, clocks, barometers, books, pictures, maps, prints, textiles, kitchenalia, lighting and furnishing accessories from the 17th–20thC.

Heanor Antiques Centre, 1–3 Ilkeston Road, Heanor, DE75 7AE Tel: 01773 531181/762783 www.heanorantiquescentre.co.uk

Matlock Antiques, Collectables & Riverside Café, 7 Dale Road, Matlock, DE4 3LT Tel: 01629 760808 www.matlock-antiques-collectables.cwc.net.
Proprietor W. Shirley. Wide range of items including collectables, mahogany, pine, oak, pictures, books, linen, kitchenalia, china, clocks, clothes and jewellery.

Devon

Quay Centre, Topsham, Nr Exeter, EX3 0JA Tel: 01392 874006 www.quayantiques.com
Antiques, collectables and traditional furnishings.

Essex

Debden Antiques, Elder Street, Debden, Saffron Walden, CB11 3JY Tel: 01799 543007 debden-antiques.co.uk
Large selection of 16th—20th century oak, mahogany and pine furniture, watercolours and oil paintings, rugs, ceramics, silver and jewellery.

The Maltings Antique Centre, Chelmsford Road, Norton Heath, CM4 0LN Tel: 07970 206682/01245 261863

Gloucestershire

Antiques Centre Gloucester, 1 Severn Road, The Historic Docks, Gloucester, GL1 2LE Tel: 01452 529716 www.antiques.center.com

Durham House Antiques, Sheep Street, Stow-on-the-Wold, GL54 1AA Tel: 01451 870404 www.DurhamHouseGB.com
Town and country furniture, metalware, books, ceramics, kitchenalia, sewing ephemera, silver, jewellery and samplers.

Hampshire

Dolphin Quay Antique Centre, Queen Street, Emsworth, PO10 7BU Tel: 01243 379994 chrisdqantiques@aol.com
Marine, naval antiques, paintings, watercolours, prints, antique clocks, decorative arts, furniture, sporting apparel, luggage, specialist period lighting, conservatory, garden antiques, fine antique/country furniture, French/antique beds.

Herefordshire

Mulberry's Antiques & Vintage Costumes, Hereford, HR1 2NN Tel: 01432 350101 mulberrysantiques@hotmail.com
Wide range of antiques and collectables - furniture, fine china, porcelain, silver, jewellery, textiles, pre-1930's clothing and accessories, objets d'art, prints, oils and watercolours.

Herts & Essex Antiques Centre, The Maltings, Station Road, Sawbridgeworth, CM21 9JX Tel: 01279 722044
Antiques, furniture, jewellery, porcelain, collectables, stamps, coins, postcards, costume, paintings, glass, ceramics and ephemera.

Kent

Castle Antiques, 1 London Road, Westerham, TN16 1BB Tel: 01959 562492.
Antiques, small furniture, collectables, rural bygones, costume, glass, books, linens, jewellery, chandeliers, cat collectables.

Nightingales, 89-91 High Street, West Wickham, BR4 0LS Tel: 020 8777 0335
Antiques, furniture and collectors items, including ceramics, glass, silver, and decorative ware.

Tenterden Antiques Centre, 66-66A High Street, Tenterden, TN30 6AU Tel: 01580 765655/765885

Lancashire

The Antique & Decorative Design Centre, 56 Garstang Road, Preston, PR1 1NA Tel: 01772 882078 www.paulallisonantiques.co.uk
Quality antiques, objects d'art, clocks, pine, silverware, porcelain, upholstery, French furniture for the home and garden.

GB Antiques Centre, Lancaster Leisure Park, (the former Hornsea Pottery), Wyresdale Road, Lancaster, LA1 3LA Tel: 01524 844734
Porcelain, pottery, Art Deco, glass, books, linen, mahogany, oak and pine furniture.

Lincolnshire

Sue's Collectables, 61 Victoria Road, Mablethorpe, LN12 2AF Tel: 01507 472406
Collectable items inc. old glass lampshades, gas & electrical fittings, breweriana, kitchenalia, Bakelite, chalk figures, Christmas lights & decorations. Pendelfins bought and sold.

London

Bourbon-Hanby Antiques Centre, 151 Sydney Street, Chelsea, SW3 6NT Tel: 020 7352 2106

Covent Garden Antique Market, Jubilee Hall, Southampton Street, Covent Garden, WC2
Every Monday from 6am.

Grays Antique Markets, South Molton Lane, W1K 5AB Tel: 020 7629 7034 www.graysantiques.com
Specialist antique dealers selling beautiful and unusual antiques & collectables.

Northcote Road Antique Market, 155a Northcote Road, Battersea, SW11 6QB Tel: 020 7228 6850 www.spectrumsoft.net/nam.htm
30 dealers offering a wide variety of antiques & collectables.

Spitalfields Antique Market, Commercial Street, E1
Every Thursday from 7am.

Norfolk
Tombland Antiques Centre, Augustine Steward House, 14 Tombland, Norwich, NR3 1HF Tel: 01603 761906 or 619129 www.tomblandantiques.co.uk

Nottinghamshire
Dukeries Antiques Centre, Thoresby Park, Budby, Newark, NG22 9EX Tel: 01623 822252 dukeriesantiques@aol.com

Occleshaw Antiques Centre, The Old Major Cinema, 11 Mansfield Road, Edwinstowe, NG21 9NL Tel: 01623 825370
Large centre with wide range of furniture, jewellery, militaria, cameras and collectables.

Oxfordshire
Jackdaw Antiques Centres Ltd, 5 Reading Road, Henley-on-Thames, RG9 0AS Tel: 01491 572289 www.jackdaw-antiques.co.uk
Collectables (modern & discontinued), furniture, books, specialist areas, Carlton ware, Doulton, Beswick.

Lamb Arcade Antiques Centre, High Street, Wallingford, OX10 0BX Tel: 01491 835166
Furniture, silver, porcelain, glass, books, boxes, crafts, rugs, jewellery, lace and linens, pictures, tin toys, motoring and aviation memorabilia, sports and fishing items, decorative and ornamental items.

Scotland
Scottish Antique and Arts Centre, Carse of Cambus, Doune, Perthshire, FK16 6HG Tel: 01786 841203 www.scottish-antiques.com
Huge gift & collectors sections. Victorian & Edwardian furniture.

Scottish Antique and Arts Centre, Abernyte, Perthshire, PH14 9SJ Tel: 01828 686401 www.scottish-antiques.com
Huge gift & collectors sections. Victorian & Edwardian furniture.

Somerset
Assembly Antiques, 6 Saville Row, Bath, BA1 2QP Tel: 01225 448488 www.assemblyantiques.co.uk

Bartlett Street Antique Centre, 5-10 Bartlett Street, Bath, BA1 2QZ Tel: 01225 466689 www.antiques-centre.co.uk

Staffordshire
Rugeley Antique Centre, 161 Main Road, Brereton, Nr Rugeley, WS15 1DX Tel: 01889 577166 www.rugeleyantiquecentre.co.uk

Suffolk
Snape Maltings Antique & Collectors Centre, Saxmundham, IP17 1SR Tel: 01728 688038

Surrey
Kingston Antiques Centre, 29-31 London Road, Kingston-upon-Thames, KT2 6ND Tel: 020 8549 2004/3839 www.kingstonantiquescentre.co.uk

East Sussex
The Brighton Lanes Antique Centre, 12 Meeting House Lane, Brighton, BN1 1HB Tel: 01273 823121 www.brightonlanes-antiquecentre.co.uk
Fine selection of furniture, silver, jewellery, glass, porcelain, clocks, pens, watches, lighting and decorative items.

Church Hill Antique Centre, 6 Station Street, Lewes, BN7 2DA Tel: 01273 474842 www.church-hill-antiques.com

West Sussex
Arundel Antiques Centre, 51 High Street, Arundel, BN18 9AJ Tel: 01903 882749

Wales
Offa's Dyke Antique Centre, 4 High Street, Knighton, Powys, LD7 1AT Tel: 01547 528635/520145
Specialists in ceramics and glass, fine art of the 19th & 20th centuries. Country antiques and collectables.

Warwickshire
Dunchurch Antiques Centre, 16a Daventry Road, Dunchurch (Nr Rugby) Tel: 01788 522450
Dealers specialising in furniture, china, glass, books, postcards, stamps, clocks, toys, trains, etc.

West Midlands
Birmingham Antique Centre, 1407 Pershore Road, Stirchley, Birmingham, B30 2JR Tel: 0121 459 4587 www.birminghamantiquecentre.co.uk

Wiltshire
Upstairs Downstairs, 40 Market Place, Devizes, SN10 1JG Tel: 01380 730266 devizesantiques@btconnect.com

Worcestershire
Worcester Antiques Centre, Reindeer Court, Mealcheapen Street, Worcester, WR1 4DF Tel: 01905 610680 ZACATWORCS@aol.com
Porcelain & pottery, furniture, silver & dining room accessories, jewellery, period watches & clocks, scientific instrumentation, Arts & Crafts, Nouveau, Deco, antique boxes, Mauchline & Tartan wares, books, ephemera, militaria & kitchenalia with full restoration & repair services on all of the above.

Yorkshire
The Antiques Centre York, 41 Stone Gate, York, YO1 8AW Tel: 01904 635888 www.theantiquescentreyork.co.uk

The Mall Antique Centre, 400 Wincolmlee, Hull, HU2 0QL Tel: 01482 327858
Georgian, Victorian, Edwardian, reproduction, 1930s furniture, silver, china, clocks, hardware, etc.

St Nicholas Antique Shops, 33-35 St Nicholas Cliff, Scarborough, YO11 2ES Tel: 01723 365221/374175 www.collectors.demon.co.uk
International dealers in stamps, postcards, silver, gold, medals, cigarette cards, cap badges, militaria, jewellery, commemorative ware, furniture, clocks, watches and many more collectables.

York Antique Centre, 2a Lendel, York, YO1 8AA Tel: 01904 641445

U.S.A.
Antique Center I, II, III at Historic Savage Mill, Savage, Maryland Tel: 410 880 0918 or 301 369 4650 antiquec@aol.com

Antique Village, North of Richmond, Virginia, on Historic US 301, 4 miles North of 1-295 Tel: 804 746 8914
Specialising in Art Pottery, country & primitives, Civil War artifacts, paper memorabilia, African art, toys, advertising, occupied Japan, tobacco tins, glassware, china, holiday collectibles, jewellery, postcards.

Antiques at Colony Mill Marketplace, 222 West Street, Keene, New Hampshire 03431 Tel: 603 358 6343
Period to country furniture, paintings and prints, Art Pottery, glass, china, silver, jewellery, toys, dolls, quilts, etc.

The Coffman's Antiques Markets, at Jennifer House Commons, Stockbridge Road, Route 7, P.O. Box 592, Great Barrington, MA 01230 Tel: 413 528 9282/9602 www.coffmansantiques.com

Fern Eldridge & Friends, 800 First NH Turnpike (Rte. 4), Northwood, New Hampshire 03261 Tel: 603 942 5602/8131 FernEldridgeAndFriends@NHantiqueAlley.com

The Hayloft Antique Center, 1190 First NH Turnpike (Rte. 4), Northwood, New Hampshire 03261 Tel: 603 942 5153 TheHayloftAntiqueCenter@NHantiqueAlley.com
Estate jewelry, sterling silver, rare books, glass, porcelain, pottery, art, primitives, furniture, toys, ephemera, linens, military, sporting collectibles and much more.

Morningside Antiques, 6443 Biscayne Blvd., Miami, Florida Tel: 305 751 2828
Specialising in English, French and American furniture and collectibles in a mall setting with many different vendors.

Parker-French Antique Center, 1182 First NH Turnpike (Rt. 4), Northwood, New Hampshire 03261 Tel: 603 942 8852 ParkerFrenchAntiqueCenter@NHantiqueAlley.com
Good mix of sterling silver, jewelry, glassware, pottery, early primitives. No crafts, reproductions or new items.

Quechee Gorge Antiques & Collectibles Center, Located in Quechee Gorge Village Tel: 1 800 438 5565
Depression glass, ephemera, tools, toys, collectibles, Deco, primitives, prints, silver and fine china.

Showcase Antique Center, P.O. Box 1122, Sturbridge MA 01566 Tel: 508 347 7190 www.showcaseantiques.com

Tennessee Antique Mall, 654 Wedgewood Ave., Nashville, Tennessee Tel: 615 259 4077

KEY TO ILLUSTRATIONS

Each illustration and descriptive caption is accompanied by a letter code. By referring to the following list of auctioneers (denoted by 🔨) and dealers (⊞) the source of any item may be immediately determined. Inclusion in this edition in no way constitutes or implies a contract or binding offer on the part of any of our contributors to supply or sell the goods illustrated, or similar articles, at the prices stated. Advertisers in this year's directory are denoted by †.

If you require a valuation for an item, it is advisable to check whether the dealer or specialist will carry out this service and if there is a charge. Please mention Miller's when making an enquiry. Having found a specialist who will carry out your valuation it is best to send a photograph and description of the item to the specialist together with a stamped addressed envelope for the reply. A valuation by telephone is not possible.

Most dealers are only too happy to help you with your enquiry; however, they are very busy people and consideration of the above points would be welcomed.

299 ⊞ 299, 299 Lillie Road, London, SW6 7LL Tel: 07860 223707

AAA ⊞ Ad-Age Antique Advertising, Maidstone, Kent Tel: 01622 670595

ABCM ⊞ A B Coins & Medals, 23–25 'Old' Northam Road, Southampton, Hampshire, SO14 Tel: 023 8023 3393

ACAC ⊞ Afonwen Craft & Antique Centre, Afonwen, Nr Caerwys, Nr Mold, Flintshire, Wales, CH7 5UB Tel: 01352 720965 www.afonwen.co.uk

ACOG ⊞ The Autograph Collectors Gallery, 7 Jessops Lane, Gedling, Nottingham, NG4 4BQ Tel: 0115 961 2956/987 6578 www.autograph-gallery.co.uk

ACOU ⊞ Acoustica Tel: 01270 619265/07947 800 543 or 07761 328 494

ADD ⊞ Addyman Books, 39 Lion Street, Hay-on-Wye, Herefordshire, HR3 5AD Tel: 01497 821136

ADV ⊞ Arlene De Vries Antiques Tel: 07850 100249 brightthingsrevisited@btinternet.com

AEL ⊞ Argyll Etkin Ltd, 1–9 Hills Place, Oxford Circus, London, W1F 7SA Tel: 020 7437 7800 philatelists@argyll-etkin.com www.argyll-etkin.com

AG 🔨 Anderson & Garland (Auctioneers), Marlborough House, Marlborough Crescent, Newcastle-upon-Tyne, Tyne & Wear, NE1 4EE Tel: 0191 430 3000

AH 🔨 Andrew Hartley, Victoria Hall Salerooms, Little Lane, Ilkley, Yorkshire, LS29 8EA Tel: 01943 816363 info@andrewhartleyfinearts.co.uk www.andrewhartleyfinearts.co.uk

AL ⊞ Ann Lingard

APC ⊞ Antique Photographic Company Ltd Tel: 01949 842192 alpaco47@aol.com

ARB ⊞ Arbour Antiques, Poet's Arbour, Sheep Street, Stratford-on-Avon, Warwickshire, CV37 6EF Tel: 01789 293453

ARo ⊞ Alvin's Vintage Games & Toys Tel: 01865 772409 alvin@vintage-games.co.uk www.vintage-games.co.uk

ASC ⊞ Andrew Sclanders, 32 St Paul's View, 15 Amwell Street, London, EC1R 1UP Tel: 020 7278 5034 sclanders@beatbooks.com www.beatbooks.com

ASHB 🔨 Stella Ashbrooke Tel: 01948 662050

ASP ⊞ Aspidistra Antiques, Tel: 07768 071948 aspidistra.pg@ntlworld.com

ATT ⊞ Rachel's Attic, P.O. Box 688, Dandridge, TN 37725, U.S.A.

AU ⊞ Auto Suggestion Tel: 01428 751397

AVT ⊞ Alexander von Tutschek Tel: 01225 465532 vontutschek@onetel.net.uk

B&R ⊞ Bread & Roses Tel: 01926 817342

BA **See BAY**

BAM 🔨 Bamfords Ltd, The Derby Auction House, Chequers Road, off Pentagon Island, Derby, DE21 6EN Tel: 01332 210000 bamfords-auctions@tiscali.co.uk www.bamfords-auctions.co.uk

BAM(M) 🔨 Bamfords Ltd, The Matlock Auction Gallery, The Old Picture Palace, 133 Dale Road, Matlock, Derbyshire, DE4 3LU Tel: 01629 57460 bamfords-matlock@tiscali.co.uk

BaN ⊞ Barbara Ann Newman Tel: 07850 016729

BAY ⊞ George Bayntun, Manvers Street, Bath, Somerset, BA1 1JW Tel: 01225 466000 ebc@georgebayntun.com

BB ⊞ Barter Books, Alnwick Station, Alnwick, Northumberland, NE66 2NP Tel: 01665 604888 www.barterbooks.co.uk

BBA 🔨 Bloomsbury, Bloomsbury House, 24 Maddox Street, London, W1S 1PP Tel: 020 7495 9494 info@bloomsburyauctions.com www.bloomsburyauctions.com

BBe ⊞ Bourton Bears

BBE **See BBe**

BBR 🔨 BBR, Elsecar Heritage Centre, Elsecar, Nr Barnsley, South Yorkshire, S74 8HJ Tel: 01226 745156 sales@onlinebbr.com www.onlinebbr.com

BCC British Collectibles, 917 Chicago Avenue, Evanston, Illinois 60202, U.S.A. Tel: 800 634 0431 kevin@britishcollectibles.com sheila@britishcollectibles.com britcol@msn.com *Photographer: David Doty*

Bea Bearnes, St Edmund's Court, Okehampton Street, Exeter, Devon, EX4 1DU Tel: 01392 207000 enquiries@bearnes.co.uk www.bearnes.co.uk

BEA **See Bea**

Bert Bertoia Auctions, 2141 DeMarco Drive, Vineland, New Jersey 08360, U.S.A. Tel: 856 692 1881 bill@bertoiaauctions.com www.bertoiaauctions.com

BET Beth, GO 43–44, Alfies Antique Market, 13–25 Church Street, Marylebone, London, NW8 8DT Tel: 020 7723 5613/0777 613 6003

BEV Beverley, 30 Church Street, Marylebone, London, NW8 8EP Tel: 020 7262 1576/07776136003

BGe Bradley Gent Tel: 07711 158005 www.antiques-shop.co.uk

BI † Books Illustrated Tel: 0777 1635 777 booksillustrated@aol.com www.booksillustrated.com

BIB Biblion, Grays Antique Market, 1–7 Davies Mews, London, W1K 5AB Tel: 020 7629 1374 info@biblion.com www.biblionmayfair.com

BKJL Brenda Kimber & John Lewis, The Victoria Centre, 3–4 Victoria Road, Saltaire, Shipley, West Yorkshire Tel: 01274 611478 or 01482 442265

Bns Brittons Jewellers, 4 King Street, Clitheroe, Lancashire, BB7 2EP Tel: 01200 425555 or 0789 008 1849 sales@brittonswatches.com www.internetwatches.co.uk www.antique-jewelry.co.uk

BOB Bob's Collectables Tel: 01277 650834

BoC Bounty Antiques Centre

BOOM Boom Interiors, 115–117 Regents Park Road, Primrose Hill, London, NW1 8UR Tel: 020 7722 6622 or 07973 114 396 info@boominteriors.com www.boominteriors.com

BRD Katherine Higgins

BrL The Brighton Lanes Antique Centre, 12 Meeting House Lane, Brighton, East Sussex, BN1 1HB Tel: 01273 823121 or 07785 564337 peter@brightonlanes-antiquecentre.co.uk www.brightonlanes-antiquecentre.co.uk

BRT Britannia, Grays Antique Market, Stand 101, 58 Davies Street, London, W1Y 1AR Tel: 020 7629 6772 britannia@grays.clara.net

BS Below Stairs, 103 High Street, Hungerford, Berkshire, RG17 0NB Tel: 01488 682317 hofgartner@belowstairs.co.uk www.belowstairs.co.uk

BtoB Bac to Basic Antiques Tel: 07787 105609 bcarruthers@waitrose.com

BuA Burgate Antiques Centre, 23A Palace Street, Canterbury, Kent, CT1 2DZ Tel: 01227 456500 vkreeves@burgate1.fsnet.co.uk

BUDD Budd Auctions Ltd, Graham Auctioneers & Valuers gb@grahambuddauctions.co.uk

BWDA Brightwells Decorative Arts Tel: 01744 24899 or 07802 561951 stanmoore@brightwells.demon.co.uk

BWH † Bears of Windy Hill, P.O. Box 51, Shipley, West Yorkshire, BD18 2YH Tel: 01274 599175 info@bearsofwindyhill.co.uk www.bearsofwindyhill.co.uk

BWL Brightwells Fine Art, The Fine Art Saleroom, Easters Court, Leominster, Herefordshire, HR6 0DE Tel: 01568 611122 fineart@brightwells.com www.brightwells.com

c20th www.c20th.com Tel: 07775 704052 simon@c20th.com www.c20th.com

CAG The Canterbury Auction Galleries, 40 Station Road West, Canterbury, Kent, CT2 8AN Tel: 01227 763337 auctions@thecanterburyauctiongalleries.com www.thecanterburyauctiongalleries.com

Cai Caithness Glass Ltd, Inveralmond, Perth, Scotland, PH1 3TZ Tel: 01738 637373 www.caithnessglass.co.uk

CAL Cedar Antiques Ltd, High Street, Hartley Wintney, Hampshire, RG27 8NY Tel: 01252 843222 or 01189 326628 ca@cedar-antiques.com www.cedar-antiques.com

CARA Cara Antiques cara_antiques@yahoo.com www.caraantiques.com

CBB Colin Baddiel, Gray's Mews, 1–7 Davies Mews, London, W1Y 1AR Tel: 020 7408 1239/020 8452 7243

CBi Collector Bits Tel: 02476 746981 or 07796 398 303 collectorbits@aol.com www.collectorbits.com

CBP Comic Book Postal Auctions Ltd, 40–42 Osnaburgh Street, London, NW1 3ND Tel: 020 7424 0007 comicbook@compalcomics.com www.compalcomics.com

CCO Collectable Costume, Showroom South, Gloucester Antiques Centre, 1 Severn Road, Gloucester, GL1 2LE Tel: 01989 562188 or 07980 623926

CFSD Clive Farahar & Sophie Dupre, Horsebrook House, XV The Green, Calne, Wiltshire, SN11 8DQ Tel: 01249 821121 post@farahardupre.co.uk www.farahardupre.co.uk

CGA Castlegate Antiques Centre, 55 Castlegate, Newark, Nottinghamshire, NG24 1BE Tel: 01636 700076 or 07860 843739

CGC Cheffins, 8 Hill Street, Saffron Walden, Essex, CB10 1JD Tel: 01799 513131 www.cheffins.co.uk

CHAC Church Hill Antiques Centre, 6 Station Street, Lewes, East Sussex, BN7 2DA Tel: 01273 474 842 churchhilllewes@aol.com www.church-hill-antiques.com

CHAM Chameleon Fine Lighting, 223 East 59th Street, New York, NY 10022, U.S.A. Tel: 212 355 6300 mail@chameleon59.com www.chameleon59.com

CHI ⊞ Chinasearch, P.O. Box 1202, Kenilworth, Warwickshire, CV8 2WW Tel: 01926 512402 info@chinasearch.co.uk www.chinasearch.co.uk

CHO ⊞ Candice Horley Antiques Tel: 01883 716056 or 0705 0044855 cjhorleyantiques@aol.com

CHTR 🔨 Charterhouse, The Long Street Salerooms, Sherborne, Dorset, DT9 3BS Tel: 01935 812277 enquiry@charterhouse-auctions.co.uk www.charterhouse-auctions.co.uk

CINE ⊞ Cine Art Gallery, 759 Fulham Road, London, SW6 5UU Tel: 020 7384 0728 info@cineartgallery.com www.cineartgallery.com

CLOB ⊞ Clobber, 920 Christchurch Road, Bournemouth, Dorset, BH7 6DL Tel: 01202 433330 or 07779 324 109 richard@vintageclobber.com www.vintageclobber.com

CO 🔨 Cooper Owen, 74 Station Road, Egham, Surrey, TW20 9LF Tel: 01784 434 900 customerservice@cooperowen.com www.cooperowen.com

COB ⊞ Cobwebs, 78 Northam Road, Southampton, Hampshire, SO14 0PB Tel: 023 8022 7458 www.cobwebs.uk.com

CoC ⊞ Comic Connections, 4a Parsons Street, Banbury, Oxfordshire, OX16 5LW Tel: 01295 268989 Comicconnections@aol.com www.american-comics.net/

COMM ⊞ Commemorabilia, 15 Haroldsleigh Avenue, Crownhill, Plymouth, Devon, PL5 3AW Tel: 01752 700795 ron_smith@commemorabilia.co.uk www.commemorabilia.co.uk

COO ⊞ Graham Cooley Tel: 07968 722269

CPCC § Cigarette Packet Collectors Club of GB, Barry Russell, Talisker, Vines Cross Road, Horam, Heathfield, East Sussex, TN21 0HF Tel: 01435 812453

CS ⊞ Christopher Sykes, The Old Parsonage, Woburn, Milton Keynes, Buckinghamshire, MK17 9QM Tel: 01525 290259 www.sykes-corkscrews.co.uk

CTO ⊞† Collectors Corner, P.O. Box 8, Congleton, Cheshire, CW12 4GD Tel: 01260 270429 dave.popcorner@ukonline.co.uk

CuS ⊞ Curious Science, 307 Lillie Road, Fulham, London, SW6 7LL Tel: 020 7610 1175 or 07956 834094 props@curiousscience.com www.curiousscience.com

CWB ⊞ www.cornishware.biz Tel: 01661 852 814 or 07979 857599 info@cornishware.biz www.cornishware.biz

CWD ⊞ Collectors World, 188 Wollaton Road, Nottingham, NG8 1HJ Tel: 0115 928 0347 markray@freeuk.com

CWO ⊞ www.collectorsworld.net, P.O. Box 4922, Bournemouth, Dorset, BH1 3JA Tel: 01202 555223 info@collectorsworld.biz www.collectorsworld.net www.collectorsworld.biz

DA 🔨 Dee, Atkinson & Harrison, The Exchange Saleroom, Driffield, East Yorkshire, YO25 6LD Tel: 01377 253151 info@dahauctions.com www.dahauctions.com

DaM ⊞ Martin's Antiques & Collectibles Jackiem743710633@aol.com www.martinsantiquescollectibles.co.uk

DD 🔨 David Duggleby, The Vine St Salerooms, Scarborough, Yorkshire, YO11 1XN Tel: 01723 507111 auctions@davidduggleby.com www.davidduggleby.com

DE ⊞ Decades, 20 Lord St West, Blackburn, Lancashire, BB2 1JX Tel: 01254 693320

DeA ⊞ Delphi Antiques, Powerscourt Townhouse Centre, South William Street, Dublin 2, Republic of Ireland Tel: 353 679 0331

DEB ⊞ Debden Antiques, Elder Street, Debden, Saffron Walden, Essex, CB11 3JY Tel: 01799 543007 info@debden-antiques.co.uk www.debden-antiques.co.uk

DEBN ⊞ Debenhams Plc

DECO ⊞ Decographics Collectors' Gallery, Arundel Antiques Centre, 51 High Street, Arundel, West Sussex, BN18 9AJ Tel: 01243 787391 www.decographic.co.uk

DeJ ⊞ Denim Junkies www.denimjunkies.com

DES ⊞ Design-Conscious Tel: 01200 427313 info@design-conscious.co.uk www.design-conscious.co.uk

DHA ⊞ Durham House Antiques, Sheep Street, Stow-on-the-Wold, Gloucestershire, GL54 1AA Tel: 01451 870404 DurhamHouseGB@aol.com www.DurhamHouseGB.com

DMC 🔨 Diamond Mills & Co, 117 Hamilton Road, Felixstowe, Suffolk, IP11 7BL Tel: 01394 282281

DN 🔨 Dreweatt Neate, Donnington Priory, Donnington, Newbury, Berkshire, RG14 2JE Tel: 01635 553553 donnington@dnfa.com www.dnfa.com/donnington

DN(HAM) 🔨 Dreweatt Neate, Baverstock House, 93 High Street, Godalming, Surrey, GU7 1AL Tel: 01483 423567 godalming@dnfa.com www.dnfa.com/godalming

Do ⊞ Liz Farrow T/As Dodo, Stand F071/73, Alfie's Antique Market, 13–25 Church Street, London, NW8 8DT Tel: 020 7706 1545

DOAN ⊞ Doll Antiques Tel: 0121 449 0637

DQ ⊞ Dolphin Quay Antique Centre, Queen Street, Emsworth, Hampshire, PO10 7BU Tel: 01243 379994 chrisdqantiques@aol.com

DRO(C) 🔨 Craftsman Auctions, Rago Arts & Auction Center, 333 North Main Street, Lambertville, New Jersey 08530, U.S.A. Tel: 609 397 9374 info@ragoarts.com www.ragoarts.com

DSG ⊞ Delf Stream Gallery Tel: 07816 781297 nic19422000@yahoo.co.uk www.delfstreamgallery.com

DuM 🔨 Du Mouchelles, 409 East Jefferson, Detroit, Michigan 48226, U.S.A. Tel: 313 963 6255 www.dumouchelles.com

DUR ⊞ Tony Durante, Alfie's Antique Market, G047/G048 - Ground Floor, 13–25 Church Street, London, NW8 8DT Tel: 020 7723 0449 or 0789 446569 durantetony@hotmail.com

DW Dominic Winter Book Auctions, Mallard House, Broadway Lane, South Cerney, Gloucestershire, GL7 5UQ Tel: 01285 860006 info@dominicwinter.co.uk www.dominicwinter.co.uk

EAL The Exeter Antique Lighting Co., Cellar 15, The Quay, Exeter, Devon, EX2 4AP Tel: 01392 490848 or 07702 969438 www.antiquelightingcompany.com

EAn Era Antiques ikar66@aol.com

Ech † Echoes, 650a Halifax Road, Eastwood, Todmorden, Yorkshire, OL14 6DW Tel: 01706 817505

EE Empire Exchange, 1 Newton Street, Piccadilly, Manchester Tel: 0161 2364445

EG Elizabeth Gibbons Antique Textiles, By appointment only Tel: 020 7352 1615/ 01989 750243 or 07754 189842 elizabeth@egantiquetextiles.co.uk

EMH Eat My Handbag Bitch, 37 Drury Lane, London, WC2B 5RR Tel: 020 7836 0830 gallery@eatmyhandbagbitch.co.uk www.eatmyhandbagbitch.co.uk

ET † Early Technology, Monkton House, Old Craighall, Musselburgh, Midlothian, Scotland, EH21 8SF Tel: 0131 665 5753 or 07831 106768 michael.bennett-levy@virgin.net www.earlytech.com www.rare78s.com www.tvhistory.tv

EV Marlene Evans, Headrow Antiques Centre, Headrow Centre, Leeds, Yorkshire Tel: 0113 245 5344

F&F Fenwick & Fenwick, 88–90 High Street, Broadway, Worcestershire, WR12 7AJ Tel: 01386 853227/841724

Fai Fair Finds Antiques, Rait Village Antiques Centre, Rait, Perthshire, Scotland, PH2 7RT Tel: 01821 670379

FC First Call, Module B2, Enterprise Point, Melbourne Street, Brighton, East Sussex, BN2 3LH Tel: 01273 202201

FD Frank Dux Antiques, 33 Belvedere, Bath, Somerset, BA1 5HR Tel: 01225 312367

FFAP Freeman's Fine Art Of Philadelphia Inc., Samuel T. Freeman & Co., 1808 Chestnut Street, Philadelphia, PA 19103, U.S.A. Tel: 215 563 9275 www.freemansauctions.com *Photographer: Elizabeth Field*

FLDA Fieldings Auctioneers Ltd, Mill Race Lane, Stourbridge, West Midlands, DY8 1JN Tel: 01384 444140 info@fieldingsauctioneers.co.uk www.fieldingsauctioneers.co.uk

FOF Fossack & Furkle, P.O. Box 733, Abington, Cambridgeshire, CB1 6BF Tel: 01223 894296 or 07939078719 fossack@btopenworld.com www.fossackandfurkle.freeservers.com

FRa Fraser's, 399 Strand, London, WC2R OLX Tel: 020 7836 9325/836 8444 sales@frasersautographs.co.uk www.frasersautographs.com

FRD Fragile Design, 8 The Custard Factory, Digbeth, Birmingham, West Midlands, B9 4AA Tel: 0121 693 1001 info@fragiledesign.com www.fragiledesign.com

FREE Freeforms info@freeformsusa.com www.freeformsusa.com

FST Frank Scott-Tomlin, The Old Ironmongers Antiques Centre, 5 Burford St, Lechlade, Gloucestershire, GL7 3AP Tel: 01367 252397 frank@scott-tomlin.fsnet.co.uk

G(B) Gorringes Auction Galleries, Terminus Road, Bexhill-on-Sea, East Sussex, TN39 3LR Tel: 01424 212994 bexhill@gorringes.co.uk www.gorringes.co.uk

G(L) Gorringes inc Julian Dawson, 15 North Street, Lewes, East Sussex, BN7 2PD Tel: 01273 478221 clientservices@gorringes.co.uk www.gorringes.co.uk

G&CC † The Goss & Crested China Club & Museum, incorporating Milestone Publications, 62 Murray Road, Horndean, Hampshire, PO8 9JL Tel: (023) 9259 7440 info@gosschinaclub.demon.co.uk www.gosscrestedchina.co.uk

GaL Gazelles Ltd, Stratton Audley, Ringwood Road, Stoney Cross, Lyndhurst, Hampshire, SO43 7GN Tel: 023 8081 1610 allan@gazelles.co.uk www.gazelles.co.uk

GAU Becca Gauldie Antiques, The Old School, Glendoick, Perthshire, Scotland, PH2 7NR Tel: 01738 860 870 or 07770 741 636 webuy@scottishantiques.freeserve.co.uk

GAZE Thomas Wm Gaze & Son, Diss Auction Rooms, Roydon Road, Diss, Norfolk, IP22 4LN Tel: 01379 650306 sales@dissauctionrooms.co.uk www.twgaze.com

GBr Geoffrey Breeze Antiques Tel: 077 404 35844 www.antiquecanes.co.uk

GEO Georgian Antiques, 10 Pattinson Street, Leith Links, Edinburgh, Scotland, EH6 7HF Tel: 0131 553 7286 info@georgianantiques.net JDixon7098@aol.com www.georgianantiques.net

GEOH Geoff Holden Tel: 020 8891 6525 Geoff.Holden@ukonline.co.uk

Getc Glass etc, 18–22 Rope Walk, Rye, East Sussex, TN31 7NA decanterman@freezone.co.uk www.decanterman.com

GLEN Glenda - Antique Dolls, A18–A19 Grays Antique Market, Davies Mews, London, W1Y 2LP Tel: 020 8367 2441/020 7629 7034 glenda@glenda-antiquedolls.com www.glenda-antiquedolls.com

GLH Glasshouse info@vmglasshouse.com www.vmglasshouse.com *Text and images courtesy of Damon Crain © 2006*

GM † Philip Knighton, 1c South Street, Wellington, Somerset, TA21 8NR Tel: 01823 661618 philip.knighton@btopenworld.com

GMI Grimes Militaria, 13 Lower Park Row, Bristol, Somerset, BS1 5BN Tel: 0117 929 8205

GOv ⊞ Glazed Over Tel: 0773 2789114

GSA ⊞ Graham Smith Antiques, 83 Fern Avenue, Jesmond, Newcastle upon Tyne, Tyne & Wear, NE2 2RA Tel: 0191 281 5065 gsmithantiques@aol.com

GTH Greenslade Taylor Hunt Fine Art, Magdelene House, Church Square, Taunton, Somerset, TA1 1SB Tel: 01823 332525

GTM ⊞ Gloucester Toy Mart, Ground Floor, Antique Centre, Severn Road, Old Docks, Gloucester, GL1 2LE Tel: 07973 768452

GWRA † GWR Auctions Tel: 01684 773487 or 01386 760109 master@gwra.co.uk www.gwra.co.uk

H&G ⊞ Hope & Glory, 131A Kensington Church Street, London, W8 7LP Tel: 020 7727 8424

H&LM ⊞ hi+lo modern www.hiandlomodern.com

HAD Henry Adams Auctioneers, Baffins Hall, Baffins Lane, Chichester, West Sussex, PO19 1UA Tel: 01243 532223 enquiries@henryadamsfineart.co.uk

HAL ⊞† John & Simon Haley, 89 Northgate, Halifax, Yorkshire, HX1 1XF Tel: 01422 822148/360434 toysandbanks@aol.com

Hal Halls Fine Art Auctions, Welsh Bridge, Shrewsbury, Shropshire, SY3 8LA Tel: 01743 231212

HANS ⊞ Hans's Vintage Fountain Pens Tel: 01323 765398 or 07850 771183 HSeiringer@aol.com www.hanspens.com

HaR ⊞ Mr A. Harris Tel: 020 8906 8151 or 07956 146083

HARP ⊞ Harpers Jewellers Ltd, 2/6 Minster Gates, York, YO1 7HL Tel: 01904 632634 york@harpersjewellers.co.uk www.vintage-watches.co.uk

HCE Hazle Ceramics Auction, Hazle Ceramics Limited, 33–35 Barleylands Craft Centre, Barleylands Road, Billericay, Essex, CM11 2UD Tel: 01268 270892 hazle@hazle.com www.hazle.com

HeA ⊞ Heanor Antiques Centre, 1–3 Ilkeston Road, Heanor, Derbyshire, DE75 7AE Tel: 01773 531181/762783 sales@heanorantiquescentre.co.uk www.heanorantiquescentre.co.uk

HEM ⊞ Hemswell Antique Centre, Caenby Corner Estate, Hemswell Cliff, Gainsborough, Lincolnshire, DN21 5TJ Tel: 01427 668389 info@hemswell-antiques.com www.hemswell-antiques.com

Her Heritage Auction Galleries, 3500 Maple Avenue, 17th Floor, Dallas, Texas 75219-3941, U.S.A. Tel: 214 528 3500/800 872 6467 bid@HeritageAuctions.com www.HeritageAuctions.com

HEW ⊞ Muir Hewitt Art Deco Originals, Halifax Antiques Centre, Queens Road Mills, Queens Road/Gibbet Street, Halifax, Yorkshire, HX1 4LR Tel: 01422 347377 muir.hewitt@virgin.net muir.hewitt@btconnect.com www.muirhewitt.com

HIGG ⊞ Katherine Higgins

HIL ⊞ Mr & Mrs Hill

HO ⊞ Houghton Antiques, Houghton, Cambridgeshire Tel: 01480 461887 or 07803 716842

HOB ⊞ Hobday Toys Tel: 01895 834348

Holl **See HOLL**

HOLL Holloway's, 49 Parsons Street, Banbury, Oxfordshire, OX16 5NB Tel: 01295 817777 enquiries@hollowaysauctioneers.co.uk www.hollowaysauctioneers.co.uk

HOM ⊞ Home & Colonial, 134 High Street, Berkhamsted, Hertfordshire, HP4 3AT Tel: 01442 877007 homeandcolonial@btinternet.com www.homeandcolonial.co.uk

HOP ⊞ The Antique Garden, Grosvenor Garden Centre, Wrexham Road, Belgrave, Chester, CH4 9EB Tel: 01244 629191/07976 539 990 antigard@btopenworld.com www.antique-garden.co.uk

HRQ ⊞ Harlequin Antiques, 79–81 Mansfield Road, Daybrook, Nottingham, NG5 6BH Tel: 0115 9674 590 sales@antiquepine.net www.antiquepine.net

HSR ⊞ High Street Retro, 39 High Street, Old Town, Hastings, East Sussex, TN34 3ER Tel: 01424 460068

HUM ⊞ Humbleyard Fine Art, Unit 32, Admiral Vernon Arcade, Portobello Road, London, W11 2DY Tel: 01362 637793 or 07836 349416

HUN ⊞ The Country Seat, Huntercombe Manor Barn, Henley-on-Thames, Oxfordshire, RG9 5RY Tel: 01491 641349 ferry&clegg@thecountryseat.com www.thecountryseat.com

HUX ⊞ David Huxtable, Saturdays at: Portobello Road, Basement Stall 11/12, 288 Westbourne Grove, London, W11 Tel: 07710 132200 david@huxtins.com www.huxtins.com

HYD Hy Duke & Son, The Dorchester Fine Art Salerooms, Weymouth Avenue, Dorchester, Dorset, DT1 1QS Tel: 01305 265080 www.dukes-auctions.com

IQ ⊞ Cloud Cuckooland, 12 Fore Street, Mevagissey, Cornwall, PL26 6UQ Tel: 01726 842364 or 07973 135906 Paul@cloudcuckooland.biz www.cloudcuckooland.biz

ITB ⊞ Inchmartine Tool Bazaar, Inchmartine House, Inchture, Perth, Scotland, PH14 9QQ Tel: 01828 686096 andrew@toolbazaar.freeserve.co.uk www.toolbazaar.co.uk

IW ⊞ Islwyn Watkins, Offa's Dyke Antique Centre, 4 High Street, Knighton, Powys, Wales, LD7 1AT Tel: 01547 520145

J&J ⊞ J & J's, Paragon Antiquities Antiques & Collectors Market, 3 Bladud Buildings, The Paragon, Bath, Somerset, BA1 5LS Tel: 01225 463715

J&S ⊞ J.R. & S.J. Symes of Bristol Tel: 0117 9501074

JAA Jackson's International Auctioneers & Appraisers of Fine Art & Antiques, 2229 Lincoln Street, Cedar Falls, IA 50613, U.S.A. Tel: 319 277 2256/800 665 6743 sandim@jacksonsauctions.com www.jacksonsauction.com

JAd — James Adam & Sons, 26 St Stephen's Green, Dublin 2, Republic of Ireland Tel: 3531 676 0261 www.jamesadam.ie/

JAM — Jam Jar Tel: 078896 17593

JB7 — James Bond Toys Tel: 01942 511912/07788 596077 bond@007lotus.co.uk www.jamesbondtoys.co.uk

JBB — Jessie's Button Box, Bartlett Street Antique Centre, Bath, Somerset, BA1 5DY Tel: 0117 929 9065

JCos — J. Costello Tel: 02476 269905 johncost@ntlworld.com

JDJ — James D. Julia, Inc., P.O. Box 830, Rte.201, Skowhegan Road, Fairfield, ME 04937, U.S.A. Tel: 207 453 7125 jjulia@juliaauctions.com www.juliaauctions.com

JEG — John English Gifts, 6 Prices Arcade (closed during Feb), Picadilly, London, SW1Y 6DS Tel: 020 7437 2082 brian@johnenglishgifts.com www.johnenglishgifts.com

JG — Just Glass, Cross House, Market Place, Alston, Cumbria, CA9 3HS Tel: 01434 381263 or 0783 3994948

JMC — J & M Collectables Tel: 01580 891657 or 077135 23573 jandmcollectables@tinyonline.co.uk

JNic — John Nicholson, The Auction Rooms, Longfield, Midhurst Road, Fernhurst, Surrey, GU27 3HA Tel: 01428 653727 sales@johnnicholsons.com

JSG — James Strang Tel: 01334 472 566 or 07950 490088 james@mod-i.com www.mod-i.com

JTB — Jim Call, Broomfield, Colorado, U.S.A. tribalam@all2easy.net www.3Gsmilkbottles.com www.milkbottleworld.com

JUN † Junktion, The Old Railway Station, New Bolingbroke, Boston, Lincolnshire, PE22 7LB Tel: 01205 480087 or 07836 345491 junktionantiques@hotmail.com

JWK — Jane Wicks Kitchenalia, 'Country Ways', Strand Quay, Rye, East Sussex, TN31 7AY Tel: 01424 713635 or 07754 308269 janes_kitchen@hotmail.com

KA — Kingston Antiques Centre, 29–31 London Road, Kingston-upon-Thames, Surrey, KT2 6ND Tel: 020 8549 2004/3839 enquiries@kingstonantiquescentre.co.uk www.kingstonantiquescentre.co.uk

KBE — Kit Barry Ephemera & Supplies, 74 Cotton Mill Hill, #A252, Brattleboro, VT 05301, U.S.A.

KKN — The Knick Knack Nook, W. Pratt Boulevard, Chicago, IL 60626, U.S.A. Tel: 773 274 9511 www.knickknacknook.com

KLH — KLH Collects Tel: 01502 582572

KMG — Karen Michelle Guido, Karen Michelle Antique Tiles, PMB 243, 1835 US 1 South #119, St Augustine, FL 32084, U.S.A. Tel: 904 471 3226 karen@antiquetiles.com www.antiquetiles.com

KTA — Kerry Taylor Auctions, in Association with Sotheby's, St George Street Gallery, Sotheby's New Bond Street, London, W1A 2AA Tel: 07785 734337 fashion.textiles@sothebys.com

KvW — Kevin Ward Tel: 01733 765548

L&E — Locke & England, 18 Guy Street, Leamington Spa, Warwickshire, CV32 4RT Tel: 01926 889100 info@leauction.co.uk www.auctions-online.com/locke

LA&I — Lewis Antiques & Interiors Tel: 07764 576106 sandie.lewis@blueyonder.co.uk

LaF — La Femme Tel: 07971 844279 jewels@joancorder.freeserve.co.uk

LAS — Reasons to be Cheerful, Georgian Village, 30–31 Islington Green, London, N18 DU Tel: 0207 281 4600

LAY — David Lay, (ASVA), Auction House, Alverton, Penzance, Cornwall, TR18 4RE Tel: 01736 361414

LBM — La Belle Maman

LBr — Lynda Brine, By Appointment only lyndabrine@yahoo.co.uk www.scentbottlesandsmalls.co.uk

LeB — Le Boudoir Collectables, The Basement, George Street Antique Centre, 8 Edgar Buildings, Bath, Somerset, BA1 2EE Tel: 01225 311061 or 07974 918630 www.le-boudoir-online.com

Lim — Limelight Movie Art, N13–16 Antiquarius Antiques Centre, 131–141 King's Road, Chelsea, London, SW3 4PJ Tel: 01273 206919 info@limelightmovieart.com www.limelightmovieart.com

LLD — Lewis & Lewis Deco Tel: 07739 904681 lewis_robin@hotmail.com

LSA — Long Street Antiques, Stamford House, 14 Long Street, Tetbury, Gloucestershire, GL8 8AQ Tel: 01666 500850 longstantiques@aol.com www.longstreetantiques.co.uk

LT — Louis Taylor Auctioneers & Valuers, Britannia House, 10 Town Road, Hanley, Stoke on Trent, Staffordshire, ST1 2QG Tel: 01782 214111

LUNA — Luna, 23 George Street, Nottingham, NG1 3BH Tel: 0115 924 3267 info@luna-online.co.uk www.luna-online.co.uk

M&C — M&C Cards, Unit 30/32 Antique Centre, Severn Road, Gloucester, GL1 2LE Tel: 01452 506361

MA&I — Moore, Allen & Innocent, The Salerooms, Norcote, Cirencester, Gloucestershire, GL7 5RH Tel: 01285 646050 fineart@mooreallen.co.uk www.mooreallen.co.uk

Mal(O) **See MAL(O)**

MAL(O) — Mallams, Bocardo House, 24 St Michael's Street, Oxford, OX1 2EB Tel: 01865 241358 oxford@mallams.co.uk

MARK ⊞† 20th Century Marks, Whitegates, Rectory Road, Little Burstead, Near Billericay, Essex, CM12 9TR Tel: 01268 411 000 or 07831 778992 info@20thcenturymarks.co.uk www.20thcenturymarks.co.uk

MCA ⚒ Mervyn Carey, Twysden Cottage, Scullsgate, Benenden, Cranbrook, Kent, TN17 4LD Tel: 01580 240283

MCS ⊞† Memories Collectors Shop, 130–132 Brent Street, Hendon, London, NW4 2DR Tel: 020 8203 1500 dave@mempics.demon.co.uk www.memoriespostcards.co.uk

Mel ⊞ Melodies Memories, 2595 FM 275 S, Cumby, TX 75433, U.S.A.

MICH ⊞ Michael Webb

MILI ⊞ Militaryman Tel: 01473 274367 militaryman@peace41.fsnet.co.uk www.dinkycollector.com

MINN ⊞ Geoffrey T. Minnis, Hastings Antique Centre, 59–61 Norman Road, St Leonards-on-Sea, East Sussex, TN38 0EG Tel: 01424 428561

Mit ⚒ Mitchells, Fairfield House, Station Road, Cockermouth, Cumbria, CA13 9PY Tel: 01900 827800 info@mitchellsfineart.com

MN ⚒ Mastro Auctions, 7900 South Madison Street, Burr Ridge, Illinois 60527, U.S.A. Tel: 630 472 1200 jmarren@mastroauctions.com www.mastroauctions.com

Mo ⊞ Mr Moore

MRA ⊞ Millroyale Antiques Tel: 01902 375006 www.whiteladiesantiques.com

MRW ⊞ Malcolm Welch Antiques, Wild Jebbett, Pudding Bag Lane, Thurlaston, Nr Rugby, Warwickshire, CV23 9JZ Tel: 01788 810 616 www.rb33.co.uk

MSB ⊞ Marilynn and Sheila Brass, P.O. Box 380503, Cambridge, MA 02238-0503, U.S.A. shelmardesign1@aol.com

MSh ⊞ Manfred Schotten, 109 High Street, Burford, Oxfordshire, OX18 4RG Tel: 01993 822302 sport@schotten.com www.schotten.com

MTB ⊞ The Magic Toy Box, 210 Havant Road, Drayton, Portsmouth, Hampshire, PO6 2EH Tel: 02392 221307 magictoybox@btinternet.com www.sindy-dolls.co.uk

MTM ⊞ More than Music, P.O. Box 2809, Eastbourne, East Sussex, BN21 2EA Tel: 01323 649778 morethnmus@aol.com www.mtmglobal.com

MTMC § Muffin the Mule Collectors' Club, 12 Woodland Close, Woodford Green, Essex, IG8 0QH www.Muffin-the-Mule.com

MUR ⊞ Murray Cards (International) Ltd, 51 Watford Way, Hendon Central, London, NW4 3JH Tel: 020 8202 5688 murraycards@ukbusiness.com www.murraycard.com/

MURR ⊞ Murrays' Antiques & Collectables Tel: 01202 823870

MYS ⊞ Antique Mystique Tel: 308 532 3404 www.antiquemystique.com

N ⚒ Neales, Nottingham Salerooms, 192 Mansfield Road, Nottingham, NG1 3HU Tel: 0115 962 4141 fineart@neales-auctions.com www.dnfa.com/nottingham

NAR ⊞† Colin Narbeth & Son Ltd, 20 Cecil Court, Leicester Square, London, WC2N 4HE Tel: 020 7379 6975 Colin.Narbeth@btinternet.com www.colin-narbeth.com

NAW ⊞ Newark Antiques Warehouse Ltd, Old Kelham Road, Newark, Nottinghamshire, NG24 1BX Tel: 01636 674869/07974 429185 enquiries@newarkantiques.co.uk www.newarkantiques.co.uk

NGL ⊞ Noble Gold Ltd Tel: 01275 464152 james.cole1@btinternet.com

NOA ⚒ New Orleans Auction Galleries, Inc., 801 Magazine Street, AT 510 Julia, New Orleans, Louisiana 70130, U.S.A. Tel: 504 566 1849 www.neworleansauction.com

NOS ⊞ Nostalgia and Comics, 14–16 Smallbrook, Queensway, City Centre, Birmingham, West Midlands, B5 4EN Tel: 0121 643 0143

NP ⊞ The Neville Pundole Gallery, 8A & 9 The Friars, Canterbury, Kent, CT1 2AS Tel: 01227 453471 neville@pundole.co.uk www.pundole.co.uk

NW ⊞ Nigel Williams Rare Books, 25 Cecil Court, London, WC2N 4EZ Tel: 020 7836 7757 nigel@nigelwilliams.com www.nigelwilliams.com

NWE ⊞ North Wilts. Exporters, Farm Hill House, Brinkworth, Wiltshire, SN15 5AJ Tel: 01666 510876 or 07836 260730 mike@northwilts.demon.co.uk www.northwiltsantiqueexporters.com

OACC ⊞ Otford Antiques & Collectors Centre, 26–28 High Street, Otford, Kent, TN14 5PQ Tel: 01959 522025 info@otfordantiques.co.uk www.otfordantiques.co.uk

OAK ⊞ Oakwood Antiques Tel: 01204 304309 or 07813 386415

OCA ⊞ The Old Cinema, 160 Chiswick High Road, London, W4 1PR Tel: 020 8995 4166 theoldcinema@antiques-uk.co.uk www.antiques-uk.co.uk/theoldcinema

OD ⊞ Offa's Dyke Antique Centre, 4 High Street, Knighton, Powys, Wales, LD7 1AT Tel: 01547 528635/520145

OH ⊞ Old Hat, 66 Fulham High Road, London, SW6 3LQ Tel: 020 7610 6558

OIA ⊞ The Old Ironmongers Antiques Centre, 5 Burford Street, Lechlade, Gloucestershire, GL7 3AP Tel: 01367 252397

OLD ⊞ Oldnautibits, P.O. Box 67, Langport, Somerset, TA10 9WJ Tel: 01458 241816 or 07947 277833 geoff.pringle@oldnautibits.com www.oldnautibits.com

ONS ⚒† Onslow Auctions Ltd, The Coach House, Manor Road, Stourpaine, Dorset, DT8 8TQ Tel: 01258 488838

OTA ⊞† On The Air, The Vintage Technology Centre, The Highway, Hawarden, (Nr Chester), Deeside, Cheshire, CH5 3DN Tel: 01244 530300 or 07778 767734 www.vintageradio.co.uk

OTB ⊞† The Old Tackle Box, P.O. Box 55, High Street, Cranbrook, Kent, TN17 3ZU Tel: 01580 713979 or 07729 278 293 tackle.box@virgin.net

OW **See STa**

PASC ⊞ Pascoe & Company, 253 SW 22nd Avenue, Miami, Florida 33135, U.S.A. Tel: 800 872 0195/305 643 2550 mike@pascoeandcompany.com www.pascoeandcompany.com

PASM ⊞ Pastimes (OMRS), 22 Lower Park Row, Bristol, Gloucestershire, BS1 5BN Tel: 0117 929 9330

PAST ⊞ Past Caring Tel: 01924 848119 chrisbates@lineone.net

PEPE ⊞ Pepe Tozzo pepe@tozzo.co.uk

PEZ ⊞ Alan Pezaro, 62a West Street, Dorking, Surrey, RH4 1BS Tel: 01306 743661

PF 🔨 Peter Francis, Curiosity Sale Room, 19 King Street, Carmarthen, Wales, SA31 1BH Tel: 01267 233456 nigel@peterfrancis.co.uk www.peterfrancis.co.uk

PFK 🔨 Penrith Farmers' & Kidd's plc, Skirsgill Salerooms, Penrith, Cumbria, CA11 0DN Tel: 01768 890781 info@pfkauctions.co.uk www.pfkauctions.co.uk

PHa ⊞ Peter Harrington, 100 Fulham Road, London, SW3 6HS Tel: 020 7591 0220/0330

PI ⊞ Pure Imagination, P.O. Box 140, South Shields, Tyne & Wear, NE33 3WU Tel: 0191 4169090 or 0771 5054919 www.pureimaginations.co.uk

PICA ⊞ Piccadilly Antiques, 280 High Street, Batheaston, Bath, Somerset, BA1 7RA Tel: 01225 851494 or 07785 966132 piccadillyantiques@ukonline.co.uk

Pin ⊞ Gazzas Pinballs Tel: 07753 949887 garypound@go.com www.gazzaspinballs.co.uk

PMa ⊞ PennyMachines.co.uk, 50 Charlemont Road, Walsall, West Midlands, WS5 3NQ Tel: 01922 621888 david@pennymachines.co.uk

POI ⊞ Sophie Tarleton, 25 Meynell Crescent, London, E9 7AS Tel: 07973 412131 srtarleton@yahoo.co.uk www.poikilia.co.uk

POL ⊞ Politico Book Shop Tel: 0870 850 1110 bookstore@politicos.co.uk www.politicos.co.uk

POLL ⊞ Pollyanna, 34 High Street, Arundel, West Sussex, BN18 9AB Tel: 01903 885198 or 07949903457

POP ⊞ James Hardwick Tel: 07768 667 986 popshopuk@aol.com

POS § Postcard Club of Great Britain, c/o Mrs D. Brennan, 34 Harper House, St James Crescent, London, SW9 7LW Tel: 020 7771 9404 drenebrennan@yahoo.co.uk

Pott 🔨 Potteries Specialist Auctions, 271 Waterloo Road, Cobridge, Stoke on Trent, Staffordshire, ST6 3HR Tel: 01782 286622 www.potteriesauctions.com

POTT **See Pott**

PPH ⊞ Period Picnic Hampers Tel: 0115 937 2934

PrB ⊞ Pretty Bizarre, 170 High Street, Deal, Kent, CT14 6BQ Tel: 07973 794537

PROP ⊞ The Prop Store of London, Great House Farm, Chenies, Rickmansworth, Hertfordshire, WD3 6EP Tel: 01494 766 485 steve.lane@propstore.co.uk www.propstore.co.uk

PSH ⊞ phil-comics auctions, P.O. Box 3433, Brighton, East Sussex, BN50 9JA Tel: 01273 673462 or 07739 844703 phil@phil-comics.com www.phil-comics.com

Q&C ⊞ Q & C Militaria, 22 Suffolk Road, Cheltenham, Gloucestershire, GL50 2AQ Tel: 01242 519815 or 07778 613977 qcmilitaria@btconnect.com www.qcmilitaria.com

Qua ⊞ Quadrille, 146 Portobello Road, London, W11 2DZ Tel: 01923 829079/020 7727 9860 (sat only)

R2G ⊞ Retro2Go, P.O. Box 1171, Sault Ste, Marie, MI 49783, U.S.A.

RB ⊞ Retrobrick www.retrobrick.com

RdV ⊞ Roger de Ville Antiques, Bakewell Antiques Centre, King Street, Bakewell, Derbyshire, DE45 1DZ Tel: 01629 812496 or 07798 793857 contact@rogerdeville.co.uk www.rogerdeville.co.uk

RETC ⊞ Retro Centre Tel: 0118 950 7224 al@retro-centre.co.uk www.retro-centre.co.uk

RETO ⊞ www.retroselect.com

RETRO **See RETO**

ROA ⊞ Roding Arts, Elsie Cottage, Church Street, Church End, Great Dunmow, Essex, CM6 2AD Tel: 01371 859359 or 07808 933862

ROK(B) ⊞ Rokit Ltd, 101 & 107 Brick Lane, London, E1 6SE Tel: 020 7375 3864

ROS 🔨 Rosebery's Fine Art Ltd, 74/76 Knights Hill, London, SE27 0JD Tel: 020 8761 2522 auctions@roseberys.co.uk

RS ⊞ Racing Stuff, P.O. Box 127, Bicester, Oxfordshire, OX26 2WL Tel: 07779 925537 www.racingstuff.piczo.com

RTo 🔨 Rupert Toovey & Co Ltd, Spring Gardens, Washington, West Sussex, RH20 3BS Tel: 01903 891955 auctions@rupert-toovey.com www.rupert-toovey.com

RTT ⊞ Rin Tin Tin, 34 North Road, Brighton, East Sussex, BN1 1YB Tel: 01273 672424 rick@rintintin.freeserve.co.uk

RTW ⊞ Richard Twort Tel: 01934 641900 or 07711 939789

RUSK Ruskin Decorative Arts,
5 Talbot Court, Stow-on-the-Wold,
Cheltenham, Gloucestershire,
GL54 1DP Tel: 01451 832254
william.anne@ruskindecarts.co.uk

RUSS Russells
Tel: 023 8061 6664

RW Robin Wareham

S&D S&D Postcards,
Bartlett Street Antique Centre,
5–10 Bartlett Street, Bath, Somerset, BA1 2QZ
Tel: 07979 506415 wndvd@aol.com

SA Sporting Antiques, 9 Church St, St Ives,
Cambridgeshire, PE27 6DG
Tel: 01480 463891 or 07831 274774
johnlambden@sportingantiques.co.uk
www.sportingantiques.co.uk

SAA Scottish Antique and Arts Centre, Carse of
Cambus, Doune, Perthshire, Scotland,
FK16 6HG Tel: 01786 841203
sales@scottish-antiques.com
www.scottish-antiques.com

SAAC Scottish Antique and Arts Centre, Abernyte,
Perthshire, Scotland, PH14 9SJ
Tel: 01828 686401
sales@scottish-antiques.com
www.scottish-antiques.com

SAFF Michael Saffell Antiques, 3 Walcot Buildings,
London Road, Bath, Somerset, BA1 6AD
Tel: 01225 315857
michael.saffell@virgin.net

SAI J. Sainsbury Plc
Tel: 0800 636 262

SAT The Swan at Tetsworth, High Street, Tetsworth,
Nr Thame, Oxfordshire, OX9 7AB
Tel: 01844 281777
antiques@theswan.co.uk
www.theswan.co.uk

SBL Twentieth Century Style
Tel: 01822 614831

SCH Scherazade
Tel: 01708 641117 or
07855 383996
scherz1@yahoo.com

Scot Scottow Antiques, Green Street Green,
Orpington, Kent Tel: 07860 795909

SDD Sandra D. Deas
Tel: 01333 360 214 or 07713 897 482

SDR Spinna Disc Records, 2B Union Street,
Aldershot, Hants, GU11 1EG
Tel: 01252 327261
sales@spinnadiscrecords.com
www.spinnadiscrecords.com

SEK Bukowskis, Arsenalsgaten 4, Stockholm, Sweden
Tel: 8614 0800
Fax: 8611 4674
info@bukowskis.se
www.bukowskis.se

SHa Shapiro & Co, Stand 380,
Gray's Antique Market, 58 Davies Street,
London, W1Y 5LP
Tel: 020 7491 2710 or 07768 439777

SHER Sherwood Golf Antiques
Tel: 07968 848448
sherwoodgolf@btinternet.com

SK Skinner Inc., The Heritage On The Garden,
63 Park Plaza, Boston, MA 02116, U.S.A.
Tel: 617 350 5400
www.skinnerinc.com

SMI † Skip & Janie Smithson Antiques
Tel: 01754 810265 or 07831 399180
smithsonantiques@hotmail.com

SOR † Soldiers of Rye, Mint Arcade, 71 The Mint, Rye,
East Sussex, TN31 7EW Tel: 01797 225952
rameses@supanet.com
www.rameses.supanet.com

SOU Source, 11 Claverton Buildings, High Street,
Widcombe, Bath, BA2 4LD
Tel: 01225 469200/07831 734134
shop@source-antiques.co.uk
www.source-antiques.co.uk

SPF Scarborough Fine Arts,
Unit 2, Grange Industrial Estate, Albion Street,
Southwick, West Sussex,
BN42 4EN Tel: 01273 870371
info@scarboroughfinearts.co.uk
www.scarboroughfinearts.co.uk

SpM The Girl Can't Help It!, Sparkle Moore & Cad
Van Swankster, Alfies Antique Market,
G100 & G116 Ground Floor,
13–25 Church Street, Marylebone,
London, NW8 8DT Tel: 020 7724 8984 or
07958 515614
sparkle.moore@virgin.net
www.sparklemoore.com

SPRI Mrs V. Sprigg

SPUR Spurrier-Smith Antiques,
39 Church Street, Ashbourne, Derbyshire,
DE6 1AJ Tel: 01335 342198/343669
ivan@spurrier-smith.fsnet.co.uk

SRH Sally's Rocking Horses, Unit 1,
The Fox Building,
Severn Road, Welshpool, Powys, Wales,
SY21 7AZ Tel: 01938 558075
sally@sallysrockinghorses.com

SSPP Stew & Simm Period Phones
Tel: 07952 836404
stewart.sutton772@ntlworld.com

SSS Susan's Selections, 2125 Tiburon Drive,
Carrollton, Texas 75006, U.S.A.

STa Starbase-Alpha,
Unit 19–20, Rumford Shopping Halls,
Market Place, Rumford, Essex, RM1 3AT
Tel: 01708 765633
starbasealpha1@aol.com
www.starbasealpha.cjb.net

StB Steven Bishop Antiques & Decorative Arts
Tel: 07761563095
meridian34all@btinternet.com
www.meridiangallery.co.uk

STBL Steve Blackham
Tel: 01302 849256

STE Stevenson Brothers, The Workshop, Ashford
Road, Bethersden, Ashford, Kent, TN26 3AP
Tel: 01233 820363
sales@stevensonbros.com
www.stevensonbros.com

SUW Sue Wilde at Wildewear Tel: 01395 577966
compacts@wildewear.co.uk
www.wildewear.co.uk

SWB ⊞† Sweetbriar Gallery Ltd, 29 Beechview Road, Kingsley, Cheshire, WA6 8DF Tel: 01928 788225 sales@sweetbriar.co.uk www.sweetbriar.co.uk

SWO Sworders, 14 Cambridge Road, Stansted Mountfitchet, Essex, CM24 8BZ Tel: 01279 817778 auctions@sworder.co.uk www.sworder.co.uk

TA ⊞ Tintern Antiques, The Olde Bakehouse, Monmouth Road, Tintern, Wales, NP16 6SE Tel: 01291 689705

TAC ⊞ Tenterden Antiques Centre, 66–66A High Street, Tenterden, Kent, TN30 6AU Tel: 01580 765655/765885

TASV ⊞ Tenterden Antiques & Silver Vaults, 66 High Street, Tenterden, Kent, TN30 6AU Tel: 01580 765885

TB ⊞ Millicent Safro, Tender Buttons, 143 E.62nd Street, New York, NY10021, U.S.A. Tel: 212 758 7004 *Author of BUTTONS*

TDG ⊞ The Design Gallery 1850–1950, 5 The Green, Westerham, Kent, TN16 1AS Tel: 01959 561234 or 07974 322858 sales@thedesigngalleryuk.com www.thedesigngalleryuk.com

TEA § Totally Teapots, The Novelty Teapot Collectors Club, Vince McDonald, Euxton, Chorley, Lancashire, PR7 6EY Tel: 01257 450366 vince@totallyteapots.com www.totallyteapots.com

TIN ⊞ Tin Tin Collectables, G38–42 Alfies's Antique Market, 13–25 Church Street, Marylebone, London, NW8 8DT Tel: 020 7258 1305 leslie@tintincollectables.com www.tintincollectables.com

TL ⊞† Telephone Lines Ltd, 304 High Street, Cheltenham, Gloucestershire, GL50 3JF Tel: 01242 583699 info@telephonelines.net www.telephonelines.net

TMA Tring Market Auctions, The Market Premises, Brook Street, Tring, Hertfordshire, HP23 5EF Tel: 01442 826446 sales@tringmarketauctions.co.uk www.tringmarketauctions.co.uk

TMa ⊞ Tin Man, 9 Church St, St Ives, Cambridgeshire, PE27 6DG Tel: 01480 463891 or 07831 274774 johnlambden@sportingantiques.co.uk www.sportingantiques.co.uk

TNS ⊞ Toy's N Such Toy's - Antiques & Collectables, 437 Dawson Street, Sault Sainte Marie, MI 49783-2119, U.S.A. Tel: 906 635 0356

TOL ⊞ Turn On Lighting, Antique Lighting Specialists, 116/118 Islington High St, Camden Passage, Islington, London, N1 8EG Tel: 020 7359 7616

TOP ⊞ The Top Banana Antiques Mall, 1 New Church Street, Tetbury, Gloucestershire, GL8 8DS Tel: 0871 288 1102 info@topbananaantiques.com www.topbananaantiques.com

TOT ⊞ Totem, 168 Stoke Newington, Church Street, London, N16 0JL Tel: 020 7275 0234 sales@totemrecords.com www.totemrecords.com

TRA ⊞ Tramps, 8 Market Place, Tuxford, Newark, Nottinghamshire, NG22 0LL Tel: 01777 872 543 info@trampsuk.com

Tus ⊞† Tussie Mussies, The Old Stables, 2b East Cross, Tenterden, Kent, TN30 6AD Tel: 01580 766244 tussiemussies@btinternet.com www.tussiemussies.co.uk

TWI ⊞† Twinkled, 1.5 Kingly Court, Carnaby Street, London, W1B 5PW Tel: 020 7734 1978/ 07940 471569/07940 471574 info@twinkled.net www.twinkled.net

UD ⊞ Upstairs Downstairs, 40 Market Place, Devizes, Wiltshire, SN10 1JG Tel: 01380 730266 or 07974 074220 devizesantiques@btconnect.com

VAN ⊞ Vanessa Parker Rare Books, The Old Rectory, Polranny, Achill Sound, Co Mayo, Republic of Ireland Tel: (098) 20984 or (087) 2339221

VAU Vault Auctions Ltd, P.O. Box 257, South Norwood, London, SE25 6JN Tel: 01342 300 900 contact@vaultauctions.com www.vaultauctions.com

VDA ⊞ Vetta Decorative Arts, P.O. Box 247, Oxford, OX1 5XH Tel: 0780 905 4969 vettaatam@aol.com

VEC Vectis Auctions Ltd, Fleck Way, Thornaby, Stockton-on-Tees, Cleveland, TS17 9JZ Tel: 01642 750616 admin@vectis.co.uk www.vectis.co.uk

VRG ⊞ Vintage & Rare Guitars (Bath) Ltd, 7–8 Saville Row, Bath, Somerset, BA1 2QP Tel: 01225 330 888 enquiries@vintageandrareguitars.com www.vintageandrareguitars.com

VSP Van Sabben Poster Auctions, Appelsteeg 1-B, NL-1621 BD, Hoorn, Netherlands Tel: 31 (0)229 268203 uboersma@vansabbenauctions.nl www.vansabbenauctions.nl

WAC ⊞ Worcester Antiques Centre, Reindeer Court, Mealcheapen Street, Worcester, WR1 4DF Tel: 01905 610680 ZACATWORCS@aol.com

WAD Waddington's Auctions, 111 Bathurst Street, Toronto, M5V 2R1, Canada Tel: 416 504 9100 info@waddingtons.ca www.waddingtons.ca

WARD ⊞ Wardrobe, 51 Upper North Street, Brighton, East Sussex, BN1 3FH Tel: 01273 202201 www.decoratif.co.uk *Costume jewellery courtesy of Philip Parfitt*

WE ⊞ Webb's of Tenterden Ltd, 45 High Street, Tenterden, Kent, TN30 6BH Tel: 01580 762133

WO ⊞ Woodville Antiques, The Street, Hamstreet, Ashford, Kent, TN26 2HG Tel: 01233 732981 woodvilleantiques@yahoo.co.uk

WOS ⊞ Wheels of Steel, Grays Antique Market, Stand A12–13, Unit B10 Basement, 1–7 Davies Mews, London, W1Y 2LP Tel: 0207 629 2813

WP ⊞† British Notes, P.O. Box 257, Sutton, Surrey, SM3 9WW Tel: 020 8641 3224 pamwestbritnotes@aol.com www.britishnotes.co.uk

WW Woolley & Wallis, Salisbury Salerooms, 51–61 Castle Street, Salisbury, Wiltshire, SP1 3SU Tel: 01722 424500/411854 enquiries@woolleyandwallis.co.uk www.woolleyandwallis.co.uk

WWB ⊞ Robert Mullin, The Wee Web, 113 Montgomery Street, Edinburgh, Scotland, EH7 5EX Tel: 0131 467 7147 contact@theweeweb.co.uk www.theweeweb.co.uk

INDEX TO ADVERTISERS

INDEX

Bold page numbers refer to information and pointer boxes

C